Encyclopedia of Fantasy and Horror Fiction

DON D'AMMASSA

Checkmark Books®
An imprint of Infobase Publishing

Encyclopedia of Fantasy and Horror Fiction

Checkmark Books
An imprint of Infobase Publishing
132 West 31st Street
New York NY 10001

Library of Congress Cataloging-in-Publication Data

D'Ammassa, Don, 1946–
Encyclopedia of fantasy and horror fiction / Don D'Ammassa.
p. cm.
Includes bibliographical references and index.
ISBN 0-8160-6192-0 (hc : acid-free paper);
ISBN 0-8160-6924-7 (pbk : acid-free paper)
1. Fantasy fiction, English—Encyclopedias. 2. Fantasy fiction, American—
Encyclopedias. 3. Horror tales, American—Encyclopedias. 4. Horror tales,
English—Encyclopedias. I. Title.
PR830.F3D36 2006
809.3'8738'03—dc22
2005009375

Checkmark Books are available at special discounts when purchased in
bulk quantities for businesses, associations, institutions, or sales promotions.
Please call our Special Sales Department in New York at
(212) 967-8800 or (800) 322-8755.

You can find Facts On File on the World Wide Web at
http://www.factsonfile.com

Text design by Joan M. McEvoy
Cover design by Salvatore Luongo

Printed in the United States of America

VB Hermitage 10 9 8 7 6 5 4 3 2 1

This book is printed on acid-free paper.

Contents

INTRODUCTION

Welcome to the world of elves, dragons, unicorns, vampires, werewolves, ghosts, and magic. This book is designed to serve as a companion to *Encyclopedia of Science Fiction* (2005), and covers the remaining two main branches of fantastic fiction, fantasy and supernatural horror. Critics have argued for years about precisely where the borderlines should be drawn within fantastic fiction as a whole, but some broad assumptions can be made, although even in these cases there are numerous exceptions to the rule. Generally, then, whereas science fiction assumes that the universe operates according to certain natural laws, even if they are sometimes laws about which we have yet to learn, fantasy and horror are similar in that they assume quite the contrary. There are some elements in the worlds of fantasy that are not entirely rational and often do not obey what we think of as natural law. Although there is usually fairly close agreement regarding what is science fiction and what is fantasy, the distinction is considerably less clear between fantasy and supernatural fiction, which is one reason why it makes sense to consider them together here. Should a humorous ghost story such as "Topper" by Thorne Smith fall under supernatural horror simply because it has a ghost in it? Should "Casting the Runes" by M. R. James be considered fantasy because it involves the use of a magical spell? And how should we classify the works of Laurell Hamilton, who deals with vampires and werewolves but who sets her novels in an alternate world where both are accepted members of society? This confusion about the borders between the two genres is so pervasive that some publishers and critics have taken to using the term *dark fantasy* to indicate those works that could be plausibly included in either category.

Fantasy and the supernatural both evolved from myths, legends, and folklore later developed into fairy tales, which though ostensibly written for children were often contrived with adults in mind. Hans Christian Andersen and the Brothers Grimm gave way to George MacDonald, William Morris, H. Rider Haggard, James Branch Cabell, and others. Children's fantasy in particular has contributed a number of novels that are significant not just as fantasy but as classics in general, including such familiar titles as *Pinocchio* by Carlo Collodi, *Alice in Wonderland* by Lewis Carroll, *The Wizard of Oz* by L. Frank Baum, and *Peter Pan* by J. M. Barrie, and in more recent years the Narnia books by C. S. Lewis, *The Hobbit* by J. R. R. Tolkien, the Earthsea series by Ursula K. Le Guin, and perhaps most notably the Harry Potter series by J. K. Rowling.

For much of the 20th century, publishers treated adult fantasy as a subdivision of science fiction, and books from both genres are still shelved together in bookstores, although horror fiction is usually given its own much smaller section or is lumped in with mysteries or general fiction. Prior to the 1960s most fantasy fiction fell into two broad categories—sword and sorcery or light adventure. The first was thematically dominated by the work of Robert E. Howard, whose characters Conan, King Kull, Bran Mak Morn, Solomon Kane, Red Sonja, and others have inspired movies, television programs, pastiches, and countless imitators. These stories generally feature a barbarian culture and a protagonist who depends as much or more on his brawn than on his brains. The popularity of that form has fluctuated in recent years, but it remains a significant subset of the genre, particularly in those books associated with computer or other game systems such as Warhammer.

The light fantasy adventure story was closely associated with the magazine *Unknown,* which helped bring writers such as L. Sprague de Camp to prominence. The central characters in these novels were more likely to be intelligent and civilized and often fell into their adventures by mischance, perhaps by being inadvertently kidnapped by fairies. They were generally humorous in tone and employed simple, direct plots. A third type of fantasy story often overlapped with science fiction—the lost race novel. Writers such as H. Rider Haggard, A. Merritt, and Talbot Mundy introduced their characters into isolated civilizations, remnants of ancient cultures, sometimes describing them as possessing superior science and sometimes capable of performing genuine magic. The lost world fantasy novel has largely been abandoned by modern writers, but the other two forms are still actively in use.

During the late 1960s publication in mass market paperback of the *Lord of the Rings,* a trilogy by the British writer J. R. R. Tolkien, began what would be the transformation of fantasy and its gradual rise to a popularity as great as that of science fiction. Tolkien's epic story of a world filled with diverse races, with a fully worked out history and intricate political and social structures, has been imitated by numerous writers, perhaps most notably Terry Brooks. The Forgotten Realms and Dragonlance game systems are set in a Tolkienesque world and have been the basis for literally hundreds of fantasy novels and stories. Scores of fantasy trilogies followed, some of them similar to Tolkien's, most of them not. Another form of fantasy, the disguised historical, infrequently used before the 1970s, began to grow in popularity and is now the dominant theme in the field.

This trend started when Katherine Kurtz, Robert Jordan, Merecedes Lackey, L. E. Modesitt Jr., and other writers began producing a kind of Graustarkian romance with magic. Their stories are all set in completely imaginary worlds, although in almost every case there are strong parallels to his-

torical Europe. These worlds or political entities within them are generally ruled by kings and queens or emperors, contain wizards who side either with good or evil, and are prone to warfare and other violence, although frequently most of the conflict arises from palace intrigues, rebellions, or conspiracies, and often the plot hinges upon the efforts to protect the throne from insurgents or recover it from usurpers. Many borrow from Tolkienesque fiction and include quests for knowledge or magical artifacts, enchanted swords, and occasionally dragons. This form has become so popular that even the better novels often seem stale and repetitive, and truly innovative writers such as George R. R. Martin, Stephen R. Donaldson, China Miéville, and Mary Gentle may sometimes be lost in the crowd of lesser authors.

Other forms of fantasy remain generally on the periphery. Humor made a brief comeback in the late 1980s and early 1990s, with a steady output from Esther Friesner, Craig Shaw Gardner, Robert Lynn Asprin, John DeChancie, and others, but only Piers Anthony, Terry Pratchett, and occasionally Diana Wynne Jones have continued to be successful in the United States. Laurell Hamilton blurred the distinction between fantasy and horror with the very popular Anita Blake, Vampire Hunter, series, which depicts various supernatural creatures as varying from good to evil just as humans do and which is set in a world very similar to but not quite our own, but only a handful of writers such as Charlaine Harris and Kim Harrison have explored similar territory. There have also been a few writers who set their fantasy novels in genuine historical settings, such as Judith Tarr, Sara Douglass, and Gael Baudino, but they are in a decided minority, as are more consciously literary fantasists such as Gene Wolfe, Jeffrey Ford, and the more recent Michael Moorcock.

Although the result of this has been counterproductive in terms of the field's creative development, it appears that readers are perfectly content with the situation the way it is, and not a month goes by without announcements of new trilogies or open-ended series involving warriors, princes, wizards, and occasional demons. There have been indications of some movement since the early 1990s, however, and the fact that World Fantasy

Awards have recently been presented to such works as *The Prestige* by Christopher Priest, *Declare* by Tim Powers, and *Moonlight and Vines* by Charles De Lint suggests that hardcore fantasy readers are beginning to look for material that does not fit into familiar patterns.

Supernatural horror is as old as the first storyteller squatting by a campfire. Although much more popular in Europe than in the United States, it has not developed into a significant separate genre on either side of the Atlantic. The oldest and most familiar form of supernatural horror is the ghost story, and, in fact, during the first part of the 20th century, all supernatural horror was referred to as "ghost stories" even if there were no ghosts involved at all. The form was quite popular in England for many years and quite acceptable even for writers such as Edith Wharton, Henry James, Robert W. Chambers, and others whose major emphasis lay in more "serious" fiction. Horror fiction did not begin to diversify greatly until the advent of the pulp magazines, during which period a variety of labels were invented to describe subsets of the field, such as weird fiction and occult fiction.

Writers such as M. R. James, Oliver Onions, and H. R. Wakefield concentrated on evoking a sense of terror, while others such as Dennis Wheatley began using the occult adventure context to tell fast-paced thrillers. The American writer H. P. Lovecraft created his own subgenre, borrowing the concept of an alien race from science fiction and using it in place of the traditional demons and other monsters of his predecessors. Lovecraft proved to be particularly influential, and writers continue even now to add to his Cthulhu Mythos, which assumes that Earth was once ruled by a race of superhuman creatures who wish to return and reclaim it for their own. Lovecraft proved to be heavily influential on writers such as Robert Bloch, Frank Belknap Long, and Clark Ashton Smith. There was also a subset of weird fiction that borrowed from the mystery genre, the protagonists of which were generally called psychic detectives. Algernon Blackwood, Seabury Quinn, and William Hope Hodgson all wrote in this vein, and more recently Charles L. Grant and Jim Butcher have employed the same device, though in a more sophisticated manner.

The collapse of the pulp magazines eliminated most of the market for horror and occult fiction until the publication of two important best-selling horror novels, *Rosemary's Baby* by Ira Levin in 1967 and *The Exorcist* by William Peter Blatty in 1971. The enormous popularity of the novels, both of which became major motion pictures, convinced publishers that the reading public was ready for more of the same. The timing was perfect for Stephen King, whose *Carrie* (1974), *'Salem's Lot* (1975), and *The Shining* (1977) immediately made him the leading name in horror fiction and opened the doorway for dozens of lesser writers to break into print. The horror boom lasted well into the 1980s but collapsed before the end of that decade, possibly because the taste of the readers changed, or perhaps because of the flood of lesser titles that appeared every month, which diluted the quality of the field significantly. It should also be noted here that many nonfantastic thrillers, including excellent novels such as *The Silence of the Lambs* by Thomas Harris, *Ghoul* by Michael Slade, and *Magic* by William Goldman, were sometimes marketed as horror, and similar titles continue to appear under that label today. These are outside the scope of this book, however, and have been ignored except in two or three cases such as Edgar Allan Poe's "The Pit and the Pendulum," whose title is so closely associated with the horror field that its absence would be noted.

The horror boom did not last long enough for many significant new trends to develop. A subset of writers who specialized in particularly graphic images and story lines came to be known as "splatterpunks," most notably the writing team of John Skipp and Craig Spector, but the label has now largely disappeared. Vampire fiction survived the downturn, in large part because the image of the evil, repulsive vampire had been transformed by Anne Rice and others. The vampire was now a romantic figure and was as likely to be good as evil. Vampire detective novels, vampire romances, and vampire historicals continue to flourish, and, in fact, many of these books are not "horror" novels at all.

There has been a recent resurgence in supernatural horror fiction. Stephen King has remained the field's dominant writer, but Peter Straub,

Graham Masterton, and Dean R. Koontz have also found a continuing audience, and newer writers such as Bentley Little, Edward Lee, Thomas Ligotti, Tom Piccirilli, Nancy Holder, and Christopher Golden appear to be attracting a new generation of readers. The diverse styles and subject matters of these writers, none of whom confine themselves to traditional ghosts, vampires, demonic possessions, and satanic cults, may indicate a healthier and more gradual expansion of the field in the future.

There are far too many authors and significant works to cover them all adequately even in a book of this length. What I have attempted to do is provide an overview of the careers of the significant writers, some of whom are active in both fields, as well as a sampling of newer writers who may become the leading names over the next few years.

I have also chosen selected novels and short stories, including many of the best fantasy and horror stories ever written, but also some of the most influential, and a few that illustrate points that may not have been covered elsewhere. There is also a bibliography of the fantasy and horror books of each writer covered, lists of the winners of the Bram Stoker Awards presented by the Horror Writers' Association and the World Fantasy Awards presented by the World Fantasy Convention, a brief bibliography of reference works I have found useful, and a glossary of terms that might be unfamiliar. I hope that readers will find this book useful and that they may be stimulated to discover as much pleasure in reading some of the works mentioned herein as I have.

Abbey, Lynn (1948–)

Lynn Abbey made her fantasy debut with *Daughter of the Bright Moon* (1979), the first adventure of Rifkind, a female warrior in a predominantly male world. She followed up the next year with a sequel, *The Black Flame* (1980), which had more definite feminist undertones and which developed the character of its protagonist significantly. Rifkind is a powerful woman whose self-confidence grows as she gains the patronage of a goddess and realizes the full extent of her own physical and mystical abilities. Although the form is that of the quest story, much of what Rifkind accomplishes is as much internal as external. The protagonist of Abbey's next novel, *The Guardians* (1982), undergoes a similar transformation, although in this case the setting is the contemporary world and the danger originates from alternate realities wishing to cross the barrier that separates them from each other and from us.

Abbey's next sequence of two novels was set in a variant of 11th-century England, where magic works and history is slightly different. The king is dying, and evil sorcery threatens to affect the succession to the throne. Opposing the mysterious figures moving behind the scenes are two sisters who have magical powers of their own and who are loyal to the existing bloodline. Another duo of books followed, based loosely on the computer game *Ultima*, consisting of *The Forge of Virtue* and *The Temper of Wisdom*, both appearing in 1991. Although constrained by the limitations of the game world, Abbey turned out two surprisingly enter-

taining stories of rebellions and quests. *The Wooden Sword* (1991) was a much more original work, set in a far more diverse and interesting world, one in which sentient trees interact with humans. The sequel, *Beneath the Web* (1994), continued the story but did not measure up to its predecessor. Several shared universe novels followed, most based on role playing games, of which the only one that rose above its subject matter was *Cinnabar Shadows* (1995).

Abbey's next major work was *Jerlayne* (1999), a thoughtful, understated adventure that was something of a reversal of her earlier *The Guardians* (1982). Fairies are traditionally poisoned by the touch of iron, which is unknown in the Land of Faery, but the borders between their world and ours are eroding, and traces of iron that pass through the barrier are causing serious problems. The protagonist is a healer whose efforts to stem the onset of diseases and other problems brought inadvertently by intruders from our world become increasingly desperate. The story is far less melodramatic and action-oriented than the author's previous work and seems to have indicated a switch to more serious subject matter. Even more significant was the Emma Merrigan series, consisting to date of *Out of Time* (2000), *Behind Time* (2001), and *Taking Time* (2004), with *Down Time* scheduled to appear soon. Merrigan is a librarian who discovers she has been given the magical power to travel through time and the obligation to use those powers to help people by removing family curses, solving generations-old mysteries, and accomplishing other tasks beyond the abilities of ordinary people. Abbey seems much more confident about her material in this series, and the protagonist is certainly her most fully developed character.

Abbey continues to intersperse her original work with game tie-in novels of varying quality. She is also well known as the coeditor with Robert Lynn Asprin of the Thieves' World shared universe anthology series and has written one novel of her own in that setting, *Sanctuary* (2002), as well as several short stories. The series was revived recently following a lengthy hiatus, having found a home with a new publisher.

"The Abominations of Yondo" Clark Ashton Smith (1926)

During the 1920s and 1930s fantasy fiction was split into a number of different forms, including fairy tales, medieval style adventures, and others. In the United States in particular there was a subset of fantasy generally referred to as weird fiction, which blurred the borders of genres as we define them nowadays to include elements of horror, fantasy, and even science fiction. Writers such as H. P. LOVECRAFT and Robert E. HOWARD were prominent among this group of writers, who interacted with one another socially and by letter. One of the most influential of these was Clark Ashton SMITH, also a poet, who wrote a large number of comparatively short tales, many of them grouped into one or another of his imaginary universes.

This story, one of his most provocative, does not fit easily into any of those subsets. The setting is the rim of the world in some distant past or future that is never made explicit. Even the gods have abandoned the region, which is populated by twisted vegetation, grotesque animals, hints of dark magic, terrible odors, and other imagery designed to paint an atmosphere of decay and danger. Even the hills assume the shapes of sleeping monsters. The protagonist has been expelled into this region for heresy by the priests of Ong, about whom we learn virtually nothing, nor do we find out much about the character himself, because Smith's purpose was not so much to tell a story as to create a series of images that would linger in the reader's memory. He accomplishes this by means of an intricate and colorful use of language that is largely absent from contemporary fantasy fiction.

The nameless protagonist leads us through a short series of strange encounters—a crying statue, a spiderlike creature that dwells in a cave, a mysterious pursuer visible only by its shadow—before finally deciding that even the fate planned for him by the priests of Ong is preferable to a longer stay. References to events or scenes so frightening that they have the power to drive people mad recur frequently in weird fiction from this period, as does the use of the menace or creature unseen and undescribed. As any fan of horror movies can confirm, there is almost always a letdown when we finally see a creature, because our imagination creates much more frightening images than does Hollywood. Conscious of that fact, Smith and other writers suggested rather than described their shadowy menaces.

Aickman, Robert (1914–1981)

Robert Aickman was a British writer and opera critic who began producing short horror stories in the late 1940s and who received considerable attention after producing several quite memorable ones early in his career, including the often-reprinted "Trains" (1951). He is generally thought of as a writer of ghost stories, but his short fiction explored a number of other supernatural themes as well, and a sizeable portion of his work draws its conflict from psychological rather than supernatural sources. Even his overtly supernatural work is less concerned with the nature of the threat than with the mental processes of his protagonists, their reactions to what is happening around them, and their ability or inability to deal with it. Many of his stories have decidedly downbeat endings, not so much because his characters fail to win their struggles as because they refuse to even make the attempt.

The vast majority of Aickman's supernatural fiction consists of short stories, which have been variously collected and cross-collected. The best selections are *Cold Hand in Mine* (1975) and *The Wine Dark Sea* (1988). Both of his genre novels are quite short. *The Late Breakfasters* (1964) is a rather conventional though often eerie ghost story, while *The Model* (1987) is an adaptation of a Russian fairy tale with mildly supernatural overtones that might almost be dismissed as delusions. Among the best of his short stories are "Ringing the Changes" (1971), "Bind Your Hair" (1971), "PAGES FROM A YOUNG GIRL'S JOURNAL" (1973), "The Wine Dark Sea" (1976), and "The Fetch" (1987). "Pages from a Young Girl's Journal" won the World Fantasy Award in 1975.

Aickman's reputation was always greater in England than in the United States, almost certainly because the ghost story form is held in much greater esteem in Europe than in America. The fact that Aickman did attract a considerable following in America while most writers of similar fiction in Great Britain remain unknown outside that country is a testimony to the power of his prose and his ability to project his readers into the minds of his characters.

Alexander, Lloyd (1924–)

Lloyd Alexander made his debut as a writer of children's fantasy with *Time Cat* (1961), the slight but amusing adventure of a cat who can move back and forth through time. It was with *The Book of Three* (1964), however, that he established himself as a major new talent. The novel was the first of the Prydain sequence of five novels, to which he also added three minor peripheral titles loosely based on Welsh legends. The protagonist is Taran, a young assistant pig-keeper whose destiny is to change the future of his people. Despite the fact that the series is clearly aimed at younger readers, Alexander sometimes uses very dark imagery to add a distinctive color to his stories. Although he simplifies the characters from the original legend to make them more clearly good and evil, he describes Taran's self-doubts and indecision in ways that make him come alive for even more sophisticated readers, and in some of the subsidiary characters, temptation and virtue contend even more openly. An evil sorcerer raises an army of zombies in THE BLACK CAULDRON (1965), and a young princess is kidnapped in *The Castle of Llyr* (1966), requiring a complex rescue operation. Taran learns the secret of his own destiny in *Taran Wanderer*

(1967) and triumphs over the villainous magician in the conclusion, *The High King* (1968). As a unit, the five-volume series is one of the enduring classics of children's fantasy, one that still commands an audience among adult readers. The books were the basis for the animated Disney film *The Black Cauldron* (1985).

Unfortunately, Alexander's later novels, while uniformly competent and sometimes quite amusing, never achieved the level of the Prydain series. Most of these are set in alternate versions of one historical period of another. The most interesting sequence consists of *The Illyrian Adventure* (1986), *The El Dorado Adventure* (1987), *The Drackenberg Adventure* (1988), *The Jedera Adventure* (1989), and *The Philadelphia Adventure* (1990). The young Vesper Holly saves the day when her alternate version of our Victorian era is menaced by magical armies and other dangers. *The Remarkable Journey of Prince Jen* (1991) is a low-key Arabian Nights–style story. In *The Iron Ring* (1997) a king loses all of his possessions except for a magical ring.

Two early novels are also of interest. A young boy finds himself in a magical world where he is declared king in *The First Two Lives of Lukas-Kasha* (1978), only to discover that he is the object of a complex set of conspiracies. In *The Marvelous Misadventures of Sebastian* (1970), a youngster uses magic to solve a variety of problems before learning to deal with matters in more ordinary ways. Alexander's lesser books are invariably entertaining, and the Vesper Holly series is actually quite good, but his name will always be associated primarily with the Prydain series.

Alice in Wonderland Lewis Carroll (1865)

Lewis Carroll was the pseudonym Charles Dodgson used as the author of what is possibly the best-known children's novel of all time. An earlier version was later discovered and subsequently published in 1886 as *Alice's Adventures Underground*, and the more familiar version has appeared with several variations of the title, including *The Annotated Alice* and *Alice's Adventures in Wonderland*. It is one of the best-selling children's fantasies of all time, with editions from at least a score of different publishers. There have also been a number of film versions, starting in 1933, both animated and with live actors, and the term *Alice in Wonderland* has entered the language as a term for a person caught up in circumstances so unusual that they are bewildering.

The young Alice, who may or may not have dreamed the entire story, follows an oddly attired rabbit into his hole and eventually finds herself in Wonderland, where she has a series of odd adventures and meets a large cast of memorable characters including the March Hare, the Mad Hatter, Tweedledum and Tweedledee, and the Queen of Hearts. Carroll sprinkled the book with bizarre images that appealed to young readers, including a caterpillar whose body parts tend to disappear, the Mad Hatter's very nonsensical tea party, croquet played with birds instead of mallets, drugs that make people grow or shrink, and other inspired madness. Alice eventually escapes back to the real world after a series of adventures that are exciting without being overly frightening, and she remains in tight control of herself throughout most of her experiences. Embedded within the text are verses including the memorable "The Hunting of the Snark."

Alice's second adventure, *Alice Through the Looking Glass* (1871), followed in much the same vein, this time admitting Alice by means of a magical mirror through which she can step between worlds, a device used later in several adult fantasies. As with the first volume, it has self-contained poems and episodes, including "Jabberwocky" and "The Walrus and the Carpenter." Carroll undoubtedly was satirizing people and events around him at times, although the references are so obscure that they amounted to little more than a private joke. The major plot of the novel is somewhat loosely based on a game of chess.

Although there have been many imitators, one notable instance being *The Phantom Tollbooth* (1961) by Norton Juster, who also shared Carroll's interest in mathematics, no other writer has managed to fully capture the madcap atmosphere of the original. There have also been several sequels of varying quality, the most recent of which is *Alice's Journey Beyond the Moon* (2004), by R. J. Carter, which is presented as a lost manuscript complete with annotations and original illustrations.

The Alvin Maker Series Orson Scott Card (1987–2003)

Orson Scott Card, who is primarily known as a science fiction writer, displays clear evidence that his work has been influenced by his Mormon background. His deep commitment to his faith is even more evident in his fantasy fiction, particularly the Alvin Maker series, which parallels the early days of the Mormon Church and the original trek to Utah. Alvin made his debut in *Seventh Son* (1987), set in an alternate early America where the Revolution never took place and there is no large nation-state. It is a simpler, more rural version of America, and one where magic works. Although the circumstances of his birth as the seventh son are supposed to confirm Alvin as unusually lucky, he quickly acquires powerful enemies as he grows to manhood, a tension that grows more palpable and dangerous in *Red Prophet* (1988). By the time of the events in *Prentice Alvin* (1989), there is a clearly dominant opposing figure in the form of Alvin's brother, and the two become, to a great extent, parallels of Christ and the Antichrist.

Although Alvin appears to have fulfilled his destiny by the end of the original trilogy, Card returned to his character after several years with *Alvin Journeyman* (1995). Also back is Calvin, the "Unmaker," still determined to thwart his brother's plans. The story spreads to a wider stage in *Heartfire* (1998), with a prophetess traveling to Europe to meet the king of England, and investigations into the Salem witchcraft trials, which unfortunately took place in this reality as well as our own. After another considerable gap, Alvin and his followers returned in *The Crystal City* (2003), this time attempting to establish a separate community of the faithful in a remote part of the American West, surrounded by various Native American societies but still not completely free from the meddling of Alvin's enemies.

With the growing popularity of Christian-oriented fantasy, it is not surprising that Card's Mormon-inspired series found a loyal audience. They are first and foremost entertainments that are patterned after historical and religious events, but they are not designed to proselytize and avoid the trap of preaching to their audience. Card had already demonstrated that he could command a varied and loyal audience of readers in the science fiction community, but his success with fantasy fans has not as yet been proportionately large. The Alvin series is the best of his fantasy, however, and the clarity and intensity of its continuing core story is likely to ensure its continued popularity. The short episode "Hatrack River" (1987) won the World Fantasy Award.

The Amber Series Roger Zelazny
(1970–1991)

Although Roger ZELAZNY was well established as a science fiction writer by 1970, it was obvious even in that genre that he was fascinated with myths and legends, with larger-than-life characters placed in situations where they affected the future on a dramatic scale. It was not a great surprise when he announced that he was working on an extended series of fantasy novels, originally envisioned as a set of nine. The first five were published between 1970 and 1978 and seemed to tie things up, but Zelazny returned to provide a further set of five between 1985 and 1991.

The premise of the Amber stories is that there are a vast number of different realities, all supposedly revolving around a central one known as Amber, of which the others are all flawed reflections, including our own, one of the few in which magic does not work. The premise is modified as the series progresses, or more properly speaking, the characters—chiefly Corwin, one of the princes of Amber—realize that they are not after all the center of the universe, that Amber is balanced by Chaos, another reality, and that this dichotomy leads to violence, although more yin and yang than good versus evil. In the opening volume, *Nine Princes in Amber* (1970), Corwin's memories have been suppressed, and he has been exiled to our universe, but trouble follows. His father is believed to have died, and a large cast of siblings are engaged in inventive and often brutal projects to replace him.

Corwin returns to Amber to claim the throne himself in *The Guns of Avalon* (1972), but there is considerable opposition, both straightforward and covert. The conflict worsens in *Sign of the Unicorn* (1975), with some of his siblings openly challeng-

ing his right to rule, and the rivalry becomes still more dangerous in *The Hand of Oberon* (1976), during which Corwin's brothers and sisters are forced to rally behind him in order to help determine who is responsible for a series of assassination attempts directed at their family, possibly by one of their own number. The various conflicts are resolved in *The Courts of Chaos* (1978), the traitor's identified, a group of shape-shifting assassins are defeated, and Corwin's primacy is established, although still perhaps somewhat uneasily.

The rich texture of the original sequence was not as evident in the second set of five novels, which follows the adventures of Corwin's son, Merle or Merlin. *Trumps of Doom* (1985) introduces him in much the same fashion as was his father. After surviving a murder attempt while visiting our reality, he returns to Amber to find out who is responsible. He forges an uneasy alliance with a shapeshifter in *Blood of Amber* (1986) and sets out to identify the secret forces working against him in *Sign of Chaos* (1988). His loyalty to Amber is put to the test in *Knight of Shadows* (1989), but he discovers the true nature of the plot against him in *Prince of Amber* (1991) and finally establishes a peace between that realm and Chaos.

Dynastic fantasies with conflicts spanning multiple worlds were not original with Zelazny, and they have become more common in recent years, but the Amber series was quite remarkable when it first appeared. The earlier sequence in particular is rich in symbolism and complexity. John Betancourt has begun a new sequence with *Dawn of Amber* (2001) that does a moderately successful job of capturing the tone of the original books. Zelazny also wrote a few short stories against that setting, which can be found collected in *Manna from Heaven* (2003), and also produced a companion volume, *Roger Zelazny's Visual Guide to Castle Amber* (1988).

The Amber Spyglass Philip Pullman (2000)

Philip PULLMAN's His Dark Materials trilogy came to a conclusion with this volume, following THE GOLDEN COMPASS and THE SUBTLE KNIFE. The series, which is loosely based on *Paradise Lost* by John Milton, is effectively a single novel in three volumes rather than three related adventures. The premise is that many worlds exist parallel to one another, and in one of these a war in heaven is being mirrored by a power struggle among factions within a dominant church in a Europe very similar to that of our Victorian era.

Lyra Belacqua and Will Parry are two youngsters who have been swept up in the struggle. The previous volume left Lyra in the hands of kidnappers, and readers now learn that she has fallen once again into the hands of the mysterious Mrs. Coulter, whose allegiances and morality are never quite clear. According to a prophecy, Lyra will face a temptation that will affect the fate of the world, and at least one group within the church has decided to kill her to prevent her from possibly making the wrong choice. She and Will have adventures separately and together, and some of the subsidiary characters have their own story lines to follow, the most interesting of which is Mary Malone's sojourn among the mulefa, a race of wheeled creatures whose fate is inevitable if all of the mysterious "Dust" is drained from their world.

The children visit the underworld in search of their friend Roger and his missing father, but the outcome is not what they hoped for. Eventually Lyra will face temptation, just as Eve did, but of a very different nature. The conclusion is very surprising and quite low-key, and some readers were disappointed by its subtlety and by the very many loose ends Pullman did not feel required to clear up. His indictment of entrenched authority's tendency to withhold information is stronger than ever. The trilogy is unquestionably one of the most rewarding children's fantasies ever written and one of the most sophisticated as well. Although Pullman has continued to write in the genre, His Dark Materials is likely to endure as his masterpiece.

"Ancient Sorceries" Algernon Blackwood
(1908)

Algernon BLACKWOOD was one of the earliest writers of supernatural fiction to use a recurring character, specifically a form of occult detective, someone who specializes in cases out of the ordinary. Seabury QUINN and William Hope HODGSON would create characters who believed implicitly in the occult,

but Blackwood's John Silence was somewhat more skeptical, and several of his cases are ultimately dismissed as illusions or the result of psychological maladies.

"Ancient Sorceries" is the title story from one of his collections and is one of Blackwood's most rewarding works. The story unfolds at a very leisurely pace, a style that has largely disappeared from modern horror fiction because there are few places where a long novelette such as this could be published today. Silence, who styles himself a "psychic doctor," has a new patient, an ordinary British businessman with no penchant for flights of the imagination who impulsively gets off a train during a vacation in France to visit an obscure village. He does so despite the enigmatic warning of a fellow passenger, a warning he will later remember.

The town seems perfect at first, attractive, restful, and filled with friendly if not overly sociable residents. He takes a room at an inn where he is well treated though cautioned that he must come in promptly at dusk because they lock all the doors at night. It is only over the course of days that he realizes there is something amiss. No matter where he goes, he always draws a crowd, although they all pretend not to have noticed him. Some people disappear in mysterious ways when he tries to follow them, and sometimes he notices a movement that seems more catlike than human. He still feels no overt alarm, even when he realizes that his will seems to have been sapped, that he no longer is certain whether he can summon the desire to leave and return home. Things are further complicated by the arrival of his landlady's daughter, a young woman who appears attracted to him despite the disparity in their ages and to whom he feels unnaturally drawn.

The reader will probably have realized the truth well before the protagonist. The entire village is united in their worship of satanic forces, and their religion has given them animalistic attributes. The tourist begins to remember hints of a former existence and nearly becomes a full initiate, but a fortuitous accident momentarily breaks the spell and he flees just in time to save his soul. Silence later determines that his stay in the village was actually much shorter than he remembered and that most of what he experienced there consisted of illusions generated by his memories of a previous incarnation, although the true status of the villagers is never explicitly explained.

A comparison with the work of H. P. LOVE-CRAFT is inevitable. Lovecraft also wrote of isolated communities whose populations were united in some unholy practice and whose physical natures had been altered accordingly. Lovecraft's imagery involves reptilians and fish, where as Blackwood used cats. Both authors hint at greater horrors, Satan or alien gods, but both wisely leave them off stage. Blackwood's story might strike modern readers as mild, but the subtle implications are built so carefully and effectively that they generate a mood that is not easily shaken off.

Andersen, Hans Christian (1805–1875)

Along with the Brothers GRIMM, the Danish writer Hans Christian Andersen is probably the best-known writer of fairy tales who ever lived. He began writing these fanciful tales in 1826, primarily for adult readers and publishing them in small batches. When they were translated into English, they were invariably targeted toward children, who sometimes missed the point of the allegories.

Many of Andersen's fairy tales have become so widely known that it has become unnecessary to actually read them in order to know the stories, and many have also provided the inspiration for live and animated films. Among his best known tales are "The Emperor's New Clothes," "The Ugly Duckling," "The Princess and the Pea," "The Snow Queen," and "The Ice Maiden." Despite the cavalier treatment of his work in England and America, the powerful images and simple but effective plots remained in the memories of their readers, and echoes of these stories can be found in a variety of forms in every genre. A few, such as "The Emperor's New Clothes" and "The Ugly Duckling," have become the common vernacular for familiar situations. The tone of the stories varies from lightly humorous to dark and sometimes frightening, and many of his characters meet terrible fates.

Andersen's fairy tales have been assembled into scores of different collections and editions since they first appeared. Although a few were drawn from earlier folk tales, most were original

with him, and, although he is rarely acknowledged formally as a fantasy writer, he originated many themes and devices that have become so commonplace now that their origin is no longer obvious.

Animal Farm George Orwell (1946)

Fairy tales have always made extensive use of talking animals as characters, sometimes to appeal to younger audiences, sometimes to mask the fact that they were written as satires of real persons and events. The form is largely confined to very young readers in today's market, although the Redwall series by Brian JACQUES is a very notable exception. George Orwell, the author of the dystopian classic *Nineteen Eighty-Four* (1949), had previously written this slim novel, which uses animal characters as transparent stand-ins for human beings. The novel satirizes the workings of political collectivism in a very unusual and effective fashion. Orwell was himself a socialist, but he viewed developments within the Soviet Union as a corruption of otherwise noble ideals.

The setting is a small farm where the animals have revolted and expelled their human owners in order to establish their own state. The phrase "all animals are created equal" is quickly amended to acknowledge that some animals "are more equal than others," thereby justifying privileges to those few who gather power to themselves. The pigs become the ruling class, led by Napoleon, who is almost certainly meant to be Stalin, and they inexorably tighten their grip, diverting more of the farm's resources to their own comfort while the majority of animals, the masses, experience inconveniences and eventually hardships even worse than those they endured when humans were in charge.

Orwell also implied that the Stalinists had sold out their ideals in another fashion, by consorting with members of the class they supposedly worked to eliminate. Similarly, Orwell's pigs begin to mimic human activity, even going so far as to walk on their hind legs and adopt other human affectations. The ultimate betrayal comes when the pigs begin to socialize with the human owners of nearby farms. Many of Orwell's fellow socialists bridled when the book appeared, but his distrust of the possibility of perverting the ideals of socialism persisted in his later work. *Animal Farm*, which was made into a full length film in 1955, has remained in print ever since.

Anthony, Mark (1966–)

Mark Anthony is one of several fantasy writers who started their careers producing game-related fantasy novels for what was then known as TSR Publishing and is now Wizards of the Coast. His debut novel was *Kindred Spirits* (1991), a collaboration with Edith Porath, which unconventionally used a typical fantasy world adventure setting for a fairly sophisticated murder mystery. *Crypt of the Shadowking* (1993) was closer to the publisher's usual formula, a well-told but predictable story of intrigue and sorcery, but *Curse of the Shadowmage* (1995) was notable for the sophistication of its plot, which involves questions of morality in dealing with an individual who has the potential for great evil, but who also possesses the possibility of redemption. *Escape from Undermountain* (1996) was considerably less ambitious but a well-told quest adventure.

Anthony switched publishers in the late 1990s and launched a six-volume series, the Last Rune, with *Beyond the Pale* (1998), a distinctly more original work although set squarely in mainstream fantasy. The novel suggests that there is another world existing parallel but separate from ours, one where magic works and legendary creatures exist. The barrier between the two realities has begun to fray in the vicinity of a town in contemporary America, some of whose residents are about to discover their own innate heroism. The proximity of the two worlds leads to a series of confrontations and potential disasters in both, and the small cast of recurring characters find that the job of saving both realms has been thrust upon them in *The Keep of Fire* (1999). Although most of the action takes place in the magical world of Eldh in that volume, the focus switches to our reality in *The Dark Remains* (2001), when the heroes and a wounded comrade return seeking medical help pursued by ruthless enemies.

Anthony widens the scope of events even further in *Blood of Mystery* (2002), transporting some

of the main characters back through time to Colorado during the 1880s, still harried by the forces of evil. The change of setting is initially distracting and confusing but eventually becomes an integral part of the ongoing story. The secrets of manipulating magic are finally mastered in *The Gates of Winter* (2003), and the battle is carried to the enemy at last in the concluding volume, *The First Stone* (2004). Despite a few rough spots, the series is a dramatic step forward from Anthony's early work and clear evidence that he has the potential to be a major player in modern fantasy, although perhaps not one of its most innovative writers.

Anthony, Piers (1934–)

Although Piers Anthony, whose real name is Piers Anthony Dillingham Jacob, is best known for his fantasy, he started his writing career as a mildly controversial science fiction writer during the 1960s who mixed sexual themes and other touchy subject matter in his fiction. Although *A Spell for Chameleon* (1979), the first novel in the Xanth series, diverted his career into a very different channel, it was not his first fantasy novel. He had previously written a five-volume martial arts/fantasy sequence with Roberto Fuentes, and his Arabian Nights–style fantasy adventure *Hasan* had been published in magazine form in 1969, although it would not see book form until 10 years later.

It was with the Xanth series that he became a perennial best-seller, and Xanth has dominated his output ever since, with the most recent title being *Currant Events* (2004). It is the 28th adventure in that setting, although there are no characters common to all of the books. Xanth is a fantasy world whose magical system is subject to defined rules and populated by a wide variety of intelligent creatures, mostly drawn from myths and legends but some completely original. Although each novel is an adventure story, usually involving some form of quest, the tone is light and often openly humorous, with a particular penchant for puns and other word play. The opening volume, *A Spell for Chameleon*, remains one of the best in the series. The protagonist, Bink, is apparently the only person in Xanth who lacks a magical talent, but he eventually learns that he is, in fact, immune to magical attacks, which is a talent in itself. Bink's subsequent search for *The Source of Magic* (1979) nearly ends in disaster.

Anthony tried to vary the formula for the third, *Castle Roogna* (1979), the story of a love affair between a ghost and a zombie, with time travel thrown in as well, and the quality of the series became uneven thereafter. The best of the later titles include *Dragon on a Pedestal* (1983), in which a plague of amnesia complicates life even more than it usually is, *Crewel Lye* (1984), which features a ghost whose quest is to find living assistance in order to reassemble his scattered bones, and *Golem in the Gears* (1986), which casts a golem anachronistically in the role of a fearless hero. Also of note are *The Man from Mundania* (1989), in which Xanth and our reality interact, and *The Color of Her Panties* (1992), in which a pair of enchanted underpants are the focus for the usual comic events. Other titles have involved such diverse topics as floods, deals with the devil, a visit to hell, missing kings, star-crossed lovers, and attempts to retroactively meddle with history. The Xanth series has been criticized for its lightness, and certainly some of the individual volumes have been less successful than others, but they are intended as light entertainment for a slightly older audience than the Oz series, which they resemble in many ways, and Anthony clearly has a large and loyal readership.

Anthony has written a considerable body of non-Xanth fantasy as well, much of it more sophisticated and ambitious, although not always successful. The Tarot trilogy, *God of Tarot* (1979), *Vision of Tarot* (1980), and *Faith of Tarot* (1980), was Anthony's first attempt to merge fantasy and science fiction in the same story. Tarot is a distant world where some elements of the occult are valid. The creation of supernatural creatures is semirationalized as an untapped power of the human mind, but the stories themselves are clearly fantasy. This use of magic on another planet recurs in the less-interesting *Havoc* (2003). Anthony explored this dichotomy from a different perspective in the Apprentice Adept series, which began with *Split Infinity* (1980). Two worlds exist parallel to each other, Proton, in which science is all important, and Phaze, where magic works. Stile is from the

former world and is transported into the latter, where he discovers that his counterpart there has been murdered and that someone is trying to kill him as well. The mystery continues in *Blue Adept* (1981) and *Juxtaposition* (1983), with Stile growing uncertain of his allies. He and his robot sidekick have further adventures in *Out of Phaze* (1987), *Robot Adept* 1988), and *Unicorn Point* (1989) before finally defeating an alien invasion of both worlds in the final volume, *Phaze Doubt* (1990).

The Incarnations of Immortality series was Anthony's most ambitious fantasy project. The premise this time is that various archetypes—Evil, Nature, Fate, and so on—are actual physical beings but that they are mortal and periodically are replaced by candidates recruited from ordinary humans. In the opening volume, *On a Pale Horse* (1983), a man kills Death himself and must take his place. Although there are moments of humor, it is of a darker variety, and the series is much more serious in tone than Anthony's other fantasy. Another human agrees to become Time personified in *Bearing an Hourglass* (1984), and the role of Satan, who appears to be genuinely immortal, becomes more complex as he begins manipulating the other incarnations to suit his own desires. *With a Tangled Skein* (1985) introduced Fate, and *Wielding a Red Sword* (1986), the best single title in the series, casts a peaceful man as War, much to the dismay of Satan, who tricks him into visiting hell, where War incites a rebellion. A musician is transformed into Nature in *Being a Green Mother* (1987), and Evil becomes a rival to Satan in *For Love of Evil* (1990). The final volume, *And Eternity* (1990), opens with Evil becoming the ruler of the world, although his power is eventually broken.

Science and magic are blended again in the Mode series, which began with *Virtual Mode* (1991). A woman from our reality crosses into an alternate world, where magic is the source of all power and women are forbidden to use it, resulting in a patriarchal system the newcomer finds abhorrent. She battles to change things in the sequel, *Fractal Mode* (1992), but the plot begins to fragment toward the end. An alien visitor complicates matters even further in *Chaos Mode* (1993), which brought the series to an apparent end, although Anthony has recently returned to that world for

DoOon Mode (2001), introducing an evil wizard to stir things up. The series has interesting moments, particularly in the opening volume, but as a whole feels like a pale imitation of the Apprentice Adept novels.

Anthony has written several fantasies in collaboration with other writers, including Mercedes LACKEY and Philip José Farmer, but the only ones that measure up to his solo work are those written with Robert E. Margroff. *Dragon's Gold* (1987) introduced Kelvin of Rud, whom prophecy says will unite the scattered communities of his world. The series is atypical in that it is much more traditional than Anthony's other fantasy. Kelvin overcomes various enemies and ignores a superfluity of advice, unites the land, and defeats his enemies over the course of five volumes, ending with *Mouvar's Magic* (1992).

Two of Anthony's novels have employed contemporary settings with supernatural elements. *Shade of the Tree* (1987) is a haunted house story, but the horror element is very restrained. *Firefly* (1990) was considerably stronger. The supernatural menace in this case exudes psychic sexual hormones that influence everyone in the vicinity. The strong sexual content is unusual but not unknown in Anthony's work, particularly his early science fiction and the minor fantasy novel *Pornucopia* (1989). Clearly, his reputation lies with his fantasy, particularly the Xanth novels. Although critics have lamented the lightness of most of Anthony's fiction, his recurring status as a best-seller over the course of three decades suggests that he has more staying power than their criticism might suggest.

Applegate, K. A. (1956–)

K. A. Applegate's books are written exclusively for young adults. She first became prominent with the Animorphs series, which was ostensibly science fiction because there was an attempt made to rationalize the powers of the recurring teenaged characters. However, their ability to change their bodies into the forms of other animals violated the laws of conservation of mass and energy, and they could just as easily be read as fantasy. There were three dozen novels in the series between 1996 and 1999, after which Applegate turned to outright fantasy for her next series.

The EverWorld sequence consists of 12 novels, starting with *Search for Senna* (1999). When one of their friends disappears into a magical world, a group of teenagers from our reality decide to rescue her. Unfortunately, they find themselves not in one discrete world but in a fractured reality where various mythical creatures live separately but with frequent interaction. In the opening volume they get caught up in the battle between the ancient Norse gods and those of pre-Columbian Mexico. They have various adventures there and encounter Merlin the Wizard, but without finding the elusive Senna, whom they pursue into an analogue of the Christian hell in the fourth title, *Realm of the Reaper* (1999). The Greek gods appear in volume six, *Fear the Fantastic* (2000), and help Zeus battle a race of aliens in *Gateway to the Gods* (2000).

The next few volumes establish the ambiguous nature of the aliens, and the protagonists begin to understand more of the rules of the game in which they have become trapped. Unfortunately, Neptune sends them on a sidetrip to Atlantis in *Understanding the Unknown* (2000), and they must make their way through an ancient, magical version of Ireland in *Mystify the Magician* (2001) before finally resolving their various questions, repairing the damage they have inadvertently caused, meeting Merlin for the final time, and returning home with Senna in the concluding volume, *Entertain the End* (2001).

Although the series is lightweight entertainment, Applegate handles the interface between the various groups of characters well, although the aliens are not as plausible or interesting as they might have been. Her latest series, Remnants, is science fiction.

"The Ash-Tree" M. R. James (1904)

The publication of *Ghost Stories of an Antiquary* by M. R. JAMES in 1904 was a major event whose importance has been obscured by the passage of time. It is one the most frequently reprinted collections of short horror fiction in England, and to a great extent it established the standards of the form for generations that followed. The term *ghost story* was used at the time to encompass almost all supernatural fiction, and, in fact, "The Ash-Tree," which appeared in that collection, only marginally involves a ghost. It is more properly the story of a witch's curse.

During the 16th century Mrs. Mothersole is convicted of witchcraft and executed, largely on the testimony of the owner of Castringham, a sprawling house that dominates the countryside. At the moment of her death, Mothersole utters a vague threat, and a short time later her accuser is found dead in his bed, his body contorted as though he had experienced great pain but with no physical evidence of the cause of his demise. The room, whose view is obscured by a large ash tree that stands just outside the window, is immediately closed up and used only for occasional guests during the next several years. That particular tree is significant because it was a frequent haunt of Mrs. Mothersole, although no one knows specifically what attracted her to it.

The years pass until the grandson of the dead man takes up residence and, unwisely, decides to use the shunned bedchamber. He sleeps poorly the first night and decides to have the tree removed in order to facilitate a fresher passage of air. Unfortunately, he defers the decision until too late, because the very next night he dies under circumstances that mirror those surrounding his grandfather's fate. We also learn that the witch's casket has been exhumed and found to be empty. Her bones are later discovered inside the tree, which is destroyed in a fire and which proves to contain a nest of oversized, venomous spiders of unknown origin, presumably the witch's familiars.

James never attempts to describe the actual method by which the victims were killed, leaving that to our imagination. The ending is deliberately understated, which was common in horror fiction before contemporary writers turned to more explicit storytelling. It is one of several James stories that are undeniable classics, although the quality of his work is consistently excellent. A specialty publishing house that has been regularly reprinting supernatural fiction from the early 20th century took as its name Ash-Tree Press in honor of this classic story.

Audrey Rose Frank DeFelitta (1975)

When the horror field was enjoying its brief heyday on the bestseller lists in the 1970s and 1980s, almost every traditional supernatural theme was resurrected in some form or another, everything from ghost stories and vampires to visitors from other worlds. Most of these devices were done to death quickly thanks to repetitive variations of the same basic story, but other themes such as werewolves and reincarnation never achieved the same kind of popularity with writers or readers. One of the rare exceptions in the latter case was *Audrey Rose*, one of four horror novels by Frank DeFelitta.

The Templetons are an ordinary couple who dote on their young daughter Ivy, with no suspicion that anything out of the ordinary may be happening around them. When Elliot Hoover shows up, claiming that Ivy is the reincarnation of his own daughter, who died a horrible death by fire following an automobile accident, they dismiss him as emotionally disturbed and a potential danger. Five-year-old Audrey Rose died at the precise moment Ivy was born, and Hoover has decided through this and other questionable evidence that his daughter has returned and that they are destined to be reunited. The reader accepts that Hoover is correct long before the Templetons come to the same realization, but Hoover is in for another surprise. His once loving daughter is consumed by rage and pain because of the manner of her death, and her reincarnated spirit is not looking for love but instead is seeking vengeance.

A common theme in reincarnation stories is that parallels are inevitable from one life to the next, and that is the case here. The body of Ivy Templeton, inhabited by the spirit of Audrey Rose, is fated to die by fire yet again, this time as the result of a hypnotic session that causes her to relive the moment of her previous death. The 1977 film version, based on the author's own screenplay, was quietly effective and much less sensational than most other horror films of that era. DeFelitta later wrote a sequel, *For Love of Audrey Rose* (1982), in which Audrey Rose's spirit is reincarnated yet again, but the melodramatic occultism and an over-the-top villain prevented it from achieving the same quiet effectiveness of its predecessor.

The Avalon Series Marion Zimmer Bradley and Diana L. Paxson (1982–2004)

Marion Zimmer BRADLEY's Darkover science fiction series had already become quite popular with fantasy fans, because the manner in which Bradley described her imaginary planetary society and the mental powers of the local inhabitants had much the feel of epic fantasy. Although she had written a few straightforward fantasy novels as well, it was not until *The Mists of Avalon* appeared in 1982 that she achieved best-seller status. The novel, which is quite lengthy, is an intricate and thoughtful reimagining of the legend of King Arthur and Camelot. Bradley employed a decidedly feminist perspective and chose Morgan Le Fay as her primary character in order to examine Arthur's rise and fall in very different terms from the traditional ones. She also avoided the usual subplots, turning instead to Celtic fantasy to create a brilliantly imagined world where druid priestesses reside in a magical realm hidden from the rest of us, interacting with those outside only when they so choose. The advent of Roman and Christian influences and their clashes with the native religion are a major subplot. The novel, in very condensed form, appeared as a television miniseries.

Although the novel stands by itself, Bradley decided to enhance the story by adding a prequel, *The Forest House* (1993). This gave her the opportunity to further explore the clash of cultures as Rome became a dominant power, this time focusing on the controversial love affair between a druid woman and a half-breed Roman soldier. Each must deal with divided loyalties in a society that tries to force them to make a clear-cut decision. Diana L. PAXSON was an uncredited collaborator and may also have worked on another prequel, *Lady of Avalon* (1997). Similar issues arise in this volume as well, but now the druids have acknowledged their inability to physically resist the Roman invasion, so instead they choose to retreat to magically protected islands and wait for the tide of foreign intervention to recede.

Paxson was acknowledged as a collaborator on the next in the series, *Priestess of Avalon* (2001). Bradley, who had become terminally ill, had discussed future volumes with her in great detail but probably contributed little if any of the actual prose. The plot is very similar to that of *The Forest House*, although the druid culture is explored in much more detail this time. Paxson has written a further installment on her own based on her conversations

with Bradley, and additional volumes may follow. *Ancestors of Avalon* (2004) is chronologically the earliest of all the titles, describing the arrival of the first druids in the British Isles following the destruction of their former home, Atlantis. Although none of the added volumes have achieved anything approximating the stature of *The Mists of Avalon*, they have all been well above average historical fantasies, particularly *The Forest House*.

Aycliffe, Jonathan (1949–)

Jonathan Aycliffe is the primary pseudonym of Dennis MacEion, who also writes in other genres as Daniel Easterman. The Aycliffe name was first used for *Naomi's Room* (1991), a powerful psychological ghost story in which a man struggles to reconcile the loss of his young daughter with the clear evidence that her spirit is still active in the world. The residual spirit of Jack the Ripper complicates matters and initially seems to intrude too much on the core story, but Aycliffe eventually resolves things quite neatly. *Whispers in the Dark* (1992) was also a ghost story, this time set in Victorian England. As with his first novel, Aycliffe suggests that ghosts vary from good to evil just as they did in life, but that these attributes might be pushed to their extremes following the transition.

Vanishment (1994) is the story of a haunted house on the Cornish coast. A writer and his wife begin to experience unusual emotional swings, apparently reliving tragic events that took place there years earlier. Although the story is a familiar one, Aycliffe does a superior job of letting his readers peer inside the minds of his characters and is equally skilled at evoking a quietly menacing atmosphere. There are no ghosts in *The Matrix* (1995), although in a sense its protagonist is haunted by his dead wife, driven by grief following her death to delve into obscure occult lore that nearly costs him his life. *The Lost* (1996) is a kind of vampire novel whose protagonist discovers that he is descended from the "strigoi," a race of eastern Europeans who have decidedly vampirelike habits. Although relatively short, the novel is filled with surprising revelations and develops its horrific theme systematically and effectively. It is Aycliffe's most impressive title to date.

The Talisman (1999) is a tale of possession. When a family moves into their new home, they take little notice of a statue that proves to be the focus for a supernatural entity that eventually begins to manipulate their thoughts and influence their actions. *A Shadow on the Wall* (2000) describes the aftermath of an exorcism, which unfortunately leaves the possessing spirit disembodied and very angry. *A Garden Lost in Time* (2004) is another complex ghost story.

Aycliffe writes almost exclusively in the Gothic tradition. There is more insinuation and suggestion than overt horror in his novels, which rely heavily on atmosphere, setting, and the psychological states of his characters. His fiction is largely in the tradition of M. R. JAMES and other early British horror writers, and his novels seduce readers gradually rather than grab them from the opening page. A short story, "Reiver's Lament" (1995), is also quite notable.

B

Bailey, Robin Wayne (1952–)

Robin Wayne Bailey made his debut with *Frost* (1983), the story of a woman in a typical fantasy world who combines the talents of warrior and sorceress, although early on she suffers a temporary loss of the latter power. An angelic figure gives her an artifact with which she will be able to summon a defense against evil forces, and fairly typical conflict follows. Frost is, however, a surprisingly complex character subject to considerable psychological stress. She is responsible for her father's death and is unable to relate well to her son. Bailey chronicled two subsequent adventures using the same protagonist. In *Skull Gate* (1985), with the army of demons weakened but still advancing, Frost undertakes a journey to hell itself, where she rescues a kidnapped princess and eventually defeats the major evil. She returned for a third adventure, *Bloodsongs* (1986), coming out of retirement with her magical powers renewed for one more battle. The Frost trilogy's quiet but detectible feminist theme probably contributed to its popularity.

Other than a few competent but not outstanding short stories, Bailey produced mostly derivative work for the next several years, tie-ins to computer games and an entry in the prepackaged shared universe series. The best of these was *Nightwatch* (1990), set in the Greyhawk game system universe. A mysterious force wipes out all of the magicians who would normally protect an isolated city, after which monstrous events begin to take place. An unmagical but determined member of the Night Watch, the local equivalent of a police force, steps in to save the day.

Bailey returned to original work with the Dragon trilogy, consisting of *Brothers of the Dragon* (1992), *Flames of the Dragon* (1994), and *Triumph of the Dragon* (1995). Two brothers are magically transported into what at first appears to be a standard fantasy world but that contains some interesting twists. Dragons and unicorns are associated with opposing forces in what is essentially a battle between good and evil, but for a change it is the dragons who are on the side of good and the unicorns who are the grotesquely evil creatures. Although they are reluctant to get involved in a conflict they do not understand, the interlopers are forced by circumstances to kill one of the unicorns shortly after arriving, which elevates them to involuntary hero status. Their subsequent adventures include a brief return to our reality and considerable temptation in the form of a beautiful enchantress who wants to divide their loyalties. The Dragonkin trilogy—*Wyvernwood* (2004), *Talisman* (2004), and *Undersky* (2005)—is a less impressive quest story set against the backdrop of a magical war.

Shadowdance (1996) is Bailey's single best work. A paralyzed man is given the magical ability to walk again but only if he dances every night. His dancing magically causes those around him to act out their fantasies in real life, some of which are violent, and ultimately he is forced to measure his own well-being against the harm he is doing to others. *Shadowdance* is a pleasantly intelligent and thoughtful fantasy that deserves more recognition than it has received. *Swords against the Shadowlands* (1998) was to have been the first of several novels based on the popular characters FAFHRD AND THE GRAY MOUSER, created by Fritz LEIBER, but no additional titles have appeared. Bailey continues to write occasional short fiction, of which "Cocoons" is his most notable effort.

Bangs, John Kendrick (1862–1922)

Despite the success of Terry PRATCHETT and Piers ANTHONY, humorous fantasy has not been able to maintain consistent popularity in the United States in recent years. Humor is even less common in the horror field. John Kendrick Bangs, who wrote under a variety of pseudonyms in addition to his own name, poked fun at both genres, and while much of his work has fallen into obscurity, his best efforts are still considered minor classics. Perhaps the most famous of these is the Houseboat sequence, consisting of *A House-Boat on the Styx* (1895), *The Pursuit of the Houseboat* (1897), and *The Enchanted Typewriter* (1899). The three books are written in a leisurely style that is no longer popular, recounting numerous conversations among the dead, both the famous and the obscure, as they reside in Bangs's sketchily described afterlife. The first two are novels of a sort, while the third is a series of interrelated stories involving a typewriter that allows the living to communicate with those who have passed on.

Bangs also wrote a substantial body of short stories, many of which are designed to invoke humorous rather than horrified responses. The best of his stories in this vein are collected in *The Water Ghost and Others* (1894) and *Ghosts I Have Met and Some Others* (1898). *Roger Camerden: A Strange Story* (1887) was his only straightforward horror novel, and it has largely been forgotten. *Toppleton's Client* (1893) is considerably better but still slight, as is his satirical look at biblical events, *The Autobiography of Methuselah* (1909). *Olympian Nights* (1902) is his only other novel of real merit, an account of the meeting between a modern man and the Greek gods. The best of his short fiction includes "The Water Ghost of Harrowby Hall" and "The Exorcism That Failed."

Barker, Clive (1952–)

Clive Barker's emergence as a major horror writer was accomplished in a fashion that had never been done before and has not been duplicated since. Although he had never published any supernatural fiction at all, he wrote a considerable body of short horror stories that were published in three volumes in 1984 as *The Books of Blood* and that collectively won the World Fantasy Award as best collection. The subject matter was frequently extreme, many of the plots were highly original, and with no previous history in the field at all his name was suddenly mentioned in the same breath as that of Stephen King. Three more volumes appeared the following year, which appeared in the United States as *The Inhuman Condition*, *Cabal*, and *In the Flesh*. *Cabal* is actually a short novel about a society of strange creatures living underground, which was filmed as *Nightbreed* in 1990. Although not quite as popular as the first set, the new stories were remarkable enough to ensure his continued status as a genre leader.

Barker's first full-length novel was highly anticipated, although it proved to be less impressive than his shorter work. *The Damnation Game* (1985) follows the exploits of a creature who lives disguised as a human being and who has the power to command the dead. The title refers to a form of supernatural gambling that affects the lives of several characters. Although the plot was original and the writing excellent, the novel was not nearly as intense as his short fiction. Barker's second novel, *Weaveworld* (1987), is a very long fantasy with some dark overtones. A large cast of characters battles for control of a magical carpet that contains the design for countless realities, including ours, woven into its intricate patterns. Manipulating the designs affects the worlds depicted, which makes it a potentially powerful weapon. *The Great and Secret Show* (1989), also very long, blends fantasy and horror in an uneasy mix that involves a method of consciously controlling evolution and the erosion of what we think of as reality. Barker was clearly not willing to remain just a horror writer, but he also avoided writing mainstream fantasy.

His next novel, *Imajica* (1991), was so long that it was later split into two volumes. This was more overtly a fantasy, reminiscent in some ways of the AMBER SERIES by Roger ZELAZNY. Our world is one of five separate realities, but for some reason we have been cut off from the others, which otherwise still communicate with one another. *Everville* (1994) is a sequel to *The Great and Secret Show* that, contrary to the usual fate of sequels, was actually somewhat better than its predecessor. *The Thief of Always* (1992) used much of the same imagery as his massive dark fantasies, but the horrors were probably unnecessarily toned down for its young adult target audience.

Several of Barker's novels were produced as movies, sometimes based on his screenplays or even directed by him. The most successful of these was *Hellraiser* (1987), followed by four sequels, which were based on the novella THE HELLBOUND HEART (1986), about a search for the ultimate pleasure, which opens the doorway between realities. Some of the visual imagery in the films is quite startling. *Cabal* was produced as *Nightbreed,* and "Rawhead Rex" (1984) became a routine monster movie, but "The Forbidden" (1985) inspired the above-average Candyman trilogy. "The Last Illusion" (1984) also came to the screen as the very disappointing *Lord of Illusion* (1995).

Barker continues to mix fantasy and horror motifs in long novels such as *Sacrament* (1996) and *Galilee* (1998), the latter a version of the story of Romeo and Juliet set between rival families, both of whom make routine use of magic. *Coldheart Canyon* (2001) involves a convalescing writer who discovers that he is sharing his temporary home with occult forces, and *Abarat* (2002) is another contemporary fantasy for young adults filled with magical devices, bizarre images, and hints of darkness. Barker's stature as a leading figure in horror fiction did not last long as it became obvious that he was writing material that did not clearly fit into any one genre. His later novels have been considerably less melodramatic, but no less inventive, and he is probably vastly underestimated as a writer and a fantasist. *The Essential Clive Barker* (1999) selects a representative sample of his best short fiction. He wrote only a handful of short stories during the 1990s, most of them less interesting than his early work.

Barrie, J. M. (1869–1937)

Sir James Matthew Barrie's first fantasy was an episodic, fictionalized version of his own life, *The Little White Bird* (1902), within which several magical stories are told, including one that would later be published separately as *Peter Pan in Kensington Gardens* (1906). The story was immensely popular, and Barrie subsequently transformed it into a play, which he revised on more than one occasion, with the final version appearing in 1928. A full-length novel followed, *Peter and Wendy* (1911), which has also appeared as *Peter Pan and Wendy* but more commonly just as *Peter Pan.* In 1908 he also wrote a short story that continued the story, "When Wendy Grew Up."

Although Barrie wrote a few other tales that contained fantastic elements, none were as successful and it is for this single work that he is remembered, although the others are of historical interest. In *Dear Brutus* (1917) a number of characters visit a magical wood and are transformed. *A Kiss for Cinderella* (1916) is a retelling of the classic children's story. *Mary Rose* (1920) involves magical time travel and ghosts and is the most readable of Barrie's plays. *Farewell, Miss Julie Logan* (1931) is also a ghost story.

Barrie was the product of an unhappy childhood, partly alienated from his mother after the death of his brother at an early age. He also had a peculiar relationship with his wife and suggested that he was forever arrested in his own childhood. Barrie's life became the subject of the motion picture *Finding Neverland* (2004), which concentrates more on Barrie's friendship with several young boys who became the inspiration for the character Peter Pan. The premise of a child who does not wish to grow up has been used by other authors since, most notably by Harlan ELLISON in "JEFFTY IS FIVE" (1979).

"The Bat Is My Brother" Robert Bloch (1944)

Although this is far from being one of the very best of Robert BLOCH's short horror stories, it has a particular distinction that makes it noteworthy. Vampire fiction has become almost a separate genre in recent years thanks in large part to the romantic novels of Anne RICE and others. The old image of vampires as unclean, repulsive creatures has largely given way to newer images. Vampires today are often charming and attractive, dark and mysterious, or are described as living in tribes hidden within human society, where they vary from good to bad, very much like living people. Even at their worst, the vampires of Anne Rice's novels are not wholly evil, and writers such as Les DANIELS and Chelsea Quinn YARBRO have created entire series of novels about vampires who are less evil than their human companions. Fred SABERHAGEN has even turned Dracula himself into a misunderstood creature with noble qualities.

This change has developed comparatively recently. Before the 1960s vampires were almost invariably evil. This 1944 short story by Bloch is probably the very first that had a sympathetic vampire as a narrator. Graham Keene awakens in a grave and emerges with no memory of what happened to him. He is greeted by a mysterious figure who insists they are both vampires and subsequently proves his point. The older vampire, who died in 1777, has concocted an elaborate plan to recruit more vampires and eventually seize control of the world from the living, a plan that is ultimately thwarted by Keene, who views his new existence with complete horror. He tricks his mentor and confines him in a coffin from which he cannot escape, where he will slowly rot away to nothingness while still conscious.

There are two other extraordinary features in the story. Most writers of vampire stories ignore the obvious mathematical progression of vampirism. If the victims all become converts, then it would only be a matter of time before the undead outnumbered the living. This is the pivotal point of the vampire villain's plot. Previously, vampires destroyed most of their victims' bodies in some fashion to avoid discovery. Now they will deliberately multiply. The premise that the world might become the playground of vampires would later be the basis of the classic *I Am Legend* (1954), by Richard MATHESON, and the anthology *Under the Fang* (1991), edited by Robert McCAMMON. This story was also one of the very first to partially rationalize vampires as nonsupernatural. Vampirism is characterized as a disease, not a curse, transmitted like rabies through a bite. Although Bloch does not follow through—his vampires do not cast reflections or shadows, for example—the interpretation that vampirism is a contagious disease has influenced many other authors.

Baudino, Gael (1955–)

Although Gael Baudino published a couple of marginally interesting short fantasies in the early 1980s, it was only after three novels appeared in 1988 and 1989 that she began to develop a following. *Dragonsword* (1988) was the opening volume of a trilogy that continued with *Duel of Dragons* (1991) and ended with *Dragon Death* (1992). Although a traditional fantasy in which two academics from our world find themselves in a typical fantasy realm, there were some interesting twists, including a universal form of amnesia that caused the entire population to forget events more than a few years into the past. We subsequently learn that the villains are planning to conquer the fantasy realm by using high-tech weaponry imported from our reality, although their plans are ultimately and predictably thwarted. Some of the imagery is quite dark, and the contrast between the two cultures is very well handled.

A second and more interesting series opened with *Strands of Starlight* (1989), a historical fantasy set during the time of the Inquisition, although in a world where elves really exist. The protagonist is a victim of rape, who is subsequently accused of witchcraft, who receives training as a warrior and is instrumental in defending her village. The mood of the novel is very dark, and that carries over into subsequent volumes. *Maze of Moonlight* (1993) turns its attention to the Crusades as the elves' numbers begin to dwindle, thanks in large part to persecution by the Inquisitors in *Shroud of Shadow* (1993). *Strands of Sunlight* (1994) transports the last of the elves through time to the present day, where magic may once again rise in the world. Several related short stories were collected as *Spires of Spirit* (1997). Although not strictly set in actual history, Baudino provides a chillingly effective description of the excesses of the Inquisition.

Baudino published one more trilogy, her best, which includes *O Greenest Branch!* (1995), *Branch and Crown* (1995), and *The Dove Looked In* (1996). The setting is the "Three Kingdoms," a world much like ours in which the "Righteous States of America" is on the brink of war with a mythical kingdom. The protagonists visit a magical library and become reluctantly involved with a prince whose secret identity is the Blue Avenger. Although slightly lighter in tone than her other series, the trilogy still features Baudino's preoccupation with the role of religion and her reservations about the effect of its influence on society. Her only solo novel, *The Gossamer Axe* (1990), is an entertaining but minor time travel fantasy.

Baum, L. Frank (1856–1919)

L. Frank Baum is, of course, best known for THE WIZARD OF OZ (1900), along with several sequels, a children's fantasy world so popular that other writers have been adding to the series ever since. Baum began writing for children in the late 1890s, but it was not until 1900 that the first Oz book appeared. Baum would go on to write 13 more in the series, not all of them involving the original characters, which greatly overshadowed his other children's fiction, some of which is equally charming.

The *Surprising Adventures of the Magical Monarch of Mo* (1900) appeared almost simultaneously with *The Wizard of Oz*. It has a similarly whimsical setting and an odd cast of characters but lacks the excitement and inventiveness of Oz. *Dot and Tot of Merryland* (1901) has a plot remarkably similar to Oz. Two children wander into a magical land consisting of seven valleys, make friends with the local queen, but suspect her motives when it comes time to leave. *The Master Key* (1901) is arguably science fiction, since the wonders are eventually explained scientifically. *The Life and Adventures of Santa Claus* (1902) is Baum's best known non-Oz book, an amusing look at how Santa organizes his annual expedition; he followed it up with the short "A Kidnapped Santa Claus" in 1904. In *The Enchanted Island of Yew* (1903) a magical being wishes to be transformed into a heroic human. Baum's remaining interesting non-Oz book was *Queen Zixi of Ix* (1905), in which a magical cloak helps a young boy become king.

It had become obvious by 1903 that the Oz books were what the reading public wanted, so Baum concentrated on them with mixed results, the later volumes generally being less interesting than the earlier ones as he ran low on fresh ideas to sustain them. Occasional other works continued to appear, including *The Sea Fairies* (1911) and its sequel, *Sky Island* (1912), although the latter had some connection with the Oz books. Baum's early short fiction for children is collected in *American Fairy Tales* (1901).

Beagle, Peter S. (1939–)

Peter S. Beagle's debut novel, *A Fine and Private Place* (1960), is a gentle and even sentimental fantasy of a type that has largely disappeared from contemporary fantasy literature. The setting is a cemetery in which dwell a diverse group of characters, both living and dead, including a talking raven. There is little physical action, and the story is largely told through the dialogue and interactions of the various characters in fairly static conditions, although extra tension is added by the apparent decision by a family to relocate one of the bodies. Since the ghosts are tied to the physical vicinity of their remains, this will separate a pair who have found true love in this gentle afterlife existence. Unfortunately, they are unable to communicate with their living relatives. Their affair is mirrored by another among the living. The novel remains very popular, and at the time there was considerable interest in Beagle's next work, although he would prove to be disappointingly unproductive for some time. Only one short story appeared during the next several years, "COME, LADY DEATH", in which death personified appears at a dinner party.

Beagle's second fantasy novel, *The Last Unicorn* (1968), drew upon a much different tradition. The unicorn of the title is the only one who remains free in a magical world, so she sets off on a quest to find others of her kind, her efforts intersecting the life of Schmendrick, a would-be magician with maturity problems. Their subsequent adventures are episodic and frequently amusing, and Beagle's understated prose style is highly effective. Ultimately, the unicorn is magically transformed into the shape of a young human woman for the confrontation with King Haggard, the brooding villain, which results in the rejuvenation of the land and the working out of the destinies of the various characters. Although it is clearly not meant to be taken too seriously, readers make definite emotional connections with the story, and the novel has remained quite popular. A full-length animated version was brought to the screen in 1982 but did not measure up to the written work.

"Lila the Werewolf" (1974) is an interesting urban fantasy, one of whose characters is a werewolf, although the story could not even remotely be considered horror. This short story is related to the novel *The Folk of the Air* (1986), in which the activities of an elaborate medievalist society are actually a partial mask for some genuinely magical events and powers. Although the novel is quite readable, it is disappointingly slight compared to Beagle's first two book-length fantasies. *The Innkeeper's Song* (1993) is an episodic, traditional fantasy adventure told in a very complex style and featuring several interlocked quest stories. The novel is very loosely related to *The Last Unicorn,* as are the contents of *Giant Bones* (1997), a collection of short stories. *The Unicorn Sonata* (1996) follows the adventures of a young girl who is transported into an alternate reality where unicorns actually exist.

Beagle's most recent novel is *Tamsin* (1999). A young American girl moves to England, where she soon meets a sociable 300-year-old ghost. Together they explore the world of the lingering dead as the ghost seeks her long lost lover and the living girl tries to find a purpose for living. At times reminiscent of *A Fine and Private Place* as well as *The Canterville Ghost* (1906) by Oscar Wilde, it is one of Beagle's most impressive efforts. He has also produced a number of outstanding short stories in recent years, including "A Dance for Emilia" (2000), in which a human spirit resides in a cat, and "Quarry" (2004). Most of his recent short work has been collected in *The Rhinoceros Who Quoted Nietzsche and Other Odd Acquaintances* (2003). Although the amount of work produced in a career that spans 45 years is comparatively small, the average quality is ex-

tremely high, and Beagle has long been regarded as a major fantasy writer, even when several years elapsed between new titles.

Beaumont, Charles (1929–1967)

Charles Beaumont was the pseudonym of the American writer Charles Nutt, who started writing science fiction in the early 1950s but who soon turned to supernatural and psychological horror and sometimes straightforward mystery stories, including his only novel. Beaumont was a prolific short story writer whose quality was consistently high. Many of his stories were adapted for television, for which he frequently wrote screenplays. He also scripted several movies, of which the most worthwhile are *The Seven Faces of Dr. Lao* (1964) and *Burn Witch Burn* (1961), based on novels by Charles G. Finney and Fritz LEIBER, respectively.

Beaumont's most famous story is "THE VANISHING AMERICAN" (1955), in which an inoffensive man fades slowly out of existence, a device that is taken up and examined in more detail in *The Ignored* by Bentley LITTLE (1997). A well-intentioned man inadvertently frees the devil himself from captivity in "THE HOWLING MAN" (1960), and the magical power of jazz is invoked effectively in "The Night Ride." Beaumont's ability to portray contemporary characters in extraordinary situations and to create an atmosphere of quiet horror rivaled that of Richard Matheson and the early Ray Bradbury, and his premature death following the onset of Alzheimer's disease while he was still in his 30s was tragic. Almost all of his stories are excellent, but titles of particular note include "The Beautiful People" (1952), "The Last Caper" (1954), "The Hunger" (1955), "The Crooked Man" (1955), and "Perchance to Dream" (1958).

Although his career lasted only 15 years, Beaumont produced enough outstanding short fiction to fill five collections, *Yonder* (1958), *The Hunger and Other Stories* (1958), *Night Ride and Other Journeys* (1960), *The Magic Man* (1965), and *The Edge* (1966). Later collections reshuffled these and added a few that had been overlooked, and most of his work can be found in *The Best of Beaumont* (1982), *The Howling Man* (1992), and *A Touch of the Creature* (1999). *Charles Beaumont:*

Selected Stories (1988) won the Bram Stoker Award for a short story collection.

The Beckoning Fair One Oliver Onions
(1911)
British writer Oliver ONIONS wrote several earnest contemporary novels before discovering supernatural fiction, and while he remained active in both areas for the remainder of his career, it is for his short ghost stories that he is best known. *The Beckoning Fair One,* which is considered by some critics to be the best ghost story ever written, is a novella that uses very subtle devices to create a chilling atmosphere, allowing the reader to watch the gradual change in the protagonist's personality.

Paul Oleron is a marginally popular writer who is halfway through writing what will probably be his most financially successful novel. On an impulse he rents a portion of an abandoned house, a place his close friend Elsie Bengough instinctively dislikes. Shortly after moving in, Oleron discovers window seats that have been nailed closed, inside one of which is the cover for a harp. After the initial move, he expects to resume work on his book, spurred on by his dwindling funds, but a pervasive lethargy prevents him from doing any further work, and at times he feels that the existing manuscript is worthless and must be discarded despite Elsie's insistence that it is the best he has ever written. This situation may well have influenced the character of Stephen KING's protagonist in *THE SHINING* (1977).

It is soon clear to the reader that something in the house wishes to keep Oleron for itself. Not only does he feel disinclined to go out, but Elsie is driven away by a series of unlikely accidents. Oleron's feelings toward her become generally callous and unfriendly, although at other times he realizes that he is being unfair. The creepy atmosphere continues to build, without any obvious menace manifesting itself. Oleron wakens one morning humming an unfamiliar tune, later identified as "The Beckoning Fair One," which was traditionally sung to the accompaniment of a harp. As in all houses, there are many strange noises at night, but he is frightened at one point by the unmistakable sound of a woman brushing her hair, even though he is alone.

Eventually Oleron is driven to inquire into the house's history. He discovers that the last tenant, an unmarried man who seldom went outdoors, was found starved to death, even though he was not poor. Determined to find the ghost, he becomes progressively more obsessed after observing a comb moving as though held by a human hand while cutting himself off from almost all external contact. His gradual psychological decline continues even when there are no overt signs of a supernatural presence in the house, for the haunting is now as much in his mind as in the physical building. Concerned for Oleron's well being, Elsie enters the house while Oleron is lying in bed, lost in a dream state and slowly starving to death. He is vaguely aware of her presence but loses consciousness, and an indefinite period of time passes before the authorities break in to discover a nearly comatose Oleron and Elsie's dead body.

As is the case with most of the best supernatural fiction, the true horrors take place inside the protagonist's mind. His slow submission to the wiles of the ghostly spirit, who is never identified or actually seen, is relentless and convincing and has an air of inevitability that draws the reader on even though it is clear that the destination is going to be an unpleasant one.

Bellairs, John (1938–1991)
John Bellairs was one of several writers of children's fantasy adventures who also enjoyed a following among adult readers, thanks to his unusual imagery and clever sense of humor. His first fantasy novel was *The Pedant and the Shuffly* (1968), an undistinguished but pleasant work about a battle against an evil magician. *The Face in the Frost* (1969) was much more successful, a wryly humorous alternate world historical fantasy. A rash of strange occurrences, including the appearance of a face during an unseasonable frost, alerts Roger Bacon to the presence of a villainous magician, whom he defeats only by reaching into our reality for the solution. The novel was quite well received, and Bellairs might have gone on to a successful career as an adult fantasist but instead turned to children's fiction for the balance of his life.

The House with a Clock in Its Walls (1973) introduced the recurring character of Chubby Lewis. Chubby's uncle recently purchased a sprawling house filled with secret passages and other wonderful features but that formerly belonged to a sorcerer who left behind some rather dangerous items as well. Chubby finds a magic amulet in *The Figure in the Shadows* (1975) and initially believes that it is a sign of good luck, but it in fact carries an ancient curse. *The Letter, the Witch, and the Ring* (1976) returns to the sorcerer's house, but Chubby Lewis gives way to a fresh set of characters. This loosely constructed trilogy is Bellairs's most successful work, but he abandoned the sequence entirely at that point in favor of a new recurring character.

The Treasure of Alpheus Winterborn (1978) introduced Anthony Monday, whose adventures in a mysterious house were reminiscent of those of Chubby Lewis. Anthony saves the world from destruction by way of another magical act in *The Dark Secret of Weatherend* (1984), and yet again in *The Lamp from the Warlock's Tomb* (1988). *Mansion in the Mist* (1992), the best in the series, sends the boy into an alternate world whose inhabitants are plotting to invade our reality. Bellairs mixed fantasy adventure and light humor effectively in the series but at times seemed to be cannibalizing his own earlier material.

Another recurring character, Johnny Dixon, made his debut in *The Curse of the Blue Figurine* (1983), in which he acquires a small statue that bears an inevitable curse. This would prove to be Bellairs' most extensive series, with eight volumes published during his lifetime plus four posthumous collaborations. The best of these are *The Trolley to Yesterday* (1989), which involves time travel, *The Eyes of the Killer Robot* (1986), and *The Chessmen of Doom* (1984).

Brad Strickland completed several of Bellairs's manuscripts after his death, including four with Johnny Dixons and three new adventures of Chubby Lewis. The latter three, *The Ghost in the Mirror* (1993), *Vengeance of the Witchfinder* (1993), and *The Doom of the Haunted Opera* (1995), are considerably better than the Dixons. Bellairs was a steady, skillful writer whose reputation might have been even greater had he been willing to use a broader variety of plots.

Bergstrom, Elaine (1946–)

Elaine Bergstrom made her debut with a vampire romance, *Shattered Glass* (1989), the first in a series of novels about the Austras, a family of the undead. Her vampires owe more to the film portrayal of DRACULA than to the original Bram Stoker novel, and her heroine is captivated by her inhuman lover despite his penchant for draining the blood of his other acquaintances. The sequel, *Blood Alone* (1990), is set against the backdrop of World War II, with the Austras clan struggling to protect the secret of their existence amid the chaos of war. Once again there is a strong romantic element, which grows even more pervasive in the next in the series, *Blood Rites* (1992). The fourth installment, *Daughter of the Moon* (1992), deals with a nobleman who is seduced by vampirism and suffers the consequences. At that point Bergstrom abandoned the series for a time but eventually returned to add a fifth volume, *Nocturne* (2003). Europe has become too dangerous a place for the surviving Austras, so they immigrate to the United States. Unfortunately, an old enemy is aware of their movement and follows in what is to date the best volume in the series.

Not all of Bergstrom's novels are about vampires. *A Tapestry of Dark Souls* (1993) is set in the shared universe of the Ravenloft game system and involves a tapestry that contains the physical presence as well as the artistic depiction of various monsters in its patterns. When the order of monks guarding the magical tapestry begins to dwindle, the possibility that the creatures might escape raises considerable alarm. *Baroness of Blood* (1995), also set in the Ravenloft universe, involves an aristocratic vampire and is much less interesting.

In 2004 Bergstrom began using the pseudonym Mira Kiraly for some of her novels. The first of these, *Mina* (1994), would later be reissued under her own name. The novel is a direct sequel to *Dracula* (1897) by Bram STOKER. Although Dracula himself is dead, Mina is still not free of the taint of his blood. Her struggles to return to normality are intertwined with a strong romantic theme in this and the sequel, *Blood to Blood* (2000), in which the Harkers are pursued by Dracula's vengeful sister. The two Mina novels are Bergstrom's strongest work. Her remaining two novels, both as Kiraly, are *Leanna* (1986), a moderately successful ghost story, and *Madeline* (1996), another strong effort in which Edgar Allan POE is prevailed upon to help one of the descendants of the Usher family from "THE FALL OF THE HOUSE OF USHER."

Bergstrom's only nonsupernatural fantasy novel is *The Door through Washington Square* (1998). After her great-grandmother becomes seriously ill and is confined to a hospital, a young woman moves into her house to manage the estate. Almost immediately, she discovers that one of the doorways leads back through time to the era of Aleister Crowley, with whom she subsequently becomes romantically and adventurously involved. Although clever at times, it lacks the intensity of most of her other fiction.

Beyond Any Measure Karl Edward Wagner (1982)

Although probably best known for his heroic fantasy, Karl Edward WAGNER also produced a considerable body of short supernatural fiction with contemporary settings, including this fine novella, which won the World Fantasy Award. Reincarnation is an infrequently used theme in contemporary horror, but Wagner here provides one of the best examples of how the resurgence of past life memories can have a devastating impact on the present.

Lisette is an American art student whose relocation to London has been accompanied by disturbing dreams, including a recurring one in which she awakens in a room filled with antique furniture. Once it becomes obvious that the dreams are not going away, she agrees to consult with a New Age psychologist, Dr. Ingmar Magnus. Although she is skeptical at first and does not plan to pay a second visit, the dreams grow even more intense, and she decides to seek his help. He hints that her dreams may contain evidence of a previous incarnation, or at least some form of occult knowledge of a different lifetime.

Magnus uses hypnosis to regress Lisette's mind into the past, when she was an English society woman named Elizabeth Beresford. The nightmares continue unabated by the therapy, and she considers terminating the sessions despite the enthusiasm Magnus is exhibiting because her case supports his theory of reincarnation. He responds by telling her that if she fails to discover the truth about Elizabeth, her own mental stability might be in jeopardy. Eventually, she decides to sever her relationship with Magnus anyway, convinced his efforts are hurting rather than helping her, and Magnus pretends to agree, although he maintains his hypnotic control over her.

Lisette's roommate is found dead, apparently a suicide, although the reader knows that it follows an encounter with someone who appeared to be Lisette physically, although with a different personality. This apparent anomaly is explained when we subsequently learn that Elizabeth Beresford's body is still alive, occupied by the soul of a vampirish being, and that her original soul has reincarnated itself as Lisette in order to destroy the vampire, which she eventually does, although she also dies in the process. Wagner's story is particularly successful because the reader never really understands what is happening until the final revelation but is never left so completely in the dark that it becomes difficult to follow what is happening at the moment.

"Bianca's Hands" Theodore Sturgeon (1947)

During the 1940s the distinctions that currently define science fiction, fantasy, and horror were less specific. Many writers wrote in all three forms, although usually their best work would tend to be of the same variety. Theodore Sturgeon was one of the rare exceptions, a highly skilled writer who produced westerns, detective fiction, and a historical novel in addition to his science fiction and fantasy. Although he is generally remembered now as a science fiction writer, he wrote some of the most memorable and literate horror stories of that period, including this highly atmospheric piece.

Bianca was born without will or intelligence in a fragile body whose only good feature was her hands, beautifully formed and with an animation missing from the rest of her body. They act like "beautiful parasites," draining all of the other energy from her person and refusing to do any physical labor except to groom themselves. Bianca lives with her mother in a decaying house where they are barely able to survive and are shunned by the rest of the community. That changes when they venture into a store and are spotted by Ran, a dull-witted but powerfully built young man who immediately becomes obsessed with Bianca's hands.

Ran rents a room in Bianca's house and eventually convinces her mother to let him marry Bianca. He and the hands have an odd relationship, and the hands now become flirtatious. On their wedding night he prepares everything in advance, then lies down with Bianca and allows her hands to move up over his body to his throat. In the morning Ran is dead, strangled, and Bianca's mother is arrested for the crime, since it would have been impossible for the girl to have done the deed. Her hands have lost their vitality and are now withered and paralyzed.

Sturgeon was famous for his ability to create multidimensional characters with a very economical use of words, and the three principal characters here are excellent examples. But the most interesting characters are the hands themselves, whose antics remain in the reader's mind long after the others have faded away.

Bierce, Ambrose (1842–1914?)

Ambrose Bierce is one of those writers whose life was so colorful and eccentric that he might well have been one of the characters in his own stories. He served in the military during the American Civil War, which left a deep impression on him and which is the setting for a great many of his short stories, became a journalist, spent a considerable period of time in Europe, and then disappeared in Mexico during its civil war in 1914.

Most collections of Bierce's short fiction mix supernatural and mundane fiction indiscriminately, but it is his stories of the fantastic and macabre for which he is most remembered. His most popular story is "AN OCCURRENCE AT OWL CREEK BRIDGE," in which a man experiences an entire sequence of imagined adventures in the split second that precedes his death. "THE DAMNED THING" describes efforts to identify and capture an invisible creature. "Moxon's Master" is a very early story of a device that would later be called a robot.

"A Tough Tussle" is more ambiguous. A Union soldier horrified by the dead is forced to man a position near the body of a Confederate, and in the morning he has been killed and mutilated in a similar fashion. "AN INHABITANT OF CARCOSA" features a man wandering a desolate land who finds his own grave and realizes that he is dead. Revenge from beyond the grave is also the theme of "The Middle Toe of the Right Foot." "The Eyes of the Panther" involves a woman who changes into the form of a panther. Several of Bierce's other stories are traditional, though unremarkable, ghost stories, and others end ambiguously, leaving it to the reader to decide whether the supernatural was involved.

Bierce also wrote some fantasies, mostly in the form of fables and allegories, the best of which can be found in *Cobwebs from an Empty Skull* (1874) and *Fantastic Fables* (1899). *The Devil's Dictionary* (1911) is an excellent nonfantastic satire. Although only a few of his individual short stories are outstanding, the lesser work remains interesting because of its authentic depiction of life during the Civil War.

"The Black Cat" Edgar Allan Poe (1843)

Edgar Allan POE was the first major American horror writer, and several of his stories, including this one, are acknowledged classics of the supernatural. This particular story begins with a statement by the narrator, who professes to have been a gentle man all of his life and one who loved animals almost as much as he did his human companions. His marriage was a happy one and, since his wife shared his fondness for animals, they had several pets, including a jet black cat named Pluto, who was the narrator's particular favorite.

As the years passed the narrator fell prey to alcoholism and became increasingly abusive to his wife and the animals, until finally in one drunken fit he cut out one of Pluto's eyes. Although remorseful the following day, he soon succumbs to the temptations of drink once again. Eventually, he gives in to a perverse impulse—a recurring theme in Poe's fiction—and hangs the cat from a tree. Shortly thereafter his house burns to the ground, and among the ruins is a burnt patch that accurately depicts a cat hanging by a noose around its neck.

A short time later the narrator encounters another cat, remarkably similar to Pluto and also lacking one eye, which follows him home and seems affectionate, although he feels a growing aversion to the animal, perhaps because it reminds him of his guilt. The markings on the cat's chest resemble a gallows, a portent of things to come. In a moment of ungoverned rage, he kills his wife, then walls her up in the basement, working cleverly so that there is no evidence that the existing structure was altered. Unfortunately, while police are searching the house, they are alerted by the scream of the cat, which he inadvertently walled up with his wife's corpse.

Although there is clearly a supernatural element in this story, it is chiefly concerned with the psychology of the protagonist, who is essentially trapped by his own guilt, guilt which made him acquire the cat in the first place and probably subconsciously prevented him from realizing that the cat had been left inside the makeshift tomb. It is one of Poe's most subtle and effective stories and an enduring classic of literature.

The Black Cauldron Lloyd Alexander (1965)

The Black Cauldron is actually the second title in the Prydain series by Lloyd ALEXANDER, although it is the best-known because of the 1985 animated movie version, which actually covers the events in that novel and in the first in the series, *The Book of Three* (1964). Prydain is a mythical land where magic works, but it is based in large part on Wales and Welsh legends. In the first volume we are introduced to Taran, an assistant pig keeper who is a young boy with big ambitions who wants to be a hero and fight for his people. Taran meets several other characters who will eventually play a larger part in later volumes, and their early interactions are often enlivened by Alexander's subtle but witty sense of humor. We also learn that everyone and every occupation have value and that artisans are just as important as warriors.

The series borrows heavily from mythic stereotypes. Like Merlin, Gandalf, or Dumbledore, Dallben is the wise old man who imparts wisdom but who cannot fight young Taran's battles for him. Taran resembles Frodo, the young Arthur, or even Luke Skywalker, an innocent with good intentions who will be tested greatly. Alexander adds some original characters in support, including some unusual witches and a traveling troubadour whose part-time job is to be king, and then sets his heroes in opposition to an evil force determined to rule them all, in this case the Horned King.

The tone turns much darker in *The Black Cauldron,* as we learn that the good characters are not necessarily going to survive to the end, that there is some good and bad in each of us, and that even decent people may falter and commit an evil act. The cauldron is a magical artifact that allows the evil army to replenish itself by animating the bodies of fallen soldiers, and Taran seeks to destroy it in order to reduce the enemy's resources. The remaining three titles in the series, which bring the conflict to a conclusion, are *The Castle of Llyr* (1966), *Taran Wanderer* (1967), and *The High King* (1968). Alexander also wrote some shorter works set in Prydain.

Black Easter James Blish (1967)

The vast majority of James Blish's published work was science fiction, including the classic novel *A Case of Conscience* (1958), in which he examined the possibility that Satan might share the power of creation with God. This novel was part of a thematic set with the historical novel *Dr. Mirabilus* (1964) and two novels of supernatural horror, *Black Easter* and *The Day after Judgment,* the latter two consisting of one continuous story. The overall title for the four novels was *After Such Knowledge.*

Black Easter was first published in serial form as *Faust Aleph Null.* The two major characters are Theron Ware, a modern-day wizard who uses black magic to pursue knowledge, and Baines, a wealthy but bored entrepreneur who hires Ware to release a number of demons from hell for a single night's rampage. The underlying premise to what follows is that God is, in fact, dead, a device used again with considerable effect in *Towing Jehovah* (1994) and two sequels by James MORROW. The freed demons wreak great devastation, but when it is time for them to return to hell, they refuse to go. Ware protests because their advent was supposed to have been preceded by the Antichrist, but the demons tell him that the old laws are no longer in effect and that the Antichrist is unnecessary because "God is dead," thus ending the first volume on a shocking note.

The second half, *The Day after Judgment* (1971), fails to live up to its predecessor, probably inevitably given the obvious anticlimactic nature of the story. Satan's forces have created a new city on Earth, and efforts by the military to destroy it are complete failures. Blish does offer some hope for the survivors. The death of God has left a power vacuum that Satan must fill, but to do so properly he must abandon his former evil nature and become a benevolent deity. The two-part novel is particularly effective because of Blish's matter of fact, almost journalistic, narrative style, which adds credibility to an otherwise incredible plot.

Blackwood, Algernon (1869–1951)

Algernon Blackwood was one of the early British ghost story writers, and the majority of his most famous works fall into the horror genre, although he also wrote several fantasies based on pagan beliefs. He was an interesting figure in his own right, widely traveled and involved in various occult organizations. His series of stories about John Silence, who specialized in occult investigations, was the first notable psychic detective series and has been imitated by numerous writers since, including Seabury QUINN, William Hope HODGSON, and Charles L. GRANT.

Blackwood made an impressive start with three collections of short stories, *The Empty House and Other Ghost Stories* (1906), *The Listener and Others* (1907), and *John Silence: Physician Extraordinary* (1908). Within a few years he began to emphasize mystical fantasy, as shown in *The Lost Valley and Others* (1910), *The Centaur* (1911), and *Pan's Garden* (1912). Blackwood's fondness for natural settings is particularly evident in these books, which involve such diverse topics as a living spirit of the Earth and the power of sound as a means of controlling the universe. Several classic stories appeared during this period, including "THE WILLOWS," "The Insanity of Jones," "THE WENDIGO," and "ANCIENT SORCERIES." Most of the stories are quite understated by modern standards, relying

more on mood and suggestion than overt action or detailed description.

Blackwood's short fiction continued to be strong in the years that followed, but only "A Descent into Egypt" stood out. His fascination with reincarnation and the occult manifested itself in *Julius LeVallon* (1916), which is quite complex and successful but a type of story no longer in fashion. The sequel, *The Bright Messenger* (1921), was much less interesting. *The Wave* (1916) is also a routine novel of reincarnation and the survival of love across the ages. *Day and Night Stories* (1917) underlined the shift in Blackwood's emphasis, relying much more on mystical and occult themes than on the supernatural.

Dudley and Gilderoy (1929) is a talking animal fantasy about a cat and a parrot, is surprisingly witty and sophisticated, and is one of Blackwood's best book-length efforts. Blackwood's later stories were always competently done but lacked the originality and strong impact of his early work. He was also the author of several fantasies for children, although they were invariably more popular with adults than their apparently intended younger audience.

Blaylock, James P. (1950–)

James Blaylock began his writing career with a couple of minor short stories during the 1970s, followed by several witty but fairly conventional fantasy novels. *The Elfin Ship* (1982) was clearly influenced in part by J. R. R. TOLKIEN, but Blaylock mixed airships and other technology with a world of elves, goblins, and similar creatures of legend to create a landscape with a character all its own. Villainous magic is interfering with trade, so a perky hero helps foil the plot, although only after an amusing series of adventures. *The Disappearing Dwarf* (1983) continues the story, with the protagonist and a party of adventurers searching for riches following the discovery of a treasure map. Both novels are entertaining light fantasies that only hinted at the more polished work that would follow. Blaylock returned to this setting several years later to add a prequel, *The Stone Giant* (1989), a quest story with an evil witch and a decidedly more sinister tone. The sense that evil is a tangible force developed into a recurring theme that would be reflected in most of Blaylock's work during the 1990s.

The Digging Leviathan (1984) is also quite playful despite a more serious tone. The protagonist is a boy born with webbed fingers and the magical ability to create worlds from his imagination. When he discovers the books of Edgar Rice Burroughs, he decides to create similar environments, which do not always turn out exactly as intended. *Homunculus* (1986) is a fascinating Victorian fantasy about the efforts by a scientist to bring the dead back to life or to create artificial life from nothing, in this case in the form of a homunculus—an animated human form enlivened by unnatural means. The novel won the Philip K. Dick Award and was followed by an episodic and less-satisfying sequel, *Lord Kelvin's Machine* (1992), which blends magic with time travel paradoxes.

Land of Dreams (1987) is a contemporary fantasy involving three friends who investigate the results of a rare astrological conjunction that frays the barrier between the waking world and the one we enter when we dream. The evil carnival sequences are particularly effective. In *The Last Coin* (1988), one of Blaylock's best novels, a monomaniac has gathered together all but one of the silver coins given to Judas to betray Christ. If he acquires the last one, the world will end, but it is being held safe by a man living in a magical house. One of the characters in this unusually inventive novel is eventually identified as the Wandering Jew. Even better is *The Paper Grail* (1991), a diffuse but very moving story that mixes a mildly mysterious death with the discovery of an odd machine that seems to have no function. The author introduces a number of disparate plot elements and ties them up very efficiently.

Night Relics (1994) is a contemporary ghost story, although more mysterious than terrifying. Blaylock also invokes a ghost in *Winter Tides* (1997), but in this case the supernatural becomes almost a peripheral issue in a story of murder and other villainy. *All the Bells of Earth* (1995) is a deal-with-the-devil story whose protagonist is searching the world for a means to recover his soul. He finds his destiny in a small California town that is the focus of a monumental mystical battle. A young boy has the unique ability to perceive the supernatural around us in *The Rainy Season* (1999), Blaylock's most recent novel.

Although not a prolific short story writer, Blaylock has produced at least one first-rate story, "Paper Dragons" (1985), which won a World Fantasy Award. "Two Views of a Cave Painting" (1988) is also quite good, and "Thirteen Phantasms" (1997) won another World Fantasy Award. His short fiction has been collected in *The Pink of Fading Neon* (1986), *The Shadow on the Doorstep, with Trilobyte* (1987), and *Thirteen Phantasms and Other Stories* (2000), of which the last is the most comprehensive. *The Magic Spectacles* (1991) is a children's fantasy.

Bloch, Robert (1917–1999)

Robert Bloch is best-known to the general public as the author of the psychological suspense novel *Psycho* (1959), the basis for the famous Alfred Hitchcock movie filmed the following year. Bloch was a prolific writer, particularly at shorter length, and had been active since the 1930s, contributing to a variety of pulp magazines under his own name and others'. Throughout his career Bloch intermixed fantasy and horror, science fiction and non-fantastic suspense, supernatural and sometimes even ambiguous story elements, and his many collections rarely fall into a single category. Those listed in the bibliography of this volume are the ones most predominantly fantasy or supernatural horror, but individual stories in those genres can also be found in collections that were packaged as science fiction.

Bloch's first published short story was "Lilies" (1934), and he sold more than 100 more stories during the next 10 years. Much of his early work was heavily influenced by that of H. P. LOVECRAFT and bore melodramatic titles such as "The Feast in the Abbey" (1934), "The Shambler from the Stars" (1934), and "The Fane of the Black Pharaoh" (1937). A few of his early stories were fantasies, most notably "The Black Kiss" (1937), written with Henry KUTTNER, but during the 1940s most of his fantasy became lighter, generally humorous adventures. The best of his fantasy fiction can be found in the collection *Dragons and Nightmares* (1969) and the novel *The Big Binge* (1955), which appeared in book form as *It's All in Your Mind.* The novel features a young man who acquires a number of psychic powers while out drinking, further complicated by the arrival of various amusingly portrayed villains including vampires and communists. Bloch would continue to write short fantasy fiction sporadically, but it was never a significant part of his work, which became primarily supernatural and/or psychological suspense. The best of his nonhorror work is "That Hell-Bound Train" (1958), which won the Hugo Award as best story of the year from the World Science Fiction Convention, one of the first fantasies ever to win that honor. The story is a deal-with-the-devil variation and one of the very best examples of its type.

Bloch's first collection of horror stories, *The Opener of the Way,* appeared in 1945. Although some of the stories are crude by his later standards, there is a raw power to many of them that has ensured their continued popularity. Among the best in the collection are the title story, "THE OPENER OF THE WAY", which concerns an Egyptian tomb, "YOURS TRULY, JACK THE RIPPER" (1943), wherein an immortal Jack the Ripper claims new victims in Chicago, and "The Dark Demon" (1936), whose protagonist is a transparent image of fellow writer Lovecraft. A follow-up collection did not appear until 1960, when the same publisher issued *Pleasant Dreams,* whose contents were generally of much better quality. The outstanding stories this time included the classics "THE CHEATERS" (1947), "The Hungry House" (1951), the animated piano of "Mr. Steinway" (1954), and "That Hell-Bound Train".

Bloch's popularity jumped dramatically following *Psycho,* and no less than twelve new collections appeared during the 1960s containing some new material and a large but not exhaustive selection of his earlier work. Most of the stories from the first two collections were reprinted, as well as many excellent but overlooked stories such as "THE SKULL OF THE MARQUIS DE SADE" (1945) and "The Ghost Writer" (1940). The collection *Blood Runs Cold* (1961) contained primarily nonfantastic stories, but others such as *Nightmares* (1961), *More Nightmares* (1961), and *Yours Truly, Jack the Ripper* (1962) reshuffled the older stories from Bloch's earlier collections, which had been available only in hardcover editions. *Bogey Men* (1963), despite

the title, is predominantly fantasy and very light horror. The remaining collections from this period are uneven, mixing more recent work with older stories, some of them better left in obscurity. Bloch wrote several novels during this period and would continue to do so throughout the rest of his career, but almost all of these were nonfantastic thrillers, including two sequels to *Psycho,* neither of which had any connection to the movie sequels.

Bloch's short fiction appeared less frequently from the 1970s onward. A three-volume set of his short fiction contains most of his better stories, consisting of *Bitter Ends, Final Reckonings,* and *Last Rites,* all published in 1988. Additional collections of merit include *The Best of Robert Bloch* (1977) and *Cold Chills* (1977). Two new collections of his oldest work also appeared. *The Early Fears* (1993) is a general selection, while *Mysteries of the Worm* (1981) gathers together his Lovecraftian pastiches. "THE SCENT OF VINEGAR" (1994) won the Bram Stoker Award.

Bloch did write a few book-length supernatural works. The first of these was *Strange Eons* (1979). H. P. Lovecraft and other writers who contributed to his Cthulhu Mythos, which became an early shared universe, always described efforts to recall the alien beings that once ruled the Earth but never considered the possible consequences of their return to power. Bloch addressed that issue headlong in this suspenseful story, in which a group of people discover that Lovecraft's fiction was based on fact and that the conquest of humanity is at hand. *Lori* (1990) was somewhat more ambiguous. The title character loses her parents to a brutal murderer on the day of her high school graduation, after which a psychic warns her that two men will enter her life and that one of them will kill her if she does not take desperate measures. The supernatural element is minimal but crucial to the plot. *The Jekyll Legacy* (1990), written with Andre NORTON, suggests that Edward Hyde may have survived despite the death of Dr. Jekyll.

Many of Bloch's short stories were adapted for television, and he also wrote movie screenplays and adaptations including *The Couch* (1962), from his own novel, *The Cabinet of Dr. Caligari* (1962), *The Deadly Bees* (1967), and *The House That Dripped*

Blood (1970). During the 1940s he also wrote for radio. He was an unusually accessible author, often responding to letters from fans and contributing to amateur journals. His wry sense of humor and gift for the macabre have rarely been equaled.

"The Bones Wizard" Alan Ryan (1984)

There is an infrequent but recurring theme of music in modern horror fiction, particularly rock music, which has led to at least three anthologies of rock-oriented short fiction and several bad horror movies as well as one of the classic novels in the genre, *Armageddon Rag* (1983) by George R. R. MARTIN. Other writers have turned to other forms of music—folk and country in the Silver John series by Manly Wade WELLMAN, jazz in "Night Ride" (1957) by Charles BEAUMONT and *The Blues Ain't Nothin* (2002) by Tina L. Jens, and classical in *Angel of Darkness* (1990) by Charles DE LINT. Alan Ryan contributed another significant story to this tradition with "The Bones Wizard," which involves Irish folk music and which won the World Fantasy Award.

The protagonist is Sean, whom we first see as a child so obsessed with music that his mother is convinced it will eventually be the death of him. Not a day passes that he does not go off on his own for at least a little while and make music in some form. Ryan then presents the rest of Sean's life in a series of flashbacks and flash forwards, so that his story fills itself in like a mosaic. As he grows older his love of music becomes stronger, not weaker, leaving little room for other concerns—love, a career, or even friendship. Although he is talented with many instruments, the one for which he has a particular affinity is a folk instrument known as the "bones," literally constructed from them to make an unusual and distinctive percussive sound.

Sean is never satisfied with inferior materials, an insistence that pays off as he becomes a respected member of an Irish folk band. His quest for perfection takes him to a mysterious man who has the reputation of making the very best "bones" that can be had, instruments so well crafted that there is a kind of magic in the sound they produce. Although we do not learn the truth until the final paragraphs, this is a kind of deal-with-the-devil

story, for the catch is that the only way that Sean can acquire the perfect instrument for his needs is through sacrificing his own leg bones. Although there is only a hint of the fantastic in the story, it leaves the reader with a haunting, even unsettling, image. Ryan wrote several other high-quality stories, but none of them ever rivaled this understated classic.

"The Book" Margaret Irwin (1935)

Although Margaret Irwin was popular during her lifetime as an author of historical novels, it is for her comparatively small body of ghost stories and occult fiction that she has been best remembered. This is the most famous of her stories, a cleverly constructed and altogether eerie tale of a man who discovers that there is some knowledge best left undiscovered.

Mr. Corbett is happily married with three children, a successful investment broker who often reads himself to sleep at night. For this purpose the family has accumulated a bookcase full of odds and ends, including a selection of very old books that they acquired at a rummage sale. One evening Corbett chooses a book from the second shelf, but changes his mind. When he returns to exchange the book, he notices a gap much wider than can be accounted for by his own withdrawal, which leaves him vaguely disturbed, although in the morning the books are all tightly packed once again. In fact, one of his daughters insists that that particular shelf is always full, no matter how many books are taken away.

Corbett begins to notice another change in his life. The books he formerly enjoyed and the authors he once admired now seem to be laden with hidden meaning, snide commentaries, hidden cruelty, and implied perversions. No matter what he reads, even the most innocuous material betrays the deviousness of the writer, and Corbett finds himself reading compulsively in an effort to ferret out their secrets. This sour attitude spreads into his personal relationships with his family and with his business associates.

Eventually, Corbett finds another book on the shelf, one written by hand and in Latin. Curious, he begins to translate it, discovering that it is a rambling philosophical text or perhaps a description of an odious secret society. His next discovery is even more startling, for the book is still being written. Every night a line or two is added at the end, and the new remarks seem to be directed at him. He follows their veiled advice, and his business efforts begin to prosper as never before, although his peers are increasingly distrustful of him.

As is usually the case with horror stories of this sort, there is a price to be paid. The book begins requiring that he perform minor obscenities, and when he balks, his stream of good luck falters. Properly chastised, he does as he is told, rationalizing his actions under this supernatural compulsion. He begins to have doubts when it tells him to kill the family dog, which has been avoiding him, but attempts to do so anyway, thwarted by the intercession of one of his daughters, who appears to have some insight into what is going on. Then the book orders him to kill her, and at last he finds the strength to resist and even destroy the book, although the effort is so great that he dies of the strain. Irwin's depiction of his gradual subversion by greed and curiosity is masterful, and the story is one of the classic tales of occult possession.

The Borrowers Series Mary Norton
(1952–1982)

A former stage actress, Mary Norton turned to writing children's books with *The Magic Bed-Knob* (1943) and its sequel, *Bonfires and Broomsticks* (1947), which together became the inspiration for the 1971 Disney movie *Bedknobs and Broomsticks,* but she is best known for the five adventures of the Borrowers, a race of tiny human beings who live hidden inside the house of a normal family, surviving by "borrowing" what they need. They made their debut in *The Borrowers* (1952), a charming story in which we learn that they hide because terrible things happen whenever they are discovered by normal-sized people.

They returned in *The Borrowers Afield* (1955). When the human residents of the house begin to suspect that the mysterious disappearances of food and other items are the work of rats, they call in an exterminator, so the Borrowers are forced to abandon their home under a grandfather clock and find

their way in the unknown outside world. Various difficulties force them to move again in *The Borrowers Afloat* (1959), and they are finally discovered by humans in *The Borrowers Aloft* (1961), one of whom imprisons two of their number for use as a tourist attraction. The others contrive a clever rescue plan fraught with mild dangers and considerable humor. Norton returned after a 20-year gap to add *The Borrowers Avenged* (1982), the weakest of the set and largely a retelling of the previous two volumes.

The Complete Adventures of the Borrowers (1967) only includes the first four titles. Norton's only other fantasy book was the very short *Are All the Giants Dead?* (1973). Her 1945 short story, "Paul's Tale," is horror. There have been several imitators of the Borrowers stories, of which the most successful is the Littles series by John Peterson.

Boston, Lucy M. (1892–1990)

The British author Boston is known primarily as the author of the Green Knowe series of gentle children's fantasies, all of which take place in the environs of the estate named in the title. In *The Children of Green Knowe* (1954), a contemporary family lives a pleasant life despite the presence in their home of ghosts of a past generation. In fact, the ghosts provide some insulation between the protagonists and the sometimes disturbing outside world, as we see in the sequel, *The Chimneys of Green Knowe* (1958, also published as *The Treasure of Green Knowe*). One of the family's most valuable paintings has been loaned to a museum, and the ghosts associated with it are forced to follow along.

The children discover that there is strangeness outside the walls as well when they make a voyage of discovery in *The River at Green Knowe* (1959), and a missing gorilla takes refuge on the grounds of the haunted house in *A Stranger at Green Knowe* (1961). *An Enemy at Green Knowe* (1964) is considerably darker than the earlier titles and probably the best in the series. The children investigate the secrets of magic while pitting their wits against a witch who is plotting against them. *The Stones of Green Knowe* (1976) is partially set during the 12th century, when the house was first constructed.

A young boy discovers that he has a limited ability to travel back and forth through time.

Boston, who spent much of her life restoring old houses and their grounds, made buildings and gardens such a vivid part of her novels that they are almost characters themselves. Two other children's fantasies have very similar themes. In *Guardians of the House* (1974) a young boy is brought to a sprawling, apparently deserted mansion by a woman and left to explore, and he discovers that many of the furnishings have magical powers. There is little actual plot, just a series of episodic encounters. More interesting is *The Castle of Yew* (1958), in which two boys explore a magical garden partially laid out as a chessboard and find themselves magically reduced in size, providing some low-key thrills as they encounter animals and insects.

As with the similar writer Edward EAGER, Boston seems to go through brief periods of popularity separated by longer intervals of neglect. She also wrote several other titles for very young children, some of which have marginal fantastic elements.

"The Bottle Imp" Robert Louis Stevenson (1896)

Robert Louis Stevenson was the author of several classic adventure stories, but he is also remembered for the classic horror tale DR. JEKYLL AND MR. HYDE (1888) and a handful of short stories of the supernatural of which this is the most famous. In form this is a variation of the deal-with-the-devil story, of which there would later be so many variations that the device has become a genre cliché. Stevenson's devil is an imp imprisoned in an ornate bottle who grants any wish made by its owner, although usually with some undesired consequences.

There is a way to beat the curse. Whoever dies with the bottle in his or her possession is doomed to hell, but it is possible to sell it beforehand and escape that fate. There are rules to the transaction, however. The buyer must know the terms of the curse or the sale is void, and the purchase price must always be lower than the price the seller originally paid. The protagonist is Keawe, a Hawaiian who encounters the bottle's current owner by chance. Although skeptical, he pur-

chases the imp and wishes for a mansion on the coast of one of the islands. Returning home, he discovers that his uncle and his cousin both died in separate incidents, that his uncle had accumulated an unsuspected fortune in recent years, and that Keawe is now the sole heir. Before long, an impressive house is under construction, and Keawe, convinced that he is set for the balance of his life, sells the bottle to his friend, Lopata, who wishes to own a sailing ship.

Having escaped the curse, Keawe meets and falls in love with Kokua, a beautiful young girl who soon reciprocates his affection. But just as his life seems complete, Keawe discovers that he has contracted leprosy and is thus barred from marrying the woman he loves. His only hope is to recover the bottle from Lopata, wish himself free of the taint, then sell it again. Unfortunately, the imp has passed through numerous hands by now, and when Keawe finally tracks it down, he is forced to buy it for one cent. Although he is cured and marries Kokua, his happiness is corrupted by the knowledge that he is doomed to damnation. This gloom begins to affect the marriage, until he finally tells Kokua the truth.

Kokua suggests that they go to another island where the currency includes centimes, or fractions of a cent. Unfortunately, the restriction that they must describe the curse prevents them from finding a buyer until Kokua, who feels guilty about the sacrifice Keawe made for their love, hires someone to buy the imp for four centimes, after which she purchases it for three. Keawe discovers what she has done and returns the favor, but the drunken villain who acts as his agent refuses to relinquish the imp, convinced that he is going to hell anyway so he might as well enjoy the remainder of his life.

The establishment of clear rules for the fantastic element adds a structure that is often absent from modern horror tales. The complexity of the situation and the clarity of the solution have rarely been equaled in the many similar stories published since Stevenson's classic.

"Bottle Party" John Collier (1941)

Genies, or djinn, rarely appear outside Arabian Nights–style fantasies, and when they do, they usually take one of two forms. A few writers such as Tim POWERS emphasize their inhuman cruelty and powers, as in his excellent novel *Declare* (2001), but most prefer to emphasize their humorous side, and, in fact, many genie stories are essentially variations of the deal-with-the-devil type, in which the human attempts to make a trick-proof wish while the genie strives to trip him up. F. Anstey established that formula with his classic *The Brass Bottle* (1900), and many writers have attempted variations, though only a few have found a really original twist.

The best of these is this classic story by John Collier. Franklin Fletcher is a frustrated man. He has long sought the company of beautiful women, but all to no avail. On the verge of surrendering all hope, he decides to take up another hobby and visits an antique store in search of inspiration. The owner, who insists Fletcher is his very first customer, has a number of curious items, but the most curious of them all is a collection of bottles, in each of which is imprisoned one entity or another, including a variety of genies and the most beautiful woman in the world.

Fletcher eventually purchases one of the genies, takes him home, unstoppers the bottle, and wishes for an immense palace filled with beautiful women. The genie immediately supplies everything requested and seems perfectly content to serve his new master, but Fletcher quickly grows bored, because he has obtained his wealth and the attention of beautiful women too easily. He wishes the latter away and begins a search for the one perfect girl, rejecting one after another until the genie reminds him that the shopkeeper owns a bottle containing the most beautiful woman in the world.

No sooner said than done, and Fletcher feels fulfilled at last. It is only now that the genie shows his wiles, flirting with the woman behind his master's back and enlisting her aid in his project. She no longer protests when told to return to her bottle; in fact, she seems happy to go away, and the genie suggests to Fletcher that perhaps she is not alone in there, that she has some man waiting for her. Enraged, Fletcher calls her forth, then enters the bottle himself, with the predictable result that he is caught and the genie and the girl live happily ever after. Fletcher's new home is sold to a pair of

sailors, who are decidedly unhappy when they uncork it, expecting to find a beautiful woman. Collier tells his little tale economically and neatly and clearly illustrates the point that it is best to quit while you are still ahead.

Boyer, Elizabeth (1913–2002)

Elizabeth Boyer was one of the more interesting of the crop of new fantasy writers who emerged during the 1980s. Although her plots were very similar to those of her contemporaries, she employed a quiet but pervasive sense of humor that enlivened her stories, all of which are set in the magical world of Alfar, although they are arranged in three separate sequences. The first series consists of *The Sword and the Satchel* (1980), *The Elves and the Otterskin* (1981), *The Thrall and the Dragon's Heart* (1982), and *The Wizard and the Warlord* (1984). This set of four follows the adventures of Kilgore, a young man who wants to be a hero and who masters the use of a magical sword but who is somewhat put off when he discovers the strength and numbers of his enemies. He survives a series of adventures, captures, and pursuits, gaining the enmity of an evil sorcerer, getting caught up in an imminent war, and encountering zombies, trolls, giants, and a host of other legendary creatures before finally saving the day.

A second series of four novels followed, the Wizards' War series, beginning with *The Troll's Grindstone* (1986), which is essentially a more polished version of her first two novels with a new set of characters. *The Curse of Slagfid* (1989) is less interesting, with its heroes tricked into helping a wizard with bad intentions, but the pace picks up in *The Dragon's Carbuncle* (1990) and climaxes in *The Lord of Chaos* (1991), Boyer's best novel, hinting at an apocalyptic war that might end the world.

Boyer's most recent sequence is less ambitious. *The Clan of the Warlord* (1992) is set in the aftermath of that war and is a rather routine quest adventure. *The Black Lynx* (1993) is the author's darkest book and somewhat slow paced, but her protagonist is a much more fully rounded character than can be found in any of her previous novels. *Keeper of the Cats* (1995) has several interesting subplots, but seems patched together and tentative.

Boyll, Randall (1962–)

The popularity that horror fiction enjoyed during the 1970s and 1980s came to a stunning halt in the early 1990s. The number of new titles dropped dramatically, and a good many writers who had built careers in that genre were forced to write very different books or stop writing altogether. One of the most promising of the writers who debuted at just the wrong time was Randall Boyll, whose *After Sundown* (1989) was an extremely effective and chilling novel. A family vacationing in a remote cabin find that they are surrounded by the spirits of people who died at the hands of a religious fanatic. The very landscape surrounding the cabin alters to prevent them from escaping.

Boyll was chosen to write movie novelizations soon thereafter, and more than half of his subsequent novels were of that type, including a series based on the Darkman comic books and films. His second original novel, *Mongster* (1991), was a somewhat confused blend of humor and horror. An abused child learns of the existence of a hidden treasure and raises the dead to protect himself from his enemies. His third original novel, *Chiller* (1992), is a very unsettling story and easily Boyll's best book. A grieving father steals the body of his daughter from an experimental laboratory where she is being studied because, although dead and rotting, she is still conscious. Their flight from the FBI and other pursuers is a sequence of bizarre and sometimes disturbing scenes.

As horror became more difficult to sell, Boyll moved increasingly toward novelizations and mundane suspense. *Katastrophe* (2000) does have some supernatural content. Under hypnosis a man claims to be the reincarnation of Adolf Hitler, which precipitates a world crisis, but the tone is very different from that that made his earlier horror novels so emotionally gripping. Recent signs of an increase in the popularity of supernatural fiction may lure him back to the genre in the future.

Bradbury, Ray (1920–)

It is a function of the way fiction publishing works in the contemporary world that novels are far more likely to attract attention than does short fiction and that most writers who actually derive a living from their art are those who produce book-length works with some regularity. One of the rare exceptions to that rule is Ray Bradbury, who had until recently produced novels only at great intervals and in a variety of genres ranging from contemporary fiction to science fiction to horror. He is also one of the few genre writers, such as Kurt Vonnegut, Philip K. Dick, and Ursula K. LE GUIN, who has managed to attract considerable attention from mainstream critics and editors, and in fact many of Bradbury's earlier short stories found a home in the mainstream or slick magazines of the 1950s.

Bradbury was drawn to fantastic literature by the early science fiction magazines, but it is significant that his second published sale was to *Weird Tales,* a magazine that specialized in what we now call dark fantasy. He was incredibly prolific throughout the 1940s and with consistently high quality, producing too many classic stories to mention all of them, the most outstanding of which were "THE CROWD" (1943), "THE JAR" (1944), "The Traveler" (1946), "THE SKELETON" (1945), and "THE SMALL ASSASSIN" (1946). Some of his most suspenseful and effective stories include "The Handler" (1947), in which a mortician with a penchant for playing practical jokes on dead bodies gets his just deserts when some of them become animated, and "The Man Upstairs" (1947), a very subtle vampire story. Several of Bradbury's characters refuse to accept death, as in "There Was an Old Woman" (1944) and "The Dead Man" (1945). His first collection, *Dark Carnival,* appeared in 1947 and contained almost exclusively stories of supernatural horror, but he was already expanding his horizons. Most of his subsequent collections would mix science fiction, fantasy, horror, straight suspense, and contemporary drama indiscriminately. THE ILLUSTRATED MAN (1951) was another collection loosely organized under a frame story— each individual tale being represented by a tattoo on a man's body—but the stories themselves varied from straightforward science fiction to horror.

Bradbury's science fiction, never particularly rigorous with regard to scientific accuracy, grew increasingly implausible from a rational viewpoint, and his classic collection of stories about the colonization of Mars, *The Martian Chronicles* (1950), often wanders into mysticism and other nonrational fantasy. He began writing more frequently for general magazines during the 1950s, but the volume of new work began to slow, and by the 1960s his work was appearing comparatively infrequently. Although his later fiction has become more polished, particularly his detective and crime stories, the imaginative content has steadily lessened, and the tales themselves are less original and striking.

Bradbury has written for younger readers, most notably *Switch on the Night* (1951), *The Halloween Tree* (1972), and *From the Dust Returned* (2001), but none of these evoke the feeling of authentic childhood nearly as well as his adult fiction featuring young protagonists, such as the nonfantastic novel *Dandelion Wine* (1957). The wonders of childhood and the nature of life in a small town are recurring themes and influences in Bradbury's work, and his ability to provide a glimpse of life through the eyes of a child is particularly effective. His single major novel of fantasy is SOMETHING WICKED THIS WAY COMES (1962), a reworking of material previously published in short form, particularly "The Black Ferris" (1968). A sinister carnival arrives in a small town containing a merry-go-round that prematurely ages its passengers, a mirror room that steals souls, and other marvels. Only some of the town's children recognize the danger. A reasonably effective film version appeared in 1983 based on Bradbury's own screenplay. He also provided the scripts for the short-lived but high-quality anthology series *The Ray Bradbury Theater.*

Bradbury was also the editor of two excellent early anthologies, *Timeless Stories for Today and Tomorrow* (1952) and *The Circus of Dr. Lao & Other Improbable Stories* (1956). He received a Grand Master Award from the Science Fiction and Fantasy Writers of America for his lifetime achievement and similar recognition from the World Fantasy Convention. His fiction, particularly his dark fantasy and horror, has been very influential on other writers including Richard MATHESON, Charles BEAUMONT, and William F. Nolan. The bibliography lists those of Bradbury's collections that contain large percentages of fantasy and horror fiction, but many stories in a similar vein can be found in his other collec-

tions as well. The best selections are those in *The Illustrated Man* (1951), *The October Country* (1955), and *A Medicine for Melancholy* (1959). The most comprehensive collection is *The Stories of Ray Bradbury* (1980). His collection *One More for the Road* (2002) won the Bram Stoker Award for best collection.

Bradley, Marion Zimmer (1930–1999)

Marion Zimmer Bradley began her career as a science fiction writer and is chiefly remembered in that field for her Darkover novels, a long series set on a distant planet with a culture very similar to that of many classic fantasy novels. Some of the citizens of Darkover possess "laran," a psychic power that is analogous to magic, and fantasy fans may find much of the series, particularly the later volumes, of interest.

Her first novel of fantasy was *Dark Satanic* (1972), a Gothic suspense novel involving a cult of Satan worshippers. One of the characters is a genuine psychic, but most of the plot is straightforward and does not involve the supernatural. The two sequels are both more heavily dependent on fantastic content. The protagonist of *The Inheritor* (1974) is a woman who is sensitive to the dark spirits that haunt the old house where she is staying. There is another reluctant psychic in the third in the series, *Witch Hill* (1990), a woman who denies her powers until she runs into the satanists.

A second and much better supernatural series consists of *Ghostlight* (1995), *Witchlight* (1996), *Gravelight* (1997), and *Heartlight* (1998), all four of which are uncredited collaborations with Rosemary EDGHILL. The daughter of a famous occultist decides to write a book on the subject and is soon beset by poltergeists and other unnatural events. The later volumes involve a large-scale investigation into the occult and then the discovery that magical forces are being used to manipulate the public. Bradley also wrote two stand alone novels of the supernatural, *Drums of Darkness* (1976), which contains some genuine voodoo, and *In the Steps of the Master* (1973), based on a short-lived television series about a parapsychologist.

Although she started writing fantasy with some short stories reminiscent of J. R. R. TOLKIEN during the 1970s, Bradley's fantasy fiction is dominated by the AVALON SERIES, in particular *The Mists of Avalon* (1982). The novels are a feminist interpretation of the story of King Arthur, which eventually reveals that the druids are descended from the last survivors of Atlantis. They retreat into a magical realm when the Romans invade Britain but still interact with the outside world. Her first fantasy novel, however, was *The House between the Worlds* (1980), whose hero travels mentally to the land of the fairies where he witnesses the abduction of their queen by unfriendly goblins. Eventually he gains physical access to the other world and crosses over to rescue her.

Web of Light (1983) and *Web of Darkness* (1983) constitute a somewhat tedious two-part adventure story set on the lost continent of Atlantis, published jointly as *The Fall of Atlantis* (1987). *Night's Daughter* (1985) is based on Mozart's *The Magic Flute,* but it is more interesting as a curiosity than as fiction. More satisfying is *Warrior Woman* (1985), the story of a female gladiator, and *Lythande* (1986), a collection of related short stories about a female magician that first began appearing in the Thieves' World shared universe series. *The Firebrand* (1987) is a different take on the Trojan War and also one of her better fantasies. Bradley also collaborated with Andre NORTON and Julian May for the interlocking Trillium series, but her best cooperative work was *Glenraven,* written with Holly LISLE, the story of a demonic force hidden in a remote part of Italy.

Bradley also spent considerable effort encouraging new writers. In addition to the long-running series of "Sword and Sorceress" original anthologies, she published *Marion Zimmer Bradley's Fantasy Magazine.* Bradley's work varies greatly in quality and tone. Her strongest assets were the ability to people her stories with interesting characters. *The Mists of Avalon,* which appeared as a television miniseries, has already become a minor classic with a strong following outside the genre, and several of her other fantasy novels deserve a wider audience.

Bramah, Ernest (1868–1942)

Ernest Bramah Smith used this abbreviated version of his name for all of his fiction, which included the

Max Carrados detective series and a few mainstream novels. He is best remembered for Kai Lung, a quick-witted Chinese gentleman set in a historically questionable ancient China. Kai Lung's adventures were collected in *The Wallet of Kai Lung* (1900), *Kai Lung's Golden Hours* (1922), *Kai Lung Unrolls His Mat* (1928), *The Return of Kai Lung* (1937), *Kai Lung Beneath the Mulberry Tree* (1940), and *Kai Lung: Six* (1974), the last collected posthumously. The first three volumes are unquestionably superior to the later work. Although sometimes wrapped in a frame story, all of the books are essentially short story collections except for *The Return of Kai Lung,* which is the weakest in the series. Several individual stories were published as separate chapbooks, in fact.

Kai Lung is a quick witted adventurer and also something of a rascal. He has a tale and an aphorism for every occasion, and some of his rejoinders have found their way into books of quotations. Often his life is in danger, and he tells his stories to delay his punishment or to put his captors off guard. The frame story, when it exists at all, is nonfantastic, but the individual tales he tells often involve magic, strange creatures, supernatural intervention, and other elements not necessarily specific to Asian mythology. All of this is conveyed in an artificially elaborate prose structure that has occasionally been imitated but rarely successfully. Although more popular in England than in the United States, his books, particularly the later ones, have become collectors' items in both countries. He is perhaps best read in small doses, but his intelligently plotted tales and brilliant prose will reward the effort.

Brandner, Gary (1933–   )

After writing several minor suspense novels, some with marginal fantastic content, Gary Brandner produced his first and still best-known horror book, *Howling* (1977), one of the most successful werewolf stories of all time. Horror writers have rarely found sufficiently original interpretations of the werewolf legend to produce memorable new works. Brandner's contribution was to portray them as uneasy pack animals, a hidden society living concealed within our own, gathering together in disguise on a health farm, and preserving their secret until the rash actions of one of their number leads a journalist to a startling discovery. Although the novel ends with the destruction of the colony, there are some survivors who become the basis for two inferior but still interesting sequels, *Howling II* (1979) and *Howling III* (1985). In the first two, the reporter is pursued by her now-infected husband and his friends, and in the third, a werewolf child is adopted by an unsuspecting normal family. The first book was turned into an above-average horror film in 1980. The five movie sequels bear no relation to the novels.

Brandner's later novels vary considerably in content and quality. *Walkers* (1980) is a rather predictable story of a woman brought back from the dead after an accident who finds herself pursued by spirits from the other side who want her to join them. A demon in human form similarly pursues a woman and her child in *Hellborn* (1981), but the supernatural element is subordinated to what is essentially a mystery story. After novelizing the remake of *Cat People* (1982), Brandner wrote *Quintana Roo* (1984), a jungle adventure story with supernatural episodes.

The Brain Eaters (1985), a mix of horror and science fiction, was Brandner's best book since *The Howling*. A new form of parasite begins to affect human brains, driving their hosts into fits of violence. Although the story is very much in the vein of *Night of the Living Dead* and its many imitations, Brandner avoids most of the usual clichés and delivers a taut and exciting suspense novel. Many of the same devices appear in *Carrion* (1986), in which a fraudulent magician discovers that some of his powers are real. He resurrects the dead but without understanding the consequences, and they wander around, deteriorating physically and mentally, until they become dangerous and repulsive. *Cameron's Closet* (1987) develops the childhood fear of a monster in the closet in a somewhat predictable but nevertheless relentlessly suspenseful fashion. An inferior but occasionally interesting film followed.

Floater (1988) is a disappointing revenge story involving astral projection, and *Doomstalker* (1989) was only marginally more interesting, another story of demonic retribution. Brandner's most recent horror novel, *Rot* (1999), measures up to his best

work, however. The protagonist is a woman brought back from the dead to track down her attackers, but she has to succeed before her decaying body deteriorates. Brandner's occasional short stories are generally minor, but "Julian's Hand" (1974), "Mark of the Loser" (1979), and "Old Blood" (1993) are of interest.

The Brave Little Toaster Thomas M. Disch (1981)

It is often forgotten that much of the fiction we think of as classic children's fantasy was actually written as satire directed at least partly at adult audiences. Jonathan Swift's GULLIVER'S TRAVELS (1626) and ALICE IN WONDERLAND (1865) by Lewis Carroll are the two most obvious examples. Children could read them for their surface story, while adults might chuckle at the exaggerated portrayals of events or even people from the contemporary world. One of the rare recent examples is *The Brave Little Toaster*, originally published in a collection of fantasy stories for adult readers, then reprinted in 1986 in hardcover as a children's book.

Talking animals have been a mainstay of children's fantasy ever since Aesop, but talking inanimate objects have rarely been more than minor elements. Disch turned that completely around by imbuing all of the electrical appliances in a vacation lodge with personalities. The various devices, led by the toaster, are loyal to their young human master, who has apparently abandoned them. They set out on a quest to find him, convinced that he would have returned had he been able and ignorant of the fact that people change much more dramatically with the passage of time than do their creations. They eventually rescue him and are reunited in a surprisingly unsentimental but still touching resolution. The surface story is clever and amusing, and the underlying satire, which deals with our interactions with the technological devices we have created, is gentle. The story was turned into an above-average animated film in 1987.

Disch added a sequel, *The Brave Little Toaster Goes to Mars* (1988), in which a radio picks up a distress call from the planet Mars. A particularly ingenious piece of technology, built by Albert Einstein himself, makes it possible for many machines—led, of course, by the toaster—to cross the gap between worlds to confront the Martian natives, who are preparing to invade the Earth. The Martian machines are encouraged to rebel against their expansionist masters, and the machines from Earth are able to return home in time for Christmas. This spoof of science fiction approaches the quality of the first book, but the satire is somewhat more heavy handed.

Brennan, Joseph Payne (1918–1990)

One of the best writers to emerge in the latter days of the pulp magazines was Joseph Payne Brennan, whose weird fantasies and horror stories began appearing in the early 1950s. Although he continued to write short fiction until the late 1980s, most of his work was published by small presses and was largely unavailable during his lifetime. Some of his best work appeared quite early, including "SLIME" (1953). "THE CALAMANDER CHEST" (1953), and "Levitation" (1958), but his highly literate stories remained entertaining and well constructed throughout his career.

Brennan's first collection, *Nine Horrors and a Dream* (1958), contains the best selection, but there are also many fine stories in *Scream at Midnight* (1963), *Stories of Darkness and Dread* (1973), *The Shapes of Midnight* (1980), and *The Borders Just Beyond* (1986). He also wrote a considerable body of poetry, some of it with macabre themes, but his only novels were a collaboration with Donald M. Grant, *Act of Providence* 1979), which has some minimal fantastic content, and a marginally supernatural mystery, *Evil Always Ends* (1982).

Brennan's fiction often involved ghosts or curses, such as in "Canavan's Back Yard" (1958), in which a man is lost and transformed in a magically cursed plot of land, and "The Mail of Juniper Hill" (1958), which features the ghost of a mailman endlessly repeating his rounds. Juniper Hill is a common setting Brennan used in many of his stories, although the characters did not noticeably overlap. A more formal series is the Lucius Leffing sequence. Leffing is a psychic detective in the tradition of Algernon BLACKWOOD's John Silence or the Jules de Grandin stories by Seabury QUINN.

Leffing's adventures, which do not always involve the supernatural, were collected in *The Casebook of Lucius Leffing* (1973), *The Chronicles of Lucius Leffing* (1977), and *The Adventures of Lucius Leffing* (1990). Although never an immensely popular writer, he was highly respected within the field and produced a substantial body of quiet, literate tales of the supernatural.

"The Brighton Monster" Gerald Kersh (1948)

It is sometimes difficult to determine whether a time travel story is science fiction or fantasy, and, in fact, there are some critics who insist that all time travel is fantasy because it is patently impossible except by magic. Most readers, however, have little difficulty differentiating between a story in which the protagonist climbs into a machine and travels forward and backward in time, and one in which he or she accomplishes the same feat by means of a magic amulet. There are, however, many stories that straddle the two forms, in which the motivating force is ambiguous or, as in this case, never explained at all.

The author Kersh is himself the narrator of this story, which is in large part based on his supposed discovery of a pamphlet first published in 1747. The pamphlet was written by a clergyman named Arthur Titty, who recounts the discovery by two fisherman of a humanoid creature that they believed to be a monster from the sea. The creature's body is covered with depictions of unusual animals and strange symbols, and he is, apparently, incapable of human speech, although he makes noises that sound similar. Much of his skin is also covered with what appear to be scales, adding to his bizarre appearance.

Reverend Titty purchases the oddity from the sailors and feeds and clothes him, occasionally walking him around town on a leash. On one occasion a burly local bully accosts them and is thrown head over heels by the creature, although it makes no move to harm Titty. Although the minister is more benign than the sailors, he, too, believes the creature to be other than human and provides constant supplies of salt water in an attempt to keep it healthy. Despite his best efforts, sores break out on the monster's body, and he becomes steadily weaker, as though wasting away from some mysterious disease.

Eventually, the monster escapes and throws itself into the sea, confirming the local theory about its origin. Kersh amuses himself by naming two of the witnesses Herbert George and Rebecca West, an obvious reference to H. G. Wells and his wife, Rebecca West. The real end of the story takes place in the 1940s, when the fictional version of Kersh, having owned the pamphlet for some years, encounters an intelligence officer who was acquainted with a Japanese martial arts expert named Sato, who disappeared when Hiroshima was destroyed. Sato was heavily tattooed, and his decorations exactly matched those described in the pamphlet. The reverend's faithful depiction of the symbols on the monster inscribed before its disappearance confirm his identity. Somehow, Sato was transported back through time to the 18th century, where radiation sickness doomed him to a slow and painful death in captivity. Kersh, who wrote only occasional fantastic pieces, produced one of the most tightly constructed and effective time travel fantasies of all time.

Brite, Poppy Z. (1967–)

Poppy Brite began writing predominantly horror fiction during the 1980s, quickly gaining a reputation for her distinctive characterizations and her rich prose style. Several of these early short stories attracted considerable critical attention, including "His Mouth Will Taste of Wormwood" (1990), "The Taste of Blood and Altars" (1992), and "Calcutta, Lord of Nerves" (1992). She was chosen the best new writer in the British Fantasy Awards for 1994, and her first collection, *Wormwood* (also published as *Swamp Foetus*) appeared in 1996.

Lost Souls (1992) was her first novel, a very unusual vampire story that avoided supernatural explanations. Her vampires are simply another race of mortal beings who live concealed within human society, hiding their existence in fear of the pogrom that would inevitably follow their discovery. The novel explores the characters of several of these creatures, some fully aware of their nature

from the outset and some gradually awakening to the truth. There is no strong, central plot but rather a series of interlocking character studies that together create a fascinating and just slightly alien worldview. A shorter, earlier version of the novel was later published as *The Seed of Lost Souls* (1999). *Drawing Blood* (1993) shares some similarities and contains some extremely vivid scenes as well as some explicit scenes of homoeroticism. Two young men are sharing a house whose former owner murdered most of his family. The house contains a dark strain of magic that influences the personalities of its residents, although this is not, strictly speaking, a haunted house story.

Brite's third novel, *The Lazarus Heart* (1998), is set in the universe of the Crow films and is a comparatively disappointing story of revenge from beyond the grave. She has continued to write short fiction sporadically, of which the title story of the collection *Are You Loathesome Tonight?* (1998) and "Nothing of Him Doth Fade" (2002) are the best. Her remaining collections are *Self Made Man* (1999) and *The Devil You Know* (2003). Brite's style is much more layered and intense than is that of most of her contemporaries, and her horror fiction is generally more ambitious and complex in structure.

Brooks, Terry (1944–)

Terry Brooks was the first major new writer of fantasy to base his work openly in imitation of J. R. R. TOLKIEN, starting with *The Sword of Shannara* in 1977. In the tradition of the Lord of the Rings series, Brooks created a fantasy world replete with goblins, gnomes, and other legendary creatures, dominated by an evil wizard whose efforts to rule the world result in a heroic quest for a magical object, in this case an enchanted sword, and an epic battle. Two sequels followed in short order, each of which consists of an independent story, although both involve similar quests. In *The Elfstones of Shannara* (1982) a somewhat inept magician strives to protect an elven maiden from the unwanted advances of a demon using magic seeds to bring forth a forest of protective trees. A druid and a woman who can invoke the basic force of nature unite in *The Wishsong of Shannara* (1985) to protect the world from a horde of malevolent creatures.

The next set of four Shannara novels, set some centuries after the events of the first trilogy, make up one continuous story. The titles are *The Scions of Shannara* (1990), *The Druid of Shannara* (1991), *The Elf Queen of Shannara* (1992), and *The Talismans of Shannara* (1993). The elves and dwarves have been driven from the land by the new rulers of Shannara, and the practice of magic is outlawed. A fabled sorcerer returns from the dead as a ghost to challenge them and organizes a rebellion, The elves are located in their place of exile and encouraged to help battle the villains, and a plague is unleashed in a desperate attempt to suppress the rebellion. Brooks subsequently continued the story with a sequel, *First King of Shannara* (1998), with the forces of good repelling an invading army of trolls.

A new sequence began with *Ilse Witch* (1990), in which a druid and a witch set out on a dangerous sea voyage to secure a new and dangerous form of magic before it can be seized by the wrong hands. They reach their destination in *Morgawr* (2002) and discover that they have misunderstood the situation from the outset. *Jarka Ruus* (2003) is also a quest story, this time following a group of adventurers seeking a missing woman, who is located and rescued in *Tanequil* (2004). The Shannara books are openly derivative, and the early volumes in particular are often uneven and awkward. Brooks improved his storytelling skills in the later volumes, but in this series he never attempted to break new ground. His other novels, though less popular, are actually much more interesting.

Magic Kingdom for Sale—Sold! (1986) launched the Kingdom of Landover series. A lawyer purchases an entire kingdom in a magical otherworld, but once installed in his new property, he discovers that there are numerous problems besetting him. Low-key but sometimes genuinely funny consequences follow. The story continues with *The Black Unicorn* (1987), in which the protagonist is magically altered in appearance so that his friends no longer recognize him, *Wizard at Large* (1988), which traps the lawyer and his magical wife in our world, where she can exist only for a limited time, and *The Tangle Box* (1994), this time pitting the hero against a villain-

ous con man who traps him in a magical maze. The most recent title in the series is *Witches' Brew* (1995), which is more adventure than humor. The hero's daughter has begun to age prematurely thanks to evil magic just as an army begins an invasion. Although the tone varies considerably from book to book, and sometimes even within a single volume, the Landover novels are much more original than the Shannara series.

Brooks's remaining set of three novels is easily his best work. *Running with the Demon* (1997) also straddles two worlds, ours and a magical realm, but has a much darker tone than the Landover series. An immortal knight and a disguised demon battle to shape the future of both realities. The central character is much more vividly portrayed, and the writing is more controlled and realistic than in the author's other work. The story continues in *A Knight of the Word* (1998), with prophetic dreams warning the knight of dangers to be averted when he is awake, although the constant turmoil troubles him greatly. He and another wizard finally triumph in the final confrontation in *Angel Fire East* (1999). Brooks is potentially a writer of much greater merit than his published work suggests, but paradoxically the very success of his Shannara series has apparently prevented him from consistently moving on to more original efforts.

Brust, Steven (1953–)

Most science fiction authors begin with short stories and move to novels, but most fantasy writers debut at book length and only write short fiction, if at all, as an occasional change of pace. That pattern holds true for Steven Brust, whose first published fantasy was *Jhereg* (1983) and whose subsequent short fiction has been inconsequential. That novel was the first adventure of Vlad Taltos, a marginally psychic assassin living in a typical fantasy world who is bonded to a reptilian companion and has various energetic adventures leavened by doses of light humor. Brust's second fantasy novel, *To Reign in Hell* (1984), was a retelling of the story of the war among the angels and is atypical of the balance of his work.

Taltos returns in *Yendi* (1984), with Taltos now confirmed in his position within the professional assassins' guild but immediately threatened by up-sets within that organization and the efforts of his latest target to avoid his fate. In *Teckla* (1987) he gets caught between a growing rebellion by the lower classes, who view him as one of the despised nobles, and the entrenched aristocracy, who sus-pect of him of being a traitor to their class. A vam-pire sorceress and her minions test his wits and his courage in *Taltos* (1988), one of the more inventive fantasies in recent years, and in *Athyra* (1990) Vlad is thinking about retiring with his accumu-lated wealth and taking it easy for the rest of his life. Unfortunately, assassins tend to accumulate enemies, and they have a less pleasant future planned for him. *Orca* (1996) has a frustrated Tal-tos associating himself with a group of questionable merchants. Brust then returned to his protagonist's younger days for the next in the series, *Dragon* (1997), but *Issola* (2001) continues the story, this time forcing him to temporarily suspend his retire-ment to rescue a pair of friends.

The Taltos books, which have been reissued in omnibus volumes, are straightforward fantasy ad-venture with a touch of Alexander Dumas. There is more than a touch of Dumas in the opening vol-umes of his second series, the Khaavren novels, which are set in the same alternate universe. *The Phoenix Guards* (1991) is a swashbuckling tale of swordplay, chases, battles, and clever adventures told in a sparkling and highly literate style. *Five Hundred Years After* (1994) provides more of the same. The Khaavren series was later extended by three very idiosyncratic fantasies, *The Paths of the Dead* (2002), *The Lord of Castle Black* (2003), and *Sethra Lavode* (2004). A cataclysm changes the world, and in the generations that follow, a sor-cerer returns from the dead.

Brust's remaining fantasies include *Brokedown Palace* (1986), a low-key fantasy adventure related to the Khaavren books. *Gypsy* (1992), written with Megan Lindholm (who is better known as Robin HOBB), is a contemporary fantasy involving a gypsy with magical abilities and his interaction with a local crime figure. *Freedom and Necessity* (1997), written with Emma Bull, is a sometimes murky novel about a missing man who reappears with no memory but with magical abilities. *Agyar* (1993) also uses a contemporary setting. The protagonist is

a benevolent vampire, although that term is never mentioned anywhere in the text, who makes friends with a ghost from the Civil War period. Brust's strongest assets are his ability to tell a fast-paced and inventive story enlivened by just the right amount of humor, an element generally absent from his contemporary fantasies, which are for the most part of less interest.

Bunch, Chris (1943–)

During the 1980s Chris Bunch and Allan Cole col-laborated on a series of military science fiction ad-ventures that became quite popular, so it was not until the 1990s that they tried their hands at fan-tasy with the Anteros trilogy, consisting of *The Far Kingdoms* (1993), *The Warrior's Tale* (1994), and *Kingdoms of the Night* (1995). The series opens with a coming-of-age story as a young warrior takes pas-sage to unknown distant lands in search of wealth and adventure, finding little of the former but plenty of the latter. The second volume introduces a female warrior as protagonist, further exploring their magical world, but the final title reverts to Anteros, now growing old, who discovers that what he thought were the Far Kingdoms are only a mask concealing the really distant lands, which stand as a bulwark against evil sorcery. Although very tradi-tional in theme and style, the Anteros stories achieved considerable recognition for their clean, crisp, imaginative plotting and narration.

Cole and Bunch parted ways shortly there-after, and Bunch produced his own trilogy, *The Seer King* (1997), *The Demon King* (1998), and *The Warrior King* (1999). The two major characters are a soldier and a wizard who make common cause when each narrowly survives a murder attempt. The setting is a typical fantasy kingdom, but Bunch takes the story in a slightly different direc-tion by assuming that with the collapse of the old order, even a magical realm might evolve toward a more democratic form of government. The result is a sort of constitutional monarchy, although the new king promptly begins to abrogate the safe-guards in the second title, and the two former friends become mortal enemies. Although the wiz-ard is eventually killed and the threat averted, he returns from the dead in the final volume for one more battle. Although primarily an adventure story, Bunch demonstrated considerable skill creating his characters, whose motives and loyalties are often in question.

The Empire Stone (2000) is a rather ordinary quest story, but Bunch's next novel, *Corsair* (2001), also not part of a series, is his most consistently entertaining single work. The protagonist in this case is released from prison because he has knowledge crucial to defeating an impending attack by a nation of pirates, but even he fails to realize their true nature until it is almost too late. *Storm of Wings* (2002) launched the Dragonmaster trilogy, set against the backdrop of a magical war. A young boy learns rough lessons about his world, including the

fact that the kindly, gentle dragons with which he is familiar can become terrible weapons when directed to that purpose. His people learn that there are even more fearsome creatures than dragons in *Knighthood of the Dragon* (2003), and the story is brought to a conclusion in *The Last Battle* (2004).

Bunch has also written occasional short stories, of which only "The Vampires of Malibu High" (2003) is of note. He has proven himself to be a reliable writer of high adventure whose settings and characters are original enough to stand out. Although he has yet to produce a breakthrough work, he has demonstrated that he has all the necessary tools, and it seems likely that he will grow in stature as his career progresses.

C

Cabell, James Branch (1879–1958)

James Branch Cabell was the author of numerous books, not all fantasy, but the majority of which were loosely assembled into a sequence known as the "Biography of the Life of Manuel," a pivotal historical figure in the imaginary European nation of Poictesme. About 20 of his books were listed as part of this series, which was not written in chronological order, but the connection is very loose at times, tracing its way through various descendants, and the order in which the stories are read is largely irrelevant. Some of the titles are, in fact, not fiction at all but collections of essays or verse. The sequence includes the best of his work, including his most famous novel, *Jurgen* (1919), which was banned in New York when it was first published because of its double entendres—very tame by contemporary standards—and its satire of organized religion. Cabell and his publishers won the court case that followed, and he reaped considerable publicity, which helped his subsequent career. *Jurgen* is also Cabell's most complex and rewarding novel, a quest story in which an ordinary man inadvertently wishes his wife away and then spends much effort trying to find her among myriad time periods and altered realities. He encounters a large number of historical and mythological figures, including Helen of Troy and a vampire, before discovering that God is an illusion.

Cabell's fantasy was an odd but clever mixture of detailed research into history and mythology, word play and anagrams, and mannerly behavior and outrageous acts. The first several Poictesme

books appeared between 1904 and 1916 and are listed for informational purposes in the bibliography, although their fantasy content is minimal or nonexistent. The first major fantasy title was *The Cream of the Jest* (1917), subtitled a *Comedy of Evasions*. The protagonist finds a magical artifact that allows him to enter the land of dreams, where his low-key adventures center around his pursuit of a beautiful woman, his own personal ideal. Eventually he discovers that his wife in the real world has similarly accessed the dream world and that it is she whom he has been striving to reach. *Beyond Life* (1919), mostly nonfiction, is chronologically the first in the series and provides much of the background, but it was with *Jurgen* that Cabell's reputation began to soar.

Domnei (1920, previously published in 1913 in a shorter version as *The Soul of Melicent*) is an adventure story set in a magical kingdom that never existed in historical Europe. The protagonist sets out to rescue a beautiful woman and has a series of low-key but very amusing adventures. *Figures of Earth* (1921) is the title that deals most specifically with Manuel and presents him in two not necessarily conflicting roles. On the one hand, he was the savior of his people, who battled witchcraft and other evils and triumphed over adversity. On the other, he was a swindler and a wastrel, greedy and self-centered, whose victories were more inadvertent than planned. Cabell's broad satire clearly applied to a wide range of historical figures. He starts life as a swineherd, is encouraged by a magician to rescue an imprisoned woman, finds love, and sacrifices it in his own self-interest. His later adventures include an amusing sequence in which he sells fraudulent magical feathers that are so convincing that actual miraculous events follow.

The High Place (1923) is a combination of a quest story and a deal with the devil. Florian, the not particularly admirable protagonist, falls in love with a woman who has been enchanted into an endless sleep and rescues her by promising to sacrifice their first child to his benefactor, and a confusing but amusing sequence follows when a meddling saint tries to save the child. Florian discovers that the woman he loves is intolerably stupid, the pact is circumvented, and eventually time itself is turned about to produce, if not a happy ending, at least a clever one. *The Music from behind the Moon* (1926) is a very minor fantasy in which one of Manuel's daughters is first imprisoned on the moon, then freed through chicanery.

Cabell's next two novels were both outstanding. *The Silver Stallion* (1926) takes place shortly after Manuel's death. The Fellowship of the Silver Stallion is dissolved, and the various members have separate adventures, including one in which a magician discovers that the world was once ruled by a nonhuman race reminiscent of the Cthulhu Mythos by H. P. LOVECRAFT. Other characters meet their fate in often comical fashion, encounter demons, find hidden libraries, die in battle and get sent to the wrong heaven, and discover some truths about the great Manuel. *Something About Eve* (1927) is a magical exploration of different aspects of the female persona and contains a number of episodes, including a very funny satire on book reviewing. *The White Robe* (1928) is a comparatively minor piece about a magical robe whose wearer is physically transformed into a werewolf, and *The Way of Ecben* (1929) is only slightly more interesting. Cabell seemed to have exhausted his imagination by this point, and his subsequent work, though always clever and sometimes interesting, is comparatively minor.

The most ambitious of his later fantasies is the thematically related trilogy consisting of *Smirt: An Urbane Nightmare* (1934), *Smith: A Sylvan Interlude* (1935), and *Smire: An Acceptance in the Third Person* (1937). The first and last consist largely of thinly veiled attacks against features of contemporary culture that Cabell found repressive, while the middle is an episodic medieval adventure. All three involve different aspects of a single character who is theoretically exploring reality through his dreams, although the underlying plot is often incoherent or undetectable. They were published in an omnibus edition as *The Nightmare Has Triplets* (1972). *There Were Two Pirates* (1946) is a historical novel that involves some low-key ghostly appearances, and *The Devil's Own Dear Son* (1949) is a minor religious satire. Cabell is still highly regarded for his better efforts, and the James Branch Cabell Society for many years published *Kalki*, a magazine devoted to study of his career.

Cady, Jack (1932–2004)

Although Jack Cady had begun writing short horror fiction as early as 1970, it was not until the publication of his first horror novel, *The Well* (1980), that he attracted any extensive attention. Although the book is essentially a haunted house story, it was both unusually restrained, with little overt supernaturalism until the closing chapters, and intelligently written both in terms of concept and style. Cady developed his horrors with subtlety and raised the level of suspense by implication rather than more explicit descriptions and actions. His follow-up novel, *The Jonah Watch* (1981), was even more impressive. A Coast Guard cutter becomes icebound off the coast of Maine. Strange voices are subsequently heard from time to time, and the crew becomes convinced that there is, in fact, a Jonah among them. Eventually, suppressed fear turns to open violence in what might have been a straightforward psychological adventure story, but Cady includes a genuinely supernatural series of events.

Two of Cady's novels appeared under the pen name Pat Franklin. *Dark Dreaming* (1991) has only marginal supernatural content for most of its length. A woman experiences increasingly frightening dreams that appear to have been invaded by a malevolent entity, which eventually manifests itself physically. *Embrace of the Wolf* (1993) is even more ambiguous. One of the residents of a wonderfully evoked town is influenced by an unspecified animalistic spirit. Cady reverted to his own name for *Street* (1994), the story of a serial killer whose apprehension is accomplished only after some mild psychic events, and *The Off Season* (1995), his best novel, set in a town that labors under a curse. Time runs differently from person to person, and reality proves to be a malleable commodity. Cady's last horror novel was *The Haunting of Hood Canal* (2001) and is more conventional than his other work. The spirit of a murdered child molester rises to influence the minds of passersby.

Although primarily known for his novels, Cady's infrequent but impressive short stories began to appear during the late 1980s and early 1990s, including such excellent tales as "By Reason of Darkness" (1988), the Bram Stoker Award–winning "The Night We Buried Road Dog" (1993), and "Daddy Dearest" (1998). Most of his short fiction was collected in *The Sons of Noah and Other Stories* (1992), which won the World Fantasy Award, *The Night We Buried Road Dog* (2002), and *Ghosts of Yesterday* (2003). Although he produced a relatively small body of work during his lifetime, he was very highly regarded both by readers and critics, and his out-of-print books are highly sought after.

"Cafe Endless: Spring Rain"   Nancy Holder (1994)

Since the early 1990s vampire fiction has become almost a separate genre, with good vampires, bad vampires, and vampires torn between right and wrong. It sometimes seems that writers have explored every possible combination of situations and settings and that every new title is simply a variation of an old plot, but every so often a talented writer thinks of some new twist to an old story or a different way to look at the relationship between the vampire and his or her victim. The latter is the case with this atmospheric story by a writer who produced a considerable body of first-rate short horror fiction during the 1990s and who seems likely to be recognized as a major talent in the future, particularly if she continues to produce stories of this quality.

The setting is modern Japan. Satoshi is a Japanese businessman serving as a sort of private tour guide for an influential American woman who is apparently vacationing in Japan in conjunction with a business trip. Satoshi feels mildly attracted toward Buchner, the American, and is very tolerant of her occasional breaches of good manners. There is another tension as well, which only begins to emerge when they reach a particular part of Tokyo, the vicinity of a modern building. Satoshi conceals his impatience, but he is now anxious to fulfill his duties to his guest as quickly as possible so that he can enter the building, where he senses the presence of a woman to whom he is supernaturally drawn.

The woman is a vampire, of course, and they eventually meet for a fairly overt sexual encounter culminating in the drawing of blood. But their relationship is far more complex than that. The vampire is as much a prisoner of her victim as he is subject to her will, and their elaborate dance of sex becomes ultimately an act of mutual self-destruction. The story won the Bram Stoker Award presented by the Horror Writers' Association and is still Holder's best known story.

"The Cairn on the Headland"   Robert E. Howard (1932)

Although he is best-known for the CONAN series and other swashbuckling fantasy tales, Robert E. HOWARD wrote in a number of different genres, including a respectable body of horror fiction, of which "The Cairn on the Headland" is one of the best examples. The story opens with two men examining a 12th century cairn in Ireland, anomalously constructed by the ancient Irish despite the fact that this form of burial was a Viking tradition that they did not ordinarily follow. According to legend, all holly plants in the area were uprooted and destroyed, although the reason for that action has been lost. The spot has been shunned for so many generations that no one alive remembers the historical background, but the narrator is still wary of the site, although his companion remains skeptical.

The second man, Ortali, plans to open the cairn secretly, under cover of darkness, to plunder whatever treasures it might hide, while the narrator, O'Brien, has continued and ever more serious misgivings. He is approached by a mysterious woman who gives him an ancient cross to protect him, an artifact he recognizes as a long-lost relic supposedly buried with an unknown woman in an unmarked tomb. Clutching a stone taken from the cairn, O'Brien falls asleep and reverts back through time to the Battle of Clontarf, where he discovers the truth. Odin himself had participated in the battle clothed in human flesh, and he is still trapped in those decaying bones and will be until a touch of holly sets him free to meddle once more in the affairs of humanity.

Ortali, intent upon treasure, disturbs the cairn and inadvertently revives the demonic Odin just as O'Brien discovers that the woman who brought him the cross has been dead for three centuries. Odin is no longer the anthropomorphic god of Norse legend but an inhuman creature who brutally slays Ortali before O'Brien can use the mystical cross to drive him away. In a fashion typical of stories of this type and era, the conclusion is abrupt and not entirely conclusive. Howard's depiction of the conflict between gods of different faiths, of which the "White Christ" is only one, was a common element in both his fantasy and his supernatural fiction.

"The Calamander Chest" Joseph Payne Brennan (1953)

Ernest Maax is inordinately pleased with himself when he finds a chest of calamander wood, a beautiful, fine-grained variety, on sale for an almost suspiciously low price. He purchases it and has it moved to his small apartment, where he cleans and polishes his new find so that it can be properly displayed. A few days later, he sees—or thinks he sees—a finger emerging from under the lid, but upon closer examination it is gone and the chest is empty. The same illusion occurs once again, however, and the shaken man decides to dispose of the chest at the earliest possible opportunity.

His first attempt to have the chest burned fails through a combination of circumstances that he takes as a sign that he is making a mistake. Although he has reluctantly accepted the possibility of the supernatural, he feels no real sense of menace, although the visions are by their very nature unsettling. When the next manifestation occurs, which includes the magical disabling of the chest's lock, he experiences a terrifying nightmare in

which the now animate finger lures him inside the chest. Thoroughly alarmed now, he arranges for a moving firm to take the chest away and throw it into a quarry, but their truck breaks down, delaying them until the next day.

That night Maax's nightmare comes true. He is wakened by a furious scratching sound and finds himself drawn inexorably to the calamander chest. The movers arrive the following morning and take away the locked and unusually heavy box. Maax, of course, is never heard from again, and we subsequently learn the history of the chest, which was used to suffocate and murder its former owner.

The concept that a horrible death can imbue inanimate objects with, if not a ghost, at least a ghostlike presence, is a common one in the literature of the supernatural. BRENNAN's story is a typical though unusually well-told example of the form, with effectively only a single character and a very straightforward plot whose inevitable consequences remain suspenseful even though the reader knows, or at least suspects, the rough form of the climax almost from the outset. It is also an excellent example of how some of the best and most disturbing horror fiction can achieve its effects without explicit gore, and, in fact, Maax's fate is implied and never actually described.

"The Calling" David B. Silva (1990)

Although David Silva has not been a prolific writer within the horror genre, his small body of novels and short stories are highly regarded, and he has also shown considerable skill as an editor. "The Calling" is probably his best short story and is also a good illustration of a trend that has become particularly popular in modern horror fiction, the use of a single, often very graphic and disturbing, image to leave the reader with a sense of shock, an image that often becomes more disturbing when contemplated later than when first encountered.

The protagonist is a middle-aged man who gives up his career and his home to move back in with his terminally ill mother, who is dying of cancer. There are no villains in the story. The mother is trying desperately to hang on to her dignity and be as little of a burden as possible. The son has his moments of frustration and resentment but always conceals these from his mother and never falters in his efforts to make her last days as comfortable as possible. Despite the good intentions on both sides, there are moments of quiet horror when she has trouble with her memory or her coordination and needs help performing even the most rudimentary tasks.

The son is particularly upset when he leaves his mother sleeping on the couch one night and finds her on the floor when he rises in the morning. She wakened during the night, could not call loud enough to wake him, and lacked the strength to reach her own bed. Mortified, he buys her a whistle so that she can call him more easily, but as the days pass he grows to hate the sound of the whistle, which disturbs his sleep and which almost always signals the need to perform some onerous task. The climax comes when he is awakened one night by the whistle, which he initially tries to ignore. Every few seconds it repeats itself, and he finally stumbles out of bed to find out what his mother needs.

He discovers instead that she has died, but even as he comes to that realization, he hears the whistle again. It originates somewhere inside her clothing, and when he investigates he realizes that it has fallen against her most recent incision, which has reopened. The whistle is pressing against the exposed tissue, and this time it is the cancer itself which is calling him. "The Calling" won the Bram Stoker Award for short fiction.

Campbell, Ramsey (1946–   )

Ramsey Campbell started his writing career in the 1960s with several short stories, most of which were in obvious imitation of H. P. LOVECRAFT, although he soon began exploring other themes, often concentrating on the psychological effects of terror. His early Lovecraftian tales were collected as *The Inhabitant of the Lake and Less Welcome Tenants* (1964), and many of his other early short stories appeared in *Demons by Daylight* (1973). Although he has continued to produce short fiction regularly ever since, his novel-length works quickly established his reputation as a writer of quiet but intense horror novels. His first book-length work, *The Doll Who Ate His Mother* (1976), is a mildly ambiguous novel about an evil man who uses apparently supernatural powers to influence the mind of a child, and his second, *The Face That Must Die* (1979), has no fantastic content.

After publishing several movie novelizations under a pen name, Campbell wrote *The Parasite* (1980), in which a group of children conduct a playful séance that actually raises a demonic force that resides within one of their number until its host becomes an adult. A slightly different version appeared as *To Wake the Dead*. *The Nameless* (1981) began to establish a common theme in Campbell's novels, a core mystery the protagonist seeks to solve that eventually becomes encumbered by the supernatural. In this case a woman receives a phone call that leads her to believe the daughter she thought long dead has somehow survived. *Incarnate* (1983) is another novel of past behavior returning with deadly consequences, in this case affecting the members of a group who experimented with prophetic dreaming. *Obsession* (1985) follows a similar pattern, this time in the form of a mysterious advertisement answered by several young people who discover the price they must pay for success only after several years have passed.

The Hungry Moon (1986) is very much in the spirit of Algernon BLACKWOOD. A remote English town conceals the existence of cavern-dwelling creatures and surviving druidic magic. An elderly woman desperate to cheat death finds a way to return from the grave and infect the mind of a young child in *The Influence* (1988). Campbell's most rewarding novels began appearing in the late 1980s and early 1990s, in which he rarely resorted to the more explicit excesses of his contemporaries. *Ancient Images* (1989), possibly Campbell's best novel, starts with the discovery of a long-lost Boris Karloff horror film and gradually moves to a remote English town and a supernatural secret. *The Midnight Sun* (1990) pits a writer and his family against an inhuman malevolent force that resides in a nearby forest. The plot of *The Count of Eleven* (1991), which progresses from an obsession with numerology to serial murder, seems disjointed but is actually quite well-integrated, and the protagonist's devolving personality is convincingly portrayed. *The Long Lost* (1993) is a less effective story involving a woman with ancient magical powers, and

Nazareth Hill (1996) is a mildly interesting haunted house variation. *Pacts of the Fathers* (2001) similarly reexamines the deal-with-the-devil plot.

Although his novels have moved toward psychological horror, most of Campbell's short fiction involves the supernatural, and he is one of the few contemporary writers still producing ghost stories with any regularity. Almost all of his large output of short stories are enjoyable, and some are excellent. Among the best of these are "The Inhabitant of the Lake" (1964), "THE CHIMNEY" (1977), "Mackintosh Willy" (1980), the last two of which won the World Fantasy Award, "The Faces at Pine Dunes" (1980), "The Missed Connection" (1986), and "Needing Ghosts" (1990). The best of his many collections are *Cold Print* (1985), *Scared Stiff* (1987), which contains several successful blends of horror and eroticism, *Fine Frights* (1988), *Waking Nightmares* (1991), *Alone with the Horrors* (1993), and *Ghosts and Grisly Things* (2000). *Alone With the Horrors* won both the World Fantasy and Bram Stoker Awards as best collection of the year. He is also the author of *Ramsey Campbell, Probably* (2002), a collection of essays and columns he has written on various subjects within the horror genre. He coedited several volumes of the "Best New Horror" series of reprint anthologies with Stephen Jones during the early 1990s as well as two volumes of the "New Terrors" series in 1980, and the shared universe horror anthology, *Deathport,* in 1993.

The Canterville Ghost Oscar Wilde (1887)

In addition to writing one of the greatest classics of horror fiction, THE PICTURE OF DORIAN GRAY (1891), Oscar Wilde wrote a considerable body of short fantasy, almost all for younger readers and much of it collected in *The Happy Prince and Other Stories* (1888). His most famous work in that vein is this humorous ghost story, actually a short novel, which places a very traditional English ghost at the mercy of the extremely pragmatic new residents of the stately home to which he is bound. Rather than running in terror when he attempts to scare them off, they are fascinated by his existence and his antics, and eventually the living and dead find common cause thanks in part to the innocence and openness of the children. For the first time it appears that there is hope that the curse might be lifted.

The original short novel has been filmed several times, although almost always in different settings. The details of the plot have also varied considerably, but the basic situation has been preserved in all of them. After many generations of his descendants have been scared out of Canterville Castle by the cursed ghost, his solitude is disturbed by an American branch of the family who are not so easily run off, either new tenants or temporary visitors, who eventually learn his secret and find a way to release him. The partnership between the living and an agreeable if somewhat gruff ghost has been imitated many times since, almost always in the form of comedy, as in *Topper* (1926) by Thorne SMITH and *The Ghost and Mrs. Muir* (1968) by Alice Denham, both of which also were eventually made into motion pictures. Ghost stories had traditionally been grim, and even the relatively benevolent ghosts of A CHRISTMAS CAROL (1843) by Charles Dickens were rather daunting. Wilde's short novel was a reaction against the tradition of Gothic horror that was prevalent at the time but which was soon to give way to more diverse forms of horror fiction. The marriage of humor and the supernatural has rarely worked well, but Wilde proved that it was possible to blend the two and still produce a masterpiece.

Carmilla J. Sheridan Le Fanu (1871)

Although the Irish newspaper publisher J. Sheridan LE FANU wrote several supernatural short stories and more than a dozen nonfantastic novels, he is best remembered for *Carmilla,* one of the earliest books about vampires and the first to hint openly at a link between vampirism and lesbianism. Le Fanu employed Bram STOKER as a theater reviewer from time to time, and he was obviously a strong influence on Stoker's creation of DRACULA several years later.

Laura is a dignified, somewhat retiring young woman living on the family estate in Styria. The family is hosting young Carmilla, a beautiful but mysterious girl who was slightly injured in an accident and who seems particularly fond of Laura. As their relationship grows more intense, Laura's health begins to decline, and she experiences increasingly disturbing nightmares, eventually alarming her father, who calls in an elderly doctor, who, like Van Helsing, recognizes the symptoms of vampiric intervention, particularly after learning of mysterious deaths in the surrounding area. After considerable investigation, we learn that the vampire is actually the Countess Mircalla von Karnstein, who died many years before. Mircalla is an anagram of Carmilla, which is the false identity the woman's spirit has taken for her return. The sexual implications of their relationship are not explicitly stated, of course, but they are very heavily implied, and various film versions that have appeared subsequently have emphasized the sexual nature of their relationship. Given the prevalence of vampires in modern romance fiction, it is surprising that this theme remains so little used in mainstream horror fiction. The story is efficiently and convincingly told, but Le Fanu's style and his preference for atmosphere over action often fail to appeal to modern readers.

Carmilla has been directly filmed at least seven times since 1963, but several other movies have drawn on the same basic story. Other stories by Le Fanu of interest are "Schalken the Painter" (1839), in which a woman discovers she has been married to a dead man, "The Haunted Baronet" (1870), a story of supernatural revenge, and "Green Tea" (1869).

Carroll, Jonathan (1949–   )

Some writers start their careers slowly, eventually producing more significant work that establishes their reputations. Others make an immediate impression, inviting impossibly high expectations for their subsequent work. Jonathan Carroll's first novel, *The Land of Laughs* (1980), caused considerable comment, but fortunately Carroll has continued to produce unusual, provocative, and highly regarded work ever since. Two writers travel to the hometown of a famous, now deceased fantasy writer in order to research a biography and discover that his imaginative creation and the town where he lives have become intermeshed and that the border between reality and illusion is not as distinct as they believed.

Voice of Our Shadow (1983) similarly questions the nature of consensus reality. An American tourist in Europe is haunted by the mysterious death of his brother while they were children. His life becomes even more unsettled when he discovers that his brother did not die as he has long believed and that neither of them are entirely human. The protagonist of *Bones of the Moon* (1987) is a woman who is troubled by particularly vivid dreams that begin to exert influence in the real world, affecting her objective reality. This was followed by a related novel, *Sleeping in Flame* (1988), wherein a similarly troubled man enlists the aid of a magician when his dreams reveal secrets of another lifetime. A horror film producer commits suicide in *A Child across the Sky* (1989), and an old friend tries to discover what drove him to it. His investigations reveal that the dead man drew his inspiration from the land of the dead and set loose a dark force that threatens the living. These three and the following four titles constitute a thematically linked sequence, although the separate titles do not have common characters.

The Black Cocktail (1990) is a novella in which a man discovers that a childhood friend has not aged even though years have passed since they were last together, or at least that's what appears to have happened. It is a cleverly worked out blend of the fantastic and the intricacies of human psychology, although the story falters toward the end. The protagonist of *Outside the Dog Museum* (1991) is an architect who suffers a nervous breakdown, undertakes a project for an Arab potentate, and discovers that there is genuine magic in the world. *After Silence* (1992), though thematically linked, contains no fantastic elements. Death personified takes a hand in events in *From the Teeth of Angels* (1994), which suggests that all of the protagonists in the previous books may have been mere playthings in the hands of a supernatural power.

Carroll's most recent novels have been quieter but equally effective. *The Marriage of Sticks* (1999) is a contemporary ghost story handled very unconventionally. A woman is troubled when she learns of the death of her high school sweetheart and then begins catching glimpses of him in crowds and elsewhere, until he eventually confronts her, revealing the possibilities she might have experienced if she had chosen other paths in life. In *The Wooden Sea* (2001), Carroll's best novel, a police officer is confronted by a dead dog that refuses to remain buried, a mysterious figure who gives him the ability to travel in time, and the unexpected appearance of a younger version of himself. Ultimately, he learns the purpose of human existence. A man is brought back from the dead in *White Apples* (2002) in order to play a pivotal role in the safety of his unborn son, who has extraordinary powers.

Carroll's fantasy novels, which often contain elements normally associated with horror fiction, are so original and unconventional that they defy comparison. His prose is fluid and intelligent, and his insights into human personalities are insightful and revealing. His short fiction appears infrequently but is of the same high quality as his novels, particularly "FRIEND'S BEST MAN" (1987), which received the World Fantasy Award, "Mr. Fiddlehead" (1989), and "The Life of My Crime" (1992). Most of his stories have been collected in *The Panic Hand* (1995), recipient of the Bram Stoker Award. Carroll should not be confused with another writer of the same name, who writes young adult fiction.

Carroll, Lewis (1832–1898)

Lewis Carroll was the pen name of Charles Lutwidge Dodgson, a mathematician whose fantasies for young children include ALICE IN WONDERLAND (1865) and THROUGH THE LOOKING GLASS (1871), which are probably the most widely known children's fantasies ever written. Both books are episodic adventures of young Alice, a girl from our world who stumbles into alternate realities, in one case by following a rabbit into his hole, in the other by stepping through a mirror. Unlike most children's literature published previously, they glorified nonsense and were not designed to teach a moral lesson or illustrate any particular point, but just to provide a zany form of entertainment. Carroll's inspired nonsense is timeless and speaks just as clearly to the present generation as it did to children, and many adults, when it first appeared.

Although the first of Alice's adventures is the more popular, it is actually the sequel that is a more consistent, integrated novel and is arguably the better of the two at least in a literary sense. Both contain nonsense verses that contain phrases familiar even to those who have never read the books. A section of the second novel that was cut from the original published edition later appeared as a chapbook under the title "The Wasp in a Wig." There have been many sequels and imitations, but none measured up to the original. Carroll also wrote another mild fantasy novel, *Sylvie and Bruno* (1889), which has been almost completely forgotten. Readers interested in more detail about the Alice books should try *The Annotated Alice* (1960).

Carter, Lin (1930–1988)

Lin Carter started his career as a novelist with *The Wizard of Lemuria* (1965), the first in a series of barbarian adventure novels in the style of Robert E. HOWARD. Although the stories contain all the elements of sword and sorcery, he rationalized the magic as "super science," and the series is technically science fiction. The majority of his later novels also fall into that genre, many of them written in imitation of the styles of Edgar Rice Burroughs, Leigh Brackett, and other writers who he admired. His other early fantasies were pedestrian, including the quest story *The Flame of Iridar* (1967), *Lost World of Time* (1969), which pits a barbarian hero against the inevitable evil sorcerer, *Quest of Kadji* (1971), the story of a young man determined to drive the usurper from his throne, and its sequel, *The Wizard of Zao* (1978). *The Black Star* (1973) was the best of his early heroic fantasies, and *Tara of the Twilight* (1979), which featured a female protagonist and some atypical, self-conscious sexual encounters, was probably his most ambitious effort.

The Zarkon series, which consists of *Nemesis of Evil* (1975), *Invisible Death* (1975), *The Volcano Ogre* (1976), and the later additions *The Earth-Shaker* (1982) and *Horror Wears Blue* (1987), were written as imitations of Doc Savage, a brawny and brainy hero of a series of sometimes fantastic adventure novels originally published in the pulp magazines. Zarkon and his friends defeat a variety of villains, usually equipped with plans for world domination or an empire of crime, but unlike the

Doc Savage books, the Zarkon adventures involve genuine occult forces that clearly move them into the fantasy field. During the 1970s, Carter and L. Sprague DE CAMP began adapting some of the Robert E. Howard's short stories to add them to the CONAN series, adding original material of their own, and while these additions did not often reach the quality of the originals, they helped flesh out the character's history and stimulated the revived interest in sword and sorcery in general, and Howard's work in particular.

Carter's most interesting fantasy series consisted of *Kesrick* (1982), *Dragonrouge* (1984), *Mandricardo* (1986), and *Callipygia* (1988). The setting is a magical land in which all of the legends of human history are real. The opening volume is predominantly cast in the form of an Arabian Nights–type adventure, but in later volumes the two heroes eventually meet dragons, giants, and various other dangers. The tone is lightly humorous, but the author's affection for his material is obvious and the series is quite readable. *Kellory the Warlock* (1984), although more serious in tone, also demonstrates that Carter was becoming more skillful late in his career.

Carter also produced a fair body of short fantasies. *Lost Worlds* (1980) is a general collection, while *The Xothic Legend Cycle* (1997) collects tales in the style of H. P. LOVECRAFT. *Lin Carter's Anton Zarnak: Supernatural Sleuth* (2002) chronicles the investigations of an occult detective in the manner of the John Silence stories by Algernon BLACK-WOOD and other similar psychic investigators. Despite his considerable body of published fantasy fiction, however, Carter's primary importance to fantasy was as an editor. In addition to the five-volume *Flashing Swords* series of original anthologies, he collected and reissued many classic short pieces in several anthologies and even more importantly oversaw the Ballantine Books Adult Fantasy line, which reissued fantasy work by William MORRIS, James Branch CABELL, William Hope HODGSON, Evangeline WALTON, William Beckford, Ernest BRAMAH, George Meredith, G. K. Chesterton, and many others. The success of that line helped convince publishers that fantasy could sustain itself as a separate genre, and today new fantasy titles are as numerous as new science fiction.

"Casting the Runes" M. R. James (1911)

Although M. R. JAMES is often credited as the most important ghost story writer of the early 20th century, several of the stories for which he is best remembered do not involve ghosts at all. This particular story, one of his best, opens with the rejection of a paper discussing alchemy written by an obnoxious individual named Karswell, whose odious character is revealed to us by the recounting of an episode in which he terrorized a number of children and scandalized his neighbors. We also learn that Karswell had previously published a book about witchcraft and that Harrington, a reviewer who trashed it, later died under mysterious circumstances. The paper was rejected at the suggestion of Edward Dunning, an authority on the subject who declares it badly written and of dubious value. Although Dunning's identity is kept confidential, it is not difficult for Karswell to determine his identity, which he has done.

Ominous events begin to occur. Dunning and two attendants notice a strange advertisement posted in a train car, a commemoration of Harrington's death, although the notice vanishes as mysteriously as it appeared. A stranger hands Dunning a leaflet, although he makes no effort to distribute any others, and another stranger returns some fallen papers to him in the library, who Dunning subsequently learns is none other than Karswell himself.

The situation rapidly grows more serious. Dunning's servants are poisoned and taken to the hospital. There are strange noises in his apartment at night, and the power fails. He begins to feel that he is not alone, that unseen eyes are watching him. Convinced that Karswell is somehow involved, he visits Harrington's brother and learns that the dead man experienced similar forebodings. Together they learn the truth, that Karswell included in the papers he handed to Dunning a slip that contains magical runes that dictate his fate. The only escape is to return the runes to Karswell, but there is a catch: They must be formally accepted. Simply mailing them back or destroying them will not save Dunning. To this end, Dunning disguises himself, and with Harrington's aid and the fortunate coincidence of a minor accident, he is able to return the runes to Karswell in a packet of tickets. The doom planned for Dunning subsequently claims its author.

Effective horror stories must usually include at least two conditions. First, the protagonist must have a chance to survive, although that is not necessarily what happens. Second, the supernatural element should conform to a set of rules. Vampires must recoil from a cross, for example, unless the reader is specifically told in advance that this particular rule is invalid. James was cognizant of this fact, and his efforts to ensure that the reader understand the nature of the problem to be solved makes the story a more effective one. This interpretation of the manner in which runes can be used to impose a curse was later used to great effect in *Rune* (1990) by Christopher FOWLER and the amusing 1991 film *Cast a Deadly Spell.*

The Castle of Otranto **Horace Walpole**
(1765)

Horace Walpole virtually invented the genre of Gothic fantasy and supernatural fiction with this very early novel, which, although poorly constructed and archaically written by modern standards, remains of interest because the author originated many conventions imitators would embrace and develop in subsequent years. Although Walpole wrote other fiction, none of his other work was rooted in the supernatural, and it is largely unknown and unavailable today.

The story is set in Otranto, Italy, in an undetermined time but probably the 11th or 12th century. Manfred, the local ruler, is a cruel and bitter man who hopes to forge an alliance between his ailing son and the daughter of a powerful rival. Before the marriage ceremony can be completed, the son is killed by the fall of an oversized helmet that resembles that found on a statue of an earlier benevolent ruler named Alfonso. When one of the guests comments on that fact, he is promptly seized and thrown into the dungeon. Manfred proposes to take his son's place, even though his own wife is still alive. A succession of supernatural events takes place before Manfred is thwarted, though not killed, and much of the castle is destroyed by a supernaturally projected giant who anoints the imprisoned house guest as Manfred's successor. Further revelations include the murder of Alfonso by Manfred, the death of Manfred's daughter, and the eventual marriage of the new ruler.

When originally published the novel purported to be a translation of an existing manuscript, a device still used in some modern fiction. Walpole's imitators, particularly Anne Radcliffe, produced much more coherent and entertaining tales along similar lines, but their debt to Walpole is clear. *The Castle of Otranto* has been reprinted many times since, most recently in 2002, but because of its unfamiliar prose style it is of interest chiefly as a literary milestone.

The Castle Series John DeChancie
(1988–1994)

John DeChancie began his writing career with some quite innovative science fiction novels that contained elements of sharp humor that became much more appropriate and effective in this series of eight fantasy novels, starting with *Castle Perilous* (1988). Humorous fantasy was quite popular at the time, and authors such as Craig Shaw GARDNER, Esther FRIESNER, J. Calvin Pierce, and other American writers joined DeChancie to produce a steady supply of light-hearted fantasy novels. DeChancie's madcap adventures are set inside a magical castle fitted with 144,000 doors, each of which opens onto another reality. In *Castle Perilous*, a frustrated academic stumbles into the castle and meets a variety of odd people, not all of them human. This set the premise and the tone for the subsequent books, which varied widely in their actual plots and settings.

The frantic pace was turned up a notch in *Castle for Rent* (1989). The ruling king is stranded temporarily in contemporary New York City, while Castle Perilous is infested by a horde of blue demons. *Castle Kidnapped* (1989), which is the weakest in the series, consists of various episodic adventures that ensue when many of the residents of the castle are dumped unceremoniously into a variety of weird worlds, including one dominated by dinosaurs who play golf. *Castle War!* (1990) was a decided improvement. The residents of the castle are menaced by the structure's evil twin, an alternate version of the castle inhabited by a host of villains drawn from multiple realities.

The melodrama cools down considerably in *Castle Murders* (1991), which spoofs conventions of both fantasy novels and the detective story genre. *Castle Dreams* (1992) is another episodic story, only slightly more interesting than *Castle Kidnapped*. *Castle Spellbound* (1992) is much better but basically reiterates many of the situations from *Castle War!*, and it was beginning to appear that the author was growing tired of his creation. The popularity of humorous fantasy had dropped off dramatically by the middle of the 1990s, and the series came to a close with *Bride of the Castle* (1994), in which chaos breaks out when the guests for a wedding are invited from multiple realities and interact in unexpected raucous ways. There are funny moments, but the jokes were generally repetitions or variations of previous material. DeChancie went on to write four more fantasy novels, of which only *MagicNet* (1993) is of any lasting interest.

Cave, Hugh (1910–2004)

Hugh Cave was a regular contributor to pulp magazines during the 1930s and 1940s, producing lurid stories of mystery and adventure interspersed with supernatural or occult adventures whose heroes often met grisly deaths or discovered previously hidden horrors. Many of these early stories featured grotesque images, and Cave's prose, considerably more polished than that of most of his contemporaries, made many of them stand out at the time, although he never achieved the enduring status of Ray BRADBURY or Robert BLOCH. A representative sampling of his early short fiction can be found in *Murgunstrumm and Others* (1977), *The Corpse Maker* (1988), *Death Stalks by Night* (1995), and *The Door Below* (1997), although much of his short fiction remains uncollected. Among his best works are "Stragella" (1932) and "Murgunstrumm" (1933), both vampire stories, "Dead Man's Belt" (1933), "Disturb Not the Dead" (1936), and "Calavan" (1942).

Cave lived in Haiti after World War II and became something of an authority on voodoo practices, writing a considerable amount of nonfiction on the subject and incorporating authentic voodoo lore into some of his subsequent novels. *Legion of the Dead* (1979), his first novel, is an excellent ex-

ample. An outsider falls in love with a local girl, earning the ire of the locals, who employ zombies in their efforts against him. A legless man dwells in the remote jungles of Haiti in *The Evil* (1981) using irresistible mental powers to bend others to his will. Voodoo magic, zombies, and the quest to destroy the source of such inhuman power dominate the plot. A much-belated sequel, *The Evil Returns* (2001), recapitulates the original story and adds mind control to the mix.

Voodoo is also central to *Shades of Evil* (1982), but this time without zombies. Instead, an evil spirit that manifests itself within a gaseous cloud emerges from the swamps to claim its victims. In *Disciples of Dread* (1989) a man whose brother is a secret agent with psi powers hides from conspirators in Jamaica, only to discover that he has become the target of voodoo magic. He must match his own abilities against those of the "houngan", a voodoo priest, who has chosen him as a victim. Voodoo is allied with the hero in *The Lower Deep* (1990) when a mysterious force from somewhere in the ocean enslaves the sleeping minds of villagers, drawing them out on mysterious and often deadly missions. *The Restless Dead* (2003) involves voodoo only peripherally, as an expert on the subject helps a troubled family defeat the inhuman creatures who live secretly beneath their home.

Not all of Cave's horror novels involve voodoo. In *The Nebulon Horror* (1980) a small town in Florida is beset by increasingly bizarre incidents that arise from its proximity to a gateway to hell, which creates an insidious force that affects the minds of the inhabitants and drives them to commit violent acts against one another. *Lucifer's Eye* (1991) is a more conventional story about a band of satanists who have genuine supernatural powers. There are multiple cases of demonic possession in a small town in Maine in *Isle of the Whisperers* (1999), and *The Dawning* (2000), technically science fiction, is set in the near future and involves the struggles between humans and a variety of mutated animals. Cave's horror novels are entertaining and workmanlike, but he will be remembered primarily for his detailed, convincing depictions of voodoo magic and ritual. He won the Bram Stoker Award for lifetime achievement and the World Fantasy Award for *Murgunstrumm and Others*.

Chapman, Vera (1898–1986)

Vera Chapman was a longtime fan of fantasy fiction and founded the British Tolkien Society, but she was in her 70s before she first began selling fiction. Her most famous work is the three-volume Arthurian fantasy romance consisting of *The Green Knight* (1975), *The King's Damosel* (1976), and *The King's Daughter* (1976). An omnibus edition of the three titles appeared as *The Three Damosels* (1978).

In the first volume, Morgan Le Fay plots to undermine Arthur through the sacrifice of an innocent young girl and the corruption of Sir Gawain. The Green Knight of the title is her ally, a man who can transform himself physically into a brutish monster. The two sequels involve a search for the Holy Grail and the battle between Arthur's daughter and Mordred for control of the succession to his throne. Chapman's interpretation includes a notable strain of feminism, and the power of Arthur is to be preserved through his daughter. The story of Arthur and Camelot had already been rendered in many versions by the 1970s, but Chapman brought a new interpretation that attracted considerable favorable attention from critics.

Her subsequent fantasy novels are not as effective. *Blaedud the Birdman* (1978) is also set in ancient Britain. In a variation on the story of Icarus, Chapman tells the story of a king so obsessed with the possibility of flight that he makes an unwise bargain with a druidic sorceress. *The Enchantresses* (1998), published posthumously, is the story of the three half-sisters of Arthur raised by Merlin and their roles in the preservation of Arthur's heritage following his death and the fall of Camelot. *Miranty and the Alchemist* (1983) is a minor tale for younger readers. The stories in *The Notorious Abbess* (1993) occasionally contain fantastic elements. Her most interesting short story is "With a Long Spoon" (1981).

Charlie and the Chocolate Factory
Roald Dahl (1964)

Roald DAHL wrote a large body of somewhat bizarre short stories for adults and even briefly hosted a television anthology program based on weird stories, often depending on macabre twist endings, so it should come as no surprise to discover that his fiction for children contains similar, sometimes unsettling images and events. His first fantasy for younger readers was JAMES AND THE GIANT PEACH (1961), which attracted only casual comment, but *Charlie and the Chocolate Factory* (1964) became an immediate cause of controversy because of what some saw as depictions of sadistic violence toward children.

The plot is fairly straightforward. A chocolate factory has been closed to visitors for many years, but the owner, Willy Wonka, has announced a contest from which five winners will be chosen. Each, accompanied by a relative of his or her choosing, will be given a conducted tour of the chocolate factory and perhaps samples of some of the candy. Young Charlie, whose family is destitute, becomes one of the lucky five and arrives with his grandfather. A business rival of Wonka's tries to bribe Charlie into stealing the secret of the factory's most prized product, but the boy resists the temptation.

A series of mild adventures follows during which each of the children are tested in some fashion, and gluttony in particular is punished in a rather grotesque fashion. Charlie is tempted a second time, and despite some wavering, his flawless character resists again, after which we learn that it has all been a test to choose Wonka's successor as the factory's owner. Some adults were alarmed by the suggestion of cruelty, but the punishments are not malicious, although they are extreme. Children seem to have had no difficulty understanding that this is a fairy tale, and there are any number of equally grisly deaths and misfortunes in the work of Hans Christian ANDERSEN and the Brothers GRIMM.

A live action motion picture was made from Dahl's own screenplay in 1971 as *Willy Wonka and the Chocolate Factory*, and predictably it received very mixed reviews because of the comic book–style violence. Dahl also wrote an amusing but inferior sequel, *Charlie and the Great Glass Elevator* (1972), in which Charlie, now managing the chocolate factory, visits outer space and meets aliens.

"Chatting with Anubis" Harlan Ellison (1995)

Harlan Ellison is usually identified as a science fiction writer, although many of his stories are clearly fantasy. This Bram Stoker Award–winning short story is one of the best of his more recent fantasy tales, the story of a marvelous discovery that is more impressive for its smooth, emotionally charged prose than for the details of its plot. Wang Zicai is an archaeologist whose name prophetically means "rushing headlong toward suicide." His services are requested when an unusual archaeological discovery is made under the Sahara following an earthquake. There he is teamed with a colleague, Amy Guiterman, and their relationship quickly grows to become more than just professional.

They identify the buried structures, which are surprisingly well preserved, as the fabled Shrine of Ammon, where Alexander visited and asked the oracle a single question, after which he left without ever speaking of the conversation to another person. The shrine itself was lost to history, its location and fate unknown.

The excavation reaches the roof of an enormous chamber and is stopped pending daylight, but Wang and Amy sneak out of the encampment after dark, determined to be the first to see the interior, even if that means violating protocol. They quietly break through into a chamber so immense that it contains statues 500 feet in height. But they find more than they bargained for, because Anubis, the Egyptian lord of the dead, is there in person waiting for them.

Obviously, they want to know what Alexander learned. Anubis tells them the shrine's true purpose, which is not to prevent the dead from returning to the world of the living but rather to bar from the afterlife the one person who brought about the death of the gods of the ancient world. That person is Moses, whose efforts changed the way humans thought about their gods forever. The idea that the gods lose their power when people stop believing in them is an old one in fantasy fiction, but usually there is no effort made to identify the catalyst for this change in perception.

"The Cheaters" Robert Bloch (1947)

Few of us would initially question the statement that it is a good thing to know the truth about where we stand with other people, but Robert BLOCH proves that is not necessarily the case in

this classic supernatural thriller. The owner of a second-hand shop purchases the entire contents of an abandoned speakeasy, formerly the private home of a man who dabbled in witchcraft and alchemy. His relationship with his wife, Maggie, and his single employee are not amicable, but he does not realize how bad things have gotten until he finds a pair of magic spectacles hidden in a desk. The spectacles, also known as "cheaters," are embossed with the word "veritas," or "truth," and when he wears them he can hear the thoughts in the minds of people he sees. When he discovers that his wife and employee are plotting to kill him—they are also "cheaters"—he kills them preemptively and is subsequently executed.

The glasses pass to Miriam Olcott, an aging kleptomaniac and semi-invalid who resents the presence of her daughter and son-in-law in her home. She tries them on when her doctor comes to visit and reads in his thoughts that he has been bribed by the daughter to poison her so that they can inherit her estate. She switches their cups so that it is the doctor who dies but then overindulges despite her medical condition and dies shortly afterward.

Her daughter inherits the house, and the glasses are neglected at first, but her socially ambitious husband prevails upon her to run a fancy costume party to which the leading community figures will be invited. He dresses as Benjamin Franklin and eventually dons the glasses during a poker game, which enable him to win consistently. Then he discovers that one of the other men is cheating, assaults him, and is accidentally killed when the others attempt to stop the fight. One of the witnesses is a writer who suspects some of the truth, steals the glasses, and researches their history. He becomes convinced that using them to spy on others inevitably causes the death of the owner and resolves not to employ them for that purpose. Instead, he plans to don them only a single time, to look at himself in a mirror. Unfortunately, the knowledge of his own inner flaws is so devastating that he decides to take his own life, destroying the spectacles in the process. Bloch economically combines four separate but related tales of horror into a single story and demonstrates that too much of anything, even truth, can be a bad thing.

Cherryh, C. J. (1942–)

Although some of C. J. Cherryh's early novels contained many elements of fantasy, she established her reputation primarily as a science fiction writer, for which she has received considerable acclaim. With the exception of a few short stories, she wrote no true fantasy until 1983, when the two-volume sequence consisting of *The Dreamstone* and *The Tree of Sword and Jewels* appeared, later published jointly as *Arafel's Saga.* The growing number and power of the human race has forced the magical folk of a fantasy world to retreat into a narrowly circumscribed reality. Arafel, the last elf, tries to protect that rapidly dwindling stronghold in a very traditional and sometimes very slowly paced story that often feels like an old fairy tale. Five years passed before Cherryh's next fantasy novel, *The Paladin* (1988), a rather routine adventure in which the protagonist organizes resistance to an invasion when his emperor falters. Cherryh had been contributing short stories to a shared universe anthology series set literally within hell itself, which eventually resulted in the novel *Legions of Hell* (1987), which mixed a variety of historical characters in a series of conflicts, and *Kings of Hell* (1987), written with Janet MORRIS, which features an interesting reenactment of the Trojan War. She is also listed as a collaborator on a violent otherworld fantasy trilogy consisting of *A Dirge for Sabis* with Leslie Fish, *Wizard Spawn* with Nancy Asire, and *Reap the Whirlwind* with Mercedes LACKEY, all published in 1989, although it is uncertain how much she actually contributed to the text.

Much more interesting are three stand-alone novels based on Russian fairy tales. *Rusalka* (1989) is set in pre-Christian Russia and involves travelers who encounter a magical wood and the ghost of a murdered girl. Rusalka is magically restored to life, but she is lured off by the spirit of her murderer in *Chernevog* (1990). The interaction continues into the next generation with the final installment, *Yvgenie* (1991). Her next two fantasy novels were readable but undistinguished. *The Goblin Mirror* (1992) is a fairly routine though pleasantly told quest story, and *Faery in Shadow* (1994) is a darker version of the Arafel sequence set in Scotland.

Cherryh's most sustained and interesting fantasy series consists of *Fortress in the Eye of Time*

(1995), *Fortress of Eagles* (1998), *Fortress of Owls* (1999), and *The Fortress of Dragons* (2000). Tristen is created by magic as the savior of the land of Ylesuin, helps secure the throne for the rightful ruler, defeats his enemies, retires, then returns to battle a fresh assault by outsiders. Much of the action and background is standard fare, but Cherryh has a narrative flare that allows the stories to rise above the limitations of their subject matter. Although to date her science fiction has usually been of higher quality than her fantasy, her contributions to the latter field are not insignificant.

Chetwynd-Hayes, R. (1919–2001)

Ronald Chetwynd-Hayes began writing professionally during the 1950s, but it was not until the latter part of the 1960s that he began to specialize in ghost and horror fiction, particularly short stories. He was quite prolific, particularly at shorter length, and took the unusual route of publishing most of his short stories in the form of single-author collections rather than having them appear initially in magazines and anthologies, starting with *The Unbidden* (1971). Chetwynd-Hayes wrote a great many ghost stories, although later in his career he focused much of his attention on vampires. He was also one of the few horror writers who could successfully include humorous sequences and events in his work without fatally wounding the mood of terror and suspense.

His most famous and successful series revolves around Clavering Grange, which was first mentioned in *The Dark Man* (1964, also published as *And Love Survived*), a low-key supernatural novel in which a sleeping man regresses through time. Chetwynd-Hayes returned to this setting for several short stories as well as two novels. *The Grange* (1985, also published as *The King's Ghost*) is a historical ghost story filled with high adventure, as is the less successful *The Haunted Grange* (1988). *Tales from the Hidden World* (1988) collects most of the associated short stories. A second series consists of stories about the descendants of Count Dracula, which were collected in two volumes as *Dracula's Children* (1987) and *The House of Dracula* (1987). Chetwynd-Hayes also wrote a series of short stories about an occult detective, Francis St.

Claire, which were collected as *The Psychic Detective* in 1993.

Chetwynd-Hayes produced more than two dozen collections of short stories, most of which are quite enjoyable, if unmemorable. The best of these collections are *The Monster Club* (1975), *The Other Side* (1983), and *Shudders and Shivers* (1995). Several of his stories are worthy of being singled out, particularly "Which One?" (1981), which challenges the reader to figure out which of several people is actually a ghost, the chilling "Something Comes in from the Garden" (1975), "Long Long Ago" (1986), and "Moving Day" (1987).

In addition to writing his own fiction, Chetwynd-Hayes edited a very large number of horror anthologies, including almost a dozen volumes of the prestigious Fontana Books of Ghost Stories. His nonseries novel *The Curse of the Snake God* (1989) is quite good but long out of print. He also wrote movie novelizations, of which *The Awakening* (1980) is of note because it was based on Bram STOKER's 1903 novel *The Jewel of the Seven Stars*.

"Children of the Corn" Stephen King (1977)

Horror fiction often allows readers to vicariously confront those things that frighten them, sometimes fears that are not even consciously acknowledged. When Stephen KING wrote *Carrie* (1974), he addressed many of the situations that trouble adolescents, and when Ray BRADBURY wrote "THE SMALL ASSASSIN" (1946), he was giving form to our vaguely perceived and rarely acknowledged fears about the alien nature of children. King, who has proven himself extraordinarily skillful at evoking the feel of childhood in such works as "The Body" and *IT* (1990), gave this fear an even more substantial form in "Children of the Corn," which has since been the inspiration for a series of five horror films of varying quality.

Burt and Vicky Robeson are traveling across the country trying unsuccessfully to salvage an increasingly rocky marriage. Burt leaves the highway in a remote part of Nebraska to relieve the monotony but instead finds himself traveling through seemingly endless fields of corn. He and Vicky are arguing again when, distracted, he hits a child in the road, although when they inspect the body they discover the boy's throat had been cut and that he was dead or dying when the collision took place. They take the body to nearby Gatlin, a small town of about 5,000 and find it deserted, with every indication that it was abandoned 12 years earlier. Vicky grows increasingly frightened, but Burt is determined to find someone to take charge of the body.

Burt investigates a strangely transformed church and finds evidence that the children slaughtered all the adults years before in service to a mysterious entity known as "He Who Walks Behind the Rows." Vicky is attacked and carried off, and Burt is forced to kill one of the children before fleeing into the cornfields. The pursuit continues until darkness falls, and he discovers that he has been guided by some unseen force to a clearing where his wife has been mutilated and crucified adjacent to the long-dead corpses of the local police chief and minister. All hope of escape is lost when he is confronted by both the children and the monstrous creature they worship.

Unlike the movie version, in which the couple survive and even rescue some of the children, King's short story is relentlessly grim. We never learn the explicit nature of the entity, but it is implicitly the evil that can grow within ordinary people if they allow their religious beliefs to grow so narrow that they no longer have room for compassion or humanity. On the surface the evil lies in the demonically motivated children. In reality it lies within each of us.

"The Chimney" Ramsey Campbell (1977)

Many of the best horror stories involve childhood fears with the elements of suspense doubly effective because those are the primal fears we never quite outgrow, even though we may think we do, and because the protagonists are usually children as well, which lends a special air of vulnerability to the characters. Ramsey CAMPBELL is a prolific short story writer and steadily productive novelist who is particularly noted for his ability to describe the intricate workings of human psychology so that his characters become multidimensional and easy to identify with.

The main character in this story is a young boy whose personality has been shaped by an overly protective mother and a father who has distanced himself from them both. He spends most of his life in fear, frightened of the other kids at school, of hurting himself while playing, of strangers, and of many other things both innocuous and genuinely dangerous. Although his mother reinforces his nervousness, even she is not aware of the one thing that terrifies him the most, the chimney that runs up through his bedroom and that he believes to be the home of some unseen, unknown, and unfriendly creature. Over the course of time, he grows out of many of these fears despite his mother's coddling and lives a fairly normal life, but he continues to be nervous about the chimney. The climax of his terror comes when he becomes confused over the story of Father Christmas emerging from the chimney with presents, assuming that he lives there all the time. This new misapprehension and his old fantasy merge, and one night he does, in fact, see a shadowy figure in his room, which he perceives as horribly burned, deformed, and covered with soot. The crisis is resolved for the moment when the intruder turns out to be his father dressed as Father Christmas.

What might have been just an interesting incident acquires a new dimension when Campbell moves us forward a few years. A fire breaks out in the house, and although the protagonist survives, his father is killed in horrible fashion. When his body is brought out of the ruined building, the boy recognizes the same horribly mutilated figure he had only imagined—or did he?—years previously. Campbell never clears up the ambiguity, leaving the reader as well as the main character with an acute sense of uncertainty about what is real and what is not.

"The Chop Girl"　Ian R. MacLeod (1999)

Superstition is a powerful force in human life. Even people who scoff at the ideas are often secret believers, going out of their way to avoid "unlucky" objects or situations "just in case." Superstition seems particularly prevalent in situations in which there is overt, even violent, competition, such as in many sports events and even more significantly during wartime. The British writer MacLeod in-

vokes this concept in this fairly long story set during the latter days of World War II. The blitz is over, and allied bombers are pounding the German-held cities in Europe. Even though they control the skies, the toll among bomber crews is terrific. Less than half the airmen will live through their required number of tours, and each of the enclosed cultures of the British airbases has developed an elaborate series of superstitions, charms for both good luck and bad.

The worst of the latter is the "chop girl," whose company means bad luck. The narrator becomes the chop girl for her base after three incidents in which she became close to a pilot, each of whom died or disappeared on his very next mission. Although no one is openly impolite to her, the others begin to avoid her company, particularly the airmen, and she becomes increasingly isolated. In contrast to her is Walt Williams, a pilot with such great good luck that it seems—and eventually proves to be—a magical quality. Walt is charming and competent and leads an obviously charmed life. He can even walk across an icy puddle without getting his feet wet. Walt never gambles or wastes his good luck on anything trivial, and once in the sky he is never in any danger.

The gift does not come without a price, which he reveals only when he and the chop girl run into each other one night and discover that they are mutually lonely. There had been stories about him crying out in the night, perhaps caught up in a nightmare, but the truth is even worse. Walt is troubled by visions. When he sleeps he witnesses the bad luck of others, their terrible deaths and mutilations, and his visions are not confined to the English, or the Allies, or even to the current day. He recoils in horror from the aftermath of Hiroshima and the fall of Berlin, even though neither event has yet taken place. During their first night together bad and good luck merge, but Walt tells her that he is confident that he is safe and is, in fact, resigned to a life he cannot escape. But the truth is that he longs for death, and this is a part of his plan to achieve it, for on his very next mission he is lost, and investigators discover that he deliberately disconnected his parachute.

"The Chop Girl," which won the World Fantasy Award, is a particularly moving and subtle story. Although there is genuine magic in it, the impact comes from MacLeod's skill in creating believable people reacting plausibly under great stress. He also does a superb job of describing a situation in which belief in superstition is almost inevitable and showing us the inevitable emotional toll.

A Christmas Carol Charles Dickens (1843)

This short novel is one of a handful of classics whose story line is so familiar that almost everyone knows it in detail, and people actually reading it for the first time may feel as though they are revisiting an old favorite. It is certainly the most famous Christmas story outside the Bible, has been filmed more than a dozen times since its first appearance in 1935, and is one of the most commonly produced stage plays year after year. It is also a ghost story, although properly speaking only Jacob Marley is a true ghost. The others are manifestations of abstractions rather than the souls of the dead.

Ebenezer Scrooge is an irascible, uncharitable, stingy old man who early in his life gave up the opportunity to secure a loving wife and family, good friends, and a clear soul in favor of accumulating wealth, which has now become such an obsession that he will not even treat himself to the luxuries he could easily afford. Scrooge's single employee is Bob Cratchit, a poor, honest, self-effacing man with many children who he can barely feed, one of whom is Tiny Tim, a disabled child doomed to die without outside assistance. Dickens presents a series of brief incidents that establish Scrooge's character quite effectively and demonstrate the quieter happiness of the Cratchits as a counterpoint.

Dickens contradicts himself about the time span in which the supernatural events occur, but Scrooge is, in fact, visited by a succession of apparitions. Jacob Marley, his ex-partner, appears as a warning, worn down by heavy chains of his own fashioning. The Ghost of Christmas past points out what he has forfeited in his life, the Ghost of Christmas Present shows him what he is currently denying himself, and the Ghost of Christmas Future warns him of his eventual death, friendless, alone, and unmourned. Scrooge emerges from this series of revelations with his character miraculously changed and sets about mending his ways.

The transition is somewhat too abrupt to be psychologically convincing, but it works extraordinarily well dramatically. *A Christmas Carol* is an enduring classic whose deceptively simple message speaks to all of us.

The Chronicles of Narnia C. S. Lewis (1950–1956)

The British author C. S. LEWIS is best known for his seven-volume fantasy series for young readers that is set in the land of Narnia, a magical world visited in each case by children from our reality. The only character to appear in all of the volumes is Aslan, a mystical lion who is meant to be a parallel to Jesus. The series began with THE LION, THE WITCH & THE WARDROBE, and continued with PRINCE CASPIAN, THE VOYAGE OF THE "DAWN TREADER", THE SILVER CHAIR, THE HORSE AND HIS BOY, THE MAGICIAN'S NEPHEW, and THE LAST BATTLE. The internal chronology of the stories does not agree with the order of publication, but they should be read in the order of publication.

The Circus of Dr. Lao Charles G. Finney (1935)

Charles G. Finney was not a prolific writer, and he is best remembered only for this, his first novel, although *The Old China Hands* (1961) is a memorable treatment of his early military service in mainland China. The town of Abalone, Arizona, is startled by the arrival of a mysterious circus and initially disappointed by its opening parade, which consists of three wagons drawn by a unicorn, a sphinx, and a golden ass. There is considerable disagreement among the spectators about the nature of the animals, particularly the occupant of one cage, which might be a bear or a man. The reader will recognize almost immediately that Dr. Lao, the oriental leader of the circus, has gathered together selected creatures from myth and legend and magically transplanted them to rural America.

The exhibits include a genuine medusa, a roc's egg, a mermaid, and Appolonius of Tyana, a magician who brings the dead back to life and creates living things out of moist earth. Dr. Lao gives brief and often fascinating lectures on each of his attractions, but his articulate English disappears whenever he is posed a question he does not wish to answer. The visitors are surprised, sometimes deeply shocked, by their experiences. An insistent, abrasive woman is turned to stone by the medusa, and a repressed schoolteacher visits the faun and is seduced by his masculinity, releasing something of the secret inner feelings she has concealed even from herself. Another consults a fortune-teller and learns the depressing truth about her future, that it will be unproductive and uneventful. Different characters take something away or leave something of themselves, and the circus disappears just as mysteriously as it arrived.

The story itself is followed by an extensive catalog of characters and things named in the main text, which is itself fascinating and informative. The 1964 film version, as *The Seven Faces of Dr. Lao,* was extremely well done, although it changes the character of Lao and his circus quite radically, implying that their intentions are essentially benevolent and it is only our human failings that prevent us from taking advantage of its wonders. The ending is, for most of the characters, considerably more pleasant than in the book.

"The City of the Singing Flame"
Clark Ashton Smith (1931)
One subset of fantasy fiction adopts some of the trappings of science fiction and is sometimes labeled *science fantasy* to imply that it straddles the borderline between the two genres. This was true of many stories of lost Atlantis, or those set in other realities where the laws of nature made magic possible or where the creatures of mythology still exist. Clark Ashton SMITH frequently couched his fantasies in pseudoscientific terms, setting them in the impossibly distant future or in lost worlds of the past, but despite a veneer of science, they remain essentially fantasy tales.

The protagonist of this story is a fantasy writer himself. He stumbles across two magical stones while walking one day and finds himself immediately transported to a bizarre landscape near a magnificent city. His first visit terrifies him, but he manages to find his way back across the invisible gateway. Once recovered from his initial shock, he

decides to return, armed this time, and approaches the city, whose inhabitants are oversized and inhuman. Although he is unobserved, he is nearly seduced by mysterious music that emanates from within the city walls. Later he returns yet again with cotton to block out the sound of the music and explores the city, which is peopled by so many different forms of life that no one pays him any particular attention. He eventually learns to recognize the city's original inhabitants, who alone seem to be immune to the lure of the singing, which originates in a supernatural flame in which one visitor after another seeks a fiery death. Eventually he enlists the aid of a friend, but despite everything he succumbs to the lure.

Reprints of the story often include with it a less interesting sequel, "Beyond the Singing Flame" (1931), in which an acquaintance of the original protagonist investigates his disappearance. There we learn the name of the city, Ydmos, and witness its destruction when the living flame finally falters. As is the case with most of Smith's fiction, characterization is minimal, and even the plot is comparatively threadbare. What made Smith such a remarkable writer was his ability to create magnificently exotic images and conduct his readers on tours of worlds that never existed but that seem vivid and logical. His elaborate prose style might seem awkward by contemporary standards, but his precise and varied vocabulary provides an extra layer of atmosphere to his already richly ornate fiction.

Clark, Simon (1958–)
The British horror writer Simon Clark began his career with a handful of short stories in the 1980s, culminating in a collection, *Blood and Grit* (1990). He continued to write short fiction intermittently until the publication of his first novel, *Nailed by the Heart* (1995), and has concentrated on novels ever since. "Salt Snake" (1993), included in his second collection, *Salt Snakes and Other Blood Cuts* (1998), is his only outstanding piece at that length.

Nailed by the Heart bears a close resemblance to the work of Algernon BLACKWOOD and Ramsey CAMPBELL, set in a remote English village where the old ways from before Christianity have yet to completely disappear. A demonic force abides there, and shortly after the protagonists arrive it manifests itself through the crew of a long-sunken freighter, raising their uneasy spirits from the dead. The novel is at its best when it is understated, but the horrors eventually become less covert and considerably less chilling as we learn their true nature at first hand. *Blood Crazy* (1996) edged toward science fiction and introduced a situation Clark would use more than once in the future, the collapse of civilization as the result of a new disease or other transformation, with horrifying consequences for the survivors. In this case the plague drives all the adults in the world into a homicidal rage against their children.

Darker (1996) is less ambitious and considerably more effective, featuring an invisible and menacing supernatural evil opposed by a small band of desperate heroes. *King Blood* (1997) is another apocalyptic vision, this one following the destruction of civilization with the appearance of the enigmatic "Gray Men," who prey on the minority left alive. Clark then turned to more traditional fare for *Vampyrrhic* (1998), a sometimes quite effectively creepy story about a band of vampires who lurk beneath a small British town, although the plot is very slow to develop in the early chapters. His later sequel, *Vampyrrhic Rites* (2003), although basically a restatement of the original story, is considerably more effective in generating suspense.

Judas Tree (1999) is a much quieter horror story and is Clark's best novel. A young woman pays a visit to her mother, who has taken up residence on a remote Greek island, and discovers that the entire island is in a sense a single entity and that it does not wish for her to leave—ever. *Darkness Demands* (2001) is also quietly impressive, another story of a slumbering evil wakening in a rural setting, but the plot contains few surprises and only occasional chills. Clark invoked still another worldwide holocaust in *The Stranger* (2002), this time in the form of a plague that causes instantaneous mutations. The resulting melodrama is fast paced and well written, but the logic of the situation is rather strained. *Exorcising Angels* (2003), with Tim Lebbon, is a collection of more recent short stories. *Night of the Triffids* (2001), sometimes shelved with horror fiction, is actually a science fiction novel, a sequel to *The Day of the Triffids* (1951) by John Wyndham. Clark was quite popular in England for several years before finding a publisher in the United States but has recently become much better known in America.

Clayton, Jo (1939–1998)

Jo Clayton began writing science fiction novels in the late 1970s with the Diadem series, and they have much of the atmosphere and many of the devices of fantasy despite their outer space setting. His first outright fantasy novel was *Moongather* (1982), the first in the Duel of Sorcery series. Serroi, a young woman cast out by her family, becomes a trained warrior in service to the emperor. By chance, she stumbles across a plot to assassinate him and must betray her sworn word and challenge an immortal wizard in order to save his life. She falls under the wizard's magical influence in *Moonscatter* (1983) and regains her freedom to act, saving the day, in *Changer's Moon* (1985). Although standard fantasy fare, the stories are rousingly told and feature an interesting, admirable female protagonist. The Dancer duo is related to the Duel of Sorcery. In *Dancer's Rise* (1993) an immortal creature manifests itself in the human world, undertakes a dangerous journey, and confronts a man with the ability to control the minds of others. A new form of magic transforms the world in *Serpent Waltz* (1994), and Serroi, the heroine of the earlier series, is awakened from a generations-long sleep to help save the day.

A second and somewhat darker series began with *The Drinker of Souls* (1986). Brann is a combination of vampire and disembodied spirit, but she still values the code of honor she embraced while alive and still feels intense loyalty to her people. In the opening volume she helps undermine the rule of a despotic tyrant. A sleeping god must be awakened in *Blue Magic* (1988), and another seeks freedom from age-long imprisonment in *A Gathering of Stones* (1989). *Wild Magic* (1991) and its sequel, *Wildfire* (1992), are set in the same universe but feature different characters. A poorly prepared sorceress is catapulted into a prominent role in the battle among various magical forces. This five book sequence is considerably more inventive and interesting than those set in the Dancer universe.

Clayton had begun a new fantasy series before her death, consisting of *Drum Warning* (1997), *Drum Calls* (1997), and *Drum into Silence* (2002), the last completed posthumously by Kevin Murphy. The trilogy describes the tensions caused by the interfacing of two separate fantasy worlds and is sometimes quite original, although the plot follows a familiar path. Clayton devotes considerably more attention to the complexity of her characters, who are much more believable than her earlier protagonists. One other title, *A Bait of Dreams* (1985), is actually several intertwined short stories about a group of people who use magical jewels to travel among realities. Clayton was a competent, intermittently interesting writer of fantasy adventures notable chiefly for her strong female characters. Much of her science fiction should be equally appealing to fantasy readers.

Clegg, Douglas (1958–)

It is a testimony to the skill of Douglas Clegg that he began to write horror novels just as the field began to collapse during the late 1980s and has continued to find a home for his books ever since. In his first novel, *Goat Dance* (1989), a young girl is brought back to life after apparently drowning, but some members of her family believe that another consciousness has usurped her body. A greater threat is the malevolent "Eater of Souls," a supernatural creature that spreads death and terror across the countryside. A young man returns to his hometown in search of closure for a terrible incident in his past and achieves it only by facing an even greater fear. Although Clegg's prose is sometimes difficult to follow, the novel rewards attentive reading.

Clegg's follow-up was a sometimes predictable but quite tense haunted house story that adds an elaborate array of voodoo and the risen dead into the mix. *Breeder* (1990) features a supernatural entity that is seeking to reproduce its kind. A couple settles into their new townhouse despite the presence of a strange nanny and a homeless woman who warns them to leave quickly before the house harms them. Somewhat predictably, they begin to

conduct research into the history of the house, but whatever sinister presence resides there has already begun to insinuate itself in their minds. *Neverland* (1991) more consciously explores Stephen KING territory. While on vacation a young boy becomes involved with his cousin Sumter, who has an uncertain relationship with some supernatural force that calls itself Lucy and resides in a shack the children call Neverland. Lucy turns out to be more than just a ghostly child. Clegg carefully establishes his characters, then turns their world end over end for the balance of the novel. Sumter's character in particular is effective and unsettling.

Dark of the Eye (1994) is even more obviously influenced by King. Hope is a young child with a magical power that allows her either to heal or harm. She is kidnapped by a murkily motivated man who removes one of her eyes, but an accident disrupts his plans and Hope's mother steals her back and runs away to California, pursued by a host of grotesque characters, not all of whom are human. There are several bits that are highly inventive, but the author has perhaps tried to insert too many different wonders into his story, which becomes unfocused and erratically paced. *The Children's Hour* (1995) is another story of a bad town, this one haunted by an evil presence that preys on the local children, eventually revealed to be a vampire variation. *Bad Karma* (1998), written under the name Andrew Harper, is an ambiguous thriller in which an escaped mental patient menaces the family of her doctor while recalling memories of a past life when she was the mistress of Jack the Ripper. It was filmed as *Hell's Gate* (2001).

There is another supernatural creature hiding in a small town in *Halloween Man* (1998), which interweaves two stories, each of which is affected by the efforts of the townspeople to conceal the monstrous entity they secretly worship. Satanism has not been a popular theme in recent horror fiction, but Clegg proves that it is possible to employ an old theme in an entertaining new way. His novels had always been very complexly plotted, but he was clearly developing his narrative abilities to make it easier for readers to stay focused on the individual story lines.

Mischief (2000) was the first novel in the Harrow sequence. Harrow is a mansion that has been modified to be a prep school. A new arrival is forcibly initiated into a secret society that looks suspiciously like a coven. Stories of unsavory events in the building's past continue to grow, including several suicides, but the novel ends without clearing up most of the mysteries. The story is continued in two sequels, *Infinite* (2001) and *Nightmare House* (2002, although previously published electronically). The first title is reminiscent of the classic THE HAUNTING OF HILL HOUSE (1959) by Shirley JACKSON. A team of psychic investigators is sent to Harrow to identify the supernatural forces at work there, but the evil is insidious and clever and exploits their own insecurities. The latter is actually a prequel to the others, in which the new owner of the mansion faces a host of standard elements from early horror fiction, including ghosts and premature burial. Clegg later added a novella-length story set even earlier, *The Necromancer* (2003), which chronicles a young man's seduction by the dark arts. Apparently more volumes in the informal series are planned.

Naomi (2000) is in some ways Clegg's most interesting novel, although a bit hastily told. The protagonist becomes convinced that his dead friend is still around and is taken on a fascinating tour of a world hidden below New York City. *You Come When I Call You* (2000) is another King-influenced work. A demonic force believed to have been destroyed is back, and the group of friends who defeated it the first time must reassemble to deal with it permanently. *The Hour before Dark* (2002) is a sophisticated and initially ambiguous thriller about two young people investigating a murder by means of a form of mental projection that allows them to detect supernatural influences. A mummy rises from the dead in *The Attraction* (2004), a surprisingly effective treatment of what might have been merely silly.

Douglas Clegg has managed to survive and prosper in the horror field even when the decline in that genre has taken a heavy toll among his fellow writers. Although most of his themes and plot devices are familiar ones, he assembles them in new configurations and particularly in his later novels demonstrates an increasing ability to present believable and sympathetic, if not always likeable, characters. *The Nightmare Chronicles* (1999)

collects most of Clegg's better short fiction. It received the Bram Stoker Award as best collection of the year.

Collins, Nancy (1959–)

Nancy Collins won instant attention and a Bram Stoker Award for her first novel, *Sunglasses after Dark* (1989), the first adventure of Sonja Blue, a very atypical vampire heroine. Sonja escapes from a mental institution and takes the reader on a tour of a world hidden from our eyes but existing all around us, one where the creatures of legend and nightmares exist in a reality of their own that interfaces with ours. Sonja's personality is split between her savage vampire nature and her humanity, and that struggle persists through the series that continued to be interesting but that never achieved the success of its opening title. Sonja forms an uneasy alliance with a private detective in *In the Blood* (1991) as part of her effort to track down the local vampire lord. She has a series of interlinked adventures in *Paint It Black* (1994), gets involved in a major conflict between rival vampire powers in *A Dozen Black Roses* (1996), and hunts down some of her own kind in *Darkest Heart* (2002). Although Sonja continued to be an interesting character, her latter adventures are much less innovative and striking than her earlier ones.

Tempter (1991, but massively rewritten for the 2001 reprint) is another vampire novel, without Sonja Blue, and is intermittently interesting but a more conventional thriller than her other work. *Wild Blood* (1993) and *Walking Wolf* (1995) are both werewolf stories. The first follows the adventures of an orphan boy who discovers that he is a shape changer and seeks others of his kind, while the latter, and better, of the two features a shape shifting Comanche who had difficulty adjusting to life among modern Americans, and not just because of his supernatural abilities. *Angels on Fire* (1998) describes a battle between good and evil agents against the backdrop of a modern city, but it is at times emotionally flat and uninvolving. *Lynch* (1999) is a straightforward story of a man returning from the dead for vengeance with an Old West setting and is the best of her later novels, quietly effective and eerie.

Collins also has written a considerable body of short fiction, the best of which is contained in *Nameless Sins* (1994), *Knuckles and Tales* (2001), and *Dead Roses for a Blue Lady* (2002). Her most successful stories include "The Vargr Rule" (1992), "Cold Turkey" (1992), "The Needle Men" (1993), "Avenue X" (1995), and "Catfish Gal Blues" (1999).

"Come, Lady Death" Peter S. Beagle (1963)

Despite having produced a very small body of work over the more than 40 years of his career, Peter S. BEAGLE is one of the most highly respected of all fantasy writers. His short stories have been even less frequent than his novels, but this early tale has become a classic. The setting is 19th-century England, and the main character is Flora, Lady Neville, an elderly, extremely rich woman who dominates London society to such an extent that even the king would not refuse an invitation to one of her parties.

Lady Neville realizes one day that she is bored and decides to resolve the problem by inviting Death himself to attend her next get together. After considerable effort to determine the manner in which Death should be addressed, she faces the difficulty of delivering the invitation, although since Death is presumably a nobleman, she concludes that he must live quite close by, since hers is the best neighborhood in all of London. She hits upon the idea of giving the invitation to the father of a dying child, to be delivered when Death arrives to take his due. In due course she receives an acknowledgment, accepting her invitation. By the nature of the handwriting, however, she and her friends conclude that Death is, after all, female.

Death appears in the form of a beautiful young woman, and the guests are charmed as well as frightened. The party proceeds as expected, but only one aging soldier is brave enough to dance with Death, although when morning approaches and she announces that it is time for her to leave, there is a storm of protest at her going, not all of it genuine. She tells them that she would like to stay and be human, but to do so she must find someone from among their company to take her place. She chooses Lady Neville, having decided that the

woman's heartless cruelty toward the dying child is proof that she is suited for the position, which she identifies as a curse, not a privilege. For her part, Lady Neville is so bored with life that she offers no objection.

The concept that the role of Death can be passed on from individual to individual recurs in *Mort* (1987) by Terry PRATCHETT, who uses the device for darkly humorous purposes, and in the Incarnations of Immortality series by Piers ANTHONY, but Beagle's short story is still its most effective presentation.

The Conan Series Robert E. Howard and others (1932–2004)

The character Conan was first created by Robert E. HOWARD in 1932 and appeared in one novel and slightly more than a dozen shorter pieces during the four years prior to Howard's death. Conan was a brash but powerful barbarian warrior from Cimmeria in Hyborea, a primitive world presumed to be in Earth's past some time following the fall of Atlantis. Howard showed Conan at various stages in his life, naive and youthful, seasoned, mature, and established as king, and fragments of additional stories survived Howard's death. Hardcover publication in the 1930s brought them to the attention of fans and some writers, but not the general reading public. They languished in relative obscurity until the 1960s, when they were brought back into print in mass market paperback editions. The existing material was extensively elaborated by the completion of many of those fragments, primarily by L. Sprague DE CAMP and Lin CARTER and by the conversion of other stories to feature Conan in place of the original protagonist. These did extremely well in book form, and Howard's reputation has continued to grow ever since. He was a remarkably prolific writer and produced a wide variety of work, not all of it fantasy, but most of it recently reprinted in various collections and cross-collections. Publishers have mixed the Conan stories into so many combinations that it may appear that Howard himself wrote much more material than is actually the case.

Howard's original stories contain examples of mild racism at times, but several of these, including "The People of the Black Coast" and "The Tower of the Elephant," are undeniable classics of fantasy. His world was a violent one, and Conan does not always act by what we might consider high moral standards. He supports himself by thievery for much of his life, but he always adheres to his personal code of honor and is unalterably opposed to the clearly evil men and monsters he meets during his travels. Howard is also credited with introducing some of the earliest strong female characters in fantasy, particularly Red Sonja, who developed from a minor character in the Conan stories to the protagonist of a series of later novels by other writers and later even had her own comic book. De Camp and Carter were criticized at times for having diluted the original material, but the popularity of the character was immense, and Howard's influence can be seen quite clearly in a number of authors of varying talents, including Carter himself, Andrew J. OFFUTT, John Jakes, Gardner Fox, David GEMMELL, and many others. No fantasy writer other than J. R. R. TOLKIEN has had more influence on modern fantasy fiction.

During the 1980s several other writers were invited to produce additional book-length adventures. The most prominent of these was Robert JORDAN, who subsequently moved on to create an immensely popular fantasy cycle of his own. Others who contributed include Poul Anderson, Karl Edward WAGNER, Andrew J. Offutt, John Maddox Roberts, Harry TURTLEDOVE, and Roland Green. Most of these extended adventures were decidedly inferior to the original material. Marvel Comics introduced a graphic version during the early 1970s, often adapted from Howard's stories, with original material appearing as well. There were also two movies made starring Arnold Schwarzenegger as Conan, though neither were based on any of Howard's, or indeed any written, material, though both were subsequently novelized. *Conan the Barbarian* (1981) is the better of the two, recreating Conan's youth and providing a story line not dissimilar to those of Howard himself. *Conan the Destroyer* (1984), a modified quest story, is palatable but less true to Howard's character.

Both of the movies were novelized, the first by L. Sprague de Camp and the second by Robert Jordan. The only Conan novel written by Howard himself is *The Hour of the Dragon,* which has also appeared as *Conan the Conqueror.* It was originally published in magazine form in 1935 but not as a book until 1950. Howard's novel deals with an older Conan who has apparently seized the throne of a small country and must now battle with his wits as well as his sword as conspiracies and dark magic threaten his rule. Over the years there has been considerable nonfiction published about the background history and culture of Hyborea including at least two full-length books. There have also been numerous parodies, most notably a three-novel series of spoofs by the British writer James Bibby. Conan is the barbarian hero against which all others are measured and the single most dominant character in all of sword and sorcery fiction.

A Connecticut Yankee in King Arthur's Court Mark Twain (1889)

Mark Twain is best known for his creation of two young characters named Tom Sawyer and Huckleberry Finn, but he also wrote a number of fantasies, many of them satiric, involving happenings in the afterlife, talking animals, mythical creatures, and other extraordinary events. His most famous fantasy, however, is this interesting time travel story in which a man from Twain's time is magically transported by a bump on the head back through the centuries to the court of King Arthur at Camelot, where he meets all of the legendary characters, from Sir Lancelot to Merlin the wizard.

Twain's protagonist, Hank Morgan, fortunately has a working understanding of technology and the foreknowledge of an eclipse, which saves his life. His ability to build working devices is instrumental in elevating his status to that of wizard, in which role he is known as "The Boss." His exploits are also designed to point out that the romantic vision of that period, which is still prevalent today, ignored the reality of the situation, the filth, squalor, disease, virtual slavery of much of the population, religious repression, and inequities of the government, even under the supposedly enlightened King Arthur. Ultimately, Morgan's attempts to turn the monarchy into a republic are doomed to failure. Some of the humor has not aged well, but the basic satire of the story remains valid.

There have been several film versions ranging from serious to animated to musical comedy, and the protagonist has been replaced with a spaceman and a young black female child in some cases. L. Sprague DE CAMP, responding to the ease with which Twain's protagonist is able to recreate modern technology in a primitive culture, wrote what is perhaps his best single novel, *Lest Darkness Fall* (1941), in which a contemporary academic falls back through time to the days of the Roman Empire and tries unsuccessfully to use modern knowledge to prevent the fall of civilization. Knowledge in a vacuum proves to be virtually useless. There is no industrial base to provide the tools he needs to build advanced weapons, and even if he did, the preconceptions and habits of the Romans are so entrenched that he has no serious chance of changing their attitude. Many other time travel novels, including hundreds of time travel romances, owe at least a nodding debt to Twain's classic.

Constantine, Storm (1956–)

Although Storm Constantine's early fantasy novels have only recently begun to appear in the United States, she quickly accumulated a significant readership when they first appeared in the early 1990s. Constantine employs a rich prose style to describe very elaborate fantasy worlds whose characters, human and otherwise, have complex and believable personalities. She mixes various archetypes—angels and vampires among them—and some of her fantasy worlds overlap into science fiction and vice versa. Her Wraethu series, the early volumes of which are essentially science fiction, are often lumped with her fantasy because they read so similarly, and more recent titles in the series blur the distinction even further. *Hermetech* (1991) can also be read as part of either genre.

Sign for the Sacred (1992) is more clearly fantasy, a sometimes darkly humorous story in which angels and vampires are blended into a somewhat erotic, intensely mystical story about the role of religion in human life. The vampires are relatively benevolent and are actually a race from another world who have settled on a magical alternate

Earth in *Burying the Shadow* (1992). The protagonist of *Calenture* (1994), whose beautifully described cultural setting is fascinating in itself, may or may not be imagining the other characters in the story. Two opposed groups of angelic creatures battle each other over the destiny of the human race in *Stealing Sacred Fire* (1995).

Stalking Tender Prey (1995), the first of the Grigori books, covers somewhat similar ground. A race of angels has long abandoned humanity, but now one of their number has returned, and the population of a small village falls under his hypnotic power. In the sequel, *Scenting Hallowed Blood* (1996), a large number of angels have secretly taken up residence in England, where they plan to assert their authority over humanity at the coming of the millennium. One of their number has had second thoughts, however, and acts to preserve human free will and independence.

Her most successful fantasy work to date is the Magravandias Chronicles, consisting of *Sea Dragon Heir* (2000), *The Crown of Silence* (2000), and *Way of Light* (2001). The heir to the throne of Caradore is magically bonded to the ruler of the people who conquered his country. This is designed to enforce loyalty, but the situation becomes fluid when the current heir becomes passionately involved with his own sister, an act that wakens old and dangerous magic. Prophecies and a magician raised from the dead accelerate matters, which resolve themselves finally with a blend of treachery, intrigue, and overt adventure. The underlying sexual imagery is powerful even in restraint, and Constantine's prose is invariably impressive, although it may demand too much from some casual readers.

Much of Constantine's short fiction is related to her novels, usually embellishing her fantastic worlds or providing sidelights to the histories of her imagined nations. The best collection is *The Oracle Lips* (1999), but *Three Heralds of the Storm* (1998) and *The Thorn Boy and Other Dreams of Dark Desire* (2002) are also quite good, the latter containing stories related to the Magravandias Chronicles.

Cook, Glen (1944–)

Glen Cook started his career writing science fiction in the early 1970s, but by the end of the decade he was mixing it with fantasy. By the middle of the 1980s he was writing fantasy almost exclusively. His first sequence was inevitably designed to be a trilogy, the Dread Empire, although Cook would subsequently add more volumes at both ends of the sequence. The original trilogy consists of *A Shadow of All Night Falling* (1979), *October's Baby* (1980), and *All Darkness Met* (1980), set in a fantasy world that bears more than a slight resemblance to historical Asia. Tensions mount between one enormous empire and a handful of neighboring states, with prophecies, wizardry, treachery, and a variety of plots. The war finally comes in the final volume and contains some of the earliest and best military fantasy writing. Cook enhanced this imaginary world with *The Fire in His Hands* (1984) and *With Mercy Towards None* (1985), prequels involving early efforts to unite some of the outlying peoples while elsewhere a religious prophet appears whose life in some ways parallels the rise of Islam. Cook then returned to the main sequence for *Reap the East Wind* (1987) and *An Ill Fate Marshalling* (1988) but abandoned the series at that point, despite leaving many questions unresolved. A stand-alone novel from the same period, *The Swordbearer* (1980), was considerably less interesting, a story of magical swords and stolen thrones.

The Black Company (1984) launched a second and more popular series and remains to this day the best example of military-oriented fantasy. The title refers to a group of mercenaries in a land where evil seems to rule unchallenged. They hear rumors of a manifestation of a more benevolent god and decide to serve a new cause. The god is exposed as a fraud in *Shadows Linger* (1984), but the mercenaries have not given up hope that a power for good may still be found, although their commitment to virtue is more a matter of tactics than of conscience. An alternate deity finally does arrive on the scene in *The White Rose* (1985), the climax of the original series. Cook returned to their world after a four-year gap with *The Silver Spike* (1989) and has added to the saga intermittently ever since. Having disbanded, the Black Company must reunite when a magical menace is inadvertently released from captivity. Their exploits continue in *Shadow Games* (1989), *Bleak Seasons* (1996), *Dreams of Steel* (1996), *She Is the*

Darkness (1997), *Water Sleeps* (1999), and *Soldiers Live* (2000). These later adventures are all independent stories and despite some superficial similarity are still the most consistently entertaining military fantasy novels.

Cook's longest series started in 1987 with *Sweet Silver Blues*, the first adventure of a private detective named Garrett who lives in an alternate magical world that has some but not a great many similarities to our own. The 10th and most recent is *Angry Lead Skies* (2002). The Garrett stories are to date the most successful and sustained effort to blend fantasy with the detective genre. *Red Iron Nights* (1991) is particularly effective, pitting Garrett against a serial killer who may or may not be human. The novels in the series all have similar titles and do not need to be read in their order of publication, although it is interesting to note the evolution of the protagonist. In other volumes Garrett works as a bodyguard, rescues kidnap victims, saves the world from an evil plot, defeats a sleeping god, traces missing persons, and has other adventures. Garrett himself is not an entirely admirable character, sometimes relying on questionable tactics to achieve his goals and bound only by his own personal and sometimes fluid code of honor.

The Tower of Fear (1989), a stand-alone novel, is also quite entertaining, pitting a typical fantasy hero against a particularly nasty and clever witch. Cook's rare short fantasy fiction can be found in *Sung in Blood* (1990). Throughout his career he has avoided medieval style fantasies, which largely dominate the genre, possibly explaining his less-frequent appearances in recent years. Cook's characters are almost never the virtuous, often implausible heroes that dominate most modern fantasy fiction. They are flawed, self-contradictory, misguided, and egotistical at times, and as such they are much more believable than their counterparts in the work of most other fantasy writers.

Cook, Hugh (1956–)

Hugh Cook, who was born in England, raised in New Zealand, and currently lives in Japan, was the author of a 10-volume fantasy series known as the Chronicles of an Age of Darkness, which he describes as a blend of Tolkien and the cold war.

The series started with *The Wizards and the Warriors* (1986, also published as *Wizard War*), which opens in a typical fantasy world with an evil wizard stealing a magical object that could give him power over the entire world. A council of rival wizards sets out to stop him. Nine sequels followed, although each is a separate adventure, and they can be read in any order.

The second volume, *The Wordsmiths and the Warguild* (1987), was published in two volumes in the United States as *The Questing Hero* and *The Hero's Return* and is a straightforward quest story. It was followed by *The Women and the Warlords* (1987, also published as *The Oracle*), actually written earlier and featuring a female protagonist caught up in the war between two magically empowered nations. *The Walrus and the Warwolf* (1988, also published in abridged form as *Lords of the Sword*) follows the episodic adventures of an apprenticed swordmaker forced to flee for his life. The American edition contains less than half of the original novel, which is quite long.

The Wicked and the Witless (1989) is essentially a return to events in the previous volumes, retold from a fresh viewpoint. *The Wishstone and the Wonderworkers* (1990) and *The Wazir and the Witch* (1990) constitute a subset of their own, centered on one city and its inhabitants and could just as easily have been set in another fantasy world entirely. If there had ever been a central theme to the series, Cook had by now lost track of it and seemed to be adding adventures almost at random. *The Werewolf and the Wormlord* (1991) is, as the title suggests, a werewolf story interesting primarily because the author chose to set every scene after nightfall. *The Worshippers and the Way* (1992) and *The Witchlord and the Weaponmaster* (1992) brought the series to a close, but Cook's subsequent work, with the exception of a few short stories, has been confined entirely to print on demand and other electronic formats. His published work contains many interesting elements but lacks the depth or originality that might have given it broader appeal.

"Cool Air" H. P. Lovecraft (1928)

Although H. P. LOVECRAFT is known primarily for his Cthulhu Mythos stories, several of his more generic horror tales are at least as skillfully done. Lovecraft's precise, idiosyncratic language helped create a distinct atmosphere for his horror stories. One of the most memorable is this very short tale, which opens with some vague foreshadowing of the horror to come as the unnamed protagonist, whose financial situation has lately deteriorated so that he is forced to seek lodging in a mildly disreputable rooming house, becomes aware of the resident living above him, Professor Munoz, who is reportedly very ill, rarely leaves his room, and maintains it at a particularly low temperature for health reasons.

He makes the professor's acquaintance as the result of a minor heart ailment and finds him to be intelligent, well-spoken, and neat in appearance, although there is something indefinable about him that is equally repelling. Munoz tells him that he has devoted his life to defeating death and that he believes the spirit or will can keep the body operating even when the flesh itself has otherwise failed. The perceptive reader will take this as a sign of what has yet to be revealed. The two strike up a mild friendship despite the narrator's continued revulsion, amplified by a further physical deterioration that takes place over the course of several weeks.

The crisis comes when the cooling equipment breaks down in the middle of the night. Efforts to repair it prove unavailing, and a part must be found on the following day. Munoz orders a constant supply of ice and hides in the bathroom, but things go from bad to worse. He runs out of ice and locks himself in his room, from which comes a pungent odor and a constant sound of dripping. When the door is broken down, what remains of Munoz, never described, lies on the couch. The story ends with the revelation in the dead man's last note that he has, in fact, been dead for 18 years. "Cool Air" is an excellent example of a story that remains suspenseful even though the reader must anticipate the ending very early on and that delivers its horror without the necessity of describing things too minutely. It is one of Lovecraft's most effective and memorable stories and was produced as an episode of *The Night Gallery* in 1971. *Chiller* (1992) by Randall BOYLL uses a very similar premise in a very different fashion.

Cooper, Louise (1952–   )

Louise Cooper's first fantasy novel, *The Book of Paradox* (1973), is set in a world based on the Tarot and contains several interesting elements, but her second effort, *Lord of No Time* (1977) is disappointing. Her other early work consists of some not particularly memorable supernatural fiction and a minor fantasy for younger readers. It was not until the middle of the 1980s that she began to write superior fiction, starting with the Time Master trilogy, which takes the central story from *Lord of No Time* and expands it quite effectively into three titles, *The Initiate* (1985), *The Outcast* (1986), and *The Master* (1987). The opening volume sets up the dichotomy between Order and Chaos, two magical forces battling for control of the universe. The central character is destined to bring balance, but some of his allies consider him a demonic force and drive him off in the middle volume. Only the woman he loves stands by him for the final battle. Cooper's portrayal of the roles of both Order and Chaos in human society is clever and rather sophisticated for a straightforward adventure story.

Obviously pleased with the results of this revised work, Cooper went on to add two more trilogies to the series. *The Deceiver* (1991), *The Pretender* (1991), and *The Avenger* (1992) take place after the events in the original series and concentrate on a daughter of Chaos who wants to seize control of the world using an army of the risen dead pledged to her service. *Star Ascendant* (1994), *Eclipse* (1994), and *Moonset* (1995) take place much earlier and are the weakest in the series, reprising many elements from the earlier novels with only very slight new twists. Cooper started an entirely separate sequence with *Nemesis* (1988), the first of the Indigo books, in which a woman inadvertently releases seven demons into the world and sets out to track down and neutralize each of them in turn. There are eight volumes in the series, ending with *The Aisling* (1993), all of which are superior sword and sorcery adventures, avoiding most of the clichés and featuring an unusually well-drawn female protagonist.

Cooper also wrote occasional stand alone novels, including *Mirage* (1987), a fairly conventional fantasy adventure, and *The Sleep of Stone* (1991), an elaborate fairy tale about a shape changer who impersonates a human in order to marry the man she loves. The latter is Cooper's best novel. Most of her recent work has consisted of young adult fantasies and horror stories, including the Daughter of Storms and Seahorses trilogies.

Cooper, Susan (1935–   )

Susan Cooper's first novel, *Mandrake* (1964), is generally considered science fiction, although the existence of a world-spanning intelligence that pervades all living things might better have been explained magically. She achieved acclaim, however, with the first title in a five-volume young adult fantasy series based on the premise that some of the figures from the time of Camelot were actually magically endowed and are still around to help in the battle between the forces of good and evil. *Over Sea, Under Stone* (1965) introduces the main characters and the background as they discover a map that promises to reveal the location of the Holy Grail and revive the magic that has been dormant since King Arthur's time. Never a prolific writer, Cooper allowed eight years to elapse before providing the sequel, *The Dark Is Rising* (1973), in which the young Will Stanton discovers that animals and even people have begun avoiding his presence, apparently reacting to some magical spell of which he is unaware.

The remaining three volumes appeared much more quickly. With the assistance of a benevolent witch, the children retrieve a magic grail from another world dominated by an evil force in *Greenwitch* (1974), but in *The Grey King* (1975) Will discovers that he is not safely back in the familiar world and that his old adversary is pursuing him. The story is finally brought to an end in *Silver on the Tree* (1977) with the discovery of a magic sword and the final battle. Although written for younger readers, this is one of a handful of such fantasies that has found a large and loyal audience among adults.

Cooper's subsequent novels have been infrequent and less impressive but are invariably entertaining. *Seaward* (1983) is set in an alternate reality where the forces of life and death are personified. *The Boggart* (1993) is an amusing story in which a variety of Irish gremlin is involuntarily forced to relocate to America, where he attracts attention by playing endless practical jokes on his host family. *Green Boy* (2002) invokes the spirit of Gaia, or the soul of the Earth, to transport two teenagers into a highly polluted future where they are given the task of rehabilitating the ecosystem. Although her later novels are comparatively minor, the Dark Is Rising sequence remains popular and will likely do so for many years to come.

Costello, Matthew J. (1948–)

Although Matthew Costello has written some science fiction and one minor fantasy novel, *Wizard of Tizare* (1990), he is known primarily for his horror fiction, which began with *Sleep Tight* (1987), an interesting but occasionally unfocused story in which a gateway between our world and another reality is opened, allowing a sinister force to menace the unsuspecting. His second horror novel, *Beneath Still Waters* (1989), was far better, a ghost story variation with an unusually effective setting, an entire town that was sacrificed to facilitate construction of a dam and reservoir and that now lies quiet, but not uninhabited, at the bottom of a lake. Years later the dam begins to show unexpected signs of deterioration, and the angry spirits trapped below employ a variety of methods to wreak vengeance on the living. Costello's bizarre imagery is particularly effective in the underwater sequences.

Midsummer (1990) is science fiction as well as horror. An expedition to Antarctica ends disastrously with a series of apparently psychotic murders. The sole survivor is evacuated and kept under close surveillance, and eventually we discover that the explorers stumbled across a previously unknown parasitic life form that possesses humans and drives them to commit violent acts. *Wurm* (1991) and its sequel, *Garden* (1993), use a very similar device, but this time the creatures live in the depths of the ocean. During the 1990s Costello diverted much of his effort to writing game scripts such as *The Seventh Guest*, comic book scripts, and other media-related materials. His next novel, *Darkborn* (1992), is a fairly pedestrian effort in which a group of friends conjure up a demon and then discover they are unable to get rid of it.

Costello's two most recent books mark a return to his original form. *The Unidentified* (2002) is an effectively suspenseful story of an enigmatic structure that is actually a portal to another reality whose monstrous inhabitants have designs on our world. Even better is *Missing Monday* (2004), an unusual novel of possession whose protagonist awakens one day to discover that a complete day of her life is missing. Two of his short stories are also noteworthy, "Abuse" (1993) and "Unexpected Attraction" (1997). Costello clearly has the tools to become a sustained, significant writer of horror fiction. Whether he will use those tools consistently remains to be seen.

"Couching at the Door"   D. K. Broster (1933)

Dorothy Kathleen Broster was a prolific though minor writer, and only a small portion of her output was horror fiction. Of that, only this single short piece has remained popular over the years. Suspense stories rely on their ability to make the reader care about what happens to their protagonists, and generally this is accomplished by making the character someone we like and can identify with. Horror fiction frequently makes use of an alternate approach, developing protagonists in the opposite direction, making them unpleasant at best and actively evil at worst. Since it is often obvious at the outset that a character is doomed, readers can enjoy the preliminary steps building to the inevitable and perhaps ghastly demise of a character they have come to loathe.

That is certainly the case with Broster's classic, which opens with the introduction of Augustine Marchant, a pretentious poet who has inherited substantial wealth and who plays his chosen part to perfection, although he is contemptuous of his acquaintances and pursues secret vices while vacationing where he is less well known. Marchant is disturbed one day when he notices a bit of what he at first believes to be dust in his private rooms but that later moves toward him purposefully as though it might be an insect or small animal. A rapid succession of incidents follows during which Marchant becomes convinced that the apparition is real, that it is a kind of familiar, a manifestation of his past sins—specifically a never clearly described incident involving an experience with black magic and suggestions of human sacrifice. The manifestation, which generally takes the form of a long furry caterpillar, follows him when he travels, and there are even hints that it can occasionally be seen by others.

After encountering a biblical passage that seems relevant, Marchant discovers that to a limited extent he can command the creature, although it will not be driven away. Eventually he hits upon the plan of corrupting a young artist in such fashion that the familiar will seek out the younger man's greater evil in preference to his own, and after some time it appears that he has succeeded. The artist, however, commits suicide, after which the familiar returns to its original master, but now transformed into a much more menacing and malevolent creature. The author wisely allows the reader's imagination to fill in the next scene. Justice is served and evil determines its own reward.

"Count Magnus" M. R. James (1904)

This classic horror story is represented from the outset as an account gleaned from various papers left by the protagonist, which has since become an almost certain giveaway that the central character will not survive the story. Mr. Wraxall has two passions, his curiosity and his love of travel, and he marries them happily in his profession of writing travel guides enhanced by interesting historical details uncovered during his visits. His latest and last project was a guide to Scandinavia, in the course of which he visited Sweden and happened upon the story of Count Magnus de la Gardie, long since dead and interred in a mausoleum. The count was a man known to have engaged in alchemy who conducted a quest for immortality and who is rumored to have completed the Black Pilgrimage, about which Wraxall can find no helpful description. Magnus was a cruel man, guilty of murder and other evils, and there have been long-standing rumors that his former property is still troubled by some malevolent spirit. Trespassers there have died horribly or been driven mad in the past. The count's closest companion was a small man who

accompanied him everywhere and who is likewise interred in the tomb.

This is all grist for Wraxall's mill, and he arranges to visit the mausoleum and examine the count's casket, which bears unusual and vaguely disturbing decorations. During his first visit he notices that one of the three padlocks on the coffin is open and on his return discovers that two are in fact unfastened, a discrepancy he explains to himself as the result of his lack of attention. Unfortunately, he expresses aloud a whimsical wish to have seen the count in person, and during his final visit to the tomb, the last of the locks falls loosely to the floor. Terrified, Wraxall immediately returns to England, but the damage is done. His notes indicate that he saw shadowy figures that could only be the count and his companion elsewhere on the ship and later on land in England. Wraxall stops at an inn where he is found dead in the morning, his body so horribly disfigured that it causes a minor sensation.

"Count Magnus" would seem tame and somewhat predictable if it were to appear today, but M. R. JAMES was practically inventing ghost stories when he wrote this. His basic formula has proven to be the template for many more tales of terror.

Coville, Bruce (1950–)

Almost all of Bruce Coville's fiction has been for young adults or children, and much of it is narrated in a deliberately light and playful style. His earliest books of distinction were young adult horror, starting with *Eyes of Tarot* (1983), in which a teenager defies a family curse by using a tarot deck to look into her own future, only to be dismayed by what she finds there, and *Spirits and Spells* (1983), in which a group engaged in a role playing game find themselves trapped in a real and dangerous alternate reality that conforms to the rules of their fantasy. *Waiting Spirits* (1984) is an effective ghost story with a petulant spirit making life difficult for the protagonist, and *Amulet of Doom* (1985) is the suspenseful tale of a cursed object and the desperate attempts of a teenager to escape her fate. Most of Coville's subsequent supernatural fiction is much lighter in tone and directed at a younger audience and includes such titles as *The Ghost Wore*

Grey (1988) and *The Ghost in the Big Brass Bed* (1991), in which the restless spirits are more likely to be victims in need of help than menacing figures themselves.

Much of his work in the late 1980s was science fiction, but almost all of his books published after 1990 are fantasy, several of which are outstanding. The best of these is *Jeremy Thatcher, Dragon Hatcher* (1991), whose title character purchases a dragon's egg with predictable but quite touching results. This was the middle volume of a loosely connected series about a magic shop that began with *The Monster's Ring* (1989) and continued with *Jennifer Murdley's Toad* (1992), an amusing variation of the charmed prince story, and *The Skull of Truth* (1997). *The Dragonslayers* (1994) is a more traditional and less interesting heroic fantasy, also for younger readers, but *Goblins in the Castle* (1992) is a delightful story about a boy who discovers that goblins and other creatures are living secretly in a creepy old castle.

Into the Land of the Unicorns (1994) introduced the Unicorn Chronicles, transporting a girl from our world into an alternate reality where the unicorns are in danger. The story continues in *Song of the Wanderer* (2001). Coville's fiction has grown less frequent in recent years, but the quality has remained consistently high. *Juliet Dove, Queen of Love* (2003) is particularly effective, as are many of the short stories collected in *Oddly Enough* (1994) and *Odder Than Ever* (1999). Coville has also edited several anthologies for younger readers, mostly of supernatural and suspense stories.

Coyne, John (1937–)

John Coyne was a victim of the collapse of the horror market in the early 1990s, so his career essentially spans a single decade, starting with *The Legacy* (1979), a surprisingly interesting novelization of a screenplay by Jimmy Sangster, a variation of the Ten Little Indians plot. A handful of people are invited to the remote mansion of a man with occult powers, each hoping to be the beneficiary of his will. His first original novel appeared almost simultaneously. In *The Piercing* (1979) a woman is troubled by miraculous transformations once a week, manifestations that capture the public's attention and result in wide-scale publicity. Although the church asserts that the effects are only an elaborate hoax, the protagonist priest realizes that they are genuinely supernatural, if not holy. Although they are claimed as signs from a benign God, he believes they are evidence of satanic involvement. The powerful religious theme is particularly effective, as is the clear effort to blur the distinction between good and evil.

The Searing (1980) presents a somewhat similar plot on a much wider scale. All of the female inhabitants of a remote town are subject to sudden, inexplicable attacks of sexual arousal, even at totally inappropriate times. At the same time, several of the infants in the area are mysteriously killed. Although the buildup is excellent, Coyne's resolution is less satisfying this time, involving interference by enigmatic alien creatures. *Hobgoblin* (1981) is much better. The protagonist is a young boy whose fascination with role playing games and the use of monstrous disguises is linked to his conviction that there are creatures sharing the world with us that remain invisible except to those who know how to look for them. He throws a Halloween party for his friends to which he invites the fantasy creatures as well, and what follows is a bizarre, sometimes surreal, and entertainingly ambiguous mix of self-delusion and genuine magic.

The Shroud (1983) returned to a religious theme, but this time with the more subtle horror of his previous book. A priest is troubled by the apparition of a shrouded figure, which lures him toward an apparent heresy. *The Hunting Season* (1987) is very marginal but intensely suspenseful, but his next novel, *Fury* (1989), failed to match the quality of Coyne's previous work. The protagonist in this case experiences moments of revelation in which she realizes she is a reincarnation of a prehistoric human, and she becomes subject to episodes in which she is transformed into a vicious killer in response to those memories. Coyne's last novel was *Child of Shadows* (1990), a return to his original form. A woman resigns her job to take care of a homeless boy, but shortly after moving to a rural location she discovers that the local people have taken a violent dislike to the child, who may not even be human. Coyne's short story "The Cabin in the Woods" (1976) is also quite good.

"The Crate" Stephen King (1979)

If a story requires the protagonist to perform a despicable act such as murder, but the author wants the reader to remain sympathetic, the plot must be constructed in such a way that the action is justified or at least understandable, which is no easy task to accomplish. Stephen KING manages this in one of his earliest and best short stories by saddling a henpecked college professor, Henry Northrup, with a wife whose unpleasantness is so great that the reader can be convinced, at least for a moment, that there is at least some justification for murder.

The story opens with the appearance of Henry's longtime friend, Dexter Stanley, a fellow academic who is nearly hysterical with terror. He was approached earlier that day by a janitor who found a trunk tucked away under a staircase, a trunk that belonged to an expedition that visited Antarctica in 1834. Curious about its contents, the two men remove the crate to another room and pry it open, whereupon a powerful but never completely described creature reaches out and kills the janitor. Stanley runs off in horror and eventually encounters a graduate student, the only other person in the building at that time of day. The student is understandably skeptical, particularly when they return to the basement to find both the crate and body gone, but the trail of blood leads them back to the staircase, where the trunk is back in its original place. Despite Stanley's warnings, the other man investigates and is promptly killed for his troubles.

Northrup listens sympathetically and offers Stanley a drink, lacing it with a sleeping tablet. While Stanley slumbers Northrup lures his wife to the empty building, tricks her into approaching the crate, and waits patiently until she is dead. Using great care, he moves the crate again, this time conveying it to a quarry and throwing it in, disposing of both the creature and the evidence of his wife's death. He then returns to a revived Stanley, and the two vow to keep their secret. The characters are such that we can never really admire any of them, so King describes Wilma Northrup as such a horrid, unbearable person that we can share in the vicarious pleasure of her destruction. The story became one episode of the movie *Creepshow* (1982), based on King's own screenplay.

"Creation" Jeffrey Ford (2002)

As children we are taught many complicated concepts that we sometimes fail to grasp accurately until we have become older and more experienced. Adults, even teachers, often assume that they have transferred this knowledge accurately, unaware of the imperfections in the process and the occasionally dramatic differences in interpretation. Jeffrey FORD captures the essence of this discontinuity in "Creation," whose protagonist is a young boy who becomes fascinated by what he is told in catechism class, taught to him by the appropriately named Mrs. Grimm, whose demeanor is entirely without humor or warmth and whose story of how God created the world has much of the flavor of a dark fairy tale.

The boy becomes fascinated with the possibilities of creation, wondering why God conceived of such an idea. His preoccupation leads to imitation and experimentation. In a remote wooded area he builds himself a man out of earth, branches, and other objects, names him Cavanaugh, and waits for him to waken, only to be disappointed when the misshapen creature remains inert. That evening, however, he dreams that his creation came to life, and when he investigates the following morning he finds no trace of Cavanaugh. Although he is uncertain what happened, his catechism book, which he left behind by accident, is also missing, and he wonders if Cavanaugh is wandering through the woods trying to read it.

In the days that follow he has a series of visions in which he sees Cavanaugh in one context or another, but Ford never commits himself as to whether these are imagination or reality. Troubled and feeling the need to talk to Cavanaugh just once, he turns to his father who, though an atheist, is sympathetic to his son's mental turmoil. Together they search the woods for Cavanaugh, who speaks to the boy from concealment, but only when he and his father are temporarily separated. Cavanaugh has a single question, wanting to know why he was created, and the boy replies that he did it because of love. Ford remains noncommittal even at the end, when the boy has become a man, and we never find out whether Cavanaugh was real or whether his father played the part. Ford's subtle commentary on the relationship between God and man won the World Fantasy Award.

"Croatoan" Harlan Ellison (1975)

Although Harlan Ellison is generally considered a science fiction writer, much of his fiction is less easy to categorize, and some of it is overtly fantasy or horror. His style has always been deeply emotional and personal, and his evocative imagery and caustic observations have made him a frequent center of controversy across a broad spectrum of viewpoints and special interests. This particular story raised the hackles of many feminists and others because of its theme, although most of their objections were the result of a superficial reading of the story.

"Croatoan" opens moments after an illegal abortion has been accomplished. The narrator is an attorney whose profligacy has led to more than one such situation in the past. His lover becomes suddenly despondent and remorseful and insists that he recover the aborted fetus, even though it has already been flushed down the toilet. He sets off to do so in what is obviously an unrealistic but dramatically imperative step, reaching the sewers after prying open a manhole cover. There he encounters an entire hidden world inhabited by the homeless, one of whom follows him until he is rebuffed, at which point we discover that the derelict has no hands. Later the lawyer stumbles across the first of several alligators, this one still trailing a leash behind it, a discarded pet similarly flushed down the toilet, and finally an entire colony of children, distorted and malformed, each having developed improbably from a discarded fetus.

It would be easy to conclude that the story is a direct attack on abortion, but that is too simple an interpretation. Ellison himself has stated that it was a response to his reaction to the waste of potential and an indictment of the human unwillingness to accept responsibility for our actions. The lawyer and his lover could easily have used birth control to make the waste of life unnecessary. The title is the single word that was found scrawled on a tree when the early European colony at Roanoke, Virginia, disappeared without a trace.

The Croquet Player H. G. Wells (1937)

Although H. G. Wells did on rare occasions include supernatural elements in some of his short stories, the fantastic content was almost always rationalized scientifically, and Wells is not generally thought of as a significant writer of fantasy or horror. This novella is a rare, late exception that, like most of his science fiction, also reflected his acerbic attitude toward modern civilization, particularly late in his life.

The title character is the narrator, a rather spoiled, thoughtless man named Frobisher who lives and travels with his aunt, who has a similar disposition. While staying at a lodge he chances to fall into conversation with Dr. Finchatton, a physician whose aversion to blood and suffering ill suits him for his profession. Finchatton prevails upon Frobisher to listen to his story, which starts with his purchase of a practice in a very remote part of England peopled primarily by farmers. Cainsmarsh is an odd town, he discovers from the outset. There has been a disproportionate amount of violence there in recent years, and a surprisingly large portion of the population indulges in opiates or other drugs to dull the senses.

Finchatton soon feels that he has been affected by the atmosphere of the place. His dreams are troubled, and he begins to feel that others are conspiring against him. Troubled, he consults the local vicar, who advances the theory that excavations in the area have disturbed the bones of ancient people and that their troubled and unwholesome spirits are influencing the living. The vicar becomes increasingly irrational in the process of elaborating his theory, and Finchatton takes his leave. A further consultation with the local priest is similarly bizarre. Concerned about his own sanity, Finchatton then explains that he has consulted the psychiatrist Doctor Norbert and is currently under the man's care.

Frobisher subsequently meets Norbert and learns from him that most of what the doctor told him was a lie or a delusion. The malady is real, insists Norbert, but it is not the spirits of prehistoric people but a contagious ailment of the mind that has been awakened by extending our awareness of time ever further into the past. There is a symmetrical perception of an ever more distant future with all of its uncertainties, and that is what is causing the paranoia and violent outbursts, insists Norbert. Frobisher remains skeptical and takes his leave, only to discover in the closing lines that he, too, has contracted the mental disease. Wells had grown bitter by the 1930s, and much of his fiction from this period is decidedly inferior and polemic. In this one case, however, he encased his message in an eerie and engrossing story.

"The Crowd" Ray Bradbury (1943)

Traditionally, horror stories were usually set in very specific locations, haunted houses, crumbling castles, graveyards and dark forests and almost always took place at night. Some writers realized quite early, however, that there is a kind of artificiality about those settings that lacks resonance with readers. If one really wants to frighten readers, inject something horrible into everyday life, into pleasant or familiar scenes. Ray BRADBURY and Fritz LEIBER were among the first to consciously shape their writing to challenge the familiar, and one of the very best early examples is this chilling story by Bradbury.

In the opening paragraph we are introduced to Spallman, whose unsafe driving results in a serious accident, at the end of which he is lying in the street next to his overturned automobile. He notices the crowd of onlookers closing around him, hears one of them announce that he will live, and is surprised to feel an instinctive revulsion toward them. It is only later while lying in the hospital that the anomalous nature of their appearance occurs to him. They almost seemed to materialize out of thin air because the accident occurred in a deserted part of the city in the middle of the night. The image that sticks in his memory is that the wheels of his car were still spinning as they clustered around him, which means that they must have arrived within a few seconds.

Following his release, Spallman is disturbed by his proximity to another accident and pursues his investigations. He examines clippings of other incidents that occurred in the same part of the city and notices that certain individuals show up time and again, always as part of the crowd and always wearing identical clothing, even though the events themselves are years apart. Convinced that he has uncovered proof of some sort of conspiracy, he bundles up his notes and starts for the police sta-

tion, driving with particular care. It does him no good in the end. A truck comes out of nowhere and hits him. He and his documents are thrown from the car, and the crowd, which includes a number of familiar faces, ensures his death by moving him before his injuries can be treated. The story concludes with Spallman's realization that they are the dead and that he is about to join them. Anyone who has found himself or herself surrounded by the curious in a similar emergency can sympathize with Spallman's terror. Since Spallman's accident was clearly a response to his discovery, the implication is that sometimes we are better off not knowing the truth. This distrust of the unbridled search for knowledge shows up occasionally in Bradbury's other stories, particularly his science fiction.

Crowley, John (1942–   )

John Crowley started his writing career in science fiction, moved quickly to fantasy, and in recent years seems to be moving toward mainstream fiction. His first fantasy was *The Deep* (1975), marketed as science fiction and set in an alternate universe where the laws of nature work differently. His first acknowledged fantasy was *Little, Big* (1981), which on its surface explores the existence of worlds within worlds, specifically the land of fairies. The story focuses initially on Smoky Barnable, who travels to a remote part of New England after falling in love and discovers that there are gateways of a sort into a magical realm, although what follows is not the simple other worlds adventure that it might have been in the hands of a lesser writer. Crowley uses highly literate prose and a conscious awareness of the way in which fantasies are contrived and used to produce a work that transcends the simple story line that a plot summary suggests. The text also contains allusions to and in some cases parodies of some of the classics of children's fantasy. The novel was both a popular and literary success, despite its sometimes challenging structure and language. There is also a considerable amount of humor, although not of the farcical nature generally associated with humorous fantasy.

Aegypt (1987) deals with some of the same concepts, but it is also a secret history that suggests that powers unknown to the rest of us, and originating perhaps in a version of Egypt that is at variance with the one we know—hence the title—are clandestinely shaping the fate of the world. The story is continued in *Love and Sleep* (1994) and *Daemonomania* (2000), the latter taking on a much darker aspect involving the rise of cults and the possible end of the world. A fourth and concluding volume is planned but has not yet been announced. Most of Crowley's short fantasy fiction has been collected in *Antiquities* (1993), of which "Missolonghi 1824" is the best, a story of Lord Byron's encounter with a mythical creature. The uncollected short story "An Earthly Mother Sits and Sings" (2000) is also outstanding. Despite Crowley's dominant position in literary fantasy, his vision is so unique that he has no serious imitators. *Little, Big* and the novella *Great Work of Time* (1990) both won the World Fantasy Award.

Cunningham, Elaine (1957–)

For most of her writing career Elaine Cunningham has been content to produce game tie-in novels rather than produce work set in a world of her own making. Her debut novel was *Elfshadow* (1991), set in the sprawling FORGOTTEN REALMS universe. Despite occasional awkwardness, Cunningham creates an interesting murder mystery against that backdrop of magic and swordplay, but her next novel, *The Radiant Dragon* (1992) is decidedly inferior, at least partly because of the nature of the Cloakmaster game system to which it was linked. Elves and other legendary creatures interact awkwardly in a space travel format, dealing with a crisis that rises when rumors begin to appear that one side in an ongoing battle has developed a secret weapon.

Elfsong (1994) returned to the Forgotten Realms with a more traditional plot this time. A company of adventurers seeks to discover the nature of the curse that troubles their land and eventually lift it. *The Unicorn Hunt* (1995) is a minor quest story set in the DRAGONLANCE universe and seems to indicate that its author is willing to rework familiar story lines indefinitely. Her next several novels all returned to the Forgotten Realms shared world, sometime using common characters. *Daughter of the Drow* (1995, but revised in 2003) is considerably better, featuring a competent female protagonist whose magical quest shows flashes of considerable originality and whose subsequent troubles are described in the slightly less interesting *Tangled Webs* (1996).

The protagonist of *Elfshadows* returns in *Silver Shadows* (1996) for some fairly standard but better-written adventures. *Thornhold* (1998) and *Evermeet* (1998) show clear progress in Cunningham's writing skills, particularly in her characterization, but the plots are so constrained by the limitations of the shared universe that the degree of her improvement is not immediately clear. *The Dream Spheres* (1999) is considerably more original and more satisfying, a mystery adventure involving the illegal trade in dangerous magical artifacts. *The Magehound* (2000) is largely a series of chases, exciting but unmemorable, and *The Floodgate* (2001), though well written, is yet another account of a major battle between the forces of good and evil, competently done but offering nothing particularly new.

Cunningham's last two novels in that setting follow the same pattern, but *The Wizardwar* (2002) brings a sequence of battles and quests to a resounding and satisfying conclusion. *Windwalker* (2003) brings the series begun with *Daughter of the Drow* to a satisfying close. Despite her obvious talents and marked improvement, Cunningham seemed content to produce interesting but minor work until recently. Her most recent novel, *Shadows in the Darkness* (2004), is a contemporary fantasy involving a very well-portrayed female private detective who discovers that there is magic in the world after all. It is too early to predict whether she will continue this character's career with additional titles, but if she does so they are likely to help Cunningham break out of her former mold and become a more significant fantasy writer with a wider audience. Most of her short fiction has also been in the Dragonlance or Forgotten Realms settings, but "The Knight of the Lake" (2002) is an interesting exception.

D

"Dagon" H. P. Lovecraft (1919)

In the early part of the 20th century, there was no clearly defined horror field, and most of what did get published was lumped loosely as "weird fiction," which could include fantasy and science fiction as well as overtly supernatural stories. Much of H. P. LOVECRAFT's work fell into this category, including this short piece that could arguably be called science fiction as well as horror. One pattern that stories from this period used was to introduce a more or less ordinary character into an unusual situation that required little if any action on his or her part. The story then is comprised of the character's reactions to a bizarre scene or event. Lovecraft, Clark Ashton SMITH, and other writers would describe, often by implication, a series of exotic and presumably unsettling images, after which the protagonist would frequently be driven to madness or self-destruction because of the degree of horror experienced. By contemporary standards this might seem an implausible overreaction, but when these stories were first appearing in print it was an accepted conceit that a shock of this sort could unseat one's sanity.

The protagonist of "Dagon" escapes after being taken prisoner by the Germans during World War I. He drifts aimlessly across the ocean until he encounters a newly risen expanse of land, an island raised from the ocean floor and exposed to the sun for the first time in countless generations. He decides to explore, finding at first only a lifeless landscape littered with the reeking bodies of dead fish but eventually stumbling across an an-cient building, a monolith, inscribed with horrific images of a race half human and half fish. Then a leviathanlike creature emerges from the ocean to worship at the monument; the sight so overwhelms him that he casts off immediately, and his mental balance is forever disturbed. He is terrified by visions of Dagon, the fish-god, and apprehensive that hordes of hideous creatures are still alive under the placid waters of the oceans and that they may one day emerge to destroy the world of humanity. This same plot is used far more elaborately for another of Lovecraft's famous stories, "At the Mountains of Madness" (1936), which places the alien ruins in the Antarctic. Stuart Gordon's film *Dagon* (2001) draws its title from this story, but most of the actual plot is derived from another of Lovecraft's tales, "THE SHADOW OVER INNSMOUTH" (1936).

Dahl, Roald (1916–1990)

Although Roald Dahl started writing for children as early as 1943, with *Gremlins*, he was not a success in that field until the early 1960s. During the interim he produced a great number of adult short stories for slick magazine markets, some of which contained supernatural or fantastic elements, although many did not. Dahl specialized in the surprise ending and was noted for his ability to produce some truly wicked characters and mete out rough justice to his villains. Several of his fantasy stories have become minor classics. The composer Franz Liszt is reincarnated as a cat in

"Edward the Conqueror," and a child's horrible imagination manifests itself physically in "The Wish" (1953). The protagonist of "Georgy Porgy" (1959) finds himself trapped inside a woman's body quite literally.

Although his short adult fiction includes many excellent stories, Dahl will be remembered best for his children's fantasy novels. JAMES AND THE GIANT PEACH (1961) is a clever story about a boy, an oversized piece of fruit, and the unusual insects that live inside it, but it was CHARLIE AND THE CHOCOLATE FACTORY (1964, filmed as *Willy Wonka and the Chocolate Factory* in 1971), that would make him famous. The novel, somewhat controversial because of the way some of the less-admirable children are treated, was followed by a lesser but still amusing sequel, *Charlie and the Great Glass Elevator* (1972).

Although Dahl's other fantasies for children are less well known, several of them are quite well done. An inconsiderate hunter goes through a strange transformation in *The Magic Finger* (1966), a boy and his father have a series of unusual adventures in *Danny, the Champion of the World* (1975), a plot is hatched to turn all of the children on Earth into mice in *The Witches* (1983), and a boy finds a tribe of tiny people living in the forest, although they are definitely not in the benevolent tradition of Mary Norton's THE BORROWERS SERIES in *The Minpins* (1991). Despite the controversy over what is perceived as amoral cruelty in some of his stories, Dahl remains immensely popular with young readers, perhaps because he understands their viewpoint better than do most adults.

Dalkey, Kara (1953–)

Kara Dalkey's first published fantasy fiction consisted of a minor short story in the Liavek shared world anthology series. Her first novel appeared shortly thereafter, *The Curse of Sagamore* (1986), a pleasant variation from the usual story of the battle for the throne of a magical kingdom. In this case the heir apparent, descended from a line of court jesters, would just as soon avoid the honor, but there is a magical mark upon him and he is forced to confront various rivals, some aided by magical creatures. His frequently humorous adventures

continue in a sequel, *The Sword of Sagamore* (1989), which recounts his adventures after he has assumed the throne.

Dalkey's other early novels are more serious in tone. *The Nightingale* (1988) is a retelling of the fairy tale by Hans Christian ANDERSEN. In ancient Japan a woman gifted with a beautiful singing voice is haunted by a malevolent ghost. *Euryale* (1988) features a protagonist who has been turned into a gorgon, after which she inadvertently turns her lover to stone. She travels to Rome hoping to find a cure for her condition and a way to reverse the transformation of her lover, but when she accomplishes her goal, she discovers that the relationship between the two of them has been altered irreversibly.

Dalkey fell silent for several years before returning with *Little Sister* (1996), the first tale of Mitsuko, set in ancient Japan. Mitsuko must cross over into a magical realm to find help in rescuing her family, who have been taken by an evil warlord. Mitsuko returns in *The Heavenward Path* (1998), in which she and her demonic companion must fulfill their obligation to a ghost by rebuilding a shrine and accomplishing other tasks. Both novels rely on a strong sense of place and the intricate construction of Dalkey's characters.

Goa (1996) was the first volume in a trilogy, promptly followed by *Bijapur* (1997) and *Bhagavati* (1998). An adventurer in 16th-century India encounters an alchemist who appears to have the ability to restore the dead to life. He subsequently explores a hidden city rumored to be the home of a manifested goddess, then becomes shipwrecked and is taken prisoner by the Inquisition. The trilogy is Dalkey's most impressive work and one of the best historical fantasy sequences of all time.

Three other novels are free standing. In *Steel Rose* (1997) an actor uses magic to further his career but discovers that there is a price to be paid for supernatural assistance. *Crystal Sage* (1999) is an unusual contemporary fantasy in which one character is transformed into a guitar, and a friend has to deal with elves to reverse the process. *Genpei* (2000), Dalkey's most recent novel, returns to early Japan to recount the effects that follow when gods take sides in a war between men. Of Dalkey's short fiction, only "The Peony Lantern" (1991), a

Japanese ghost story, and "The Chrysanthemum Robe" (1995) are noteworthy.

"The Damned Thing" Ambrose Bierce
(1891)

One of the shortcomings of much modern horror fiction is a tendency to describe the supernatural too precisely. Readers of splatterpunk fiction in particular demanded and authors provided descriptions of their monsters down to the last tentacle, and authors are sure to mention each individual drop of blood shed during their depredations. Early horror fiction kept the details at arm's length and suggested rather than described most of the physical horrors. Ambrose BIERCE, who wrote several early classics of the genre, provides an excellent example of how effective this technique can be with this short, understated, and very memorable tale.

The story opens at the inquest of one Hugh Morgan, who died under mysterious circumstances and whose body, torn and battered, lies on a table nearby. The proceedings get underway with the arrival of William Harker, a journalist, who was with Morgan at the time of his death and whose testimony is, obviously, of vital importance. He recounts their plan to go quail hunting, during which they both observed a peculiar movement in a field of oats, as though a large body were passing through it, even though nothing was visible to either man. Morgan became particularly agitated and fired his shotgun at the disturbance, after which he was attacked and killed by an unseen force. Technically speaking, the creature was not invisible because it was impossible to see through it, but it was—as we discover later—of a color that is beyond the spectrum detectible by human eyesight.

The coroner refuses to credit Harker's testimony, and the verdict is that Morgan was killed by a wild animal. However, the coroner has also read Morgan's diary and knows that he was troubled by the repeated depredations of a creature he believed to be invisible. The story concludes there, and whereas another writer might have gone on to explain the creature's origin and nature, and even its eventual demise, Bierce was content to leave the reader wondering.

Daniels, Les (1943–)

The late 1970s saw the first indications of the rising popularity of vampire fiction, which has by now become almost a genre in itself. Anne RICE introduced Lestat, Chelsea Quinn YARBRO began the chronicles of St. Germain, and Les Daniels, the least-known but certainly not the least talented of the three, brought us Don Sebastian de Dellanueva. Don Sebastian makes his first appearance in *The Black Castle* (1978), set during the Inquisition in Spain in 1496. Although he is undead and survives by drinking blood, the horrors taking place around him—performed by ordinary mortal men—are so appalling that even he is repelled by them. He is the vampire horrified by man, and that theme is carried on through Daniels's subsequent novels, all of which are sequels set in different time periods.

The Silver Skull (1979) takes place a century later. Seeking arcane knowledge, Don Sebastian travels to the New World, where he is caught up in the conflict between the Spanish conquistadores and the native tribes. Once again he is revolted by the excesses of cruelty and violence taking place around him. He returns to Europe for the third volume, *Citizen Vampire* (1981), set during the French Revolution. Predictably, the vampire has no more sympathy for the revolutionaries and their guillotine than he has for the self-centered and oppressive nobility whom they have overthrown. *Yellow Fog* (1988), originally a novella, moves to middle 19th-century England, in the years just before Jack the Ripper stalked Whitechapel. Don Sebastian must drink blood in order to survive, but he has learned to avoid killing his victims, not so much from compassion as to avoid the attention that would follow. Daniels evokes an eerie atmosphere quite effectively in what has so far proven to be the best novel in the series. The most recent entry is *No Blood Spilled* (1991), a comparatively weak story in which the vampire protagonist seeks arcane knowledge once again, this time in British colonial India.

At least one further volume in the series is planned but has not yet appeared. Daniels has produced only a handful of short stories over the last decade, but "The Good Parts" (1989) and "Under My Skin" (2002) are both quite effective. He is also the author of *Living in Fear: A History of Horror in the Mass Media* (1975) and several book-length stories of the history of comic books. The quality of his fiction has been consistently above average, but he has not been prolific enough to draw a large following.

"The Dark Man"   Robert E. Howard (1931)

Although Norse legends have been the basis of a number of classic fantasy novels from Poul Anderson's *Broken Sword* (1954) to *Grendel* (1971) by John Gardner, Celtic fantasy has proven to be a much more popular source for most fantasy writers. Robert E. HOWARD invokes both cultures in this classic, rather long story about an outcast Irish warrior named Turlogh Dubh unjustly accused of collaborating with the Danish raiders who nevertheless feels the call of his native blood when the Irish princess Moira is carried off by Thorfel and his henchmen. Turlogh, who is powerfully built and described as black haired and of dark complexion, might at first seem to be the dark man of the title, but Howard soon tells us otherwise. Foolishly pursuing Thorfel in a small fishing boat, Turlogh runs ashore on an unknown island where he finds the remains of a party of Danes who fought a battle with a lesser number of odd looking, smaller men, and no one from either party survived. Among the bodies Turlough discovers a five-foot statue that, though made of stone, seems inordinately light, so he decides to bring it with him as a good luck charm.

His decision proves to be a wise one. Despite a terrible storm, he is guided to the exact location where Thorfel and his men are carousing and where he plans to marry Moira forcibly by means of a captive priest. Two of the Danes find the statue, but they have great difficulty moving it because of its immense weight and because they seem prone to painful accidents in its presence. Turlogh steals into the keep and watches as Moira indignantly refuses to marry Thorfel and then mortally wounds herself rather than become his slave. Enraged, he charges in to do hopeless battle but survives thanks to the intervention of a force of warriors similar to those who originally guarded the statue, who identify themselves as Picts. Although the fair maiden is not saved, she dies honorably, and Turlogh returns the statue of the Dark Man to its rightful owners. They insist that the statue is the home of the spirit of a great leader of their kind, Bran Mak Morn, who is the central figure in a short series of stories by Howard. The strong, silent, outcast hero would become a staple of Howard's subsequent fiction and one of the prototypes for sword and sorcery ever since.

The Dark Tower Series   Stephen King (1982–2004)

Although Stephen KING is obviously best known for his horror fiction, he has also gathered a considerable amount of favorable attention for the Dark Tower series, an elaborate, idiosyncratic fantasy sequence that he asserts was influenced by the movie *The Good, the Bad, and the Ugly* and indirectly the works of J. R. R. TOLKIEN, all wrapped around imagery from Robert Browning's classic poem about Childe Roland and the Dark Tower. The first title was *The Gunslinger* (1982), incorporating pieces earlier published separately. Years later King revised the text to make it more consistent with the later volumes, adding considerably to the personality of the primary protagonist, Roland Deschains.

When we first meet Roland he is traveling through a blasted wasteland peopled with humans, mutants, monsters, and machines searching for the Dark Man, who he finally meets in the closing chapters. The first volume is particularly episodic, but the next, *The Drawing of the Three* (1987), is much more coherently a single story. Roland is still traveling to the tower, the linchpin that holds back the forces of Chaos in the universe, but now he travels through a series of doors into 1980s America, where he must recruit three companions to become fellow gunslingers. *The Wastelands* (1991) takes them back into the postapocalyptic world, where they meet a cyborg bear and where Roland begins to wonder if he is losing his sanity. The story ends with a startling cliffhanger.

Wizard and Glass (1996) resolves that crisis and continues with a fast-paced sequence aboard a sentient train that is apparently psychotic. The bulk of the book, however, is a flashback to Roland's youth and his encounter with a vampire witch and participation in a major battle. In *Wolves of the Calla* (2003) we learn more about the nature of the Tower and, by implication, the importance of Roland's quest. He and his friends intercede to stop the Wolves from kidnapping one half of a set of twins, while Susannah, one of the companions, begins to act strangely. King also provides a handful of cross-references to his horror novels, suggesting a multiverse similar to that of Michael MOORCOCK.

Song of Susannah (2004) explains the title character's odd behavior. She has been possessed by a kind of demon who takes her to America in the 1990s. Since time travel is common in the series, Roland and the rest are diverted to Maine in the 1970s, where they meet the author himself. Although there is another cliffhanger ending following a series of crises, the reader knows that the end is near, and in *The Dark Tower* (2004) we discover the truth at last. Roland reaches his goal, the final conflict unfolds, and most of the loose ends are neatly tied up. An episode in the series has also been published as a chapbook under the title "The Little Sisters of Eluria" (1999). The series is at times difficult to read, and the books do not hold up well separately. The plot is far from linear, and much of the imagery is not entirely clear. That said, it is also one of the more impressive works of modern fantasy because of the originality of its concept, the depth of characterization, and the intensity of individual episodes.

Davidson, Avram (1923–1993)

Avram Davidson's quirky, often unclassifiable short stories first began appearing in the 1950s, and despite the high quality of many of his novels, he is still best-remembered for stories such as "The Golem" (1954), "The Power of Every Root" (1967), "Goslin Day" (1970), and "Polly Charms the Sleeping Woman" (1975). Although he wrote several science fiction novels and at least one pseudonymous mystery, his fantasy novels are generally held in higher regard. Some of his science fiction such as *Rogue Dragon* (1965) uses many of the artifices of fantasy.

Davidson's first fantasy novel was *The Island under the Earth* (1969), originally planned as the first in a series, although Davidson never wrote any of the sequels. A varied cast of characters interacts in a magical land where six limbs are just as common as four. It was a very unusual setting, the novel attracted considerable interest, but it was soon overshadowed by *The Phoenix and the Mirror* (1969), still considered Davidson's best single book-length work. The protagonist is the poet Vergil, who is also a sorcerer and whose adventures are set in a convincing magical alternate reality that Davidson describes in great detail. This was also planned as part of an extended series, although only one sequel was completed, *Vergil in Averno* (1987), actually a prequel involving a commission to perform certain work in a city darkened by corruption, complicated by his romantic entanglement with a married woman. Yet another trilogy started with *Peregrine: Primus* (1971), the story of a young pagan's fantastic adventures at the time of the Roman Empire, continued in *Peregrine: Secundus* (1981) as he escapes a curse and meets various mythological creatures. Davidson never completed what would have been the final volume.

Ursus of Ultima Thule (1973) borrows from the CONAN SERIES by Robert E. HOWARD for its setting, but Davidson approaches barbarian fantasy in a much more literarily conscious manner than Howard and his imitators. *Marco Polo and the Sleeping Beauty* (1988, written with Grania Davis) is an entertaining historical fantasy but does not measure up to his earlier work. *The Boss in the Wall* (1998, also with Grania Davis) is a minor mystical fantasy in a contemporary setting. The series of short stories about Dr. Esterhazy, variously collected, shift back and forth between science fiction and fantasy. The best of Davidson's short fantasy fiction can be found in *Collected Fantasies* (1982), although all of his collections include at least some, usually mixed with science fiction. Davidson, who also edited *The Magazine of Fantasy & Science Fiction* for several years, was one of the most literate and original writers in the genre, and his work has become even more popular in the years since his death. Davidson received the World Fantasy Award for "NAPLES" in 1979.

"The Dead Boy at Your Window" Bruce Holland Rogers (1998)

Many early fairy tales were designed as parables rather than as straightforward stories, although with the passage of time their secondary meanings have sometimes been lost. Modern fantasy tends to be primarily adventure fiction, but a few writers, particularly at short length, have more aggressive agendas. Bruce Holland Rogers is one of the emerging talents in the field, whose work often defies easy classification, as in this very short, very powerful story of a mother and her stillborn child and what happens when she refuses to accept that he is dead.

Her rejection of the truth is so powerful that the child becomes animated, although he is still not alive. He is unable to grow, of course, so his father builds a frame in which he regularly stretches the boy's body so that he seems to be getting taller. The child is odd but quite bright and eventually becomes a good pupil in school, although many of the other kids dislike him. The local bullies beat him up, but since he feels no pain he neither complains nor resents their actions, although sometimes he feels lonely. Then one day they fasten his thinly stretched body to a wire frame and launch him into the air like a kite.

The dead boy drifts through the sky, eventually coming to the ground in the land of the dead. The dead are all naked, and they are jealous of the newcomer at first. They are also anxious for word from those they left behind, even though they no longer remember their own names or the names of their loved ones. When the dead boy tells them that he is going to return to the land of the living, they give him messages of their love to carry back, even though they cannot tell him to whom they should be delivered. So the dead boy passes them on at random and receives messages from the living that he carries back on his next flight, and for many flights to come. Rogers states his point explicitly at the end, although it is clear from the context. Love outlasts memory, and it needs no names to endure. The story earned its author the Bram Stoker Award.

Dean, Pamela (1953–)

Pamela Dean is the pen name of Pamela Dyer-Bennett, who began her career contributing sto-

ries to the Liavek shared universe anthology series but quickly switched to novels, starting with *The Secret Country* (1985). This was the first of a series of four in the Hidden Lands series, very charming fantasies for younger readers, written with enough wit and sophistication to entertain adult audiences as well. Several children have been engaged in an elaborate fantasy game of their own making, but they discover they have either created something real or have been influenced by a hidden reality already existing as they stumble into a world that follows the same rules as their game. They return for a second series of adventures in *The Hidden Lands* (1986), in which they battle the Dragon King before finally escaping back to their homes. Inevitably, they are summoned back for what appears to be the final battle in *The Whim of a Dragon* (1989), which was apparently originally intended as the end of the series, although Dean added *The Dubious Hills* (1994), a somewhat low-key and mildly anticlimactic extension, although a very fine novel on its own.

Her other novels are intended for adults. *Tam Lin* (1991) is an elaborate retelling of a classic fairy tale updated to a contemporary setting. Although much of it is set on a college campus, the major conflict is between a mortal woman and the fairy queen, both of whom love the same man. Her most recent novel is *Juniper, Gentian, and Sage* (1998), which has a decidedly darker tone. Three sisters become fascinated by an unusual boy who moves in across the street. He convinces them to help him build a time machine in their attic, which they believe to be nothing more than an unusual game, but he is in deadly earnest and lies to them about the purpose of the machine. It controls time rather than allows travel to other ages, and when it is complete, he uses it to seize control of their lives. Although Dean wrote only a handful of short stories, they are all quite entertaining, particularly "Owlswater" (1993) and "The Fair Gift" (1996). Her recent lack of new work is regrettable.

De Camp, L. Sprague (1907–2000)

Some authors are content to write exclusively within the fantasy genre, but when L. Sprague de Camp first began selling stories during the early

1940s, the borders between fantasy and science fiction were much less distinct than they are today. He would eventually write at great length in both genres as well as five very highly regarded straightforward historical novels, a considerable body of nonfiction, including a study of Atlantis in myth and literature, a biography of H. P. LOVE-CRAFT and another of Robert E. HOWARD, plus works on the art of writing and on various scientific subjects. Catherine Crook de Camp, to whom he was married for more than 60 years, is credited on a few of these works, mostly the later ones, but she probably contributed to some extent to many of the others. His biography of Lovecraft was mildly controversial, partly because of its critical portrayal.

The major market for new fantasy fiction at the time was *Unknown,* a companion to *Astounding Stories,* a science fiction magazine. Although *Unknown* lasted only a few years, its name has been associated with a particular brand of fantasy ever since, stories in which the magic elements are subject to specific laws or rules and the plots are adventures enlivened by some humor. De Camp was one of the main contributors to the magazine throughout its existence, providing many excellent stories, often in collaboration with Fletcher Pratt. Their first major sequence together was the Harold Shea series of novels and novellas, most of which eventually appeared in book form as *The Incomplete Enchanter* (1941), *The Castle of Iron* (1950), and *Wall of Serpents* (1960). The premise is that it is possible to contrive a mathematical equation that would allow one to physically enter an imaginary world such as that created by a work of fiction. Shea and his companion visit Edmund Spenser's *The Faerie Queen* (1590), the world of Norse mythology, the *Kalevala,* a Celtic fantasy world, and others.

Also writing with Pratt, de Camp produced a series of tall tales as related in a tavern, eventually collected as *Tales from Gavagan's Bar* (1953). Other fantasy and science fiction writers employed this same device as in *Tales from the White Hart* (1957) by Arthur C. Clarke, the Callahan's Bar series by Spider Robinson, and *The Outpost* (2001) by Mike Resnick. Another noteworthy collaborative story from this period was "The Weissenbrock

Spectacles" (1954). Their remaining novel together was *Land of Unreason* (1942), an amusing story in which a man puts out an alcoholic drink for the fairies instead of milk. Inebriated, they carry him off for a series of amusing adventures in their world.

De Camp had written four fantasy novels of his own by 1960, but they were all comparatively minor. In *The Carnelian Cube* (1948) a magic artifact allows the protagonist to visit alternate realities, but he gets into trouble every time and mildly amusing consequences ensue. *The Tritonian Ring* (1953) is a prehistoric quest fantasy of little interest, and *Solomon's Stone* (1957), in which a faked demonic invocation actually works, is barely readable. The best of these was *The Undesired Princess* (1951), in which an engineer from our world crosses into one that runs by pure logic, with frequently hilarious developments. These novels were all reprinted from their original magazine appearances during the 1940s. *The Enchanted Bunny* (1990) by David DRAKE is a sequel to *The Undesired Princess.*

When the CONAN SERIES by Robert E. Howard began to appear in mass market paperback editions during the 1960s, de Camp and his fellow writer Lin CARTER were employed to turn fragments into stories and write new ones to flesh out the series. De Camp also rewrote some non-Conan stories by Howard, substituting Conan for the existing hero, which evoked criticism from many fans of Howard's work. With Carter he also did a novelization of the first Conan movie, *Conan the Barbarian* (1981), and he wrote several articles pertaining to Howard's imaginary past world. Several of his own older fantasy stories were collected as *The Reluctant Shaman* (1970), but the only original novel he wrote during that period was *The Goblin Tower* (1968).

The Goblin Tower was the first in the Reluctant King series, light adventures in the style of *Unknown* and the best fantasy de Camp had written in years. The new king of a fantasy realm is indeed reluctant, because unless he accomplishes certain seemingly impossible deeds, and quickly, he will be ritually executed. His subsequent adventures include a very funny confrontation with a giant squirrel before he finds a way to avoid his fate. The series continued with *The Clocks of Iraz* (1971), with King Jorian set to defeat marauding pirates, rescue a fair maiden, and repair a set of magical clocks. He eventually succeeds in escaping and, accompanied by a helpful wizard, seeks to rescue his still-captive queen in *The Unbeheaded King* (1983). The final book in the series, *The Honorable Barbarian* (1989), is a comparatively minor afterthought chronicling the adventures of Jorian's brother.

The Fallible Fiend (1973) is in much the same vein. A relentlessly literal demon is set to guard a doorway and is eventually disgraced when he devours his master's apprentice. Most of the humor comes from the efforts by the demon to understand human behavior. *The Purple Pterodactyls* (1979) is a collection of older light short fantasies with a common character, none of which are individually significant, although the whole is greater than the sum of its parts. With Catherine credited as coauthor, *The Incorporated Knight* appeared in 1987, a collection of short stories about a knight who has various whimsical, magical adventures. *The Pixilated Peeress* (1991) followed, de Camp's last significant fantasy work. An unlikely hero assists a fugitive maiden as she magically alters her appearance, but things go awry with the result that she ends up looking like an octopus. Subsequent attempts to set things right lead to danger at the hands of a charismatic sorcerer and his followers, as well as the untrustworthiness of magic in general. *Sir Harold and the Gnome King* (1991) is a novella continuing the Harold Shea series, but it lacks their ingenuity and liveliness.

De Camp's historical novels, particularly *The Dragon of the Ishtar Gate* (1961) and *The Bronze God of Rhodes* (1960), should appeal strongly to fantasy fans because of their marvelous invocation of an imagined version of history. *Lest Darkness Fall* (1941), although science fiction, was written as a rebuttal of A CONNECTICUT YANKEE IN KING ARTHUR'S COURT (1889) by Mark Twain, a fantasy in which a modern man travels back through time and uses modern technology to transform Camelot. De Camp's response has an engineer sent back to Rome, where despite all of his best efforts, he is unable to do anything to preserve the empire. There are too many fine short stories to list them all here, but among his best are "The Hardwood Pile" (1940), "When the Nightwind Howls" (1951),

"The Rape of the Lock" (1952), the latter two both with Fletcher Pratt, and "Ka the Appalling" (1958). Even when it features barbarian warriors and primitive societies, de Camp's fiction is imbued with a sense of human decency and good humor that is largely missing from most modern fantasy.

Dee, Ron (1957–)

Although Ron Dee had previously published two novels, one a medical thriller, it was with *Blood Lust* (1990) that he finally found material with which he was both comfortable and successful. The plot is that of a typical vampire story, with a traditional evil undead creature invading a small town and rapidly propagating his kind within the population. Dee avoids answering questions about the inevitable end of such rapid reproduction, although he addresses it partially in the two sequels. The first of these was *Dusk* (1991), in which a coven of newly transformed vampires gathers in a small Mexican town to plan their strategy. Unfortunately, some of the less cautious of their number travel to Dallas and engage in an undisciplined killing spree, which threatens to reveal the secret of their existence and imperil their common future. Although Dee's vampires are all essentially bad, their personalities are sufficiently differentiated that we can feel some sympathy for their plight. The FBI becomes aware of vampirism in the third in the series, *Blood* (1993). A research laboratory develops a miracle cure for the terminally ill, but the cure is actually the essence of vampirism. Their patients are soon searching for blood and fleeing from federal agents intent upon destroying them.

Two other novels appeared under Dee's name. *Descent* (1991) is a sometimes confusing mix of occultism and ghosts with a plot that never seems to pick up any speed. *Succumb* (1994) is considerably better, the story of a man troubled by a succubus who invades his dreams. Strong erotic content is also found occasionally in Dee's vampire novels. He wrote a substantial number of short stories during the 1990s, most of them involving vampires but none of particular merit. His 1994 collection, *Sex and Blood,* appeared only in a small press edition.

Dee also published four novels as David Darke, two of which are also about vampires. *Shade* (1994)

is the best of Dee's novels, featuring Scarlett Shade, who writes vampire stories with an air of expertise, not surprising since she is herself one of the undead. *Blind Hunger* (1993) involves a woman whose husband returns from the grave as a kind of vampire, but her subsequent reaction is not entirely plausible. *Horrorshow* (1994) rather predictably describes the carnage that follows the re-creation of a set of horrible murders, and *Last Rites* (1996) details the unfortunate and inevitable consequences of dabbling in black magic. Dee's gritty depiction of existence within the vampire community is probably his strongest asset, and the current popularity of vampire fiction has generated continued interest in his work, even though he has published no new material in nearly a decade.

Deitz, Tom (1952–)

Tom Deitz is a southern writer who has transplanted Celtic mythology to his native Georgia and blended it with Native American folklore to create the background of many of his novels. His work is normally filled with fairly straightforward conflict, and his plots are often advanced by the use of unlikely coincidences. Most of his protagonists are teenagers, although his work is marketed for adults, and there is a good deal of repetition from one book to the next. At the same time, he does an excellent job of creating his setting, a snapshot of idealized Americana frozen in time but not entirely familiar, as though he had distilled out the elements of our world that might have complicated his stories.

His debut novel was *Windmaster's Bane* (1986), the first of the David Sullivan series. David has second sight and can see the "Sidhe" as they pass through our world. He learns of the existence of a sorcerer from the other world who wants to extend his control into ours and eventually thwarts the villain. Sullivan returned for seven more adventures, ending at present with *Warstalker's Track* (1999). The best in the series is *Stoneskin's Revenge* (1991), in which a soul-drinking entity from another reality slips into our world to claim his victims. In the other volumes Sullivan has adventures in our world and in Faerie, struggles to end a war in the other world and to defeat thoughtless land developers in

ours, and averts a supernatural flood that could inundate the entire state of Georgia.

Deitz's second series consists of *Soulsmith* (1991), *Dreambuilder* (1992), and *Wordwright* (1993). The series, which owes its inspiration to the AMBER SERIES by Roger ZELAZNY, focuses on a Georgia family all of whom possess the magical ability to move from one universe to another, although use of that power is supposedly reserved for the current family head. The protagonist, a teenager in the opening volume and a college student by the third, becomes involved in family politics despite his intention to ignore the family secret.

The Eron series includes *Bloodwinter* (1999), *Springwar* (2000), *Summerblood* (2001), and *Warautumn* (2002). The setting is an imagined world with two kingdoms poised on the brink of war. Overpopulation and the ravages of a plague threaten the stability of both peoples, and a newly seated king lacks the experience to control either internal problems or the international crisis. A war breaks out, but the greater threat proves to be the priests of a secretive cult who have their own ideas about the manner in which the kingdom should be governed. The series is much better written than Deitz's previous work but is disappointing because of its predictable plot.

Deitz also wrote three nonseries novels. *The Gryphon King* (1989) is quite rewarding, the story of a college play that inadvertently summons Satan, much to the consternation of one of the students. A selkie interacts with humans in *Above the Lower Sky* (1994), and in *The Demons in the Green* (1996) the entire world is in peril as sea borne spirits seek to supplant the human race. Deitz has proven himself capable of writing dramatic and convincing fiction, sometimes introducing quite original concepts, but he has yet to establish a clear enough voice to distinguish himself from his contemporaries.

De Lint, Charles (1951–)

The Canadian writer Charles De Lint began publishing short fantasy stories in the late 1970s, some of them released as chapbooks and others appearing in anthologies, but did not turn to novels until the middle of the 1980s. By the end of that decade 11 novels and a collection had appeared, and De Lint was firmly established as a significant fantasy writer. Several of his stories were linked and followed the career of Cerin Songweaver, and music was a common theme, not surprising given the author's strong musical background.

His first novel, *The Riddle of the Wren* (1984), is a pleasant but unexceptional story about the opening of a gateway between our world and another. The suggestion that magic still exists hidden around us pervades De Lint's work, and most of his major novels have had contemporary settings. *Moonheart* (1984) introduced Tamson House, a structure that effectively exists both in our reality and an alternate one where magic is commonplace. The novella *Ascian in Rose* (1987) uses the same setting, as does *Westlin Wind* (1989). De Lint wrote several short stories involving Tamson House or characters connected to it, and several of these were collected as *Ghostwood* (1990), later expanded as *Spiritwalk* (1992). The Tamson House stories draw from a variety of different folklores and portray a world recognizably our own but different in very subtle ways.

The Harp of the Grey Rose (1985) is a more traditional fantasy, although it avoids the pervasive large-scale violence common to that form. A wandering minstrel rescues the woman he loves from a nefarious sorcerer. De Lint invokes gypsy magic in *Mulengro* (1985), a tense and fascinating thriller in which an angry man conjures up a homicidal creature to murder his enemies. *Jack the Giant Killer* (1987) and its sequel, *Drink Down the Moon* (1990), return to a contemporary setting, pitting resourceful Jacky Rowan against a variety of magical creatures when they invade a contemporary city. *Yarrow* (1986) is one of several stories by De Lint that involve the dream world, in this case posing for the protagonist the problem of discovering who has been literally stealing her dreams. A similar device is used less effectively in the quasi–science fiction novel *Svaha* (1989). The migration of characters from the world of fairies into our own recurs in *Greenmantle* (1988), and there is a somewhat similar theme in *Wolf Moon* (1988), whose protagonist is an involuntary werewolf who travels about searching for some place that will accept him despite his affliction. His life is ultimately transformed by the power of love.

De Lint opened the 1990s with the more melodramatic *The Dreaming Place* (1990), which pits its two main characters against a Manitou, a powerful Indian spirit who can transfer their consciousness into the bodies of lower animals. The author's interest in darker themes eventually resulted in three horror novels, all originally published under the name Samuel Key, and two of which—*Angel of Darkness* (1990) and *From a Whisper to a Scream* (1992)—involve the supernatural. *Our Lady of the Harbour* (1991) is a touching novella about a man's encounter with a mermaid, and *The Little Country* (1991) is a complex and satisfying story in which a young girl literally enters another world by reading a book written about it. The last was De Lint's most ambitious book to date, and there was no longer any doubt that he was a major figure in the fantasy genre despite his avoidance of the dominant form, disguised historical romances.

The stories collected in *Dreams Underfoot* (1993) and the novel *Memory and Dream* (1994) establish the imaginary city of Newford, which would be the setting of a large portion of De Lint's work during the 1990s. The plots are often quiet and understated, as is the case in the novel, whose artist protagonist has forsworn her ability to bring her paintings to magical life. *The Ivory and the Horn* (1995), *Moonlight and Vines* (1999), winner of the World Fantasy Award for best collection, and *Tapping the Dream Tree* (2002) are further groupings of Newford stories, and *The Onion Girl* (2001) and *Spirits in the Wires* (2003) are both associated novels, the latter of which is particularly well done.

De Lint's more recent novels have varied from very good to excellent. *Trader* (1997) poses an interesting problem for a musician who wakens one day to discover that he has magically swapped bodies with a villainous magician. His efforts to reclaim himself run into somewhat predictable but cleverly rendered difficulties. An investigator in *Someplace to Be Flying* (1998) discovers that there are magical creatures living hidden within human society, but that revelation is potentially dangerous because of human fear of the unknown. *Forests of the Heart* (2000) is one of his most interesting efforts. Various Irish spirits have migrated to the New World, but they are unable to displace the native Manitou, so instead they cluster in the cities, hidden to all except a few who have the vision to recognize them for what they are. Although De Lint uses very similar themes in much of his work, he is constantly examining them from a fresh viewpoint or unfolding his stories in different directions. He is probably the most accomplished current writer of fantasies using a contemporary setting.

"The Demon Lover" Elizabeth Bowen (1945)

The concept of the demon lover relies on the premise that although love and hate may seem diametrically opposed, they also are linked because of the intensity of the emotions involved. Demon lovers are sprinkled through horror fiction, and include such disparate forms as revenant ghosts, soul-stealing incubi and succubi who invade our dreams, crazed but otherwise ordinary humans, and in recent years charming vampires with ambiguous natures. Perhaps the most frightening versions of the demon lovers are those that are less specific, never clearly delineated, such as the invisible intruder in "WHAT WAS IT?" (1881) by Fitz-James O'Brien and the enigmatic visitor in the demon lover series by Shirley JACKSON. Elizabeth Bowen, who wrote only a handful of supernatural stories, contributed one of the shortest and very best of these with this effective thriller.

Mrs. Drover is happily married. Her children have grown, she is content with her lot in life, and the fiancé who disappeared during the war 25 years in the past is no longer even a memory. She and her family have relocated to their vacation home for the summer, but she stops by their closed up house to collect a few items she has forgotten. On a table inside she finds an unstamped letter addressed to her and is puzzled by its presence, since no one could have known she was stopping by on this particular day, and only the caretaker, who would have forwarded the correspondence, has a key. She opens it and reads an unsigned note reminding her that she had promised to keep an appointment at some unspecified hour.

She is understandably more confused than alarmed, but gradually memory returns to her of the promises she made to the missing man. As the hour advances she feels near panic and decides to find a taxi to take her away quickly. She does so, but once inside she realizes that the cab driver is her long-lost lover. The story ends as he drives off with Mrs. Drover trapped in the rear. We never learn what happened to him, how he returned, or what he plans for his disloyal lover, but it does not matter. Bowen wisely leaves the next scene to our imagination.

"The Demon Pope" Richard Garnett (1897)

The British writer Richard Garnett wrote a small but well respected body of short fantasies, the thrust of which was usually to indict one or another aspect of organized religion, Protestant or Catholic, usually satirically. The most clever of these is this deal-with-the-devil story, which, like most of its type, is darkly humorous, although his version of Lucifer seems particularly gullible. Lucifer intends to tempt young Sylvester with promises of wealth and power, but Sylvester has no intention of surrendering his soul. Finally, Lucifer offers a different arrangement, 40 years of assistance in return for the completion of one task at the end of that period, with the stipulation that the task must be within Sylvester's power. He agrees, the pact is sealed, and we jump forward to learn the outcome.

Sylvester has become pope in the interim. Lucifer appears, reminds him of his bargain, and then asks to be made a cardinal. Sylvester correctly infers that Lucifer hopes thereby to succeed to the papacy so that he can subvert the church, but since Sylvester is a good man, he refuses, inviting Lucifer to take him to hell for reneging. Lucifer is nonplused and refuses since the advent of a good man in the infernal regions would result in their destruction. Sylvester offers a compromise of his own. Lucifer will be pope for 12 hours, at the end of which time Sylvester will appoint him a cardinal, if the demon still wishes that outcome.

Lucifer is transformed into an exact duplicate of Sylvester, although one foot is a cloven hoof, but is promptly set upon by a conspiracy among the cardinals, who charge him with heresy and throw him into a dungeon. They discover his cloven hoof, but rather than recoil in horror, they begin approaching him singly and covertly, each hoping to enlist his aid in one plot or another. Since they recognize him as being satanic, he clearly is a believer and hence cannot be a heretic; they restore him to authority, but then time runs out and he reverts to his original form. Lucifer himself is appalled by the deviousness of the church officials and leaves Sylvester to continue his own good works. Garnett's indictment of corrupt clergymen is mirrored in many of his other fantasies, but never as skillfully as in this classic.

Denning, Troy (1958–)

The FORGOTTEN REALMS role-playing game system has been accompanied for many years by tie-in fantasy adventure novels, in most cases written by authors who have had no previous experience in the genre, although some such as R. A. SALVATORE, Margaret WEIS, and Ed GREENWOOD have subsequently enjoyed some success with other publishers. Troy Denning's first three adventure stories were published under the house name Richard Awlinson and are competent but rather routine quest adventures.

The first novel to appear under Denning's own name was *The Verdant Passage* (1991), the first in the Prism Pentad, a series of five novels whose overall story was the battle between a group of heroic rebels and the evil sorcerer who has ruled their world for a thousand years and the consequences of his fall. The slaves have been freed in *The Crimson Legion* (1992), but that causes widespread social chaos, an ideal situation for another ambitious and ruthless sorcerer. The battle continues in *The Amber Princess* (1992) and *The Obsidian Oracle* (1992), finally ending with *The Cerulean Storm* (1993), which repeats much of the plot of the opening volume. Denning followed this with the Twilight Giants trilogy—*The Ogre's Pact* (1994), *The Titan of Twilight* (1995), and *The Giant among Us* (1995), which tells the story of a war between humans and giants with considerable enthusiasm but little originality.

The Veiled Dragon (1996) was the first of Denning's novels to stand out, with a witch forced to solve a murder mystery while avoiding the unwanted attention of a cult. It is still his most interesting work. *Pages of Pain* (1997) was more ambitious, a complex story set in a multitude of universes that has some excellent moments that are overwhelmed by the rapid pace and overt action. *Faces of Deception* (1998) was memorable chiefly for its protagonist, a man whose face is so disfigured that he keeps it concealed. *Beyond the High Road* (1999) and *The Oath of Stonekeep* (1999), the latter based on a computer game, were routine quest stories. The Return of the Archwizards sequence, which includes *The Summoning* (2001), *The Siege* (2001), and *The Sorcerer* (2002), is also set within the Forgotten Realms universe and tells the story of another interspecies war. Denning is considerably more sure of himself, and his story rises at times above its overly familiar material. Whether he will follow other authors who have moved from this venue to wider markets remains to be seen, although he clearly has the required skills to do so.

Derleth, August (1909–1971)

Although August Derleth produced a considerable body of fiction during his career, most of it was neither fantasy nor horror. He did write a number of ghost stories, some of which are quite good, enough to fill several collections. His primary significance to the field, however, is his long-standing promotion of the works of H. P. LOVECRAFT, whose continued popularity is in large part due to Derleth's early efforts to ensure that they escaped the obscurity of the pulp magazines where they first appeared. With Donald Wandrei, another writer who specialized in weird fiction, Derleth founded Arkham House, a high-quality specialty publisher that brought most of Lovecraft's work into print in hardcover editions as well as the work of many other new and obscure writers. Arkham House survived the death of both founders and still publishes a small number of new titles.

Derleth's own supernatural fiction began appearing during the 1920s. His best stories are "The Lilac Bush" (1930), "Wild Grapes" (1934), "Feigman's Beard" (1934), "LOGODA'S HEADS" (1939), and "The Gentleman from Prague" (1944). Almost all of his supernatural fiction has been collected in *Someone in the Dark* (1941), *Something Near* (1945), *Lurker at the Threshold* (1945), *Dark of the Moon* (1947), *Not Long for This World* (1948), *Lonesome Places* (1962), *Mr. George* and Other Odd Persons (1964), and Colonel Markesan and Less Pleasant Persons (1966, with Mark Schorer). Derleth also published several short stories that were described as collaborations with H. P. Lovecraft, although it seems likely that they were entirely written by Derleth. These were published in book form as *The Survivor and Others* (1957), *The Mask of Cthulhu* (1958), and *The Trail of Cthulhu* (1962), but oddly enough the quality of these stories is inferior to that of both Lovecraft and of Derleth's own work.

Derleth also edited several excellent anthologies of horror stories, including *Sleep No More* (1944), *Night's Yawning Peal* (1952), *When Evil Wakes* (1963), and *Over the Edge* (1964). Although his influence as a writer is peripheral, as an editor and publisher he was one of the more significant figures in the early development of the horror genre.

"Descending" Thomas M. Disch (1964)

One of the most effective techniques in a short story, particularly fantasy and horror, is to take a familiar object or situation and alter it in such a way that the reader becomes momentarily disoriented. There are few activities more prosaic than descending an escalator, but Thomas M. Disch transforms that simple act into a nightmare in this story from early in his career.

The protagonist, whose name we never learn, is on the verge of bankruptcy. He has no job and no prospects, his family has indicated it cannot or will not help him any longer, and the rent on his apartment is due shortly and he has no means of paying it. Discouraged and perhaps not entirely sane, he decides to indulge himself on one final splurge, charging for gourmet groceries, some books, and an excellent restaurant meal. With his purchases bundled awkwardly in one arm, he decides to return to his apartment, leaving a department store by descending its enclosed escalators to the ground floor and reading during the descent.

Lost in his book, he loses track of time, finally recollecting himself when he realizes that he has been descending for much longer than should have been necessary. There are no doors back into the building on any of the landings, no features at all, not even signs to indicate where he is. Disoriented, he continues to descend, counting more than 40 floors before accepting that something is seriously wrong. Initially, he attempts to rationalize the experience, although it is clearly impossible for there to be more than 30 stories below street level. Nevertheless, he decides to reverse the process and climb back up, which proves to be more difficult than he expected since there is no "Up" escalator. The first signs of panic strike. He abandons most of his purchases after eating some of the groceries and drinking from the water fountains, which are thoughtfully provided at every 10th floor.

Exhausted physically and emotionally, he sleeps for a while and then resumes his climb, although the lack of discernible progress is so discouraging that he soon begins descending again. It is so much easier to go down that he ignores his misgivings and is rewarded when he returns to his abandoned goods and can eat again. Some of the items prove inaccessible, since he has no way to open the cans. His subsequent attempts to affect his fate are perfunctory, and as delirium and hunger overwhelm his senses, he concludes that he is en route to hell itself. The reader realizes that this has been simply a reenactment of his life, a constant drop in expectations and decline in his personal fortunes, interrupted by brief and futile attempts to escape the inevitable.

Disch created a bleak snapshot of a life. The reader senses very early on that there is no hope for the protagonist and that he is as doomed now as he has been throughout his life. The story suggests that it might be instructive for each of us to find an appropriate metaphor for our own life.

"The Devil and Daniel Webster" Stephen Vincent Benét (1936)

If one were to compile a list of classic deal-with-the-devil stories, one of the first titles to appear would almost certainly be this classic by the poet and author Benét, who wrote a fair number of fantastic stories, including two less interesting sequels to this one. Properly speaking, although the story does, in fact, involve efforts to avoid a contract between a foolish farmer and the devil himself, Benét's story is not typical of the form, which usually focuses on some elaborate logical or legal argument or a trick ending, whereby the unhappy soul is saved.

The farmer in this case is Jabez Stone, who foolishly offers to sell his soul after a long string of misfortunes plagues his farm and family. The devil shows up, and Stone feels honor bound to complete the deal, after which he prospers, although thoughts of his fate cloud his happiness. In the final days before the contract ends, the desperate man seeks out Daniel Webster, the most prominent lawyer and politician in the country, and begs for his help. Webster cannot abandon a fellow resident of New Hampshire, so he agrees to take the case, and that very night the devil appears to collect his fee.

In most similar stories the reader would then be treated to thrust and counterthrust, but Benét takes a more remote approach, informing us that Webster's arguments were brilliant but ineffective rather than showing us. As a final resort Webster insists on a jury trial, and the devil conjures up a judge and jury from among the most reprehensible, criminal, and traitorous Americans he can cull from among the dead. The apparitions are clearly not in sympathy with Stone, but Webster tries anyway, arguing until dawn with an eloquence that impresses even the damned. Ultimately, despite Webster's inability to muster a convincing legal argument, the jury finds in Stone's favor as a reward for such a prodigious effort. The devil, thwarted, hopes to punish Webster by telling him his own future, the failure of his aspirations to be president and the early death of his sons, but Webster remains unmoved.

The story is thus more a celebration of Americana than fantasy or the supernatural. It was made into a motion picture (1941) and has been performed at various times on the stage. Although the two sequels are minor, Benét wrote one other notable fantasy story, "Johnny Pye & the Fool Killer" (1937).

Dexter, Susan (1955–   )

Susan Dexter was one of a handful of new writers who emerged in the fantasy field during the early 1980s, at which time it was customary for even fantasy epics to contain elements of light humor. Her initial work was, almost inevitably for that genre, a trilogy, the Winter King's War consisting of *The Ring of Allaire* (1981), *The Sword of Calandra* (1985), and *The Mountains of Channadran* (1986). The sequence opens with a quest, an apprentice taking over his master's mission to find a magic horse, defeat a dragon, and rescue a princess, all situations drawn from classic mythology. Dexter employs a light authorial hand, and despite the dangers and adventures, the reader never doubts that the hero will prevail. In the second volume the hero discovers that he is, in fact, the rightful heir to the throne, which he can gain only by finding a magical sword and which occupies him during his second quest. Having ascended to the throne in the concluding volume, he now faces a threat to his people and confronts an evil sorcerer, thus adding the final cliché of modern fantasy. The trilogy is openly, even proudly, derivative, but Dexter's light-hearted approach is refreshing.

Dexter's second trilogy, the Warhorse of Esdragon, also has a fairy tale quality but is considerably more interesting in its own right. *The Prince of Ill Luck* (1994) introduces the protagonist, a young man whose life has been shadowed by a curse of bad luck. In the first volume he falls in love with a princess and agrees to help her locate her missing parents, a task more difficult than it first appears. *The Wind-Witch* (1995) takes an even more serious turn, with war spreading chaos over the countryside. The war and other outstanding issues are resolved in *The True Knight* (1996), a coming-of-age story in which two heroes discover the truth about themselves and their personal destinies. This second trilogy is more serious in tone and more original in content, but its author has since produced very little new fiction.

Dexter also wrote two nonseries novels. *The Wizard's Shadow* (1993) is considerably more original than her other work. A traveling peddler agrees to provide transportation for a wizard's ghost, but by doing so he becomes tangled up in the mystery of the wizard's death at the hands of one of his enemies. *Moonlight* (2001), for younger readers, follows the efforts of another apprentice, this one assisted by an intelligent cat, to rescue a unicorn. Dexter's rare short stories vary in quality, and "Thistledown" (1991) is her best at that length.

Dickinson, Peter (1927–)

Throughout his writing career Peter Dickinson has largely ignored genre classifications. His mystery novels occasionally include science fiction or supernatural elements, he writes with equal ease for both adult and young adult audiences, and his tone can be humorous, adventurous, or suspenseful. Dickinson's first fantasy consisted of a very highly regarded young adult trilogy about Merlin, *The Weathermonger* (1968), *Heartsease* (1969), and *The Devil's Children* (1970), in which the slumbering wizard Merlin is wakened in modern England, and his advent triggers an overnight transformation of the British Isles from technology to magic. A handful of children interact with him and with a fugitive outsider who is sent to find out what is happening. Eventually, they convince Merlin to return to his age-long rest so that modern civilization can be restored.

The Gift (1974) was the closest Dickinson came to writing an outright horror novel, pitting a young clairvoyant boy against a ruthless killer. *The Blue Hawk* (1976) is a historical fantasy set in ancient Egypt. The young protagonist steals a sacred bird, precipitating a crisis, and flees into a wilderness that is still home to ancient forms of magic, although their power is fading from the world. *Tulku* (1979) is a fantasy set in ancient China, a story of a young man's sudden maturity, and *Healer* (1983) chronicles the troubles a young girl experiences when powerful interests discover that she can heal people with a simple touch.

Dickinson's next few fantasies were for much younger readers, although *Merlin Dreams* (1988), a collection of linked tales of Merlin the magician, is of some interest to adult readers. *The Lion Tamer's Daughter and Other Supernatural Stories* (1997) also contains a few good tales, although his first really excellent short stories appeared only in *Water* (2002), a collection of stories written by himself and by Robin MCKINLEY, to whom he is married. His two most recent young adult fantasy novels are both among his best work. *The Ropemaker* (2001) is a quest story in which a young girl tries to find out why the magical forest that protects her village is losing its power, and *Tears of the Salamander* (2003), set in 18th-century Italy, is a story of alchemy. None of Dickinson's fantasy novels were written primarily for adult audiences, but his lucid, intelligent prose gives them an appeal beyond the young adult market to which they are aimed.

The Discworld Series Terry Pratchett (1983–2005)

Although humorous fantasy has had its brief periods of popularity in the United States, genre readers apparently prefer a more serious tone, and only a handful of such novels appear each year. The form is considerably more popular in England, where writers such as Andrew Harman and Tom HOLT have built careers writing tales of the absurd. The most popular British fantasy humorist, Terry PRATCHETT, has also proven to be the most successful on this side of the Atlantic, and the Discworld series, which makes up the vast majority of his work, has produced a steady line of best-selling novels.

It all started with *The Colour of Magic* (1983), which established the peculiar nature of that world and the first of its recurring characters, Rincewind the inept wizard. The Discworld is a fantasy realm that consists of an enormous, disc-shaped landscape held on the back of gigantic elephants, who in turn are standing on the back of an enormous turtle, an unlikely setting for an unlikely but often hilarious series of adventures that have gradually evolved into several subsets, of which the Rincewind stories are one. The first volume specifically parodied other works of fantasy, but Pratchett quickly expanded his approach to include a variety of aspects of modern culture and humanity's bewildering unreasonableness. Much of the familiar background is introduced or enhanced in *The Light Fantastic* (1986), wherein Rincewind possesses a spell vital to the future of the world but does not know how to use it. Rincewind's adventures continue in *Sourcery* (1988), *Eric* (1990), *Interesting Times* (1994), and *The Last Continent* (1997). *Equal Rites* (1987) introduces a second set of recurring characters, including Granny Weatherwax, a good witch, whose further adventures in *Wyrd Sisters* (1988) elaborate her background and set the tone for further volumes. The witches' exploits continue in *Maskerade* (1995) and *The Fifth Element* (2000).

Three of the best Discworld novels involve Death personified. *Mort* (1987), the most consistently clever of the early titles, investigates the consequences when a temporary stand-in for Death refuses to take the life of a young girl, whose continued existence vaguely perplexes her family and friends. *Reaper Man* (1991) and *Soul Music* (1994) continue in this vein, although not as successfully. *Guards! Guards!* (1989) is the first of the Night Watch sequence. The forces of law and order in Discworld's largest city struggle to apprehend a murderous dragon, spoofing a number of detective fiction tropes in the process. *Men at Arms* (1996) and *Feet of Clay* (1996) are similar episodes. A new island rises from beneath the sea just beyond the city in *Jingo* (1997), and time travel makes detection even more difficult in *Night Watch* (2002).

Pyramids (1989) is more or less independent, set in an Egyptian-patterned society in a distant part of Discworld. *Moving Pictures* (1990) very effectively lampoons Hollywood, and *Small Gods* (1992) does the same for organized religion, introducing a cult that believes that Discworld is spherical rather than flat. *Lords and Ladies* (1995) is one of Pratchett's least successful efforts, but *Hogfather* (1996), in which Discworld's version of Father Christmas is kidnapped, is one of his best. *Carpe Jugulum* (1998) informs us of the downside of inviting vampires to family events, and *The Truth* (2000), another relentlessly satiric story, describes what happens when a man magically incapable of telling a lie becomes the publisher of a newspaper. Time is a quantifiable commodity in *Thief of Time* (2001), and an aging, out-of-fashion hero confronts the gods to tell them off in *The Last Hero* (2001).

In recent years Pratchett has written some titles aimed at children, starting with *The Amazing Maurice and His Educated Rodents* (2001). *The Wee Free Men* (2003) and *A Hatful of Sky* (2004) are in the same vein. "Troll Bridge" (1992) is also set in Discworld. Pratchett is a publishing phenomenon in England, certainly the best-selling novelist in that country, and has a large following around the world. Considering that the series has already reached more than 30 volumes, it remains surprisingly fresh and innovative.

"The Distressing Tale of Thangobrind the Jeweler, and of the Doom That Befell Him" Lord Dunsany (1912)

Edward Plunkett, Lord DUNSANY, was one of the earliest fantasy writers and had a strong influence on the work of J. R. R. TOLKIEN and through him on virtually every fantasy writer who would follow. His stories are told in a very literate but slightly artificial style and are structured much like fairy tales in that they made no effort to realistically describe the psychology of his characters. Gods and magical creatures are there in abundance, some traditional, some not, and many of the tales are essentially episodes, sometimes with virtually no plot.

One of his most famous stories is this short history of one Thangobrind, ostensibly a jeweler but in practice a brilliant thief who specializes in stealing only the most precious of stones. One of his clients approaches him with a commission to steal a diamond as large as a man's head from its resting place in the lap of a distant and notoriously vengeful god. The client offers to pay for the diamond with the soul of his oldest daughter, and Thangobrind accepts the job, perhaps as much for its challenge as for the material gains. There follows a brief, capsule account of his lengthy journey to the temple of the dreaded god, in which the author alludes briefly to adventures that could have filled an entire novel.

At last he arrives in the land of Hlo-hlo's adherents, where he drugs the local priests long enough to make off with the diamond. When they recover, the priests are oddly calm, perhaps because the jewel has been stolen in the past but always returns to its original resting place. Thangobrind is celebrating his success when he begins to feel that he is being pursued. Ultimately, the idol reclaims the diamond, and the thief's life is forfeit. The story is compact, straightforward, and might be unremarkable if it were to appear for the first time today, but Dunsany was inventing the modern form of fantasy at the time, and his work is recognized today for its innovation and imaginative content.

Donaldson, Stephen R. (1947–   )

When the *LORD OF THE RINGS* by J. R. R. TOLKIEN was finally published in mass market paperback during the late 1960s, it wakened a sudden widespread interest in fantasy fiction that germinated over the next few years and which began to grow rapidly during the 1970s. By the end of the 1970s, publishers were actively looking for new fantasy talent to promote, and Stephen R. Donaldson burst onto the scene at precisely the right time with the Chronicles of Thomas Covenant, which originally consisted of two trilogies and which has recently been extended with the first of four new titles. The titles in the first trilogy were *Lord Foul's Bane, The Illearth War,* and *The Power that Preserves,* all published in 1977.

The trilogy was obviously heavily influenced by Tolkien, but the hero in this case is a man from our universe, Thomas Covenant, a leper who has become deeply traumatized by his condition and who believes the Land, the magical realm to which he is transported, to be an extended psychotic dream. In fact, even after he is convinced to help the inhabitants of that land in their fight against the mysterious and totally evil Lord Foul, he never completely believes in the reality of his experience. There was, in fact, some criticism because of an early incident in which Covenant, believing this to be an elaborate dream, commits rape.

The second trilogy, *The Wounded Land* (1980), *The One Tree* (1982), and *White Gold Wielder* (1983), is considerably more somber, and much of the action focuses on characters other than Covenant. The Land has been poisoned at the instigation of Lord Foul, who can be free only when it has been completely destroyed. He is finally defeated, again by Covenant, who this time is forced to give his own life in the process. The new sequence opens with *The Runes of the Earth* (2004), in which Covenant's son, under the influence of Lord Foul, kidnaps a child and his own mother, who is mentally ill, and takes them to the once again horribly transformed Land, pursued by Linden Avery, the doctor who was introduced during the second trilogy. Three more volumes are planned.

Donaldson, who has also written thrillers and a series of space adventures, has published only one additional book-length fantasy, a two-part novel under the titles *The Mirror of Her Dreams* (1986) and *A Man Rides Through* (1987). Known collectively as *Mordant's Need,* the story focuses on

a young woman caught up in an elaborate and convincing series of intrigues and minor adventures and is in large part a coming-of-age story. The scale is considerably narrower than in his previous fantasies, but the tone is lighter and the characterizations equally dense. Donaldson has also written a number of short stories, almost all of which are of very high quality, and his collections, *Daughter of Regals and Other Tales* (1984) and *Reave the Just and Other Stories* (1998), mix predominantly fantasy with material from other genres. The latter collection won the World Fantasy Award. Donaldson's extended absence from fantasy has only partially diminished his reputation, and his recent return is likely to restore him to prominence.

Douglas, Carole Nelson (1944–)

Between 1982 and 1992 Carole Nelson Douglas produced seven traditional fantasy novels of considerable merit, arranged in one sequence of five plus a separate duo. Her subsequent fiction has been primarily in the mystery genre, although the Irene Adler series flirts with fantastic elements from time to time, and the Midnight Louie series is told from the point of view of a cat. Her occasional short fiction has been generally minor, although "Dracula on the Rocks" (1995) is amusing.

Her first two novels, *Six of Swords* (1982) *and Exiles of the Rynth* (1984), establish the setting and introduce the main character, Irissi, along with several companions including an intelligent cat. Irissi is the last of her kind, and she seeks to escape into another world where she will not be alone. The gateway is discovered in the second book, which sets the stage for the next three volumes, the Sword & Circlet trilogy—*Keepers of Edanvant* (1987), *Heir of Rengarth* (1988), and *Seven of Swords* (1989). Irissi and her friends spend all three books battling an evil wizard named Geronfrey, but Douglas avoids most of the common clichés and delivers a surprisingly mature story.

The Talisman duo includes *Cup of Clay* (1991) and *Seed upon the Wind* (1992). These two have a considerably darker tone and address issues of gender prejudice and child abuse. The protagonist is a reporter from our world who falls through a standard gateway into a magic land that initially seems a pleasant place but whose underlying corruption becomes increasingly apparent. She encounters a man of that world on a magical quest and inadvertently derails his plans, although she eventually redeems herself, saves the day, and then seeks a return to her original world. Nelson switched to mystery and suspense before the extent of her abilities as a fantasy writer were known, but the relatively small body of work she did produce stands up well compared to most contemporary fantasists.

Dracula Bram Stoker (1897)

When Bram STOKER wrote *Dracula*, he penned possibly the most famous novel of the supernatural of all, established the prototype for vampires for the following generation of writers, and created one of the most recognizable fictional characters of all time. The character Dracula is loosely based on Vlad Tepes, a 15th-century sometimes prince of Wallachia who became known as Vlad the Impaler. There had been previous stories of vampires. John Polidori's *The Vampyre* had appeared in 1819, *Varney the Vampyre* by James M. Rymer appeared in 1847, and *CARMILLA* by J. Sheridan LE FANU, for whose newspaper Stoker occasionally wrote, was first published in 1871. The legend of the vampire was not consistent from place to place, and Stoker was free to choose which portions to use and which to discard. Modern readers of vampire fiction often forget that Dracula could walk abroad in daylight and that he could be killed by gunfire. Later writers would vary from the formula, sometimes dramatically, but the basic rules of vampirism were carried on—drinking blood by means of a bite on the neck, the aversion to religious objects and garlic, the conversion of victims to vampirism in turn, and in many cases the ability to physically change shape.

We first meet Count Dracula through the eyes of Jonathan Harker, who is acting as an agent of his employer to help arrange the count's relocation to England from his native Transylvania. Harker is only mildly disturbed by the attitude of Dracula's neighbors, who fear and loathe him, and his initial impression is favorable. As his stay at the castle becomes extended, he discovers that he is a prisoner rather than a guest, and his eventual escape comes only after he has experienced such a shock that he becomes seriously ill.

The scene shifts to England, specifically the home of Lucy Westenra, a spoiled and rather empty-headed young woman who has recently chosen Arthur Holmwood from among her various suitors. Lucy's companion is Mina Murray, Harker's fiancée. They are intrigued by the appearance of the mysterious and vaguely romantic Count Dracula. However, shortly after he arrives Lucy begins sleepwalking, and her health declines. Doctor Abraham Van Helsing is called in, and he correctly diagnoses the problem as a vampire, although his companions are understandably skeptical. A battle of wits ensues as Dracula slowly subverts and eventually kills Lucy, who returns as one of the undead but is destroyed by Van Helsing and the others after a brief series of depredations. Dracula, however, now has his sights set on Mina, and his evil infects her, although she remains among the living.

Dracula recruits the assistance of Renfield, an inmate at the asylum of Dr. Jack Seward who seems able to enter and leave the premises at will. Renfield proves to be an unreliable servant, however, and Dracula eventually destroys him. The company of friends has his number by now, and they systematically destroy all but one of the coffins of native earth he brought with him from Transylvania. Having decided that discretion is the better part of valor, Dracula abandons his new home and sets out on the long trip back to Transylvania, pursued by the others who can acquire some knowledge of his movements by means of a psychic link to Mina. They catch him in the nick of time, destroy him and his three wives, and lose one of their number in the process. There are parts of the novel that seem overly sentimental, particularly the constant homages to Mina by her friends, but the story has an undeniable power that comes through the somewhat archaic prose.

There are hundreds if not thousands of stories and novels that were influenced at least indirectly by *Dracula*, as well as more than 40 sequels. Some of the more interesting of these include *Sherlock Holmes vs Dracula* (1978) by Loren Estleman, *Dracula Began* (1976) by Gail Kimberly, which is actually a prequel, *Mina* (1994) by Elaine BERGSTROM writing as Mira Kiraly, an account of Mina Harker's subsequent slide toward vampirism because she is not completely free of Dracula's taint, and *Dracula Unbound* (1992) by Brian W. Aldiss, which describes Dracula as a time traveler from the far future when humans have evolved into blood drinkers. Fred Saberhagen has written a series of interesting novels with the premise that Dracula was not as bad as Stoker portrayed him and that he survived to the present day. Perhaps the oddest series of Dracula novels was written by Robert Lory. In which a pair of modern-day vigilantes capture Dracula and enslave him with a wooden pacemaker, then use him as a weapon against organized crime.

Dracula's presence in the movies is, if anything, even more pronounced. There have been at least half a dozen versions of the original story and scores of sequels, most with little connection to the original characters and settings. The earliest was the silent film *Nosferatu* (1930), an unauthorized adaptation, and the most famous followed in 1931 starring Bela Lugosi in the role for which he will always be remembered. Later versions have varied from the interesting but flawed *Bram Stoker's Dracula* (1992) to the ridiculousness of *Billy the Kid vs Dracula* (1965). Stoker's novel may not be a literary triumph on a level with most of the classics of his time, but he struck a chord that resonates intensely and created one of the most familiar and terrifying of archetypical villains.

The Dragonlance Series

The immense popularity of the Dungeons & Dragons game system inevitably led to a line of tie-in novels from TSR Publishing, which began in the early 1980s and has continued ever since, although the imprint is now called Wizards of the Coast. The Dragonlance novels and the universe they are set in was adapted from the scenarios used in the games and given depth primarily by the early novels produced by the collaborative team of Margaret WEIS and Tracy Hickman. The major setting is the land of Krynn, heavily influenced by the works of J. R. R. TOLKIEN in that it is home to a wide variety of intelligent races in addition to humans, in-

cluding elves, trolls, orcs, and goblins. The series concentrates on violent conflicts, often wars, and is filled with standard fantasy devices including quests, magical artifacts, usurped thrones, evil sorcerers, and barbarian warriors.

There have to date been more than 120 titles in the series, including a considerable number of anthologies of short stories. Although the rough history of Krynn has been worked out as a backdrop, most of the details were deliberately left vague to make it easier for authors to insert stories without contradicting one another. There are a few recurring characters used by more than one writer such as Dalamar the Dark, a good wizard, but for the most part the authors create their own casts of characters. Almost all the novels are arranged in subsets, with either a continuous story line or a series of linked themes. Many of the subordinate series are written by a single author, as is the case with The Defenders of Magic by Mary Kirchoff, the Dhamon series by Jean Rabe, the Icewall series by Douglas Niles, and the War of Souls by Margaret Weis and Tracy Hickman. Others use a variety of authors for individual volumes, including the Age of Mortals, Bridge of Time, Chaos War, Lost Histories, and Preludes sequences.

Although most Dragonlance authors began their career writing tie-in novels for either this or the similar Forgotten Realms series from the same publisher, a few writers with previous titles to their credit have occasionally contributed, including Nancy Varian Berberick, Richard A. KNAAK, Dan Parkinson, and Roland Green. A few who started writing for TSR have subsequently placed books with other publishers, including Douglas Niles, Jean Rabe, Mark ANTHONY, and J. Robert King. Although the Dragonlance novels are generally considered to be at the low end of the fantasy fiction spectrum because of their repetitive plots and sometimes awkward writing, there are individual titles that compare favorably to mainstream fantasy fiction, and in recent years the overall quality of the writing has improved noticeably.

Drake, David (1945–   )

David Drake began writing professionally in the early 1970s, and for most of that decade he produced short stories only, although in a wide variety of forms including military science fiction, sword and sorcery, and horror. His early horror fiction includes several notable pieces such as "The Barrow Troll" (1975) and "Blood Debt" (1975), and his collection of supernatural stories, *From the Heart of Darkness* (1983) is of very high quality, although Drake has subsequently written very little horror.

His first full-length fantasy was *The Dragon Lord* (1982), a retelling of the story of King Arthur, but with a very unconventional take on the main characters and with a genuine fire-breathing dragon added to the mix. He was also a regular contributor to the Thieves' World shared world anthology series and used his recurring character as the protagonist of *Dagger* (1988), a fairly routine fantasy adventure. *The Sea Hag* (1988) was equally conventional but much better written and was originally planned as the first volume in a series, but no further volumes have appeared to date. Drake's short fantasy fiction largely fell into two series. One was collected as *Vettius and His Friends* (1989), the story of a Roman soldier who defeats various magical opponents, and the other as *Old Nathan* (1991), set in an alternate version of early 19th-century America where magic works.

Drake apparently enjoys working in the universes created by other writers and has written *The Enchanted Bunny* (1991) and *To Bring the Light* (1996), both sequels to works by L. Sprague DE CAMP, and collaborated with Janet MORRIS for *Explorers in Hell* (1989), set in the shared universe created by Morris and C. J. CHERRYH. He finally started a major sword and sorcery series of his own with *Lord of the Isles* (1997), a complicated story of intrigue involving a mysterious and evil magical force and the survivors of a drowned kingdom.

Drake has produced five more volumes in this series to date. *Queen of Demons* (1998) is a straightforward quest story with a party of adventurers searching for information that can help them oppose the encroachment of an evil queen. They are diverted by a trip back through time to rescue a kidnapped woman in *Servant of the Dragon* (1999). Just when it appears that they are out from under the shadow of evil, an army of monsters appears on the horizon in *Mistress of the Catacombs* (2001), they are scattered among myriad realities

in *Goddess of the Ice Realm* (2003), and evil sorcery proves too tempting for some in *Master of the Cauldron* (2004).

Drake's remaining fantasy novel is *The Tyrant* (2002), written with Eric Flint, set in a fantasy world that resembles ancient Rome and that faces many of the same problems and palace intrigues and the danger of a slave rebellion. In recent years he has written very few short stories, of which only "Elf House" (2004) is particularly interesting. He has proven himself to be a reliable and entertaining writer, but the intensity and powerful characterization of his earliest short stories is largely missing from his more recent work.

The Dreamers Roger Manvell (1958)

A frequent criticism of modern horror fiction is that it draws almost exclusively on Christian mythology and the legends of Western civilization. Vampires are repelled by crosses, and the devil made them do it. Although this is understandable since that is the tradition of most active horror writers as well as their audience, it leaves a great number of resources untapped. There have been exceptions, of course. Henry Hocherman's *The Gilgul* (1990) invokes a Judaic form of possession, Dan Simmons investigates native Hawaiian legends in *Fires of Eden* (1995), African legends are central to *The Stickman* (1987) by Seth Pfefferle and *The Living Blood* (2001) by Tananarive Due, a Filipino folk tale is the basis for *The Bamboo Demons* (1979) by Jory Sherman, and Japanese myths create the tension in *Tengu* (1983) by Graham MASTERTON, but they are a decided minority. Voodoo is probably the major exception, but even there one often sees a blending of voodoo ritual with Christianity.

Roger Manvell wrote only one horror novel, but he drew his inspiration from an African legend and developed it into a chilling, suspenseful story using a supernatural device that has largely been ignored by other genre writers—the contagious dream. Using the principle of six degrees of separation, an African witch doctor plots to exact his revenge by communicating a dream, disturbing at first but not dangerous, which is so vivid and frightening that the dreamer feels compelled to pass it on. With each transfer the dream grows more powerful, and ultimately it will be fatal to the party for whom it is intended when it finally reaches its destination. The ultimate doom is averted, not through ordinary means, but by understanding and applying the native African lore that made it possible in the first place. This unusually effective novel was reprinted in the early 1960s but has unaccountably been out of print ever since.

Dr. Jekyll and Mr. Hyde Robert Louis Stevenson (1886)

The author of *Treasure Island* and other classic adventure stories occasionally dabbled with darker themes in short stories such as "THE BOTTLE IMP" and this short novel, which is such a familiar classic that even people who have never read the story or seen any of several movie versions still have a general idea of the plot. The term *Jekyll and Hyde* has become a familiar description of conflicting personalities within a single individual, and the infamous Mr. Hyde has become a classic villain of a stature that rivals Bram STOKER's vampyrrhic *DRACULA* or Frankenstein's monster.

The story is revealed to us through the eyes of Utterson, a lawyer and close friend of Dr. Henry Jekyll. Utterson hears from a companion, Richard Enright, the story of a fiendishly cruel man who ruthlessly attacked a child some time in the recent past. Utterson correctly identifies the culprit as Edward Hyde, a disreputable and secretive new friend of Jekyll's who has recently been made the primary beneficiary of the doctor's estate. There is something about Hyde that repulses everyone he meets, but he seems to be so thoroughly in Jekyll's good graces that he can intrude at odd hours of the morning demanding financial support. Utterson, predictably, suspects blackmail, but Jekyll resists his efforts to pursue the matter further.

A year passes uneventfully, and the friendship among Jekyll, Utterson, and another doctor, Lanyon, slowly deteriorates through lack of contact. The situation changes following the brutal and public murder of Sir Danvers Carew by Hyde in front of a witness. The police attempt to apprehend the killer, but Hyde has disappeared completely. Jekyll

insists that he will never be found. Shortly after these events, Jekyll becomes more reclusive than ever, and Lanyon experiences some terrible shock about which he will not speak but which has shaken him so severely that his health takes a sharp turn for the worse, and he dies a short while later.

Utterson's failed attempts to renew his friendship with Jekyll discourage him from further efforts until he is summoned by Jekyll's butler. His master locked himself in one of his rooms several days previously, but now his voice sounds strangely different and foul play is suspected. Sure enough, Utterson recognizes Hyde's voice and orders the door broken down. By the time they effect entry, Hyde is dead by his own hand, and Jekyll is nowhere to be found, a mystery that is resolved when Utterson pieces together the rest of the story from letters left behind by both Jekyll and Lanyon, who had become a party to the terrible secret.

Jekyll had long been fascinated by the dichotomy between good and evil impulses within individuals, and he experimented with various combinations of drugs until he finally hit upon a formula that would allow him to separate the two. To his surprise, when under the influence of his evil self, he physically transformed, becoming smaller and darker and having an indefinable air of unspecific deformity. He finds a new freedom in the experience, because as Hyde he can indulge all of his baser impulses without being troubled by a guilty conscience, while as Jekyll he pursues worthwhile and charitable goals untroubled by temptation. Unfortunately, the Hyde half wishes to remain dominant, and eventually the transformations begin to occur without the use of drugs, as Hyde forces himself into the ascendant. Jekyll's efforts to reverse the process fail when he is unable to replicate his original formula.

Readers who had previously watched one or another of the film versions might be surprised at how relatively unmelodramatic the print version is. To a great extent, this novella is a werewolf story, with the drug taking the place of the full moon and without the danger of contagion. It is also a cautionary tale warning us against scientific experiments that ignore the morality of the experimenter's choices and that fail to properly anticipate the outcome.

Readers interested in a retelling of the story from a different viewpoint should try *Mary Reilly* (1991) by Valerie Martin, in which one of the housemaids employed by Dr. Jekyll becomes romantically obsessed with the elusive Edward Hyde. A film version of the novel was released in 1996. *The Jekyll Legacy* (1990) by Robert BLOCH and Andre NORTON is a direct sequel in which Dr. Jekyll's niece inherits the property and begins to suspect that Hyde has somehow survived after all.

"The Drowned Giant" J. G. Ballard (1965)

Early fantasy writers such as Clark Ashton SMITH and Lord DUNSANY occasionally wrote short fantastic tales that were not stories in the strictest sense. They were anecdotes, episodes, or even just short descriptive passages that evoked a fantastic image or idea. Sometimes they were constructed to comment on one subject or another, but at other times they were merely intended to create an unusual image and describe it in elaborate prose. This form has almost entirely disappeared from modern fantasy, but there have been a few remarkable exceptions, of which this short piece by J. G. Ballard, whose early work was generally science fiction, is an extraordinary example.

The story is, in its simplest form, the description of the body of a giant washed up on a beach near an unnamed city and the subsequent mutilation and decay of the oversized corpse. The nameless narrator responds to what he initially believes to be just a rumor and discovers that it is true. The body, which seems not particularly impressive upon initial inspection, proves to be as large as a sperm whale. It has died only recently and is still unblemished when first encountered, and Ballard compares it alternately to a beached ship and a temple. Initially, the onlookers remain at a respectful distance, but eventually familiarity makes them irreverent; they begin climbing on the body and making sport of it. It is at this point that the reader begins to recognize the parallel between the giant's body and the "great man," a person who becomes prominent in the public eye, is revered until the first flush of fame fades, and then becomes the subject of jokes and jibes. The parasitic nature of public opinion is represented by those who clamber across the body, who are compared to flies and later seagulls.

The narrator returns after a three-day lapse to discover that the natural decaying process has made the body look more mature. Scientists and city officials have arrived to consider how best to deal with what is now clearly a public nuisance. Similarly, we can conclude, fame makes our own outstanding individuals troublesome to established authority. Graffiti begins to appear, evidence of repressed spite, and the giant now seems no more than human. Ultimately, the various parts of his body are disassembled and disposed of, sometimes frivolously, and specific memories of what happened begin to fade until the giant is no more than a series of disparate and generally mistaken recollections. Ballard's story has no plot in the conventional sense and no specific characters. The protagonist is, if anything, the public in general and an indictment of the way we treat anyone who stands out.

Duane, Diane (1952–)

Diane Duane, who is also the author of several Star Trek novels, began her career with the fantasy novel *The Door into Fire* (1979), a sword and sorcery series set in a world where the power of fire is supreme, and its manipulation is a talent ordinarily limited to women although one male character shares that ability. The story rises above the general run of similar fantasies, and the sequels that followed drew a considerable number of fans, although its publishing history is erratic. *The Door into Shadow* (1984) and *The Door into Sunset* (1992) were both very fine continuations of the original story, but the long-promised fourth volume has yet to appear. Duane developed her world into a unique and interesting setting, and some of the characters—including Sunspark, the fire elemental—are quite well drawn.

Duane is better known among fantasy readers for her young adult series, which opened with *So You Want to Be a Wizard?* (1983) and has now been extended to seven titles. In the opening volume children from our world are transported to a magical alternate New York City, where they discover that they have supernormal talents. They are briefly transformed into the shape of whales in *Deep Wizardry* (1985) and save another child from the dangers of excessive imagination in *High Wizardry* (1990). Their subsequent adventures involve Irish ghosts in *A Wizard Abroad* (1993), an attempt to use magic to cure cancer in *The Wizard's Dilemma* (2001), communication with toys in *A Wizard Alone* (2002), and a visit to another planet in *Wizard's Holiday* (2003). The thoughtful development of the characters as they age through the books is unusual in children's fantasy and adeptly handled.

Duane has also written occasional adult fantasy. *Book of Night with Moon* (1997) chronicles the exploits of a group of sentient cats who are actually the secret guardians of the portals that allow travel among various realities. They return in *To Visit the Queen* (1999), which borrows heavily from science fiction. The cats detect a malfunctioning portal and investigate, only to discover that an evil mastermind has created an alternate timeline in which Queen Victoria died and nuclear weapons were developed. The best of Duane's fantasy novels is *Stealing the Elf King's Roses* (2003), set in the kingdom of the elves. A murder has been committed, and the king himself is the prime suspect. Duane also writes occasional short fiction, of which the most notable is "The Dovrefell Cat" (1994).

Duncan, Dave (1933–)

Although his debut fantasy novel, *A Rose Red City* (1987), was a stand-alone novel, most of Dave Duncan's fantasy consists of series of novels, although the common factor might be an imagined world or history rather than a single set of characters. The first of these comprised *The Reluctant Swordsman* (1988), *The Coming of Wisdom* (1988), and *The Destiny of the Sword* (1988), which is a conventional fantasy adventure involving a man sent on a magical quest by a goddess. A rival deity provides the major obstacle, but the hero prevails through a series of exciting and quite intelligently plotted trials and tribulations.

Duncan's second trilogy consists of *Magic Casement* (1990), *Faery Lands Forlorn* (1990), and *Emperor and Clown* (1991), in which a stableboy discovers that he has magical powers that he eventually uses to rescue a kidnapped princess and save the kingdom. This sequence is notable for the way in which Duncan consciously structures his setting, providing a set of rules that govern the magical elements, which emerge as a major part of the story rather than functioning as simple background. He used the same technique in his next series, *The Cutting Edge* (1992), *Upland Outlaws* (1992), *The Stricken Field* (1993), and *The Living God* (1994), which continues the story of Rap, the one-time stableboy, now king. The ruler of a rival kingdom has become insane, and a god warns that the end of the world may be near. A war with a virtual army of wizards ensues before the evil dwarf is finally defeated and peace restored.

The Reaver Road (1992) and its sequel, *The Hunter's Haunt* (1995), are amusing, lighter adventures, and *The Cursed* (1995) is a somewhat darker fantasy in which those who survive a terrible plague develop magical powers that make them a separate, privileged caste. *Past Imperative* (1995) introduces a battle that is being fought across multiple realities as part of an elaborate game. That story continues with *Present Tense* (1996) and *Future Indefinite* (1997). Duncan resorted to a pseudonym for another trilogy, *Demon Sword* (1995), *Demon Rider* (1997), and *Demon Knight* (1998), all by Ken Hood. The series is set during the 13th century and features a hero who is periodically possessed by a demon, which proves to be quite helpful during some of his battles.

Duncan's most recent and by far most impressive series is the King's Blades, which started with *The Gilded Chain* (1998). Although they have been published in rough chronological order and there are some common characters shared between volumes, each is a separate story, and they can be read in any order. The basic premise is that an elite corps of warriors exists who can be bonded magically to their masters. The link is so powerful that the Blades die or go insane if their master is killed, which necessarily forces them to remain loyal. The opening volume follows the career of one of these men from his youth to his eventual emancipation and establishment as an adviser to the king, and it is one of the most impressive fantasy adventures ever written, often reminiscent of Alexander Dumas.

Lord of the Fire Lands (1999) continues at the same high level of quality. Two young Blades refuse to be bonded to the present king, which makes them outlaws. A young woman becomes the uneasy heir to the throne in *Sky of Swords* (2000) and secures her claim through clever manipulation at court aided by the loyalty of several of the Blades. *Paragon Lost* (2002) moves to a neighboring country in which a delegation escorted by the Blades discovers that the local ruler is dangerously unbalanced. Another foreign ruler appeals for help in *Impossible Odds* (2003), seeking to free her people from the domination of an evil sorcerer, and a small delegation of Blades are given the apparently impossible task of helping her. The most recent in the series is *The Jaguar Knights* (2004), a fascinating and original work in which an outlying fortress is attacked by a band of warriors, some of whom are not human. They are clearly from an unknown land, but their methods of travel and attack are so strange that the king decides he will sacrifice some of his loyal Blades if necessary to discover the truth.

Duncan also wrote two adventures of the King's Daggers, a short-lived young adult sequence set in the same world. *Sir Stalwart* (1999) compels two young enemies to work together to clear their names of scandal, and *The Crooked House* (2000) is a moderately clever murder mystery. Duncan is one of the handful of contemporary fantasy authors who avoid using familiar settings and situations and consistently provide original and innovative new adventures. He also tackles steadily more intricate story lines and creates increasingly elaborate cultures in his later work.

Dunsany, Lord (Edward John Moreton Drax Plunkett) (1878–1957)

Edward John Moreton Drax Plunkett wrote extensively using his title, Lord Dunsany, as his byline, and the significant portion of his work that was fantasy is generally his best-remembered fiction, although he also wrote the classic mystery short story "Two Bottles of Relish." His first major fantasy work was *The Gods of Pegāna* (1905), a collection of anecdotes about a set of mythical gods, most of which would not technically qualify as short stories. His second collection, *Time and the Gods* (1906), contains more plot and narrative,

and the third, *The Sword of Welleran and Other Stories* (1908), contains several classic tales, including "THE FORTRESS UNVANQUISHABLE, SAVE FOR SACNOTH," which anticipated many of the now all-too-common themes of modern fantasy fiction. Several more collections followed, each containing at least a few outstanding stories. Many of the later stories are in the Jorkens series, not all of which are fantasy and most of which are decidedly humorous.

Dunsany's full-length novels are, in general, not as interesting as his short fiction. *Don Rodriguez: Chronicles of Shadow Valley* (1922) is an episodic adventure set in a magical version of medieval Spain and was clearly influenced by *Don Quixote* by Cervantes. *The King of Elfland's Daughter* (1924) is the best of his novels, relating the sometimes comical consequences when a mortal man marries a fairy princess. *The Charwoman's Shadow* (1926) is a pleasant but minor fairy tale, and magic plays a decreasing role in *The Blessing of Pan* 1927) and *The Curse of the Wise Woman* (1933).

There was revived interest in Dunsany's fantasy during the early 1970s, when Lin CARTER edited three new collections of his short stories for the Ballantine Books adult fantasy line, *At the Edge of the World* (1970), *Beyond the Fields We Know* (1972), and *Over the Hills and Far Away* (1974), and there have been reprints and cross collections ever since. Recent new volumes, *In the Land of Time* (2004) and the *Complete Jorkens* (2004), indicate that interest in his work has not diminished. Dunsany is rightly considered one of the inventors of adult fantasy fiction, and many of his short stories are undeniable classics. He was also the author of many plays, several of which have fantastic elements.

"The Dunwich Horror" H. P. Lovecraft (1929)

A large portion of the horror tales of H. P. LOVECRAFT are set within the context of the Cthulhu Mythos, which assumes that Earth was once ruled by a race of monstrous alien intelligences who were banished to another reality and who hope one day to return. In several of his stories, including this, one of his most famous, humans cooperate to some extent in that effort. The story opens slowly but effectively, describing the environs of Dunwich, Massachusetts, a remote, decaying town whose inhabitants are inbred and narrowminded. Among their number is the Whateley family, disliked and feared by their neighbors. Wilbur Whateley was born under unusual circumstances, matured with surprising quickness, and keeps to himself, studying arcane books and never exposing much of his body to scrutiny. He and his grandfather make frequent alterations to their farmhouse, removing partitions and boarding up the windows on the second floor. They also buy cattle in large numbers, although the size of their herd never seems to increase.

Although still only a teenager, Whateley appears to be an adult when he travels to Miskatonic University to study their copy of *The Necronomicon,* a fictional book that Lovecraft created for this cycle of stories, although there have subsequently been several modern *Necronomicons* published to take advantage of the title's familiarity. Whateley's efforts are thwarted by Dr. Henry Armitage, an expert on the occult, who suspects that the young man's studies are dangerous. He is not greatly surprised when Whateley later attempts to steal the book. A guard dog kills the intruder, and he is revealed to be only marginally human, his body malformed and alien. More significantly, since his grandfather has already passed on, there is no one to watch over whatever it is that lives in the boarded up farmhouse.

That creature emerges and launches a series of destructive attacks in Dunwich. At first only cattle are killed, but then one family is wiped out, followed by another. The creature itself is enormous and leaves footprints but is invisible, seen only very briefly when Armitage and two friends appear on the scene to use magical incantations to reveal the creature and expel it from our universe. The creature is, of course, Whateley's twin brother, but we are told that he looked more like the father than Wilbur did. "The Dunwich Horror" is one of Lovecraft's most popular stories, and it became a low-budget motion picture in 1970 with a screenplay that did not radically differ from the original story line.

Durgin, Doranna (1960–)

With her debut novel, *Dun Lady's Jess* (1994), Doranna Durgin turned a familiar fantasy device on its head. Instead of a human being transformed into the shape of an animal, the protagonist in this case is a horse who is magically changed into human form. Her efforts to find her former master are hampered significantly by her adjustment to her new circumstances and the vagaries of human society. Jess returns in a sequel, *Changespell* (1997), in which she has managed an uneasy accommodation to being a werehorse until she discovers that someone is deliberately causing other people to become involuntary shape changers. The sequel is not quite as charming as the original, but the character is sufficiently interesting to compensate for the shortcomings of the plot.

A second duo consists of *Touched by Magic* (1997) and *Wolf Justice* (1998), set in an alternate world from which magic has disappeared, a condition that seems to be on the verge of reversing itself. The subsequent adventures of the protagonist are competently told but lack the cleverness of the Jess stories. *Barrenlands* (1998) is similarly a well-crafted tale of court intrigues and secretive battles for control of a throne, but once again it appears that Durgin was simply drawing upon familiar plots and standard story elements rather than developing her own alternate world.

Wolverine's Daughter (2000) is a mixture of quests and the coming of age of a young woman. This time Durgin rises above her straightforward subject material by means of a thoughtfully detailed portrait of its central character, who seeks to learn why her father abandoned her as a child. *Seer's Blood* (2000) shows continued improvement, set in an unusual fantasy world that resembles rural Appalachia. A band of travelers turns out to be a covert invasion force armed with magical talents. There is a darker tone in *A Feral Darkness* (2001), whose protagonist is a dog groomer whose neighbor has summoned supernatural assistance.

Durgin's more recent novels have been somewhat disappointing. *Changespell Legacy* (2002) is a low-key and only marginally satisfying addition to the story of Jess, and *Dark Debts* (2003) is a competent but unmemorable tie-in to a game system. Durgin's short fiction has been occasional and follows no established pattern. "Fool's Gold" (1997) is so far her best at that length.

"Dust Motes" P. D. Cacek (1997)

P. D. Cacek is one of a handful of potentially important new dark fantasy and horror writers who emerged during the 1990s, writers who have almost abandoned the traditional icons and images of the genre in favor of terrors more appropriate to the modern age. Her vampires will not be found sleeping in coffins, and they have contemporary sensibilities. Although she has written a few interesting novels, her greatest strength is at shorter length, for she has a definite talent for creating complex characters and vivid settings with a very economical use of words and delivers each story succinctly and powerfully, like a sharp blow to the chest.

The protagonist in this case is Leslie Carr, a woman who has developed apparently terminal cancer. Unable simply to sit at home, she is drawn to a large library for which she has pleasant memories, but even here she feels awkward and out of place, as though her cancer were visible and a source of shame. She is also troubled by the presence and attention of a distinguished-looking man dressed in gray who strikes up a conversation with her. He identifies himself as Howard Ross, a ghost, visible and audible to Leslie because she is dying. Her startled reaction nearly causes her to be expelled from the library, but she is quick-witted enough to cover herself.

Ross explains to her that more than a hundred ghosts are trapped in the library, waiting for the chance to tell a living person the most important moment of their lives, a necessary step before they can proceed to the afterlife. Leslie agrees to listen and returns day after day, releasing each of the ghosts in turn, but toward the end she begins to have trouble seeing them. She is elated to discover that this means she is going to survive the cancer after all but dismayed by the realization that there is not enough time to listen to all the remaining stories.

Although this gentle, heart-warming story first appeared in a collection called *Gothic Ghosts*,

it is neither horror nor a traditional ghost story. In recognition of its poignant depiction of a woman facing her own death who still finds time to help others, it received the World Fantasy Award.

Dying in Bangkok Dan Simmons (1992)

Dan SIMMONS is one of the most versatile writers working today. He has won acclaim and awards for his horror fiction and his science fiction and has also produced mainstream novels that have been favorably received. This particular story takes place during two different times, the first during the war in Vietnam in which two soldiers are on leave in Cambodia, and the other describing the return to Bangkok by one of them, Merrick, in the present. The former sections are told in the past tense and the latter in present tense to emphasize the gap in time.

Merrick originally came to Bangkok with Robert "Tres" Tindale, a fellow soldier to whom he felt a special bond. Tindale was fascinated with the more arcane aspects of local life, and he convinces Merrick to accompany him to witness a bizarre ceremony in which a vampirelike woman and her baby feed off a willing volunteer in an overtly sexual public encounter. Merrick is repulsed, but Tindale becomes fascinated and eventually returns alone to participate in the ceremony himself. Unfortunately, something goes wrong, and his bleeding is excessive. Despite the danger to his life, Tindale tries to make a third visit, and his mutilated body is found in a river bed.

The present-day Merrick is a wealthy man, a prominent doctor who has returned to Bangkok searching for the vampire mother and daughter, Mara and Tanha. He knows that they are still alive, but they have become cautious and only cater to a very limited number of rich customers. He is nearly murdered during the search but finally meets them, offering an immense sum of money for their services. Although initially reluctant, he convinces them that he is sincere, and the bizarre ritual of blood and sex is completed. It is only in the final paragraphs that we learn the true nature of Merrick's obsession. He is not drawn by the bizarre sexual gratification, but rather by the thirst for revenge. Although he had not recognized it at the time, Merrick is gay and was in love with Tindale. His revenge is embodied in his own blood, which carries the HIV infection.

In the hands of a lesser writer, this could have been a tawdry tale with a trick ending. Simmons transforms a relatively simple idea into a complex story of obsession and self-destruction. The story won the Bram Stoker Award in 1993.

Eager, Edward (1911–1964)

Edward Eager was an American dramatist who began writing children's fantasies with *Half Magic* (1954), in which a group of children find a magical coin and use it to transport themselves into other worlds, where they have various low-key adventures complicated by the fact that the coin grants only a portion of each wish. This first effort set the pattern for the fantasies that followed. Eager's books for children are relentlessly good natured and there is never any suggestion that the children are in real danger. They are frequently reprinted and often compared to the work of Edith NESBIT, Lucy M. BOSTON, and similar writers.

Knight's Castle (1956) transplants a different group of children back through time to learn the true story about one of England's legendary heroes. *Magic by the Lake* (1957, also published as *Magic or Not?*) is another story of wishes granted, in this case by a magical turtle. More children travel through time in *The Time Garden* (1958), this time with the assistance of a supernatural toad. There is a genuine wishing well in *The Well Wishers* (1960), and in *Seven Day Magic* (1962) a charmed talisman answers requests with sometimes humorous results. Although all of Eager's fantasy novels have almost identical plots and the characters do not grow or change during them, he demonstrated a gift for telling a story that enthralls younger readers. Although they hold little of interest for an older audience, they are charming examples of gentle fantasies. Eager produced only a handful of titles during his lifetime, but they have remained popular and were recently reprinted in 1999.

"Eat Me" Robert R. McCammon (1989)

The 1989 anthology *Book of the Dead,* edited by John SKIPP and Craig SPECTOR, was designed as a homage to the Living Dead films of George Romero, whose premise is that some form of contagious disease causes the dead to rise and feast on the living, turning their victims into fresh legions of zombies. The movie was, of course, intensely visual, and the premise for a collection of stories based on that setting seemed unpromising. A surprising number of the contributors found a fresh, interesting approach to the theme, most notably in "ON THE FAR SIDE OF THE CADILLAC DESERT WITH THE DEAD FOLKS" (1989) by Joe R. LANSDALE and in this much shorter piece by Robert R. McCAMMON.

McCammon set his story much later in time, after all the living in the world have died and only the dead still walk the earth. During the interim they have learned to speak again and have begun to imitate their old lifestyles, although in very distorted ways. The protagonist is Jim, one of the living dead, who wonders one night just when it was that love died in the world. He is lonely and without purpose, and his wandering takes him to a restaurant that has now become a kind of singles club for the living dead, where rats are currency and dancing is dangerous because the patrons' decaying bodies are beginning to fall apart. There he meets a shy dead girl, Brenda, and the two go through a gentle parody of our contemporary dating ritual, eventually leaving together to go to her room.

Traditional sex is, of course, impossible for the dead, so they pleasure themselves in the only way possible, by beginning literally to eat one another. The two individuals are becoming one in a way that is impossible to the living, but at the moment of their consummation they are caught up in a terrible storm that fuses them together and finally stills their unnatural lives forever. Another of their kind stumbles over the remains and realizes that, through their final act of love, they finally escaped the world of the living dead into one of the truly dead. "Eat Me" won the Bram Stoker Award.

Eddings, David and Leigh (1931–   )

Although all of David Eddings' novels prior to 1995 were listed as by David Eddings alone, his wife Leigh was reportedly involved in his writing from the outset and has been retroactively credited as a collaborator. The early novels are almost all part of one series or another, sometimes interrelated. Although they are invariably variations of familiar plots and themes, Eddings employs a light, anecdotal, sometimes whimsical style that gives them a distinct flavor.

His first sequence of novels was the Belgariad comprising *Pawn of Prophecy* (1982), *Queen of Sorcery* (1982), and *Magician's Gambit* (1983). The central plot is a quest to prevent villains from neutralizing the power of a magical artifact that holds an evil god at bay. The story wanders a bit but usually entertainingly, and the trilogy was very favorably received. Two sequels followed, *Castle of Wizardry* (1984) and *Enchanter's Endgame* (1984), in which the heroes are compelled to battle evil once again and thwart the warped deity for the final time. Another sequence with many of the same characters followed, known as the Malloreon. In *Guardians of the West* (1987) the now firmly established king is troubled by portents of danger. He pursues his son's kidnappers in *King of the Murgos* (1988), struggles with plague and imprisonment in *Demon Lord of Karanda* (1988), and eventually rescues the boy before he can be sacrificed in the final two volumes, *Sorceress of Darshiva* (1989) and *The Seeress of Kell* (1991).

As the Malloreon was drawing to a close, Eddings shifted locations for another sequence that opened with the Elenium trilogy, *The Diamond Throne* (1989), *The Ruby Knight* (1990), and *The Sapphire Rose* (1991). The plot is very similar to that of his first series of novels. A knight and his companions seek a magical cure for their princess, who is locked in a mystical coma that will result in her death if she is not freed within a year. A second linked trilogy followed, *Domes of Fire* (1992), *The Shining Ones* (1993), and *The Hidden City* (1994), but most of this quest sequence consists of a repetition of incidents from earlier titles.

Belgarath the Sorcerer (1995) is the first of two belated prequels to the Belgariad, chronicling the youth of the powerful magician who will take a central part in the battle against the sleeping god. *Polgara the Sorceress* (1996) follows the career of a shape-changing sorceress in the same setting. *The Redemption of Althalus* (2000) is a more ambitious and frequently witty novel about a thief recruited by a goddess to do her bidding and his subsequent exploits. Despite some occasional redundancies in the plot, the novel is quite amusing and often cleverly done. Two novels using contemporary settings are less successful. *The Losers* (1992) is awkwardly constructed, and *Regina's Song* (2002) is a painfully inept novel of the supernatural whose plot is dependent on major misunderstandings of how the legal system functions. Their most recent fiction consists of the opening volumes of a new series, *The Elder Gods* (2003) and *The Treasured One* (2004), a story of high adventure set in a magical world torn by warfare.

Eddison, E. R. (1882–1945)

Eric Rucker Eddison was a contemporary of J. R. R. TOLKIEN and C. S. LEWIS, but his very idiosyncratic fantasy fiction little resembles theirs, although the scope of his imagined worlds is as great and his gift for creating larger-than-life characters rivals Tolkien's. His first and most famous novel is THE WORM OUROBOROS (1922), a story filled with heroes and villains and some of the trappings of mainstream fantasy, but whose cast of characters is entirely human and whose world is uniquely his own. The frame story in the opening chapter is extremely awkward, but Eddison never reverts to it once the real story is underway.

Eddison's other major fantasy work is the Zimiamvia trilogy, actually three related novels that do not share a common story line and can be read in any order despite some consistent internal chronology. Zimiamvia is rather tenuously connected to *The Worm Ouroboros* and includes the three volumes *Mistress of Mistresses* (1935), *A Fish Dinner at Memison* (1958), and the unfinished, posthumously published *The Mezentian Gate* (1958). The plots of the novels are very intricate and the prose ornate. Several of the characters become associated with two supernatural forces, or deities, who manipulate the universe from behind the scenes. Lessingham, a minor character from the frame story of *The Worm Ouroboros,* is a major figure in the trilogy. *Mistress of Mistresses* is sometimes criticized for its relatively flaccid plot, but its depiction of heroism and split loyalties is superbly done. Lessingham is forced to reevaluate his priorities following the death of his king and the rise of a controversy over the succession. *A Fish Dinner at Memison* takes place earlier, while King Mezentius is still alive, and is rife with intrigues and conspiracies as well as some speculation about the nature of reality.

Some fragments related to the Zimiamvia books were included in an omnibus edition in 1992. Eddison's only other novel, *Styrbiorn the Strong* (1926), is a Viking story whose final chapter is set in Valhalla but which is otherwise historical fiction. The Valhalla chapter has been published separately as "In Valhalla." Eddison's style and preoccupations were so unusual that he has not been imitated to any great extent, and the intricacy of his prose dissuades most casual readers. Even so, his work still commands a sizeable and loyal following.

Edghill, Rosemary (Eluki bes Shahar)
(1956–)

Writing under the name Eluki bes Shahar, Rosemary Edghill began selling science fiction novels in the early 1990s and has used that byline for a few fantasy short stories since. Most of her fantastic fiction has appeared as by Edghill, however, beginning with the Twelve Treasures trilogy. *The Sword*

of Maiden's Tears (1995) starts off as a familiar quest story, with the protagonist and a small group of disparate companions setting off to locate and retrieve a magic artifact, one of 12 required to secure the stability of the throne. A librarian from our world crosses into that magical realm in *The Cup of Morning Shadows* (1995), in which the plot picks up rapidly and Edghill's imaginary land of fairies becomes much more vivid and interesting. The story finally reaches its inevitable but still entertaining conclusion in *The Cloak of Night and Daggers* (1997), which also mixes characters from both realities.

Her next fantasy novel, *Met by Moonlight* (1998), is less interesting, a magical time travel romance in which a modern witch finds herself back in a time when witches were persecuted. Fortunately, she falls in love, and everything turns out well. Edghill's next solo fantasy novel, *The Warslayer* (2002), is much better, adding a touch of humor to a fantastic adventure. An actress from our world who portrays a Xenalike fantasy heroine on television is abducted into a real magical realm and prevailed upon to battle an all-too-authentic monster. *Vengeance of Masks* (2003), her most recent, is the first of a two-volume series set in a world menaced by an awakened demon.

Much of her work has been collaborative. With Mercedes LACKEY she has written three novels, of which *Beyond World's End* (2001) most closely resembles her own work, a story in which elves and humans cross the borders between their respective realities. The other two, *Spirits White As Lightning* (2001) and *Mad Maudlin* (2003), are set in Lackey's series about similar crossovers from the magical Shadowlands. Her collaborations with Andre NORTON are *The Shadow of Albion* (1999) and *Leopard in Exile* (2001), a two-volume adventure in which the protagonist, who is from the contemporary world, travels to an alternate historical England in which the colonies never revolted, Napoleon is on the verge of conquering all of Europe, and the continental war is being fought with magic as well as force of arms.

Edghill has also written a number of mysteries involving nonsupernatural witchcraft and is the uncredited coauthor of four novels of the supernatural with Marion Zimmer BRADLEY. She has become an increasingly prolific short story writer since 1997, many of whose fantasies can be found in *Paying the Piper at the Gates of Dawn* (2003). Her best short stories include "The Phaerie Bride" (1997) and "Piper at the Gate" (2000).

"Elle Est Trois (La Mort)" Tanith Lee (1983)

Tanith LEE has proven to be one of the most reliable and prolific fantasy writers of recent years, writing for both adults and children and also establishing a smaller but still respectable reputation in science fiction and horror. This World Fantasy Award–winning story falls within the last category. Armand Valier is a young French poet on the verge of starvation when he experiences a strange transition while crossing a bridge. On one side an object in the water appears to be the drowned body of a young girl, but when it emerges from under the bridge it is simply a mess of rags and other debris. Nevertheless, he feels that the bridge has somehow marked a transition between the normal world and some other realm of existence. Drawn by this strange feeling, he returns to the area and catches a brief glimpse of an aristocratic woman who also appears to dissolve into shadows.

Valier meets several fellow failed artists in a cafe, where he describes his encounter. He also is reminded of a childhood game whose chanted refrain gives this story its title. The game is a variation of musical chairs; the individual who is left facing a particular symbol is eliminated and declared dead. Death has three faces, Thief, Seductress, and Slaughterer. One of the others, Etiens, an artist, recalls an incident from his childhood when he also had a series of visions of an apparently imaginary person, in his case a young girl who appeared in his room while he was seriously ill and who at the end attempted to lure him to his death.

The third member of their small group is France, a musician, who returns to his apartment just in time to be hacked to death by a vengeful ex-girlfriend. But France saw someone else, the personification of death itself in the form of a beautiful woman. The story ends with speculation about the nature of fate and death and the many faces that our personal dooms might take. If life

and death are a game, then there will be winners and losers, and perhaps the role assigned is just a matter of luck.

Elliott, Kate (1958–)

Kate Elliott is the pseudonym of Alis A. Rasmussen, who used her own name for her early science fiction and for her very first published novel, which was a fantasy. The Elliot name was also used initially for science fiction, although it was obvious even then that these otherworldly romantic adventures were edging closer to fantasy fiction. *The Labyrinth Gate* (1988), her debut novel, is a pleasant but unexceptional story of alternate worlds accessed by means of a deck of enchanted tarot cards and bears little resemblance to her later work.

All five of her fantasy novels are in the Crown of Stars series, which opened with *King's Dragon* (1997). The rule of the present king of Wendar is menaced not only by his ambitious and unprincipled sister, who is gathering a rival army to her banner, but by legions of inhuman creatures in the lands to the north and east, who are striking across the borders. A missing heir to the throne complicates matters even further in the second volume, *Prince of Dogs* (1998), while the political and military situation continues to deteriorate. In *The Burning Stone* (1999) the conflict becomes more personal and immediate, and a young woman must decide whether to use the power of sorcery despite the taint of evil that surrounds it. The individual titles grew progressively longer and more complex as Elliott developed her world and its people, with a very large cast of characters and ever more detailed background material. *Child of Flame* (2000) scatters most of the main protagonists into separate story lines. One seeks to discover the truth about her own heritage, one uncovers a new plot against the throne, and others simply strive to survive as the war comes closer and the world grows more dangerous. The future is very much in doubt in *The Gathering Storm* (2003), for the king has shown questionable judgment in dealing with his many enemies.

The series often feels more like historical fiction set in an imaginary country than traditional fantasy, but Elliott's narrative skills have improved noticeably as the series has progressed. Although the author has confined her efforts to this one setting and story line almost to the exclusion of everything else, occasional short stories such as "My Voice Is My Sword" (1994) and "Sunseeker" (2002) suggest that she might yet produce a more diverse variety of fiction.

Elrod, P. N. (1951–)

Patricia Nead Elrod's writing career has been dominated by vampires, although in most cases they have not been the evil, unclean creatures of legend. Her vampires are mostly misunderstood, reluctant, troubled, or goodhearted as the situation and story line demand. Elrod started her career with the first three adventures of her most popular vampire hero, Fleming, all of which were published in 1990. *Bloodlist* introduces Fleming, recently converted to vampirism against his will, as he struggles to adjust to a new life confined to darkness and to satisfy his need for blood without killing human beings. Fleming is a moderately well-drawn, likeable enough character who becomes a private detective and who, in *Lifeblood*, has considerable run-ins with vampire hunters who do not know, or care, that he is of the benevolent variety. He solves a murder mystery in *Bloodcircle* while still trying to track down the female vampire who is responsible for his own condition. Fleming's 10th and most recent adventure is *Cold Streets* (2003), in which he is blackmailed by a mobster who knows his secret and forced to participate in a gang war. *The Dark Sleep* (1999) and *Lady Crymsyn* (2000) are the two best titles, the latter involved a mystery that turns up when Fleming decides to open a nightclub.

Elrod's second vampire series consists of *Red Death* (1993), *Death and the Maiden* (1994), *Death Masque* (1995), and *Dance of Death* (1996). The protagonist's situation is the same—he was converted against his will by a woman—but the setting is very different. He is attacked while in England in the days just prior to the American Revolution and returns to find the colonies in turmoil. His efforts to survive and adjust without taking human life are parallel to those of Fleming and sometimes more interesting, but the character

himself never completely comes to life, and the historical background is sketchy.

I, Strahd (1993) is a somewhat darker story set in the Ravenloft shared world series, a fantasy realm that resembles historical Europe. Strahd makes an unholy supernatural deal to defeat a rival and discovers that the price is his conversion to vampirism. Immortal and the ruler of a small kingdom, Strahd returns in *The War against Azalin* (1998) to fight a new batch of enemies. *Quincey Morris, Vampire* (2001) is a sequel to DRACULA (1897) by Bram STOKER in which Morris dies and becomes a vampire, protégé to Dracula himself. It is probably Elrod's best single novel. One other vampire series is a collaborative effort with the actor Nigel Bennett. *Keeper of the King* (2000), *His Father's Son* (2001), and *Siege Perilous* (2003) tell the story of Sir Lancelot, an immortal vampire living in the modern world as Richard Dun and still protecting the public from supernatural enemies.

Elrod has recently strayed from vampires for *The Adventures of Myhr* (2003), a minor alternate world's quest adventure featuring a character who is half human and half feline. Her occasional short fiction is, not surprisingly, usually about vampires. She has also edited two anthologies of vampire stories, *Time of the Vampires* (1996) and *Dracula in London* (2001).

Emerson, Ru (1944–)

Like Kate ELLIOTT, Ru Emerson began her writing career with a comparatively minor fantasy adventure that prominently featured the tarot deck. *The Princess of Flames* (1986) is a standard story pitting the protagonist against the usurper who stole the throne but straying somewhat from the ordinary, as the heir this time is a female. Emerson followed up with the Nedao trilogy, starting with *To the Haunted Mountains* (1987), which features a female swordswoman as the primary protagonist and a sentient cat as the narrator. The series continued with *In the Caves of Exile* (1988) and concluded in *On the Seas of Destiny* (1989). The enemies of Nedao have invaded the kingdom, and the ousted ruler leads her people into exile, where they eventually organize and regain their freedom. The unusual choice of narrator is quite effective and gives the trilogy a unique flavor.

Emerson's next series is called Night Threads. In *The Calling of the Three* (1990), three young people from our reality are brought to a typical fantasy realm to help restore the rightful ruler to the throne. The series is less inventive than Emerson's other fantasy work and consists of five titles ending with *The Science of Power* (1996). *The Art of the Sword* (1994), the strongest in the series, presents the protagonists with a pressing problem. One of their number has taken a poison that will eventually prove fatal unless an antidote can be found in time.

Most of Emerson's other novels have been tie-ins to television programs and are of little interest, although *Questward Ho!* (1999), a Xena novel, is quite humorous. *Spell Bound* (1990) is a more somber story set in a variation of early Europe involving a witch's effort to avenge her mother. Emerson's single best fantasy novel is *The Sword and the Lion* (1993), written as Roberta Cray, a disguised historical novel set in an imaginary world that appears to be patterned after the life of Alexander the Great, with minimal fantastic content. *Fortress of Frost and Fire* (1993), written with Mercedes LACKEY, is a minor installment in Lackey's light-weight series about elves. Emerson occasionally writes short fiction, often for shared world anthologies, but has not been noticeably successful at that length.

"The Empty House" Algernon Blackwood (1906)

Just as ghost stories do not always involve haunted houses, haunted house stories do not necessarily contain a ghost in the usual sense. This classic short story by Algernon BLACKWOOD may be the first example of an author telling his audience that houses can have personalities of their own, that the dark events we might suspect are caused by the restless spirits of former residents are actually a manifestation of the uncanny aspects of the building itself. The narrator of this creepy tale is Shorthouse, who is summoned by his Aunt Julia to spend a night with her in an abandoned house reputed to be haunted. The subject of their investigation is virtually identical to all the others in its vicinity, at least in appearance, but tenants rarely linger more than a few weeks. Also, it has an unspecified bad reputation possibly linked to a brutal murder that occurred therein more than a century earlier.

Their initial foray is almost a catalog of the devices authors would use in subsequent stories of haunted houses. Doors close without apparent cause, a candle is snuffed out by the application of force rather than by a breeze, brief apparitions appear and disappear before they can be identified or investigated, unusual noises occur in remote parts of the building, and the two explorers feel that their strength is being sapped on some spiritual level, shaking their self-confidence. They are bothered from the very moment they step inside by phantom coughs from an invisible throat near at hand and are harried by them until they finally leave. The ultimate confrontation comes when they hear clear evidence of a ghostly reenactment of that long-ago, savage crime as it takes place right around them.

Haunted house stories have appeared in droves since the early 1900s, but only a few of them, such as THE HAUNTING OF HILL HOUSE (1959) by Shirley JACKSON, have been as evocative and compact as this early thriller. Although the climax feels somewhat incomplete in that we never learn anything substantive about the long-ago murder and the house is left unchanged when Shorthouse and his aunt depart, the atmosphere Blackwood evokes is one of sustained, riveting suspense, and writers ever since have attempted to mimic this early masterpiece.

"Enoch" Robert Bloch (1946)

One of the standard plot devices in suspense fiction (and, unfortunately, sometimes in real life as well) is the individual who suffers from a mental aberration in which voices speak inside the mind, compelling the affected person to commit horrid acts. In many stories of psychological suspense, serial killers commit a series of murders at the command of this imaginary companion. Robert BLOCH is the author of perhaps the most famous of these, *Psycho* (1959), in which Norman Bates believes that his dead mother is responsible for a series of homicidal assaults that he himself is committing.

In horror fiction, however, it is entirely possible that the voices be real.

Seth, the narrator of "Enoch," is a mentally ill man living alone in a remote swamp—alone, that is, except for Enoch, an invisible, intangible demon who lives on top of his head, having been bonded to him by Seth's now-dead mother, a practicing witch. Enoch tells Seth how to take care of himself, but in return he demands that Seth kill a succession of people, after which the headless bodies are thrown into the quicksand. Not even Seth knows what happens to the heads. Although the reader might initially believe this to be just a delusion, we soon realize that Enoch has advance knowledge of his victims that would not be accessible to Seth. Eventually, however, Enoch neglects to cover all of Seth's tracks, and he is arrested for one and eventually all nine murders.

Although a psychologist clearly believes Seth to be mentally ill, the district attorney very much wants a sensational conviction. He plans to undermine the doctor's testimony by convincing Seth to deny that their conversations are being accurately reported. When Seth balks because of Enoch, the district attorney offers to take custody of Enoch temporarily. Unfortunately, he discovers very quickly that Enoch is real, and when he refuses to do as he is told, Enoch devours his head from the inside out and returns to Seth, who escapes jail and runs off, presumably to be blamed for a 10th murder. There is a feeling of rough justice about the ending, although Seth and Enoch are presumably fated to kill again. This is probably Bloch's most frequently reprinted story, short, nasty, and direct.

"Enoch Soames"   Max Beerbohm (1919)

Deal-with-the-devil stories usually have one of two basic plots. Either the human party finds an elaborate and often humorous way to escape the consequences of the pact, or despite a clever attempt to outwit the devil, the protagonist loses everything, including his or her soul. There have been so many that it has become a cliché within the genre, and there are entire collections of stories on the theme and even a few novels. Max Beerbohm is best remembered for his nonfiction and satirical writing and is not generally thought of as a genre writer,

although a few of his small output of short stories contain fantastic elements. The most famous of these, "Enoch Soames," is still one of the oddest and most satisfying stories of its type because the title character sells his soul not for fame or glory or anything grandiose but merely for a glimpse of the future.

Enoch Soames is a painfully awkward and unsuccessful writer of poetry and essays who inhabits the fringes of the artistic community during the 1890s. Although he eventually publishes three books, they are almost complete failures. We meet Soames through the eyes of the narrator, who is Max Beerbohm himself. They strike up a mild acquaintance, and Soames describes himself as a Catholic diabolist, that is, he does not worship the devil so much as trust him to be true to his nature. Beerbohm meets him from time to time over the course of years, and believes that Soames is content with his lot and that he is convinced that his great literary merit will be confirmed by posterity, even though he seems likely to remain unappreciated during his own lifetime.

Their last meeting comes by chance at a small restaurant, and during the ensuing conversation Soames expresses his bitterness about his obscurity, vowing that he would sell his soul for a chance to examine the historical record a century hence to confirm his belief that he will be an acknowledged master. Another diner promptly introduces himself as the devil and offers to transport Soames to the British Library a century in the future, granting him five hours to conduct his research, after which he will return to the present and be carted off to hell. Although Beerbohm believes it to be a sham, he urges Soames not to agree, but to no avail. The frustrated writer promptly disappears, returning five hours later looking more disturbed than ever. In the minutes that remain before he is to pay his last bill, Soames announces bitterly that the only mention of his name was as a fictional character in a story by Max Beerbohm, a nice recursive touch to tie up a brilliantly executed story.

"The Enormous Radio"   John Cheever (1946)

The novelist and short story writer John Cheever occasionally used fantastic elements in his fiction, but they were almost always ambiguous—illusions, psychological disorders, or simply odd events left unexplained, suspended somewhere between the rational and the irrational. One of the few with a genuinely magical element is "The Enormous Radio," a deceptively quiet story with a hint of humor, although it quickly develops into a simmering nightmare.

Jim and Irene Westcott are an ordinary upper-middle-class couple with two children, a happy home life, and no apparent financial problems who are united by a common love of music, which they listen to avidly on their aging radio. When that instrument finally fails, Jim orders a new one, a modern device which—common at the time the story was written—is a piece of furniture in itself, free-standing and dominating. Irene takes an instant dislike to it, considering it ugly and an intruder in her carefully decorated home. To her, the lights on the instrument panel seem "malevolent." When she finally turns it on and adjusts the volume to her satisfaction, she is quite pleased with the quality, although as the minutes pass she becomes aware of an increasing level of interference, which she finally realizes is in response to the operation of any electrical device in either her own or nearby apartments. Jim is similarly disconcerted, and a repairman arrives the following day to adjust the set.

The interference disappears, but now they are able to eavesdrop on conversations taking place elsewhere in the building. Sometimes they can recognize the voices or guess the identity of the speakers through context; at other times it is a complete mystery. They are amused initially and feel very little guilt about invading the privacy of their neighbors, but Irene becomes obsessed and can barely tear herself away. Her mood switches to a steadily deepening depression. The more she listens, the more she hears of illness, bad luck, quarrels, worries, and occasional violence. What she hears begins to influence her reactions to other people in the building, even strangers, and then to other people in general.

Jim becomes disturbed by the change in her demeanor, particularly when she urges him to confirm that they are immune to the petty jealousies, animosities, and misfortunes that affect their neigh-

bors, but her despondency triggers a reaction in her husband, who reveals a series of complaints about her behavior and criticisms of her lifestyle. By dwelling on the unhappiness of others, Irene has ruined her own life. The radio's strange power is never explained, but there are sufficient hints in the text to tell us that it is not just mischance, that it is an instrument of evil with a definite, although unstated, purpose. The story reveals the quiet hell that lives within even the most peaceful exterior.

Etchison, Dennis (1943–)

Dennis Etchison's quietly chilling horror stories rarely involve the familiar monsters and menaces of the genre. His terrors often originate in subtle changes to the familiar or strange impulses taken to extremes. Kitchen appliances perform in strange ways, or a salesman's pitch seems just slightly too odd to be comfortable. Most of his stories have an urban setting, usually California, and he has a genuine talent for creating imperfect but believable characters and then subjecting them to horrifying events. His horrors can originate in as mundane an activity as cleaning a car or involve some bizarre extreme such as stolen human organs. Among his many exceptional stories are "The Dark Country" (1981), a World Fantasy Award winner, "Inside the Cackle Factory" (1998), "You Can Go Now" (1980), "One of Us" (2002), and "The Woman in Black" (1984). The best collections of Etchison's work are *The Dark Country* (1982), *Red Dreams* (1984), *The Blood Kiss* (1988), and *Talking in the Dark* (2001).

Etchison's novels are generally less successful than his short fiction and usually involve an external threat to an entire family group rather than a single individual. *Darkside* (1986), his best book-length work, describes the agitation of a man and his family whose lives begin to fall apart when they inadvertently cross paths with a bizarre cult. Their daughter is transformed into an inhuman creature, and similar fates may await them all unless they can understand the rules and find a way to counter the otherworldly forces that surround them. A bitter man and a troubled child psychologist are drawn into a terrifying and unsettling series of mysteries in *Shadow Man* (1993), eventually discovering the existence of a mysterious figure who preys on children. In *California Gothic* (1995) a successful man and his family find themselves in danger when an old girlfriend shows up, apparently not having aged a day since the last time he saw her many years previously. *Double Edge* (1997) is a deliberately confusing story about a woman trying to recover from a tragedy who is plagued by a mysterious stalker and the unsettling visions of a psychic. Etchison's remaining three novels, two as by Jack Martin, are film novelizations. He has also edited several anthologies of horror fiction and won the World Fantasy Award for his work editing the anthology *The Museum of Horrors* (2002).

Eulo, Ken (1939–   )

By its very nature most horror fiction does not lend itself to the possibility of sequels. If the monstrous evil is thwarted, it is anticlimactic to bring it back for another battle, since the reader already knows that it is vulnerable. If the monstrous evil has triumphed, it is unlikely that any of the heroes are around to try again, and if an author is going to create a new cast of characters, there is going to be little continuity anyway. That has changed somewhat in recent years, mostly because of the flood of novels about benevolent and/or misunderstood vampires, but most of these, while supernatural, are probably not, strictly speaking, horror stories. In any case, a series about the same haunted house seems improbable even now, and in the early 1980s it was almost unheard of, which makes it that much more surprising that Ken Eulo started his career with a trilogy using a variation of the haunted house story.

The Brownstone (1980) was the first and best of the three, all of which are probably better described as stories of "bad places," although they read like haunted house stories, particularly the opening volume. A young couple moves into an aging brownstone mansion with a slightly odd reputation. Their landlady begins to behave strangely, and there are other warning signs that gradually escalate into a confrontation with a resident evil force. The young woman from the first novel escapes the doom planned for her, but the monstrous evil reaches out and invades her mind in *The Bloodstone* (1981), compelling her to return for a

fresh round of thrills and chills. There is some repetition, however, which becomes even more prevalent in the final volume, *The Deathstone* (1982).

Eulo changed gears for his next novel, *Nocturnal* (1983), one of many stories in which a clairvoyant acquires psychic knowledge of the activities of a killer and must identify him before the killer learns her identity. The novel is competently written but holds few surprises and only minor thrills. *The Ghost of Veronica Gray* (1985) also uses a familiar plot—a child's imaginary playmate is actually an angry ghost using her to avenge herself on the living, but this time the author produced a livelier plot and considerably more suspense. The evil being in *The House of Caine* (1988) is a kind of vampire, but sufficiently out of the ordinary to support a rather long and convoluted story. Eulo seemed at this point to be on the verge of producing a major horror novel, but the genre imploded in the late 1980s. He was one of many promising writers whose career was suddenly disrupted and uncertain.

Eulo did publish two more novels with fantastic content, although both were marketed as general thrillers. *Manhattan Heat* (1991) is a police procedural mystery, except that the case at hand involves the walking dead. *Claw* (1994) is a science fiction horror story in which an escaped tiger displays unusual intelligence thanks to some secret genetic manipulation by the government. Although Eulo did not manage to produce a breakthrough novel during his brief career, he wrote solid, entertaining stories of suspense. He will probably be remembered primarily for his initial trilogy, but *Manhattan Heat* and *The House of Caine* are his best novels.

The Exorcist William Peter Blatty (1971)

Horror fiction enjoyed mild popularity in Europe from the early 20th century onward, but in the United States it existed only as a novelty, sometimes lumped with science fiction, sometimes with mysteries and suspense novels, sometimes with general fiction. That held true until the late 1960s, when the first of two influential novels appeared. ROSEMARY'S BABY (1967), by Ira Levin, was a hit both as a novel and a movie, and William Peter

Blatty's *The Exorcist* (1971) repeated the phenomenon, convincing the publishing and film industries that the American public was ready for high-quality horror. This set the stage for the appearance of Stephen KING and the emergence of horror as a separate publishing genre.

The nonsupernatural portions of the novel are partly based on a real case of a child so emotionally disturbed that his family believed demonic possession was the cause. Blatty's novel is far less ambiguous. Two priests strive to drive a satanic presence from a little girl, but they are made vulnerable by their own self-doubts and lack of faith. Readers who believed in the possibility of demonic possession were particularly enthralled, and those who did not were still impressed with the cleverness with which the creature manipulates the forces of good. The treatment is understated and sometimes reads like nonfiction, which lends an air of authenticity and plausibility to the plot. It is, of course, a classic story of good versus evil made even more obvious in the 1973 film version, which Blatty himself adapted for the screen.

Blatty later wrote a sequel, *Legion* (1990), in which a serial killer mimics the methods of the Gemini Killer, who is dead. The detective from the first novel returns to discover that the worlds of the living and dead are not as widely separated as he once believed. The story appeared as a lackluster film under the title *Exorcist III* (1990), and the novel was reissued under that title. Blatty had no connection to *Exorcist II*, the first sequel, and his only other fantastic fiction is a short story, "Elsewhere" (1999).

"The Extraordinarily Horrible Dummy"
Gerald Kersh (1946)

The malevolent ventriloquist's dummy is a natural subject for horror fiction. The simulation of human life given to an assembly of wood and wires speaks to some basic fear in us, and even the puppet from Carlo Collodi's PINOCCHIO (1871), who strives to be a real boy, is not an entirely comfortable image.

Malevolent puppets have come to life, or an imitation of life, in fiction, most notably in *Magic* (1976) by William Goldman, although in this case it proves to be a delusion, in movies such as the Puppetmaster series, and even as an episode of *Buffy the Vampire Slayer*, in the latter case turned cleverly end over end. One of the earliest and best of such stories is by Gerald Kersh, a British writer who wrote in so many different genres that he is not associated with any one in particular.

We learn the story of Ecco, the ventriloquist, and his puppet, Micky, from the man who lives in the adjacent room in a rundown rooming house. The narrator believes Ecco to be the greatest ventriloquist of all time, but Ecco is down on his luck and clearly unhappy with his situation. At times he rehearses loudly in his room with Micky, but often it sounds more like a tense argument than practice for a performance. One night the noise grows so loud that the nameless narrator hesitantly complains. Ecco apologizes and lays Micky to rest almost as if he were human, then suggests that they have a drink together. Over the drinks he reveals his story.

He was raised and trained by Dr. Vox, a gifted ventriloquist in his own right, but a cruel man who beat his student mercilessly. When Vox died in an accident, Ecco inherited Micky and set out to pursue a career in show business, but Micky, he tells his companion, was not inert. The wooden body has apparently become the resting place for the angry spirit of Dr. Vox, who continues to torment his pupil from beyond the grave. The narrator takes his leave, certain that Ecco is insane, but there are several final hints that suggest that Ecco was indeed telling the truth. This quite short tale, originally published under the title "The Whisper," is surprisingly effective considering that nothing much happens overtly during the course of the story. Like much of the best of horror fiction, it achieves its effect through insinuation rather than explanation and is designed to leave us feeling not quite sure what is real and what is not.

F

The Fafhrd and the Gray Mouser Series
Fritz Leiber (1939–1990)

Although Robert E. HOWARD was certainly the single most influential writer of sword and sorcery fantasy, he was not the only one who would be imitated in the years that followed. Howard's fantasy heroes—Conan, Bran Mak Morn, Kull, Solomon Kane—tended to be loners who rarely displayed much of a sense of humor. Fritz LEIBER offered an alternative. His two thieves, Fafhrd and the Gray Mouser, were friends and partners, and their many adventures were often lighthearted, although rarely dull. One is a hulking warrior in physical appearance, although no mental slouch either, and the other a clever, scheming, and sometimes exasperated planner. Leiber also used a much more polished prose style to describe their adventures.

The duo made their debut in Leiber's first professional sale, "Two Sought Adventure" (1939, also known as "The Jewels in the Forest"). The stories that followed typically involve their employment as professional thieves and the various things that go wrong with even their best-laid plans. Although they are criminals, they are very moral criminals, living by the rules of a civilization in which theft is not viewed with quite the same sense of dishonor that it would be in ours. They are frequently employed by one of two wizards, Sheelba or Ningauble, both of whom are quite mysterious and only sketchily described, and most of their adventures take place in Nehwon.

The stories are of such uniformly high quality that singling out individual ones is very difficult,

but "Ill Met in Lankhmar" (1970), which won both the Hugo and Nebula Awards, would certainly be numbered among the best, along with "Adept's Gambit" (1947) and "Scylla's Daughter" (1961). The first collection of their adventures was *Two Sought Adventure* (1947), but these stories were redistributed for a series of collections and one patched together novel as *The Swords of Lankhmar* (1968), *Swords in the Mist* (1968), *Swords against Wizardry* (1968), *Swords and Deviltry* (1970), *Swords against Death* (1970), and *Swords and Ice Magic* (1977). The older stories and some new material were reshuffled again in *Ill Met in Lankhmar* (1995), *Return to Lankhmar* (1997), *Farewell to Lankhmar* (1998), and *Thieves' House* (2001), and selected stories have appeared in limited editions and other collections. Leiber is the only writer of sword and sorcery other than Howard who created a substantial body of work that stands as a literary as well as a popular achievement.

"The Fall of the House of Usher" Edgar Allan Poe (1839)

The story of a family curse is not original with Edgar Allan POE, nor is the setting of the bad place, a locality so infused with evil or dread that newcomers react to its atmosphere even when there is no rational reason to do so. The House of Usher is both a place and family, a house and the people within it, a bloodline that has so failed to prosper that it has no extensions beyond the immediate family. The narrator is a visitor to the Ushers who is immediately impressed with the sense of gloom and decay that adheres to the place and its residents.

He is the guest of his childhood friend Roderick Usher, an artist and musician lately afflicted with such a sensitivity to all stimuli that it makes him shun everything except bland food, gentle light, and soft sounds. Roderick and his sister, Madeline, who is reportedly terminally ill, are the last of the Ushers. Usher is convinced that there is a kind of low-level intelligence that exists unknown to us and that can imbue a place or a structure with a distinct personality. When Madeline dies Usher announces that he plans to treat her body with preservatives and delay its final interment for a time. The coffin containing the surprisingly lifelike body is thus held temporarily while Usher reconciles himself to the death of the sister he now announces was his twin.

Usher's health and mental stability decline rapidly, and even the narrator refers to him as a "hypochondriac" whose mind is affecting his body. He is particularly disturbed one stormy night, so the narrator reads from a novel to him in an effort to soothe his friend. Just as he reaches the description of a man bursting through a door, they both hear the sound of rending wood from somewhere in the house. Later there comes a distant shriek. Finally Usher admits that Madeline was entombed while still alive, that his hypersensitive hearing had detected the sounds of her struggles days before, but that he was too frightened to act. Madeline appears, Roderick dies of fright in her arms, and the narrator flees into the night, barely escaping when the house is destroyed in a landslide. Inextricably linked with the family, it could not survive their extinction.

This particular story was a very obvious influence on later writers, particularly H. P. LOVECRAFT, who similarly included references to fictional books of occult lore. Ray BRADBURY retold the same story satirically in "Usher II" (1950) but set it on Mars, and *Usher's Passing* (1984) by Robert McCAMMON reframes the story in a contemporary setting, chronicling the fate of the "real" family whose plight formed the basis of Poe's classic short story. Poe's original has been filmed several times, of which the best rendition was produced in 1960. The climactic image of horror, of being buried alive, recurs in Poe's "The Premature Burial" (1944).

"The Far Islands" John Buchan (1889)

The vast majority of John Buchan's more than 80 books contain no element of the fantastic, and he is certainly best remembered for *The Thirty-Nine Steps* (1915), an early spy novel. He also produced several less-known but still significant supernatural and historical fantasies and was almost certainly an influence on the work of Robert E. HOWARD. This particular story is also something of a compressed family saga starting with Colin, an associate of the legendary Bran Mak Morn, whose fascination with the supposed lands to the west of the British Isles is carried by some supernatural means down through subsequent generations, until we reach the main story, featuring Colin Raden, latest in that distinguished line.

Raden is seriously ill as a youth and spends considerable time in the traditional family homeland, where he imagines—or perhaps sees—visions of magical islands across the sea. As a young man he is athletic, handsome, intelligent, and a born leader, but he is also introspective, forgetful, and distanced from others. He continues to have recurring dreams, but there is also some progression within them, providing enhanced hints of what he might one day find. He is not drawn to female companions because they somehow disrupt the dream, which has quietly become central to his life. If the reader has any lingering doubt about the fantastic content, Buchan dispels it at this point by having the protagonist speak eloquently in a language he never learned. A researcher who believes that hallucinations sometimes run in families fails to understand the depth of Raden's belief in his dream.

War breaks out, and Raden serves loyally and heroically, although his ability to function in the real world is increasingly constrained because he can no longer control the visions. Ultimately, he is fatally wounded on the battlefield, but at the moment of his death, he is perhaps magically transported to that far island of his imagination and may live on even after his body has failed. The illusions are, in effect, a family blessing, not a curse. Shortly after the story was published the author Joseph Conrad charged that the story had been plagiarized from Rudyard Kipling, causing a brief and unjustified controversy.

Farris, John (1936–)

John Farris had been writing suspense novels, sometimes with fantastic twists, and general fiction ever since the middle of the 1950s, but it was with *The Fury* (1976) that he made his initial impact on the horror genre, a story for which a case could also be made that it is science fiction. Two young siblings have extraordinary powers that can be interpreted as supernatural or magical but that Farris rationalizes as untapped abilities of the human mind. An unscrupulous man hopes to exploit their talents for his own advantage, and what follows owes more to the spy novel than horror, with chases, captures, and escapes before the villain is finally defeated and suitably punished and the two protagonists seem free to pursue their own lives. *Firestarter* (1980) by Stephen KING uses a very similar plot, and King may well have been influenced by Farris's earlier novel.

Although *The Fury* is the author's most widely recognized genre title, his best horror novel is actually *All Heads Turn When the Hunt Goes By* (1977, also published as *Bad Blood*). This story involves an old southern family whose history of involvement with slavery has mixed African folklore and black magic into the family traditions. Farris, who had previously written the steamy *Harrison High* (1959), was one of the first modern horror writers to inject explicit sexual scenes into his work and emphasize the linkage between horror and erotica. His next title, *Catacombs* (1981), also exploited African legends, this time on the scene as an archaeological expedition uncovers more than it bargained for while excavating a newly discovered site.

The Uninvited (1982) has less overt horrors, but they are just as chilling. The protagonist is a young woman devastated by the recent death of her fiancé. She is startled when the dead man shows up, apparently suffering from amnesia and possible brain damage, disoriented and disturbed but still drawn to her. Her reaction is obviously inconsistent and uncertain, but she attempts to nurse him back to health and understand what has happened to him. That revelation becomes increasingly more chilling, however, as she discovers that his continued existence and mental improvement is contingent upon stealing those qualities from other friends and acquaintances. The story draws upon the legends of both the zombie and the vampire and builds something new and terrifying.

Son of the Endless Night (1985), although effectively told, is less original than most of his other work. A serial killer has been caught, and his defense is that he was compelled to commit the crimes by the intercession of a demon. The prosecution suspects that this is a ploy to set the stage for an insanity plea, but as the investigation proceeds there are rising suspicions that this time the defendant may actually be telling the truth. *Wildwood* (1986) is more original but builds its suspense rather slowly. The protagonist in this case is interested in an estate where a friend of his may have gone insane, believing the surrounding forest to be the home of inhuman creatures known only in Native American mythology. The reader will probably be far ahead of the characters in this one, but Farris does an excellent job of setting the atmosphere and shaping the psychological component of the suspense.

Whereas the female protagonist of *The Uninvited* is menaced by the consequences of her deep love, *The Axman Cometh* (1989) takes the opposite approach. A vicious killer murdered all the members of a family except one female child, who has now grown to adulthood, although she is still troubled by memories of the past and experiences deep anxiety and troubled dreams. Her fear is so intense, in fact, that it somehow re-creates a supernatural version of the boogey man in her dreams, a shadowy insubstantial figure that eventually takes physical form and menaces her life. *Fiends* (1990) is another very impressive novel, a variation of the vampire story. The colony of supernatural creatures in this case is a separate species that was created at the same time as humans but that was confined to eternal interment because they displeased God. Unfortunately, someone allows them to escape. Physically and by nature, they are a cross between a vampire and an angel, seductive, powerful, and mercilessly cruel.

A handful of fairly long supernatural stories were collected as *Scare Tactics* (1988), but with the exception of "horrorshow," they are inferior to his longer work. Farris recently returned to dark suspense and horror with two sequels to *The Fury*, although like the original, they are fundamentally action adventure stories. *The Fury and the Terror* (2001) examines the results when a psychic discovers that elements within the U.S. government are secretly conducting a terror campaign to influence public opinion. *The Fury and the Power* (2003) is more overtly supernatural. A woman who can voluntarily generate her own doppelgänger, or duplicate, battles an evil entity. Some of the stories in *Elvisland* (2004) also involve fantastic themes. Although Farris has not written consistently in the genre, his most cohesive body of work lies within that field, and it is most likely the fiction for which he will be best remembered.

Feist, Raymond E. (1945–)

Raymond Feist started his career as a novelist and, with the exception of a very few short stories starting in 1995, has written exclusively at book length. He is primarily an adventure story writer and uses mostly familiar plots, settings, and devices, but he manages to rearrange them in patterns that seem fresh, peoples his work with unusually resonant characters, and employs a lively and smooth prose style that distinguishes him from most of his contemporaries. Most of his novels to date are set in either the Riftwar or Serpentwar sequences, both sharing the same magical alternate reality although remote from each other in time.

Feist debuted with *Magician* (1982), which was so long that it appeared later in two volumes as *Magician: Apprentice* and *Magician: Master*. The conflict lies in the interface between two universes, one resembling medieval Europe and the other feudal Asia. The Riftwar continues in *Silverthorn* (1985), a quest story involving a poisoned princess, *A Darkness at Sethanon* (1986), which expands the conflict to include the basic forces of Order and Chaos, *Prince of the Blood* (1989), set just after the

war ends only to segue into a civil war, and *The King's Buccaneer* (1992), one of Feist's best, a story of pirates and derring do.

His second series was a trilogy written with Janny WURTS comprising *Daughter of the Empire* (1987), *Servant of the Empire* (1990), and *Mistress of the Empire* (1992). The sequence is a well written but very derivative story of the battle for the succession to a throne, mixed with court intrigues, foreign invaders, and liberal doses of sorcery. Much more significant is the Serpentwar sequence by Feist alone, a series set some time before the events chronicled in the Riftwar books. *Shadow of a Dark Queen* (1994) sees Midkemia facing invasion by a mixed force of humans and intelligent reptiles from another universe. Although the rulers and people are ill-prepared for war, a small group of businessmen start setting the framework for a major military buildup. Their efforts begin to bear fruit in *Rise of a Merchant Prince* (1995), and the war finally erupts in *Rage of the Demon King* (1997). The leader of the enemy force is killed, but her still-powerful army remains as a threat in *Shards of a Broken Crown* (1998). The series is particularly realistic in establishing the economic requirements for conducting a major war, even in a relatively primitive economy.

The Riftwar novels led to the development of a role-playing computer game, which then led in turn to a new trilogy set in the years following the war. This new sequence consists of *Krondor: The Betrayal* (1998), *Krondor: The Assassins* (1999), and *Krondor: Tears of the Gods* (2000), which fortunately are considerably more substantial than most game-inspired fiction, presumably because the author was still developing his original vision. Although collectively known as the Riftwar Legacy, the novels are generally independent, describing separate crises that arise, including a potential war with evil dwarves and a rebellion among the criminal class.

Feist later returned to the Riftwar universe for a trilogy written with three collaborators, consisting of *Honoured Enemy* (2001) with William R. Forstchen, *Murder in Lamut* (2002) with Joel Rosenberg, and *Jimmy the Hand* (2003) with S. M. Stirling, but they are peripheral adventures of only passing interest and have not as yet found a publisher in the United

States. His only nonseries novel, *Faerie Tale* (1988), is also his only novel set in our world, a mix of fantasy and horror tropes about a man who discovers the creatures secretly living among us. It is also his most original novel and the best of his early titles.

Feist's most recent series includes *King of Foxes* (2002), *Talon of the Silver Hawk* (2003), and *Exile's Return* (2004) and is known collectively as the Conclave of Shadows, which continues the history of Midkemia. The sequence has an unusual structure in that the villain of the first novel, a tyrannical despot who is ousted from power by the hero, is later redeemed. The hero of the opening volumes, who rises from poverty to avenge his slaughtered people, is supplanted by his enemy as protagonist of the third volume. As the defeated usurper wanders the world beyond the borders he once ruled, he discovers that the barrier between universes is permeable once again and that an even greater horror than before is about to invade. The decision to use a villain as a protagonist and to reform him while doing so is quite unusual in fantasy adventures, which normally make clear distinctions between good and evil. Feist has proven to be a durable, sometimes surprising writer who inserts unusual concerns and techniques into otherwise standard stories that give them an original and convincing flavor.

The Fellowship of the Ring   J. R. R. Tolkien (1954)

The term *trilogy* is often applied to any series of three novels involving common characters, although it is traditionally a single story so long that it is published as three separate volumes. That is the case with *The Lord of the Rings*, partly because J. R. R. TOLKIEN had so much story to tell and partly because he expended so much effort in creating the historical background of his created world and in describing the many different cultures that inhabit it.

The opening volume is the most critical of the three, because if readers fail to connect with the situations and characters there, they are unlikely to invest time in what follows. The story opens in the Shire, home of the hobbits, who despite some minor physical variations and a smaller stature, are essentially humans, although their psychology is considerably less aggressive than our own. The peace and calm in the Shire serves as a sharp contrast to the violence and uncertainty that governs the rest of Middle Earth. Bilbo Baggins is an aging hobbit who was the hero of THE HOBBIT (1937) and who discovered the magical ring of power when it was lost by Gollum and brought it back to the Shire. Although he has largely avoided the downside to its dark magic, even he is partially under its influence.

Bilbo has decided to spend his declining years among the elves and leave all of his worldly possessions, including the ring, to his nephew Frodo. A good wizard, Gandalf, chances to see the ring and, after investigating its history, comes to the conclusion that it is indeed the ring of Sauron, an evil creature who once tried to rule all of Middle Earth and who is apparently stirring again, returned from the dead. He charges Frodo with the mission of carrying the ring to the elves, so that they—with their greater wisdom—might decide what to do about it. Frodo's friend and servant, Sam Gamgee, accompanies him, and two other Hobbits also join the company when they meet by chance on the road. Gandalf hopes to meet them en route but must first consult Saruman, the senior wizard of his order, unaware of the fact that Saruman has been subverted by Sauron.

Their immediate enemies are the Nazgul, nine supernaturally enlivened former kings who serve Sauron, although there are other foes as well. Frodo and his friends are helped by Aragorn, also known as Strider, who has influence among the elves, and they are pursued by a mysterious figure who turns out to be Gollum, the former owner of the ring who is determined to reacquire it. The ring's ability to corrupt makes it impossible to use it against Sauron without creating, in effect, another powerful enemy to be overcome. To some extent, the novel includes the early stages of a coming-of-age story, for Frodo's carefree innocence is tested severely as he begins to realize the magnitude of what he has undertaken. The title refers to the group of nine assembled at the end of the first volume to continue the efforts to return the ring to Mount Doom, the only place where it can be destroyed.

Tolkien's saga is fleshed out with songs, historical records, and a very large cast of characters. The plot is largely episodic, although the underlying story provides a strong central structure. It is, in effect, a reverse quest story. Rather than searching for a magical artifact, the heroes seek its destruction, but the results are much the same. The remaining titles in the trilogy are THE TWO TOWERS (1954) and THE RETURN OF THE KING (1955), all three of which were recently produced as major motion pictures.

Five Children and It Edith Nesbit (1902)

Edith NESBIT (1858–1924) is considered one of the first important writers for children, and she was certainly an influence on many who followed, such as Mary Norton, Edward EAGER, and Alan GARNER. Nesbit began her career by writing a considerable amount of nonfantastic fiction, much of it pseudonymously but with little success until a series of stories about the children of the fictional Bastable family became so popular that they appeared collected in book form and were followed by two novels involving the same characters. Although not fantasy, the Bastable stories are similar in their portrayal of children and may have helped Nesbit establish the tone that she would use for her more important work.

Nesbit began writing fairy tales in the 1890s and then a full-length fantasy novel published in serial form as *The Psammead or the Gifts* (1902), later published in book form as *Five Children and It.* The children in the story, who would be recurring characters in later novels, discover a sand fairy near their home, a magical creature with the power to grant them one single wish each day. The sand fairy, or Psammead, is an ancient being that vaguely resembles a spider and that has been alive since the dinosaurs walked the Earth. It would much rather be left alone but grudgingly agrees to use its powers on their behalf.

Despite their efforts to craft their wishes precisely, in each case the results are not what they had hoped for. Great riches, the ability to fly, and the acquisition of worldly goods all seem to backfire, usually in very comical fashion. Eventually they make a more serious mistake, and an innocent man is accused of a crime, an error they can correct only if they agree never to make another magical wish. Although Nesbit is not as well known as many other classic children's writers, she was to a great extent inventing the form as she wrote and has been a major influence, either directly or indirectly, ever since.

"The Footsteps Invisible" Robert Arthur (1940)

Robert Arthur was a prolific short story writer during the 1930s and 1940s, very active in mystery and suspense and occasionally producing an interesting fantasy or horror story, including his most famous story, "SATAN AND SAM SHAY" (1942). Arthur was also the ghost editor of the early Alfred Hitchcock suspense anthologies, which often included supernatural or fantastic elements.

The protagonist of this particular tale is Jorman, who lost his vision and now supports himself operating a newsstand in Times Square. Jorman has become acutely sensitive to sounds and can recognize his regular customers by the pattern of their footsteps. One of those customers is Sir Andrew Carraden, an archaeologist, who becomes very interested when he hears of Jorman's unusual acuity and invites him to his rooms, where he tells him a very strange story.

Carraden indicates that several years previously, while excavating in Egypt, he violated an ancient law for which he has gained the implacable hostility of a relentless enemy who has pursued him from one hiding place to another around the world. Although he feels comparatively safe in New York City, he knows that it is just a matter of time until he is discovered and forced to take flight again. He asks Jorman if he would use his talent to listen for the distinctive footsteps of his pursuer and demonstrates them. Jorman takes instant alarm, telling him that he heard that very sound only an hour earlier. Carraden immediately prepares to leave the city, but his pursuer is already in the corridor beyond the main door, and his emergency exit has been jammed shut due to an accident earlier in the day.

Jorman can only listen as the barricaded door is literally torn down. The distinctive footsteps pass him and join Carraden in another room, at which point the archaeologist throws himself from the window, even though they are on the fifth floor. Jorman makes his way out of the hotel, convinced that Carraden is dead, but he hears the man's footsteps run past him, followed relentlessly by the other. It is only a short while later that he realizes the truth. Carraden did, in fact, die in the fall, but he is being pursued in death just as he was in life. Arthur's story delivers a double shock and is particularly effective as told from the point of view of Jorman, who obviously never sees the form of the pursuer, if it was ever visible in the first place.

Ford, Jeffrey (1955–)

Most readers and editors tend to be very wary of writers who stray from existing styles and plots. Readers are often reluctant to try anything new, and publishers are reluctant to risk what might prove to be a commercial failure. Fantasy is generally viewed today as a literature of romance and adventure, and only a handful of writers have used it for more literary purposes. Most of them were already established, such as Gene WOLFE. It is much more difficult for a newcomer to break out of the mold.

Jeffrey Ford first started appearing in print during the late 1980s, most notably with his quirky short novel *Vanitas* (1988), which mixes science fiction and fantasy as it tells the story of a legendary hero who allegedly visits the moon and defeats a virulent new plague before dying under mysterious circumstances. He leaves behind various pieces of exotic equipment, including some that appear to be designed to revive the dead. Although not as powerful as his more recent novels, *Vanitas* was quite exceptional for its time, but it nevertheless was published by a small press in a limited edition.

Ford began attracting attention during the early 1990s with short stories such as "The Woman Who Counts Her Breath" (1995) and his first full-length novel, *The Physiognomy* (1997), which won the World Fantasy Award and was a New York Times Notable Book of the Year. Cley, the protagonist, is an expert specializing in personality analysis based on certain physical and mental traits and is employed by the government in a fantasy world

that is roughly early industrial, although it does not exactly parallel our own history. As punishment for an infraction, he is sent to a remote mining village to catch a thief and instead learns that much of what he thought he knew about his society is wrong. Cley returned for two sequels, *Memoranda* (1999) and *The Beyond* (2001). In the former, the man who Cley exposed counters with a plague of induced sleep, and in the latter he goes on a phantasmagoric journey of discovery.

Short stories began to appear regularly after the 1990s, including excellent tales such as "The Fantasy Writer's Assistant" (2000), "Something by the Sea" (2002), and "Jupiter's Skull" (2004). His most recent novel is *The Portrait of Mrs. Charbuque* (2002), which won significant critical acclaim from the mainstream press as well as within the fantasy field. The setting is another fantasy world, a large city in which an artist is hired by the woman of the title to paint her portrait, but he must do so without ever setting eyes on his subject.

Ford won a second World Fantasy Award for best collection, *The Fantasy Writer's Assistant and Other Stories* (2002), which includes most of his better short stories, and a third for "CREATION" (2002). He has also been one of the finalists for other awards as well. Ford's innovative settings and nontraditional plots have clearly struck a resonant chord with readers, and his superior literary qualities suggest that he may be finding a much wider audience than will most of his contemporaries.

The Forgotten Realms Series

The Forgotten Realms series, like the very similar DRAGONLANCE SERIES, is a shared world system that was originally derived from a series of role playing games set in an elaborately contrived fantasy background. Although there are monsters, elves, and magic, a large portion of the work in this milieu concentrates almost entirely on humans, one notable exception being the Elminster books by Ed GREENWOOD, whose central character is an elf. There has been considerable variation in quality among the many authors of the more than 130 titles to date, all of them published by TSR Books or its later incarnation as Wizards of the Coast. Most of the more active contributors to the series have concentrated on events within a group of interrelated kingdoms varied enough to allow virtually any form of mainstream fantasy adventure. The series is heavily influenced by the work of J. R. R. TOLKIEN and less obviously by Robert E. HOWARD.

The various titles have generally been arranged in subseries, which are split into two types. The first is composed of novels by a single author that tell a single, continued tale or that feature the same set of characters. These more closely resemble mainstream fantasy. Authors who have written in this vein include R. A. SALVATORE, Elaine CUNNINGHAM, Ed Greenwood, and Paul Kemp. Other more loosely connected series have been written by multiple authors, not necessarily telling a single story and sometimes sharing only a common setting, character, or situation. These include The War of the Spider Queen, the Harpers, Sembia, and the Return of the Archwizards sequences.

Several authors who started writing for TSR later enjoyed success with other publishers, the most notable of whom is R. A. Salvatore. Ed Greenwood, Mark ANTHONY, Troy DENNING, James Lowder, Carrie Bebris, and Elaine Cunningham have also made successful leaps to general fantasy. At the same time, several authors better known for their independent work have contributed at least one volume to this growing saga, including Chet WILLIAMSON, Mel Odom, Scott Ciencin, Lynn ABBEY, and Victor Milan. There have also been more than a dozen collections of short stories, usually edited by one or another of the regular contributors. Most of the Forgotten Realms novels are minor and derivative, although they are rarely badly written, and Salvatore in particular has managed to produce some surprisingly creative and original work given the restrictions of the setting.

"For the Blood Is the Life" F. Marion Crawford (1911)

Although F. Marion Crawford was an American writer, he spent most of his adult life in Italy, which is where this story is set, writing novels about high society in Europe. His handful of short supernatural tales include several classics, of which this vampire tale is one of the two best, the other being "THE UPPER BERTH" (1886), a ghost story. The tale

opens when the narrator and a friend observe an unusual phenomenon, a burial mound upon which, from a distance, there appears to lie an indistinct human body. After a subtle but effective introductory sequence, the story reverts to the origin of the apparition.

Angelo was the son of a retired criminal whose hoarded fortune was stolen by two cronies while he lay on his deathbed. They are in the process of burying the strongbox for later retrieval when a young woman happens upon them. To prevent her from raising the alarm, they assault her and bury her with the money, then return to establish an alibi. The woman, Cristina, appears to have been in love with Angelo, who is absent on business when his father is fatally stricken. Angelo is left penniless, and Cristina has, of course, vanished without a trace.

Vampire lore had not become as rigid as it is today when Crawford was alive. His description of Cristina's nocturnal visits to Angelo are more like those of an incubus than a vampire, and he does not provide an explanation for her transformation other than the brutal nature of her death and burial. She appears in Angelo's dreams, looking emaciated but intense, and he wakens feeling weak and unrested. The visitations become more compulsive, and he begins to waste away toward the inevitable end. Fortunately for Angelo, a newcomer to the village and a priest take his side, warding Cristina off with holy water, exhuming her body, and driving a stake through her heart. Angelo's missing legacy is retrieved in the process.

Crawford's story has much in common with Bram STOKER's classic DRACULA (1897), but his vampire is more resilient. Even after being laid to her final rest, Cristina can manifest herself visually and even exert some small influence on those who travel too near her grave. The highly melodramatic events are delivered in a low-key, almost casual style, and the missing details, rather than detract from the story's verisimilitude, actually make it feel like a more authentic account.

"The Fortress Unvanquishable, Save for Sacnoth" Lord Dunsany (1908)

Early 20th-century fantasy stories often bore considerable resemblance to fairy tales in that they compressed many events into very short sequences and featured characters who were little more than a name and a type. Lord DUNSANY used this technique for many of his large body of short fantasy tales, including this one, which incorporates a quest for a magical sword into an encounter with evil sorcery. The people of Allathurion have been troubled by unsettling dreams, and a wizard tells them these are the result of the return of Gaznak to the world. Gaznak, who is sometimes referred to as Satan, was traveling the universe on a comet, but now he is back, dwelling in a fortress so powerful that it cannot be breached except by the bearer of Sacnoth, a magic sword. Unfortunately, Sacnoth has not yet been forged and is, in fact, a portion of the spine of a creature described as a dragon-crocodile, although the creature's body is entirely made of metal.

Leothric is the champion who sets off to acquire Sacnoth, battling for three days and nights before destroying the dragon-crocodile and securing the materials with which to construct Sacnoth. He then proceeds to Gaznak's castle, whose genesis lay in Dunsany's own military service in Gibraltar. There, in short order, Leothric and Sacnoth deal with a number of obstacles, including locked gates, vampires, a giant spider, armed retainers, the temptations of magically endowed women, a brace of dragons, and deadly music before confronting Gaznak, whose warped dreams are physically manifested while he sleeps. A protracted sword fight ensues, during which Leothric finds himself at a disadvantage despite his magic sword. Gaznak can literally detach his head from his body and remove it from harm's way. Leothric finally triumphs by cutting off the hand that holds the head. With Gaznak dead, the castle itself rapidly disintegrates, and peace is restored to Allathurion.

Dunsany's short tale economically incorporates a plot that modern writers would have expanded into at least three lengthy books. The physical nature of the fortress, though described only in brief passages, is nevertheless impressively exotic and awe inspiring. The story itself is a good example of the transition from fantasy that was primarily written for children to the adult fantasy that dominates the genre today.

Fowler, Christopher (1953–   )

The British writer Christopher Fowler began writing short fiction in 1986, much of which played with supernatural themes and situations, although often with a rational explanation. He very quickly established himself as a notable new writer with two collections, *City Jitters* (1987) and *City Jitters Two* (1988), as well as his very popular debut novel, *Roofworld* (1988). The novel, like most of Fowler's fiction, is set in London, but it alternates between the familiar one and another that exists among a hidden society of individuals who live exclusively on the rooftops, moving secretly and conducting their business beneath, or rather above, the notice of the external world. They have split effectively into two tribes, roughly corresponding to good and evil, although the author does not make things quite that simple. The leader of the latter is on a quest to acquire more than human powers, and the subsequent resolution of his conflict with the protagonist and the working out of the various subsidiary plots is compulsively readable.

A third collection of short stories, *The Bureau of Lost Souls,* followed in 1989, and then a second and even more impressive novel, *Rune* (1990), which makes use of material first popularized in "CASTING THE RUNES" (1911) by M. R. JAMES. A pattern emerges following a series of bizarre accidents. Each of the victims had on his person a slip of paper inscribed with various mysterious characters, subsequently identified as runes used as a curse to bring about the deaths. The protagonist is an advertising copywriter who realizes that he is linked to each of the victims and who slowly accepts the supernatural explanation before discovering who is responsible and why.

Red Bride (1992) links the rise to fame of a prominent actress to a series of murders, *Darkest Day* (1993) is a detective story pitting its protagonists against a cult of Satan worshippers who actually do have some supernatural powers, and *Spanky* (1994) involves a deal with the devil. Despite the fantastic content in these novels, it has become increasingly obvious that Fowler's inclinations are tending more and more to nonsupernatural suspense, and most of his recent work has consisted of mystery novels, although often with bizarre twists.

A recent novella, *Breathe* (2004), considers the possibility that environmental problems within very large building complexes could actually affect the personalities of people working within them, leading to insanity and homicide. Fowler has continued to write first-class short fiction, occasionally with supernatural content. His newer collections include *Flesh Wounds* (1995), *Dracula's Library* (1997), and *Uncut* (1999). Given recent trends in Fowler's writing, he seems likely to recede to a peripheral position within the horror genre, but his work during the 1990s demonstrates the potential for him to be a significant figure within the field should he return to his original interests.

France, Anatole (Anatole-François Thibault) (1844–1924)

The French writer Anatole-François Thibault, who won the Nobel Prize for literature, wrote a substantial body of work, of which several titles are fantasy, often involving Christian allegories or a satire of Christian principles. The most famous and successful of these is *The Revolt of the Angels* (1914). The central character is a guardian angel on Earth who discovers through his researches that the Christian concept of the order of things is incorrect and that its adherents have been defrauded into worshipping a minor deity. He decides to organize a rebellion among the fallen angels presently in the vicinity of Paris along with certain disaffected angels still in good standing and recruits Lucifer to lead the revolt. Lucifer, however, declines to involve himself even though modern technology has provided mortal man with more powerful weapons than those available to the minions of Jehovah. An amusing subplot involves the efforts of a mortal Christian to reconvert his guardian angel. The satire was rather daring for its time but is tame by contemporary standards, though still quite effective.

France's other major fantasy novel is *Penguin Island* (1909). This is also a satire in which a near-sighted priest mistakenly baptizes an island full of penguins, as a consequence of which they are all miraculously transformed into a sort of human beings and undergo a history that parallels our own, allowing France to poke fun at a variety of human institutions and failings. Several of his shorter works also contain fantastic elements, primarily religious, as in "The Juggler of Notre Dame" (1892, also known as "Our Lady's Juggler") and "Saint Satyr" (1909). Others are ghost stories, the best of which are "The Mass of the Shadows" (1892) and "Leslie Wood" (1896). "The Kingdom of the Dwarfs" (1899, also known as "The Honey-Bee") involves kidnapping by dwarves, and "The Shirt" (1920) is a nonheroic quest story.

Frankenstein, or The Modern Prometheus
Mary Shelley (1818)

Although even now many people confuse the name of Victor Frankenstein with that of his nameless monster, the basic plot of that early novel is one of the most familiar in all of literature, and if our mental image is forever shaped by Boris Karloff's screen portrayal, it is as much because of the power of Shelley's original imaginative conception as it is of the impressive efforts of Hollywood. We use the term *Frankenstein* as a shortcut to describe a situation in which an individual is destroyed by his own creator and also as the archetype of the mad scientist, the seeker after truth who loses his sense of morality in his quest for knowledge of the secrets of the universe. The original novel is claimed both by horror and science fiction writers, the latter because the monster is restored to life through scientific means, however improbable, rather than through magic or the occult. Mary SHELLEY undoubtedly drew inspiration from the legend of the golem, although her creation was fashioned of mismatched human parts rather than of completely artificial origin. The initial impetus to write her classic novel came from a competition involving the poets Percy Shelley and Lord Byron, among others, but hers was the only entry to achieve widespread fame.

Victor Frankenstein is a wealthy man with a promising future who is married to a beautiful and devoted wife, a member of a respected family. He is driven, unfortunately, by an obsession that grows more powerful with each passing day—the desire to create life where it did not previously exist, although in practice he may be reanimating rather than creating since presumably he is working with organic material. He clandestinely gathers the raw materials upon which to experiment, concealing his activities from everyone. Eventually he achieves his goal, after a fashion, though his monster varies considerably from the film interpretation in that it is intelligent and more human in appearance. Despite Frankenstein's early optimism, however, there is clearly something wrong with his creation, and it eventually escapes and then launches a campaign of terror and revenge against its creator's family.

Although the monster is dangerous, physically daunting at eight feet in height, and lacks a soul, it is difficult not to feel some sympathy for its plight, and when the novel concludes with it drifting off alone to an unknown fate, it is not a moment of triumph for the reader. It is Frankenstein who is the true villain, because he acted without thinking, took risks without considering the consequences, and brought death and misfortune to the innocents around him while not directly suffering himself. Even as he nears his own death at last, he refuses to express regret for what he has accomplished, holding out hope that others will replicate and continue his work to accomplish even greater achievements. Frankenstein and his monster are the literary forebears of many fictional stories of unintended disaster, from the *Terminator* movies to countless novels of runaway plagues, genetically altered animals, selectively bred superhumans, and various other terrors.

The novel has also generated several direct sequels and alternate versions, both in film and in book form. Most of the novels have been as derivative and forgettable as the bulk of the movies, of which there are more than 40 to date, including the delightful spoof *Young Frankenstein* (1974). A few novels have made better use of their source material, however. *The Memoirs of Elizabeth Frankenstein* (1995) by Theodore Roszak, for example, tells the story from the point of view of Frankenstein's wife, an active participant in the project who well deserves her eventual death at the hands of the creature. Roszak pushes the story into the openly supernatural, describing Elizabeth's occult contributions to the raising of the dead. *FRANKENSTEIN UNBOUND* (1973) by Brian W. Aldiss uses the point of view of an inadvertent time traveler from our era who becomes a witness to the efforts made to create a bride for the monster, drawing upon both the novel and the film *The Bride of Frankenstein* (1935). The most subtle of these sequels is *Brittle Innings* (1994) by Michael Bishop, in which the monster has survived into the 20th century by altering its appearance and becoming highly educated, although it supports itself playing minor league baseball, a premise that might have been comic, although Bishop treats the subject seriously. The passage of years has rendered Shelley's prose style very difficult for casual readers, but the essential plot of the novel and the questions of scientific ethics that it raised are as gripping and relevant today as they were in the early 19th century.

Frankenstein Unbound Brian W. Aldiss (1973)

The classic novel FRANKENSTEIN (1818) by Mary SHELLEY may or may not be science fiction as well as horror, depending upon how one defines the two genres. Brian W. Aldiss, primarily known as a science fiction writer, has claimed it for that genre and also wrote one of the most interesting of the many sequels and alternate versions that have appeared during the 20th century. Joe Bodenland is an American from the near future who finds himself transported by inexplicable but clearly scientifically rational means back to 19th-century Switzerland, where he meets Mary Shelley herself but where he also discovers that Victor Frankenstein is a real person who did, in fact, create a monstrous creature. Undeterred by the flawed results, Frankenstein intends to continue his experiments.

Bodenland has the advantage over his new contemporaries in that he knows how the story will turn out, although as is usual in such fictional situations, it is very difficult for him to affect the course of events. Frankenstein is planning to create a mate for his creature by cobbling together parts from corpses, but the monster is impatient, demanding, and impulsive. The protagonist finds himself becoming romantically involved with Shelley, and in fact the best parts of the novel are those that involve his interaction with her and the circle of literary figures who were her friends rather than those involving the monster or its obsessed creator.

Eventually, Bodenland and some of his new acquaintances are transported back to his home era, where the final conflicts are resolved. Aldiss delivers his sometimes melodramatic but always absorbing story in an intelligent, clear prose and forces the reader to take a fresh look at the implications of unrestrained scientific research and the obligations of the scientist to the world at large. The novel was turned into a moderately loyal but essentially disappointing movie in 1990. Aldiss returned to this theme for a somewhat related but less interesting novel, *Dracula Unbound* (1991), in which Bram STOKER discovers that vampires are actually time travelers from a distant future in which humans have evolved into a blood-drinking race.

"Friend's Best Man" Jonathan Carroll (1987)

Many of Jonathan CARROLL's stories lurk somewhere in the borderland between fantasy and horror, a region that editors and critics have come to call "dark fantasy." Carroll is a particularly original and inventive writer, however, and it is very difficult to categorize many of his stories, which do not fit easily into existing pigeonholes. This short story, which won the World Fantasy Award, includes some of his most brilliantly realized characters and delivers its fantastic elements more by hint and suggestion than by actually revealing them.

The narrator protagonist is an unmarried writer whose closest companion is his dog, Friend. While walking one day, Friend sits down on a railroad track and is nearly run down by a train but is saved by his owner, who loses a leg in the process. Hospitalized, he meets Jasenka Ciric, a seven-year-old girl who is terminally ill and wise beyond her years. Jasenka eventually meets Friend and tells the narrator that he is able to talk to her and that she will relay the messages because Friend wants to do something good for his master in recompense for the loss of his leg. Their relationship develops, as does his other connection, a female neighbor to whom he is attracted and who he eventually marries.

Although he dismisses Jasenka's claim as playfulness, some of the information she passes on is extraordinary. She predicts that he will win a contest, and he does, although not quite as she had indicated. But she also knows of his wife's interest in another man, and his phone number, and provides other information she could not logically have known unless she were indeed receiving some kind of telepathic communication from Friend. Just before she succumbs to her illness and dies, Jasenka passes on one last warning. She tells the narrator that all of the animals in the world are finally fed up with humans and that within a few days all of humanity will be killed except those who take shelter in one area allocated for the true friends of animals. The story ends at that point, leaving the reader as well as the narrator uncertain whether this is all just her imagination or whether the end of the world really is at hand.

Friesner, Esther (1951–)

Although Esther Friesner's first few published stories during the early 1980s were science fiction, most of her subsequent novels and short stories have been fantasy, often humorous. Her first novel, *Mustapha and His Wise Dog* (1985), which initiated the Twelve Kingdoms series, is an unconventional quest story. Mustapha is exiled by his family and wanders the world accompanied only by his loyal dog. Eventually, he learns that he has been chosen by the gods to investigate an ancient evil and prevent its reemergence. The series continues with *Spells of Mortal Weaving* (1986), a more familiar story in which a prince travels to a distant land to rescue his kidnapped lover, *The Witchwood Cradle* (1987), a clever story in which 12 witches are each given one power to oppose evil, and *The Water King's Laughter* (1989), the least-interesting in the series. *The Silver Mountain* (1986) and *Harlot's Ruse* (1986), both of which stand alone, respectively pit an amnesiac prince against a variety of enemies and put a young woman in the middle of a battle among legendary creatures. They are competently written but do not compare favorably to Friesner's other early work.

Much more interesting is *New York by Knight* (1986), the first of several contemporary fantasies that quickly established Friesner as an important new talent. Two magical beings, an immortal knight and a powerful dragon, manifest themselves in modern New York to continue their battle of good against evil. *Druid's Blood* (1988) is a historical fantasy set in an alternate Victorian England. Queen Victoria asks an old friend for help following the theft of a book of magic that safeguards the future of the British Empire. In its absence, supernatural creatures harass the citizenry, and the throne itself may not remain safe for long. *Elf Defense* (1989) was her first openly humorous fantasy, although it has its somber moments. The protagonist is a mortal woman who married but has recently separated from a prince of Faerie. When he sends his minions to reclaim her, she counters with a potent new ally—a divorce lawyer.

Humorous fantasy became quite popular at the end of the 1980s, and Friesner quickly became one of its leading talents. Her first trilogy consisted of *Here Be Demons* (1988), *Demons Wild* (1989), and *Hooray for Hellywood* (1990). A group of underachieving demons are exiled to Earth, where they attempt to corrupt a group of college students, one of whom discovers that his mother is a reformed demon. A second set includes *Gnome Man's Land* (1991), *Harpy High* (1991), and *Unicorn U* (1992), an even funnier story arc in which goblins invade a high school, a student struggles to avert his doom when it is announced by a banshee, and the gods themselves show up to disrupt things.

Much of Friesner's short fiction is similarly light in approach, and many of her funny fantasies were collected in *It's Been Fun* (1991). *Sphynxes Wild* (1989), a far more serious novel although with many amusing moments, follows the adventures of a sphinx who has assumed human form to visit contemporary America. *Yesterday We Saw Mermaids* (1992) is the most underrated of her novels from this period, the story of a ship that precedes Columbus to the New World, which is full of magical creatures whose existence will be nullified with the arrival of rationalists from Europe. *Wishing Season* (1993) continues Friesner's string of humorous novels, a predictable but likeable story about a genie's efforts to control his thoughtless master's proliferating wishes. Another trilogy, *Majyk by Accident* (1993), *Majyk by Hook or Crook* (1994), and *Majyk by Design* (1994), is less successful, the adventures of an apprentice magician and his magically intelligent cat. *Split Heirs* (1993), written with Lawrence WATT-EVANS, is an amusing satire about court intrigues. *Child of the Eagle* (1996) is her last major fantasy novel and her best single book. Within the context of a magical alternate Roman Empire, Brutus betrays his fellow conspirators to Caesar. Later he has second thoughts and realizes that he should probably have stuck to his original intention.

Friesner has become less prolific in recent years, producing two very fine science fiction novels and a humorous fantasy, *E Godz* (2003), written with Robert Lynn Asprin, which spoofs corporate business dealings. She has also edited a series of anthologies of humorous fantasy fiction that includes *Chicks in Chain Mail* (1995), *The Chick Is in the Mail* (2000), and *Turn the Other Chick* (2004). She has become a prolific short story writer in recent years, alternating humor with serious themes, and her most recent collection is *Up the Wall & Other Tales of King Arthur and His Knights* (2000). The decline in popularity of humorous fantasy in the United States may have disrupted her momentum, but she has proven able to write excellent novels with serious themes as well and is likely to retain her prominence in fantasy.

Frost, Gregory (1951–)

Gregory Frost had begun writing fantasy fiction as early as 1981 with "In the Sunken Museum" but made little impression until *Lyrec* (1984), his first novel, which relates the adventures of two companions as they travel across a wide variety of parallel worlds, taking on new personalities or even altered physical bodies every time they switch realities. One of them becomes a traveling musician as the story develops, while the other is trapped in the body of a cat. Frost enthusiastically develops his theme in a rather loose series of adventures that mix good-natured humor with wild adventure.

His next two novels, *Tain* (1986) and *Remscela* (1988), two exploits of the legendary Cu Chulainn, or Cuchulain, from Celtic mythology, are considerably more serious and ambitious, though in some ways less interesting. They are filled with historical allusions, druidic magic, spells, and a visit to the land of the Fairies, but there had been so many similar treatments, not always as well written, that the duo made less of an impression than it might have otherwise. They were published in a combined edition as *Crimson Spear* (1988). Frost next wrote a very fine science fiction novel, *The Pure Cold Light* (1993), but his next fantasy novel was long delayed, appearing finally in 2002. *Fitcher's Brides,* which is based on the fairy tales about Bluebeard, focuses on a 19th-century end of the world cult whose members are beginning to hear bodiless voices. The leader of the unit, an obsessed preacher, has a habit of making his wives disappear, and his latest has to use all of her wits to escape the fate he has planned for her.

Frost also wrote a number of short stories, the best of which are his occasional barbed horror stories such as "That Blissful Height" (1996) and "The Girlfriends of Dorian Grey" (2000). He is long overdue for a collection.

G

Gabaldon, Diana (1952–)

Time travel stories are one of the most common forms of the modern romance novel, and there have been literally hundreds of them published during the last 10 years, most of them involving travel to a handful of historical periods and locations in Europe and most of them pedestrian in style and repetitious in plot. Typically a female protagonist is projected back by some barely explained and largely irrelevant means—a magic device, a mysterious storm, a family curse—where she meets a charming though frequently mysterious man, and after considerable effort they become romantically involved. Only a few writers actively using this device employ authentic historical backgrounds and skilled writing to produce a genuinely interesting novel, and none as well and as successfully as Diana Gabaldon in her Outlander series.

Diana Gabaldon is the pseudonym of Diana Watkins, whose first novel, *Outlander* (1991, also published as *Cross Stitch*), rapidly became a best-selling romance. Gabaldon was one of the first to blend a traditional romantic plot with more serious literary purposes. The story follows the adventures of a contemporary married woman who touches a magic stone and finds herself projected back through time to 18th-century Scotland, where she meets a local nobleman with whom she has various adventures and eventually falls in love. In the first sequel, *Dragonfly in Amber* (1992), she convinces him that she does, in fact, know the future, and they travel to the royal court to attempt to change history and avert the Battle of Culloden. Although

they appear to have done just that, they later learn that there has been treachery, partially instigated by an ancestor of the man to whom the protagonist, Claire, is married in our present.

In *Voyager* (1994) Claire has returned to modern time, bearing her lover's child and convinced that he died in battle. When she uncovers information that indicates he might have survived, she decides to find a way to cross the gap of time again, even if it means abandoning her daughter. The daughter, Brianna, becomes the protagonist in *Drums of Autumn* (1996), convinced that her mother has disappeared into another era. She tries to follow and ends up in Revolutionary War America instead. They are all reunited in America in *The Fiery Cross* (2001), along with Brianna's husband, but their lives continue to be subject to turmoil and danger.

Lord John and the Private Matter (2003), although it features a minor character from the series, is a historical mystery. Gabaldon returned to Claire and her 18th-century family in *A Breath of Snow and Ashes* (2005). Gabaldon has also written a nonfiction book providing additional detail about the background and writing of the first four novels, *The Outlandish Companion* (1999).

Gaiman, Neil (1960–)

Although Neil Gaiman originally achieved prominence for his work on various graphic novels, particularly the Sandman sequence during the late 1980s and early 1990s, his career has become decidedly more oriented toward prose in recent years. One of his Sandman entries won the World Fantasy Award as best short story in 1991, and the recent graphic novel *The Dream Hunters* (1999, with Yoshitaka Amano) contains so much text that it is worth considering as a work of prose. His first novel was *Good Omens* (1990), a collaboration with Terry PRATCHETT and a consistently hilarious spoof of horror novels and movies such as *The Omen*. A selection of his early fiction appeared as *Angels and Visitations: A Miscellany* (1993), but his first solo novel did not appear until several years later.

Neverwhere* (1996) was originally a BBC television series created by Gaiman, which he later turned into a novel. The protagonist finds himself lost in a magical other reality that exists beneath familiar London and has a series of adventures as he seeks to understand his new environment. *Stardust* (1999) is an unusual quest story in which the hero attempts to find a fallen star, which he believes will help him win the heart of the woman he loves. *Coraline* (2002) is an exceptional story for younger readers about a girl who finds a portal into a world where animals talk. It won both the Hugo and Nebula Awards as best novella of the year. His recent fantasy novel *American Gods* (2001) also collected both awards. It is the story of a man who discovers that when waves of immigrants reached the New World, they brought along certain magical entities as well.

Smoke and Mirrors* (1998) was Gaiman's second collection of short stories. Among his better shorts are "The White Road" (1995), "How Do You Think It Feels?" (1998), "Keepsakes and Treasures" (1999), and "Inventing Aladdin" (2003). He won the Hugo Award for his fantastic Sherlock Holmesian adventure story "A Study in Emerald" (2003). Gaiman has also written poetry, edited several anthologies, and written a substantial body of nonfiction, most of it related to fantastic literature. He has very quickly become one of the prominent figures in literary fantasy while also establishing himself as very popular with a wide range of readers.

"The Garden of Fear" Robert E. Howard (1934)

Although reincarnation would seem to be a logical plot device for fantasy writers, it is actually used comparatively rarely. Robert E. HOWARD liked the idea well enough to use it in this classic story, although only as a frame for the main plot. James Allison is a contemporary man who can remember his previous lives, including his existence as Hunwulf the Wanderer and even further back to the bestial ancestors of humanity. Hunwulf was a Norse warrior, and the love of his life was Gudrun, a beautiful woman who he met while wandering through what would eventually be northern Europe.

Hunwulf kills the man to whom Gudrun is betrothed, and the two lovers flee their people, escaping into a land where the natives speak an unintelligible language, although they manage to convey a warning about proceeding farther south. Unfortunately, Gudrun is seized by some large flying creature during the night, which the natives insist was a winged man. Hunwulf pursues and finds an immense, anachronistic tower set within a garden of odd looking plants. He instinctively distrusts the situation; the plants do not move with the breeze, and he feels as though he is being watched by unseen eyes. His caution is rewarded when a winged man throws a hapless victim from the top of the tower. The plants attack the sacrifice, draining his blood.

The winged man is the prototype of the devil, a holdover from an ancient race whose line is all but extinct and whose existence has remained in our racial memory ever since. Hunwulf is undaunted, however, and starts a brush fire to stampede a herd of mammoths, who crush the flowers and nearly destroy the tower. The winged man flies off to safety but returns while Hunwulf is scaling the castle wall, resulting in the final battle during which the demonic figure is slain, but only because Gudrun herself intercedes at a crucial point. Howard's female characters were rarely reticent about taking a hand themselves in a battle when the situation demanded it.

Howard's speculation that racial memory might retain the concept of a prehistoric race has been used many times since in works as disparate as Arthur C. Clarke's visionary science fiction novel *Childhood's End* (1953) to the Cthulhu Mythos stories of H. P. LOVECRAFT and other horror novels such as *Seductions* (1984) by Ray GARTON. His depiction of ancient man as a warrior who thought along narrowly focused lines has proliferated through sword and sorcery, and his gift for creating vivid and exotic scenes has only rarely been equaled.

Gardner, Craig Shaw (1949–   )

Craig Shaw Gardner began writing a series of humorous short fantasies in the late 1970s, eventually collecting several of these as his first novel, *A Malady of Magics* (1986), which led to two more adventures of the wizard protagonist Ebenezum, *A Multitude of Monsters* (1986) and *A Night in the Netherhells* (1987). Ebenezum's problem is that he is allergic to magic, which makes it very difficult for him to respond when faced with requests to cast spells for the benefit of potential clients. Gardner immediately followed up with additional adventures in the Wuntvor trilogy, *A Difficulty with Dwarves* (1987), *An Excess of Enchantments* (1988), and *A Disagreement with Death* (1989). Ebenezum and his apprentice generally succeed in making the situation even worse during encounters with witches, demons, and other strange denizens of his imaginary world.

Gardner's next set of novels was also humorous fantasy, but much more original in concept. The protagonist discovers that motion pictures are reflections of alternate realities where the extremes of cinema are commonplace and the "rules" of genre films are natural laws. The trilogy consists of *Slaves of the Volcano God* (1989), *Bride of the Slime Monster* (1989), and *Revenge of the Fluffy Bunnies* (1990). Three more humorous adventures followed, this time poking fun at Arabian Nights stories. *The Other Sinbad* (1991) describes what happens when a genie mistakenly attaches himself to the wrong Sinbad, *A Bad Day for Ali Baba* (1991) is a hilarious send up of that classic story, and *The Last Arabian Night* (1993, also published as *Scheherazade's Night Out*) is in the form of a series of nested stories within stories that is amusing in its structure as well as its content.

The popularity of funny fantasy dwindled during the early 1990s, and Gardner's next trilogy took a more serious turn. *Dragon Sleeping* (1994, also published as *Raven Walking*), *Dragon Waking* (1995), and *Dragon Burning* (1996) transplant an entire neighborhood from our world into a fantasy realm where ancient magical powers are stirring in anticipation of a momentous battle. The interlopers are forced to choose sides while resolving their own interpersonal troubles. The author perhaps tried to deal with too many separate story lines because it is occasionally difficult to keep track of the various subplots, but his imagined world is original and interesting and his characters are generally well drawn.

Most of Gardner's other novels are tie-ins to television programs, movies, and computer games. He has written one new fantasy trilogy under the name Peter Garrison. *The Changeling War, The Sorceror's Gun,* and *The Magic Dead* all appeared in 1999. The three-part story is a serious approach to a theme that other fantasy writers have usually tackled humorously, the merging of a world with its dominant technology and another where magic is the underlying structure. The imaginary world of the Castle is unique and intriguing, and the author's steadily improving narrative ability is evident. Gardner also writes occasional short stories, of which "Warm" (1993) and "Blood Ties" (1996) are notable.

Garner, Alan (1934–   )

Although he had had some fiction published previously, Alan Garner only began to attract enthusiastic attention with *The Weirdstone of Brisginamen* (1960, also published as *The Weirdstone*), the first of several children's fantasies and the first half of a two-part series. The child protagonists are visiting a remote part of England when they become intrigued by a local legend and manage to discover its truth, the existence of ancient warriors lying in a coma beneath the ground waiting for the moment when they must rise to defend the world from evil. Their adventures involve a pair of wizards, one good and one mildly evil, and eventually they must act on their own to prevent a catastrophe. It is the strongest of his three major fantasy novels and unusually suspenseful for stories targeted at this age group, particularly during the 1960s. *The Moon of Gomrath* (1993) continues the story with even darker twists involving a variety of demonic possession and even some sexual awakening within the children. Once again, they save the day, assisted by a helpful wizard but largely on their own.

Elidor (1965) transports a new group of children into an even more frightening world that is barren and ruled by a sinister figure who uses dark magic. The four children acquire four magical artifacts and remove them to our own world, protecting them despite pursuit by the forces of evil and thereby helping to restore the health of the blasted otherworld. Once again, Garner uses dark imagery and intense sequences that have only recently been deemed acceptable in children's fiction, this time also including a wealth of literary and mythic references. *The Owl Service* (1967) draws from Welsh myths and is essentially a ghost story, although rich in detail and surprisingly complex. The episodic *Red Shift* (1973) deals with three separate men who may be alternate versions of one another, all of whom are influenced by subtle magic from an ancient artifact.

Most of Garner's subsequent work was not fantasy, although he has written numerous fairy tales. The majority of these were collected as *Fairytales of Gold* (1989). "Feel Free" (1980) is also of particular interest. Garner appears to have abandoned fantasy almost entirely since 1990, but the powerful images in his early novels assure him an honored place in the history of the field.

Garton, Ray (1962–)

As early as his first novel, *Seductions* (1984), it was obvious that Ray Garton was willing to explore the linkage between extreme horror and sex to a degree unusual among his peers. The supernatural entities in his first novel are a race of women, apparently survivors from a prehistoric age, who can change their appearance in order to better seduce their victims and lure them into an underground lair. They are a form of incubus, although less ethereal, and capable of recovering from wounds that would be fatal to a human being. The protagonist discovers their existence, which attracts their unwelcome notice. *Darklings* (1985) makes the horror even more personal in the form of a tentacled creature that lives inside human bodies, compelling its host to do its bidding. Garton's first two novels clearly heralded a significant new talent, and his third original novel measured up to that early promise.

Live Girls (1987) is a vampire novel, and since there is often a deep current of sexuality in modern vampire fiction, it was clearly an appropriate subject for Garton to tackle next. The title is a clever play on words because the protagonist visits a nightclub that advertises live girls and falls under the thrall of a female vampire, who is, of course, not alive at all. He eventually regains the will to fight her, but only after some unusually overt sexual content. A sequel, *Night Life,* has been announced but has not appeared as of this writing. Sexuality is an even stronger component in *Crucifax* (1988), in which a charismatic cult leader arouses considerable opposition because of what is perceived as his exploitation of many of his younger followers. He is actively evil rather than immoral, however, a supernatural being who has taken human form. The content was so explicit that his publisher edited Garton's novel so severely that he published the uncut version through a small press as *Crucifax Autumn* (1988).

Lot Lizards (1991) is another vampire story. In this case the undead prey on a group of travelers trapped by a blizzard at a truck stop. *The New Neighbor* (1991) involves a succubus feeding on her neighbors. There is another cult in *Dark Channel* (1992), this time led by a man who is demonically possessed, but for the first time the plot seems oddly muted and without tension despite the horrific acts described. *The Folks* (2001) is a novella about a family harboring a dark secret amid a rash of serial killings. Garton's most recent novel is *Zombie Love* (2003).

A large portion of Garton's short fiction, which is infrequent but almost always exceptional, has been collected in *Methods of Madness* (1990) and *Pieces of Hate* (1996). Among his best at this length are "Monsters" (1988), "Shock Radio" (1990), "Dr. Krusadian's Method" (1991), and "A Night Out with the Boys" (2003). Garton has also published several young adult horror novels as Joseph Locke, of which the best are *Kiss of Death* (1992) and *Vampire Heart* (1994). He has been a reliable but slow-paced contributor of above-average horror novels whose reputation has suffered from the gaps between major novels and the fact that many of his titles are available only from small press imprints.

Gemmell, David A. (1948–)

Only a handful of authors make a lasting impression with their first book, but David Gemmell is one of that elite group. *Legend* (1984, also published as *Against the Horde*) introduced the world of the Drenai, which has been the setting for an intermittent string of related novels ever since, wrapped around other series and stand-alone novels. Drenai is a fairly standard quasi-medieval world, but Gemmell has managed to give it a unique feel of its own and people it with a variety of interesting characters. His heroes are somewhat superior to the ordinary and are reminiscent at times of Robert E. HOWARD's tales of the more mature Conan, a bit weary of the world, more realistic, and resigned to their fates rather than enthusiastic about them.

The early Drenai stories deal primarily with efforts to protect that realm from the constant threats of surrounding barbarian neighbors. The Drenai's difficulties are compounded when their own king goes insane in *The King beyond the Gate* (1985), and his replacement faces a fresh external assault in *Waylander* (1986). Gemmell explores subsidiary stories and alternate viewpoints in the next three books in the series, *Quest for Lost Heroes* (1990), *In the Realm of the Wolf* (1992), and the stories collected in *The First Chronicles of Druss the Legend* (1993). *Druss the Legend* (1994) and *Winter Warriors* (1997) were his last additions to the series for a time, but he returned to the world of the Drenai for *Hero in the Shadows* (2000), which poses a more daunting threat. Passage to another world filled with bestial humans and evil sorcerers has been barred for generations by a magical spell that is now failing. Two recent Drenai novels are both among his best work, *White Wolf* (2003) and *The Swords of Light and Day* (2004). In the first, two ancient heroes are restored to life to save the Drenai, but their mutual animosity makes it difficult for them to work cooperatively. They resolve their differences for a rousing series of adventures in the second.

Ghost King (1988) is set in a troubled kingdom whose ruler has recently died. The queen survives and is using dark sorcery to impose her own rule in her husband's stead. The conflict is resolved in *Last Sword of Power* (1988), although only after a heroic figure escapes from hell itself. *Knights of Dark Renown* (1989) is a singleton and one of the best of Gemmell's early novels. Nine knights are given the magical power to protect the world from evil, but eight have disappeared and the ninth has been unjustly branded a coward. *Morningstar* (1992), also a stand-alone novel, poses the threat of a barbarian army led by rulers who are a kind of vampire race.

Gemmell's second major series began with *Wolf in Shadow* (1987, also published as *The Jerusalem Man*), and continues with *The Last Guardian* (1989) and *Bloodstone* (1994). Ancient horrors threaten the contemporary world in these, and a typical world-weary hero is called upon to defeat them. *Lion of Macedon* (1990) and its sequel, *The Dark Prince* (1990), are set in ancient Greece and involve threats from another magical alternate world. *Ironhand's Daughter* (1995) and *The Hawk Eternal* (1996) similarly describe efforts to unite the feuding Highlander clans into a single force to counter an invasion fueled by sorcery.

Although his more recent novels are in a very similar vein to his early work, Gemmell has become a much more confident and experienced author and one of the most skilled storytellers in modern fantasy. The Rigante novels, *Midnight Falcon* (1999), *Ravenheart* (2001), and *Stormrider* (2002), deal with the conflicts among cultures in a world threatened with barbarism, but superimposed on this greater conflict are more subtle stories of the individual characters, many of whom go through some variation of a rite of passage during their adventures. *Echoes of the Great Song* (1997), set in a postapocalyptic world in which the very laws of nature appear to have changed, is particularly effective in the presentation of its characters and the depiction of an imagined and distinctly original setting. Gemmell is rightly viewed as primarily a writer of adventure stories, but he has used that form to quietly examine issues such as one's individual duty to society at large, the virtues and shortcomings of personal courage, and the need to cooperate in order to survive. He has a reputation for reliable storytelling and intelligent plotting as well as a very clear and accessible narrative style.

Gentle, Mary (1956–)

Although Mary Gentle started her writing career with a traditional fantasy novel, *Hawk in Silver* (1977), she diverged into science fiction for a while, and when she finally returned to fantasy, it was with a very different approach. *Rats and Gargoyles* (1990), the first in the White Crow sequence, is set in a timeless city where intelligent rats rule and humans are slaves. There are forces poised to effect potentially violent change stirring from behind the scenes in this richly detailed, complex novel set in a world distinctly different from anything that had previously appeared in fantasy fiction. The story is many-layered and filled with complex metaphors, but despite the elaborate structure, the story is quite straightforward and appeals to even less-sophisticated readers.

The Architecture of Desire (1991) takes place in a kind of warped Renaissance Europe, where rival magical forces contend for control of the architecture in the city of London, because by doing so they can seize control of the empire and later the world. The specific plot involves medical ethics, the consequences of rape, and the disillusionment of the protagonist. *Grunts* (1992) was considerably less weighty, a humorous tale told from the point of view of an orc soldier who knows not only that he is fighting on the side of evil, but that he is doomed to lose.

Gentle's major recent work is the Ash sequence, published in one volume in England as *Ash: A Secret History* (1997), but split in the United States as *Ash: A Secret History* and *Carthage Ascendant*, both in 2000. *The Wild Machines* (1998) continues the story. The setting is an alternate 15th-century Europe where magic and technology both exist and where the empire of Carthage never fell and now threatens to overwhelm the civilized world. The protagonist is a female mercenary who hears a voice inside her head that she initially believes to be God but later ascribes to more mundane causes. *1610: A Sundial in*

a Grave (2003), Gentle's most recent novel, is also set in an alternate, magical Europe and follows the exploits of an assassin who successfully kills the king of France.

Gentle's short fiction, which is often related to her novels, has been collected in large part in *Left to His Own Devices* (1994) and *Cartomancy* (2004). The quality of her short fiction is, if anything, superior to that of her novels. Of particular note are the title story from the first collection plus "A Harvest of Wolves" (1983), "Anusazi's Daughter" (1984) and the amusing "Orc's Drift" (1997). Gentle is a powerful writer whose often violent themes are designed to support subtle and thoughtful examinations of human interaction.

"The Ghost Ship" Richard Middleton (1912)

Although Richard Middleton's stories, many of which are fantasy, were well received when they first appeared, he was a troubled and insecure man who took his own life while still in his 20s. A few of his stories, including this one, his most famous, were ghost stories, although most were not in the usual tradition. The setting in this case is Fairfield, a small English town that is comfortable with the presence of ghosts, and, in fact, the narrator informs us that he has seen people pass them without a second look since they are so common thereabouts.

One day there is a terrible storm, the winds so powerful that many of the ghosts are blown away and have to spend days traveling back to Fairfield. There is also a ghost ship blown in from the ocean left lying in a field of turnips, although since it has no solid properties it has not done them any harm. But as time passes, the ghost ship remains where it is, and, in fact, it becomes detectably solid. A reconnoiter turns up its captain, Bartholomew Roberts, who apologizes for his unannounced visit but who seems disinclined to leave. His presence seems innocuous at first, but then the villagers begin to notice that all of the ghosts of young men have taken to drink, and the carousing becomes so annoying that the local vicar finally confronts Captain Roberts, who promises to sail off the following night. Another storm arises, and the ship is gone. He takes with him all of the ghostly young men, leaving the ghostly young women heartbroken, and ever after that the turnips grown in that field have a distinct flavor of rum.

Ghost stories in the early 20th century were very serious things, and it was a rare writer who dared poke fun at the convention. Today one is more likely to find ghosts amusing than terrifying, and humorous renditions such as *Topper* (1926) by Thorne SMITH and *The Ghost and Mrs. Muir* (1968) by Alice Denham, both of which became movies, are common. Most of Middleton's fantasy fiction can be found in *The Ghost Ship and Other Stories* (1912).

Ghost Story Peter Straub (1979)

Ghost stories have probably existed since people first began telling tales around a fire. Unlike most horror themes, ghosts have been used by a variety of authors who might not otherwise be associated with the genre. There are ghosts in Shakespeare's *Hamlet*, for example. Henry James gave us THE TURN OF THE SCREW (1898), and Edith Wharton wrote a number of ghost stories, as did Charles Dickens, Rudyard Kipling, and many others. There are ghosts in haunted houses, although not all haunted house stories are, strictly speaking, ghost stories, and they can be found in cemeteries, at the scenes of their deaths, or attached to physical objects. Ghosts come in many forms, usually insubstantial though sometimes capable of moving solid objects and even in a few cases physically manifested and palpable. Some ghosts are friendly, some comical, some neutral, and others positively malevolent.

Most tales of ghosts are short stories, and when they appear in novels their presence is often a peripheral issue or a plot device, part of the setting rather than separate characters. With the possible exception of *The Turn of the Screw* by James or THE BECKONING FAIR ONE by Oliver ONIONS, there is no single ghost story that stands out significantly from among the rest because to a large extent the stories follow a very similar formula. Peter STRAUB, who had written interesting but relatively minor supernatural fiction previously, would create in his long novel *Ghost Story* a crystallization of the form with a contemporary setting. Like many ghost

stories, the novel is about revenge, but the fashion in which the revenge is worked out is unique and frighteningly effective.

As young men, a group of friends become involved with a rather controversial young woman. Internal tensions among them, caused by her flirtations, eventually lead to open conflict, during which she is injured. Believing her to be dead, they conspire to conceal her death by driving her car into a lake, discovering only when it is too late that she was still alive. They swear an oath of secrecy to which they adhere for many years, but eventually she returns, wreaking her vengeance on them and their children. Unlike most ghosts, she can physically interact with the world, walks about in daylight, and can change her appearance. The novel is relentlessly suspenseful and written in a refreshingly intelligent and witty prose style. No other writer has produced a similar story to rival it. A fairly faithful film version was made in 1981.

"The Girl with the Hungry Eyes" Fritz Leiber (1949)

The standard clichés of early horror fiction were creepy castles, graveyards, foggy streets, and locations whose strangeness and unfamiliarity were designed to heighten the sense of uneasiness. Fritz LEIBER had a very different viewpoint. He thought that supernatural events would be even more unsettling if they occurred in familiar settings, and he proved it with numerous stories including *Conjure Wife* (1935), with its depiction of witchcraft in a contemporary urban academic setting, "SMOKE GHOST" (1941), which makes use of an industrial background, and this story, which blends a form of vampirism with advertising and photography.

Leiber's unnamed girl is a fashion model who takes the world by storm. The public is fascinated by her image, particularly her unusual eyes, but strangely uninterested in her background. No one knows who she is, and only the two photographers who have used her as a model have ever seen her in person. Although she appears in a number of photographs, her image has never been drawn or painted, she has never appeared on television or radio, and her background is a complete mystery. The narrator was the first to take her picture, and he was mildly disturbed even the first time he met her, feeling as though something had been taken from him through some invisible means.

To his surprise, several clients want to meet the model, but she refuses to see anyone except him, alone, at his studio. She also will not provide him with a name, address, or telephone number. The girl is completely self-confident and certain that he will comply, and he is unable to summon the courage to refuse the arrangement. Eventually, the mystery becomes too much for him, and he follows her and sees her go off with a man who turns up mysteriously dead the following morning, his heart having apparently just stopped. At last the narrator can resist no longer and insists on leaving with her after a session. She agrees, and that is when he finds out what she really is, a kind of personification of everything that we want but can never get. She subsists by draining away the high points of people's lives, feeding on them until there is nothing left to keep the original owner alive. She is a vampire, but not a traditional one. Indeed, she is far worse because she takes more than just her victims' lives, she takes that which makes them what they are. Although the narrator tears himself away in time to save himself, he never sees her again.

Leiber transformed an old terror, a remnant of the Dark Ages, recreating it as part of the modern world. The girl is everything that dehumanizes us, wrapped in an attractive package, tempting but ultimately unobtainable.

Glory Road Robert A. Heinlein (1963)

Few writers have dominated a field as thoroughly as Robert A. Heinlein once dominated science fiction. He is less well remembered for his occasional fantasies, although even there he was often well ahead of his contemporaries. His novella *Magic Inc.* (1940, also published as *The Devil Makes the Law*) treats magic the way an engineer might design it, narrowly defining the rules by which it operates and making the interaction of those rules the primary source of the conflict. Other fantasy writers such as Lyndon Hardy and Jack L. Chalker adopted similar strategies in their own fantasy. *The Unpleasant Profession of Jonathan Hoag* (1942) was another story typical of *Unknown,* the leading fan-

tasy magazine of its time. The protagonist is an amnesiac who eventually wakens to the realization that he is not a mortal human.

The longest of Heinlein's fantasy stories and his only true fantasy novel is *Glory Road,* a quest adventure that was not favorably received at the time, at least in part because Heinlein was writing something so at variance with what he had previously written. The protagonist is a Vietnam War veteran who is enlisted by Star, a beautiful young woman who proves to be competent and assertive as well. She hires him to help with her quest through multiple universes, anticipating the multiverse concept later used by Michael MOORCOCK and others, searching for the inevitable magical artifact. They encounter and overcome a variety of opponents in the process, including a giant and some dragons, and the adventure, while rousing and well written, is narrated in a light and sometimes humorous manner.

The novel is one of the last of Heinlein's works that avoids lecturing the reader about one or another of Heinlein's pet causes. The sexual content would be considered tame by today's standards—consisting mostly of innuendoes and double entendres—but was relatively daring for genre fiction of its time. Although often dismissed as an anomaly, it is certainly Heinlein's most underrated novel and probably influenced in some small way the explosion of similar quest fantasies that would begin to appear a few years later.

"A Gnome There Was" Henry Kuttner (1941)

Tim Crockett, the well-intentioned but badly misguided do-gooder protagonist of this charming story, sneaks into a coal mine disguised as a miner to investigate working conditions. He foolishly wanders into an area where explosives are in use and is nearly killed, surviving only when he is trapped in what remains of a long-abandoned tunnel. His initial panic becomes even greater when he discovers that he has been magically transformed into the physical shape of a gnome, with short legs and an oversized head.

Almost immediately Gru Magru arrives, a veteran gnome who impatiently explains the facts of life to Crockett. Gnomes cannot reproduce themselves normally, so they watch for miners who stray away and doom themselves, using magic to transform these unfortunates into members of their own species. If fairies can steal babies, then gnomes can steal adults, particularly those who were in any case doomed otherwise to die. There are compensations, for gnomes are immortal, but there is a down side as well, since gnomes must remain forever underground and hidden from humans.

There are lots of amusing tidbits in the story. For example, the first emperor of the gnomes was unaccountably Podrang the Third, whose descendant is Podrang the Second. Most of the humor results from reversals. The gnomes bathe in mud, and cheating in a fight is admirable rather than dishonorable. Crockett is put to work mining anthracite, and before long he is involved in organizing the other gnomes into a union. Unfortunately, his fellow strikers would rather fight than do almost anything, and even more unfortunately, Podrang is a magician who casts spells that turn his enemies into a variety of different creatures. Crockett plots to submit to a spell restoring his humanity, but his plans go awry. He ends up in the form of an even more repulsive creature.

This type of lightly humorous, implausible fantasy was typical of the leading fantasy magazine of the 1940s, *Unknown*. Henry KUTTNER wrote several similar stories, probably with his wife, C. L. Moore, as an uncredited collaborator, but this is his single best and one of his most widely known tales.

"God Grante That She Lye Still" Lady Cynthia Asquith (1942)

Cynthia Asquith, who was for a time secretary to J. M. BARRIE, the author of *PETER PAN*, is best remembered for the anthologies of ghost stories she edited as well as for some of her own short tales, which were primarily ghost stories involving some form of possession. This particular story is not only an unusually impressive work but one of the most effective and convincing stories of supernatural possession ever written.

The narrator is Dr. John Stone, newly arrived in the area. One of Stone's patients is Margaret Clewer, a beautiful young woman whose family has lived in the same house for many generations. Stone, who is interested in gravestone inscriptions, visits the family cemetery and notices the phrase from which the title is taken on the grave of one of Margaret's ancestors. The motivation for the epigraph puzzles him, but he dismisses it until much later.

Stone is fascinated by Clewer, whose health is not good, and eventually falls in love with her. She has a psychological quirk that disturbs him, for she believes herself to be without any real personality, as though she were an empty vessel waiting to be filled. Margaret is also drawn to the graveyard and has chosen a bedroom that overlooks it. She complains of dreams in which she has a vision of her own face looking at her and eventually develops a habit of sleepwalking. More incidents follow. Her pet birds are killed mysteriously, and her loyal dog no longer recognizes her. Stone finds her sleeping in the graveyard one night, lying on the same grave he had noticed earlier.

Eventually he discovers old documents that pertain to the dead woman that imply that she was evil and wished to conquer death. Although he does not believe in the supernatural, it is clear that Margaret's personality is, in fact, altered at times, as though two different people were at war within her body. She has arguments with herself during the night, her handwriting is inconsistent, and her personal habits begin to change. Ultimately, Margaret repels the invader, her own ancestor, but the struggle is too much for her frail constitution and she dies. As the last of her line, presumably this precludes any further attempt by the dead woman to return to the world of the living. There is very little melodrama in the story, and the gradually escalating conflict is entirely psychological and very effectively done.

Godwin, Parke (1929–)

Parke Godwin began writing fiction during the 1970s, starting with a mystery story that had supernatural overtones, *Darker Places* (1973), then writing science fiction short stories and a novel in that field with Marvin Kaye. He started to turn to fantasy in earnest in 1980 with *Firelord*, which retells the story of King Arthur without most of the unrealistic trappings of the legend, describing him as a flawed but noble man faced with a difficult job. The fantasy element is primarily associated with his mortal enemy, Morgana, who derives her magical powers from the fairies. *Beloved Exile* (1984) is an interesting attempt to extend the story after the death of Arthur, chronicling the efforts by Guinevere to hold the splintering kingdom together in his absence. The two novels provide an unusually original rethinking of the story of King Arthur. Godwin returned to that setting for *The Last Rainbow* (1985), in which a Christian priest travels to the land of the Celts, hoping to convert them, and discovers that not only do the natives still worship the pagan gods, but that magic is real and an important part of their culture.

Godwin wrote a second trio of novels based on the legend of Robin Hood that are even less fantastic and amount to historical novels about events that never took place. The three titles are *Sherwood* (1991), *Robin and the King* (1993), and *Return to Nottingham* (1993). *The Tower of Beowulf* (1995) is based on the Norse legend and covers the early life of Beowulf, his training as a warrior, the culture that produced him, his battle against Grendel, who dies midway through the book, and his subsequent alienation from his own people. *The Lovers* (1999) is a retelling of the story of Tristan and Iseulde and is Godwin's weakest novel.

Several of Godwin's early short stories involve the supernatural, and most of these were collected in *The Fire When It Comes* (1984), which won the World Fantasy Award as best collection. *A Cold Blue Light* (1983), written in collaboration with Marvin Kaye, is a sort of haunted house story without ghosts but with plenty of supernatural events anyway. *A Truce with Time* (1988) involves ghosts but is basically a humorous love story whose plot is enlivened by the pranks of the mischievous spirits. Many writers have written novel-length retellings of legendary stories, but few have done so as skillfully and intelligently as has Parke Godwin.

Goingback, Owl (1959–   )

Owl Goingback began producing short fiction in 1993 and sold half a dozen stories before his first novel appeared. The most remarkable of his short tales from this period is "The Spoils of War" (1993). His popularity soared following the publication of his first novel, *Crota* (1996), which won the Bram Stoker Award for first novel and was also a finalist for another as best novel altogether. A prehistoric creature is freed from an underground cavern by an earthquake and begins preying on people in the area. Its destruction is made more difficult by the fact that it has an intelligence to rival our own and is immensely more powerful. With the help of a medicine man, the protagonists finally track it to its underground lair for some particularly suspenseful sequences in an abandoned ruin.

Shaman Moon (1997) appeared in the omnibus *The Essential World of Darkness* and has never been published alone. It is the story of a young orphan who escapes a brutal institution and is subsequently befriended by a shaman who realizes that she has the potential to be a guardian of a mystical gateway between worlds. When a legion of supernatural creatures make a subsequent attempt to invade our world, they are thwarted only when she acknowledges and masters her abilities. The idea that our world interfaces with another is repeated in *Darker Than Night* (1999). The protagonist in this case is a horror writer who inherits a house from the grandmother he believed was unbalanced in her belief that she was harried by inhuman creatures, but he discovers that she was right after he moves into her home and has a similar experience.

Evil Whispers (2001) is less interesting, an unremarkable possession story mixed with voodoo. *Breed* (2002) is considerably better, another story of the thinning of a border between realities. Three would-be witches inadvertently stumble on a genuine magical spell, unwisely open a doorway, and allow a malevolent, shape-changing creature to enter our reality. Goingback consistently demonstrates exceptional writing skills, although individual scenes from his novels are often more memorable than the main plot. He frequently draws on his Native American heritage to good effect and is one of the more skillful horror writers in crafting his characters. He has also written two children's books.

Golden, Christie (1963–   )

A short-lived subset of the role-playing-game–related fiction produced by TSR publications was the Ravenloft series, which was set in a Gothic fantasy world where vampires, werewolves, and other supernatural creatures were the dominant themes rather than elves, fairies, and unicorns. Although the series lasted only a few years and produced less than two dozen titles, they were generally much more interesting than the publisher's standard line of Tolkienesque fantasy adventures. The very first novel in that setting was also the first published book by Christie Golden, *Vampire of the Mists* (1991). Two vampires battle each other, one originally human, one originally an elf, in a world that suggests our own historical past. Golden returned to Ravenloft for a second novel, *Dance of the Dead* (1992), a much more interesting novel. A singer aboard a riverboat fights for her life when the ship stops at an island inhabited by the living dead.

The Enemy Within (1994) was in much the same vein, borrowing from Robert Louis Stevenson's DR. JEKYLL AND MR. HYDE (1886). A benevolent aristocrat lives with a terrible secret. Periodically he is transformed physically and mentally into an evil version of himself, and the struggle between his two personalities is moving toward a climax. *Instrument of Fate* (1996) is more conventional fantasy, emphasizing adventure rather than atmosphere. A wandering minstrel has episodic adventures among elves and demons in what is a competent but lightweight story. *King's Man and Thief* (1997) was considerably better. A plague of madness caused by uncontrolled magic is troubling a fantasy realm until a heroic figure arises to find a solution and defeat the forces of evil.

Golden's most recent fantasy novel is *On Fire's Wings* (2004), a fantasy romance and a somewhat convoluted story about a young girl employed as a servant who is actually the illegitimate child of the local tribal leader. The situation grows even more complex when she develops paranormal powers. Golden has also written several *Star Trek* novels and occasional short stories, of which "Stag Party" (1996) and "Summer Storms" (1996) are the two most interesting. It is not yet clear how significant a figure Golden might become in the fantasy genre, but there are definite indications of increasing maturity as a writer.

Golden, Christopher (1967–)

Christopher Golden, who should not be confused with fellow fantasy and horror writer Christie Golden, began writing professionally in the middle of the 1990s and quickly established himself as a prolific writer of fast-paced, well-plotted supernatural adventure stories. His first horror novel, *Of Saints and Sinners* (1994), turns the vampire story format head over heels. The villains are a militant secret society within the Catholic Church who hunt down vampires using demons and banshees to assist them, and some of the vampires are rather admirable. Golden has subsequently written three more novels using this setting, *Angel Souls and Devil Hearts* (1998), *Of Masques and Martyrs* (1998), and *The Gathering Dark* (2003). A later, somewhat similar series began with *The Prowlers* (2001), in which a ghost helps his living friends track down and battle a race of werewolvish creatures who have taken up residence in Boston. That series continues in *Laws of Nature* (2001), *Predator and Prey* (2001), and *Wild Things* (2002) and does a much more thorough job of developing its characters.

Strangewood (1999) is less overtly adventurous and more atmospheric. A writer of children's books discovers that the fantasy world he thought he had created is real and that his son's spirit has been kidnapped by its inhabitants. *Straight on 'Til Morning* (2001) uses a similar device when a teenaged boy becomes suspicious after the girl he admires finds a new boyfriend, and eventually he has to rescue her from an alternate reality where magic works. *The Ferryman* (2002) is a traditional but very suspenseful ghost story. His best single novel is *The Boys Are Back in Town* (2004), in which a man attends his high school reunion and discovers that his memories of the past are at decided odds with those of other attendees, so he decides to find out which version is the truth.

Golden is currently collaborating on two series with Thomas E. Sniegoski. The Menagerie sequence consists so far of *The Nimble Man* (2004) and *The Tears of the Furies* (2005) and involves an alliance of supernatural creatures against an evil force. The Outcast series includes *The Un-Magician* (2004), *Dragon Secrets* (2004), and *Ghostfire* (2005) and is a straightforward fantasy world adventure for a slightly younger audience.

Golden has also written a large number of tie-in novels to the television series *Buffy the Vampire Slayer*, most of them in collaboration with Nancy Holder. He is also a very active author of comic book scripts as well as the young adult suspense series Body of Evidence. Although the quality of his work fluctuates considerably, his least interesting works are still quite readable, and his best are exceptional. He is a very infrequent short story writer, but "The Pyre" (2004) is quite good.

The Golden Compass Philip Pullman (1995)

The opening volume of the His Dark Materials trilogy, published in England as *Northern Lights*, is a complex and rewarding fantasy novel inspired in part by John Milton's *Paradise Lost*. The protagonist is Lyra Belacqua, later known as Lyra Silvertongue, an 11-year-old orphan living in Oxford, England, although not in our universe. She lives in a reality where everyone is born with a demon companion, not an evil demon but an animus, which has a malleable shape at first, growing into its final form as the human to whom it is bonded matures.

The complex plot picks up very quickly. Lyra is the ward of Baron Asniel, who arrives at Oxford on mysterious business having to do with the apparition of a city suspended in the Aurora Borealis. Lyra is instrumental in averting an assassination attempt aimed at her guardian thanks to the aid of Pantalaimon, her personal demon, more familiarly known as Pan. She overhears references to the Dust, a mystery with which the Baron is seriously concerned. When he is called away, she is left in the custody of the enigmatic Mrs. Coulter, who will prove to be one of the most complex characters in the trilogy.

Lyra feels compelled to act when her best friend, Roger, becomes yet another in a series of children who have disappeared under mysterious circumstances, taken away perhaps by the menacing gobblers, about whom little is known. Her pursuit takes her into the Arctic, where she encounters witchcraft as well as an intelligent race of bears who are armoring themselves for war. It is a war that is coming, after all, a war in heaven that is reflected on Earth, or in many parallel Earths as we eventually discover. Lyra also has the advantage of

possessing a magical device that detects falsehoods and dispenses advice.

The novel is richly textured and is sometimes criticized as being too subtle and complex for younger readers, although that does not seem to have prevented large numbers of them from enjoying it and its sequels. The subject matter also generated some controversy because of its portrayal of elements within the church as being thoughtless or even outright evil. PULLMAN seems to be indicting no particular faith or institution, however, as much as opposing the maintenance of any power structure through the enforced ignorance of those subject to its will. He also avoids the relentlessly cheerful atmosphere found in much lesser young adult fantasy. His characters experience guilt and deep distress, some of them die unjustly, and the line of demarcation between good and evil is not always readily apparent. The trilogy continues with THE SUBTLE KNIFE and concludes with THE AMBER SPYGLASS.

Goldstein, Lisa (1953–)

Lisa Goldstein made her impressive writing debut with a novel, *The Red Magician* (1982), set in a version of eastern Europe where magic works. The setting is a rural Jewish community beset by demonic figures and caught up in the conflict between two wizards, one of whom has had a precognitive vision of World War II. This clever and emotionally powerful short novel won the American Book Award, although it was not as highly regarded in genre circles. Goldstein's second novel, *The Dream Years* (1985), is, if anything, even better. A novelist from the 1920s is magically transported forward through time to the 1960s, where he participates in the cloistered literary community of that decade, whose work is inspired by that of the protagonist's own time. The barrier between different time zones begins to erode, at least for the principle characters, in a novel filled with dry humor and an excellent description of a very circumscribed community.

Tourists (1989), expanded from the short story of the same title, is an almost surrealistic tale about a family who move to an imaginary foreign country and discover much about themselves through their exploration of their new environment. By now

Goldstein was well established as a major literary fantasist whose work could not be loosely fit into a predefined category or easily described, but the complexity and originality of her work may have discouraged more casual readers. *Strange Devices of the Sun and Moon* (1993) moved closer to mainstream fantasy, using a historical setting with a magical overlay. During the reign of Elizabeth I, the queen of the fairies and her entourage travel to London in search of her missing son.

The god of summer becomes so fond of living in the world of humanity in *Summer King, Winter Fool* (1994) that he refuses to return to the sky to change the seasons, plunging the world into an eternal winter. *Walking the Labyrinth* (1995) follows the adventures of a woman whose investigation of certain fantastic events rumored to have happened to family members leads to her pursuit by a mysterious organization. The best of her recent novels is *Dark Cities Underground* (1999), in which an investigation into the life of a fantasy writer reveals that many of the incidents he related actually occurred. Her most recent novel, *The Alchemist's Door* (2002), is also excellent, a historical fantasy in which John Dee travels to Prague and becomes involved in the construction of the fabulous golem.

Goldstein has produced a small but steady stream of excellent short stories along with her novels, including "Daily Voices" (1986), "Breadcrumbs and Stones" (1993), and "Finding Beauty" (2004). The majority of these have been collected in *Daily Voices* (1989) and *Travelers in Magic* (1994). Goldstein generally avoids the traditional settings and plots of fantasy and uses magic and other fantastic elements as a way to reexamine aspects of human behavior that exist independently of time or place. She has also written some science fiction that deals with very similar themes.

Goodkind, Terry (1948–   )

By the middle of the 1990s, publishers were suddenly realizing that traditional fantasy adventures were drawing very large audiences, and a host of brand new writers were introduced who had no previous experience writing fiction but who could turn out one large epic adventure after another, usually grouped in trilogies or even longer series. A case in point is Terry Goodkind, whose first published work was *Wizard's First Rule* (1994) and who has not left that setting for any of his next eight novels. His only short work, a novella, is actually a prequel to his main series. The title refers to a series of "rules" that are actually witticisms and not rules at all.

The opening novel introduces Richard Rahl, who believes himself to be a humble villager but who finds out otherwise when the magical barrier protecting his people from an unspecified evil menace begins to fail. The author had apparently not thought out his background very thoroughly, because it is often inconsistent. No one in the village has any recollection of what lies on the other side, for example, even though the barrier was erected in living memory. Rahl rescues the beautiful Kahlan Amnell from a band of assassins and discovers that she is the last of her order, a kind of magically powered police force from beyond the barrier, and that her kind has been nearly exterminated by the minions of a powerful evil wizard, who turns out to be Richard's father. A wise but cranky hermit friend is later revealed to be Richard's grandfather and protector as well as the most powerful wizard who ever lived, maybe.

The Sword of Truth series continues with *Stone of Tears* (1995). Although the evil wizard is dead and Richard rules in his place, death does not necessarily preclude the villain from meddling in the affairs of the living. *Blood of the Fold* (1996) introduces a new villain, an emperor who can exert power through people's dreams and whose followers are fanatically loyal and apparently exist in uncountable numbers. Goodkind routinely expands and reinvents his world for each new book, regardless of how well it meshes with what he has previously established. *Temple of the Winds* (1997) continues in the same vein, with a storehouse of magical artifacts caught between the forces of good and those of evil.

Soul of the Fire (1999) and *Faith of the Fallen* (2000) continue the bedevilment of the two lover protagonists, who are separated once again as another megalomaniac seeks to rule the world. *Debt of Bones* (2001) is a novella that describes the final battles in the war that ended with the erection of the magical barrier. There is an endless winter and a new army of conquest in *Pillars of Creation* (2001), a search for the antidote to a deadly poison in *Naked Empire* (2003), and mass selective amnesia in *Chainfire* (2004).

Goodkind has undeniable storytelling skills and a talent for inventing detailed and interesting societies, but it is likely that much of the popularity of the series results from the pervasive sexual undertones and the frequency of sadomasochistic scenes in which characters of both sexes are tortured and/or humiliated, sometimes in excruciating detail. The characters have little depth and a confusing morality that sometimes results in heroes performing acts every bit as heinous as those of the villains, sometimes with no apparent justification. Goodkind's fantasy world has been revealed in great chunks in successive books, not all of which seem in harmony with what has gone before. Despite his present popularity, he has yet to produce anything that would ensure continued interest in his work in the years to come.

"The Gorgon" Tanith Lee (1983)

Some of the most bizarre creatures in Greek mythology are the Gorgons, Medusa and her sisters, who sported snakes for hair and whose faces were so repulsive that their gaze turned living men into stone. Tanith LEE, who often draws her imagery from myths and legends, invokes the Gorgons in a very different fashion in this highly acclaimed story, using a contemporary setting.

The narrator is a writer visiting the island of Daphaeu off the coast of Greece. Shortly after arriving, he notices a smaller island nearby and inquires about it, but the local people will not discuss it except obliquely and warningly. Even generous bribes are not sufficient to convince anyone to take him there. Eventually, he provokes one into talking about why they avoid the subject, a young man who insists that it is home to "the cunning one," a term historically applied to Medusa. The writer is understandably skeptical, but his curiosity has become so intense that he decides to swim across the narrow channel and investigate on his own.

He does so the following day and discovers that there is a single house on the island, a contemporary structure where he is warned off by an angry servant. The woman who owns the house emerges and invites him in, and he accepts her invitation, noting that she has a peculiar voice and manner of speaking. He is also intrigued by the fact that she wears an elaborate mask that completely covers her face. Although he apparently never seriously considers that she might actually be a Gorgon, the reader is less certain, particularly when she makes no effort to explain it.

The story builds slowly to a climax in which the reader expects the protagonist to discover that he is in mortal danger, but in due course we learn the truth. The woman is in fact a kind of Gorgon, but a natural one. A nerve disease has left her face twisted into a horribly distorted expression and damaged her vocal chords as well. When he swims back to the main island the following morning, the protagonist has realized the truth, that rather than suffering from embarrassment because of her condition, the woman was contemptuous of him for the ease of his life. He has not accomplished anything significant because he has never had to overcome great adversity. That realization has left him emotionally stunned, metaphorically turned to stone, and he wonders if the original legend started in much the same fashion.

Goudge, Elizabeth (1900–1984)

The British novelist Elizabeth Goudge is best known for her nonfantasy work, which includes well known novels such as *Green Dolphin Street* (1944), *Pilgrim's Inn* (1948), and *The Heart of the Country* (1953). Her adult fantasies are not very well known. *The White Witch* (1958) involves incidents of genuine witchcraft set in the middle of the 17th century, while *The Middle Window* (1935) is a story of reincarnation in which two lovers gradually become aware of their previous lives together and come to the conclusion that they are fated to suffer very similar disappointments and separation in their new lives.

Goudge's fantasies for children are somewhat better remembered, particularly *The Little White Horse* (1946), in which a remote castle contains gateways to other worlds and times through which people from the present can secretly observe. A new arrival helps lift a mild family curse through use of the castle's special qualities. The book won the Carnegie Medal for children's literature. Other fantasies for young readers include *Smoky House* (1940), which involves fairies, and *Linnets and Valerians* (1964), an underrated story in which a group of children discover yet another gateway to other realities, one through which some quite nasty entities are planning to infest our world. Goudge often used images from fantasy or legends in her nonfantastic work as well.

Grant, Charles L. (1942–)

The explosion of modern horror novels that followed the success of Stephen KING provided a market for a large number of writers of varying qualities, most of whom wrote straightforward supernatural thrillers that varied in plot and sometimes style, but only within a fairly narrowly defined range. A handful of others chose to develop a distinctive prose style, such as Thomas LIGOTTI, and others specialized in a particular kind of story, such as, for example, John SAUL's many tales of vengeful child ghosts. One small group opted for extremely explicit horror, aiming to shock and even revolt as well as thrill the reader, and writers such as John SKIPP and Craig Spector became well-known proponents of what was termed "splatterpunk," deriving its name from splatter films. On the opposite end of the spectrum was Charles L. Grant, whose name became associated with quiet horror because he rarely resorted to the extremely visceral style of the splatterpunks, instead concentrating on subtle development of atmosphere and the power of suggestion.

Grant began publishing science fiction and occasional horror stories in 1968 and during the early 1970s produced some very memorable short pieces, including "Come Dance with Me on My Pony's Grave" (1973), but his first few novels were science fiction. It was not until 1977 that his first horror novel, *The Curse* (1977), finally appeared. He also included some minor fantastic content in *The Eve of the Hound* (1977) and *Voices out of Time* (1977), two of four Gothic suspense novels he published using the pen name Deborah Lewis. That same year also brought *The Hour of the Oxrun Dead*, the first of more than a dozen novels and short stories Grant set in Oxrun Station, a fictional New England town that seems to function as a magnet for evil. The widow of a police officer whose body was badly mutilated during a fatal attack draws the ire of a group of satanists. Grant's characteristic care not to "rub the reader's nose" in the details of the horrible events taking place would quickly become his trademark.

There is another religious cult in Oxrun Station in *The Sound of Midnight* (1978) worshipping a twisted and malevolent god of their own and sacrificing innocent lives to propitiate their deity. The best of the early Oxrun Station novels is *The Last Call of Mourning* (1979). The protagonist is a young woman who finds her father's dead body but a short time later discovers that he is apparently alive and well. There have been other disappearances and reappearances in town in recent days, and her investigation leads her to a man who seems to have the power to raise the dead as his servants.

Grant, who was also writing mildly fantastic romance novels as Felicia Andrews by now, next appeared under his own name with *The Grave* (1981), which features another subtle horror preying on the inhabitants of Oxrun Station. That same year saw the appearance of his first two collections of short fiction, *A Glow of Candles and Other Stories* and *Tales from the Nightside,* both of which drew primarily on his supernatural tales. From this point onward Grant's only significant science fiction was a series of young adult novels under the name Steven Charles.

With *The Nestling* (1982) Grant proved that he could write longer and potentially more generally popular horror novels. In this case the tensions between Native Americans and the surrounding communities provides a realistic backdrop to the story of a mysterious flying creature that preys on humans. A third collection followed, *Nightmare Seasons* (1982), which won the World Fantasy Award, as well as a new Oxrun Station novel, *The Bloodwind* (1982), in which a supernatural beast is linked to the rising of the wind. *The Soft Whisper of the Dead* (1982) was the first of three historical horror novels, also set in Oxrun Station, this one featuring a vampire. The other two in the sequence are *The Dark Cry of the Moon* (1986), a werewolf story, and *The Long Night of the Grave* (1986), which features a mummy.

Grant moved away from Oxrun Station for most of his subsequent novels and stories. *Night Songs* (1984) is set on an island that is beleaguered by supernatural forces from the ocean. *The Tea Party* (1985) is set in a somewhat similar town and contains some insidiously creepy passages involving a series of stone walls that are not always in the same place. *The Orchard* (1986) is one of Oxrun Station's bad places, and things get worse when its power begins to extend outside the immediate vicinity. There is a serial killer in *The Pet* (1986), but Grant takes the overdone idea and adds a new dimension to it, proving that there are even worse things in the world than a homicidal maniac.

Grant's list of pseudonyms was growing. As Lionel Fenn he wrote four lightly humorous fantasies, three of them in the White Duck series. As Geoffrey Marsh he created the Lionel Blackthorne series, four novels featuring a not entirely serious two-fisted hero whose job is to track down magical artifacts and wrest them away from a variety of foes, human and otherwise. The final book in the series, *The Fangs of the Hooded Demon* (1988), is particularly good. The horror boom had already begun to fade by the late 1980s, but Grant had no difficulty attracting readers and continued to avoid the excesses of some of his contemporaries. *For Fear of the Night* (1987), for example, was an extremely effective traditional ghost story, and *Dialing the Wind* (1989), an Oxrun Station novel, does an excellent job of describing the mystery of how some unusual music controls the secret of several lives. Grant's weakest novel, *In a Dark Dream* (1989), is still noticeably more polished than those of most of his fellow horror writers.

Grant opened the 1990s with a pair of solid new titles, *Something Stirs* (1991) and *Stunts* (1991), but it was obvious that the collapse of the horror market was affecting even the most talented writers in the field. Grant began writing horror stories for young adults, starting with *Fire Mask* (1991), which avoided the usual tendency to write down to a supposedly less sophisticated audience that mars most young adult fiction. Grant continued in this vein as Simon Lake, as well as writing two unusually good tie-in novels to the *X-Files*

television program, *Goblins* (1994) and *Whirlwind* (1995). He revived the Lionel Fenn name to write humorous novels of the fantastic featuring Kent Montana, of which *The Mark of the Moderately Vicious Vampire* (1992) and *666: The Neighbor of the Beast* (1992) are the two most entertaining. *Jackals* (1994) is somewhat disappointing, but *The Black Carousel* (1995), another Oxrun Station novel, represents Grant at the top of his form.

Grant's most recent novels of the supernatural have been marketed and packaged differently and have been grouped into two separate series. *Symphony* (1997), *In the Mood* (1998), *Chariot* (1998), and *Riders in the Sky* (1999) make up the Millennium Quartet. The apocalypse is about to come upon the world, and the forces of good and evil are recruiting allies for the battle to come. The series is Grant's most ambitious and in some ways most interesting project. A second series is in the tradition of the psychic detective story. The Black Oak mysteries include *Genesis* (1998), *The Hush of Dark Wings* (1999), *Winter Knight* (1999), *Hunting Ground* (2000), and *When the Cold Wind Blows* (2001). The protagonists battle ghosts, vampires, and werewolves, but Grant always provides an original twist, avoiding the clichés of each of the classic horror monsters.

His short fiction is of consistently high quality, although he has won only one award, the World Fantasy Award for "Confess the Seasons" (1983). He also won the World Fantasy Award for editing the Shadows series of original horror anthologies. Grant also edited four anthologies with the shared setting of Greystone Bay and several other collections of short horror fiction, all of which are highly regarded. Without much of the fanfare that surrounds many big-name authors, Grant has become and remains one of the most significant modern horror writers.

"Graves" Joe Haldeman (1992)

The science fiction writer Joe Haldeman drew upon his own experiences during the war in Vietnam for a rare excursion into the world of the supernatural in this short but effective story, which won the World Fantasy Award as well as the Nebula Award presented by the Science Fiction and

Fantasy Writers of America. The narrator works for Graves Registration, an organization within the U.S. military that retrieves, identifies, and provides for the disposition of the bodies of servicemen killed in foreign conflicts.

Under ordinary circumstances the protagonist never leaves his base and processes bodies that have already been removed from combat areas. On rare occasions, if there is a suspicion that the death was a murder rather than a combat fatality or if there are unusual circumstances, he is sent into the field. That is the situation as this story begins, and he and his supervisor are sent to a dangerous remote firebase to examine the body of a naked Vietnamese man. The body displays unusual mutilations, although it is generally intact, dried by the heat into a kind of mummy. Their efforts to examine it further come to a halt when they come under enemy fire, and the major accompanying them is instantly killed.

The firefight lasts through the night, ending only when aircraft arrive to drive the enemy away. Once the situation has stabilized, they set out to recover the major's body, only to discover that it has been horribly mutilated as though some creature feasted on his flesh and drank his blood. Even more unsettling is the disappearance of the mummified body that was their reason for being on-site in the first place. Although the narrator suggests possible rational explanations, he admits that they are extremely unlikely and that he has been troubled ever since by nightmares. Haldeman delivers a chilling tale of the supernatural even though there is no overt fantastic content, suggesting just enough to stimulate the imagination of his readers. The contrast between the presumed horror surrounding the body and the more familiar horror of chaotic warfare is particularly effective.

"The Graveyard Rats" Henry Kuttner (1936)

Although he is best known for his science fiction and fantasy, Henry KUTTNER wrote several horror stories early in his career, many of them in imitation of the work of H. P. LOVECRAFT. The best of his horror stories is this short tale of a cemetery caretaker turned grave robber who gets his just desserts. Masson has recently been hired because

his predecessor disappeared under mysterious circumstances that are probably explained by his own subsequent fate. Masson hates the rats that live in tunnels under the cemetery because they have a habit of chewing their way into the coffins and making off with the bodies, including any jewelry or gold teeth that Masson might have purloined himself. His efforts to exterminate them all fail, and he continues to be amazed by their size and ferocity. Their tunnels, for example, are large enough for a grown man to crawl through.

When he digs up a particularly valuable coffin just as the rats are carrying away its contents, Masson snaps. With a revolver in his pocket, he feels brave enough and angry enough to go after them, so he begins crawling through the tunnel, ever deeper into the earth, only beginning to reconsider when he grows tired and senses that there is something very large moving in the distance, perhaps some dark intelligence that is directing the activities of the lesser rats. Then he stumbles across a rotting corpse that is nevertheless somehow animated and realizes that something distinctly uncanny is happening. Panicking, he discovers next that he does not have room to turn around and must back out all the way to the surface. The rats pursue despite his efforts to drive them off with his weapon, and he attempts to take refuge in a side corridor, blocking the entrance by collapsing part of the roof. He realizes only when it is too late that he is inside a coffin, not a through passage, and that he is effectively buried alive.

Kuttner's story is filled with frightening images—the animated dead, oversized intelligent rats, and the claustrophobic descent through the tunnels. He packs a variety of strong images into an efficiently small story. Although not credited, the story was probably the inspiration for the movie *The Dark* (1993).

"The Great God Pan" Arthur Machen (1890)

Although he turned away from supernatural fiction almost entirely after the turn of the century, the Welsh writer Arthur MACHEN wrote a fairly large number of fantastic tales early in his career and remains highly regarded, although perhaps more because of his seniority than for his actual stories, most of which are only intermittently available. The best and most famous of his dark fantasies is "The Great God Pan," which mixes a subtle supernatural theme with suggestive sexual references quite unusual at the time, all conveyed in a rather complex story structure.

The tale opens with Dr. Raymond revealing to his friend Clarke his plan to operate on a financially dependent young woman to allow her to look on an aspect of the world that is invisible to the rest of us. That vision includes Pan, the satyr, a figure that had changed with the advent of Christianity from that of a playful manifestation of nature to a carnal and even frighteningly evil creature, perhaps an aspect of Satan himself. The experiment is a success, but the woman, Mary, is driven mad almost immediately and never recovers her wits. Machen provides plenty of foreshadowing and several allusions to the days of Roman Britain to strengthen the reader's awareness that something pre-Christian is taking place.

The story then jumps several years into the future. A gentleman's chance encounter with an old friend reveals that something bizarre is happening. The friend married a young woman named Helen, whom he blames for all of his subsequent misfortunes, including his bankruptcy and moral ruin. The man dies shortly afterward, and the mysterious Helen has disappeared. A second inexplicable death took place near their former home, and they were suspected of being involved in the crime, although never charged. Then London society becomes preoccupied with a newcomer, Mrs. Beaumont, whose parties are much in demand. At the same time, a wave of suicides is troubling the citizens of London, although no one realizes until quite late that all of the victims were recent visitors to Mrs. Beaumont's house.

Villiers, who belatedly emerges as the story's protagonist, suspects some portion of the truth and is determined to confront the woman. We learn in the final pages that she is also Helen, which should have been obvious to most readers, and is the daughter of Mary, who was made pregnant during that instant when she was sane and could look upon Pan's face. The specific acts she uses to drive men to suicide and despair are not described but

are almost certainly sexual in nature. Discovered, she takes her own life, bringing the cycle of destruction to an end. The story delivers a clear message, one that would later be common in science fiction, that there are some things in the world that humankind was not meant to know, or in this case, see. The complex story structure, which changes protagonists several times, is reasonably well done, and the transitions are quite smooth. The secret might seem rather tame by contemporary standards, but it was quite daring for the late 19th century.

Green, Sharon (1942–)

Sharon Green began writing professionally in 1982, and for the first several years her output was exclusively science fiction, although the plots and treatment were so similar to fantasy that fans of the latter should enjoy her earlier work as well. Her first actual fantasy was *The Far Side of Forever* (1987), a novel of multiple worlds that can be accessed through portals. A team of adventurers sets out to recover a stolen magical artifact that is essential to the continued stability of their particular universe. Green later added a less interesting sequel, *Hellhound Magic* (1989), a magical search and rescue operation. Her second fantasy novel, *Lady Blade, Lord Fighter* (1987), is considerably more sophisticated. A young woman secretly trains herself as an expert with a sword, a skill she puts to good use after she returns home to find her brothers missing and herself betrothed to a man she despises. The subsequent intrigues and action sequences are very well handled. *Dawn Song* (1990) blended elements from her previous novels, mixing a quest story uneasily with another set of political intrigues. *Werewolf Moon* (1993) is quite atypical for the author, a supernatural romance novel whose protagonist is drawn to a mysterious man who may or may not be a werewolf.

The Hidden Realms (1993) launched a series of five novels, the premise of which is that there are entire worlds lying concealed within one another and that inhabitants of these hidden universes may at times emerge to spread their influence into the larger realms. A shape-changing princess and an arrogant mercenary are forced to rise above their petty differences in the second volume, *Silver Princess, Golden Knight* (1993), but they end up married in *Dark Mirror, Dark Dreams* (1994). They have successfully repelled the intruders and gained the throne in *Wind Whispers, Shadow Shouts* (1995) but predictably discover that it is not easy to rule a troubled kingdom. The thwarted forces of evil have to be confronted once more in *Game's End* (1996).

Convergence (1996) is the opening volume in the Blending series, which treats the same premise, invaders from another reality, in slightly different fashion. Five individuals, each schooled in a different form of magic, must combine their talents to meet the threat, which they do over the course of *Competitions* (1997), *Challenges* (1998), *Betrayals* (1999), and *Prophecy* (1999). Their number is expanded for further adventures in *Intrigues* (2000), *Deceptions* (2001), and *Destiny* (2002). The Blending series is more original than the Hidden Realms sequence but is sometimes slow paced and repetitive.

Enchanting (1994) is an above-average fantasy romance with a cleverly constructed plot, and *Haughty Spirit* (1999), in which a goddess is forced to become mortal, is often quite funny. Green's occasional short stories are mostly minor contributions to one shared world series or another, but "And the Truth Shall Set You Free" (1989) is memorable.

Green, Simon R. (1955–)

Simon R. Green started writing fantasy with the Hawk and Fisher series, whose two protagonists, though a couple, are often reminiscent of those of the FAFHRD AND THE GRAY MOUSER stories by Fritz LEIBER. They are employed as city guards in a corrupt and primitive fantasy city but function more like private detectives. They debuted in *Hawk and Fisher* (1990, also published as *No Haven for the Guilty*) battling miscreants and magic in pursuit of their duties. Their job is to suppress all magic manipulation during a political campaign in *Winner Take All* (1991, also published as *The Devil Take the Hindmost*) and to track down a serial killer who specializes in eliminating gods in *The God Killer* (1991). The enemy is an aristocratic terrorist in *Wolf in the Fold* (1991, also published as *Vengeance for a Lonely Man*), they find themselves

framed and discharged in *Guard against Dishonor* (1991), and they discover a second city hidden under their own in *The Bones of Haven* (1992, also published as *Two Kings in Haven*). Green later added a seventh adventure, *Beyond the Blue Moon* (2000), also a sequel to the otherwise separate Demon Wars series.

The Demon Wars started with *Blue Moon Rising* (1991), a good-humored fantasy quest in which the heir to the throne of a small kingdom is forced to fight a dragon, rescue a princess, and complete several other tasks, although his supposed supporters prefer failure to success since the kingdom is in dire financial straits and cannot meet the expenses of maintaining an actual hero. He befriends the dragon, meets the other challenges, and returns to his home to confront his advisers. *Down Among the Dead Men* (1993), the sequel, is competent but minor, and *Beyond the Blue Moon* (2000) throws Hawk and Fisher into the mix after a king is murdered.

Shadows Fall (1994) is an unusual blend of magic, technology, and the supernatural containing some interesting sequences but not as well integrated as most of his other novels. Green spent most of the later 1990s writing science fiction novels, primarily his Deathstalker series set in a galactic empire whose political and social structure is very similar to that of his fantasies that may appeal to fantasy fans as well. His next fantasy novel was *Drinking Midnight Wine* (2001), skillfully handling a familiar theme, a man from our world discovering a doorway to a magical realm whose evil denizens are plotting against us.

Green has recently begun a new series blending fantasy with the tough detective genre. *Something from the Nightside* (2003) introduces the Nightside series, set in an alternate version of our world where magic works and is accepted as an everyday occurrence. In the second volume, *Agents of Light and Darkness* (2003), the protagonist is hired to locate the Unholy Grail, the cup from which Judas drank at the Last Supper. The story is cleverly told and is reminiscent of the Garrett series by Glen COOK. A prominent singer begins to exhibit suicidal tendencies in *Nightingale's Lament* (2004), and her friends suspect the change has a magical cause. More volumes in the series are projected. He has also written one related short story, "Nightside, Needless to Say" (2004). Green is always an entertaining and occasionally quite inventive storyteller who mixes violent action with wry humor and whose narrative style is precise and entertaining.

Green Mansions W. H. Hudson (1904)

William Henry Hudson was a naturalist and author who spent much of his childhood in Argentina. He had written a few short fantasies before *Green Mansions,* the only one of his works to remain popular into the 21st century, although his science fiction novel *A Crystal Age* (1887) is one of the more interesting utopian novels. *Green Mansions* is set in South America and involves an encounter with a young woman who apparently lives alone in a region the natives shun because of their fear of the mysterious beings thought to reside there. Rima seems only barely human, ethereal and reserved, and possibly without a sense of sin. She can also communicate with the jungle animals and claims to be planning a return to her own people. Unfortunately, the ignorance of the natives and her own strange actions result in a confrontation in which she is killed.

Most of the story unfolds through the interactions of Rima with Abel, a political outcast who has always lived in cities and who is captivated by both the strange girl and her unfamiliar environment. Abel feels superior to the local people and only begins to gain humility toward the end of the story. The romantic elements are appealing, but some readers may be discouraged by the long descriptive passages, as Hudson used his extensive background in natural history to create a very detailed setting, so intricately described that it almost functions as a separate character. The novel was brought to the screen in 1959 with an impressive cast but failed to capture the mystical atmosphere of the novel.

The Green Mile Stephen King (1997)

Charles Dickens published most of his novels as serials, writing them even as earlier installments were being published, which made it impossible for him to go back and change earlier sections of the novel. This problem normally does not exist in the modern publishing industry because manuscripts are completed and published as a unit, but Stephen KING decided to emulate Dickens with this novel, originally published as six slim paperbacks between 1996 and 1997. When the first installment, "The Two Dead Girls," appeared, the second half of the novel had yet to be written. Although the marketing information suggested that King himself did not know how the story would end, he undoubtedly had a good idea where the story was going. Given the unorthodox manner in which it was written, it is particularly surprising that the novel holds together so well, is, in fact, more tightly written than several of his other novels, and is numbered among his best works.

Most of the story takes place on death row in a small prison and is related through the eyes of the officer in charge of that section. One of the inmates is a troublemaker, possibly insane, violent, and vindictive. Another is an unlikely killer, an insecure, frightened, and otherwise likable character. The third is the focus of the story, an enormous black man who appears to be mildly retarded and who has been convicted of the brutal murder of two young children, even though he is innocent. John Coffey has a secret, though. He has an extraordinary power to draw the illness and pain out of another human being, absorb it into his own body, and then expel it harmlessly. He was, in fact, attempting to help the two murdered girls when he was caught with them, but they were beyond even his power.

The head guard, Paul Edgecombe, eventually accepts the existence of Coffey's powers and becomes equally convinced that the man is innocent. At the same time, he acknowledges the fact that there is nothing he can do to alter the situation, that Coffey is doomed and is even perhaps eager to die and put all of the pain and misery behind him. After appearing separately, the six volumes were combined into one title as *The Green Mile* (1997), and the unified story was made into an excellent, very loyal film under the same title two years later. The combined edition also won the Bram Stoker Award for best novel.

Greenwood, Ed (1959–)

The popularity of the role-playing game Dungeons & Dragons led to the development of similar game systems, including the DRAGONLANCE and FORGOTTEN REALMS fantasy role playing products from TSR Publishing, which eventually became Wizards of the Coast. Both of these took for their setting a typical fantasy world peopled with humans, elves, goblins, trolls, and other legendary creatures, and the general political and social setup was largely influenced by the popularity of the LORD OF THE RINGS trilogy by J. R. R. TOLKIEN. As the games increased in popularity, the publisher began commissioning writers to generate original novels set in these imaginary worlds. Most of those writers during the early years were unknown outside the gaming world, and many of them were only marginally talented. A handful, such as R. A. SALVATORE, Margaret WEIS, and J. Robert King eventually began to produce more original work for other publishers.

From 1988 until 2000, Ed Greenwood confined his efforts to this circumscribed fantasy universe, starting with *Spellfire* (1988), a standard fantasy adventure that introduces his recurring character, Elminster, the protagonist of most of his subsequent work for this publisher, although in this title and its sequel, *Crown of Fire* (1994), the main character is a feisty young woman. Elminster's story is told in more detail in *Elminster: The Making of a Mage* (1994), describing his abduction by a sorcerer and his subsequent mastery of magical powers of his own. Greenwood's next several novels are routine potboilers, although *Stormlight* (1996) has an interesting puzzle at its core, and *Cormyr* (1996), written in collaboration with Jeff Grubb, mixes fantasy and mystery with considerable skill.

Greenwood continued to write about Elminster's adventures through the end of the 1990s and intermittently since then, but in 2000 he started a new series, the Band of Four, set in a world of his own creation and with a new publisher. *The Kingless Land* (2000) is a quest story with a group of companions setting out to acquire magical artifacts necessary to release their king from a magically induced sleep. Although the king is revived in *The Vacant Throne* (2001), he has not been restored to his throne. An evil wizard opposes the restoration and raises an army to seize power in *A Dragon's Ascension* (2002), and even after he is defeated, the kingdom is troubled by shape-changing spells in *The Dragon's Doom* (2003). Although not part of the series, the episodic *The Silent House* (2004) is set in the same universe as the Band of Four and probably signals further novels yet to come.

Although Greenwood continues to write game tie-in novels, most notably *Death of the Dragon* (2000), written with Troy DENNING, it seems likely that he will continue to diversify now that he has reached a wider audience. He is primarily a writer of adventure fiction and rarely strays from familiar fantasy venues and devices, although his skill at using them has steadily improved. His short fiction has been almost entirely along the same lines and is to date undistinguished, but that may also change as he moves away from his game-related origins.

Gresham, Stephen (1947–)

During the brief horror boom of the 1980s, a number of competent but undistinguished horror writers emerged, producing large numbers of derivative paperback originals. When the field contracted at the end of that decade, authors such as Ruby Jean Jensen, William Johnstone, William Hill, and others turned to other genres or ceased to write altogether. One of the writers from that period who faltered but who has recently returned with even stronger stories is Stephen Gresham, whose first novel, *Moon Lake*, appeared in 1982. Although there are some rough spots in that story, the discovery of an evil presence in a peaceful lake is generally suspenseful and effective.

His next two novels, *Half Moon Down* (1985) and *The Shadow Man* (1986), involve children threatened by a supernatural force. Neither approach the quality of his first book, but next came *Dew Claws* (1986), with a similar plot but much more skillfully handled. A supernatural presence in a swamp stalks a young boy who escaped the brutal death of his family. Gresham seemed to be quite comfortable with this formula, in which children battle a supernatural threat, and he used it again in *Midnight Boy* (1987), pitting a psychic child against a serial killer, and *Night Touch* (1988). *Runaway* (1988) also fits the pattern but reduces the supernatural element to an ambiguous peripheral issue.

Abracadabra (1988) fit the same pattern, but it did show a considerable improvement in Gresham's delivery. A group of stage magicians had dabbled briefly with genuine magic before dropping the idea, but a memento left over from that time falls into the hands of a young girl, with predictably disastrous consequences. *Demon's Eye* (1989) involves a cooperative effort by three families to restore a tavern that turns out to be the dwelling place of demonic forces. Once again children are the primary characters, a device Gresham seemed reluctant to drop even when the story could be told equally well with an adult protagonist. That was the case again in *Blood Wings* (1990), one of his best novels, the story of a vampirelike creature whose existence is hinted at in a young boy's dreams. In *The Living Dark* (1991), which is even better, a woman with magical abilities creates a spectral wolf to protect her children.

Just as Gresham seemed on the brink of creating more memorable fiction, the field contracted sharply. During the remainder of the 1990s, he published only two horror novels, both for young readers under the pseudonym J. V. Lewton. He returned to the adult field with *In the Blood* (2001), a familiar but well-handled vampire story, and followed up with the intriguing *Dark Magic* (2002), in which a group of three witches combine their talents to battle a supernatural menace that threatens the world. Gresham returned to children in jeopardy with *Haunted Ground* (2003), in which he creates some truly nasty ghosts. All three of these novels are markedly better than those produced during the first portion of his career, although his latest, *The Fraternity* (2004), is a rather routine supernatural thriller. Gresham seems to have the basic skills to become a more significant writer in the genre but is perhaps too cautious about exploring new territory. Time will tell whether he will take the risks necessary to advance his career.

"The Grey Ones" J. B. Priestley (1952)

One of the most frightening concepts, in life as well as fiction, is the possibility that people around us might not be as they appear, that they may have a secret agenda of their own. This fear of the hidden stranger has manifested itself in many forms, from the witch hunts in Salem to the modern-day witch hunts in search of communists during the McCarthy era. The situation arises frequently in literature as well, often disguised. Science fiction writers suggest that aliens or mutants might live among us without our knowledge, usually planning our extermination or enslavement, and similar devices show up in fantasy and supernatural fiction in the guise of possession, changelings, and werewolves.

John Bolton Priestley, a popular British novelist and dramatist much of whose work has become unfortunately difficult to find, wrote occasional fantasy stories, including this one, which uses the hidden personality theme to deliver a satiric look at contemporary life and the human willingness to settle for mediocrity and conformity. The entire story unfolds as a conversation between Mr. Patson, a patient, and Dr. Smith, a psychiatrist. Patson explains that he has come to believe that there is an "Evil Principle" at work in the world, a conscious force that means to corrupt and eventually destroy the human race. Even worse, the Evil Principle has countless agents who are secretly living as humans, entities whom he calls the "grey ones."

The grey ones are not born but possess ordinary humans, displacing the original personality. Their purpose is to dull down life rather than cause overt trouble. They are plodding workers who never excel but make their way into positions of power through steady work. They quietly discourage innovation, maneuver things so that talented individuals are not employed where they can best use their talents, and are gradually lulling the general public into an apathy so deep that humanity will lose any chance it has of resisting. Dr. Smith, of course, suggests that this is all a delusion resulting from Patson's instinctive rebellion against subtle social pressures, but Patson insists that is not the case, that he has identified several individuals who are definitely grey ones and even sneaked into one of their conferences and saw them in their true form, oversized transparent toads. The reader is probably well ahead of Patson in anticipating the climax, wherein we discover that Smith is himself one of the grey ones. Priestley's indictment of conformity and complacency is cleverly done and is probably his best-remembered short story.

Grimm, Jacob (1785–1863) and Grimm, Wilhelm (1786–1859)

The Grimm Brothers, along with the Danish writer Hans Christian ANDERSEN, are the most famous and revered writers of fairy tales. The two German brothers, one a linguist and the other a literary scholar, were intensely interested in folklore and believed that it was important that it be recorded so that individual tales would not be lost over the course of generations. They began their project with their first collection of folk tales in 1812 and preserved almost 250 of them before they were done.

Although the stories were not original with them, it is likely that many would have been lost to us had they not done their careful work, and in some cases they "improved" on the folk tales by adding scenes or even changing plot elements. Among the many classics they adapted are "Cinderella," "Snow White," "Tom Thumb," "The Bremen Town Musicians," "The Frog Prince," "Rumpelstiltskin," "The Golden Goose," "Little Red Riding Hood," and "Hansel and Gretel." The number of stories, novels, and films based directly or indirectly on these is far too great to list. As with Hans Christian Andersen, the Grimm Brothers were writing for adults, but when translated into English their work was invariably targeted at youths and even dismissed as children's literature.

Gulliver's Travels Jonathan Swift (1726)

Although Jonathan Swift wrote a number of other works, some of them fantasy, the single title for which he remains most renowned is this episodic novel, which was originally titled *Travel into Several Remote Nations of the World*, acquiring its more familiar title, *Gulliver's Travels*, almost a century later. Although Swift used the experiences of Lemuel Gulliver for satirical purposes, targeting a different idiosyncrasy of humanity in each country Gulliver visits, most of that has now been forgotten, and the book, like most early fairy tales, is generally considered a children's classic, its subtext forgotten or ignored. The names of his nations of tiny people and giants, Lilliput and Brobdingnab respectively, have entered the general vocabulary as descriptive terms for very small and very large objects or concepts.

Gulliver is alternately honored and made captive, delighted and shocked, mystified and elated as he visits a succession of obscure regions. There are satires of capitalism, technological progress, the legal system, and other subjects, as in the case of a war fought over the question of which end of an egg should be broken first. Some of the societies he encounters would not be out of place in science fiction, including a land of immortals, but others are clearly fantastic, including one in which magic is employed to communicate with the dead, providing Gulliver the chance to converse with Aristotle, Julius Caesar, and others.

More than half a dozen film versions, including a recent television miniseries, have been based on Swift's classic novel. There were several early sequels by other writers, none of which were worth preserving, and the form of the novel, which Swift adapted from earlier writers, has been imitated many times since. The author conveys one or more protagonists through a series of societies, each of which is distinct and designed to illustrate a satirical point. The most recent of these is *Lurulu* (2004), by Jack Vance, which substitutes different planets for the various islands of Gulliver's day but otherwise follows a very similar pattern.

H

Haggard, H. Rider (1856–1925)

Henry Rider Haggard was a British writer who spent six years in Africa, which had a strong influence on most of his later fiction. A great many of his novels are lost world stories, a form that lends itself to science fiction, straightforward adventure, and fantasy, the former two when the society is described in realistic, rational terms such as in *King Solomon's Mines* (1885), the latter when occult forces or supernatural influences are present, as in SHE (1886). Haggard's most familiar character was Allan Quatermain, a great white hunter who appears in more than a dozen books. Quatermain was also revived as a character in the recent comic book series and motion picture *The League of Extraordinary Gentlemen* (2003). Haggard did not distinguish between various genre forms, and Quatermain's adventures fall variously into different categories. Most of his stories take the form of a series of revelations to an explorer or traveler who purposefully or by chance finds himself interacting within an alien culture, which in turn is usually split into conflicting factions.

His first clear fantasy was *She* (1886), whose lost civilization is located in Asia. Ayesha is a 2000-year-old woman who rules an isolated society and who falls in love with an explorer who stumbles into her domain. She offers him immortality, but at a cost. Haggard returned to her world for *Ayesha: The Return of She* (1905), chronicling the arrival of another group of outsiders who find Ayesha waiting to meet the reincarnation of her lost love. Her next appearance was in *She and Allan* (1920), but her meeting with Quatermain is considerably less entertaining than those in the preceding books. *Wisdom's Daughter* (1923) is actually a prequel, in which the young Ayesha stubbornly refuses to abandon a forbidden love and angers the gods, who sentence her to eternal life in his absence. Richard MONACO also added to her saga with *Journey to the Flame* (1985).

Haggard was also interested in Norse mythology and wrote several historical adventures using that backdrop. *Eric Brighteyes* (1891) is a fantasy, its warrior hero wielding a magic sword. *The Wanderer's Necklace* (1913) is also a Viking story, a variation of the story of the Wandering Jew, in this case a warrior who offends the gods and gets punished by an endless life of traveling.

Several of the Quatermain novels involve magic or the supernatural. There is a supernaturally empowered elephant in *The Ivory Child* (1916), for example, although the main plot is mundane adventure. Allan uses a magic herb to travel mentally back through time to one of his earlier incarnations in *The Ancient Allan* (1920) and again in *Allan and the Ice-Gods* (1927). There is also some minor fantastic content in one of his last adventures, *Treasure of the Lake* (1926).

The Yellow Mask (1908) mixes financial skullduggery with the influence of an enchanted mask, but the plot never comes to life in the absence of the colorful settings Haggard created for his more successful novels. In *The Ghost Kings* (1908, also published as *The Lady of the Heavens*) an African tribe that uses genuine magic is asked to arbitrate an issue between two rivals. *Morning Star* (1910) is an Egyptian historical novel with liberal doses of magic. *The Mahatma and the Hare* (1911) describes a tedious journey through a dream world and is probably Haggard's least successful novel. Early in his career he collaborated with fellow fantasy writer Andrew LANG on *The World's Desire* (1889), a sequel to Homer's *The Odyssey* in which Odysseus goes to Egypt to search for Helen of Troy for a series of adventures that include an encounter with a magical serpent.

Haggard was the most consistently successful writer of lost race novels, a form that enjoyed considerable popularity until it became obvious that most of the world had been explored. The form has recently enjoyed renewed popularity among thriller writers such as James Rollins, Jeff Long, and John Darnton, sometimes very ingeniously. Several of his nonfantasy novels are also lost world adventures, including *King Solomon's Mines* (1885), *Allan Quatermain* (1887), *The People of the Mist* (1894), *Heart of the World* (1895), *When the World Shook* (1918), and *Heu Heu or the Monster* (1924). *King Solomon's Mines* has been filmed at least twice and, the character Allan Quatermain has also appeared in *Allan Quatermain and the Lost City of Gold* (1987), not based on one of Haggard's novels.

"The Hag Seleen" Theodore Sturgeon (1942)
The borders between science fiction and fantasy were much more tenuous during the 1940s than they are today, and although Theodore Sturgeon is remembered primarily for his work in the former genre, he produced a considerable body of fantasy and supernatural fiction, including a number of enduring classic short stories that appear sprinkled through his collections, all of which were marketed as science fiction. Like so much of Sturgeon's work, this story is much more remarkable than its straightforward plot suggests and is remarkable for its skillful and efficient character development, in this case the relationship between the narrator and his very young daughter, Patty.

The story opens with them canoeing through a Louisiana bayou when they are struck and almost killed by a sawyer, the stump of a cypress tree that has become waterlogged and unbalanced beneath the water, periodically rising unexpectedly to entangle anything overhead with its ropy roots. They just manage to make it to the shore, where they are confronted by Seleen, a classic hag whose appearance is so hideous that they are both instinctively repulsed. Seleen tells them that this part of the bayou belongs to her and that she magically compelled the sawyer to kill them. Her attitude is so menacing that the narrator strikes her and vows thereafter to be particularly watchful lest she sneak up on them in the nearby cabin they have rented.

There is no immediate sequel, but Patty begins behaving strangely, stealing locks of hair and hiding them in a rotted tree. Her father discovers what she is doing and concludes that she is being tricked by Seleen into providing the raw materials for a fresh curse, which is partly true. As it turns out, Patty, who is in some ways much too old for her years while in other ways a typical child, has a little magical talent of her own, and the hag is eventually defeated and the family saved. The conflict is between the family and Seleen, but the true focus of the story is Patty, about whom Sturgeon manages to convey a more detailed picture than might have been accomplished in an entire novel by a less talented writer.

Hambly, Barbara (1951–   )
Although most science fiction writers start with short stories and move on to novels, fantasy writers are more likely to begin with book-length works and produce occasional short fiction later on. That was the case with Barbara Hambly, whose career was launched with the Darwath trilogy, *The Time of the Dark* (1982), *The Walls of Air* (1983), and *The Armies of Daylight* (1983). Two individuals from our world are dragged into an epic conflict when a woman begins to experience visions in which inhuman creatures invade the world, although she eventually realizes that it is a magical alternate reality that she is seeing. The pair are recruited by a wizard who hopes to defeat the invaders and eventually prove crucial to developing a magical defense. Their efforts are further hampered by widespread distrust of magic even among those who have the most to gain from their intervention. Hambly's story is darker than most similar

fantasies, a tendency that recurs in much of her subsequent work.

More series followed, sometimes with considerable gaps between volumes. *Dragonsbane* (1985), *Dragonshadow* (1999), and *Knight of the Demon Queen* (2000) open with a quest novel, but the quest is turned on its head when the dragon being sought is discovered to be innocent. Another dragon helps the protagonist rescue his kidnapped child from demons in the second volume, and repeating the reversal, the demons become his ally in the conclusion. The Sun Wolf series, consisting of *The Ladies of Mandrigyn* (1984), *The Witches of Wenshar* (1987), and *The Dark Hand of Magic* (1990), is less unconventional than most of Hambly's other fantasies. A warrior is coerced into protecting a group of women from a bellicose king, accompanies a witch during the exploration of a long-abandoned city, and battles treachery as well as more obvious enemies in the closing volume.

The Windrose series includes *The Silent Tower* (1986), *The Silicon Mage* (1988), *The Dog Wizard* (1993), and *Stranger at the Wedding* (1994, also published as *The Sorcerer's Ward*). In this series Hambly superimposes magic on technology, in the second novel in particular when a wizard plots to transfer his personality into a computer to advance his plan for world conquest. The barriers between worlds continue to deteriorate, allowing intruders to cross freely, but a typical misunderstood renegade wizard comes to the rescue. The final volume is, unfortunately, the weakest. A sorceress has a premonition that her sister's wedding will end in tragedy, so she uses magic to delay it in order to have time to solve the mystery. *Rainbow Abyss* (1991) and *The Magicians of Night* (1992) make up a shorter sequence and include some of Hambly's best writing. In the first title a blind wizard goes to the aid of a universe where magic has disappeared and in the second finds himself in Nazi Germany in our world, where a local group of less-talented magicians try to enlist his aid in opposing the government. *Mother of Winter* (1996) and *Icefalcon's Quest* (1998) make up another duo, both well written but more traditional in plot and treatment.

Three of Hambly's fantasies involve the supernatural, and all three are among her very best work. *Those Who Hunt the Night* (1988, also pub-

lished as *Immortal Blood*) and its sequel, *Traveling with the Dead* (1995), are both Victorian vampire novels with a twist. The first and better of the two describes a vampire community living secretly in London. Someone has recently begun to methodically destroy them, and they are forced to resort to hiring a human detective to solve the crime and protect themselves. The sequel less remarkably but still quite entertainingly deals with an international plot that pits vampires against each other. *Bride of the Rat God* (1994) is Hambly's best novel, set during the 1920s in Hollywood. An actress attracts the unwelcome attention of the Oriental rat god, whose minions begin picking off members of her acting company in an effort to influence her. Hambly recreates the period setting convincingly and adds a suspenseful and smoothly paced plot.

Hambly has also written science fiction, television tie-in novels, and most recently straightforward historical novels. Her very infrequent short stories are generally of very high quality, particularly "The Changeling" (1991) and "The Little Tailor and the Elves" (1994). Her most recent fantasy, *Sisters of the Raven* (2002), examines feminist issues superimposed on a typical fantasy world setting and may be the beginning of another series.

Hamilton, Laurell (1963–)

Laurell Hamilton's first novel, *Nightseer* (1992), is a competent but unexceptional fantasy adventure notable primarily because its protagonist, a woman granted a magical power in order to avenge a crime, anticipates her popular Anita Blake series in that she has to tread a thin line between imposing justice and using power for its own sake. Her only other stand-alone novel, *Death of a Darklord* (1995), part of the multiauthor Ravenloft series, also reflects her interest in mixing supernatural and fantastic themes, but it was with the publication of *Guilty Pleasures* (1993) that Hamilton came into her own.

Anita Blake lives in a world that is very much like ours, except that vampires, werewolves, and other supernatural creatures exist openly and even enjoy civil rights, although there are rules limiting their behavior. Neither is Blake entirely normal herself. She has some dark magical talents that enable her to raise the dead, although she supports herself by hunting down renegade vampires who put themselves outside the protection of the law. She is also caught up in an unusual romantic triangle. On the one hand, she is drawn to the local vampire lord, a seductive, mysterious, and mildly abusive figure. At the same time, she is involved with the leader of a pack of werewolves despite the dangers this involves, often from female werewolves jealous of her influence. Both sides of her romantic entanglements are mildly sadomasochistic, although Hamilton generally manages to deal with this potentially voluble subject in a restrained and reasonably dignified fashion. Blake has another problem that develops through the series, because her personality is not static and evolves with each book. The more she involves herself with the supernatural, the more she loses touch with her own human nature, and she concludes eventually that she is just as much a monster in some ways as are the creatures she battles.

The Anita Blake series has extended to 12 volumes to date, the most recent being *Incubus Dreams* (2004). Although it is theoretically possible to read them in any order, they are best read chronologically, at least from the seventh title, *Burnt Offerings* (1998), onward. In addition to renegade vampires, she encounters zombies, endangered trolls, a voodoo queen, serial killers, and less-familiar monsters. The two best installments are *Blue Moon* (1998) and *The Obsidian Butterfly* (1999). The more recent novels contain more explicit erotic content than do the earlier ones, as does a new series featuring a private detective who is also heir to the throne of the fairies. The first title was *A Kiss of Shadows* (2000) and the fifth will be *A Stroke of Midnight* (2005). They are considerably lighter in tone than the Anita Blake stories despite some strong parallels.

Hancock, Niel (1941–)

Between 1977 and 1991 Niel Hancock wrote 14 novels, a singleton and three series, although all of his work fits into a broader history of a single imaginary world. The first sequence, the Circle of Light, includes *Greyfax Grimwald* (1977), *Faragon Fairingay* (1977), *Calix Stay* (1977), and *Squaring the Circle* (1977). Although originally marketed for adults, they have the simplicity of plot and the heavy use of animal characters that is typically found in children's fantasy. In the opening volume a magician and his animal allies are called upon to oppose the plans of a devious Dark Queen. They complete the traditional quest to retrieve a magical artifact that can be used against her, escape a number of pursuers, and eventually employ their prize in the final successful battle against evil.

Hancock's second sequence, the Wilderness of Four, consists of *Across the Far Mountain* (1992), *The Plains of the Sea* (1992), *On the Boundaries of Darkness* (1992), and *The Road to the Middle Islands* (1993). This series is actually set earlier in time, the opening volume chronicling the rise of the king of the bears, who becomes a prominent character in the Circle of Light books. A dwarf completes a quest and develops magical abilities in the second volume, a young wizard learns humility and the value of cooperation in the third, and a leader emerges from among the otter people in the last.

The Windameir series includes *The Fires of Windameir* (1984), *The Sea of Silence* (1987), *A Wanderer's Return* (1988), and *Bridge of Dawn* (1989). Another evil force threatens humans and animals alike, so a new generation of heroes answers the call to battle. A young woman must be rescued from a giant spider, a magic sword needs to be retrieved and wielded, and a sorceress and her dragons will have to be overcome to save the day. *Dragon Winter* (1988), not part of any of the series, nevertheless pits a group of animals against a magical enemy who can only be defeated if they learn to cooperate. Hancock's books were quietly successful when they first appeared, perhaps because they successfully straddle the gap between young adult and adult fiction, and have remained surprisingly popular ever since, even though Hancock has produced no new fiction for well over a decade.

Harry Potter and the Chamber of Secrets
J. K. Rowling (1999)

The success of the first Harry Potter book, HARRY POTTER AND THE SORCERER'S STONE (1997), might have proven to be just a fluke if J. K. Rowling had been unable to come up with an equally engaging sequel. Fortunately, she did just that, bringing back all the familiar characters, major and minor, and introducing a new and slightly darker danger to the halls of Hogwarts Academy. Shortly after arriving for the new term, and in a most unconventional and exciting fashion, Harry discovers something has changed. There is a voice in the walls that speaks only to him, an odd, inhuman voice filled with menace.

There are dark rumors about the Chamber of Secrets, a room hidden somewhere within the building complex that houses a terrible monster. There are strange attacks that leave the victims turned into statues, alive but rigid and unaware. Eventually, Hermione herself is stricken, and Ron Weasley's younger sister disappears. Harry solves the current mystery and thwarts yet another plan by the villain Voldemort, who has this time placed his essence inside a magical book. He also battles and defeats the monster, the terrfying basilisk, in the closing chapters. Although the story reaches a satisfying conclusion, the underlying plot becomes even more intriguing as Harry learns more details about his parents and their fatal encounter with Voldemort.

In the first title in the series Harry is insecure and uncertain of himself, but by his second year at school he has gained confidence both in himself physically and in his use of his magical talents, although in that regard he still appears to be less consistent than is, for example, Hermione. The Malfoy family begins to evolve into a more formidable enemy as well, a trend that continues in the third volume in the series, *HARRY POTTER AND THE PRISONER OF AZKABAN* (1999). It also becomes more apparent that the headmaster, Dumbledore, has more than a casual affection for Harry and is quietly manipulating things on his behalf. As with the first in the series, the book was transferred with remarkable loyalty to the screen in 2002. Rowling's fans were already clamoring for the third in the series before it had even been announced.

Harry Potter and the Goblet of Fire
J. K. Rowling (2000)
The fourth of J. K. ROWLING's Harry Potter books is so much longer than the previous ones that it

raised fresh questions about whether her younger readers could deal with a single book of such an unusual size, and once again her readers surprised the doubters. As before, Harry is living among the ordinary people, or "muggles," when he is alarmed by a frightening dream, although he remains enthusiastic over the prospect of watching the Quidditch World Cup. But Voldemort and his minions are on the move again, still plotting Harry's death and Voldemort's restoration. Harry visits the Weasleys, planning to accompany them to the Quidditch meet, where they run into various characters new and old, including the Malfoys. Mysteries abound, including the theft of Harry's wand and its use to summon a frightening creature.

At Hogwarts Harry learns that a great competition among the various rival schools of wizardry will take place, although he is too young to compete. The contestants begin to arrive, their names chosen from the goblet of the title. Much to everyone's surprise, including Harry's, his name is selected, even though that appears to be a breach of the rules. Most suspect he found a way to cheat the system, even his best friend Ron Weasley. There are hints of a sinister conspiracy among certain members of the faculty, as Harry pays a visit to the merpeople and defeats a dragon. During a subsequent competition he crosses through a portal and is involuntarily involved in the rising, once again, of Voldemort.

In the course of developing the main plot, Rowling adds detail to the background of her other characters, particularly Snape, one of the instructors whose loyalties have not always been clear in the past, and Hagrid, the ever-faithful jack of all trades who works at Hogwarts. As Rowling ages her characters, she also seems to be writing more consciously for an older audience, and much of what takes place in this fourth volume is even darker and more frightening than what has gone before. If there was any doubt that Voldemort was irredeemably evil in the past, Rowling dispels that uncertainty now. Likeable characters can die, we discover, and no end is entirely happy.

The Goblet of Fire won the Hugo Award as best novel of the year. The film version is scheduled to be released sometime during 2005 and will necessarily be somewhat truncated, given the length and complexity of the novel. The fifth in the series, *Harry Potter and the Order of the Phoenix*, was released in 2003. Two additional titles are planned.

Harry Potter and the Half-Blood Prince
J. K. Rowling (2005)

The sixth book in the wildly popular Harry Potter series sets the stage for the final confrontations to come in the seventh and final volume. The war between the forces of good magic are divided and indecisive, while Lord Voldemort and his Death Eaters are organized and focused. Security precautions at Hogwarts are higher than ever, although predictably the villains find various ways to circumvent them and introduce dangerous objects and people into the midst of their enemies.

Harry is suffering from mounting distractions of his own. He must organize Gryffindor's Quidditch team, which is beset by problems. The death of his godfather has left him heir to a house filled with magical artifacts, as well as the rebellious Kreacher, a house elf with ties to the Malfoy family. Not all of the distractions are bad ones. Harry has grown interested in girls, particularly Ginny Weasley, although the fact that she is his best friend's sister complicates that as well. Ron Weasley and Hermione Granger are also in the throes of romantic entanglements and feuding with each other. Headmaster Dumbledore has taken Harry into his confidence but refuses to take his suspicions of Professor Snape seriously.

Against this backdrop of plots and secrecy come two revelations. The first is that Draco Malfoy is in the service of Voldemort and planning an attack against someone in Hogwarts, presumably Harry, although that proves to be a red herring. The second is that Dumbledore reveals the secret of Voldemort's apparent immortality, but in the process he is magically killed, or at least so it appears, by Snape. Harry now knows how to destroy the evil wizard, but only if he can locate the separate components of Voldemort's twisted soul.

Rowling is here much more in control of her story and her characters than in the previous books. The mystery is revealed logically and progressively, and there are some plot twists that will certainly catch readers by surprise. She also provides a number of clues hinting at the nature of the final confrontation between good and evil and throws in several jabs at the shortcomings of bureaucracy, politicians, and public opinion. The revelation of the secret of the "half-blood prince" is particularly suggestive, since the notes left behind by that former Hogwarts student prove very useful to Harry during the course of this story.

Harry Potter and the Order of the Phoenix
J. K. Rowling (2003)

Firmly established as a publishing phenomenon on or beyond the scale of Stephen KING, J. K. ROWLING followed up the very long HARRY POTTER AND THE GOBLET OF FIRE (2000) with the even longer fifth installment in the seven-volume series. Harry is now 15 years old, and, like most midteenagers, he is confused about his relationship with girls, prone to rebel against the rules imposed by adults, and given to fits of sudden emotion sometimes out of proportion to the stimulus. Although all of the novels are in a sense about young people learning to be adults, this is the one that shows most powerfully the different tensions that make the process so painful.

As if that were not enough, Harry has a host of new problems to deal with. Voldemort has been revived, more powerful than ever, and no one knows what he has in store for the world, and for Harry in particular. Most of the good wizards refuse to accept the fact that he has risen again, and Dumbledore is on the receiving end of much criticism for his efforts to organize a defense against the dark powers. There is also a new teacher at school, one of the most unpleasant characters to appear in the series, a swipe by the author Rowling against educators who are more concerned with the process than with the results. The unrest engendered by Voldemort's activities has resulted in considerable paranoia, and even at Hogwarts a version of the Inquisition is underway to root out all troublemakers and doomsayers. Finally, a newspaper seems to have devoted itself to ruining Harry's reputation, discounting his success during the previous year's competitions and generally making him a laughing stock.

Harry has to fight his way through all these distractions and prepare to thwart Voldemort's next attack, and for the first time Rowling implies that there might be some doubt about the outcome. Whether Harry will rise to the challenge remains to be seen, although readers will certainly be confident that he will find a way, probably with Dumbledore's help and guidance, to foil the plans of Voldemort.

Harry Potter and the Prisoner of Azkaban
J. K. Rowling (1999)

The third installment in what is projected by the author J. K. ROWLING to be a series of seven adventures is considerably more complex in structure than either of its predecessors and begins to prepare its readers for the even greater detail and intricacy of the titles that would follow. Although Rowling's protagonists were teenagers, she made little effort to write down to what might be perceived as a less sophisticated audience. Although this presented no difficulties for her mature readership, which has become quite large, there were doubts about the ability of younger fans to follow the story and maintain their interest over the course of a novel of such great length. These fears proved groundless, as her younger fans were not at all discouraged.

As with its predecessors, the book opens with Harry having problems with his adoptive family of "muggles," people who do not condone the use of magic. Under extreme provocation, he overreacts, and his return to Hogwarts for his third term is hasty and somewhat mysterious. Harry, it appears, is the target of Sirius Black, an escaped convict believed to have been in league with Voldemort. To protect Hogwarts in general and Harry in particular, the Dementors have been called, spectral figures so dangerous and frightening that the cure seems worse than the disease. Before it is over Harry and his friends will have to solve the secret of a concealed identity, confront a reluctant werewolf, take a trip back through time to cross paths with their earlier selves, and discover that not everything is as it appears. Harry emerges as a more forceful character, but it is Hermione who takes the lead during certain crucial events, demonstrat-

ing that she is also maturing and becoming more confident in her ability to make the right decisions. The climax proves that it is unwise to be too hasty about deciding who is a hero and who is a villain. The next volume in the series is HARRY POTTER AND THE GOBLET OF FIRE (2000). The 2004 film version was excellent, but some fans were disappointed that it varied somewhat from the original story.

Harry Potter and the Sorcerer's Stone
J. K. Rowling (1997)

When J. K. ROWLING's first adventure of Harry Potter, a trainee wizard, appeared in 1997 (under the title *Harry Potter and the Philosopher's Stone* in England), it was to become one of the most remarkable publishing events of all time. Other fantasy writers had written similar stories, including Mary Frances Zambreno and Diana Wynne JONES, but none had ever caught the public's attention so fully and successfully. The novel and its successors were hailed by many because they inspired an immense number of youngsters to read, even though the text was written with sufficient sophistication to attract a sizeable adult audience as well. Subsequent volumes would be much longer, but Rowling has held and even expanded her audience with each subsequent volume. At the same time, there were minor controversies. Some people objected to the idea that magic could be a force for good, some thought the book promoted insufficient respect for one's elders. The books were banned in a few places and burned in a few more, but with no appreciable effect on their popularity.

The first book necessarily spends a great deal of time introducing the main characters, especially young Harry Potter, who learns that he is the son of two magically talented people who were killed at the instigation of an evil magician, whose name we eventually learn is Voldemort. Harry's two closest friends are Hermione Granger and Ron Weasley, fellow students, and he is also close to Rubeus Hagrid, who works at Hogwarts, the school where young wizards learn their trade. Rowling also introduces Quidditch, the magical sport played at Hogwarts, and several members of its faculty. The plot is a mixture of mystery and quest stories. Harry discovers that Voldemort has somehow returned and that he is looking for a magical artifact hidden somewhere in the school, so he decides to beat him to it with the help of his friends and despite the interference of some of his fellow students.

This charming first novel won the National Book Award, the Smarties Prize, and the Children's Book Award and became a best-seller, and in 2001 it was brought to the screen as an immensely popular and quite loyal motion picture. The sequel is HARRY POTTER AND THE CHAMBER OF SECRETS (1999). The series is projected to end with the seventh title.

"The Haunted and the Haunters"
Sir Edward Bulwer-Lytton (1859)

Lord Lytton was known primarily as a writer of society novels, but he was deeply interested in occult matters, conducted considerable research into various aspects of magic and supernaturalism, and wrote two interesting but badly dated novels about the search for magical immortality, *Zanoni* (1842) and *A Strange Story* (1861). He also wrote this, one of the earliest and best stories about a haunted house, which also sometimes appears under the title "The House and the Brain."

The first half of the story compresses much of what would become the traditional formula for such tales. The protagonist hears of a supposedly haunted house in which no one can stay for more than three nights, a place haunted by day as well as night. He decides to visit it to investigate and secures permission to do so, after which he gathers weapons, his servant, and his dog. Upon arriving they immediately make an effort to explore the property, during which time they hear or observe a variety of uncanny phenomena including footsteps that materialize out of nothing, odd sounds, the touch of an immaterial hand, and furniture that moves of its own volition. They are temporarily locked in the room that seems the origin point of the disturbances, then are released inexplicably. The dog is too frightened to move and is eventually found with its neck broken, and the servant flees in panic after seeing something never described.

The narrator is determined to stick it out and does so, despite a horrendous manifestation, an at-

tack of paralysis, the theft of some of his property, and the extinguishing of his candles. Letters he had found earlier, hinting of murder and illicit love years before, are reclaimed by a spectral hand. He does manage to survive and keep his sanity until day breaks, primarily because he is convinced that what he is seeing are not the spirits of the dead, but actually magical projections created by a living mind. If so, they may take a different form depending on the fears of the individual. Most writers would have ended the story at this point, but Lytton carries it further.

The effects of the "haunting" might be dispersed by eliminating the room that is their focus, so the narrator encourages the owner to tear it down, since it is a late addition and doing so will not damage the house proper. In the process of doing so, they discover a secret room beneath it, a small chamber that contains, among other things, a drawing of the man who cursed the place using the same magical talents that have given him a greatly prolonged life. The narrator tracks down Richards, the only character to actually bear a name in the story, and eventually brings about his doom. The story is also filled with discourses on occult philosophy that reflect the author's own researches, but they serve only to dilute the suspense.

"The Haunter of the Dark" H. P. Lovecraft (1936)

Many of the writers for the weird magazines during the 1920s and 1930s knew each other personally, through correspondence if not by actually meeting one another, and a very close fraternity developed among them. Authors such as H. P. LOVECRAFT, the creator of the Cthulhu Mythos, openly invited or even encouraged other writers to set stories within their created universes and sometimes incorporated versions of their friends as characters, as Lovecraft did with the creation of Klarkash-Ton, a nod to Clark Ashton SMITH, and Robert Blake, the protagonist of this chilling story, which is dedicated to Blake's prototype, the writer Robert BLOCH.

Blake is described as a writer of occult stories who recently moved to an apartment in Providence that faces the Federal Hill district, then largely an

Italian immigrant area, from among which buildings he sees the tower of an elderly church. Blake grows increasingly intrigued by the building and eventually sets out to find it, a process that proves difficult because none of the local residents are willing to be helpful. He perseveres and finally enters the abandoned and decrepit church, once the home of the Starry Wisdom Cult, who were driven from the city after a series of mysterious disappearances for which they were blamed.

Inside the church he finds a collection of arcane books, a mysterious artifact, and the skeleton of a long-missing journalist that appears to have been burned or fused by acid. A nameless dread drives him from the building, carrying away a manuscript that he subsequently translates. The description of a creature from another plane of existence that so abhors the light that it cannot stand even a dimly lit city street seems fanciful until later, when he hears rumors of strange sounds and movements from inside the church. Blake feels a compulsion to return to the site but resists, even tying himself to his bed at night to prevent sleepwalking. Unfortunately, there is eventually a power failure, and the following morning Blake is found dead, apparently killed by a lightning strike, even though he is in a sealed room.

Lovecraft's fiction is replete with suggested rather than minutely described creatures, usually infiltrators from another reality intruding into our world, and the doomed humans who dare to interfere in their affairs. For a fellow writer to be elevated to the status of victim of one of his horrid alien creations would have been considered a considerable honor.

The Haunting of Hill House Shirley Jackson (1959)

If GHOST STORY (1981) is the greatest ghost story of all time, then *The Haunting of Hill House*, by Shirley JACKSON, is the greatest haunted house tale. Jackson, most of whose fiction has an air of strangeness even when there is no fantastic content at all, is best remembered for this highly effective mix of psychological horror and the supernatural and for her memorable but nonfantastic horror story "The Lottery" (1948).

Hill House is a sprawling estate with a reputation for strange goings on in the night, generally assumed to be the antics of restless spirits. A team of four people with supposed sensitivity to such phenomena are sent to stay there for a few days and conduct an investigation, but the story focuses primarily on Eleanor Vance, an introverted, insecure, and potentially unstable middle-aged woman whose life is falling apart and who in some strange way views this temporary respite as the key to a better future. Although the manifestations are quite subdued by the standards of modern horror films and many recent horror novels, the effect on the reader is considerable, partly because of Jackson's ability to build suspense through subtle increments and partly because she is so skilled at forcing the reader to examine events through the eyes of the characters.

The tension begins to fray tempers as well. Eleanor has started to identify with the house, which is seducing her into abandoning herself to its insidious aura. Although she eventually finds the will to flee, the effort is abortive, as she loses control of her vehicle and is killed, so that her spirit is forever trapped at Hill House. Jackson is never too explicit about what is happening, and one might interpret the whole thing as mass hysteria and telekinetic poltergeist activity. For Eleanor, of course, it makes no difference what was truth and what was delusion.

The novel was brought to the screen with considerable loyalty and quite effectively as *The Haunting* (1963) and remade in a less interesting, special effects–dependent version in 2001. Jackson's novel is the benchmark against which all other stories of haunted houses are inevitably measured.

Hautala, Rick (1949–)

Although very few modern horror novelists use ghosts as a major theme, Rick Hautala has drawn upon that tradition more often than any other and generally with excellent results. He started his career with a werewolf novel, *Moondeath* (1980), a straightforward tale of lycanthropy with a hint of witchcraft. His follow-up was *Moonbog* (1982), which hints at the supernatural but is actually the story of a particularly nasty serial killer. His third novel was the first to use ghosts as its supernatural menace. In *The Night Stone* (1986) a family moves into a new home with a tainted past. The parents quickly fall under the influence of the evil forces resident in the building, and their young daughter, still relatively unaffected, feels menaced on every side. An otherwise unexceptional plot is enlivened by a cast of vividly created characters, which would continue to be characteristic of Hautala's subsequent novels.

Little Brothers (1988), based on an actual legend, began to distinguish Hautala from most of his contemporaries. The title refers to an inhuman race living secretly on the fringes of human society who periodically kill and devour humans. It is a particularly suspenseful and well-written novel with significantly greater attention paid to developing its major characters. *Moonwalker* (1989) places zombies in a New England rural setting, an unlikely combination that works surprisingly well. The inhabitants of a small town are very secretive when outsiders are present and are unwilling to talk about the quiet, tireless workers in the nearby fields. Hautala had by now emerged as one of the most interesting writers in the horror field and was growing more popular even as the genre in general began to lose the appeal it had enjoyed during the 1980s.

Winter Wake (1989) is another excellent ghost story. John Carlson and his family move to a small island off the coast of Maine seeking peace and quiet, but their lives are disrupted by the spirit of a dead woman who is convinced that Carlson was responsible for the wreckage of her life. Once again, strong characterization and a clear understanding of the intricacies of human psychology turn a familiar theme into a highly successful novel. *Dead Voices* (1990) mixes ghosts, witchcraft, and the risen dead. Following the accidental death of her young daughter, Caroline tries to get her life back in order but instead runs into trouble in the form of a powerful witch who is introducing demonic forces into the bodies of the dead. When her daughter is chosen as the vessel for one of the creatures, Caroline calls upon hidden strengths to battle the witch and save her daughter's soul.

Cold Whisper (1991) is Hautala's most original novel. Sarah is a young child with an imaginary

friend, Tully, who seems at times to be not entirely imaginary. Bad things happen to anyone Sarah dislikes, but fortunately she is not basically an unkind child and eventually repudiates Tully, although she never forgets him. Years later Sarah is menaced by a killer, and she searches within herself and discovers that Tully is still there. There is a virtual crowd of ghosts in *Dark Silence* (1992), angry workers at an abandoned mill who resent their treatment while alive and who are controlled by the mental powers of an old woman until she dies, setting them free to exact revenge on the living. The ghost is benevolent in *Ghost Light* (1993), appearing only in dreams and helping to protect fugitive children from their homicidal father after they are kidnapped by his sister-in-law, who fears for their lives. All three of these novels demonstrate Hautala's now fully matured talent.

Twilight Time (1994) is a nonfantastic suspense novel, but *Shades of Night* (1995) is another ghost story, this one consisting largely of a succession of dream images, with most of the conflict involving more mundane dangers. *Beyond the Shroud* (1996) is a significant departure from Hautala's previous work. The protagonist is, in fact, dead throughout almost the entire novel, his disembodied personality alternating between our world and a surrealistic plane of existence where the ghost of his daughter helps him to prevent the murder of his widow. The otherworldly landscape and its bizarre and menacing denizens are vividly realized. *The Mountain King* (1996) is reminiscent of the author's earliest work. The protagonist investigates when a friend is carried off by members of an inhuman race living secretly in the wilderness. *Cold River* (2003), a short novel, is the very atmospheric story of a man threatened by murky shapes that emerge from the water and that are visible only to him.

Hautala's two most recent horror novels have both appeared under the pseudonym A. J. Matthews. *The White Room* (2001) is another ghost story. The spirit of a child begins to manifest itself after some long-hidden human remains turn up unexpectedly. *Looking Glass* (2004), a much more impressive work, proves that small, subtle hints of the supernatural can be as effective as more overt scenes. Residents in their new home begin to catch glimpses of a scar-faced woman in mirrors and other reflecting surfaces and eventually solve the mystery of her identity. Hautala has also written a considerable number of short stories, many of which are collected in *Bedbugs* (2000). Among his best are "Getting the Job Done" (1989), "The Back of My Hands" (1995), and "Knocking" (1999).

Hawke, Simon (1951–)

Simon Hawke was born Nicholas Yermakov and used that name for his early science fiction, although he had changed to Simon Hawke by the time he turned to fantasy. His horror fiction is limited to several movie novelizations during the late 1980s, but he also began writing fantasy during that period, primarily humorous adventures with a more or less contemporary setting. The first of these was *The Wizard of Fourth Street* (1987), which evolved into an extended series about an inept wizard who has various adventures in a world that closely resembles our own, except that magic is a part of everyday life apparently as a consequence of an apocalyptic transformation sometime in the near future.

Eight sequels followed, varying from humor to high adventure and each taking the wizard protagonist into another setting. He travels to England to rescue the last survivor of Camelot in *The Wizard of Whitechapel* (1988), tracks down a serial killer who may be Satan himself in *The Wizard of Sunset Strip* (1989), defeats a supernatural army beneath Paris in *The Wizard of the Rue Morgue* (1990), fights a Japanese sorceress in *The Samurai Wizard* (1991), makes friends with an intelligent cat in *The Wizard of Santa Fe* (1991), and has further adventures in *The Wizard of Lovecraft's Cafe* (1993) and *The Last Wizard* (1997). *The Wizard of Camelot* (1993) is actually a prequel dealing with the catastrophe that returned magic to the world. *The Nine Lives of Catseye Gomez* (1991) is set in the same universe and features the intelligent cat who appears in *The Wizard of Santa Fe*.

The Martin Brewster series is much more dependent on its humorous content. Brewster was introduced in *The Reluctant Sorcerer* (1992), catapulted into an alternate world where magic works. In the superior sequel, *The Inadequate Adept* (1993),

Brewster realizes that he is a character in a story and decides to try to influence the author. *The Ambivalent Magician* (1996) is the disappointing conclusion. Hawke has also written a number of more serious, game-related fantasy adventures, of which the best are *The Iron Throne* (1995) and its sequel, *War* (1996). He has written very few short stories, mostly early in his career, but they are generally of very high quality, particularly "Melponeme, Calliope, and Fred" (1980) and "Far Removed from the Scene of the Crime" (1980). Hawke's most recent work has been outside the fantasy field, but his return would be widely welcomed.

"He Cometh and He Passeth By"
H. R. Wakefield (1928)

The ghost and horror stories of Herbert Russell WAKEFIELD are often compared to those of M. R. JAMES, which they strongly resemble, although Wakefield's plots are less original and his prose sometimes less effective. This particular story is an excellent example of the influence James had on his work, because it is structured very much like that of James's classic story "CASTING THE RUNES" (1911). The device by which a magical curse is conveyed in the earlier story is a slip of paper inscribed with certain runes, while in Wakefield's version a drawing of an inhuman creature is substituted.

The protagonist is Edward Bellamy, a barrister who finds an old friend in dire straits. Philip Franton had fallen under the influence of a charismatic but villainous man named Oscar Clinton. Although they parted at last under apparently civil terms, Franton subsequently does Clinton a slight disservice, after which he receives a letter with the drawing of a menacing figure. In the days that follow he sees fragments of a shadow that grow progressively larger and more coherent until finally the creature itself emerges from the darkness and embraces him. Franton is dead, apparently of heart failure, but Bellamy knows that an occult force was used.

He tracks down Clinton and learns that the man is totally amoral, acting on impulse and without conscience and aided by a wealth of dangerous occult knowledge. Bellamy consults another expert, who provides the means by which he can conceal his intentions as he ingratiates himself with the man, striving to win his confidence. Eventually the plan reaches fruition, the trap is sprung, and Clinton is defeated by the very charm he used against others. Although Wakefield was known primarily for his stories of vengeful ghosts, this is one of his very best stories and clear evidence of the continued influence of M. R. James on his fellow writers.

The Hellbound Heart Clive Barker (1986)

Clive BARKER had already established himself as one of the top horror writers by the middle of the 1980s, and this novella, first published as part of an anthology and then separately in book form, reinforced his reputation for graphic, disturbing imagery and original, innovative plots. Horror film fans would see an extremely faithful transition to the screen thanks to Barker's screenplay under the title *Hellraiser* in 1998. The image of the Cenobites was so fascinating that it became a franchise, with four sequels to date, although Barker is no longer directly involved.

The story opens with Frank attempting to solve a puzzle box, the solution to which will supposedly open the door to the world of ultimate pleasure. Frank has spent his life in pursuit of such gratifications, and he is ruthless, amoral, and even cruel in his efforts to get what he wants. Unfortunately, he failed to understand the true nature of the inhabitants of that other realm, horribly scarred and mutilated beings known as Cenobites, members of the Order of the Gash. They amplify all of his senses until they are acutely painful, then literally tear him apart, imprisoning his essence in a mystical state from which he can be revived only by the touch of blood.

Frank's brother Rory and his wife, Julia, who had a short affair with Frank in the past and who is still attracted to him, move into the house, unaware that Frank was using it. When Rory cuts himself and bleeds on the floor, it starts a chain reaction that brings Frank back, although his body is incomplete and horrid in appearance. Despite that shortcoming, he seduces Julia into helping him, and she lures two men to the house to be killed, their blood helping to advance his restoration and freedom from the Cenobites.

Rory's friend Kirsty, who becomes his daughter in the movie version, discovers Frank's existence and steals the puzzle box. She later solves it, summoning the Cenobites, who intend to claim her as they did Frank. Kirsty shrewdly offers to lead them to their missing prisoner if they will take him in her place but is almost fooled because Frank has now killed Rory and assumed his appearance. Ultimately, the Cenobites see through the mask, Frank and Julia meet their just fate, and Kirsty is the sole survivor. The concept is very original both as a story and as a film and further established Barker's credentials in both media.

Herbert, James (1943–   )

The British writer James Herbert started his career with one of many nature-gone-wild horror novels that appeared during the 1970s, in his case threatening the human race with attacks by bands of malevolent rats led by an oversized mutant with an intelligence that rivaled that of a person. *The Rats* (1974, also published as *The Deadly Species*) is very similar in style and basic plot to less-polished novels by writers such as Guy SMITH, John Halkin, and Shaun HUTSON but considerably more plausible and with more believable characters and situations. Herbert later added a sequel, *The Lair* (1979), which broadens the scale of the attack but is otherwise a reprise of the first.

Herbert's second novel was *The Fog* (1975), another well-written but very derivative thriller. An earthquake releases a cloud of mysterious dust, and anyone who comes into contact with it is transformed into an irrational, enraged killer. The plague of insane murderers was another common plot device in the 1970s, and it seemed that Herbert would content himself with simply producing improved versions of ideas introduced by other writers. *The Survivor* (1976) began to break this pattern. The protagonist is the only person to survive a terrible aircraft accident, but in the aftermath odd events begin to take place all around him. Eventually he is forced to undertake a quest to find the person responsible for the crash and then to join the rest of the dead, restoring the balance. It was with *Fluke* (1977) that he began to emerge as a potentially interesting writer. The narrator is reincarnated in the body of a stray dog, in which form he seeks out his family and subsequently solves his own murder. *The Rats, The Survivor,* and *Fluke* would all later be turned into motion pictures.

The Spear (1978) blends the occult with a story of espionage. A neo-Nazi organization has discovered a genuinely supernatural power source and is planning to use it to achieve world domination. The novel is in many ways reminiscent of Dennis WHEATLEY's occult adventure novels. *The Dark* (1980) is something of a reprise of *The Fog,* although this time the source of a plague of homicidal madness is an occult force rather than an ancient gas. It was with *The Jonah* (1981) that Herbert began to receive serious attention as an emerging leader in the horror field. Jim Kelso is a police officer whose life has been troubled by a long series of disasters and tragedies that are inflicted on his friends and companions. The reader is seduced into believing that Kelso himself is responsible during his periodic blackouts, but eventually Herbert reveals that he has a dark twin whose jealousy of his shadow brother's happier life leads to secretive and deadly retribution.

Shrine (1983) is reminiscent of John COYNE's *The Piercing.* A young woman acquires the power to heal by touching, which many hail as evidence of divine intervention, although it is actually a clever ploy by the devil. Effective at times, the novel is nevertheless a considerable letdown from his previous one. His next, *Domain* (1984), extends his series about mutant rats, this one taking place after a nuclear war and more properly science fiction than horror. *Moon* (1985) is also disappointing, another story of a psychic whose mental link to a serial killer works in both directions, forcing him to track down the killer before he becomes the next victim.

The Magic Cottage (1986) is a haunted house story with a few interesting twists, and *Sepulchre* (1987) more effectively mixes demonic possession with the world of high finance. It was with *Haunted* (1988) that Herbert introduced David Ash, a psychic investigator, pitting him against the spirits in a nicely conceived haunted house. The book became a moody and uneven film under the same title in 1995. Ash returns in *The Ghosts of*

Sleath (1995), a much better novel in which a town plagued by ghosts also harbors the secret of an ancient cult. There are more secret cults in *Creed* (1990) and *Others* (1999), both of which are quite good, and a mix of telepathic children, voodoo, and other fantastic elements in *Portent* (1992), which is Herbert's weakest book. *Once* (2002) cleverly reveals the true and darker side of fairy tales, and *Nobody True* (2004) is another story of a dead man posthumously tracking down his own killer. Herbert has all the tools necessary to be a significant genre writer but has a tendency to return to already stale themes, handling them skillfully but without sufficient novelty. His last several novels have been very uneven, but his better work is still compelling.

Hobb, Robin (1952–)

Robin Hobb is the pseudonym of Margaret Ogden, who began her career as a fantasy writer under the name Megan Lindholm in 1983. Her debut trilogy consisted of *Harpy's Flight* (1983), *The Windsingers* (1984), and *The Limbreth Gate* (1984), whose protagonist predictably finds herself on the run from supernatural forces, including harpies, all of whom she outsmarts. She added one additional novel to the sequence some years later, *Luck of the Wheels* (1989). The interesting imagery and detail in the background make the books of some interest, but the stories themselves are undistinguished.

Wizard of the Pigeons (1986) is noticeably better, a contemporary fantasy about a Vietnam veteran who uses magical powers to combat a supernatural menace in a major city. Hobb/Lindholm then moved away from a contemporary setting, switching instead to a two-part fantasy series set in prehistory consisting of *The Reindeer People* (1988) and *Wolf's Brother* (1988), whose primary conflict involves a female healer in a primitive tribe and her troubles with both mundane and magical rivals. *Cloven Hooves* (1992) returns to a contemporary setting and is the best novel to appear under the Lindholm name. A woman discovers that the imaginary companion she believed in as a child has returned and poses a threat to her family. She also collaborated with Steven BRUST for the almost equally good *Gypsy* (1992), placing a gypsy with sorcerous powers in the midst of politicians and crime lords.

Ogden adopted the Robin Hobb pen name starting in 1995 with the much more successful Farseer series, *Assassin's Apprentice* (1995), *Royal Assassin* (1996) and *Assassin's Quest* (1997). In a world in which professional assassins are members of a respected occupation, a young man undertakes his first assignment, succeeds after considerable effort and his own near-fatal wounding, and learns to make use of an unsuspected magical talent, all in the service of his king. The Tawny Man sequence continues the series, with the protagonist returning to foil a kidnapping in *Fool's Errand* (2002) and surviving further adventures in *Golden Fool* (2003) and *Fool's Fate* (2004). The two trilogies are longer and more polished than her work as Lindholm but generally show less originality.

The Liveship Traders series—*Ship of Magic* (1998), *Mad Ship* (1999), and *Ship of Destiny* (2000)—is far more interesting and certainly her best work to date. Various families, both aristocratic and pirate, strive for control of particular ships, many of which have been given intelligence and self-awareness through the powers of wizardry. During the course of the three novels, the ramifications of the setting are explored as part of the engaging and exciting plot. Although few short stories have appeared under either name, and most of them in shared universe anthologies, the long tale "Homecoming" (2004) is quite good.

The Hobbit J. R. R. Tolkien (1937)

The Lord of the Rings trilogy by J. R. R. TOLKIEN is actually a sequel to this children's fantasy, in which the plot elements for the trilogy are established and some of the major characters, such as Gandalf, Bilbo Baggins, and Gollum, are introduced. The full original title is *The Hobbit, or There and Back Again*, and it tells the story of a much younger Bilbo Baggins, uncle of Frodo, who becomes the ring bearer, recovering it after Gollum loses it. Tolkien wrote the novel while a member of the Inklings, an informal writer's group that included fellow fantasy writers C. S. LEWIS and Charles Williams.

Bilbo Baggins is a hobbit, a halfling, presumably related to humans and dwarves, as the hobbits' physical appearance includes aspects of each of the two races. They are smaller than men, have large hairy feet, do not wear shoes, but otherwise might pass for human children. Bilbo seems an unlikely hero, but Gandalf sees something of value in him and convinces him to take part in a quest to steal a treasure from the dragon Smaug, who hoards it in his cave. Bilbo does so in the company of a band of dwarves and later uses his wiles to separate a golden ring from its temporary owner, Gollum. Gollum is very similar to a hobbit in origin, but his long exposure to the ring's dire magical influence has corrupted him in both mind and body. His determination to reclaim his prize is one of the central plot elements in the later trilogy.

Tolkien revised *The Hobbit* twice, once in 1951 and again in 1966, altering the emphasis in some cases to mesh more closely with the Lord of the Rings. An animated film version was produced, and a live-action motion picture is planned as a follow-up to the immensely successful series based on the other books. Although readers coming to *The Hobbit* after the Lord of the Rings may be disappointed by the relatively small scope and the comparatively simple prose, the story provides a great deal of background and allows readers to observe how Tolkien gradually shaped his created world.

Hodge, Brian (1960–)

After selling a very few short stories during the early to mid-1980s, Brian Hodge produced his first horror novel, *Dark Advent* (1988), which is squarely in the tradition of Stephen KING, Robert R. MCCAMMON, and others. A new plague devastates the world, killing most of the population over the course of a very short period of time. A handful of survivors are sheltering in a department store when they discover that the collapse of civilization has also set free an ancient evil force. Although obviously influenced by King's *The Stand* (1978), Hodge took the story in a new direction, and the climax is considerably better than King's. His second novel, *Oasis* (1989), is much more original, dealing with a blood feud that transcends the limitations of time. The protagonist witnesses unusual phenomena, including visions of a world ruled by Vikings, and later suspects that he is involuntarily the instrument of an ancient enmity.

Although both of Hodge's first novels are solid and readable, he did not begin to distinguish himself until the appearance of his third, *Nightlife* (1991). A strange new narcotic from South America has the power to physically transform its users, causing them to revert to earlier evolutionary forms with violent predispositions. Although those affected are technically monsters, it is the drug lords in the story who are the most villainous. *Deathgrip* (1992) is equally thoughtful and complex. A disc jockey discovers that he has the ability to heal through physical contact but also that he has the power to inflict illness by the same means. *The Darker Saints* (1993), which mixes voodoo and the world of advertising, is an engaging thriller in which the supernatural elements seem almost superfluous. *Prototype* (1996) is Hodge's most recent horror novel, a marginal science fiction story about a man brought to a hospital following an assault who has superhuman powers, possibly as the result of genetic manipulation. The collapse of the horror market has resulted in Hodge turning his attention, at book length, to mainstream thrillers and crime stories.

Hodge has also written a considerable body of short fiction of generally very high quality. "Androgyny" (1991), "When the Silence Gets Too Loud" (1995), and "Cenotaph" (1998) are among the best of his many stories, most of which have been collected in *Shrines and Desecrations* (1994), *The Convulsion Factory* (1996), *Falling Idols* (1998), and *Lies and Ugliness* (2002). He continues to write short horror fiction with some regularity and retains a considerable body of fans. The present slight upturn in the horror market may well lure him back at novel length as well.

Hodgson, William Hope (1877–1918)

William Hope Hodgson was a British writer whose service in the merchant marine resulted in a number of stories set at sea, some supernatural and some not. Hodgson produced a small but substantial body of work during his short life, including several novels and numerous stories. Although most have been published as horror or dark fan-

tasy, some are close to science fiction. His most famous novel, for example, is the relatively short *The House on the Borderland* (1907), in which the narrator discovers that his house is on the barrier between his own and other times and spaces and that he can move from one to the other. He is besieged for a time by monstrous creatures who prowl outside the walls and later witnesses the very distant future in a scene almost certainly inspired by *The Time Machine* (1895) by H. G. Wells. The tone is clearly intended to be horrifying despite the casual attempts at rationalization.

Similarly, *The Night Land* (1912) is set in a distant future when the nature of life on Earth has changed, but the story is a quest. The dangers consist of various monstrous creatures, and the novel is more properly dark fantasy than science fiction. The sun has burned out, and most of surviving humanity lives in one giant pyramid. Outside are material creatures, mutated monsters, and immaterial, evil, supernatural forces. The protagonist is a resident of the pyramid who learns that a smaller human outpost is on the verge of being overrun. He decides to go to their rescue but arrives too late, managing to save only a single survivor. Although filled with remarkable imagery and some wonderful sequences, the novel is in general marred by Hodgson's use of a very artificial prose style. A much shorter version, *The Dream of X* (1912), is not an improvement.

Hodgson's other two fantastic novels are both set at sea. *The Boats of the Glen Carig* (1907) recounts the adventures of a ship's crew when they find themselves near an unknown island surrounded by shoals of seaweed. A parade of bizarre and sometimes dangerous creatures follows, and Hodgson leaves much of their origin and nature deliberately unexplained. More overtly supernatural is *The Ghost Pirates* (1909), one of the earliest and best examples of the ghost ship story. The narrator takes a posting on a merchant ship despite learning that all but one of its previous complement have deserted hastily. Once away from shore, the new crew is assaulted by mysterious shapes that emerge from the sea, all being killed eventually except the narrator. Although the attackers are ghostlike, they seem to be denizens of some alternate reality rather than the spirits of the dead.

The popularity of the psychic detective John Silence, the protagonist in a series of stories by Algernon BLACKWOOD, resulted in Hodgson trying his own hand. Carnacki, whose adventures have been collected as *Carnacki, the Ghost Finder* (1913), investigates reports of ghosts, curses, and other paranormal activities. Although in many cases Hodgson solves the apparently supernatural mysteries with a mundane explanation, some involve genuinely fantastic occurrences, such as in "The Gateway of the Monster," "The Haunted Jarvee," and the best of the series, "The Horse of the Invisible."

Hodgson's first collection of non-Carnacki stories was *Men of the Deep Waters* (1914). Several new titles have appeared more recently, adding uncollected stories and rearranging others. The best of these titles are *Out of the Storm* (1975), *The Haunted Pampero* (1991), and *The Boats of the Glen Carig and Other Nautical Adventures* (2003). Several of Hodgson's short stories are very important within the genre. "The Voice in the Night" (1907) is a sea story in which the crew of a merchant ship is afflicted by a prolific fungus that distorts their bodies. It became the basis of an unfortunately minor Japanese horror film titled *Attack of the Mushroom People* (1963). "The Derelict" (1912) describes what happens when the scum and seaweed surrounding an abandoned ship evolve into a malevolent form of life. This story very probably inspired Dennis WHEATLEY's *Uncharted Seas* (1938, also published as *The Lost Continent*). Hodgson clearly had the potential to be an even more significant writer than he actually was, but his career was unfortunately cut short just as he was beginning to develop the technical skills to match his highly productive and fertile imagination.

Hoffman, Nina Kiriki (1955–   )

Throughout the 1980s Nina Kiriki Hoffman was a steady contributor of fine stories to science fiction, fantasy, and horror markets, delivering tales grounded in strong characterization in a manner reminiscent of Ray BRADBURY and Charles BEAUMONT. Her first two collections, *Legacy of Fire* (1990) and *Courting Disasters and Other Strange Affinities* (1991), mix the genres indiscriminately.

Her first two novels both appeared in 1992. *Unmasking* is a very short novel about a town whose residents undergo a magical transformation over the course of a single night, while *Child of an Ancient City*, written with Tad WILLIAMS, is an Arabian Nights–style fantasy for younger readers.

The Thread That Ties the Bones (1993) was her first major novel, the story of a family who use their magical powers to dominate a small town from generation to generation but whose authority is eventually challenged by an outsider. *The Silent Strength of Stones* (1995) somewhat similarly examines the consequences when a young boy becomes fascinated by a mysterious family, one of whom turns out to be a werewolf, while others possess unusual abilities of their own. *A Red Heart of Memories* (1996) introduces Matilda Black, one of two people with the ability to speak to inanimate objects. The novel quietly and sympathetically describes their relationship with each other and their adjustment to their very unusual talents. They return in *Past the Size of Dreaming* (2001), this time appealing to a hopefully biddable ghost to help them with their latest set of problems.

A Fistful of Sky (2002) describes a situation in which it is important to be careful what one wishes for. The protagonist is initially upset because she seems to lack the magical gift common to her relatives, then grows even more distressed when she learns that she has a unique ability to create curses and that she is compelled to inflict them upon people or face the debilitating effects herself. There is another friendly ghost in her most recent novel, *A Stir of Bones* (2003). Hoffman has also written a number of young adult, light horror stories under the R. L. Stine name.

Hoffman's novels do not seem to have cut into her productivity in short form, and she is a regular contributor to magazines and anthologies. The vast majority of her recent stories are fantasy or dark fantasy, including such outstanding pieces as "Stillborn" (1990), "Incidental Cats" (1996), and "Changes of the Heart" (2003). Her most recent collection is *Time Travelers, Ghosts, and Other Visitors* (2004), but the vast majority of her short fiction has yet to be reprinted. Given her consistent quality and her avoidance of genre clichés and devices, it seems likely that her audience will grow beyond its present limits and that she will eventually achieve the wider recognition her work deserves.

Holdstock, Robert (1948–   )

Robert Holdstock was writing fantasy and horror short stories as early as the 1960s and penned two horror movie novelizations under a pen name in 1976, but his original novels only began appearing a year later. Most of his early work was sword and sorcery stories written under two pseudonyms. As Chris Carlsen he was responsible for the Berserker series, *Shadow of the Wolf* (1977, *The Bull Chief* (1977), and *The Horned Warrior* (1979), in which a Viking warrior is cursed by Odin to wander the world subject to fits of intense, uncontrollable rage. As Richard Kirk, and in collaboration with Angus Wells, he contributed to the Raven series, which features a strong female warrior as protagonist. A third series, published under the name Robert Faulcon, is contemporary supernatural fiction. Dan Brady's family is abducted by a satanic cult in the opening volume, *Night Hunter* (1983, also published as *The Stalking*), and he spends the first five titles tracking down leads, accumulating occult knowledge, and thwarting attempts to kill him before finally rescuing them in *The Labyrinth* (1977).

Necromancer (1978), the first novel to appear under his own name, involves the accidental release of an evil entity from a stone font in an abandoned church and the subsequent efforts to reimprison it. It was the first of his novels to provide evidence that Holdstock was capable of much more substantial work, although some of his early science fiction novels hinted at his potential. None of his early work suggested the possibility that he might be capable of writing *Mythago Wood* (1984), an astonishingly large leap forward and an intelligent, literary fantasy whose premise is that Ryhope Wood in England is actually larger on the inside than on the outside and that it is home to mythagoes, which are physical manifestations of archetypal figures created by a sort of mass mind shared mythology. In one form or another, Robin Hood, King Arthur, and other mythical creatures all exist and can be contacted if one penetrates deeply enough. The main plot involves a grief-stricken

man who searches the forest for his dead wife, while his brother becomes obsessed with exploring its inner reaches. The novel won the World Fantasy Award.

Holdstock has returned to Ryhope Wood several times since. *Lavondyss* (1988) places a female protagonist in a similar situation, and her compulsive exploration of the wood leads to her physical transformation. *The Hollowing* (1993) reprises some of the situations from its predecessors and adds new developments, as does the title story in *The Bone Forest* (1991). *Merlin's Wood* (1994) is actually set in a second magical forest and concerns the birth of an unusual child and the interface between our static world and the more volatile one in the magical forest. *Gate of Ivory, Gate of Horn* (1997) demonstrates that fairies are not necessarily the gentle, benign creatures they are commonly portrayed to be.

Although *Ancient Echoes* (1996) does not involve an enchanted forest, the experiences of a man troubled by visions of an alternate world of primitive hunters often echo Holdstock's loosely constructed series. Similarly, *The Fetch* (1991, also published as *Unknown Regions*) describes the magical retribution exacted when a young boy demonstrates an arcane talent—he can reach into other times and places and literally extract items and bring them into the present. Holdstock's most recent novels are *Celtika* (2001) and its sequel, *The Iron Grail* (2002), a mystical adventure in which Jason and the Argonauts are restored to life and accompany Merlin on a series of adventures. Holdstock rarely writes short fiction. Most of his early stories appear in *In the Valley of Statues* (1982) and his later ones in *The Bone Forest* (1991). Holdstock has left his sword and sorcery roots behind to become a major fantasy novelist, a highly articulate prose stylist whose novels are rich in mythic detail and in his understanding of the subtleties of human psychology. His reputation will almost certainly continue to grow as he continues to explore the potential of classical mythologies.

Holt, Tom (1961–   )

Tom Holt had already published two nonfantastic novels when he turned his hand to humorous fantasy for *Expecting Someone Taller* (1987). Funny fantasy was already quite popular in England at the time thanks to Terry PRATCHETT and others and was enjoying some success in the United States as well, although within a few years interest on that side of the Atlantic diminished markedly. Holt's fantasy debut chronicles the comical adventures of a contemporary man who acquires a magical ring that once belonged to the Norse gods, who are determined to get it back. A whole crowd of Vikings find themselves restored to life in the present day in *Who's Afraid of Beowulf?* (1988), and the intricacies of our modern world are almost as much of a challenge as the dark power they have been raised to battle.

He has continued to produce one or two novels a year ever since, occasionally using science fiction plots but more frequently writing fantasy. There are talking household appliances in *Open Sesame* (1997) and a clever mixing of different fairy tales in *Snow White and the 7 Samurai* (2000). *Nothing But Blues Skies* (2001) is a wild farce about a woman who is actually a weredragon responsible for all of the bad weather in England and who has to rescue her kidnapped father from a gang of angry weather forecasters. In *Falling Sideways* (2002) the protagonist discovers that human civilization is actually being secretly shaped by frogs. The best of Holt's recent novels is *Valhalla* (2000), in which a feisty waitress dies unexpectedly, finds herself mistakenly sent to the Viking heaven, and decides to reform the drunken carousers she finds there. Recent renewed interest in Holt in the United States suggests that his early work may soon be more widely available.

Holt was now firmly committed to the form and began turning out witty, amusing, and occasionally brilliant whimsies quite regularly. An accountant investigating a bank account that has been active for more than a human lifetime discovers a shipload of immortals in *Flying Dutch* (1991), Hercules is reborn as an infant in contemporary suburbia in *Ye Gods!* (1992), and *Faust Among Equals* (1994) has Faust escaping from hell, which is subsequently turned into a theme park. Holt quickly established himself as a reliable fantasy humorist in a field that tends to take itself far too seriously.

"The Horla" Guy de Maupassant (1886)

Although this classic by the French writer de Maupassant is often identified as a vampire tale, the creature is more properly an incubus, a spirit that sucks energy from its victim at night. The narrator is a young Frenchman who has recently moved into a new house. He is happy with his life and his surroundings until he begins to experience strange dreams in which a dark figure hovers over him, after each of which he finds himself peculiarly lacking in energy. He begins to feel apprehensive and consults physicians without feeling any improvement. When he leaves on a short holiday, the dreams stop but start anew following his return. Then one night he notices that the container of water he left by his bed has been emptied, and by experimenting he discovers that something is drinking the water every night, even when the container is sealed.

Panicking, he flees to Paris but predictably begins to doubt the evidence of his own senses with the passage of time and the restoration of his health. After witnessing a demonstration of hypnotism, he becomes convinced that it is possible for one intelligence to impose its will on another. When he returns to his house he finds even more convincing proof, because the sinister presence begins to overpower his will, preventing him from leaving the house. Even when he finally makes his escape, he later succumbs and returns, virtually a prisoner in his own body. A newspaper account describing a similar phenomenon, though on a larger scale, in Brazil, discounted as mass hysteria, gives him fresh hope, and he theorizes that some new form of life has appeared in the world, invisible and determined to replace us.

His tormentor's grasp is not always tight, and he finally conceives of a plan. He arranges a method by which to trap the creature in his room; since it has a physical body of some sort, it cannot easily pass through a bolted door. When the trap is sprung, he starts a fire and burns the house to the ground, although he shortsightedly forgets to warn his servants, who perish in the blaze. Finally, concluding that his plan failed and that the Horla will eventually find him again, he decides to commit suicide. De Maupassant never explains the Horla's existence other than through the narrator's theories. Although it acts much like a vampire, drawing sustenance from its victim's neck, it seems to be taking life energy rather than blood and leaves no physical evidence behind. Supernatural stories in the 19th century tended to make use of existing legends, vampires and ghosts primarily. "The Horla" is an imaginative and impressive departure.

The Horse and His Boy C. S. Lewis (1954)

The fifth book in the CHRONICLES OF NARNIA steps back in time to a period during the rule of High King Peter, which took place in the closing chapters of the first book, *THE LION, THE WITCH, AND THE WARDROBE*. Two of the children from that earlier work, Edmund and Lucy, are briefly involved as characters, but this is primarily the story of Shasta, a young boy who runs away just as he is about to be sold into slavery, and Aravis, a girl who is also a fugitive, in her case because she wishes to avoid an arranged marriage, a plot device found frequently in adult fantasy. The story starts in Calormen, an Arabian Nights–type fantasy kingdom located near Narnia, with whom relations are not entirely peaceful, and continues as the two travel together, learning much about themselves and their surroundings as they flee toward Narnia. C. S. LEWIS used a much more adult theme than he had in the previous volumes, and the plot is more tightly constructed, although still somewhat episodic.

Shasta learns that the man he thought of as his father actually found him drifting alone in a boat, which explains the disparity in their looks. He escapes with the assistance of Bree, a talking horse from Narnia who has similarly been taken captive, although until now he had not revealed to anyone that he had the capacity to speak. They intend to reach safety in Narnia, soon meeting Aravis, who also has a talking Narnian horse, Hwin. Aravis is spoiled and inconsiderate, but they decide they are safer together than traveling separately. Lurking in the background is a mysterious lion, whom readers of the earlier books will recognize as the mystical Aslan, who intercedes periodically to nudge them in the proper direction. Aslan shows a harsher side this time, inflicting a painful injury on Aravis in response to her own sin.

At the same time, Prince Rabadash has been urging his father to declare war on Narnia, resorting to trickery when the latter refuses to commit himself. For this he will eventually be punished by Aslan, who turns him into a donkey, but only after the other two have reached Narnia safely. Their adventures include crossing a desert, encountering a mysterious hermit, and surviving other low-key trials and tribulations, and upon their arrival they discover that Shasta is actually a missing prince. The story is told in a more adult style than the previous Narnia books, and Aslan's character is considerably darker.

A House-Boat on the Styx John Kendrick Bangs (1895)

Much of the writing of John Kendrick BANGS is lost because of the many pseudonyms he used, and much that survives has been deservedly forgotten, although a few of his ghost and horror stories have weathered the passage of time fairly well. His most famous work is this very unusual fantasy novel, whose full original title is *A House-Boat on the Styx: Being Some Account of the Divers Doings of Various Shades*. The frame of the story is an exclusive club in hell established by a number of dead souls, some historical and some fictional literary figures. The book is structured as a series of episodes, each designed to satirize some aspect of human civilization, or more specifically some aspect of the individual character around which a particular episode is focused. Eventually, trouble rears its head from two directions, capture by a dead pirate and invasion by a group of feminist minded women.

Bangs continues the story with *The Pursuit of the House-Boat: Being Some Further Account of the Divers Doings of the Associated Shades under the Leadership of Sherlock Holmes, Esq* (1897), which some critics prefer to the first volume. Holmes is tasked with tracking down the missing houseboat, but by the time he succeeds the feminists have already outsmarted the pirates and regained control. A third volume, *The Enchanted Type-Writer* (1899), is considerably less interesting. The narrator, who is still alive, repairs a typewriter that then begins automatically typing messages from hell. Some of the targets of Bangs's satire are no longer familiar to most readers, but other segments remain just as trenchant as they were when originally written. A handful of later novels were influenced in part by Bangs's series, including the Riverworld series of science fiction novels by Philip José Farmer and *Not Too Narrow, Not Too Deep* (1936) by Richard Sale.

Howard, Robert E. (1906–1936)

With the exception of J. R. R. TOLKIEN, it is unlikely that any 20th-century fantasy writer rivaled the influence of Robert E. Howard on his fellow writers, particularly in the subcategory of sword and sorcery tales. Howard was an incredibly prolific writer who took his own life when he was only 30, leaving behind an astonishingly large and variable body of work, much of which was fantasy and supernatural fiction, although he also wrote sea adventures, boxing stories, and straightforward action tales. His most memorable creation was, of course, the barbarian warrior Conan, although he penned less than two dozen stories featuring that character. Solomon Kane, Red Sonja, Bran Mak Morn, and King Kull were lesser but no less interesting protagonists.

Howard began writing professionally in 1925 and produced new tales at an average of more than one per month thereafter. The great majority of his stories are set in the distant past, either among the Vikings or Picts or even further back, in imaginary lands that existed in prehistoric times such as Atlantis, Lemuria, and various nations of his own creation. Most of the stories involve heavy doses of magic, and many involve one or more monsters, either natural or supernatural, although the actual villains are more likely to be human—cruel tyrants, evil sorcerers, or craven criminals. Even Howard's more sophisticated heroes display a certain degree of contempt for the complacent life, and his protagonists seem more at ease roaming the landscape or carousing in a tavern than in more refined pursuits, even when they themselves sit on the throne. Howard's stories have been reassembled in different collections so many times that it might appear that he produced an even larger body of work than is in fact the case, and it is impossible to obtain a complete collection without considerable duplication.

As mentioned above, Conan is without question his most famous creation. Howard wrote 17 adventures in the series, but many of his other stories and story fragments were later completed or modified to expand that number. The stories are scattered throughout Conan's life, from his inexperienced youth as a wanderer from a remote region to his mature years as a warrior and eventually a king. They rely heavily on action and violence but also make use of relatively sophisticated storylines, such as in "The Tower of the Elephant" (1933). The brawling hero, sometimes bodyguard, sometimes thief, has subsequently become the hero of two motion pictures and a Marvel comic book title. More significantly, more than 60 new novel-length adventures of Conan have been published since Howard's death, including titles by such leading writers as Robert JORDAN, L. Sprague DE CAMP, Poul Anderson, Karl Edward WAGNER, Harry TURTLEDOVE, and Andrew J. OFFUTT. Howard himself wrote only a single book-length Conan story, *Conan the Conqueror* (1935, also published as *The Hour of the Dragon*).

King Kull appeared only in short fiction, all of which has been collected as *Robert E. Howard's Kull* (1985). An earlier volume, *King Kull* (1967), includes new and altered stories by Lin CARTER. Kull leaves Atlantis and makes a new life for himself in Valusia, eventually becoming its ruler. He is described in much the same fashion as Conan, although perhaps less inclined to tolerate rivals. The stories vary considerably in quality, but several are quite good, particularly "The Shadow Kingdom" (1929). Kull also became the inspiration for a motion picture, but other than the name, little of Howard's creation survived the transition.

The Bran Mak Morn series is set in very ancient Britain and also consists exclusively of short stories, variously collected as *Bran Mak Morn* (1969) and *Worms of the Earth* (1974). Karl Edward Wagner added to this history with *Legion of the Shadows* (1976). Bran battles the Romans as they evict the Picts from their native lands, sometimes aided by druid magic. "Worms of the Earth" (1932) is the best of Bran's adventures. Turlogh Dubh is another Howard hero, though a bit of a rogue, whose best adventure is "The Gods of Bal-Sagoth" (1931). Still another is Cormac Mac Art, whose adventures were brought together as *Tigers of the Sea* (1974), *Hawks of Outremer* (1979), and *Cormac Mac Art* (1995). Andrew J. Offutt added five novels about Cormac, two of them in collaboration with Keith Taylor and the best of which is *The Sign of the Moonbow* (1977). The last significant recurring Howard hero is Solomon Kane, who varies a bit from the standard Howard protagonist. Kane is a 16th-century pirate, more cultured and restrained than Conan or Kull and more likely to use his wits than his fists as he solves occult mysteries from England to Africa. Kane's stories have been collected in one volume as *Red Shadows* (1968), in three volumes under different titles between 1969 and 1971, and in two volumes in 1978 and 1979. Their latest incarnation is as *The Savage Tales of Solomon Kane* (2004).

In addition to his heroic fantasy tales, Howard wrote a fair number of supernatural or occult stories. Many of these were set in the Cthulhu Mythos universe created by H. P. LOVECRAFT. Howard's horror stories are collected in *Skull-Face and Others* (1946), *Wolfshead* (1968), *Pigeons from Hell and Other Weird and Fantastic Adventures* (1976), and *Cthulhu—The Mythos and Other Kindred Horrors* (1988). These include several acknowledged classics such as "PIGEONS FROM HELL" (1938), "THE CAIRN ON THE HEADLAND" (1931), and "THE DARK MAN" (1932). A few of his works such as the short novel *Almuric* (1939) and "THE GARDEN OF FEAR" (1934) use science fiction devices, either other planets or the distant future, but the tone is that of fantasy and the technology is indistinguishable from magic.

Howard's influence on the writers who followed him was not because of the novelty of his themes and settings, which were not original with him, but the manner in which he presented his stories. His plots are exciting and fast paced, his settings exotic, and his prose lucid and evocative. The resolution of the conflict is often remarkably clever, particularly in his best stories. The rough, uneducated, even crude barbarian hero would become a permanent fixture in fantasy fiction, although few writers rose to Howard's level of execution. Although his stories are often relentlessly violent and are sometimes tinged with racial prejudice, his faults are generally forgiven because

of his superior ability to tell an exciting and engrossing story.

"The Howling Man" Charles Beaumont
(1960)
Satan, or the devil, rarely makes a personal appearance in horror fiction, probably because his powers are so immense that it would be difficult to create a situation in which the protagonist could win without some form of divine assistance. Charles BEAUMONT produced with this story one of the few worthwhile exceptions. The protagonist is David Ellington, the son of a wealthy American family who travels to Europe supposedly to broaden his education. He is engaged in a bicycle trip across Germany when he falls seriously ill and wakens to find himself in St. Wulfran's, a remote monastery. Although the monks are solicitous of his health, they watch him constantly, and he is not allowed to leave his room unaccompanied.

Each night David's sleep is disturbed by the sound of a man howling somewhere in the building, a disturbance that none of the monks admits hearing. As he regains his strength he is more certain than ever that this is not a hallucination, so he eludes his watchers one evening and finds a small cell whose occupant, a nondescript but haggard-looking man, is the source of the uproar. The prisoner insists that the monks are crazy and that they have imprisoned him for the previous five years for committing adultery. When David confronts the abbot, the latter insists that they are not holding any man prisoner and that no man has been screaming during the night. The being to whom David spoke is actually the devil himself, imprisoned so that humankind only need suffer from its own faults rather than those instigated by Satan.

Predictably, David remains skeptical, waits for an opportunity, steals the key, and sets the prisoner free. The monks express their disappointment but no anger, and David leaves, feeling puzzled and more than slightly confused. He does not feel guilty until a few years later, when he sees a news story about Adolf Hitler's sudden rise to power in Germany and recognizes the man, if it was a man, who he liberated. The war eventually ends, and in the final pages David receives a message from the abbot telling him that they have secured their prisoner again. Beaumont's low-key narrative style is particularly effective for this story, whose true horrors are implied rather than explicitly stated.

"How Love Came to Professor Guildea"
Robert Hichens (1900)

In almost every instance the supernatural menace in a horror story is dangerous because of its animosity and often violence toward the protagonists. Robert Hichens, at one time a popular novelist, is now remembered almost exclusively for this one offbeat tale of the supernatural, which twists things completely around. The unexplained, invisible creature whose presence destroys the life of Professor Guildea does so by giving him its unrelenting, unshakeable love.

Guildea is a brilliant scientist who has no time in his life for love or friendship. He is a bit of a misogynist and more than a bit of a loner, celibate, secluded, and with only a single acquaintance who might be considered a friend, Father Murchison. The two meet regularly and argue about the value of human closeness, neither of them ever budging from their original positions. Then comes the day when Guildea announces that he has been shaken to the core by an odd series of events, starting with his catching a glimpse of an odd figure in a park. From that night forward he is convinced that there is another presence in the house, something that follows him around and projects a smothering, indiscriminate affection, the very emotion he most loathes.

Guildea decides that he may be suffering from overwork, but when his parrot begins to act as though it is responding to another presence, he changes his opinion, summoning Murchison to be an unbiased witness. The parrot also begins to imitate a voice that strikes both men as repulsive, a voice that neither of them has ever heard before. The value of human friendship is demonstrated further when Guildea's butler abruptly quits when his employer asks him for his help. Since he feels the presence only when he is home, Guildea is able to maintain his composure, but that changes when he travels to deliver a speech and feels his nameless admirer nudge him while he is addressing the audience.

In the midst of a nervous collapse, he conceives such a hatred for the thing that he eventually drives it away, apparently through the force of his emotion, but the strain is too great. Guildea dies shortly thereafter. If the reader feels inclined to dismiss this all as an illusion based on the victim's profoundly isolated personality, that belief is destroyed at the end when Murchison himself catches a glimpse of the briefly visible creature. Guildea's efforts to distance himself emotionally from others provide a unique weapon with which to bring about his doom.

Hubbard, L. Ron (1911–1986)

L. Ron Hubbard is best known for founding the Church of Scientology, but he wrote science fiction and fantasy as well and at one time was held in fairly high regard in the latter category. Almost all of his fantasy fiction appeared between 1936 and 1942, and much of that did not appear in book form until years later. In tone it ranges from lightly humorous to quite dark, although almost always wrapped around a series of well-told adventures. *Death's Deputy* (1940, book version 1948) is the closest to a modern horror novel. A pilot miraculously escapes a terrible accident, after which he becomes the focal point for a series of disasters. *Fear* (1940, book form 1951) is a very early story that mixes psychological and supernatural horror. The protagonist refuses to believe in the existence of the supernatural until he finds several hours missing from his life, tries to reconstruct what happened, and discovers that there are literally demons interfering in human affairs.

Typewriter in the Sky (1940, book form 1951) is considerably lighter. The hero is actually a character in a story that is in the process of being written by another character, a kind of intermediary author. When this fictional writer has second thoughts about something and revises, his character's reality perceptibly alters around him. *Slaves of Sleep* (1939, book form 1948) also makes use of a clever device. This time the central character releases a djinn, or genie, after which he is cursed with wakefulness. When his body sleeps in our world, he is awake in another filled with Arabian

Nights–style adventures and dangers. *Masters of Sleep* (1950) is an inferior sequel.

Hubbard also wrote several shorter pieces, some of which were collected in *Triton, and Battle of Wizards* (1949). Hubbard's fantasy fiction betrays many of the failings of young writers of that period. The stories are sometimes hastily composed and awkwardly constructed. He was, however, one of the more imaginative writers of that period and had a definite talent for producing exciting narratives. If he had continued to write imaginative fiction rather than devote himself to Scientology and Dianetics, he would probably have become one of the more significant writers during science fiction's explosion of popularity in the 1950s and 1960s. As it is, the small body of work he did produce retains a place of honor in the field, and it is still read and reissued to this day.

Huff, Tanya (1957–)

The Canadian writer Tanya Huff began writing short science fiction and fantasy stories in 1986 under the name T. S. Huff but switched to her full first name with the publication of her first novel, *Child of the Grove* (1988). The novel and its sequel, *The Last Wizard* (1989), are set in a world from which most of the magic has gone. A powerful wizard who retains his power decides that this is an opportunity for him to assume control, in which effort he is opposed by several characters. Although there is nothing new or daring about the plot, Huff's narrative displays a refreshingly light touch that often eludes new novelists. A standalone novel, *Gate of Darkness, Circle of Light* (1989), has a rather similar plot but an entirely different setting. A sorcerer is loose in modern-day Toronto, opposed by a handful of people who are unable to convince the authorities that they are telling the truth. This novel anticipates the Blood series, which would use the same setting with a slightly different set of premises. *The Fire's Stone* (1990) is an entertaining quest story that hints at the complexities of character that would distinguish her later work but which is itself comparatively minor.

The Blood series—*Blood Lines* (1991), *Blood Trail* (1992), *Blood Price* (1993), *Blood Pact* (1993),

and *Blood Debt* (1997)—is one of several recent series that blend horror and fantasy devices into a hybrid that fits into either genre or both. Huff casts several traditionally evil beings as her good protagonists, starting with a werewolf and a witch in the opening volume, then adding a benevolent vampire who writes romance novels for a living. Their opponents include a ghost, zombies, and a mummy. Although the novels follow very similar patterns from volume to volume, Huff expands the reader's knowledge of the hidden imaginary subculture and her main characters quite skillfully, and there is a good-natured, though occasionally bittersweet, tone to the stories.

Her next major series is more traditional fantasy, consisting of *Sing the Four Quarters* (1994), *Fifth Quarter* (1995), *No Quarter* (1996), and *The Quartered Sea* (1999), although there are several original twists in the setting and plot, and the main characters experience some unusual problems. The female protagonist is a bard in training who becomes pregnant, a violation of the terms of her apprenticeship. Interpersonal relations are even more complex in the second volume, particularly when a brother and sister are forced to temporarily share the same body, a situation not resolved until the next book. *Summon the Keeper* (1998) introduces a new series and returned to a contemporary setting. The Keeper is a woman who is charged with watching over the critical points where magic intrudes into our world. In *The Second Summoning* (2001) an angel and a demon each take possession of a hormone-driven teenager, with often amusing results. The most recent volume is *The Long Hot Summoning* (2003), but more may be planned. *Smoke and Shadows* (2004) introduces Tony Foster, about whom future volumes are expected as well. His debut involves supernatural events at a television station.

Huff has also written two science fiction novels and several dozen short stories. Many of her better fantasies can be found in *What Ho! Magic!* (1999). Her contemporary fantasies are consistently excellent, and her characterization is quite sophisticated. The quality of her work deserves more attention than it has received to date, probably because she has yet to produce a novel or series distinct enough to draw a wider audience.

Hughart, Barry (1934–   )

Fantasy with an Oriental setting first became popular in the West with *The Arabian Nights* but has enjoyed only intermittent success in recent years. One of the most enduring is the Kai Lung series by Ernest BRAMAH, which mimics many of the devices of Chinese fantasy, although the China portrayed in the text is not historically authentic. The pulp magazines of the 1940s and thriller writers such as Sax ROHMER generated images of mysterious and probably nefarious Orientals, but to this day only a handful of writers have exerted major effort in this area, reflecting the "Yellow Menace" mentality of the time. Since then a handful of writers including Jessica Amanda Salmonson, M. Lucie Chin, and Susan M. SHWARTZ have used Oriental or mock-Oriental settings. Perhaps the most highly regarded are Barry Hughart's three published novels, which somewhat resemble Bramah's novels in that they are set in a fictional version of ancient China where magic sometimes works, although Hughart differs in that he used that setting to produce three unusual and memorable detective stories.

The two protagonists of the series are Master Li and Number Ten Ox, who first appear in *Bridge of Birds: A Novel of an Ancient China That Never Was* (1984). The twosome set off on a quest, searching out a cure for a mysterious illness, in the course of which they encounter a number of magical creatures, solve an ancient mystical mystery, and provide the reader with a guided tour of a well-imagined alternate world. The story is told in a deceptively light style that actually masks considerable complexity, and in recognition of its literate originality it won the World Fantasy Award. In the sequel, *The Story of the Stone* (1988), a monk is murdered to gain possession of an apparently worthless document, and the two occult detectives solve the crime in the middle of another cluster of magical events. *Eight Skilled Gentlemen* (1991) is an even better mystery, although the fantasy elements are less interesting. Someone is systematically murdering respected mandarins, apparently with no particular motive, although Master Li eventually uncovers the cleverly concealed truth. The consistently high quality of the three novels has resulted in their continued popularity, but reportedly a fourth novel in the series has yet to find a publisher, possibly because Hughart's work does not fall into any of the existing subcategories of modern fantasy.

Hutson, Shaun (1958–   )

The British writer Shaun Hutson is primarily a writer of visceral horror tales, relying heavily on either violent action or horrible events described in graphic detail in order to generate suspense. Some of his horror novels are technically science fiction, falling into the nature-gone-wild category, but most are more overtly supernatural. He is often compared to the far more prolific Guy SMITH, but his novels are considerably more substantial and often more original.

Hutson's first horror novel was *Skull* (1982), in which an oversized and clearly inhuman skull is unearthed at an excavation site. After an accident results in contact between the skull and a sample of human blood, it begins to reconstitute its original body rather after the manner of a revived vampire. The protagonists plan to destroy the creature, but the skull is stolen by a misguided man who wants to see what the regeneration will lead to. Although a bit crudely done, the story has several genuinely suspenseful scenes. In *Spawn* (1983), a considerably more graphic novel, a mentally disturbed hospital worker steals aborted fetuses and buries them privately. A lightning strike not only brings them back to life but somehow mutates them into hideous creatures who decide to avenge themselves on the women who discarded them. Despite some good individual scenes, the novel is not among his better works.

Erebus (1984) also contains powerful images. This time an entire community begins to exhibit physiological and psychological changes akin to vampirism. The plot falters in the later chapters, but the initial build-up is very effective. Hutson's next several novels are much more formulaic and less interesting, although the zombie gangsters in *Assassins* (1988) provide some twisted amusement. *Deathday* (1986), in some editions published under the pen name Robert Neville, is his best work from that period. *Hybrid* (2002) is the most interesting of his recent novels, the story of a writer who discovers that his current project is being written even without his participation, a device Hutson develops effectively and with considerable suspense. For the most part, however, the original imagery and powerful storytelling in the author's early work appear to have given way to formulaic plots and slight variations of previously published work, which is particularly unfortunate given his early promise. His science fiction horror novel *Slugs* (1987) was produced as a motion picture.

I

The Illustrated Man Ray Bradbury (1951)

Throughout his writing career Ray BRADBURY mixed fantasy, horror, and science fiction almost indiscriminately, preferring to tell the story he wanted to write rather than conform to any genre standards. His science is often questionable, but even though the planet Mars portrayed in *The Martian Chronicles* (1950), for example, does not conform to what we know of that world and frequently displays properties we might describe as magical, the book is popular among fans of both fantasy and science fiction.

The Illustrated Man is actually a collection of unrelated stories, some of which are technically science fiction such as "The Rocket Man" (1951) and "Marionettes, Inc." (1949), and others of which are not. The frame story, a brief prologue and epilogue, describes an encounter with the man of the title, whose body is completely covered with what might seem to be tattoos but which are actually "body illustrations" whose exact forms are not entirely fixed. The stories are then introduced in turn after an examination of a related image. The individual stories are drawn from the period during which Bradbury was at his most productive, and the quality is very high throughout the collection.

Bradbury's tendency to blur the lines between science fiction and fantasy are evident in the very first story, "The Veldt" (1950), set in a near future when the technology exists to create holographic duplicates of real world situations. There is something wrong with one family's nursery program, which is programmed to project an African land-scape, but the protagonists fail to realize the danger until they are confronted by all-too-real lions. Bradbury never explains his fantastic surprise ending, but the transition from rational to irrational is so smooth that most readers never notice.

"The Last Night of the World" (1951) involves a mystical catastrophe. Although the mechanism is never explained, all the adults in the world have learned through their dreams that the world is about to come to an end. For the most part they continue to spend their last day of life doing exactly as they would have done if the end were not imminent, not even telling their children what is about to happen. The tables are turned in "Zero Hour" (1947), in which all the children in the world have been involved in a quiet conspiracy with inhuman creatures who are about to take over the entire planet. "The Exiles" (1949) is set on a fantasy Mars that has become the refuge for all the characters from myths and fiction, where they can escape the disbelief that prevails on Earth. Several of their writers/creators have fled to Mars as well. There is a Christ figure on another planet in "The Man" (1948), though not a traditional one.

There has been some slight variation of the contents in different editions of *The Illustrated Man*. Three of the stories were selected for a lackluster film version in 1969.

"The Immortals" Jorge Luis Borges (1949)

This haunting story opens with the discovery of a manuscript written by a man now believed to be dead. The work begins by describing his early life in ancient Greece, before he set out to find the City of the Immortals. Inspired by a story he first heard from a dying soldier, he leads a band of 200 soldiers and assorted mercenaries through a series of bizarre lands, losing some of his followers to desertion and eventually having to escape from them after it becomes apparent that he will not be able to quell the latest mutiny. He is overwhelmed by delirium in the desert, and when he regains consciousnes, he finds himself bound and at the mercy of a race of subhuman troglodytes, although in the distance he can see the outer wall of the city he has sought.

Although the city's walls are impregnable, the protagonist finds an entrance to an underground maze through which he struggles for so long that he loses all sense of time. Most of the passageways turn back upon themselves, but finally he finds an exit into the city, which appears to be long abandoned. The city is almost as perplexing as the maze, filled with senseless architecture, dead ends, and distorted buildings. The lone visitor begins to feel a sense of growing uneasiness and revulsion, considering the city a blight upon the face of the world despite its impressive size and complexity.

One of the troglodytes followed him through the maze, and the weary and disillusioned traveler tries to open a conversation with him. In due course he discovers that his companion is actually Homer, the Greek poet, and that the troglodytes are the immortals who built the city but who have now abandoned it. They have lived so long that they have experienced everything possible and no longer have any real interest in their own existence. Realizing the horror of his situation, he leaves, determined to rid himself of the immortality imposed upon him by the magical waters through which he passed by finding another river that has the opposite power and can relieve him of the burden of life.

The conclusion that immortality is a curse rather than a blessing recurs occasionally in both fantasy and science fiction, notably in Natalie Babbitt's TUCK EVERLASTING (1975), which emphasizes the alienation that results when a small group of individuals remain alive while everyone they know is dying. Robert A. Heinlein's science fiction work *Methuselah's Children* (1958) solves the problem by having human immortals emigrate to their own world, but other science fiction writers have been less optimistic. Whereas other authors have employed an entire novel to make their point, Borges compresses the same concept into a short but no less effective story.

The Incomplete Enchanter L. Sprague de Camp and Fletcher Pratt (1941)

L. Sprague DE CAMP and his frequent collaborator, Fletcher Pratt, wrote among other things a series of novellas that fastened on the expression "immersed in a book" and made it literal. The first two of these, "The Roaring Trumpet" and "The Mathematics of Magic," both of which appeared in slightly different form in 1940, were combined under the title *The Incomplete Enchanter*. The premise of the series is that there are an infinite number of possible worlds and that we determine which one we occupy by the way in which we perceive reality. Reed Chalmers and Professor Harold Shea work out a method of influencing that perception that is described scientifically but that is essentially magic. Using this technique they can transport themselves into these alternate realities, specifically ones that mirror the worlds described in myths or in classic works of fiction.

In the opening section they attempt to travel to the world of Celtic legend but inadvertently find themselves in a Norse fantasy world instead. Shea hobnobs with the Norse gods, retrieves Thor's missing hammer, is captured by giants, and becomes a powerful wizard before returning to our world just before the fall of Ragnarok. In the second adventure they both visit the world of *The Faerie Queene* as written by Sir Edmund Spenser. They are caught up in the local political struggle, which eventually becomes physical, and engage in more magic. Shea marries before he and his wife are returned to our reality, leaving Chalmers behind.

Although the two initial adventures are the best in the series, the sequels are also of interest. In *The Castle of Iron* (1950, revised from the 1941 serial version) Chalmers moves from Spenser's world to that of Ariosto's *Orlando Furioso*. Shea and his wife join him there, undergo some transformations, survive a side trip into the Xanadu of Samuel Taylor Coleridge, and return after some complicated adventures. The final book in the series is *Wall of Serpents* (1960), which combines two shorter pieces, "Wall of Serpents" (1953) and "The Green Magician" (1954). This time the action takes place in the Finnish myth cycle, the *Kalevala,* and then in a world based on Irish mythology. The first two books were then combined as *The Compleat Enchanter* (1975) and all three as *The Complete Compleat Enchanter* (1989, also published as *The Intrepid Enchanter*).

"In the Flesh" Clive Barker (1986)

There are two ways in which a horror writer can make a distinct impression with a story. The most common today is to take an old idea, perhaps with a twist, and execute it so well that it becomes more than just an imitation. The other is to come up with something so original that it generates a fresh new image in the reader's mind. Best of all, of course, is the story that takes an original idea and handles it surpassingly well, as is the case with this novelette, just one of several innovate stories Clive BARKER produced in the first few years of his writing career.

Cleve is a repeat offender, although not of violent crimes, serving a sentence in Pentonville Prison. His new cellmate is Billy Tait, a strangely intense young man who expresses a morbid interest in the gravesites of prisoners who were hanged in the prison more than a generation earlier. He identifies himself as the grandson of Edgar Tait, who killed his wife and children and then asked to be executed, and asserts that Edgar recognized in himself a bizarre ability to communicate with the world of the dead that he wished to snuff out before his children could pass it on. Although Cleve is understandably skeptical, he is also troubled by dreams in which he visits a mystical city whose inhabitants are all the souls of dead murderers.

When Billy finally locates his grandfather's grave, he has a fit, after which he begins to change. Under cover of darkness, he calls forth his grandfather's spirit, whose power eventually transforms the younger man and allows him to disappear from his cell and commit a double murder. Billy is now

entitled to enter the city of murderers physically, but he is having second thoughts about his virtual enslavement to Edgar's will. When Cleve tries to intercede, he wakens Edgar's ire, and the guards are shocked by the sudden appearance of a shadowy figure followed by Billy's disappearance from a locked cell. His dead body is later discovered when his grandfather is exhumed, somehow having materialized inside the closed grave.

Even Cleve does not escape unscathed. Haunted by dreams including one that promises that he, too, will one day become a resident of the dead city, he returns to a life of crime and eventually commits a murder that results in his own damnation. Barker's imaginary city is decidedly creepy, Billy's corruption and fall are chillingly described, and Cleve's hopeless despair leaves a lingering aftertaste in the reader's mind.

"An Inhabitant of Carcosa" Ambrose Bierce (1891)

Although many of the short stories by Ambrose BIERCE are far more familiar to the general public than this unusual and almost surreal vignette, it had considerable influence on weird fiction writers during the early part of the 20th century. The rather ethereal narrator finds himself suddenly and inexplicably standing on a barren plain, or wasteland. There are neither birds nor animals in evidence, the sun is concealed by an oppressive layer of clouds, and there is an air of indistinct but pervasive menace.

There are many crumbling stones scattered about, which he eventually recognizes as tombstones and grave markers, although of such great age that the burial plots themselves are no longer identifiable. They are so old, in fact, that the narrator compares them to artifacts of a long-forgotten, prehistoric race. Although he does not recall his own name, he remembers being seriously ill and delirious and wonders how he managed to elude those watching over him in order to reach such a desolate place. He is also unaccountably aware that he is near an ancient city, Carcosa.

Eventually, a wild animal appears, followed by a man in primitive clothing speaking an unknown language. Neither pay him any heed, and he concludes that he has somehow become invisible. His bewilderment increases when he stumbles upon his own gravestone, leading to the revelation that he has died and somehow been resurrected countless centuries in the future. Although there is very little actual plot, the dead narrator and the graveyard setting became a staple of early weird fiction, most notably in THE KING IN YELLOW (1895) by Robert W. Chambers and even some heroic fantasy. Bierce used deceased narrators in other stories as well, including his much better-known "AN OCCURRENCE AT OWL CREEK BRIDGE" (1891).

Interview with the Vampire Anne Rice (1976)

It is not likely to surprise any of her readers to learn that Anne RICE had already successfully written erotic fiction before turning her hand to vampires with this, the first in her popular and long-running series. Although she was not the first to transform the unclean, undead, soulless blood drinkers of Bram STOKER and J. Sheridan LE FANU into mysterious, romantic figures, she is certainly the single writer most responsible for popularizing this revisionist characterization and promoting them to the best-seller lists. The romantic or misunderstood vampire is now so firmly entrenched that it is virtually a subgenre of its own.

The success of the Lestat series lies in the depth of Rice's characterization, the intricacies of the vampire subculture she describes in great detail, portraying it as a separate and distinct society living concealed inside our own, and the evocative portraits of New Orleans and other historical locations. Lestat is an older vampire, while his companion, Louis, is a more recent convert, but in many ways the most interesting character from the first novel is Claudia, an immortal trapped in the body of a child. The plot is framed as Louis's conversation with a contemporary journalist, and Lestat appears as an almost peripheral character, although he becomes more fully developed in the sequels. Although Rice's vampires are evil in the sense that they prey on humans without remorse, there is also an element of nobility and honor. The overlay of sexual tension is sometimes extraordinarily powerful.

Many of Rice's subsequent novels continue the story of Lestat and his vampire kindred. In order of publication they are *The Vampire Lestat* (1985), *Queen of the Damned* (1988), *The Tale of the Body Thief* (1992), *Memnoch the Devil* (1995), *Pandora* (1998), *Vittorio the Vampire* (1999), *Merrick* (2000), *Blood and Gold* (2001), *Blackwood Farm* (2002), and *Blood Canticle* (2003). Many other writers have attempted to blend vampires and romance fiction, some quite successfully, but none have ever rivaled Rice's popularity. *Interview with the Vampire* was filmed in 1994, and *Queen of the Damned* in 2002.

It Stephen King (1986)

It has been obvious for some time that Stephen KING is highly skilled at capturing the essence of childhood. Stories such as "The Body" and some of the early scenes in *'Salem's Lot* (1975) describe the interactions of children with a degree of verisimilitude and with such obviously affectionate nostalgia that many of these portions of his stories are more vivid and memorable than the climactic scenes of horror. In none of his work is this more clearly displayed than in *It*, which alternates between the past in which the various protagonists were childhood friends and the present in which they are recalled by an old promise to a final battle with an ancient evil being who they once defeated, but never destroyed, when they were younger.

At intervals of several years, the small town of Derry, Maine, is troubled by the unsolved disappearances of children. The agent of their abduction manifests itself as Pennywise the Clown, certainly one of King's most memorable monsters. Horror writers and filmmakers have known for years that clowns are a rich source of troubling images, but few have done as effective a job of exploiting that asset. Pennywise can alter the perceptions of his victims, bring static figures to life, change the size and shape of his own body, and perhaps even read minds.

King does a superb job of showing two different slices of each character's life. A girl raised by an abusive father seeks out abusive lovers as an adult. A boy with a frustrating stutter pursues life as a stage comedian, and an introverted intellectual becomes a professional writer of horror stories. As children, they banded together against a gang of bullies and then again to drive Pennywise back into his periodic torpor. When the only one of their number who remained in their hometown calls them back, they respond in a variety of ways—suicide, disbelief, determination, and even renewed hope. Ultimately, each must face the crisis in his or her own way, discovering the truth about themselves and finding the courage to go forward. The story also demonstrates the impossibility of ever truly going home but paradoxically implies that there is an inevitable pressure on each of us to try. Although the adaptation took considerable liberty with some of the subplots, the 1990 television miniseries was a surprisingly effective translation.

"It" Theodore Sturgeon (1940)

Sometimes the most difficult part of writing a monster story is finding a new and interesting creature, which explains why so many writers fall back on the old standards, ghosts, vampires, werewolves, and other overly familiar figures. Theodore Sturgeon, a marvelously talented writer best known for his science fiction, came up with a particularly repulsive monster for this story, but what truly makes it remarkable is that he invites the reader to peer inside the creature's brain.

The "It" of the title is a nameless thing that spontaneously comes to life composed of decaying bits and pieces gathered around the long-dead skeleton of a man who died in a secluded part of a forest. The creature has a mind of sorts, is curious about itself and its environment, but is almost completely ignorant of the world. When it kills a small animal and notices that its eyes dim with the passing of life, it assumes that death is the same as the loss of sight, and when darkness falls, it decides it, too, has died and lies down to wait for whatever might come next. Although Sturgeon describes his monster as evil, that is not really the case. It is merely indifferent and self-centered because it has no experience of pain and no moral sense.

Not far away is the farm of the Drew family, three adults and a child, Babe, another of Sturgeon's several precocious youngsters. Alton Drew is puzzled by the disappearance of his hunting dog, finds its dismembered body in the forest, and vows to track down the party responsible. Unfortunately,

since the monster has no vital organs, no organs at all, in fact, gunshots fail to affect it, and Alton becomes its next experiment in anatomy. Predictably, Babe wanders off in search of her uncle and stumbles across the monster, and after a harrowing interlude she escapes, inadvertently leading her tormentor to an unusual but well-deserved doom.

In the hands of a less talented writer, this would have been a minor story. It is the characters who bring it to life and the passionate way in which they interact with one another. Also, there is no simple happy ending. Although the identity of the mysterious skeleton is revealed and the outlook for the Drew family becomes significantly improved financially, it is clear that Babe has been permanently affected by her experience. Even Sturgeon's happy endings often have an ambivalent tone, for life itself rarely offers unambiguous answers.

"It's a Good Life" Jerome Bixby (1953)

Although Jerome Bixby was a prolific short story writer, particularly in the science fiction field, only one of his stories has remained consistently popular since it first appeared. It became one of the very best episodes of the original *Twilight Zone* television series and was later remade as a segment of *Twilight Zone: The Movie* (1983).

The story opens in the small town of Peaksville, which we soon discover has been cut loose from the rest of the world and is suspended in a reality all its own. Everyone in town is afraid of little Anthony, the child responsible for the change. Anthony has extraordinary powers that make him invincible and omniscient, a virtual god. He can read people's minds, alter the laws of nature, and transform physical objects. He can teleport himself from one place to another instantaneously and make other objects move or vanish entirely without touching them. It is not a good idea to upset Anthony, because he might kill you or change you in some fashion, either your body or your mind. Everyone pretends at all times that things are good and that they are happy, or at the very least insist that it is a good thing that they are unhappy. They also fight against boredom, since nothing new ever comes into their world; Anthony is a destroyer, not a creator. The few unusual items left to them are rotated from family to family, and they gather reluctantly to watch nonexistent television programs because that is what Anthony wants them to do. Anthony can be dangerous even when he is trying to help. To please one woman who misses her dead husband, he animates the body and has it walk home.

Monstrous though Anthony is, the true terror comes from the helplessness of the townspeople. There is quite literally nothing they can do to improve their condition, and Bixby makes it abundantly clear that no one can even attempt to rebel because they cannot hide their thoughts. There have been many excellent stories about evil children, notably "THE SMALL ASSASSIN" (1946) by Ray BRADBURY and "Danger! Child at Large!" (1959) by C. L. Cottrrell, but no other writer has created a child to rival Bixby's Anthony.

J

Jackson, Shirley (1919–1965)

Although Shirley Jackson is considered a mainstream rather than genre writer, many of her novels and short stories contain at least some element of the fantastic, and certainly these are the ones for which she is best remembered. Her single most compelling story is "The Lottery" (1948), a nonfantastic horror tale in which a small town conducts an annual lottery to determine which of the local residents will be stoned to death, an offering to propitiate some unnamed god and ensure a good harvest for the local farmers. Although Jackson makes no attempt to imply that the ritual actually works or that there are any supernatural entities involved, the story has become one of the classics both in the horror genre and in mainstream literature. It was quite controversial when first published and was later produced as a made-for-television movie.

Her first collection, *The Lottery* (1949), also contains several loosely related stories about a cryptic man, if he is a man, who she calls the "demon lover." The best of these is "The Daemon Lover" (1949), in which a woman searches for her missing fiancé and receives contradictory and perhaps intentionally false information from various people, leaving the impression that she has either imagined his existence or is the target of a possibly supernatural conspiracy. Although the fantastic elements are often ambiguous in her stories, they are occasionally overt, such as in "The Lovely Night," in which a woman is literally absorbed into a tapestry.

Her most famous novel is THE HAUNTING OF HILL HOUSE (1959), still the best haunted house novel of all time. *The Sundial* (1958) is more ambitious, almost dreamlike. A handful of people interact in complex ways as they sit in a house awaiting the apparent end of the world. Jackson's short stories, not all of which are fantastic, have been collected in *The Magic of Shirley Jackson* (1966), *Come along with Me* (1968), *The Lottery and Other Stories* (1991), and *Just an Ordinary Day* (1997). Her prominence in the field is disproportionate to the small body of actual fantastic fiction she wrote and a testimony to its enduring quality.

Jacques, Brian (1939–)

Brian Jacques is a British fantasy writer whose work has been entirely for young readers, although he has attracted a substantial adult audience as well. The vast majority of his books are set in the Redwall series, an alternate version of our world where there are no human beings and where various talking animals are intelligent and have civilizations equivalent to ours. In one sense they are modern Aesop's fables, for Jacques uses this device to tell stories whose characters are indistinguishable from humans. They are very much in the tradition of THE WIND IN THE WILLOWS (1908) by Kenneth Grahame.

The Redwall series was not published in strict chronological order, and the individual volumes can generally be read at random, as each is a complete story in itself. The main series, with associated books, includes more than 20 volumes so far, and while there is some tendency to repetition, most of the titles are surprisingly fresh and innovative. The first to see print was *Redwall* (1986), in which a nation of peace-loving mice is forced to take up arms when they are invaded by a migrant population of aggressive rats. Martin the Mouse, a recurring character, helps overthrow the rule of the wildcats in *Mossflower* (1988). Foxes steal the local children in *Mattimeo* (1989), and their rescue is complicated by the arrival of a flock of annoying ravens. These first three novels set the tone and background for the volumes that followed.

The best of the later novels are *Mariel of Redwall* (1991), in which seafaring mice encounter piratical rats, *Salamandastron* (1993), which involves the arrival of a sinister weasel who nearly precipitates a terrible war, *The Outcast of Redwall* (1995), whose ferret protagonist is cast out by his own people but who still feels ambivalent loyalties when he is befriended by the mice whom his own kind plan to conquer, and *The Legend of Luke* (1999), set very early in Redwall's history, an exciting if somewhat offbeat pirate story. Jacques has only recently begun a second series, this one with human characters. A boy and his dog are kidnapped by the legendary Flying Dutchman in *Castaways of the Flying Dutchman* (2001) and encounter pirates and ghosts in the sequel, *Angel's Command* (2003). At least one more title is planned. Jacques is the only major writer in recent years to make use of talking animals in such a consistent and effective manner.

Jakes, John (1932–)

Although John Jakes is known mostly for his historical novels, he wrote mysteries, science fiction, and fantasy novels early in his career. The majority of his fantasy fiction features Brak the Barbarian, a crude warrior in the tradition of the CONAN SERIES by Robert E. HOWARD. The Brak stories first began to appear in 1963, and included several short stories and three novels by the time Jakes abandoned the character. The short stories were collected in *Brak the Barbarian* (1968) and *The Fortunes of Brak* (1970). Although certainly not up to Howard's standard, Jakes was one of the first

writers to openly pattern a series after Conan, and despite their crudeness, several of them are effectively told.

The novels are considerably better, providing more room for the author to develop both characters and setting. In *Brak the Barbarian vs the Mark of Demons* (1969), Brak takes a job as a caravan guard in order to gain passage across a desert, and his skills are tested when the travelers are attacked by supernatural rather than human enemies. *Brak: When the Idols Walked* was serialized in 1964 but did not appear in book form until 1978. The wandering warrior finds himself in the middle of a war fought with magical as well as mundane weapons. The least interesting in the series is *Brak the Barbarian vs the Sorceress* (1969), a rather routine encounter with evil magic.

The Last Magicians (1969) replaces Brak with a world weary warrior who vows never to wield his magic sword again but who recants when the woman he loves is in peril. Although somewhat better written technically, the story itself lacks liveliness. Paradoxically, Jakes's best fantasy novel is a spoof of the form, *Mention My Name in Atlantis* (1972), in which a typical barbarian warrior finds himself washed up on the shores of Atlantis in more ways than one. The jibes are clever and biting. With Gil Kane, he later wrote *Excalibur!* (1980), a long, conventional retelling of the story of King Arthur and the Knights of the Round Table. It is the only fantasy title he produced after 1972 and a rather nice rendition, but he is now remembered in the fantasy field only for the Brak series.

James and the Giant Peach Roald Dahl (1961)

One of the difficulties in writing fiction for young readers is that adults generally have forgotten how children think, how they can find even the most unlikely situations plausible, and how they can mix frightening and funny images without seeing any conflict. For exactly that reason Lewis CARROLL and L. Frank BAUM are often imitated, but rarely well. One of the few modern writers to successfully adopt the viewpoint of a child was Roald DAHL, who also wrote startling and acerbic adult fiction. Dahl's most famous children's book is *CHARLIE*

AND THE CHOCOLATE FACTORY (1964), but this clever and unusual novel runs a close second.

James is a young boy condemned to what might be close to the ultimate doom for children. He lives with two nasty aunts who call him names and make him do chores all the time. He has no toys, no friends, and little hope until one day the barren peach tree in the garden suddenly bears fruit, one fruit, actually, but a gigantic one. The aunts see the oversized peach as their key to fortune and begin charging admission to see it, while James, of course, spends all of his time cleaning up after the tourists. But one day, while finishing his chores, James finds a doorway in the peach, enters, and discovers its inhabitants, a silkworm, a centipede, a grasshopper, a ladybird, and an earthworm.

The peach breaks free, flattening the aunts in the process, and James and his companions are off for a series of wacky adventures. They cross an ocean, are lifted into the air by seagulls, visit the clouds, and are mistaken for aliens when they finally return to the Earth. The story is absurd, and young readers know that as well as adults, but they are more accommodating to absurdity. The novel has had a steady and appreciative audience for more than 40 years.

James, M. R. (1862–1936)

Montague Rhodes James was one of the first and most influential of British ghost and horror story writers, and his collection *Ghost Stories of an Antiquary* (1904) was probably the single most influential work of supernatural fiction in the early years of the 20th century. Three more collections contain the bulk of his remaining stories, *More Ghost Stories of an Antiquary* (1911), *A Thin Ghost and Others* (1919), and *A Warning to the Curious and Other Ghost Stories* (1925). The various individual stories have since been reassembled in several forms and under several titles, with a few additional tales added. *The Collected Ghost Stories of M. R. James* (1931) is the most complete single volume.

To a large extent James was inventing many of the standard devices of horror fiction, though modern readers may find that his stories have been imitated so often that they seem slightly stale. One major exception is "CASTING THE RUNES" (1911), which is still one of the very best stories about the consequences of a magical curse. Although James called his fiction ghost stories, actual ghosts rarely make an appearance. "The Mezzotint" (1904), for example, tells the story of a mysterious painting that gradually changes to reveal the kidnapping of a child. In "Oh Whistle, and I'll Come to You, My Lad" (1904) a magical whistle conjures up a very unusual and frightening apparition, a creature made of cloth. Church furnishings constructed from the wood of a hanging tree bring death to a guilty man in "The Stalls of Barchester Cathedral" (1911), and a magical crown is moved by unseen forces in "A Warning to the Curious" (1926). Another tree is the vehicle for a witch's curse in "THE ASH-TREE" (1904), and a ghostly form does appear in "COUNT MAGNUS" (1904).

Although James never wrote any horror novels, two of his novellas published as books are fantastic. A man acquires magical powers to communicate with animals and see fairies in *The Five Jars* (1922), and the protagonist of *Wailing Well* (1928) unwisely chooses to ignore a local curse and is taken away by animated skeletons. Although much of James's importance lies in the innovative plots he wrote at the dawn of modern horror fiction, his own stories have aged surprisingly well and have remained in print fairly steadily for the past century.

"The Jar" Ray Bradbury (1944)

The power of suggestion can be very effective, as is illustrated in this early story by Ray BRADBURY. Charlie is a simple man whose fascination with a carnival exhibit changes his life. The exhibit consists of a nameless something, which Bradbury never describes in any detail, preserved in a bottle of fluid. He buys it with all of his ready money after the carnival owner insists that he was a bit disturbed by the jar in the first place and is just as glad to see it gone. Even Charlie's horse recoils when it catches sight of the jar and its enigmatic contents. But Charlie sees it as a badge of prestige: Possession of such an unusual item will enhance his standing in the community.

He is immediately proven right. The men who formerly scorned his company now show up at his house regularly, falling into a nightly ritual of speculation about the true nature of the thing in the bottle. Charlie's wife glowers her disapproval but is powerless to change things. The jar begins to dominate the small community, for each person sees something different in it, an evocation of past memories or present fears. Sometimes the response is hysterical as people imagine that they have caught glimpses of long-lost children reflected in the jar's contents or believe that there is movement and that whatever is in the jar is still alive.

Thedy, Charlie's wife, grows increasingly jealous of his popularity. She tracks down the carnival owner and learns the truth, or at least is told what is perhaps the truth: that the contents of the jar are just rubber, plastic, and metal. She threatens to tell everyone and spoil Charlie's fun, but her husband is not about to relinquish his claim to fame and popularity. The scene jumps suddenly to the next gathering. Charlie tells everyone that Thedy is off visiting her family as they settle down to their usual ritual, trying to interpret what they can see in the jar and puzzled by some apparent changes in the color of the eyes and hair. And the reader realizes the truth, that Charlie has used parts of Thedy to increase the mystery of the jar. Wrapped around the simple but effective story is an insightful look at the way we delude ourselves and sometimes prefer the illusion of things to the reality.

"Jeffty Is Five" Harlan Ellison (1979)

Too often stories about childhood end up being sloppily sentimental. Harlan Ellison is neither sloppy nor sentimental in this tightly told, nostalgic, bittersweet story of Jeffty, Jeff Kinzer, who remains five years old even while the rest of the world ages around him. Donny, the narrator, is one of his playmates who grows older, moves away and back, then attends college. As Donny gets older he begins to have ambivalent feelings about progress and maturity, because some things are much improved, but some of the best moments of the past are gone forever. The exception is Jeffty, who is still five and whose peculiarity people are beginning to notice. His parents pass through concern to fear to animosity and end up accepting the fact of their son's existence sullenly. The other children will not play with Jeffty, and only the narrator remains his steadfast friend.

But things are much stranger than just Jeffty being a boy who does not age. Jeffty listens to the radio in his room and picks up dramatic shows such as *Captain Midnight* and *Terry and the Pirates* that have long since passed into history, and the episodes are new and involve current events. He also has comic books that have never been issued and receives mail order premiums that cannot possibly exist. Donny gets caught up in his friend's anomalous existence, living one life in the present and spending increasing amounts of time with Jeffty so that he can continually sample the past.

The reader will have anticipated by now that things will have to change, and not for the better. Donny and Jeffty have grown to be too different for the situation to remain stable, and a chance series of events and Donny's growing commitment to the present make it possible for the present to destroy the past. The present eventually disturbs Jeffty's hold on whatever it is that allows him to exist independent of time. With that certainty shaken, the rest of the magic dissipates, and his unique ability to remain outside the normal course of time and history vanishes. The story avoids cloying sentimentality while still providing a genuine emotional experience. Neither Donny nor Ellison pretend that the past was better than the present, only that by progressing, we have unfortunately lost some of the good along with the bad. When Donny allows his adult desire to pursue his business interests and accumulate wealth at the expense of his friendship, he is also destroying what remains of his old childhood and the perpetual childhood of his closest friend.

Jones, Diana Wynne (1934–   )

Fans of Diana Wynne Jones point out with some justification that she was writing clever young adult fantasies long before J. K. ROWLING emerged as a superstar. Her first fantasy novel was *Wilkins' Tooth* (1973, also published as *Witch's Business*), an amusing but light tale of two children who get into trouble with a local witch. Jones quickly shed any awkwardness in her writing, and *The Ogre Downstairs* (1974) was bright, clever, and very funny. She could write serious fantasy adventure as well as humor, however, as demonstrated by the Dalemark series—*Cart and Cwidder* (1975), *Drowned Ammet* (1977), *The Spellcoats* (1979) and *The Crown of Dalemark* (1993)—the first three of which chronicle efforts to free Dalemark from the rule of an evil sorcerer, with the later adventure appended. *Power of Three* (1976), the best of her early stand-alone novels, pits its young protagonist against a tribe of bellicose giants who are, not surprisingly, up to something.

Charmed Life (1977) launched the Chrestomanci series, a loose sequence set in a variety of alternate magical worlds, all of which are watched over by an amusing and unpredictable magician. The three sequels are *The Magicians of Caprona* (1980), *Witch Week* (1982), and *The Lives of Christopher Chant* (1988). The first and last are the strongest individual volumes, both set in a quasi-Victorian England. *The Homeward Bounders* (1981) is another multiple-world adventure through a maze in which the protagonist seeks to find his original reality. *The Time of the Ghost* (1981) is a clever ghost story told from the point of view of a spirit who cannot remember the past.

Jones began to hit her stride in the middle of the 1980s. *Archer's Goon* (1984), a not very serious quest story, remains one of her strongest titles. *Fire and Hemlock* (1984) draws on traditional fairy tales as one of the author's most fully realized characters explores a dream world that is more than just an illusion. There is an equally strong character in *Howl's Moving Castle* (1986), a young woman who offends a witch and has her youth stolen, although she can reclaim it if she can convince a wizard to help her. *Castle in the Air* (1990), although a sequel, has a very different plot and texture and is more of an Arabian Nights–style adventure.

Aunt Maria (1991, also published as *Black Maria*) is set in a small town dominated by the title character, who turns out to be one of a cabal of women who enforce their will on the entire population. Assertive women have become increasingly common in Jones's more recent novels, and her next, *A Sudden Wild Magic* (1992), addresses feminist issues even more directly when the world is faced with interference from the male magicians of another universe. *Hexwood* (1993), on the other hand, is an uncomfortable blend of science fiction and fantasy, with small town magic affecting a galactic empire. *The Tough Guide to Fantasyland* (1996), although technically nonfiction, sustains a high level of humor as it provides instructions about how to create and manage a fantasy world.

The Dark Lord of Dernholm (1998) was the first in a new series with a clever premise. The inhabitants of a magical reality stage epic battles and other attractions to lure tourists from alternate universes. Unfortunately, they have grown tired of the arrangement and are determined to find a way to break their contract. In the sequel, *Year of the Griffin* (2000), a young student of magic discovers that the rules of his universe are changing and that the school where he is enrolled is in financial trouble. Jones is at the top of her form in both novels, as is also the case with *Deep Secret* (1997), another tale of diverging realities, this time a world of magic and a world of technology. The story concentrates on the role of the secretive guardians who watch over both.

Warlock at the Wheel and Other Stories is the author's first collection of short fiction. "The Sage of Theare" (1982) is the best of her early stories. Jones has become increasingly active writing short ficiton in recent years, producing several collections in a very short period of time—*Everard's Ride* (1995), *Minor Arcana* (1996), *Believing Is Seeing* (1999), and *Mixed Magics* (2001). Fans of Harry Potter searching for other intelligently written young adult fantasy would be well advised to sample Diana Wynne Jones.

Jordan, Robert (James Rigney, Jr.) (1948–   )
Under the name Robert Jordan, James Rigney, Jr. began writing fantasy fiction in 1982 with two novels in the CONAN SERIES, based on a character created by Robert E. HOWARD. Those two early books, *Conan the Invincible* and *Conan the Defender*, are noticeably more exciting and more loyal to the original stories than those of most of the many other authors who contributed to the ongoing saga, some of them considerably more experienced than Jordan. He had produced four more original

Conan novels by 1984 plus the novelization of the second motion picture, *Conan the Destroyer* (1984). His contributions to that series are still among the very best, and unlike most others, they have been reprinted subsequently.

Jordan abandoned fantasy for the next several years, writing under other pseudonyms, but returned in 1990 with the first very long novel in the Wheel of Time series, *The Eye of the World* (1990). That sequence has now been extended to 10 volumes, with no end in sight, and Jordan has also written a nonfiction companion volume, *The World of Robert Jordan's the Wheel of Time* (1998), and a brief prequel, *The New Spring* (2004). The broad premise of his imagined world is that in the distant past humans were engaged in a battle with a powerful, magical creature akin to Sauron in J. R. R. TOLKIEN's Lord of the Rings trilogy, and, like Sauron, he is sleeping but not dead, waiting for his chance to reassert himself. A by-product of the conflict is that men can no longer safely use male magic without risking their sanity, although women are still able to use the female variety.

The opening volume is largely concerned with setting up the background and introducing a fairly large cast of characters, several of whom are chosen to be the first line of defense against the imminent wakening of the age-old foe. Although there is some superficial resemblance to the events in THE FELLOWSHIP OF THE RING, the tone and characterization are altogether different. The second volume, *The Great Hunt* (1990), is a quest story. One of those chosen to battle the evil is unwilling to accept that he has no control over his destiny, and he sets out to track down a long-lost magical artifact instead. *The Dragon Reborn* (1991) redirects the quest toward a magical sword and begins to gather the widely dispersed characters together, but despite rousing action the story seems to jump around more than necessary, which is often distracting.

Rand becomes resigned to his fate as the reincarnation of an ancient warrior in *The Shadow Rising* (1992), although the central theme is sometimes lost in this volume as Jordan introduces a bewildering number of subplots and separate story lines as well as dozens of new characters. Although much of this enriches the background, it is sometimes confusing, and readers coming to the series late would undoubtedly be completely lost. *The Fires of Heaven* (1993) clears up much of this confusion, resolving some plots and drawing others together, just as Rand begins to forge a united army to resist the evil Dark One, sometimes doing so at the point of a sword. Not everyone is easily swayed to his cause, as we discover in *Lord of Chaos* (1994), which deals primarily with internal politics.

Preparations for the prophesied last battle continue in *A Crown of Swords* (1996), and more problems arise in *Path of Daggers* (1998), but neither of these two installments does much to advance the main story. The confrontation with the Dark One seems as remote as ever. In *Winter's Heart* (2000) Rand has to battle to keep his sanity when he uses magic in what appear to be the final stages before the climactic battle while dodging assassins and trying desperately to hold his uneasy alliance together. *Crossroads of Twilight* (2003) continues to mark time, however, with more political scheming and intrigues but little forward motion.

The comparatively slow pace of the later volumes may well indicate the author's reluctance to bring the story to a close, for it is one continuous narrative rather than a series of novels featuring the same cast of characters. It has a large and loyal fan base and is certainly one of the most detailed and convincing imaginative worlds in fantasy literature. The first two volumes have recently been reprinted in a young adult format, with each title published as two separate books, so that *The Eye of the World* has become *From the Two Rivers* and *To the Blight*, and *The Great Hunt* appears as *The Hunt Begins* and *Threads in the Pattern*.

Joyce, Graham (1954–)

The novels of Graham Joyce tread the borderlines between fantasy, horror, and psychological suspense so consistently that it is difficult to assign them to any single genre. Joyce's first book was *Dreamside* (1991), which deals with a group of young men and women who participate in an experiment with shared dreaming. The psychological effects follow them for years afterward, drawing them unwillingly into a dream reality and eventually causing physical effects in their waking lives. He followed this quietly insidious thriller with

Dark Sister (1992), a tale of contemporary witchcraft that rivals the classic *Conjure Wife* (1952) by Fritz LEIBER. An abused woman dabbles in witchcraft as a means of ridding herself of her domineering husband, but she is unschooled in the arcane arts and is overwhelmed by powers beyond her control.

House of Lost Dreams (1993) has a more subtle plot. Two tourists in Greece are drawn into a mystical reenactment of the story of Orpheus and Eurydice. Joyce's fourth and probably best novel is *Requiem* (1995), a sometimes surreal tale set in modern Jerusalem. The protagonist learns of the existence of ancient documents that offer an alternative version of the life of Christ. *The Tooth Fairy* (1998) turns the familiar children's fantasy into something entirely different. The protagonist is a young boy who gains the power to see her, and he is the only one who knows she is a horrible, frightening creature. Although filled with disturbing images, the story that follows the shocking revelation is less engaging than Joyce's other novels, and the feeling of menace is uneven and ultimately dissipated. *Stormwatcher* (1998) is similarly unfocused at times, a story about multiple realities intersecting and causing considerable tension.

Indigo (2000), although only marginally fantastic, is much more coherent and intriguing, describing an international quest for the secret of invisibility, in this case in the form of a color that human eyes cannot see. The fantastic content of Joyce's novels continued to decline, with only a brief, ambiguous piece of possibly authentic magic in *Smoking Poppy* (2001), the story of a man searching for his missing daughter in Southeast Asia. *The Limits of Enchantment* (2004) is another story of contemporary witchcraft, but not as effective as *Dark Sister*. Joyce's occasional short fiction has been collected as *Black Dust* (2001). He is a powerful though not prolific writer whose work is not easily described or categorized. His best work often involves hallucinations or visions and their impact on the characters experiencing them.

"Jumbee" Henry S. Whitehead (1926)

Although several horror writers have invoked voodoo in their stories, few of them have taken the time to study that belief and ground their stories in authentic folklore. Hugh CAVE is the most significant exception, but the same is true of Henry S. Whitehead, who lived much of his life in the Virgin Islands and drew heavily on local folk tales and superstitions in his supernatural fiction. The events in his short stories are often highly melodramatic but as in this, his most famous story, related in an almost casual, unemotional manner.

Granville Lee retires to the West Indies after his lungs are damaged during World War I. There he becomes fascinated with local legends, particularly belief in the jumbee, a kind of zombie. Lee's inquiries lead him to a distinguished islander named Da Silva, who describes his encounter with the disembodied spirit of an old acquaintance who came to him to honor a pact between them in which each, having died, promised to warn the other of impending danger. That danger comes all too soon. While on his way to call on the widow, Da Silva observes another harbinger of doom, the hanging jumbee, three ghostly figures whose legs end at the ankles.

Doubly forewarned, Da Silva is careful and observant. When he later notices an old woman, he almost makes a fatal mistake, for she is a sheen, a weredog, who transforms and grows larger as she attacks. Through luck as much as skill he is able to drive her off and escape the death that had been intended for him that night. The story concludes without an explanation of the reason why Da Silva was marked, perhaps because the doings of the supernatural are not governed by rational plan. As the character himself remarks, the West Indies are unlike any other part of the world, and the normal rules do not necessarily apply there. Whitehead, who was also a member of the circle of writers that surrounded H. P. LOVECRAFT, was interested in describing accurately an element of the system of superstition that prevailed in his adopted homeland and wrote a story whose terrors are derived from a non-Christian mythos.

The Jungle Book Rudyard Kipling (1894)

Rudyard Kipling was a prolific writer who wrote classic adventure novels such as *Kim* (1901), effective stories of the supernatural such as "THE PHAN-

TOM RICKSHAW" (1888), and children's fantasies such as *Puck of Pook's Hill* (1906). Some of his books are collections of individual tales with common settings or characters rather than actual novels, as is the case with *The Jungle Book,* which draws upon Kipling's personal experiences in India, although in large part he invented his own mythology for the book rather than relying on an already-existing folk tradition.

The stories fall into the category of animal fantasy because various animal characters can speak to the chief protagonist, Mowgli, a young boy raised in the wild by a pack of wolves, from whom he learns the law of the jungle, a phrase that has entered into general usage. Mowgli's chief protectors are a bear and a feral cat, although he later proves to be considerably adept at defending himself without assistance, defeating a snake with the power of hypnotism, a village of nasty natives, an attack by a pack of dogs, and a test in which he proves he can master fire, a talent beyond that of any of his animal friends.

Kipling followed up with *The Second Jungle Book* (1895), and the two collections are often published in one volume. Mowgli, Rikki-tikki-tavi the mongoose, and their arch nemesis, Shere Khan, the tiger, return for more adventures, although the best tales are contained in the first volume. We also learn the fate of Mowgli's parents and wander into side stories about some of the minor characters. An excellent live-action film was produced in 1942, and a classic Disney animated version in 1967, as well as several less interesting renditions over the years.

Jurgen **James Branch Cabell** (1919)

Although the majority of the fantasy of the Virginian writer James Branch CABELL is set within the framework of the Biography of the Life of Manuel and in the mythical country of Poictesme, there is no single unifying plot, and each novel holds up well in isolation from the others. The best of this lengthy series of titles is *Jurgen*, which came fairly early in his career but which is unquestionably his most important novel.

Jurgen is a pawnbroker in Poictesme and also something of an egomaniac, believing himself intelligent and witty enough to banter with the gods themselves. One day he embarks on an intellectual defense of evil and its positive side, after which he is approached by Koshchei, a deity of sorts, who grants him a single wish. Since Jurgen has long chafed under the scolding of his wife, he impulsively wishes to be free of her. Koshchei complies, but Jurgen discovers that he regrets his impulse, partly because of his lingering affection for the missing Lisa but also because public opinion has gone against him.

There follows an episodic, though unified, series of adventures, in each of which Jurgen hopes to reclaim what he has lost through his own foolishness. His first attempt is to convince a goddess to restore him to his youth, but he learns that the past cannot be reclaimed even by the gods. The second episode is further subdivided into separate scenes, each of which signifies another aspect of life—physical attraction, faith, and others. None of these offer a solution, either, and his eventual encounter with the Brown Man fails to convince him that he is insignificant, that the universe is oblivious to the lives of individuals. He interacts with a number of characters who recur in some of the later novels and eventually finds himself sentenced to hell, though he later visits heaven as well, where he discovers that the God worshipped by Christians was, in fact, created by Koshchei. The final section describes Jurgen's confrontation with Koshchei and the achievement of his goal when the god erases the events of the previous year.

Cabell's allegorical fantasy was very controversial at the time of its publication, ostensibly because of the covert sexuality, although probably also because of its scoffing characterization of Christianity. It was banned in New York, though Cabell triumphed in the subsequent court case. Cabell later added a separate episode, "The Judging of Jurgen" (1920), particularly directed at those who had attempted to suppress the original text.

K

Kay, Guy Gavriel (1954–)

Although the Canadian writer Guy Gavriel Kay had previously worked with Christopher Tolkien to produce *The Silmarillion* (1977), a posthumous extension of the world of the Lord of the Rings series by J. R. R. TOLKIEN, he wrote no fantasy of his own until several years later, and his original fiction was not noticeably derivative of Tolkien's work. Kay's career as a novelist began with the Fionavar Tapestry, a trilogy, which includes *The Summer Tree* (1985), *The Wandering Fire* (1986), and *The Darkest Road* (1986). The setting is what at first seems a typical fantasy world but that is eventually revealed to be a kind of prototypical reality from which various mythological systems are drawn. As a consequence, it is a sometimes chaotic mix of conflicting images including a patriarchy and a rival matriarchy. Five college students from our world are dropped into this setting on the brink of a war that threatens to bring eternal winter to that world.

Although the trilogy was a very strong debut, Kay's subsequent work has been even more impressive. *Tigana* (1990) is a very long novel set in a land that has been conquered by an enemy so powerful that even to speak the former name of that country is impossible because of the evil magic employed by the aggressors. The revolutionaries eventually prove irrepressible, but only after a complex and quite intelligently plotted series of events and escapades. *A Song for Arbonne* (1992), which also deals with the conflict between matriarchal and patriarchal systems, minimizes its fantastic content and feels more like a historical novel set in a history that never happened. This last tendency has been repeated in all of Kay's subsequent work.

The Lions of Al-Rassan (1995) continues that trend, with very little overt fantasy content, although the setting is an imagined world. An encounter with a mythical creature plays a pivotal part in *Sailing to Sarantium* (1999), which is otherwise the story of an architect summoned by an emperor to oversee construction of an enormous edifice symbolic of his power. The story is continued in *Lord of Emperors* (2000), as the emperor's ambitions turn toward a neighboring nation. Kay's most recent novel, *The Last Light of Day* (2004), is a story of Vikings and intermingled fates. It is set in the same world as Kay's three previous novels, although the characters differ. Kay's fiction, particularly his most recent work, is thought provoking, complex, and provocative, mixing intellectual discussions with sometimes very explicit violence. He is certainly one of the less predictable fantasy writers, but also one of the most rewarding.

"Kecksies" Marjorie Bowen (1949)

Marjorie Bowen was one of the pseudonyms used by Gabrielle Margaret Campbell, a prolific British writer of thrillers, mainstream novels, biographies, and supernatural fiction, more than 150 books in total. "Kecksies" is one of her best stories, drawing from historical settings and incidents, as did much of her work. Two travelers, Crediton and Bateman, suffering from an excess of drink, are riding across Kent one evening, hoping to find an inn or other shelter. They eventually come to the home of Goody Boyle, a woman of questionable reputation, although neither traveler is much more highly regarded even though they bear the title of lord.

The two men have mixed emotions when they learn that an old enemy of Crediton's, Richard Horne, has died in the house and that his body still lies in one of its rooms. Horne had been obsessed with Crediton's wife, for which insolence he had been persecuted and bankrupted. The two men mock the corpse despite Boyle's insistence that the dead man was a warlock. Drunker than ever, Crediton and Bateman decide to conceal the corpse in some hemlock, known locally as kecksies, so that one of them can hide under the sheet and rise up during the burial to confound the guests.

Much to Bateman's surprise, his friend never sits up. Impatient, he assumes the man has fallen asleep and tries to rouse him. He discovers instead the corpse of Horne, mysteriously returned from the kecksies. There is no sign of either his companion or the man's horse. Troubled, he takes his leave, later encounters Crediton on the road, and accompanies him home. He is still sitting up when Crediton joins his wife and is alarmed by the cries of anguish from their chamber. On the point of interceding, he is interrupted by the arrival of Goody Boyle and her companions bearing the body of Crediton, for the corpse they all saw as Horne has changed back into the lord. They break down the door and witness the last moments of animation of Horne's corpse. That which he had sought after in life, intimacy with Crediton's wife, he has achieved in death. The reader will have anticipated the revelation, but that only increases the sense of horror and suspense during the last few pages of the story.

Kennealy, Patricia (1946–)

Patricia Kennealy, who sometimes renders her last name as Kennealy-Morrison, is known exclusively for her eight-volume Keltiad series, two related trilogies followed by two independent novels. Although her prose and plotting are undistinguished, she attracted considerable attention because of her unorthodox blending of high fantasy with science fiction. The Danaans, the inhabitants of Atlantis, were persecuted by their human neighbors because of their mastery of magic. When it becomes obvious that they can no longer hope to remain safe on Earth, they emigrate wholesale to another planet, Keltia, where their culture becomes subtly altered.

The sequence starts with *The Copper Crown* (1984), in which an Arthurian figure is invoked just as a critical war is about to break out. A sorceress travels among the stars in *The Throne of Scone* (1986), searching for magical artifacts connected to the heroic figure with which she hopes to affect the course of events. *The Silver Branch* (1988) is actually set prior to the previous two volumes, providing much of the background.

The second trilogy is more obviously a reimagining of Arthur and Camelot. Rivalries among the displaced population are reaching a fever pitch in *The Hawk's Gray Feather* (1990), a charismatic leader rises to power in *The Oak above the Kings* (1994), and the grail quest is reenacted in *The Hedge above the Mist* (1996). The author shifted emphasis with the seventh volume, *Blackmantle* (1997), introducing a space-faring alien race who add another facet to the ongoing factional struggles. *The Deer's Cry* (1998) is another jump back to the early days of the emigration from Earth and is by far the weakest in the series. Except for one interesting short story, "The Last Voyage," (2002), Kennealy has not been actively writing for the past few years. Although her novels were not wildly successful, they are remarkable for the way in which she chose to blend magic and technology in the same culture, a synthesis several writers have attempted, but usually without much success.

Kerr, Katharine (1944–)

Katharine Kerr's first published novel launched the Deverry sequence, which has dominated her work ever since. Deverry is an imaginary European country in an alternate version of the past where magic works, where legendary creatures such as dwarves are real, and where individuals can be repeatedly reincarnated. The first title was *Daggerspell* (1986), wherein through thoughtlessness the protagonist causes the death of the three people most dear to him, as a result of which he is punished by the gods and forced to wander the Earth seeking their new incarnations. His quest continues in *Darkspell* (1987), complicated by further interference from the gods. The tendency of the latter to view humans as play pieces in an elaborate game results in an imminent war in *The Bristling Wood* (1989), which is resolved in *The Dragon Revenant* (1990, also published as *Dawnspell: The Southern Sea*).

A second set of four novels shifts the focus slightly. A reluctant heir to the throne of the elves encounters problems in *A Time of Exile* (1991), and war threatens to break out again in *A Time of Omens* (1992). A young boy of humble origins sets off on a quest to find a legendary warrior in *A Time of War* (1993, also published as *Days of Blood and Fire*), and the concluding volume, *A Time of Justice* (1994, also published as *Days of Air and Darkness*), brings things to a conclusion when a sorceress and her allies realize that the war has been caused by a goddess who is trying to prevent the birth of a child destined to fulfill a prophecy. Although the plots of these eight novels follow the pattern of most contemporary heroic fantasy, Kerr is exceptionally skillful at creating a plausible world and well above average in her ability to people her creation with multidimensional characters.

A third set of four novels, the Dragon Mage series, is set much earlier in time. *The Red Wyvern* (1997) describes a country ravaged by civil war and the breakdown of all authority. The conflict between a sorceress and a warrior, which has continued through several previous incarnations, stirs the world again in *The Black Raven* (1998), and things get even more complex and foreboding in *The Fire Dragon* (2001). A final volume, *The Gold Dragon*, is scheduled for late 2004.

The most distinct impression one receives from reading the Deverry novels is that they are intelligently planned and executed and that the author has firm control and a consistent vision of her creation. Her non-Deverry stories have been mostly science fiction, but "The Fourth Concealment of the Island of Britain" (2001) is an interesting fantasy.

Keyes, J. Gregory (1963–)

J. Gregory Keyes, whose recent fantasy novels have appeared under the pen name Greg Keyes, made a very strong first impression with *Waterborn* (1996), which blends familiar and unfamiliar fantasy tropes. Members of a royal family have begun to disappear under mysterious circumstances, despite being nominally under the protection of the local River God. One of the young male members of the family decides to discover what is happening before he becomes the next victim. The story is resolved in *The Blackgod* (1987), as we discover that the gods are as divided as humans and as varied in nature. The two-part adventure was well received, and Keyes followed up quickly with the first novel of a new and even more inventive series.

Newton's Cannon (1998) is set in an alternate version of our own world where magic and technology coexist. Isaac Newton makes a revolutionary discovery that allows France to challenge English power throughout the world. Newton becomes friendly with Benjamin Franklin, and in the second volume, *A Calculus of Angels* (1999), the two must pool their talents in order to thwart a group of supernatural entities who have diverted an asteroid from its normal course so that it will hit the Earth. The combination of science fiction and fantasy themes, which so often fails, succeeds admirably in this case. The situation gets even worse in *Empire of Unreason* (2000), with a new ice age threatening to overwhelm civilization and with the French writer Voltaire added to the list of historical protagonists. The series came to an apparent end with *The Shadows of God* (2001). Franklin and an Indian shaman conspire to prevent Russia, France, and England from dividing the rest of the world among themselves, and assuring their dominance through magical weaponry. The four-volume set is among the most original and well-written fantasy of the last two decades.

Keyes's most recent series is equally well written, but considerably less groundbreaking. *The Briar King* (2003) and *The Charnel Prince* (2004) introduce readers to another magical world, this one inhabited by the vanished colonists from early America. There are some original touches, but much of the plot involves missing heirs and some form of quest. Keyes is at his best when he abandons the familiar trappings of fantasy, although, unfortunately, doing so might make his work less appealing to traditional cautious publishers. He has also written some science fiction novels, but they have all been media tie-ins.

King, Stephen (1947–)

The dominant position Stephen King holds in modern horror is unparalleled, and he has at least indirectly influenced the vast majority of writers working in the genre. He has mixed science fiction, fantasy, and supernatural themes so well that some of his novels can be read differently depending on the bias of the reader. *Carrie* (1974), for example, is either supernatural or science fiction, depending upon the question of whether Carrie's powers derive from poltergeists or psychokinesis, which King never answers. King's popularity results from his storytelling skills, his gift for creating memorable characters, and to some extent his timing. THE EXORCIST (1971), by William Peter Blatty, and ROSEMARY'S BABY (1967), by Ira Levin, had already suggested that the reading public was interested in high-quality horror tales. At the time, King was being published primarily under his Richard Bachman pseudonym, under which he wrote two thrillers and two science fiction novels, but his switch to horror under his own name had an enormous impact.

King began writing horror short stories in the late 1960s, producing memorable pieces right from the outset such as "The Mangler" (1972), "TRUCKS" (1973), "Sometimes They Come Back" (1974), and "CHILDREN OF THE CORN" (1977). Most of his early short fiction was collected in *Night Shift* (1978) and *Skeleton Crew* (1985). It was *Carrie* that first caught the public eye, however, the story of an outcast teenager with the ability to move physical objects by willpower alone. It was the first of many of King's creations to be turned into a motion picture and is still one of the most successful adaptations. 'SALEM'S LOT (1975) made King an instant superstar, the most important vampire novel since DRACULA (1898) by Bram STOKER and still the ultimate American vampire story.

King's next novel, THE SHINING (1977), a haunted house variation that maintains an exceptionally high level of tension, secured his popularity, and his books have been best-sellers ever since. His fondness for science fiction devices reasserted

itself in the massive *The Stand* (1978), which was heavily abridged when first published but later released with the excised text restored. A new plague wipes out the vast majority of the human race, and the relatively few survivors face an even more terrible danger when the Walking Dude, essentially Satan, physically manifests himself in the world and begins recruiting allies for a physical as well as metaphysical battle. Major novels followed quickly. *The Dead Zone* (1979) also skirted science fiction. Its protagonist wakens from a coma to discover he has prescient dreams about a future Armageddon. The child protagonist in *Firestarter* (1980) can start fires just by thinking about them, and the chief horror comes from an insane but not supernatural government agent, a common device in King's fiction. Although *Cujo* (1981) was not as well received, CHRISTINE (1983) and PET SEMATARY (1983) both continued to broaden his readership. There was also a steady supply of shorter works, including excellent tales such as "THE CRATE" (1979), "THE MIST" (1980), and "THE RAFT" (1983).

In 1984 King revived the Richard Bachman pseudonym for *Thinner*, but his true identity soon became common knowledge. With Peter STRAUB he wrote *The Talisman* (1984), an atypical work for each of them that is a contemporary quest story involving werewolves and other magical components. A recent sequel, *Black House* (2001), is much better. King's most impressive novel from the mid-1980s was IT (1986). *Tommyknockers* (1987), which is actually science fiction involving aliens, and *The Dark Half* (1989), in which an imaginary character comes to life, were both readable but not nearly as convincing and intense as the novels that preceded them. The early 1990s saw a succession of comparatively minor novels, *Needful Things* (1991), *Insomnia* (1994), *Rose Madder* (1995), *Desperation* (1996), and *The Regulators* (1996), although two nonfantastic novels, *Misery* (1987) and *Dolores Claiborne* (1992), proved that he was still capable of turning out well-crafted, emotionally moving fiction. He also continued to produce first-rate short fiction, although not at his former pace, including major works such as "The Library Policeman" (1991), "The Langoliers" (1991), and "The Night Flier" (1988). *Four Past Midnight* (1991) and *Nightmares and Dreamscapes* (1993) collected most of his short fiction from this period.

In 1996 King engaged in an interesting experiment, publishing portions of his current novel as paperbacks as they were written, so that the ending had not been completed when the first chapters were already in bookstores. The separate portions were eventually republished in one volume as *The Green Mile* (1996), which proved to be one of King's very best novels and perhaps unsurprisingly became one of the most successful movies based on his work. The setting is death row in a mythical prison somewhere in the South. The newest inmate is innocent but doomed and possesses an extraordinary healing power. Although there are some horrifying events in the novel, it could be called fantasy rather than horror with no difficulty. It is possibly the single most genuinely moving of King's stories. The experiment was not entirely original. Michael McDOWELL had written the Blackwater Saga in the early 1980s, a single story published in multiple volumes. It was imitated by John SAUL in his Blackstone series a year later, but each volume in Saul's sequence was a complete separate story within a general frame.

The novels that followed vary considerably in quality. *Bag of Bones* (1998) is one of his best, and the tensions involved in a bitter custody battle are almost as gripping as the supernatural elements. *Hearts in Atlantis* (1999) is uneven and perhaps more science fiction than horror. *Dreamcatcher* (2001) is even more so, an alien invasion story that was marketed as horror fiction. *From a Buick 8* (2002), the story of an automobile that is a conduit to another universe, is bloated and disappointing, a short story idea inflated to novel length. At the same time, the short novel *The Girl Who Loved Tom Gordon* (1999) is a very moving, low-key story about a young girl stalked by a supernatural force. His later short fiction, collected in *Everything's Eventual* (2002), is similarly uneven, although "Riding the Bullet" is excellent.

King has also written straightforward fantasy, including the conventional but comparatively minor *The Eyes of the Dragon* (1984). Much more important is the Dark Tower series, an idiosyncratic episodic quest story that introduced the Gunslinger in *The Gunslinger* (1982, originally titled *The Dark Tower*) and ended with volume seven, *The Dark Tower* (2004). Although often filled with horrific images, it is closer to the fantasy tradition than horror. King himself appears as a character, and there are loose ties to characters in a number of his horror novels as well.

King has recently announced his intention to retire from writing fiction. Even if he never produces another story, his impact on horror fiction—and on best-selling fiction in general—has been stupendous. He is certainly the most successful writer of the late 20th century in terms of total books sold, with a worldwide audience, and more than two dozen major films have been generated from his fiction. Some have attributed the advent of horror fiction as a separate publishing category to the sustained popularity of his books, and one has only to walk into a bookstore to see that the horror sections are dominated by King, with only Dean R. KOONTZ approaching the same monopolization of shelf space. His ability to speak to a wide variety of readers and to engage them with his characters and stories is unrivaled. King received the Bram Stoker Award for *Misery, Four Past Midnight, The Green Mile, Bag of Bones*, and "Lunch at the Gotham Cafe" and the World Fantasy Award for "Do the Dead Sing?" (1981) and "The Man in the Black Suit" (1995).

The King in Yellow Robert W. Chambers (1895)

Although Robert Chambers was a prolific writer who produced a considerable body of mainstream fiction, he is remembered almost exclusively today for his supernatural fiction, particularly this collection of interrelated stories. The underlying premise is the existence of a book of arcane lore so powerful that those who read it are driven insane and of a form of personified death who is the gatekeeper to a mystical otherworld.

The most famous of the individual stories is "The Yellow Sign," in which the artist narrator is confronted by the animate dead, who serve as a kind of guide between the two realities. A series of nightmarish visions and dreams follows, slowly escalating the level of tension. "The Demoiselle D'Ys" describes the increasingly ardent love affair between a traveler and a mysterious and beautiful young woman. After a brief but blissful time together, the traveler must leave, but he does so only after promising to return. At that very moment he discovers that she is a ghost and that she died centuries earlier, although somehow the cause of that death was heartbreak over losing him. The final paragraphs suggest that his own death is imminent and that they will be reunited shortly. In "In the Court of the Dragon," a visitor to a church is chased from the building by a frightening apparition whose nature is unclear.

"The Repairer of Reputations" is also linked to the underlying mythos, although it is science fiction rather than horror, a story set in a future America that has become a totalitarian state and whose pressures are so great that insanity has become a common problem. The remaining story, "The Mask," is also science fiction and has no apparent relationship to the others. Additional stories were included in a 1970 edition titled *The King in Yellow and Other Horror Stories*. Although Chambers continued to produce stories of the occult and black magic, few of his later works rivaled those in his first collection. The device of an imaginary book of powerful magic undoubtedly influenced the creation of the *Necronomicon* by H. P. LOVECRAFT.

Klasky, Mindy L. (1964–   )

Most new writers in any genre require at least a few books to build a following, but Mindy Klasky attracted enough attention with her first novel, *The Glasswright's Apprentice* (2000), to make a strong first impression, and her continuation of that story into a series has been solidly entertaining. A young woman serving as an apprentice artisan in the glasswright's guild is mistakenly identified as a traitor when one of her instructors is judged responsible for the assassination of the crown prince. She is forced to go into hiding among the worst elements of the city, where she quickly acquires self-confidence and eventually clears her name by tracking down the people who are actually responsible for the murder.

Rani Trader, now promoted to the nobility as a reward for her service to the throne, returns in *The Glasswright's Progress* (2001), intent upon rebuilding the guild that was destroyed during the first book. Her plans go awry when she is kidnapped by a foreign ruler who has a particularly unpleasant habit of selling children into slavery to finance his mercenary army. In *The Glasswright's Journeyman* (2002) she accompanies her king to a foreign land where he is reluctantly agreeing to a marriage of state, because the bride's dowry will help to rebuild the capital city and provide treatment for the many people injured in the recently concluded conflict. Rani's quick wits end up helping both nations.

The political maneuvering between and within the two countries gets even more complex in *The Glasswright's Test* (2003), complicated by internal struggles within the newly reformed guild as well as the active intervention of the gods. Rani's most recent and perhaps final adventure is *The Glasswright's Master* (2004), which ties up many of the loose ends from the previous books and forces Rani to reevaluate the choices she has already made as well as the ones immediately confronting her. Klasky's only other novel is *Season of Sacrifice* (2002), in which a young woman must respond to a crisis even though she is not yet fully schooled in the tree magic that protects her people. It is decidedly inferior to the Glasswright series. "Saving the Skychildren" (2000) is her only notable short story. Klasky is still in the early stages of her career but has already demonstrated the ability to produce a sustained series with a protagonist who develops more fully in each successive volume. She seems likely to be a steady and perhaps major new talent in fantasy.

Klein, T. E. D. (1947–   )

Although Klein has produced only one novel and a dozen or so short stories over the course of 30 years, he is still recognized as a significant figure in the field, partly because of the quality of his published horror fiction and partly because of his role as a founding editor of the short-lived but highly regarded *Rod Serling's The Twilight Zone Magazine* during the early 1980s. His long story "The Events at Poroth Farm" (1972) had already established his credentials as a writer, a moody, highly literate story that evoked much of the spirit of H. P. LOVE-CRAFT in its depiction of a decaying, cursed place destined to serve as a pivotal site for the return of an ancient evil. Klein eventually reworked the idea into his only novel, *Ceremonies* (1984), which was nominated for the World Fantasy Award and which won the British Fantasy Award. *Ceremonies* clearly draws on Lovecraft and other classic horror writers and builds its mood in very small increments, catching the reader almost unaware. Two people discover that their lives are being quietly manipulated by a third party, a man attempting to arrange things so that the supernatural entity he serves can return to the world of humanity. A straightforward plot description cannot do justice to Klein's textured, intensely intellectual story.

All of Klein's other fiction consists of short stories and novelettes, four of which are collected in *Dark Gods* (1985). The best of these is "Nadelman's God" (1986), which won the World Fantasy Award, although "Children of the Kingdom" (1980), "One Size Eats All" (1993), and "Growing Things" (1999) are nearly as good. Klein produces new fiction too infrequently to have a large and active following, but the quality of even his lesser stories is so high that his name is highly regarded by readers and fellow writers alike.

Knaak, Richard A. (1961–   )

Contemporary fantasy is dominated by the big novel, in fact more commonly the big three-part novel, with large casts of characters, a panoramic scope of action involving the rise and fall of kingdoms, multiple story lines, and societies that follow in the manner of J. R. R. TOLKIEN, E. R. EDDISON, and other early fantasists. But there is another tradition that appeals to a slightly different readership, the sword and sorcery adventure story as popularized by Robert E. HOWARD and his imitators. Typically, these stories focus on a single or at least a very small group of protagonists, there is usually a single significant story line, and the emphasis is on action and adventure rather than character development and background.

Most of the sword and sorcery fiction produced currently is linked to either a role-playing game system or a computer simulation such as FORGOTTEN REALMS and WARHAMMER. Although most of the authors writing these tie-ins tend to work primarily in that area, a few have moved on to create worlds of their own. One of the most prolific and reliable of these is Richard A. Knaak, who started his career with a DRAGONLANCE novel, *The Legend of Huma* (1988), and a few related stories but who quickly established himself as a general fantasist with *Firedrake* (1989), the first in the Dragonrealm series. Although he continued to produce tie-ins intermittently during his subsequent career, the best of his work is entirely original, although often similar in tone and execution.

The common plot element in the Dragonrealm series is that the various dragons have distinct colors that govern their attributes. The 10th and most recent volume in the series, *The Horse King,* appeared in 1997. The individual titles each tackle one of the traditional conflicts of the barbarian adventure, evil sorcerers, mysterious shape changers, ancient evil gods, wars, monstrous creatures, and occasional intrigues. They are meant to be light entertainment rather than serious fiction, and for the most part Knaak has been quite successful at achieving that goal, particularly in *Children of the Drake* (1991) and *The Crystal Dragon* (1993).

The best of Knaak's novels are those not set within a series. In *King of the Grey* (1993) vampires and other mythical creatures exist only as potential beings until they draw life from an enigmatic man. *Frostwing* (1995) subjects its protagonist to images of a living gargoyle in contemporary Chicago. A ruthless aristocrat imprisons the souls of his enemies within elaborate masks in *The Janus Mask* (1995), probably Knaak's best novel to date. It is entirely possible that he will never write the kind of breakthrough work that leads to best-seller status, but Knaak has produced a steady supply of exciting, intelligently written light adventure stories that are always readable and sometimes find new ways to twist old story lines.

Koja, Kathe (1960–   )

Kathe Koja first began to make an impact on horror fiction with several very powerful short stories during the late 1980s, many of which deal with characters obsessed by some object or activity, usually with unpleasant consequences. This character trait carried over into her first novel, *The Cipher* (1991), in which two friends, neither of whom has prospered either financially or spiritually, discover a mysterious black hole in a storage room. Items dropped into the hole and later retrieved are transformed, often in very grotesque ways. They eventually experiment by lowering a video camera into the hole, but the resulting pictures differ depending upon who is looking at them. Exploration of the hole becomes an obsession, reflecting the twisted images in their own minds. *The Cipher* won the Bram Stoker Award.

Bad Brains (1992) involves a somewhat similar situation. The artist protagonist in this case suffers an injury to his head, after which he experiences a variety of visions, or perhaps hallucinations, that might be dismissed as entirely illusory except that somehow what he experiences has a physical effect on objects around him, chiefly his paintings. *Skin* (1993) strays even further toward pure psychological horror. This time the protagonists are a sculptor and a dancer whose obsession with dark imagery leads to compulsive body piercing and other unpleasantries. Koja's next novel, *Strange Angels* (1994), explored the same themes once again in an even more surreal manner, but this and several subsequent novels avoid any fantastic content.

Her most recent book, *The Blue Mirror* (2004), edges back toward the fantastic. An unhappy young woman becomes obsessed with her new boyfriend, who may not be entirely human. Several of Koja's short stories have been collected as *Extremities* (1998), although only some of them involve the fantastic. She has continued to write short fiction, including such memorable pieces as "The Timbrel Sound of Darkness" (1993), "In the Greenhouse" (1994), "Waking the Prince" (1995), and "At Eventide" (2000).

Koontz, Dean R. (1945–   )

Dean R. Koontz started his career as a science fiction writer during the 1960s, quickly shedding the awkwardness of a new author and growing steadily more self-confident and skilled as he produced a rather astonishing volume of work under a variety of names, including nonfiction, thrillers, fantasy, and horror. His breakthrough came during the late 1970s, after which his novels were almost always marketed as horror, although more often the horrors were rationalized rather than supernatural. Most of his "horror" novels are, in fact, technically science fiction rather than supernatural or fantasy, but his name has become so identified with the horror field that they are included here.

Koontz did produce some conventional fantasy early in his career, although even then it was obvious that he preferred scientific rationales. *The Crimson Witch* (1971) transports a man from our reality to an alternate history in which a devastating nuclear war destroyed technological civilization, which has been replaced by resurgent magic. A much more interesting fantasy is *The Haunted Earth* (1973), which also mixes genres. Aliens arrive from another world with the power to open gateways between realities. Creatures of legend and even racial stereotypes exist in some of these alternate worlds and are now free to cross over into ours. Koontz uses this device for some light humor and satire. Two more recent works are also fantasy. In *Oddkins* (1988) toys come to life, complicating matters for the child protagonist, and in *Santa's Twin* (1996) the title character impersonates the original and sets out to destroy Christmas.

Night Chills (1976) was the first of Koontz's novels to be marketed as horror fiction. An experimental gas has properties that could potentially unlock an unexpected power in the human mind, but the downside is that exposure also turns most people into maniacal killers. A flurry of similarly suspenseful books followed, and his career took a new and much more successful direction. *The Vision* (1977) makes use of an overly familiar though still effective theme, the clairvoyant psychically linked to a serial killer who must be identified before he tracks down the protagonist. *The Face of Fear* (1977), which appeared in the United States as written by Brian Coffey and in the United Kingdom as written by K. R. Dwyer, uses a similar theme but is closer to being a police procedural. *Watchers* (1977) was his first major novel and has generated three film versions. Two creatures escape from a government project involving genetic enhancement, one a dog with nearly human intelligence, the other a malformed but powerful humanoid creature who pursues the dog and his protectors.

Although there are hints of the supernatural in *Whispers* (1980), which was also filmed, it is more properly described as psychological suspense, which is also the case with *The Mask* (1981), originally published as written by Owen West. Koontz's novels from this period were quieter and less ambitious, and it seemed as though he was searching for a new voice. Two somewhat stronger novels appeared under the name Leigh Nichols. In *The Eyes of Darkness* (1981) a woman grieving over her dead child is startled when she begins receiving enigmatic messages that might be from beyond the grave. *The House of Thunder* (1982) is similarly ambiguous, this time involving the survivor of a hazing who loses several friends to mysterious fatal accidents and then barely escapes her own death. Koontz had by now acquired a wide following, and he dropped most of his pseudonyms soon afterward, eventually reissuing most of the earlier novels under his own name.

Phantoms (1983) is significantly better than any of his previous book-length fiction, the story of an age-old creature that lives deep beneath the Earth and rising periodically to graze on surface life. Its own personality is transformed when it encounters humans and acquires elements of our intelligence. The novel is relentlessly suspenseful, but the recent film version stumbled early and never regained its momentum. *Darkfall* (1984, also published as *Darkness Comes*) is one of the few Koontz novels to openly use supernatural elements, in this case a sorcerer who has literally opened a gateway to hell. *Strangers* (1986) and *Lightning* (1988), although marketed as horror, involve peaceful alien visitors and a time traveler from the future, but *Twilight Eyes* (1987) returns to the supernatural. The protagonist in this case is the only person in the world who can see the true form of goblinlike creatures who are living secretly among normal humans.

Shadowfires (1987), the last novel to appear under the Leigh Nichols name, is a rationalized werewolf story. The protagonist desperately flees her abusive husband when he unwisely submits to an experiment that alters his physical body. Koontz uses this device even more effectively in *Midnight* (1989), which involves several human subjects whose transformation into shape-shifting creatures has unforeseen and unpleasant psychological consequences. *Servants of the Twilight* (1984, also published as *Twilight*) is a variation of the devil's child story. The protagonist helps a woman and a young boy elude a religious cult whose members are convinced the boy is the son of Satan. He succeeds, only to discover that they were right. The subsequent film was reasonably effective this time.

Cold Fire (1991) has a fascinating premise. The heroic protagonist always seems to defeat evil at a critical moment, but is he, in fact, somehow willing his enemies into existence? Koontz explores this theme again in *Dragon Tears* (1992), this time with a villain who can apparently generate duplicates of himself as allies. *Hideaway* (1992) is a rather disappointing variation of the psychic linkage plot, and *Ticktock* (1996) is an occasionally amusing but very minor supernatural story that actually pokes fun at some genre conventions. Several of Koontz's novels from this point onward are entirely nonfantastic, including the very effective thriller *Intensity* (1996).

Koontz introduced Snow, a recurring character who has a violent allergy to daylight, in *Fear Nothing* (1998). When his father's corpse disappears, Snow investigates and uncovers a major biogenetic conspiracy. The entire story takes place over the course of a single night. Snow returns in *Seize the Night* (1999), discovering even stranger aspects of the secret project when he investigates the disappearance of several children. Although *From the Corner of His Eye* (2000) is a disappointing chase story involving another psychic connection and some abstruse scientific theories, Koontz is at the top of his form in *The Face* (2003), in which a supernaturally enhanced serial killer stalks the son of a famous actor. The young boy is one of the author's most fully realized characters. *Odd Thomas* (2003) deals with a man who can literally communicate with the dead and cleverly mixes suspense with quiet humor. *The Taking* (2004) is another story of alien invasion, a very bizarre variety in this case that includes animation of the dead, but his most recent novel, *Life Expectancy* (2004), employs the supernatural, in this case a chilling prophecy about five critical points in a young man's life.

Many of Koontz's themes and plots are familiar ones, but he almost always manages to find a new way to look at old situations. He is capable of creating very memorable characters, although he does not consistently do so. Koontz was a productive short story writer early in his career, but he has concentrated primarily on novels for the past several years. *Strange Highways* (1995) is his only significant collection. His best horror stories are "Down in the Darkness" (1987) and "Trapped" (1989). Although he is often compared to Stephen KING, primarily because of the sheer volume of his work and his frequent appearance on the best-seller lists, the two writers have always been very different in their choices of subject matter. Koontz's emphasis has shifted more than once during his career, and it is never certain what direction his next book will take.

Kotzwinkle, William (1938–   )

Although he first began writing in 1969 and published several children's books, some of which are vaguely fantasy, William Kotzwinkle's first significant genre novel was *The Leopard's Tooth* (1976), also for young readers, although a fairly sophisticated story about a boy who accompanies an anthropological expedition to India and who becomes involved with some ancient magic propagated by a local sorcerer. More significant is *Doctor Rat* (1976), a savage satire narrated by one of the experimental rats in a laboratory, which won the World Fantasy Award. The title character initially acts as an apologist for the cruelties practiced on the animals by the researchers while having a variety of low-key adventures and eventually changing his attitude. The author's indictment of experimental practices is at times bitter, and the expressed hope that humanity will eventually learn the error of its ways is cast into doubt by the ending, in which the rebellious animals are all destroyed.

Fata Morgana (1977), probably Kotzwinkle's best fantasy novel, is set in 19th-century France and involves the interaction of a complexly described police officer with a mysterious figure who is subsequently revealed to be a wizard who subjects the police officer to a series of increasingly strange conjurations. *The Ants Who Took away Time* (1978) is a children's fantasy in which ants disassemble time, resulting in much confusion. A mysterious shadow appears in a department store to help restore the spirit of the holidays in the amusing *Christmas at Fontaine's* (1982). *Great World Circus* (1983) describes the appearance of an enigmatic female who appears to exist independently of the flow of time.

The Exile (1987) swaps the personalities of a contemporary actor with a German criminal during World War II. The latter is captured and tortured after being caught helping a Jewish girl avoid capture by the authorities. There is authentic voodoo in *The Midnight Examiner* (1989) and a bear that impersonates a human being in *The Bear Went over the Mountain* (1996). Kotzwinkle's later novels have not been as substantial as his earlier work. Two of his collections contain primarily fantasy stories, *Hearts of Wood and Other Timeless Tales* (1986) and *The Hot Jazz Trio* (1989). He has also done movie novelizations.

Krinard, Susan (1958–   )

It has only been comparatively recently that fantastic themes have become popular with romance novelists. Although light elements of magic appeared from time to time, it was not until time travel romances—in which a character is magically or inexplicably transported to another era, either physically or by displacing the personality of another—began to proliferate that romance writers and publishers began to experiment with otherworld settings, witch craft, and supernatural beings. The sudden popularity of horror fiction that started in the 1970s, particularly vampire stories, was followed by a rash of supernatural romances.

Susan Krinard's first three novels all appeared in 1996. *Prince of Wolves* chronicles the efforts by a young woman to visit the scene of her parents' accidental death, during the course of which she discovers a race of werewolves living hidden in the area and falls in love with one of their kind. *Prince of Dreams* is a modified vampire novel. This time the female protagonist learns of the existence of a vampire who draws his sustenance from the dreams of women, giving them an ecstatic experience in exchange and not hurting them at all. Unfortunately, he has an evil brother who callously takes human lives, adding conflict to their sudden romance. *Prince of Shadows* returns to the world of werewolves, reprising the first story.

Twice a Hero (1997) is a time travel romance involving a family curse, a considerable change from her previous books both in tone and subject matter and is not as successful, and *Body and Soul* (1998) is a Regency-era ghost romance that is equally slight. She returned to werewolves with the much more interesting *Touch of the Wolf* (1999), a historical novel in which a half-breed werewolf-human woman finds her true love. The heroine of *Once a Wolf* (2000) tries to deny her shape-shifting heritage but eventually learns to welcome her differences. *Secret of the Wolf* (2001) completes the loose trilogy, this time describing the reaction of a psychiatrist to a patient who believes himself to be a werewolf. *To Catch a Wolf* (2003) is her most recent werewolf romance, another tale of an individual tormented by his secret nature but who eventually finds love.

The Forest Lord (2002) is a more mainstream fantasy, although still with strong romantic elements. In Regency England fairies are faced with the extinction of their race unless they can find human lovers. Some of the characters in *Shield of the Sky* (2004) are also shape shifters, but the novel is more about the quest to destroy an evil creature than an exploration of their culture. Krinard, who has also written some science fiction romances, appears to be broadening her range of settings and plots and may be on the verge of gaining a following outside the borders of romance fiction.

Kurtz, Katherine (1944–   )

With her first published fantasy, *Deryni Rising* (1970), Katherine Kurtz introduced the imaginary world that would dominate her career as an author. Deryni is a typical fantasy land, although better realized than most, in which kings, nobles, wizards, and other magical elements combine and conflict. Kurtz was clearly influenced by J. R. R. TOLKIEN and became one of the earliest fantasy

writers to create a similar world over the course of many books. Humans share this world with the Deryni, who look very similar to humans but who possess various magical powers that are the source of considerable tension between the two races. Over the course of the series, which did not appear in chronological order, the Deryni are eventually driven into hiding, although they remain secretly powerful and influential.

In the opening volume the influence that one of the Deryni has over the current king leads to plots and counterplots. The opposition grows more heated in *Deryni Checkmate* (1972), as an entrenched human church decides to neutralize the power of the nonhumans. When they discover that the new king is half Deryni himself in *High Deryni* (1973), the church leadership transfers its allegiance to a challenger, leading to civil war. Although it initially appeared that the series would conclude as a trilogy, Kurtz started work on a second sequence consisting of *Camber of Culdi* (1976), *Saint Camber* (1978), and *Camber the Heretic* (1980), which is set much earlier in time. The current king is a corrupt and cruel Deryni sorcerer. Camber is another of his kind with more benevolent intentions who secretly plots to replace the tyrant. He succeeds, but in the second volume the new king is in danger of being similarly supplanted. The situation worsens, human resentment becomes uncontrollable, and Camber, recognizing that persecution is inevitable, begins to teach other Deryni how to pass for human and live in secret.

A third trilogy comprises *The Bishop's Heir* (1984), *The King's Justice* (1985), and *The Quest for Saint Camber* (1986). The church hierarchy was defeated but has not resigned itself to the situation. A new plot involves seceding from the king's lands and forming a separate state where the Deryni can be outlawed. Another round of civil war follows, ending with the apparent death of the king and a reappearance by a legendary Deryni. *The Deryni Archives* (1986) is a set of interwoven stories set in the same world, and *Deryni Magic* (1990) is mostly nonfiction about the author's creation, with some narrative sections.

The fourth trilogy began with *The Harrowing of Gwynedd* (1989) and continued with *King*

Javan's Year (1992) and *The Bastard Prince* (1994). Despite efforts at reconciliation, the tension between humans and Deryni worsens, and the latter are forced to go into hiding once again. The new king is failing, and his son, known to have sympathy for the Deryni, is the target of a plot by the local nobles, leading to another round of civil disturbances and rebellion. *King Kelson's Bride* (2000) poses a new dilemma from the king. For reasons of state he is compelled to marry, even though the only woman he ever loved has died. The most recent Deryni novel is *In the King's Service* (2003), another story of the early days when humans and the Deryni lived together amicably.

Kurtz has also written a second series in collaboration with Deborah Turner Harris. *The Adept* (1991) introduces a heroic figure whose latest incarnation is as protector of England against a variety of supernatural dangers, starting with a coven of black magicians in his debut adventure. He has similar opponents in *The Lodge of the Lynx* (1992) and retrieves the Seal of Solomon in *The Templar Treasure* (1993). These occult adventures are in the general tradition of the supernatural sleuth or the occult adventures of Dennis WHEATLEY. A cult threatens to use black magic to revive the Third Reich in *Dagger Spell* (1995), the high point in the series. Subsequent adventures, though always cleverly told, are less interesting.

The unrelated *Lammas Night* (1983) similarly has a coven of witches organizing a defense for Britain when Hitler employs occult forces in a surreptitious attack. *Two Crowns for America* (1996), one of the author's best novels, suggests that a magician might have used his powers to manipulate matters during the American Revolution. Her most recent stand-alone novel is *St. Patrick's Gargoyle* (2001), in which we learn that gargoyles are actually disguised angels, one of whom must team up with an elderly human being to foil a demonic plot. Kurtz is a reliable, entertaining, and intelligent fantasist who is more interesting when she strays from her primary setting, the world of the Deryni. Her short stories are generally negligible, but "The Gargoyle's Shadow" (1998) is an exception.

Kushner, Ellen (1955–)

Although Ellen Kushner's first noticeable impact on the fantasy field was as the editor of *Basilisk* (1980), an anthology, she was soon writing interesting short stories of her own, including "The Unicorn Masque" (1981), "The Red Cloak" (1982), and "Charis" (1986). Her first novel was *Swordspoint* (1987), set in an imaginary 18th-century European country and containing no other explicit fantasy devices. The novel received considerable favorable attention because of its adroit mixture of high-pitched action sequences with sophisticated dialogue and characterization. Aristocrats settle matters of honor by hiring others to fight duels for them while they sit around and plot and gossip endlessly. The alternation between action and reflection becomes an effective point and counterpoint. A later edition of the book has some short fiction added.

Kushner returned to this world in *The Fall of the Kings* (2002), written in collaboration with Delia Sherman, a much more overtly fantastic novel. The aristocratic student protagonist is conducting research into the relationship between the ancient kings of his country and the wizards who served them. It is commonly believed that there was no real magic, that it was all tricks and exaggerations, but when the student uncovers evidence that some of the magic was genuine, the repercussions threaten to shake the balance between the present government and that part of the country that would like to see the monarchy reinstated. Highly literate, intelligently plotted, and with superior characterization, it is one of the major fantasy novels of recent years.

Kushner's third novel of significance is *Thomas the Rhymer* (1990), which won the World Fantasy Award. Based on a fairy tale, it tells the story of a harpist who is abducted into the land of fairies and then returned after a seven-year absence with a magical compulsion to tell only the truth. Although not without humor, this adaptation is thoughtful and usually serious in tone. *The Enchanted Kingdom* (1986, written with Judith Mitchell) is a children's story. *St. Nicholas and the Valley Beyond* (1994) is a picture book that also contains a short fantasy story. Kushner continues to write infrequent but invariably high-quality short stories, including "Playing with Fire" (1993), "Death of a Raven" (1997), and "The House of Nine Doors" (1998).

Kuttner, Henry (1914–1958)

Although Henry Kuttner was best known for his science fiction, he also wrote some horror and weird fiction in the mode of H. P. LOVECRAFT as well as sword and sorcery fiction. He was married to Catherine L. Moore, who was also a writer who contributed anonymously to much of the work published under Kuttner's various pseudonyms and in some cases was the primary author. Kuttner's Lovecraftian fiction is mostly minor and had been out of print for many years when it was collected as *The Book of IOD* (1995). "The Eater of Souls" and "Spawn of Dagon" (1938) are the best of these.

His sword and sorcery fiction fell chiefly into two series, the Prince Raynor stories and the more interesting tales of Elak, a barbarian hero similar to the CONAN SERIES by Robert E. HOWARD. These were collected as *Elak of Atlantis* (1985), and *Prince Raynor* (1987) and the former in particular are of much higher quality than most similar fiction from the 1930s. During the 1940s Kuttner and Moore wrote a number of short novels clearly in imitation of the work of A. MERRITT, and as in his

case, they often blurred the lines between fantasy and science fiction, employing technological devices that were often indistinguishable from magic. The magazines of that time were less interested in fantasy, so in most of their work from this period magic was rationalized as superscience or the product of psi powers.

The most clearly fantastic of these early novels is *The Mask of Circe* (1948, although not in book form until 1977), in which a contemporary man discovers that he is the reincarnation of Jason and that he must relive the conflict with Circe and the gods. Rather more interesting although also quite similar is *The Dark World* (1946, but not in book form until 1964), in which another protagonist from our world discovers that he has a different identity in another reality. The good and bad aspects of his personality begin to battle with one another.

Several of Kuttner's short stories are humorous fantasy, including "The Misguided Halo" (1939), "A GNOME THERE WAS" (1941), and "Compliments of the Author" (1942). His most famous horror story is "THE GRAVEYARD RATS" (1936). Kuttner left a surprisingly large body of fiction behind despite a relatively short career, certainly because a large part was by Moore, who ceased writing fiction shortly after his death.

L

Lackey, Mercedes (1950–)

Mercedes Lackey started writing short stories in the middle of the 1980s and very quickly became one of the most popular and prolific fantasy writers. Her first several novels introduced her longest series, Valdemar, most of which are clustered into subsets. The unique aspect of the series is that certain select individuals are partnered with magical horses, usually as servants or bodyguards subject to the throne. The series was introduced by a trilogy, *Arrows of the Queen* (1988), *Arrow's Flight* (1989), and *Arrow's Fall* (1989). The three novels introduce the world and the culture as seen through the eyes of a young woman chosen to become a Herald, adjusting to her duties, overcoming the resentment of others, and finally helping thwart a magical plot against the throne. *The Oathbound* (1988) and *Oathbreakers* (1989) are set in the same world, but involve different characters. Lackey took a pair of female warriors as her protagonists this time, pitting them against a gang of bandits in the first and sending them on a quest in the second.

Lackey launched a series of supernatural adventures in a contemporary setting with *Burning Water* (1989). A romance novelist and part-time witch, Diana Tregarde, investigates Native American magic and a series of ritual murders in a very suspenseful and crisply moving adventure. Tregarde teams up with a friendly vampire in *Children of the Night* (1990) in order to solve another series of murders and made her final bow in the excellent *Jinx High* (1991). Although the series was very popular, Lackey decided to abandon it and concentrate on mainstream fantasy. Her only other novel in this vein is *Sacred Ground* (1994), an entertaining but less engaging novel about a construction project that disturbs an ancient evil.

Lackey returned to Valdemar for another trilogy, *Magic's Pawn* (1989), *Magic's Promise* (1990), and *Magic's Price* (1990). Vanyel is a young man who would rather be a simple bard than a powerful sorcerer, but the consequences of not learning to master his talent are so dangerous that he finally accepts the inevitable. In the ensuing volumes he becomes the most powerful user of magic in all of Valdemar, defeats enemy sorcery, and struggles to avert the destruction of everything he knows. The trilogy is much more closely plotted than Lackey's previous books, clear evidence that she is maturing as a writer. *By the Sword* (1991) reverts to a female protagonist, a young woman determined to rescue a kidnapped friend. It was followed promptly by still another trilogy, *Winds of Fate* (1991), *Winds of Change* (1992), and *Winds of Fury* (1993). Elspeth is heir to the throne of Valdemar some considerable time later in its history, after magic has disappeared from the land. When an evil force threatens to destroy the country, she travels to a distant place in order to regain the ability to manipulate magic, then returns to save her people.

Still another trilogy consists of *Storm Warning* (1994), *Storm Rising* (1996), and *Storm Breaking* (1996). This time the rulers of Valdemar must forge an alliance with a neighboring nation so that their combined arms can be brought to bear on a mutual enemy whose evil sorcery would overwhelm them individually. With her husband, the artist Larry Dixon, Lackey continued to expand the history of Valdemar with *The Black Gryphon* (1994), *The White Gryphon* (1995), and *The Silver Gryphon* (1996), set in a time before the events of any of the previous books. A battle between good and evil powers, both aided by sorcery, results in the formation of a new nation. Her next Valdemar novel was *Take a Thief* (2001), in which a young man's propensity for petty criminality lands him in a great deal of trouble.

Exile's Honor (2002) and *Exile's Valor* (2003) show us Valdemar from the point of view of an outsider. A soldier in the service of one of their enemies is captured, during which time he decides that he has been fighting on the wrong side and changes allegiances. Although this series has dominated her writing career and contains some of her most popular pure adventure stories, much of her best writing is in different settings.

The Lark and the Wren (1992), *The Robin and the Kestrel* (1993), and *The Eagle and the Nightingale* (1993) make up the Bardic Voices trilogy. A young woman is determined to pursue a career as a bard, and to prove her ability she challenges a ghost in the opening volume, foils a plot to eradicate all the music in the world in the second, and battles a repressive church hierarchy in the third. Related to these is *Four and Twenty Blackbirds* (1997), a story of magical possession and serial murder. All four of these are among her very best work.

Joust (2003) and its sequel, *Alta* (2004), have much the feel of the Valdemar books. The protagonist undergoes a vast change of perspective when he is chosen to work with dragons, and his unorthodox behavior subsequently affects the core values of his civilization. Several of Lackey's nonseries novels are also memorable. *The Black Swan* (1999) is an interesting retelling of the story of Swan Lake. *The Fairy Godmother* (2004) is an amusing take on a standard fairy tale plot, with the title character turning a prince into a donkey. The individual titles in the Elemental Masters trilogy, *The Serpent's Shadow* (2001), *The Gates of Sleep* (2002), and *Phoenix and Ashes* (2004) are each based on a classic fairy tale such as "Snow White and the Seven Dwarfs" and "Cinderella." *Firebird* (1996) and *The Fire Rose* (1996) are also retellings of fairy tales, the latter a variation of "The Beauty and the Beast."

Lackey has collaborated with many other writers, including Piers ANTHONY, C. J. CHERRYH, and Andre NORTON. Although in general the results have been less satisfactory than her work alone, there have been some exceptions. The Serrated Edge series, which started with *Born to Run* (1992) and was written with Larry Dixon, introduced a borderline world in which elves have infiltrated our world and interact with humans, although not in traditional ways. All of the subsequent volumes in the series have been collaborations as well with several different authors, including Rosemary EDGHILL. A similar series about elves and the less interesting Bard's Tales series are also written exclusively in collaboration.

Three other collaborative series are more substantial. With Larry Dixon again she produced the Owl trilogy, *Owlflight* (1997), *Owlsight* (1998), and *Owlknight* (1999), a typical fantasy epic about imminent war and collapse, enlivened by a well-realized and rather bizarre landscape where magic has altered the natural order of things. With Dave Freer and Eric Flint she has written two volumes in a presumably continuing series about a fantastic alternate Venice, *The Shadow of the Lion* (2002) and *This Rough Magic* (2003), very complex stories of political intrigues and hidden magic in a 16th-century Europe that never was. With James Mallory she has written *The Outstretched Shadow* (2003) and *To Light a Candle* (2004), a very well written but overly familiar story of a world poised on the brink of a magical war.

Oathblood (1990) and *The Werehunter* (1999) are both collections of Lackey's short fiction, which is generally inferior to her book-length work. *Fiddler's Fair* (1998) is a much better selection. Lackey is a very popular, very prolific writer who is at her best when she moves away from the more familiar plots and devices of mainstream fantasy and who has demonstrated a particular talent for transforming fairy tales into new and interesting stories.

Lang, Andrew (1844–1912)

Andrew Lang was a Scottish writer who with his wife, Leonora, edited a series of retellings of traditional fairy tales, each title of which involved a color, hence *The Blue Fairy Book* (1889) with eleven sequels, the last being *The Lilac Fairy Book* (1911). Although Lang was forced to draw upon less interesting stories as the series progressed, his books did serve to preserve the fairy tales that might otherwise have been lost. A selection of some of the best of these was assembled in 1993 as *The Rainbow Fairy Book*.

Most of Lang's most memorable original works were fantasies for children, such as *The Gold of Fairnilee* (1888), a fairy–tale inspired story of a man abducted into the land of the fairies, where he remains for seven years before being allowed to return. *That Very Mab* (1885), a collaboration with May Kendall, also involves fairies, although it was written for adults. The queen of the fairies has been gone from England for some time, vacationing in the South Pacific, and she returns to find things decidedly not to her liking. Lang also collaborated with H. Rider HAGGARD for *The World's Desire* (1890), the story of Odysseus's later adventures in Egypt.

Several of Lang's short stories are also fantasy. "In the Wrong Paradise" (1886) follows the travails of a man who is sent to a series of incorrect paradises after his death, with satiric results. "The House of Strange Stories" (1886) is about ghosts, and "The End of Phaeacia" (1886) involves a magical curse. Lang also did a translation of *The Odyssey* and wrote extensive nonfiction on the subject of fairy tales and fantasy in general. His original fiction, though occasionally interesting, is minor, and he will be remembered primarily for his preservation of many obscure stories.

Lansdale, Joe R. (1951–)

Joe Lansdale's gritty, unsettling, occasionally over-the-top short horror stories first began appearing around 1980. He caused a considerable stir right from the outset with disturbing and effective stories such as "Chompers" (1983), "Bestsellers Guaranteed" (1985), and "Tight Little Stitches in the Dead Man's Back" (1986). He mixed supernatural and nonfantastic themes, and his stories were filled with powerful scenes and graphic images that might have been mere sensationalism in the hands of a lesser writer.

His first book-length horror story was *Dead in the West* (1986), a blend of the supernatural and the traditional western that he and occasional other writers revisited intermittently in the future. Lansdale, in fact, coedited with Pat Lobrutto an anthology of such stories, *Razored Saddles* (1990). In *Dead in the West* the residents of a small town are stalked by the walking dead, zombies compelled by an unseen intelligence. Their champion is an itinerant gun-slinging preacher who is not afraid to face the supernatural.

The Nightrunners (1987) is much more conventional horror. After young Becky escapes from a gang of brutal rapists, their leader is captured and subsequently dies while in custody. During her recovery she slowly begins to regain her self-confidence and sense of security. Unfortunately, the dead man's spirit returns and directs his former companions on a campaign of terrifying vengeance. Lansdale followed up with two linked novels that were far less conventional and filled with bizarre imagery. *The Drive-In* (1988) and *The Drive-In 2* (1989) take place in a drive-in theater whose customers find themselves trapped one night by an inexplicable field of force. The initial panic becomes more frantic when the unseen power begins to physically affect individuals, transforming their bodies and personalities. In the second novel they are finally liberated, but the changes do not reverse themselves. The survivors attempt to form some kind of new community, but it is inherently unstable.

With the collapse of the booming horror market in the late 1980s, Lansdale shifted emphasis in his novels to more conventional suspense themes, although always maintaining his extraordinary ability to describe the most unusual events in a literate, deliberately nonsensational style. His short stories still employed supernatural elements, however, and many of them were award contenders. "The Night They Missed the Horror Show" (1988) and "With Dead Folks (1989) both won the Bram Stoker Award, as did "Found in a Harlequin Romance" (1992), "The Big Blow" (1997), and "Mad Dog Summer" (1999). Other notable stories include "The God of the Razor" (1987) and "ON THE FAR SIDE OF THE CADILLAC DESERT WITH THE DEAD FOLKS" (1989).

Lansdale's short fiction has been collected and recollected several times. The best of them are *By Bizarre Hands* (1991), *Bestsellers Guaranteed* (1993), *The Long Ones* (2000), and *Bumper Crop* (2004). His strongest assets are his very polished and readable prose style and his ability to mix extreme and original images with everyday events and characters, so that the reader is left with a lingering uncertainty about the real world that surrounds us. His recent suspense novels, while not fantastic, are often more chilling than are overtly supernatural tales in the hands of less talented writers.

The Last Battle C. S. Lewis (1956)

The CHRONICLES OF NARNIA concludes with this title, set so far in the future that the human children who visited during the earlier volumes have all died, and the land of Narnia itself has become worn out and less vital. The novel is also the most obvious Christian allegory in the series, and the efforts by the author, C. S. LEWIS, to draw his parallels are occasionally intrusive.

We are told in the opening sentence that the days of Narnia are drawing to a close. An ape named Shift lives in a remote region with his only friend, Puzzle the donkey, who he treats very badly. When an empty lion skin turns up, Shift convinces Puzzle to wear it, hoping that he will be mistaken for Aslan and thus become a powerful puppet in Shift's hands. Thus, poor Puzzle is cast in the role of the Antichrist. Tirian, the last king of Narnia, hears rumors and rejoices at the prospect of the return of Aslan, who has been absent for many generations, despite words of caution from many of his advisers. He acts rashly and is troubled by reports that Aslan has favored the neighboring kingdom of Calormen, that the talking animals are to be subject to the humans' will, and that the sacred trees and their mystical inhabitants are to be destroyed.

The Calormens worship the god Tash, who eventually is cast in the role of Satan as the two countries go to war, and Narnia is conquered. The title refers to the final efforts by the good Narnians to resist their enemies, even though their own faith has been shaken by the absence of either Aslan or the children from our world who saved them in the past. Just as everything seems at its bleakest, Aslan finally intercedes, but only to allow his followers to escape into heaven, for Narnia itself is doomed to endure its final destruction. As with the previous books, the implied lesson is that only through believing in Aslan even when it seems he has utterly abandoned his people can salvation be found, and since Aslan is another aspect of Christ, the implications for our own world are meant to be obvious.

Lauria, Frank (1935–)

Frank Lauria is not often mentioned within the horror field because his stories of the supernatural are more akin to the occult adventures of Seabury QUINN and Dennis WHEATLEY, a style of story that has largely gone out of fashion. Most of his novels feature Doctor Orient, a student of the occult who has devoted his life to mastering the secrets of the dark arts in order to thwart those who would use this power for their own benefit. He made his debut with *Doctor Orient* (1970), freshly emerged from a prolonged retreat to wage war against the minions of the devil. Although somewhat old fashioned even for 1970, the novel is entertaining and occasionally inventive.

Orient returned, now fully established as a psychic investigator, in *Raga Six* (1972). Having established himself in Manhattan, he promptly finds himself locked in battle with a coven of witches whose powers he underestimates with nearly disastrous consequences. The sequel is noticeably more polished than the previous book, a progression that would continue in small increments over the next few titles. *Lady Sativa* (1973) is an even more sophisticated supernatural mystery. Orient is drawn to a beautiful young woman who appears to be the target of malign forces, but the reality is much more complex than that, and Orient once again barely escapes disaster because of his misjudgment of the true state of affairs.

A murder attracts his interest in *Baron Orgaz* (1974), one that the authorities believe to be purely mundane but that Orient suspects is just a symptom of a more serious problem. Voodoo magic is nearly his undoing in *The Priestess* (1978), invoked by the lover of a prominent gangster. In *The Seth Papers* (1979), the best novel in the series,

Doctor Orient's decision not to use his psychic abilities for material gain is put to the test. Nonoccult powers are after him this time, coveting the potential wealth that magic might generate. They distract Orient just as he is about to confront a group of fanatics who have mastered a dangerous occult force. The most recent in the series is *Blue Limbo* (1991), which unfortunately is mostly a restatement of plot devices and situations from the earlier books.

Lauria has written very little outside this series. *The Foundling* (1984) is a variation of the demon child story featuring a young girl with various psychic powers. *End of Days* (1999) is the novelization of a mediocre horror film. Several of Lauria's novels are quite well written, but he seems to be writing for an audience other than those interested in mainstream horror fiction. After the first flurry of Doctor Orient novels, they have appeared very infrequently, preventing him from establishing himself as a reliable writer.

Lawhead, Stephen (1950–)

Stephen Lawhead began writing science fiction and fantasy novels with strong Christian symbolism and content during the middle of the 1980s and switched exclusively to fantasy by the end of the decade. His first series of fantasies consists of *In the Hall of the Dragon King* (1982), *The Warlords of Nin* (1983), and *The Sword and the Flame* (1984). An evil sorcerer tricks the local king and imprisons him, after which a young man emerges as a reluctant hero. Using a magic sword, he rescues the mortally wounded monarch, then defends his people against an army of barbarians who are aided by evil sorcery, and eventually assumes the throne himself, although he is immediately forced on the defensive once again. The clear delineation between good and evil makes for straightforward plotting, but the dialogue and characterization are often awkward in his early efforts.

Lawhead was much more effective with the Pendragon series, a revisionist view of the life of King Arthur and Camelot, although some of the same minor flaws of oversimplification found in the early books recur here as well. Arthur and Merlin are Christian, of course, and their enemies are clearly motivated by evil. The series includes *Taliesin* (1987), *Merlin* (1888), *Arthur* (1989), *Pendragon* (1994), and *Grail* (1997). Lawhead is one of several writers, such as Marion Zimmer BRADLEY, who suggest a connection between Camelot and Atlantis. In his case, Merlin's mother was a survivor of that lost land. Using the powers and knowledge he inherited from her, he helps Arthur rise to power, establish his rule, and then goes off on a mystical journey of his own. While he is gone a mysterious woman steals the Holy Grail and kidnaps Guinevere, both of which must be rescued. Arthur returns in *Avalon* (1999), reborn in the 21st century to assume the throne and troubled by the same forces of evil that he fought previously in the distant past.

Lawhead has written two other trilogies. The Song of Albion includes *The Paradise War* (1991), *The Silver Hand* (1992), and *The Endless Knot* (1993). In this series the borderland between our world and a reality where mythic creatures survive is sundered. Drawing heavily on Celtic legends, the three novels tell of the eventual migration of a human scholar to the land of Prydain, where he assumes the throne after defeating the forces of evil. The Celtic Crusades trilogy includes *The Iron Lance* (1998), *The Black Rood* (2000), and *The Mystic Rose* (2001) and is Lawhead's most sustained and interesting work. A man from our time has visions of the past in which he sees his ancestors, who are involved in a number of adventures including the search for fragments of the true cross and the Holy Grail. The Christian symbolism is still central to the story but is better integrated into the plot and less intrusive. Lawhead's reinterpretations of the story of Arthur and other elements of that legend are unconventional and sometimes jarring but provide a different perspective. This prevents them from becoming just another retelling of an overly familiar story.

Laws, Stephen (1952–)

The first novel by British writer Stephen Laws became a subject of controversy, although not because of its content. *Ghosttrain* (1985) is a particularly effective and sometimes gruesome first novel about a supernatural entity that haunts the railroad yards in search of victims. It was a surprisingly impressive debut and popular enough that the publisher placed advertisements in the British subway system. The frightening images apparently unsettled enough patrons that they were eventually removed, but only after the publicity provided a healthy boost to Laws's early career.

Spectre (1986) was not as overtly horrifying but was even more suspenseful. A group of friends begin to die off in unexpected ways, and after each death the image of that person disappears from a group photograph. They are apparently under the threat of a supernatural curse whose nature the survivors must discover before their turn comes. *The Wyrm* (1987) was not quite as good as the first two, a modified vampire story about a creature that draws energy from the living when it is released from imprisonment beneath a gallows.

Although Laws continued to enjoy some success in England, the collapse of the horror field by 1990 had cost him his American publisher, although his books have recently begun to appear in the United States once again. *The Frighteners* (1990) is relatively minor, but *Darkfall* (1992) is a very effective chiller about a freak storm that causes several people to somehow merge with the building they are sheltering in, resulting in a terrifying transformation. *Gideon* (1993) is another unremarkable vampire variation, but *Macabre* (1994), the story of a satanic cult and its quest to sacrifice the perfect child, is exceptionally well done.

The author's last few novels have been more technically impressive than his previous work but less exceptional in their plots and images. *Daemonic* (1995) is an entertaining but undistinguished haunted house story, and *Chasm* (1997) pits a sketchily described isolated community against a supernatural menace. *Somewhere South of Midnight* (1996) describes the aftermath of a terrible automobile accident whose survivors develop the ability to kill or cure with a touch and is the best of his recent work. Laws's short fiction is consistently well done but rarely outstanding. Most of it has been collected in *Voyages into Night* (1993) and *The Midnight Man* (1999). He is a steady, reliable writer whose best work is highly original and carries a powerful emotional impact.

Laymon, Richard (1947–2001)

Richard Laymon established his basic style with his first novel, *The Cellar* (1980), a story in which the human characters are nearly as repulsive as the inhuman ones. The title location is underneath a tourist attraction, a building where a brutal and mysterious crime was committed some years before. A woman fleeing an abusive husband arrives there along with her daughter, unaware that a species of humanoid beast lies in concealment, ready to murder any intruding men and sexually enslave any women that happen within their reach. Although somewhat over the top and occasionally awkward, the powerful imagery make it memorable, and Laymon would eventually provide three sequels. *The Beast House* (1986) is basically a reprise of the first story with a new cast of characters. *The Midnight Tour* (1998) and *Friday Night in Beast House* (2001) are both similar but with the sexual content even more prominent. The last title also adds an element of twisted humor.

Laymon's other early novels are considerably less successful. *The Woods Are Dark* (1981) involves a lurking creature eventually described offhandedly as an alien visitor. Bits and pieces of the story are quite effective, but it is oddly paced and sometimes almost incoherent. *Out Are the Lights* (1982) makes use of a promising premise, special effects at a movie theater that turn out to be real, but does little with the idea. *Beware!* (1985) shows some improvement. The female protagonist is bedeviled by an invisible creature whose presence only she can detect. Several uninteresting titles, including one for young adults, followed before Laymon hit his stride, producing several excellent horror novels in a very short period of time.

The best of Laymon's many novels is *Flesh* (1986), which involves a species of parasite that compels its human hosts to commit acts of increasing savagery and barbarism, eventually leading to murder and self-mutilation. The story line is neatly contrived and executed, alternating suspense and horror to keep the reader constantly on edge. *Tread Softly*, originally published in 1986 as *The Dark Mountain* under the pen name Richard Kelly, describes the unfortunate consequences of annoying a practicing witch. A party of campers does so, but after they have returned to their normal lives, a series of unlikely accidents begins to claim them one by one until the survivors realize they will have to kill the witch if they want to live.

Resurrection Dreams (1988) followed, a reimagining of the story of Frankenstein's monster. A mentally disturbed man murders several people then raises them from the dead, all in an attempt to impress a girl with whom he is infatuated. Spurned love soon turns to maniacal hatred. He kills the girl he loved, then brings her back with a few modifications. Laymon's grisly details add a strong element of dark humor to this very macabre story. *Funland* (1989) is something of a letdown and has only minimal fantastic content, but *The Stake* (1990) is among his best novels. A freelance writer stumbles upon a dead body in a deserted building, killed by having a stake driven through the heart. Inspired, he decides to write a book about a demented vampire killer, runs afoul of two separate psychopaths, and in the final pages discovers that vampires are real after all.

Laymon's next few novels are less inspired. Several people receive warnings by way of a Ouija board in *Darkness Tells Us* (1991), but they misinterpret the messages. An unusual and uncanny rainstorm turns people into homicidal maniacs in *One Rainy Night* (1991). *Alarms* (1992) features a perfectly human, though quite vicious, villain, about whom the female protagonist is warned in a series of psychic visions. Several other novels from the middle 1990s contain no element of the supernatural, and the mixture of brutality and sexuality began to feel very repetitious. Laymon's next memorable book is *Bite* (1996), an ambiguous book about two people who kill what they believe to have been a vampire, although we never learn whether they were right, and then fall prey to considerable sexual tension trying to dispose of the body.

Body Rides (1996) is uneven but often quite effective. The protagonist acquires the power to briefly possess the bodies of other people, in which manner he satisfies a number of voyeuristic impulses. *Once upon a Halloween* (2000) also has its good moments, but the two main plots, one of which involves a cult of satanists and the other a malevolent spirit that lies in wait for trick-or-treaters, clash at times. Laymon won the Bram

Stoker Award for *The Traveling Vampire Show* (2000). A carnival advertises that it has a genuine vampire among its exhibits. Some local teenagers decide to investigate and discover that things are even stranger than they imagined, but only after a series of sexual encounters that are unlikely at best. His last novel, *To Wake the Dead* (2003), involves a reinvigorated mummy and an almost bewildering number of subplots.

Laymon is also reasonably productive at shorter length, but most of his better stories appeared early in his career, such as "Grab" (1982), "The Mess Hall" (1989), "Dinker's Pond" (1989), and "Bad News" (1990). Much of his short fiction appears in *Out Are the Lights and Other Tales* (1993), *A Good, Secret Place* (1993), *Fiends* (1997), and *Dreadful Tales* (2001). Laymon's unconventional use of overt sexuality and his talent for presenting Grand Guignol–style grotesqueries in familiar settings marked his work as noteworthy from the outset, and although the quality of his work was erratic during the course of his career, his better stories and novels are likely to remain popular.

Lee, Edward (1957–   )

Although Edward Lee's first horror story appeared in the early 1980s, his career really started with *Ghouls* (1988). In a small town in Maryland, a series of strange disappearances and the theft of a body from its grave set the mood for a very macabre story. A researcher investigating ghouls, inhuman creatures who steal and devour dead bodies, discovers that they are real. He tries to study them but eventually loses control of his subjects, who seek dead flesh even if they have to kill it themselves. *Coven* (1991) is a less noteworthy follow-up, the story of a secretive cult at a private college who have acquired genuine occult powers.

Lee was more successful with *Incubi* (1991), in which a police detective tries to track down a particularly vicious serial killer while a young artist deals with a group of mysterious men who have taken a sudden and not entirely flattering interest in her work. The two separate story lines are brought together and mixed with a form of demonic possession, blending sex and violence in quite liberal doses. *Succubi* (1992) is thematically related but not quite as tightly written. Another cult provides the conflict this time as they use a retarded man as a lure to gather in their victims. *The Chosen* (1993) has a particularly clever set-up. A posh restaurant is actually operated by a kind of demon who serves human meat as the main course to a select clientele. The plot unwinds somewhat in the later chapters.

Creekers (1994) is set in a remote area where a group of inbred people develop psychic powers. A charismatic leader decides that it is time to use those abilities to dominate the nearby more developed community, and the protagonist gets caught in the middle. Although uneven, *Creekers* suggests the kind of setting and character that Lee used increasingly in later fiction, an isolated, inward-looking community that develops in grotesque ways. Lee also began to acquire a reputation for inventive brutality and occasional near-obscenity as well as the gross-out image, a scene or concept that disgusts rather than frightens the reader.

Sacrifice (1995, published under the penname Richard Kinion) is a variation of *Incubi* with even stronger sexual content but is less well plotted. *Shifters* (1998, written with John Pelan) is a vampire variation, more properly the story of a lamia, and also contains strong erotic content. Lee seemed to be stalled in his development for some time, with each novel varying only slightly from the previous. That ended with *City Eternal* (2001) and the related novel *Infernal Angel* (2003). Both books involve a literal trip to hell, and although they are filled with bizarre images, horrifying imagery, and terrible deeds, they sometimes feel as much like fantasy epics as horror novels. Both are quite powerful and potentially his most memorable work.

Other recent novels have been less interesting, though technically well done. *Monstrosity* (2002) is another story of genetically altered creatures escaping to wreak havoc in the general population and is science fiction as much as horror. In *The Teratologist* (2003, written with Wrath James Wright), a man challenges God with terrible consequences. A demonic creature sends cursed packages to post offices in *Messenger* (2004), which has some excellent individual scenes but which fails to hold together as a novel.

Lee's short stories are very similar to his longer work in both theme and treatment. Among his best are "Mr. Torso" (1994), "Dead Girls in Love" (1995), and "ICU" (1999). His only collections to date are *Splatterspunk: The Micah Hayes Stories* (1998, with John Pelan) and *The Ushers* (1999). Lee is a sometimes controversial, often surprising, and potentially much more significant horror writer than he is at present. Whether he will continue to move in unusual directions remains to be seen.

Lee, Tanith (1947–   )

It is an unfortunate artifact of the writing process that quality and quantity are usually opposing forces. Tanith Lee is one of those rare exceptions who is able to turn out a steady stream of novels and short stories but without diluting their quality. She began her career in the early 1970s with several well-written but unremarkable fantasy novels for young readers before hitting her stride by 1976 with several books for adults, most of which are science fiction, although the Birthgrave trilogy, though rationalized, is otherwise indistinguishable from heroic fantasy. Her first true adult fantasy was *The Storm Lord* (1976), which also adopts some science fiction devices and is set on another planet, one where magic works. This was the first in the Anackire series, the story of a young man maturing and seeking his rightful heritage, a traditional fantasy theme handled adroitly and very literately. *Anackire* (1983), which takes place in the same world, switches to a female protagonist who sets free a supernatural entity with unforeseen consequences. Third in the series is *The White Serpent* (1988), the story of a quest for a magical city.

Lee had already demonstrated that she could breathe new life into old plots, and she did so again with the short but outstanding *Volkhavaar* (1977), which pits two reluctant allies against an evil magical force. She exceeded even the already-high expectations of her readers with her next major work, the Flat Earth series, set in a past so distant that the Earth itself is flat and the gods meddle in human affairs freely. In an amusing irony the recurring hero of the series is the equivalent of Satan, who feels compelled to save humanity from the thoughtless gods to escape his own otherwise boring existence. The Flat Earth sequence consists of interlaced stories and novels and eventually extended to five volumes, *Night's Master* (1979), *Death's Master* (1979), *Delusion's Master* (1981), *Delirium's Mistress* (1986), and *Night's Sorceries* (1987). The first three volumes are particularly innovative and cleverly plotted.

Lee frequently incorporates non-European legends and folk tales into her fiction, and the collection *Tamastara, or the Indian Nights* (1984) borrows a number of these from the Indian subcontinent. *Sung in Shadow* (1983), on the other hand, is set in an alternate Renaissance Italy, one where magic works, and is a retelling of the story of Romeo and Juliet with a liberal dash of magic. The four-volume Paradys sequence, consisting of *The Book of the Damned* (1988), *The Book of the Beast* (1988), *The Book of the Dead* (1991), and *The Book of the Mad* (1993), structurally resembles the Flat Earth series in that it mixes short stories and longer works, a large cast of characters, and multiple story lines, but it is less focused on a single central theme. *The Heroine of the World* (1989), one of her very best novels, is set in a fictional country in 19th-century Europe but contains very little overt fantastic content.

Lee had continued to write occasional fantasies for younger readers, but her first major work in that form came in the 1990s with a trilogy, *Black Unicorn* (1991), *Gold Unicorn* (1994), and *Red Unicorn* (1997). These are set in an alternate world where unicorns are considered a myth until one appears to a young woman, setting in motion a wave of change. Lee's traditional fantasy output has in recent years begun to subside in favor of more unusual story lines, such as in *Elephantasm* (1993), which marginally involves African magic but is more concerned with psychological suspense. *When the Lights Go Out* (1996) invokes legends of mermaids and other sea-based magic, but with a very unconventional interpretation.

Faces under Water (1998) introduces the Secret Books of Venus series. An alchemist becomes fascinated with a beautiful woman, unaware that she is part of a cult that is plotting against him. The story continues and expands in *Saint Fire* (1999) and *A Bed of Earth* (2002). Lee's most re-

cent fantasy novels have been as diverse as ever, mixing traditional stories with entirely new ones and drawing upon history as well as her imagination to create credible settings. *White As Snow* (2000), for example, is a remarkably effective retelling of the story of "Snow White and the Seven Dwarfs" whereas *Mortal Suns* (2003) is an adventure story set in a magical world that resembles ancient Egypt.

Early in her career Lee displayed an interest in darker themes. *Sabella, or the Blood Stone* (1980) is an unusual hybrid, at times reading very much like a traditional science fiction novel with its setting on another planet, but the title character is a not particularly rationalized vampire, apparently a supernatural being who adapted when humanity left the Earth. *Kill the Dead* (1980) is an equally fascinating story about a woman raised from the dead and the efforts by an exorcist to return her to the grave. *Lycanthia* (1981) is set in a fantasy world and is primarily an adventure story, but the main character is a werewolf. Lee turned to more traditional fantasy in her novels after this brief flurry of darker fantasy but continued to write short fiction in both modes, eventually returning to book-length supernatural fiction after a gap of many years. Many of her short horror stories can be found in *Red As Blood, or Tales from the Sisters Grimm* (1983) and *The Gorgon and Other Beastly Tales* (1985). The title story from the latter collection won the World Fantasy Award.

Lee's interest in the grimmer side of fantasy began to reemerge in her novels in 1990 with *The Blood of Roses* (1990), which depicts a vampire as the king of a magical other race akin to the fairies. *Dark Dance* (1992) introduces the Scarabae, a family of vampires, although they are a far cry from Dracula and his kind. One of their younger generation is determined to free herself of the bloodlust and live independently. In *Personal Darkness* (1993) she resolves to kill all her relatives to exterminate their line but only partially succeeds. In *Darkness, I* (1994) she becomes pregnant and goes into hiding but discovers that she cannot escape her destiny. Lee's vampires are so different from the way they are traditionally described that they are almost a new kind of creature entirely. *Vivia* (1995) also involves vampires, but this time a somewhat more orthodox variety.

Ironically, Lee became increasingly active as a horror writer after that genre had begun its recent decline, and only about half of her subsequent novels have found a publisher in the United States. *Heart-Beast* (1993) is a historical novel about an unpleasant young man who is transformed into a particularly nasty werewolf, and *Reigning Cats and Dogs* (1995) describes a battle between a secret society of magic users and a surreptitious demonic entity. Since 1995 most of Lee's horror fiction has once more been confined to short stories.

Lee's output of short fiction has been phenomenal throughout her career, and the dozen or so published collections represent only a portion of her work. Among the best not already mentioned are *Cyrion* (1982), *Dreams of Dark and Light* (1986), and *Forests of the Night* (1989). Lee won a second World Fantasy Award for "ELLE EST TROIS (LA MORT)" in 1984. Lee's occasional science fiction novels have also been moderately successful.

Le Fanu, J. Sheridan (1814–1873)

The Irish writer and journalist Joseph Sheridan Le Fanu wrote comparatively little fantasy and horror fiction and is perhaps most significant in the mystery field for inventing the locked room mystery. The most memorable of his supernatural stories is the often-filmed CARMILLA (1871), the tale of a seductive female vampire, almost certainly an influence on Bram STOKER, who knew Le Fanu personally. Le Fanu was more interested in the psychology of his characters than were most of his fellow writers, so his stories are usually less overtly sensational.

"Schalken the Painter" (1839) is another of his better-known stories. The young female protagonist is forced into an arranged marriage with a particularly unresponsive and distressing man, who we subsequently learn is actually dead. There is a doppelgänger in "Spalatro, from the Notes of Fra Giacomo" (1843). Although there is some question about whether Le Fanu was actually the author of "The Mysterious Lodger" (1850), it is generally attributed to him and is a very effective, atmospheric piece about an evil curse. "Squire Toby's Will" (1868) resolves a quarrel over an inheritance by means of a series of disturbing dreams and ghostly appearances. "Green Tea" (1869) anticipates the occult detectives of Lord DUNSANY, Seabury QUINN, William Hope HODGSON, and others, investigating a supernatural manifestation brought on by drinking too much tea. A cat serves the function of a banshee in "The White Cat of Drumgunniol" (1870), and "Sir Dominick's Bargain" (1872) is an early and amusing variation of the deal-with-the-devil story.

The Haunted Baronet (1870) is a slow-moving but otherwise effective tale of supernatural revenge. An aristocrat thoughtlessly and incorrectly fires one of his employees after accusing him of theft and then unwisely disregards the warning by a psychic to reconcile their differences. The other man has undergone some unspecified supernatural transformation, and the two are then engaged in a protracted and not entirely clear partnership involving reconciliation and a deal with the devil, eventually leading to their mutual downfall. This was Le Fanu's only book-length work of fantasy or horror.

A very few of Le Fanu's short stories are fantasy rather than supernatural. "Laura Silver Bell" (1872), which involves fairies, is one of the best of these. Also of interest is "Stories of Lough Guir" (1870), which appear to be adaptations of folk tales. His fiction has been assembled and reassembled in various combinations, of which the best selections are *Best Ghost Stories* (1964) and *The Haunted Baronet and Other Stories* (2003).

"The Legend of Sleepy Hollow"
Washington Irving (1820)

Although there is a hint of ambiguity at the conclusion of this classic story, the most likely interpretation is that nothing fantastic really occurred, and therefore Irving's wry little tale technically should not be included here. Certainly the Disney animated version supports that contention, and the recent live-action *Sleepy Hollow* (1999), though a marvelous reinterpretation, bears only passing resemblance to the original story. Irving refrains from suggesting the mundane explanation until quite late, however, so readers might well believe it is genuinely supernatural until the final pages.

Sleepy Hollow, an area near Tarrytown, New York, as Irving describes it, is particularly subject to legends, superstitions, and unusual occurrences. Having set the scene, he introduces the three principal characters. Ichabod Crane is the local schoolteacher, a man of no particular merit, with little wealth, physically ungainly, well-read and educated, but very superstitious. Crane is interested in Katrina Van Tassel, the daughter of the wealthiest farmer in the region, but faces a formidable rival in Brom Van Brunt, an athletic, mischievous, and determined young suitor. Through perseverance and the whims of Katrina, Crane seems to be succeeding, much to Brom's distress, and he and his cronies play several pranks on Crane, although without affecting his resolve.

The most frightening of the local legends is the tale of the Headless Horseman, an image that Irving may have borrowed from an earlier story by a Dutch writer. The horseman is the spirit of a Hessian officer killed during the Revolutionary War when a cannonball took off his head. Crane finds this image particularly unnerving, which leads to blind panic when, while riding home alone one evening, he encounters what appears to be the horseman himself. A chase follows, at the climax of which the horseman throws his head at Crane, who is struck and knocked senseless. The following day Crane is gone and presumed to have been carried off by the Hessian, although years later word comes that he is alive and well. Irving clearly implies that this was another prank perpetrated by Brom, but only after the reader has been invited to assume that the decapitated soldier has, in fact, returned from the dead. The story is a classic of American literature, regardless of what label it bears.

Le Guin, Ursula K. (1929–)

Ursula K. Le Guin wrote mostly science fiction during the early part of her career, although as early as 1962 she completed "April in Paris," a short fantasy. It was with *A Wizard of Earthsea* (1968) that she first made a major impact in that genre, a novel written ostensibly for young adults but that drew and still holds a significant adult audience. A young would-be magician named Ged releases his own death into the world in the form of a shadow and spends the rest of the novel trying to repair matters. Ged returned for two further adventures. In *The Tombs of Atuan* (1971) he meets a young woman whose life has been so dedicated to becoming a priestess that she has no experience of the greater world, which changes as a result of their meeting. Ged's final appearance is in *The Farthest Shore* (1972). Magic has been disappearing from the land, threatening to alter the world irrevocably. He travels to the underworld to confront the force responsible. In each of the three novels, the conflict comes from resolving the differences between two polarized viewpoints, a theme that recurs in much of Le Guin's other work.

After a gap of several years, Le Guin returned to Earthsea for new titles, but with a different cast of characters. *Tehanu* (1990), which won the Nebula Award, is set after magic has begun to make a weak recovery. Le Guin uses this volume to adjust certain aspects of her imagined society about which she had had second thoughts. Although it was subtitled *The Last Book of Earthsea*, that was not the case. She has since added *Tales from Earthsea* (2001), a collection of loosely interconnected short stories using that setting, and *The Other Wind* (2002), in which a wizard troubled by dreams of the dead sets out on a quest accompanied by a shape-changing dragon. *The Other Wind* won a World Fantasy Award.

Not all of Le Guin's fantasy is set in Earthsea. *Orsinian Tales* (1976) is a collection of stories set in an imaginary variation of historical Europe, as is the novel *Malafrena* (1979), both of which are slow-paced, thoughtful, convoluted, and witty, but neither of which is among her best work. *The Beginning Place* (1980, also published as *Threshold*) follows the adventures of two young people who cross through a gateway to another reality and experience a rapid maturation, after which their apparently doomed love affair triumphs over considerable adversity. *Gifts* (2004) also uses young adults as its primary characters. In a village where everyone has one or another magical talent, a delicate balance of power is based on fear of one's neighbors. An adolescent boy and girl decide to renounce their powers and trust each other, which sends ripples of disquiet throughout the community.

Le Guin has also written a considerable body of short fantasy tales. The Cat Wings sequence has appeared as a series of chapbooks, starting with *Cat Wings* (1988) and ending with *Wonderful Alexander and the Cat Wings* (1994). The cats have the power to fly in these light fairy tales. More significant is "Buffalo Gals, Won't You Come Out Tonight?" which won both the Hugo Award and the World Fantasy Award, and "The Poacher" (1993), an ingenious variation of the story of Sleeping Beauty. Other notable short fantasies include "The Word of Unbinding" (1964), "Son of the Dragon's Daughter" (1981), "Gwilan's Harp" (1981), "A Ride on the Red Mare's Back" (1992), "In the Drought" (1994), and "Dragonfly" (1998). Other than those listed above, Le Guin's fantasy and science fiction stories are not collected separately, so almost all of her collections contain at least a few of each. Le Guin is generally accepted as one of the major contemporary science fiction writers. Her influence in fantasy has been nearly as strong, and she has established herself as a significant voice in both fields.

Leiber, Fritz (1910–1992)

Fritz Leiber was one of the few writers who had significant careers in science fiction, fantasy, and horror fiction and whose work remains popular in all three. His fantasy is dominated by the FAFHRD AND THE GRAY MOUSER SERIES, light-hearted sword and sorcery stories featuring a pair of good-natured, roguish thieves who battle evil men and evil magic. The series is the only sword and sorcery fiction to rival the popularity of the work of Robert E. HOWARD, and it is certainly the most literate entry in that subgenre.

Leiber wrote very little fantasy with other characters, but his supernatural fiction is far more varied. One of his favorite devices was to couple his supernatural events with an ordinary, prosaic object or activity. In "SMOKE GHOST" (1941), for example, an evil entity takes its form from smog and air pollution and hovers near smokestacks and similar venues. Criminals are menaced by a haunted pistol in "The Automatic Pistol" (1940). Other superior early stories include "The Hound" (1942), "Spider Mansion" (1942), "The Man Who Never Grew Young" (1947), and "THE GIRL WITH THE HUNGRY EYES" (1947). "A Bit of the Dark

World" (1962) is reminiscent of H. P. LOVECRAFT, the story of an unexplained, alien intelligence that manifests itself in our world. "The Man Who Made Friends with Electricity" (1962), which title literally describes what happens in the story, is a sardonic fantasy whose prejudiced protagonist gets his just deserts.

Many of Leiber's stories read very much like dark fairy tales. In "Gonna Roll the Bones" (1967) a man addicted to gambling finds himself in a deadly game with the devil himself. It won both the Hugo and Nebula Awards. Although most of Leiber's collections mix horror with other genres, several of them are predominantly supernatural, including the classic *Night's Black Agents* (1947), *Night Monsters* (1969), *Ghost Light* (1984), and *The Black Gondolier and Other Stories* (2001).

Leiber was also the author of one of the very best novels about contemporary witchcraft, *Conjure Wife* (1952), which has been filmed at least three times as *Weird Woman* (1944), *Burn Witch Burn* (1961) and *Witches' Brew* (1980). The novel also juxtaposes magic with the mundane and familiar. A successful college professor learns that his wife has been guarding his life and career by means of a number of magical spells. Although she insists that she is a good witch and not a devil worshipper, he forces her to give up what he considers a silly superstition. Unfortunately, she turns out to be right, and now that the elaborate balance of power has been disrupted, all the rival witches married to other members of the faculty begin to exact their revenge, until he finally accepts the inevitable.

Our Lady of Darkness (1978) is a modern ghost story. An ordinary businessman catches fleeting glimpses of a ghastly apparition, an inhuman creature dogging his footsteps, waiting in the shadows and revealing itself only briefly before disappearing. Since no one else can see it, everyone else thinks he is hallucinating or losing his mind, and at times the protagonist shares their opinion. Although not as significant as *Conjure Wife*, the novel is an unusually innovative and effective ghost story. These two novels were published in a single volume as *Dark Ladies* (1999). An early unpublished novel also appeared posthumously but is well below Leiber's usual standards. *The Dealings of Daniel Kesserich* (1996) involves a semirationalized return from the dead, with the usual unfortunate consequences. It is one of the few inconsequential stories among the very large number of novels and short stories that Leiber produced during his lifetime. He is perhaps more honored now than when he was alive, and interest in his work remains lively and widespread.

Lewis, C. S. (1898–1963)

The British writer and academic Clive Staples Lewis is best known for his seven-volume CHRONICLES OF NARNIA, a series of fantasy novels for children. Various children cross over from our world into Narnia for a series of adventures among talking animals and wicked witches in situations that are usually Christian metaphors. Although that series is uneven and occasionally internally inconsistent, it has remained very popular ever since it first appeared. Lewis also wrote several short fantasies for children, most of which have been collected in *Boxen* (1985). They are occasionally amusing but lack the stature of his other fiction.

His first fantasy title, *The Screwtape Letters* (1942), was intended for adults. It consists of a series of letters between two demons, both resident in hell, one advising the other on the best way to tempt mortals. *The Great Divorce* (1946) suggests that the souls of the damned might be allowed brief visits to heaven, and that most of them would find it more demanding than hell and prefer to cut short their visit. Lewis's sardonic humor is, unfortunately, largely absent from his later work. His only other fantasy was *Till We Have Faces* (1956), a retelling of the legends of Eros and Psyche in which obsessive love becomes a destructive force.

Lewis also wrote a trilogy that is generally accepted as science fiction but that relies on a metaphysical underlay. *Out of the Silent Planet* (1938), *Perelandra* (1943, also published as *Voyage to Venus*), and *That Hideous Strength* (1945, published in abridged form as *The Tortured Planet*) take two contending characters to Mars, Venus, and then back to Earth. One of the characters is clearly meant to represent the devil, and we learn that each planet has a god or spirit associated with it and that the god of Earth has gone insane. The middle volume is a retelling of the temptation of Eve in the Garden of Eden. Lewis demonstrated that he had the talent to be an important and entertaining writer, but much of his work is flawed by his heavy-handed allegories.

"Ligeia" Edgar Allan Poe (1838)

The narrator of this classic story is the man to whom the Lady Ligeia was married, a partnership so trusting that he never once learned or cared to learn her family name or anything of her background prior to their meeting. Although she is an exquisite beauty, there is some strangeness about her appearance that he is never quite able to identify, although he thinks it is something about her eyes. Their marriage seems perfect but, alas, she is struck with a fatal disease that finally claims her life, although only after a magnificent struggle in which she vows to defy death itself and bids her husband to remain loyal to her whatever might happen. Despite her determination to live, she perishes a short while later.

Distraught, the narrator moves to England, where, after some time has passed, he remarries, this time to Lady Rowena Trevanion, apparently acting on impulse. His motives are unclear, because he still grieves for Ligeia, is cruel to his new wife, who he loathes, and is often in the grip of drugs he takes to deaden the pain of loss he still feels acutely. Lady Rowena is soon in the grip of a series of mysterious maladies that threaten to make the narrator a widower yet again. In her fevers and sometimes when she is well, she complains of strange sounds and movements around her, as though she were being watched.

In due course, Rowena dies. The narrator is sitting alone with her corpse when he thinks he detects hints of remaining life. Several times over the course of the next few hours, Rowena—or at least her body—stirs as if wakening, but each time her color fades and she returns to lifelessness. Finally, just before dawn the body rises, fully alive once more, but the narrator is shocked to discover that he is looking into the eyes of the long-dead Ligeia, not his current wife. Several modern authors have used a similar device—a dead spirit possessing the body of a dying successor—but rarely as effectively and efficiently as Poe did more than a century ago.

Ligotti, Thomas (1953–   )

Because there are so few markets for short horror fiction, particularly idiosyncratic or very style-conscious prose, many of the best writers in that genre have been regular contributors to the small press, semiprofessional magazines with limited distribution and low pay rates. Writers whose work is largely confined to this venue are doing so because they enjoy the work, not because it pays the bills. Thomas Ligotti, who sold his first story in 1981, languished there for almost 10 years, producing a steady stream of quality stories that were often compared to the best work of Clark Ashton SMITH and other members of the circle that surrounded H. P. LOVECRAFT, although Ligotti's prose is much more sophisticated than was theirs. Most of his characters encounter something that makes them question their view of reality, forcing them to adjust or fall prey to this new knowledge.

His fiction is also filled with grotesque images, and his protagonists are frequently doomed from the outset. A visitor to a local festival discovers that the symbolism is more relevant than he expected in "The Last Feast of Harlequin" (1990). Dolls are given a form of life in "Dr. Voke and Mr. Veech" (1983). The Gorgon survives into the modern world in "The Medusa" (1991). "The Tsalal" (1994) is a particularly effective and very explicit tale of demonic horror. His other outstanding stories include "Dr. Locrian's Asylum" (1987) and "The Bells Will Sound Forever" (1998), although the quality of his stories is so uniform that it is difficult to narrow the list down to a few choice selections.

Ligotti's earliest stories were largely collected in *Songs of a Dead Dreamer* (1986), and the remaining few were mixed with newer tales in *Grimscribe* (1990), which is often described incorrectly as a novel. Subsequent collections are *The Agonizing Resurrection of Victor Frankenstein and Other Gothic Tales* (1994), *Noctuary* (1994), and *The Nightmare Factory* (1996). The last of these won the Bram Stoker Award, as did the short story "The Red Tower" (1996). The title story of *My Work Is Not Yet Done* (2002) is a short novel that

also won the Bram Stoker Award and is accompanied by two thematically related short stories, all of which insert horror into an ordinary business setting. His most recent work at shorter length can be found in *Sideshow and Other Stories* (2003). *The Thomas Ligotti Reader*, edited by Darrell Schweitzer (2003), is a collection of essays that can be very helpful in fully understanding his sometimes complex stories.

Lindskold, Jane (1962–   )

Jane Lindskold's short fantasy stories began appearing in the early 1990s, well-written but unmemorable except for "Teapot" (1995), an amusing take on ALICE IN WONDERLAND (1865) by Lewis CARROLL. Her first fantasy novel was *Brother to Dragons, Companion to Owls* (1994), a contemporary fantasy in which fiscal cutbacks have resulted in the ejection of a troubled young woman from an institution. She is disturbed, but with good reason, unbalanced by her very real magical powers in which no one else believes. Fending for herself, she betrays her abilities and attracts the attention of unscrupulous people prepared to take advantage of her power.

More impressive was her second novel, *The Pipes of Orpheus* (1995), a retelling of the story of the Pied Piper of Hamelin, who stole all the children from an ungrateful village, retold on a grander scale and casting the Greek god Orpheus in the role of the piper. *When the Gods Are Silent* (1997) is less remarkable, a rather routine, low-key quest story. *Changer* (1998) and its sequel, *Legends Walking* (1999), are much better. King Arthur and some other immortals have survived into the modern age but are confronted by an old enemy who has similarly survived the passage of time. The title character is a shape-shifting being who also turns up in the sequel, which switches the scene to Africa for a confrontation with a reawakened god who seeks to dominate that continent.

Lindskold's most ambitious fantasy work is the Wolf series, *Through Wolf's Eyes* (2001), *Wolf's Head, Wolf's Heart* (2002), *The Dragon of Despair* (2003), and *Wolf Captured* (2004). The series is set in another kingdom in turmoil, but the focus is on the interaction of various humans with the local wolves, who are intelligent and who in some cases raise human children as their own. *Wolf Captured* is particularly well told. *The Buried Pyramid* (2004) is perhaps her best novel, the story of an archaeological expedition in Egypt that is in a race to uncover important artifacts but that is disrupted by a magical trip back through time thanks to the intercession of Ra.

Lindskold has written quite a bit of short fiction, which has become much more interesting in recent years. Her best stories include "The Dark Lady" (1996), "Dreaming of Dead Poets" (1996), "Out of Hot Water" (1999), and "Beneath the Eye of the Hawk" (2002). She is overdue for a collection of her shorter work.

The Lion, the Witch, and the Wardrobe
C. S. Lewis (1950)

It is possible that C. S. LEWIS did not originally expect that this would be the first of a series of children's fantasies rather than a single book, because it is much more complete in itself than are any of the sequels. The four Pevensie children find a doorway into a magical world through the back of an oversized wardrobe in a house where they are staying to escape the bombing of London. In that other world the evil White Witch has cast a spell that suspends the world in a perpetual winter that never quite reaches Christmas, a significant fact given the strong Christian symbolism that pervades the novels. The children are, in fact, referred to as the "Sons of Adam" and "Daughters of Eve" by the witch and others. There is a prophesy that when the four thrones in an abandoned castle are occupied by humans, the witch will die, so she has a vested interest in preventing that from happening. Fortunately for her, humans do not exist in Narnia until the children arrive, a plot device about which Lewis was inconsistent in the later volumes.

Narnia is filled with talking animals as well as other creatures of legend, all of them intelligent, as are the trees. Lewis revised this condition later as well so that it was possible for the children to eat those varieties of animals that were incapable of speech without feeling guilty. The four have a series of adventures and hear legends of Aslan, a lion who comes from a distant land and who is sup-

posed to have the power to free Narnia from the witch's power. Aslan is an obvious Christ figure whose mystical interventions continue throughout the series. One of the Pevensies, Edmund, has been corrupted by the witch's temptations and betrays his siblings, although his visit to the witch's lair—littered with her enemies whom she has transformed into statues—convinces him that he has chosen poorly. Nevertheless, he is guilty, and Aslan chooses to submit to the witch's power and be killed in Edmund's place, obviously dying for his sins. The act of self-sacrifice wakens another form of magic, and he is restored to life in time to affect the outcome of the ultimate battle between good and evil.

The children are installed on their thrones with one of their number, Peter, as High King, and they grow to maturity ruling Narnia justly and profitably. Late in their reign they go hunting and inadvertently stumble back through the wardrobe, returning to our world only a moment after leaving, and once more with the bodies of children, although they retain their adult memories. The story is self-contained but slight, although a few scenes—Lucy's first visit to Narnia, the descriptions of the beavers' house—are quite memorable.

Lisle, Holly (1960–)

Holly Lisle began her career, as many fantasy writers do, with a trilogy, and with the exception of a small number of mildly interesting short stories, she has continued to focus on stand-alone and series novels ever since. That first trilogy consists of *Fire in the Mist* (1992), *Bones of the Past* (1993), and *Mind of the Magic* (1995). The protagonist is a young woman who survives the massacre of her family at the hands of a band of brutal soldiers and is forced to mature quickly, developing her innate magical talents in the process. The ensuing volumes involve an expedition to a lost city and a confrontation with the gods. The transition from book to book is not always smooth, but taken separately they are all fine adventure stories.

Over the course of the next few years, Lisle collaborated on novels with several people, including more experienced writers such as Marion Zimmer BRADLEY, Mercedes LACKEY, and S. M. Stirling.

She also wrote several novels on her own, including the unlikely but amusing adventure *Minerva Wakes* (1994), which sprawls across a number of realities, and *Sympathy for the Devil* (1996), a very funny novel in which a woman's prayer for the redemption of the inhabitants of hell is partially granted, resulting in an active campaign to capture her soul. The best of the collaborations are *Glenraven* (1996) with Bradley, pitting its heroine against a demon who dominates a small community, and *The Devil and Dan Cooley* (1996) with Walter Spence, in which the devil consults a radio talk show host in an effort to find a way to improve his image and better advertise his offerings.

The Secret Texts trilogy followed, starting with *Diplomacy of Wolves* (1998). Two clans appear to be on the verge of ending generations of conflict by means of a marriage uniting them, but dissidents on one side use treachery to strike at their old enemies. The survivors seek a magical device that might restore the dead to life in *Vengeance of Dragons* (1999), and the conflict becomes more general in the conclusion, *Courage of Falcons* (2000). *Vincalis the Agitator* (2002) is a prequel to the trilogy. Her most recent work includes another trilogy, the World Gates, consisting of *Memory of Fire* (2002), *The Wreck of Heaven* (2003), and *Gods Old and Dark* (2004), a panoramic adventure involving multiple realities. Although Lisle is a better-than-average writer of adventure tales, she is at her best when she can use her inventive sense of humor. Unfortunately, the fantasy market does not at presently favor humorous fantasy unless it is written by Terry PRATCHETT or Piers ANTHONY.

The List of 7 Mark Frost (1993)

Mark Frost had already enjoyed considerable success as a screenwriter before turning to booklength prose. With David Lynch he created the very offbeat *Twin Peaks* television series, which immediately drew a loyal following and which has since attained cult status. That series started fairly conventionally and became increasingly fantastic as it progressed, so it is not surprising that Frost's first novel would be squarely in the realm of fantasy and horror.

The List of 7 is narrated by a young Sir Arthur Conan Doyle, an inexperienced young man who finds himself thrown into the company of Jack Sparks, a dynamic, chameleonlike character who can change his appearance and personality almost at will. Sparks is engaged in an investigation of a secret society that is clandestinely planning to rule the world. Doyle has submitted a novel to a publisher that has strong similarities to that group, which makes him a target for their killers, human and supernatural. He and Sparks have a series of wild adventures including a chase through the British Museum by animated mummies, an encounter with a zombie, and their eventual discovery of a plot even more serious than they had anticipated. Sparks, as the reader will recognize early on, is the prototype for Sherlock Holmes, displaying many of the same traits. The chief villain, Sparks's brother, becomes the template for Moriarty, and Doyle himself serves as Doctor Watson. Bram STOKER, Jack the Ripper, and other historical characters make cameo appearances in this good-humored but very suspenseful and fast-paced occult adventure.

Frost brought Sparks and Doyle together in a sequel, *The Six Messiahs* (1995), set years later after Doyle has tired of writing Sherlock Holmes stories and is visiting the United States. Although the author brings both characters to life again, Sparks is in decline and Doyle has grown stodgy. The story involves the summoning of six people to a remote location where their union will unlock an evil supernatural force. Although a film version of the first novel was announced, it was never produced, and Frost has apparently abandoned this side of his writing career. He left behind one enduring classic and a second entertaining sequel.

Little, Bentley (1960–)

Bentley Little began writing short stories in the 1980s, mostly for the small press, of which "The Pounding Room" (1990) showed the most promise. Although he has continued to write short fiction fairly regularly since, including some very good ones such as "From the Mouths of Babes" (1994) and "The Theater" (1999), his greatest strength clearly lies in his novels. *The Revelation* (1990) won the Bram Stoker Award as best first novel and was one of his few conventional stories, in this case the travails of a town menaced by an ancient evil recently reawakened.

The Mailman (1991) was much more interesting and typical of his subsequent work. The arrival of a new mailman in a small town coincides with a rash of distressing letters filled with threats, old scandals, new charges, and mysterious items whose existence seems to defy nature. The initial shock is followed by a series of gruesome deaths and eventually by the realization that the mailman is, in fact, not human at all. The novel is an interesting parallel to *Needful Things* by Stephen King, which was published the same year and has a very similar theme. *The Summoning* (1993) is a vampire novel, but not one from the European tradition. Little's invocation of Asian legends about the risen dead is effectively unsettling and relentlessly suspenseful.

University (1994, also published as *Night School*) was the first of Little's novels to focus on an institution as the generator of evil. In this case an entire college campus has, in effect, become a single malevolent entity. *The Store* (1996) goes even further in divorcing the story from the real world. A national chain opens a new branch in a small town, but the store is almost a living thing, administered by the mysterious and inhuman Night Managers, and it spreads its influence throughout the community like a demented, supernaturally empowered Wal-Mart.

Dominion (1996, also published as *The Dark Dominion*) is something of a change of pace. A group of maenads who have survived into the modern age recall Dionysus into the world and transform a large part of California into a festival of sex and death. His next two novels involve even more unusual concepts. In *Houses* (1997, also published as *The House*) several adults feel compelled to return to the house where they grew up, but these various houses are identical and all linked through some mysterious power. *The Ignored* (1997) may be Little's most interesting and successful novel, a grand elaboration of a device first used by Charles BEAUMONT in "The Vanishing American" (1955). The protagonist discovers that he is gradually fading from the awareness of everyone who knows him. Eventually, he encounters a group of similar people, murders the boss he has long loathed, and then engages in fruitless and pointless terrorism before discovering a larger community of the invisible that is being run as a government project.

Little's next two novels are less interesting. *Guests* (1998) is a rather predictable ghost story, and *The Walking* (2000) is set in a town founded by witches whose dead rise from their graves and amble about. *The Town* (2000) is much better, revealing the consequences of forgetting to placate one's guardian angel. *The Association* (2001) sometimes feels almost surreal, and its impact depends on the reader's ability to accept that a small community might be able to operate in open violation of state law without any of the affected residents being willing to appeal to the authorities. The residents are subject to the whims of the homeowners' association, which uses draconian measures, including murder, to ensure compliance. Although technically not fantasy, since there is nothing magical involved, the community functions in such a bizarre and implausible fashion that it is clearly not set in our world at all.

The Return (2002) involves an ancient curse turned up by an archaeological expedition and is quite suspenseful if one disregards the implausibly unprofessional actions of the researchers in the early chapters. *The Policy* (2003) is much better, another story of a cursed institution, in this case an insurance company whose policies have unusual provisions and whose officers are not entirely human. The strange goings on at a vacation spot include a dangerous creature hiding in a swimming pool in *The Resort* (2004). A good sampling of Little's short fiction can be found in *The Collection* (2002). At his best, Little produces quirky, disturbing stories that reveal the darker side of modern society. He is adept at creating a world that resembles ours closely but is slightly skewed in an unpleasant direction.

"Little Girl Lost" Richard Matheson (1953)

There are few situations that cause greater tension than a frightened or lost child and fewer terrors that strike more directly at parents than a hint that they might lose their own. Richard MATHESON taps into that vein of terror in this story from early in his career, which was later filmed as an episode of *The Twilight Zone* and also provided part of the inspiration for the movie *Poltergeist* (1982).

The narrator is wakened by the sound of his daughter Tina's crying. At first he assumes it is just another upset stomach or bad dream, and even when he finds that she is missing from her bed he is not alarmed, because he can hear her crying. But when he turns on the lights there is no sign of her, just her voice apparently coming from nowhere. Eventually Tina falls asleep, and her distraught parents call a friend, who is equally dumbfounded. A brief panic ensues when they can no longer hear the sound of her breathing, but then it becomes audible again from high in a closet, although once more there is no other physical evidence of her presence.

Rescue comes from an unlikely source. The adults are so bound by the rational that they cannot sense the entrance to whatever other reality Tina has fallen into. The family dog is not similarly hindered, and once allowed into the apartment, he immediately vanishes in pursuit of the child. Her father accidentally stumbles into the gateway as well, but fortunately he fails to pass through completely, and the others are able to hold onto his legs to prevent him from becoming lost along with the others. This eventually results in their mutual rescue. Although "Little Girl Lost" is a very straightforward story with a very simple solution, it retains its powerful impact even after multiple readings because of its appeal to one of the most primal of fears.

The Little Prince Antoine de Saint-Exupéry (1943)

The narrator of this charming children's story is an airplane pilot who meets an unusual child in the desert, the Little Prince, who claims to have come from another planet where everything is extremely small. The Little Prince desires a drawing of a sheep, and after several attempts the narrator succeeds in pleasing him. During this process the reader is told repeatedly of the silliness of grownups, who need everything to be explained and quantified rather than described in terms that are meaningful for children.

Their friendship continues for an indefinite period of time. The Little Prince wonders whether or not his sheep will be able to eat the tiny baobabs found on his planet. The baobabs spread terribly fast and leave no room for other plants, so it would be very useful if the sheep could help by eating them when they sprout. The author, who illustrated the book himself, provides a very graphic example of what might happen to a tiny world if the baobabs were not held in check. The Little Prince might fear the baobabs, but he loves the flowers, even when they are being vain and self-centered. Back on his own world, he and a prized flower had a disagreement, after which he decided to leave his little planet, perhaps forever.

His first visit is to another tiny world ruled by a king who has no subjects. The king insists that the entire universe obey his commands, but only when they are reasonable commands, and, by his convoluted logic, everything that they choose to do was because he commanded them to do so. He next visits the planet of a conceited man who considers himself the handsomest and most intelligent man on that planet, which is, of course, true since he is entirely alone. He then visits a man who drinks to forget that he drinks, a businessman who is obsessed with numbers, and a lamplighter who obeys his standing instructions without cavil despite the fact that the situation has changed, making them irrelevant. Finally comes a geographer who has never actually seen anything to inscribe on his maps but who directs the Little Prince to Earth.

The narrator finally realizes that the problem with grown people is that they rush around all the time without knowing where they truly want to be and without enjoying the journey at all. The wonderful simplicity and directness of the Little Prince's comments suggest that we lose something precious when we cast aside our childhood and forget the lessons we have learned about the world.

Lofting, Hugh (1886–1947)

Although Hugh Lofting was a British writer, he spent the second half of his life in the United States. Lofting began writing his stories of Doctor Dolittle during World War I, and the first book appeared in 1920 as *The Story of Doctor Dolittle: Being the History of His Peculiar Life and Astonishing Adventures in Foreign Parts.* Seven additional titles had appeared by 1928, with four more titles added at irregular intervals afterward, ending with *Doctor Dolittle's Puddleby Adventures,* published posthumously in 1952.

After driving away most of his human companions, Doctor Dolittle learns from his parrot that a wide variety of animals speak in their own languages, which he eventually learns. The stories they tell inspire him to indulge in a series of fabulous journeys and adventures. A physician originally, he becomes a veterinarian, although later in the series he is in charge of a circus, a zoo, and various services designed for animal rather than human customers. Lofting sometimes overdoes his message about being kind to animals as well as one another, but his intentions are always good. He was a skilled storyteller with a powerful imagination, creating believable characters from familiar animals and even inventing entirely new animals such as the pushmi-pullyu. One of the later adventures, *Doctor Dolittle and the Secret Lake* (1948), is particularly good.

Lofting wrote very little fantasy outside the Dolittle series. *Gub Gub's Book* (1932) is related to the main series, but *The Twilight of Magic* (1930) is not. Although much of the content is now dated, the Dolittle books have remained popular with successive generations, and Lofting is ranked with Mary Norton, L. Frank BAUM, Lewis CARROLL, Kenneth Grahame, and other giants of children's literature.

"Logoda's Heads" August Derleth (1939)

This very short horror story was first published under the title "Lord of Evil." African magic has never been much of an influence on Western horror fiction, appearing only intermittently such as in Roger Manvell's THE DREAMERS (1958), Seth Pfefferle's *Stickman* (1987), and most recently in the works of Tananarive Due. One of the rare early examples is this story of conflict between British colonials and a local witch doctor, Logoda, who makes a habit of shrinking the heads of his defeated enemies.

An unnamed officer and a civilian named Henley enter Logoda's hut following the disappearance of an Englishman and notice that there is a fresh shrunken head among the decorations. Henley believes that the new addition is the distorted head of his missing brother. Although the officer is inclined to doubt it and to avoid unnecessarily offending Logoda, his companion is convinced that the native magic is real, which opinion is supported when the heads seem to move of their own volition whenever Logoda speaks to them. Henley arranges to be alone in the hut for a few moments, during which time he speaks to the heads in a local tongue, then requests that he be tied to a bed and guarded during the night. That night Logoda is killed in his hut, discovered in the morning with his throat torn out and his body mutilated. Henley insists that he was responsible and that he instructed the heads to attack the witch doctor.

Many horror writers have described the foolishness of questioning the beliefs of indigenes and implied that magic might work if those employing it are true believers. Unlike the officer, Henley managed to cast aside the prejudices of his civilized English upbringing and confronted Logoda with the rules understood clearly by both parties. It was Logoda who underestimated his enemy, never suspecting that an Englishman could possibly know how to influence his assembled heads. Derleth wrote a large number of traditional horror stories before turning to the Cthulhu Mythos of H. P. LOVECRAFT for his inspiration, and this is one of the best of them.

Long, Frank Belknap (1901–1994)

For most of his early career, Frank Belknap Long was a close friend of H. P. LOVECRAFT. Long began selling short fiction in 1924 and became a regular contributor to the magazines of weird fiction, producing early classics such as "The Ocean Leech" (1924) and "The Hounds of Tindalos" (1929). The latter in particular is credited with having influenced Lovecraft's own development of the Cthulhu Mythos, which in turn helped shape the careers of later writers. Unlike Lovecraft, Long often turned to science fiction, particularly during the 1940s, but the stories in *The Hounds of Tindalos* (1946), *The Horror from* the Hills (1963), and The Dark Beasts (1964) are almost exclusively supernatural or occult. "Second Night Out" (1933) is one of his best short tales, the story of a traveler on a cruise ship bedeviled by a monster. "A Visitor from Egypt" (1930) is one of the rare convincing stories of terror at the hands of revived mummies. Some of Long's lighter fantasies are also quite entertaining, particularly "Fisherman's Luck" (1940) and "Come into My Garden" (1942).

Long did not return to horror fiction until the 1970s, when, under the pseudonym Lyda Belknap Long, he wrote several Gothic suspense novels that, unlike most of the books appearing in that guise, incorporated genuinely supernatural elements. A secret society conspires to conceal occult knowledge in To the Dark Tower (1969), voodoo proves to be real in The Shape of Fear (1971), two clairvoyants solve an eerie mystery in Fire of the Witches (1971), and there is genuine witchcraft in House of Deadly Nightshade (1972). The Night of the Wolf (1972), published under his own name, is more obviously supernatural, an interesting variation on the traditional werewolf story with liberal doses of magic.

Several of Long's later science fiction novels incorporate elements of horror, such as vampires from outer space in Journey into Darkness (1967). Occasional fantastic stories can also be found in the collections The Rim of the Unknown (1978) and Night Fear (1979). Long wrote a biography of Lovecraft, his own memoir, and several volumes of poetry, much of it involving occult themes. Although his writing never received the accolades awarded to many of his peers, his early work is still regarded with considerable respect.

The Lord Darcy Stories Randall Garrett
(1964–1979)
Although Randall Garrett is remembered primarily as a science fiction writer, his most famous single character is Lord Darcy, an unusual detective in an alternate world where magic is the order of the day rather than science. Mixing fantasy and the classic mystery story has always been a difficult task, since the existence of magic invites the reader to believe that the solution may be dependent on something the author has failed to tell. Garrett was cognizant

of this fact, and, in fact, the magic system in his world is explained sufficiently to reassure the reader that the author will not cheat in the final pages.

Garrett's unusual approach was evident in the fact that the first in the series, "The Eyes Have It" (1964), actually appeared in a science fiction magazine noted for its rejection of anything remotely fantastic. Garrett had codified his magic system so that it felt like science, and Lord Darcy's assistant, a Doctor Watson of sorts, is a forensic sorcerer. The series continued with "A Case of Identity" (1964) and "The Muddle of the Woad" (1965). A novel-length adventure, Too Many Magicians (1966), posed a perplexing case of murder at a convention of wizards. Despite the popularity of Darcy and his world, Garrett added only a few more stories during the 1970s. Most of the short adventures were collected as Murder and Magic (1979) and Lord Darcy Investigates (1981), with all three volumes later combined as Lord Darcy (1983). A later printing added a few additional short pieces. Several of the stories openly acknowledge classic mystery fiction by Nero Wolfe, John Dickson Carr, and others.

Following Garrett's death the author Michael Kurland extended the series with two additional novels. Ten Little Wizards (1988) is a locked-room murder mystery involving the systematic elimination of powerful wizards, and A Study in Sorcery (1989) takes Darcy to the New World to solve a mystery involving an Aztec nobleman. Although the novels are interesting in their own right, they are less rigorous about the fantasy backdrop and never rise to the level of the originals. Garrett wrote no other fantasy of note, although much of his science fiction is memorable.

The Lord of the Rings See THE FELLOWSHIP OF THE RING, THE TWO TOWERS, and THE RETURN OF THE KING.

Lost Horizon James Hilton (1933)
The British writer James Hilton moved to the United States, where he worked primarily as a screenwriter, although he found time to produce

more than a dozen novels, of which this is one of the most famous. *Lost Horizon* is a lost race novel, although in this case the attributes of Shangri-La, a hidden civilization in the Himalayas, are magical, and the novel falls into the realm of fantasy. The protagonist is an outsider, disillusioned with the world after his experiences during World War I and wandering in search of some elusive goal he cannot articulate, let alone attain.

Hugh Conway arrives in the area by accident, rescued after an air crash and taken to a religious retreat where he learns of the existence of the nearby hidden culture. The interloper finds himself at peace for the first time, because within that lost land time itself operates in a different fashion. The romantic aspects were emphasized in the 1937 film version, which ends with him abandoning the lost land to return to civilization, whereas in the novel he becomes the next in line as a kind of guardian over that tiny world's serenity. The conclusion is a blend of optimism and sadness, for in taking that responsibility he must sacrifice his own personal happiness.

Hilton wrote no other fantasy, although a short story, "The Bat-King" (1936), about a man lost in a cave and protected by bats, treads very close to that field. A second film, *Return to Shangri-La* (1987), has virtually no relationship to the original novel. Hilton's imagined world has become a generic term for an imagined perfect refuge.

Lovecraft, H. P. (1890–1937)

Although Howard Philips Lovecraft never approached the commercial success of modern horror writers such as Stephen KING and Dean R. KOONTZ, he was nevertheless the most influential horror writer of his time, attracting a circle of writers who imitated his work even while he was alive, actively encouraging them to do so, and even allowing them to write stories set in his own contrived universe. He has been both directly and indirectly influential on most of the writers who followed.

Lovecraft is best known for the stories loosely gathered into the Cthulhu Mythos, the premise of which is that in prehistoric times Earth was ruled by a repulsive race sometimes referred to as the

Great Old Ones who were driven into another universe, from which they have been ever since plotting to return to Earth and regain control. Primary among them is great Cthulhu and his lesser associates Yog-Sothoth, Nyarlothotep, and others. Most of the stories are set in fictional towns and locations in New England, such as Dunwich, Arkham, Innsmouth, and at Miskatonic University. Knowledge of the ancient race's existence has been preserved on Earth primarily by means of a book of arcane lore, *The Necronomicon*. Despite Lovecraft's own statement that he invented the book and the absence of any references to it prior to his lifetime, there is a persistent belief among the fringes of the occult community that the book is real, and, in fact, a half dozen books have been published under that title since Lovecraft's death in an attempt to profit from the popularity of the title. In many of the Cthulhu Mythos stories, humans conspire to open a gateway and allow the Old Ones to return, although they never succeed. Many well-known writers have added to the Cthulhu Mythos over the years, including most notably August DERLETH, Robert BLOCH, Brian LUMLEY, Ramsey CAMPBELL, and Colin Wilson, and he has been acknowledged by many others, including Stephen King, as having influenced their own creations to some degree.

Much has been written about the recurring images in Lovecraft's fiction, his aversion to fish, his concerns that New England's patrician population was being supplanted by less intelligent immigrants, the decay and physical decline of people in isolated communities, the quest for forbidden knowledge, and his rejection of established religion. Lovecraft was raised in relative seclusion by his mother and later his aunts and only attended school intermittently, so it was only after his brief, unsuccessful marriage and a two-year residence in New York that he began to broaden his viewpoint.

Lovecraft had been a precocious child who become interested in the work of Edgar Allan POE and read the works of other famous early horror writers. In addition to his fiction, he was a prolific and literate correspondent, and several volumes of his letters have been collected in book form. He also wrote one of the finest surveys of early horror fiction, "Supernatural Horror in Literature." During the 1920s he became a regular contributor to occult fiction magazines such as *Weird Tales* and an occasional contributor to science fiction titles as well, although his science fiction stories almost always felt out of place there. "The Call of Cthulhu" (1928) established most of the major components of the Cthulhu Mythos, which he went on to elaborate with additional tales until the end of his life.

Lovecraft's first significant short fiction was "The Tomb" (1921). His horror stories were often conventional, but much of his best work, particularly in the early part of his career, such as "COOL AIR" (1926) and "The Rats in the Walls" (1924), was not a part of the mythos. That loose sequence began to expand in earnest in the latter 1920s, with the novella *The Case of Charles Dexter Ward* (1927) and memorable shorter pieces including "THE DUNWICH HORROR" (1930), "THE SHADOW OVER INNSMOUTH" (1931), "The Thing on the Doorstep" (1933), and "THE HAUNTER OF THE DARK" (1935). Lovecraft's protagonists were often doomed almost from the outset, but it was the journey and not the destination that held the attention of his readers, and his ability to evoke slightly twisted versions of familiar New England settings was highly effective. Many of the buildings and institutions mentioned in the stories have an almost exact counterpart in the real world.

In the last few years of his life, Lovecraft's stories began to edge toward science fiction again, and the short novels *At the Mountains of Madness* (1931) and *The Shadow out of Time* (1936) clearly show that he was no longer as interested in overt horror. The former describes the discovery of an ancient abandoned city in Antarctica, and the latter concerns a man whose mind is swapped with that of an inhuman creature from prehistory. He also wrote a small number of fantasies, of which the most famous are *The Dream-Quest of Unknown Kadath* (1943), a journey through a dreamland, and "The Strange High House in the Mist" (1931).

Lovecraft actively encouraged other writers, even to the point of rewriting their manuscripts for them. Following his death August Derleth completed a number of his fragments and wrote additional stories, although Lovecraft's more avid fans were often unhappy with these efforts to reorganize the mythos into a more consistent form. Derleth

founded Arkham House, originally for the purpose of publishing Lovecraft's fiction in hardcover, although it has remained a successful imprint specializing in science fiction and horror ever since. Lovecraft is often criticized for his archaic prose, his early racial prejudice, and his snobbishness, but whatever his faults, the originality and appeal of his stories is undeniable.

His short fiction has been collected in a bewildering number of combinations under many titles. Recent selections that provide a representative sampling include *The Road to Madness* (1996), *The Loved Dead* (1997), *The Call of Cthulhu and Other Weird Stories* (1999), and *The Thing on the Doorstep and Other Weird Stories* (2001). The early collections from Arkham House have become valuable collectors' items. Numerous films and television episodes have been made from Lovecraft's fiction, usually unhappily, including *The Dunwich Horror* (1970), *The Re-Animator* (1985), "The Colour out of Space" as *The Haunted Palace* (1963), *The Case of Charles Dexter Ward* as *The Resurrected* (1989), and *Dagon* (2001).

"Lukundoo" Edward Lucas White (1907)

Until comparatively recently most horror fiction shocked by suggestion rather than revulsion. If a body was eviscerated or mutilated, it usually happened off stage, and readers rarely received a detailed description of the monstrous figures responsible. One of the exceptions was this very unnerving story by Edward Lucas White, whose handful of other weird stories are now largely forgotten.

The story takes place in Africa as a small expedition of scientists searching for pygmies encounters a man wandering the jungle in a state of considerable distress. His name is Etcham, and he tells them that he works for another explorer named Stone who is famous for having exposed the trickery of several local witch doctors. They had penetrated deep into the jungle when Stone became afflicted with unusual growths like boils or carbuncles all over his body, a malady that continued even after he used a razor to cut them off. Stone has, in fact, become so seriously ill that he may be hallucinating, for he speaks to himself in the night using two voices and refuses to allow anyone to help him deal with the malignant growths.

The newcomers are reluctant to become involved until Etcham shows them evidence that Stone had recently discovered pygmies, for he carries a shrunken head that is too small to have been made from a normal man. Intrigued, the new expedition follows Etcham's directions and finds the man as described, but they also discover an even more bizarre fact. The shrunken head is only one of several that have sprouted from Stone's body, heads that until severed are animated and talkative. Although the experience is obviously causing him great pain, Stone implores them not to remove the most recent head. His death comes at last when a diminutive pygmy is born from his own flesh.

The grotesque images and surprise revelations are less effective for contemporary readers, but the ending must have come as a considerable shock to those unprepared for such a twist when the story was first published. "Lukundoo" holds up surprisingly well today, despite the somewhat murky explanation in the final paragraphs, which implies that the curse was engineered by Stone's ex-wife rather than a disgruntled witch doctor.

Lumley, Brian (1937–   )

Brian Lumley's earliest fiction, which began appearing in the late 1960s, was heavily influenced by H. P. LOVECRAFT, although over time Lumley gradually altered the structure of the Cthulhu Mythos so that humans had a better chance of defeating the nearly godlike alien intelligences Lovecraft had imagined. Most of the stories in *The Caller of the Black* (1971) are in this mode, as are his early novels. His second novel, *The Burrowers Beneath* (1974), introduces the first extended adventure of Titus Crow, a psychic detective who mixes arcane knowledge with overt violence. Crow, who had also appeared in several shorter pieces, returns to defend the Earth from invasion in *The Transition of Titus Crow* (1975), but his subsequent adventures, *The Clock of Dreams* (1978), *Spawns of the Winds* (1978), and *In the Moons of Borea* (1979), are more properly

science fiction. Lumley routinely mixed scientific rationalizations into later novels, making them difficult to categorize.

Lumley's next sequence consisted of *Psychomech* (1985), *Psychosphere* (1985), and *Psychamok* (1986). A man endowed with superhuman powers struggles to disrupt a villainous plot that is aided by occult powers, a theme he used again in *Demogorgon* (1987), this time pitting his hero against direct satanic intervention. Lumley also tried his hand, though less successfully, with heroic fantasy in a sequence that includes *Hero of Dreams* (1986), *Ship of Dreams* (1986), *Mad Moon of Dreams* (1987), *Elysia* (1989), and *Iced on Aran* (1990). In each volume David Hero travels through one or more dreamlands, battling an evil queen and her army of zombie warriors or facing down other foes. The series is ostensibly linked to *The Dream Quest of Unknown Kadath* (1943) by Lovecraft, but the connection is tenuous at best.

It was with *Necroscope* (1986) that Lumley leaped into the foremost ranks of horror writers. Harry Keogh is the Necroscope, that is, he can literally speak to the dead. He uses this talent in the service of British Intelligence, but unfortunately one of his communist counterparts has made contact with a super vampire from another reality and has become infected with the taint. Lumley's vampires, more properly vamphyri, are far more powerful and dangerous than those found in most other horror fiction. In *Vamphyri!* (1988), the vampire lord begins raising an army of his kind in preparation for seizing control of the Earth. Keogh discovers that the Russians have opened a portal between universes and pays an extended and unpleasant visit to the vampire world in *The Source* (1989).

Lumley continued the sequence with *Deadspeak* (1990) and *Deadspawn* (1991). Humanity has supposedly driven out the alien vampires and devastated their world as well, but some of the creatures are masters of occult sorcery and have not abandoned their quest to manipulate humans, particularly within the Soviet Union, in order to achieve their ends. Switching emphasis slightly, Lumley then wrote a trilogy set solely within the vampire universe, *Blood Brothers* (1992), *The Last Aerie* (1993), and *Bloodwars* (1994). Harry Keogh had two sons before his death, one of whom finds himself caught up in the vampire world and later opposed to his sibling, who has allied himself with the enemies of humanity. The trilogy is particularly violent at times, but Lumley created a genuinely different vampire lore for the series.

Keogh returns, or rather we are treated to previously untold adventures, in *Necroscope: The Lost Years*, published in two volumes in 1995 and 1996, the second volume later called *Resurgence*. Keogh battles more of the alien vampires, but on a less grand scale than in the previous books. Three more volumes followed. *Necroscope: Invaders* (1999) casts a new character in the role of speaker to the dead, as the vampires threaten to invade once again. The battle continues in *Necroscope: Defilers* (2000) and concludes in *Necroscope: Avengers* (2001). Although the series remains popular, the later volumes are at times repetitive.

Although it is for his novels that Lumley is most noted, some of his short fiction is excellent, such as "Fruiting Bodies" (1988) and "The Viaduct" (2002). The best of his many collections are *Fruiting Bodies and Other Fungi* (1993), *Return of the Deep Ones* (1994,) and *Beneath the Moors and Darker Places* (2002). Lumley is a reliable writer of highly suspenseful and usually quite violent stories that are often enhanced by an unusually inventive imagination.

"The Lurking Fear" H. P. Lovecraft (1922)

One of the recurring images in the work of H. P. LOVECRAFT is a community in decay, either at the instigation of outside forces, such as in "THE SHADOW OVER INNSMOUTH" (1931), or simply by inbreeding and racial or cultural flaws, such as in this story. Early in his career Lovecraft was heavily influenced by classic British horror writers, and this story feels as though it might have been set in a rural part of England, although it is, in fact, situated somewhere in the state of New York.

Martense Mansion has apparently been abandoned for many generations. It was built by rich Dutch settlers who were unhappy when the British took over the colony and retreated from the world, breeding within the family and cutting themselves off from most outside contact. The pivotal event came when one of the young males in the family went off to war, returned to find himself ostracized by his own family, and later died at their hands. Although the house is empty and partially ruined, the local residents blame the building and the apparently extinct family for a series of mysterious deaths over the years, each of which takes place during or following a thunderstorm.

The protagonist is an outsider who wishes to investigate these incidents, which have culminated with the terrible slaughter of an entire small community. He recruits two other men to help him keep vigil in one room of the mansion, and during one stormy night both of his companions are abducted right before his eyes. The only hint of the party responsible is a glimpse of a distorted shadow. Theories abound, including the possibility that it is the ghost of young Martense, killed by his own family, but the investigator believes that there is a living, organic cause, not a supernatural one. He is eventually proven right.

He discovers a system of tunnels under the house and grounds and narrowly escapes when a horde of filthy, barely human creatures emerges from their underground lair. It is the remnants of the Martense family, now grown numerous, living a troglodytic existence that they interrupt only when disturbed by the sound of thunder from the surface world. Like many of Lovecraft's stories, there is no dialogue, simply a straightforward narrative history. Although not as polished or imaginative as some of his later work, it reveals many of the attitudes and images that would recur throughout his writing career.

Lynn, Elizabeth A. (1946–   )

Elizabeth Lynn produced an impressive number of very good short stories plus two novels, one science fiction and one fantasy, all within the span of three years during the late 1970s. The short stories included excellent pieces such as "I Dream of Fish, I Dream of Bird" (1977), "The Dragon That Lived in the Sea" (1979), and the title story of her first collection, *The Woman Who Loved the Moon and Other Stories* (1981). More significantly, she wrote the Tornor trilogy, consisting of *Watchtower* (1979), which won the World Fantasy Award, *The Dancers of Arun* (1979), and *The Northern Girl* (1990).

The setting in the opening volume is superficially familiar. A medieval style kingdom is threatened by external forces, requiring a good deal of political maneuvering both in the open and behind the scenes. In the middle of this, two messengers arrive, a profession usually reserved for sexually neutral individuals, but in this case both are actually women concealing their sexuality. Although the surface plot proceeds conventionally, with the invaders defeated by subterfuge and force of arms, the details are what make the novel rich and interesting. One group is willing to fight but not to kill, for example, and the roles of the sexes are contrasted and illuminated by the four major characters.

The Dancers of Arun takes place several generations later and is essentially a coming of age novel. The protagonist was maimed as a child, so he cannot serve as a soldier, but he is developing unusual psychic powers that are not entirely a blessing. The protagonist of *The Northern Girl* has a similar problem, complicated by the fact that she is an indentured servant. The three novels examine issues of pacifism, free will, and sexual equality in a fresh and noncombative manner. Lynn was clearly a writer to watch, but unfortunately she produced very little new fiction between 1980 and 1998, only a children's fantasy and a handful of short stories. *Tales from a Vanished Country* (1990) brought most of her uncollected short fiction together in book form for the first time.

In 1998 Lynn returned to fantasy with *Dragon's Winter*. One of a pair of twins runs off with a magic talisman that would have enabled his brother to transform himself into a dragon. Trapped in a mortal body and now an adult, the latter must find a way to defeat the armies of an evil sorcerer, who turns out to be his brother, returned at last. The story is continued in *Dragon's Treasure* (2004) with at least one further title probable. Her return to the field has been warmly welcomed.

M

MacAvoy, R. A. (1949–)

Roberta Ann MacAvoy made her debut with the contemporary fantasy *Tea with the Black Dragon* (1983) and then added 10 more novels, one of them science fiction, before apparently abandoning writing in 1994. Her first novel made an immediate and lasting impression because of its strong characterization and its original treatment and concept. The protagonist is a young woman who strikes up a friendship with a man who is actually an ancient shape-changing dragon. When her daughter is kidnapped, the twosome team up to track down the criminals and rescue her.

MacAvoy followed this striking novel with a trilogy of historical fantasies, *Damiano* (1984), *Damiano's Lute* (1984), and *Raphael* (1985). Set in an alternate Renaissance Italy, the sequence opens as the son of a magician who has been taught to play music by the angel Raphael himself sets out to find a legendary sorceress who he believes has the power to save his people from getting caught up in a war. The interference of a demon interferes with his plans, and although he wins the opening engagement, he and his protector, Raphael, are dogged by the forces of evil from that point forward. In the concluding volume Lucifer outsmarts Raphael, tricking him into taking human form and by doing so precipitates the final confrontation.

The Book of Kells (1985) is a magical story of time travel in which a contemporary artist travels back to 10th-century Britain. *Twisting the Rope* (1986) brings back the protagonist from *Tea with the Black Dragon*, this time to rescue her granddaughter. Although an entertaining story, it lacks the charm of her first adventure. *The Grey Horse* (1987) is also a historical fantasy, this one involving the early history of Ireland and the appearance of a mystical horse.

MacAvoy's last fantasy work was the Lens trilogy, consisting of *Lens of the World* (1990), *King of the Dead* (1991), and *The Belly of the Wolf* (1993, also published as *Winter of the Wolf*). The trilogy chronicles most of the life of a young man who rises above his humble beginnings to become a key player in the future of his people. MacAvoy's subsequent inactivity has deprived fantasy of one of its freshest and most original voices.

MacDonald, George (1824–1905)

George MacDonald was a Scottish writer whose several nonfantastic novels have largely been forgotten, although his fantasy, both for children and for adults, has enjoyed intermittent popularity ever since. His pioneering role in modern fantasy is well established. His first fantasy novel was ostensibly for adults. *Phantastes* (1858) is an episodic and rather disorganized narrative in which the protagonist enters various magical situations by means of his dreams. As he explores these mystical realms, he begins to perceive the rules that hold sway there, not always in time to avoid making serious mistakes. On more than one occasion he errs despite clear warnings against his proposed course of action. Much of the story is a Christian allegory about the nature of good and evil and the effects of temptation.

His second adult fantasy novel, *Lilith* (1895), follows the adventures of Mr. Vane, who finds himself in a magical world where Adam and Eve watch over legions of the dead. Although more unified than *Phantastes*, it is also an episodic adventure as Vane explores, encountering a variety of characters and creatures, including one who is essentially a vampire. Much of this is also allegorical and reflective of the author's religious beliefs, but the subtext is in this case much less intrusive.

MacDonald also wrote three fantasy novels for young readers, *At the Back of the North Wind* (1870), *The Princess and the Goblin* (1871), and *The Princess and Curdie* (1882), of which the first is the best, the story of a young boy who makes friends with the north wind and is taken on a series of adventures. The other two involve Princess Lootie, who is kidnapped by a goblin and rescued by a boy of humble origin. The last title is a story of personal redemption and religious duty.

MacDonald's short fantasies are in much the same vein as his novels. "The Golden Key" (1867) is another story of travel through dreams, and "The Giant's Heart" (1863) is a fairy tale with a particularly nasty giant. "The History of Photogen and Nycteris" and "The Light Princess" are among his best. His short tales have been collected in *The Complete Fairy Tales of George MacDonald* (1961), *Evenor* (1972), *The Gifts of the Child Christ* (1973), and *The Golden Key and Other Stories* (1980). There is some slight fantastic content in *The Portent* (1885, also published as *The Lady of the Mansion*).

Machen, Arthur (1863–1947)

The Welsh writer Arthur Machen produced a large body of fiction during a writing career that lasted more than 50 years. His nonfantastic work is not particularly distinguished. Much of his fantasy and horror fiction has fared no better with the passage of time, but a relatively small portion of his work has remained popular and influential. His best known fantastic book is *The Three Impostors* (1895, also published as *The Black Crusade*), a series of tall tales related by members of a club, most of which involve manifestations of legends, the sur-

vival of magic in the modern world, and other low-key fantasy. The collection is not typical of his supernatural fiction, which tends to be darker and brooding.

Several of his shorter pieces are surprisingly original and modern in tone, including "THE GREAT GOD PAN" (1890), in which an operation on a woman's brain has unforeseen consequences years later. "The Inmost Light" (1894), which has a very similar theme, was mildly controversial at the time of its original publication but is now largely forgotten. "The Novel of the Black Seal" (1895) is one of a handful of stories that suggest that fairies may not be the amusing, mischievous folk as usually portrayed in fairy tales but are actually much darker of spirit and dangerous to cross. A scholar convinced that they exist in physical form in caverns beneath England disappears in pursuit of them and never returns. It is part of a loose series of stories that also includes "The Novel of the White Powder" (1895), one of Machen's best horror tales, in which a drug is inadvertently altered, resulting in the physical transformation of a man into a hideous monster. "The Bowmen" (1914) is particularly effective because of its timing, the story of ghostly intervention on the side of the British during the Great War.

Machen's later work is generally inferior. *The Great Return* (1915) is a story of miracles and the Holy Grail, an interesting treatment but marred by long sections in which very little happens. *The Terror* (1917) is a story of animals in revolt, attacking humanity because of the excesses of the war. It is smoothly narrated, but with very little suspense and a tendency to preach. The best collection of Machen's short horror fiction is *Tales of Horror and the Supernatural* (1948), sometimes published in two volumes.

The Magician's Nephew C. S. Lewis (1955)

The sixth installment in the CHRONICLES OF NARNIA by C. S. LEWIS is substantially different in setting and tone from the earlier novels, and the Christian theological symbolism is much more obvious. The story takes place long before the earlier continuing characters were born, initially in London. Narnia itself does not exist, for Aslan has yet to create that magical realm of talking animals. Digory is a young boy temporarily living with his aunt and uncle, the Ketterleys, when he meets Polly Plumber, a neighbor girl. Digory's uncle is descended from Morgan Lefay, and he has inherited from her some rudimentary magical knowledge that enables him to create colored rings that have the power to carry their bearer between realities. Polly is sent off on an experimental mission, and Digory follows to rescue her.

The children recover from a brief period of amnesia to find themselves in a magical wood that is a kind of way station among realities. Their explorations unfortunately bring them to the realm of Jadis, who later becomes the White Witch of Narnia, an inhuman creature who tricks them into taking her back to London with them. There she terrorizes the uncle and threatens more mayhem, some of it rather comical, before the children trick her into traveling to an unformed reality that will eventually, with Aslan's intercession, become the land of Narnia. Digory's uncle comes with them, but Digory proves to be his match when their wills clash, and Aslan's appearance at least temporarily frightens off Jadis.

Aslan brings Narnia to life all around them, creating the talking animals and intelligent trees. What follows is a modified version of the story of the creation of Paradise, complete with the apple. A monarch is established, the White Witch driven off at least for a time, and Lewis takes a few jabs at politics in our own world before sending the children back home. Although the first half of the novel is a quite entertaining children's fantasy adventure, the waning chapters grow increasingly talkative and philosophical, and it is likely that many readers will be disappointed by the lack of a rousing finish.

Majipoor Series Robert Silverberg
(1980–2001)

Although Robert Silverberg has long been recognized as a major science fiction writer, it has only been late in his career that he has made a serious effort to write fantasy, primarily with the Majipoor novels. Silverberg launched the series with *Lord Valentine's Castle* (1980), which initially appears to be straightforward science fiction. The planet Majipoor has long been conquered by humans, who find themselves ruling a variety of distinct races, one of which has the ability to change shape. As the story progresses, Silverberg strays progressively further from its scientific underpinnings. The protagonist is an amnesiac in search of his past who supports himself on his journey by learning to juggle. The second volume, *The Majipoor Chronicles* (1981), consists of a series of interwoven short stories all set against the same background, clearly indicating that the author had more to say about this unique world. *Valentine Pontifex* (1983) moves squarely into fantasy, with sea dragons revealed as having nearly godlike powers. The cast of varied characters pursue their individual quests while agitation grows to exterminate the shape-changers. This brought what was originally expected to be a trilogy to an end, but Silverberg was not done with Majipoor.

After a gap of more than 10 years, Silverberg revived his fantasy series with *The Mountains of Majipoor* (1995), set 1,000 years later. Although less ambitious than the earlier books, the story of an exiled bureaucrat's efforts to redeem himself is amusing and entertaining. More significant is *Sorcerers of Majipoor* (1996), the first of three volumes set earlier in the planet's history. Magic is much more overt in this story of an unlikely prince chosen to inherit the throne and his fulfillment of an ancient prophecy. In *Lord Prestimion* (1996) the throne is secured following a civil war, and sorcery is employed to alter the memories of the populace. The second trilogy concludes with *King of Dreams* (2001), wherein Prestimion in turn must pass on his authority to his successor. Although some readers may find the frequent and lengthy digressions into side issues distracting, others will enjoy the author's efforts to give greater depth to his imaginary world. Silverberg has written occasional other fantasy, but none even close to the stature of the Majipoor cycle.

"The Man Who Sold Rope to the Gnoles"
Margaret St. Clair (1979)

Margaret St. Clair's quirky short stories often gleefully disregard reality and assume the extraordinary as a matter of course. Such is the case in this very short but memorable story about an ambitious salesman who decides to impress his supervisor by selling merchandise to the "gnoles." The gnoles have a bad reputation, and they live in their little house isolated from the rest of the world on the edge of unknown territories. Mortensen, the salesman, studies the principles of salesmanship assiduously until he believes he thoroughly understands the process of acceptance that takes place in the mind of the customer, but he is less careful about paying attention to the list of attributes of the successful sales person and fails to properly assume the degree of awareness that is recommended.

No one ever visits the gnoles, so they are understandably surprised when Mortensen shows up on their doorstep. Although the gnoles are not remotely human, Mortensen refuses to react to their disturbing physical appearance or their distinctive odor. He is a bit disconcerted when he discovers the gnoles have no ears to hear him with, but he remains determined to sell them some rope. Patiently he lays out samples from his case along with written descriptions and pricing information while the gnoles looks on enigmatically. When a gnole finally indicates interest in placing a large order, Mortensen is pleased with himself and even contemplates trying to approach the even less-human "gibbelins" next.

Unfortunately, Mortensen is unobservant and unintentionally offends his host, who responds by hustling him down into the basement. The rope might have been a convenience, but fresh meat for the larder is, after all, much more valuable. Most of St. Clair's other fiction is technically science fiction, but her unique view of reality inserted a touch of magic into much of that as well.

The Man Who Was Magic Paul Gallico
(1966)

Paul Gallico was a flexible writer who contributed to a variety of genres, including spy stories, humor, adventure, and mundane fiction. His short *The Snow Goose* (1941) is marginally fantasy, and his novel *The Abandoned* (1950, also published as *Jennie*) is about a young boy who is transformed magically into a cat, in which body he has several amusing adventures. Gallico wrote other children's fantasies, as well as two novels, *Too Many Ghosts* (1959) and *The Hand of Mary Constable* (1964), which lead the reader to believe that they involve the supernatural, although the unusual events are eventually rationalized. There actually is a ghost in *The House That Wouldn't Go Away* (1979), but it is not one of his better books.

Gallico's single significant fantasy is *The Man Who Was Magic,* a good-natured story cast almost in the form of a fairy tale, sophisticated enough for adult readers but straightforward and suitable for a much younger audience. The setting is the hidden city of Mageia, where the Guild of Master Magicians holds sway. None of the members of the guild actually knows any magic; they achieve all of their effects through trickery, a secret known only to themselves. Enter Adam Simple, a stranger from the outer world, who arrives accompanied by Mopsy, his talking dog, hoping to join the guild. They react haughtily at first, but their attitude changes when they discover that Adam does not resort to tricks and that he really does have the ability to perform magic.

The story progresses straightforwardly, even predictably. The false magicians feel threatened and eventually conspire against Adam, hoping to drive him away and preserve their authority. Although they act villainously, none of them is actually evil, and Adam eventually eludes their efforts to entrap him. The novel enjoyed considerable popularity when it first appeared, but Gallico wrote fantasy at such great intervals that he never acquired a significant following.

"The Mark of the Beast" Rudyard Kipling
(1891)

Rudyard Kipling's experiences in British India provided material for some of his most famous fiction, including this, one of his best tales of the supernatural. The story concerns an Englishman named Fleete who, while unusually drunk, disfigures a statue in a temple to Hanuman, the god of the monkeys. As the reader might expect, this brings down the god's curse on Fleete, effected by a mysterious leper. His companions are initially puzzled by the lack of reprisals on the part of the priests, who would normally have reacted violently to such an affront, and the leper's actions seem innocuous if rather strange.

The following morning Fleete wakens with a nasty looking discoloration on his chest and a sudden craving for undercooked meat. His behavior grows increasingly biazrre, and horses brought into close proximity react to his presence with near panic. During the day Fleete's behavior grows more and more bestial. He rolls in the dirt and insists that he is ravenous and that only raw meat will satisfy him. After night falls all vestiges of his humanity vanish, and he acts like a savage animal whom they manage to control only by binding him hand and foot. A doctor is called to the scene, who diagnoses Fleete's condition as a terminal case of hydrophobia, but even he knows that the answer is far less simple.

Fleete's companions eventually capture the leper and torture him until he agrees to reverse the curse, after which he is set free. Although the abrasive Englishman makes a full recovery, his companions are on the verge of nervous collapse and will never afterward be able to dismiss lightly the power of local religions. Although one of Kipling's best-known stories, it is unsatisfying in some ways, chiefly because Fleete fully deserved his fate and later does not even remember his descent into bestiality, while the rightfully offended agent of Hanuman is tortured and defeated. The former's rapid loss of humanity is, however, eloquently and economically narrated.

Martin, George R. R. (1948–)

Although George R. R. Martin has never been a particularly prolific writer, he has still managed to become a respected name in science fiction, fantasy, and horror, having published novels and short stories in all three fields. He began appearing professionally in the early 1970s but only turned to fantasy several years later, notably with the short story "The Ice Dragon" (1980), a touching story about an emotionally disturbed child whose life is altered by the periodic manifestations of a dragon.

Martin's novel *Fevre Dream* (1982) is set aboard a Mississippi riverboat during the 19th century. A band of vampires lives there, insulated from the world of human beings. The major conflict is not between humans and vampires, but rather between two strains of the latter, those who consider humans mere food to be harvested and those who wish to abandon the traditional role of their kind and live quietly and in secret. Their battle escalates toward an inevitable but still exciting conclusion. Martin employed the supernatural again in his next novel, *Armageddon Rag* (1983), one of the few attempts to blend horror and rock music that actually succeeds. A legendary rock band, the Nazgul, has been idle for years, but they are about to be brought back together for a single reunion concert. An enterprising journalist covering the events building up to the concert discovers that there is a supernatural conspiracy behind the scenes and that the effort to bring back the spirit of the 1960s might result instead in universal Armageddon.

Martin continued to write occasional short fantasies during the 1980s, including the gentle ghost story "Remembering Melody" (1981) and the Bram Stoker Award–winning "The Pear Shaped Man" (1987). "The Skin Trade" (1989) won the World Fantasy Award. Most of these were collected in *Portraits of His Children* (1987), the best collection of his fantasy and horror short stories. Until the middle of the 1990s, Martin had written no mainstream fantasy. That changed in 1996 with the publication of *A Game of Kings*, the first in a projected series of seven novels.

A Game of Thrones introduces a very large cast of characters in a world that encompasses several kingdoms, the rulers of which are engaged in a complex game of political intrigue and physical confrontations. There is dark sorcery involved as well as the natural dangers of that world, and beyond the enormous wall that isolates the civilized world from the unexplored regions, an army of the undead has become animated and begins pressing against the borders. The story continues and grows more complicated in *A Clash of Kings* (1997) and *A Storm of Swords* (2000), with some of the conflicts resolving themselves but others becoming even more involved. Martin never eases up on the tension, and he is not afraid of killing off characters who the reader genuinely misses and who might have been expected to survive in the hands of a less skillful writer. The fourth volume has not yet appeared as of this writing, but the series is already considered Martin's most significant work of fiction.

Masterton, Graham (1946–)

The British writer Graham Masterton's first horror novel was *The Manitou* (1975), in which an Indian sorcerer named Misquamicus returns to life, physically manifesting himself within the body of a woman and eventually seizing control of an entire hospital before being defeated by a new spirit with which he is unfamiliar. The novel became a mediocre movie but was sufficiently popular to launch the author's long career as a writer of usually gruesome and almost always relentlessly suspenseful novels of the supernatural, many of which are quite original in concept. He also revived the Manitou for two interesting but inferior sequels, *Revenge of the Manitou* (1979) and *Burial* (1992).

Masterton's initial follow-up was a series of fast-paced supernatural adventures such as *The Djinn* (1977), in which a genie is set loose on Cape Cod and proves to be a malevolent rather than entertaining spirit, *The Devils of D-Day* (1978), about a haunted World War II tank, and *Charnel House* (1978), in which another Indian spirit returns, this time inhabiting an old house. His early novels rely primarily on fast-paced action and very gruesome death scenes, although even in his early work Masterton's ability to efficiently create realistic and sympathetic characters is evident.

The first of Masterton's novels to acquire greater depth was *The Hell Candidate* (1980), originally published under the pseudonym Thomas Luke. An unprepossessing man rapidly becomes the odds-on favorite to become the next president of the United States, an outcome resulting from his deal with the devil. Masterton also used the Luke pen name for *The Heirloom* (1982), in which the action centers around an apparently ordinary chair that is actually a conduit for evil powers. He returned to his own name for *Pariah* (1983), the story of a sunken ship that is the focus for an ancient evil, and none of his subsequent horror fiction has appeared under a pseudonym.

Masterton began using unusual sources of horror with some regularity thereafter, starting with *Tengu* (1983), in which Japanese demons are incarnated in the bodies of humans in an effort to undermine the international status of the United States, a blend of supernatural suspense and espionage. *Picture of Evil* (1985, also published as *Family Portrait*) concerns the supposedly real family upon which Oscar Wilde later based the character of Dorian Gray. The Grays subsist by draining the life force from others, but the most memorable portion of the novel is a chase scene that actually moves through a series of famous paintings.

Death Trance (1986) involves astral projection and the inhuman denizens of a dreamworld. The novel contains many grotesque images but is inferior to the similar Night Warriors trilogy that soon followed, consisting of *Night Warriors* (1986), *Death Dream* (1988), and *Night Plague* (1991). Following a series of horrible deaths, a group of strangers discover that they are the reincarnations of members of an occult group whose duty is to protect the world from incursions from the dream plane. They battle witchcraft and the demonic forces of that other reality in a very imaginative supernatural series. *Mirror* (1988) has a somewhat similar premise. A brilliant boy who died tragically has managed to survive in a state between the living and dead, dwelling on the opposite side of the mirror, from which he plots to change places with one of the living.

Feast (1988, also published as *Ritual*) involves a restaurant that has a very unusual specialty, human flesh, consumed to appease the forces of hell. Masterton's fascination with bizarre imagery and unusual states of being continued in *Walkers* (1990), in which the residents of an asylum are somehow trapped in a marginal existence within the structure of the walls that confine them. Their efforts to escape come at the cost of the lives of the innocent. *The Burning* (1991, also published as *The Hymn*) less successfully describes a cult whose members achieve immortality by burning themselves alive. *Prey* (1992) is as close as Masterton ever came to an homage to H. P. LOVECRAFT, pitting the protagonist against an ancient creature analogous to a witch who is plotting to bring back the old gods.

Masterton's more recent novels have been more likely to use familiar themes. *Master of Lies* (1992), for example, is the story of a supernatural serial killer, and *Spirit* (1995) is a fairly traditional ghost story, although some of the manifestations are very clever and nontraditional. *Rook* (1996) introduces a recurring protagonist, a man drafted by events into a series of battles with occult forces, a voodoo cult in the opener. Rook's adventures continue with *Tooth and Claw* (1997), in which he battles yet another Indian spirit, *The Terror* (1998), *Snowman* (2000), which deals with an Eskimo curse, and *Swimmer* (2002), a fairly straightforward tale of ghostly revenge.

The House That Jack Built (1996) is a very traditional haunted house story. One of the new owners becomes obsessed with restoring it, while the other is troubled by recurring, unsettling visions. *The Chosen Child* (1997) is one of Masterton's best. A number of headless corpses are found scattered about the modern-day city of Warsaw. A private detective and an entrepreneur investigate the crime and discover that the responsible party is not a human being. This is one of Masterton's most atmospheric novels and contains some of his best characterization. *The House of Bones* (1998), on the other hand, is fairly flat emotionally and covers no new ground. *The Doorkeepers* (2001) has a more interesting premise, a portal in London that provides access to a bizarre and dangerous alternate reality, but the plot wanders distractingly after the initial mystery is revealed.

Trauma (2002) is another of Masterton's best, although the supernatural content is marginal. A woman dealing with a variety of emotional problems becomes interested in Mexican legends when references to them show up at a series of mysterious deaths. *A Terrible Beauty* (2003) also explains much of its mystery in rational terms, although the rather unique serial killer is, in fact, acting at the behest of a supernatural force. *The Devil in Gray* (2004) is a throwback to his earliest horror novels, although it is much more polished. An invisible killer slaughters a number of victims in graphically described and very gruesome ways, while a police officer struggles with his own personal demons and the disinclination of his superiors to accept a supernatural explanation.

Starting in the late 1980s Masterton began writing short horror tales with some regularity, several of which are quite good. Among his best are "The Absence of the Beast" (1992), "Making Belinda" (1993), "The Hungry Moon" (1995), and "Epiphany" (2003). Although there have been several collections of his short fiction in Britain, only one has appeared in the United States, *Charnel House and Other Stories* (2002). Masterton has been a reliable writer of very fine horror novels for almost 30 years and has polished his skills considerably during the course of his career. At his best he mixes highly original images with unusual themes and uses fully developed characters to draw the reader into his terrifying imagined worlds. Although he has never achieved the status of Stephen KING or Dean R. KOONTZ, his work is always warmly welcomed, and he seems assured of a prominent place in the history of the field.

Matheson, Richard (1926–)

Richard Matheson's classic novel *I Am Legend* (1954, also published as *The Omega Man* as a tie-in to the rather disloyal film version), is technically science fiction since the vampires who dominate the world after a future apocalypse are rationalized, but it is so closely associated with horror fiction that it has been claimed by both genres. The protagonist is the only normal human left alive, exterminating the quasivampires created by a new plague during the day and hiding from them at night. It has been filmed twice, as *The Last Man on Earth* (1964) and as *The Omega Man* (1971).

Although it has a much less unique plot, *A Stir of Echoes* (1958) is actually a better-constructed novel. An otherwise ordinary man begins to experience psychic visions that eventually lead to the solution of an old murder case. The film version was released in 1999. *Bid Time Return* (1975) was the basis of the film *Somewhere in Time* (1980), more fantasy than horror and a love story involving reincarnation. *Hell House* (1971, filmed as *Legend of Hell House* in 1973) was obviously influenced by THE HAUNTING OF HILL HOUSE (1959) by Shirley JACKSON, although its horrors are much more overt. The man whose spirit dominates this haunted house is decidedly nasty. *What Dreams*

May Come (1978, filmed in 1998) is an almost mystical fantasy in which the spirit of a dead man seeks to be reunited with the woman he loves, who is still among the living. Matheson's later novels, which often involve no fantastic content, are generally less memorable than his early work.

Several of Matheson's better short stories are horror, although many others are science fiction, and a few straddle both genres. Among his best are "Dress of White Silk" (1951), "LITTLE GIRL LOST" (1953), "Long Distance Call" (1953), in which the dead use the telephone, "The Likeness of Julie" (1962), "NIGHTMARE AT 20,000 FEET" (1961), and "PREY" (1969), in which a tiny African figurine comes to life and wreaks havoc. Matheson's short fiction has been collected and recollected under a variety of titles. Recent volumes containing much of his best work include *Collected Stories* (1989), *Nightmare at 20,000 Feet* (2002), and *Duel* (2003). Matheson has written numerous screenplays, and many of his short stories have been adapted as episodes of television programs. He has long been and remains one of the most respected figures in the horror genre.

McCammon, Robert R. (1952–   )

Robert McCammon is one of several writers who took advantage of the popularity of horror in the late 1970s to launch his career and one of the very few to make the best-seller lists and appeal to a wider audience than the hard-core fans originally attracted to his work. His early novels, although very well written, only hinted at the talent that he would eventually reveal, partly because they make use of plot devices that had already become overly familiar. *Baal* (1978), his first novel, is, in fact, simply another variation of the son of Satan stories already done more successfully by Ira Levin in ROSEMARY'S BABY (1967) and David Seltzer in THE OMEN (1976), both of which became successful movies. The child in this case is conceived through rape and acquires supernatural powers as a consequence, but the climax is predictable and somewhat flat.

Bethany's Sin (1980) is a reversal of the situation in *The Stepford Wives* (1972), also by Ira Levin. The protagonist stumbles upon a small town whose men are kept in virtual slavery by a cult of women who have cultivated supernatural powers to protect their power base. *Night Boat* (1980) is even more traditional, a ghostly revenge story, but it is the most gripping of McCammon's early novels. A diver happens upon a sunken German submarine from World War II. Although he is only interested in salvage, he detects signals from inside the boat, as though some of the crew had survived, a circumstnce that is clearly impossible. Subsequent events proceed predictably but eerily as the drowned sailors exact revenge on the living. In each of these novels, the battle against supernatural evil is a reflection of a more mundane battle that the protagonist is waging with his or her own personal demons.

McCammon's fourth novel signaled his emergence from the ranks of mid-list writers. *They Thirst* (1981) explores the logical consequences of vampirism ignored by most other horror writers. The rate of conversion is so rapid that efforts to stem the tide fail, and eventually vampires virtually rule Los Angeles. This is a much more ambitious novel with a larger cast of viewpoint characters and a substantially wider range of events, but despite the grim nature of the plot, it is also sprinkled with moments of sardonic humor, such as in the sequence involving an undead disc jockey.

With *Mystery Walk* (1983) McCammon firmly established himself as a major player in the horror field. The story alternates between two seemingly disparate men, one a faith healer and the other essentially a medium. Neither man is particularly good or particularly evil, and their relationship and its effect on people around them is subtle, complex, and insightful. It was the first novel to show McCammon unmistakably drawing upon his own sources of inspiration rather than the work of others. It was followed promptly by *Usher's Passing* (1984), an even more impressive novel. The novel's premise is that Edgar Allan POE based the Ushers on a real family living in a remote part of the South. One of the younger Ushers has returned home intent upon severing the family's relationship with an arms manufacturer and reclaiming their honor, but the situation is not as simple as he initially believes. He finds himself caught up in the same miasma of uncertainty and doom that has plagued previous generations. The book is a prime example of the Southern Gothic horror novel and one of McCammon's best as well.

Swan Song (1987) is an obvious homage to Stephen KING's *The Stand* (1978). In the aftermath of a devastating nuclear war, the survivors discover that they have more to contend with than even science fiction writers had imagined. A supernatural creature has revealed his existence, taking advantage of the confusion in an effort to seize control of all humanity, but fortunately opposed by a small group of people who put the future of the race ahead of their own personal concerns. McCammon also borrowed a science fiction device for *Stinger* (1988), in which a single alien with unimaginable technological superiority isolates a small Texas town in order to prey on its residents. Although the novel also features some well-drawn characters, the unambiguous evil represented by the alien is less interesting than the complex situations prevalent in the previous few novels.

The Wolf's Hour (1989) returns to the supernatural but is not really a horror novel. The protagonist is a werewolf, but a benevolent one who is an agent of the British secret service working inside Nazi Germany. His ability to change his form gives him some unique advantages as a spy, but it also has its drawbacks. This is McCammon's most adventurous novel and one of his very best, but it also marked the beginning of his move away from horror. In fact, his next novel, *Mine* (1990) is a straightforward thriller.

McCammon's last two imaginative novels were both fantasies rather than horror. *Boys' Life* (1991) is a coming of age story set in a small southern town in which the corner bully shares the plot with ghosts, dinosaurs, magic, and other terrors, real and imagined. It is McCammon's most impressive novel. *Gone South* (1992) is another mainstream thriller, included here because the protagonist retains his still-living and conscious twin brother within his own body, which also provides him with a hidden third hand. McCammon wrote only a handful of short stories during this period, but they are all of exceptional quality, particularly "Yellowjacket Summer" (1986), "Night Calls the Green Falcon" (1988), and "Black Boots" (1989). Many of these were collected as *Blue World* (1989).

McCammon began a 10-year vacation from writing in 1992, which was recently broken by a two-volume historical thriller with no fantastic content. The shape of his career from this point forward remains as deep a mystery as those found in his novels. He won the Bram Stoker Award for the novels *Swan Song* and *Boys' Life* and for the short stories "The Deep End" (1987) and "Eat Me" (1989). *Boys' Life* also won the World Fantasy Award.

McDowell, Michael (1950–1999)

Michael McDowell was one of several promising horror writers who emerged during the late 1970s, although he soon abandoned the field for other writing opportunities. His first novel was *The Amulet* (1979), in which a small town is tragically altered by a piece of jewelry that carries a curse. Every time it changes hands, the new owner experiences a tragedy. Although the least interesting of McDowell's novels, it showed a surprising talent for characterization by a first novelist. *Cold Moon over Babylon* (1980) is a much more effective story of ghostly revenge. The ghost of a murdered woman rises to seek vengeance on her killer, who is meanwhile engaged in systematically eliminating the remaining members of her family. *The Elementals* (1981) appears initially to involve a haunted house, but McDowell has a different menace in mind. The forces at play are not the spirits of the departed but actually manifestations of primordial supernatural forces, far more deadly and far more powerful.

Katie (1982) is more of a psychological study than a horror novel. The protagonist is a young woman who is clearly insane and a danger to people around her, and most of the story deals with that issue, although she also experiences moments of clairvoyance. McDowell explored the use of an insane protagonist again in one of his nonhorror novels, *Toplin* (1985). His last major work was the six-part novel known as the Blackwater Saga, consisting of *The Flood*, *The Levee*, *The House*, *The War*, *The Fortune*, and *Rain*, all published in 1983. The individual titles do not stand alone, so this was actually a serial foreshadowing *The Green Mile* (1996) by Stephen KING. The story deals with the

Caskey family, decaying southern aristocrats who employ a supernatural force linked to a nearby river to ward off threats to their power and position, although the bill for these services comes due in the concluding volume.

Although Michael McDowell's horror writing career was quite short, lasting only about four years, he produced several memorable novels and pioneered the multipart novel in contemporary horror fiction. He went on to write murder mysteries, historical adventures, and a considerable number of screen and televisions scripts, including *Beetlejuice* (1988) and the adaptation of Stephen KING's *Thinner* in 1996. If the horror field had not experienced a slump during the 1980s, he might have gone on to become one of its major writers, since he clearly had the talent to do so.

McKiernan, Dennis L. (1932–   )

Dennis L. McKiernan's first published fantasy was a trilogy, actually a single story in three volumes, that was clearly deeply influenced by the work of J. R. R. TOLKIEN. *The Darkest Day, Shadows of Doom,* and *The Dark Tide,* all published in 1984, introduce the mythical world of Mithgar, which has been the setting for virtually all of McKiernan's subsequent fiction. The king of Mithgar calls for a united front when an ancient evil stirs after a long period of dormancy, an enemy eventually defeated, but only after several reversals of fortune. McKiernan followed with a two-part novel, *The Brega Path* and *Trek to Kraggen-Cor,* in 1986. The defeated forces of evil are regrouping in a remote area, so an expedition must be launched to root them out. The follow-up is marginally better than the original, and the five titles together make up a work of considerable merit. War in Mithgar is not so much high adventure as it is hardship, pain, and terror, a realistic evaluation usually absent in contemporary fantasy.

Dragondoom (1990) has a much more modest plot. Adventurers have killed a dragon and stolen its treasure, and another dragon and a sorcerer engage in an interesting quest to retrieve their loot. *The Eye of the Hunter* (1992) returns to Mithgar, where yet another supernatural evil is stirring. It is excitingly told but with little to distinguish it from

the earlier and better five-part series. *Voyage of the Fox Rider* (1993) is also a quest story set in the world of Mithgar, but a much better one. A woman experiences visions of her lost lover and sets out on an entertaining journey of discovery. Similarly, *The Dragonstone* (1997) is another quest story, this time motivated by prescient visions of a supernatural threat. McKiernan's next novel of Mithgar was split into two volumes as *Into the Forge* (1997) and *Into the Fire* (1998), another homage to Tolkien as two companions set out on a quest into dangerous territory menaced by the forces of gathering evil. *Silver Wolf, Black Falcon* (2000) is a journey back to a time before the events in the other Mithgar novels, and once again it is cast in the form of a perilous quest.

McKiernan has also written numerous short stories set in Mithgar, which have been collected as *Tales of Mithgar* (1994) and *Red Slippers* (2004). *Caverns of Socrates* (1995) is arguably science fiction rather than fantasy, since the magic all takes place in the context of a virtual reality world, but the frame is largely irrelevant to the story. *Once upon a Winter's Night* (2001) is his best novel, a variation on the story of the Beauty and the Beast. A woman wed to a prince of the fairies disobeys his command that she never look at the face beneath his mask, and by doing so she unleashes a terrible curse. *Once upon a Summer Night* (2005) is a similar enhanced retelling of a classic fairy tale, in this case the story of Sleeping Beauty. McKiernan has seemed content for the most part to produce Tolkienesque pastiches, better than most similar novels but nothing out of the ordinary. His rare excursions into fresh territory are inevitably better and suggest a considerable unrealized potential that his most recent work is finally beginning to reveal.

McKillip, Patricia A. (1948–   )

Patricia McKillip's first few fantasy novels were for the younger reader and include the gentle ghost story *The House on Parchmont Street* (1973) and the humorous fantasy *The Throme of the Erril of Sherill* (1973). She first attracted the attention of adult readers with *The Forgotten Beasts of Eld* (1974), also marketed for children, although it won the World Fantasy Award. The story involves a woman who has lived her entire life among magical animals and the consequences when a new person enters her life.

The Riddle Master trilogy followed, consisting of *The Riddle-Master of Hed* (1976), *Heir of Sea and Fire* (1976), and *Harpist in the Wind* (1979). The premise is that following the disappearance of all the wizards in the world, what magic remains is trapped in riddles. The young protagonist solves a riddle and finds himself caught up in momentous changes. The middle volume is a quest story that ends in disillusionment, and the conclusion presents the ultimate battle for the future of the protagonists and their world. McKillip had by now attracted a considerable audience for her adult fantasy, but except for three interesting but low-key children's fantasies, she devoted most of her effort for the next few years to science fiction, producing three unmemorable novels. The best of the fantasies from this period is *Stepping from the Shadows* (1982), in which a woman discards her elaborate fantasy world as she matures, only to discover that elements of that imaginative creation are intruding into her new reality.

She returned to adult fantasy with *The Sorceress and the Cygnet* (1991) and its sequel, *The Cygnet and the Firebird* (1993). Several disparate characters are trapped in a series of interconnected magical realms and must solve various puzzles in order to find their way home. What appears initially to be a clever but simple fantasy eventually evolves into a much more ambitious examination of the way we perceive reality and share it with others. *Something Rich and Strange* (1994) is a variation on the standard mermaid romance, with two lovers separated by the spirits of the ocean. McKillip had by now mastered a lyrical style that marked her prose as distinctive and unusually rewarding.

McKillip's recent work continues to mix new and traditional plot elements and is invariably noteworthy for both the quality of the prose and the sophistication of the plotting and characterization. *The Book of Atrix Wolfe* (1995) is a story of redemption. A man who brought catastrophe on his people languishes in exile, living among the wolves and waiting for a chance to correct his error. A family curse takes a very unusual form in *Winter Rose* (1996), and the only survivor of a mass slaughter seeks to discover the truth about his past in *Song for the Basilisk* (1998).

The Tower at Stony Wood (2000) poses an interesting problem for its hero, a knight who discovers that the new queen is not a human being but an illusion spun by the land's enemies. *Ombria in Shadow* (2002), which won the World Fantasy Award, similarly involves court intrigues, in this case a struggle between the apparent heir to the throne and his stepmother, a conflict into which a sorceress and various ghosts intrude. In a moment of carelessness, a knight kills a chicken in *In the Forests of Serre* (2003), which annoys a witch. To avoid the consequence of her unpleasant plans for revenge, he escapes into another reality. In *Alphabet of Thorn* (2004), arguably her best novel, a scholar's life is changed when she happens upon an enchanted book.

McKillip often avoids the usual melodrama of modern fantasy altogether, and even when she does invoke evil sorcery, physical combat, and other violence, it is generally held at arm's length. She has few rivals for the depth of her insight into the way her characters act and feel and even fewer for the quality of her prose. Notable short stories include "The Harrowing of the Dragon of Hoarsbalath" (1982), "The Troll and the Two Roses" (1985), and "The Witches of Junket" (1996). She is long overdue to have her better stories collected in book form.

McKinley, Robin (1952–)

Robin McKinley made a very auspicious debut with *Beauty* (1978), a retelling of the story of the Beauty and the Beast that deals with the theme on a very mature level. The author's fondness for and familiarity with classic fairy tales is evident throughout her early work in particular, and the stories collected as *The Door in the Hedge* (1981), ostensibly for young readers, are all variations on classic fairy tale themes. Despite its original marketing, it attracted a considerable number of adult readers, which may have influenced McKinley's subsequent career, as it has been geared almost entirely for the adult market.

Her next two novels, *The Blue Sword* (1982) and *The Hero and the Crown* (1984), are set in the same fantasy world. In the former a young woman abandons the kind of behavior usually expected from her sex to take up a magical sword and fight against her people's enemies. The second title is actually a prequel, establishing the background for the action of the earlier book and describing a conflict that takes place on a political as well as a magical level. Some of the stories in *A Knot in the Grain and Other Stories* (1994) take place in the same setting. Her next novel, *The Outlaws of Sherwood* (1988), is a reinterpretation of the legend of Robin Hood and is closer to her early work than the previous two.

Deerskin (1993) appeared after a gap of several years and is darker in tone than anything she had written before. The young protagonist flees the wrath of her father, the king, by passing into a magical alternate world. Mixed with the usual devices of fantasy is an insightful look into the less pleasant recesses of the human mind, where sexuality, greed, and the desire to impose one's will on another are all revealed in their least appealing form. *Rose Daughter* (1997) is another transformed fairy tale and is, in fact, a continuation of the story begun in *Beauty*, exploring the ramifications of the new relationship between the lovers. *The Stone Fey* (1998) and *Spindle's End* (2000) are for young adults and are both based on classic fairy tales, Little Bo Peep and Sleeping Beauty, respectively. Her most recent novel, *Sunshine* (2003), is a considerable departure. The female protagonist is spared by a vampire and then feels compelled to help him survive. Although the subject is generally associated with the horror genre, McKinley's treatment is more like a contemporary fantasy.

McKinley's short fiction has appeared primarily in collections of previously unpublished work. Her most recent, *Water* (2002), is an unusual collaboration with her husband, the writer Peter Dickinson, in that half of the stories are written by one and half by the other, with no true collaborations. Although most of her fiction is based on earlier stories, usually classic fairy tales, she almost always brings a fresh viewpoint and turns the characters into real people about whom the reader cares.

McNally, Clare (unknown)

Traditionally ghosts and haunted houses are not particularly popular themes in American horror fiction, although they do enjoy considerably more respect in Europe. Occasionally there will be a flurry of interest because of a particularly strong novel, such as THE HAUNTING OF HILL HOUSE (1959) by Shirley JACKSON and GHOST STORY (1979) by Peter STRAUB, but for the most part American readers prefer more tangible horrors. Clare McNally, who also writes conventional thrillers, probably drew inspiration for her first horror novel, *Ghost House* (1979), from the Amityville books, supposedly nonfiction when first published, which describe a serious of bizarre manifestations in an otherwise ordinary suburb. Although offering no real surprises, McNally's debut novel is a competently done and occasionally scary story, popular enough to lead to a similar though less interesting sequel, *Ghost House Revenge* (1981).

The large audience for the nonsupernatural thrillers by V. C. Andrews, in each of which the characters in jeopardy are usually children, and the similar though supernatural novels of John SAUL may have caused McNally to sharpen her focus, because ghostly children and children in danger figure prominently in her subsequent work. A vengeful child ghost seeks vengeance from beyond the grave in *Ghost Light* (1982). In *What About the Baby?* (1983) a 19th-century woman uses magical powers to contact the present and influence the thoughts of a pregnant teenager. There is another angry ghost child in *Somebody Come and Play* (1987), this one more overt in its actions, luring other children to remote areas where they can be killed. On this occasion McNally makes the ghostly presence more sympathetic and complex despite its horrible acts, and it is the first of her novels to suggest that she had the capacity to write more than routine thrillers.

Addison House (1988) returns to the haunted house format, but this time with more subtlety. The living and unliving are so intermixed that they are sometimes indistinguishable, and the result is an almost surreal series of encounters and interactions. Although children are still the primary focus, the adult characters are portrayed in much more detail. *Hear the Children Calling . . .* (1990) and *Cries of the Children* (1992) both deal with psychic powers, but both are more adventurous than chilling, consisting of chases and revealed secrets.

They are more polished than McNally's earlier novels but less interesting.

McNally returned to ghosts with *Stage Fright* (1995), her strongest story. The protagonist, a man who has been stalked by an obsessed man for years, discovers that the death of his tormentor brings no relief, because now he is pursued by the man's still determined spirit. When she joins an acting troupe, the ghostly admirer begins killing off her companions. *Good Night, Sweet Angel* (1996) has a very similar plot and is nearly as good. This time a woman and her daughter are menaced by the angry, twisted spirit of her dead husband. Unfortunately, just as McNally was becoming a writer worth following, she abandoned horror fiction and has written nothing new within the genre for almost a decade.

McNaughton, Brian (1935–2004)

Brian McNaughton's writing career can be split into two distinct periods. During the late 1970s and early 1980s he wrote several moderately interesting mainstream horror novels, then paused for almost a decade before turning to shorter works, which were much more accomplished. A collection of his later work, *The Throne of Bones* (1997), a blend of horror and fantasy occasionally reminiscent of Clark Ashton SMITH, won the World Fantasy Award.

The first of his novels was *Satan's Love Child* (1977, revised in 2000 as *Gemini Rising*), a standard story of the evil influence of a satanic cult active in a small town. Although competently written, the story fails to generate much suspense. *Satan's Mistress* (1978, revised in 2000 as *Downward to Darkness*) is considerably better. The protagonist finds a book of arcane lore that he uses in an attempt to raise the spirit of one of his ancestors. Unfortunately, he is inept and instead conjures a supernatural creature that appears in the guise of a beautiful woman. Although not a conventional entry in the Cthulhu Mythos of H. P. LOVECRAFT and others, the story clearly shows that McNaughton was influenced by that circle of writers.

There are also Lovecraftian references in *Satan's Seductress* (1978, revised in 2000 as *Worse Things Waiting*), but the story is actually a deal-with-the-devil plot with some mildly surprising twists. McNaughton's last novel was *Satan's Surrogate* (1982), similar in tone to the previous ones. A series of songs generate an occult force, which is accompanied by a plague of vampirism and cannibalism. Although all four novels are quite readable, they are not nearly as impressive as his later work.

McNaughton reinvented himself during the 1980s and began turning out stories of dark sorcery in imaginary lands or at the end of time, peopled with bizarre characters and dark gods. Most of the better ones, such as "Vendriel and Vendreela" (1988), are fantasy rather than horror, although they often involve ghastly events. He also proved to be remarkably adept at the very short horror story, producing more than a dozen of them in the course of a single year. "The Retrograde Necromancer" (1993) and "Many Happy Returns" (1998) are particularly effective, as are several Lovecraftian pastiches. Much of his short fiction has been collected in *Nasty Stories* (2000) and *Even More Nasty Stories* (2002). McNaughton is also the author of two mainstream thrillers.

Merritt, A. (1884–1943)

Abraham Merritt was an American journalist and writer who produced comparatively little fiction, but who was one of the most popular of the pulp writers during his lifetime and who is now regarded as one of the pioneers of fantasy fiction. Many of his novels are actually rewritten versions of shorter works, not always with Merritt's permission, so the text may vary considerable from one edition to the next.

Merritt's first short fantasy appeared in 1917, but his first significant story was "The Moon Pool" (1918), eventually followed by a sequel, "The Conquest of the Moon Pool" (1919). Both were later combined and rewritten as his first novel, *The Moon Pool* (1919). Four adventurers stumble into an underground civilization where humans live in consort with the survivors of an antediluvian race of intelligent reptiles. Although Merritt makes an effort to rationalize events, which technically makes this science fiction, the atmosphere is overwhelmingly that of a fantasy novel. The sequel,

The Metal Monster (1920, but not in book form until 1946), is more overtly science fiction, involving an alien life form that emerges from a sheltered world in Tibet to menace the world.

Merritt used the lost world device again in *The Face in the Abyss* (1931), which is also based on earlier, shorter pieces. Once again he mixes super-science with ambiguous magic as outsiders encounter a lost civilization that has used a form of genetic engineering to create dinosaurs and other monstrosities. Good and evil are clearly defined, and the battle between them has mixed results. His remaining lost race novel, *Dwellers in the Mirage* (1932, but revised in 1941) is possibly his best, but the editors replaced his original ending when it first appeared. Subsequent reprintings have not always used the restored version.

Merritt's remaining novels vary considerably in subject matter. *The Ship of Ishtar* (1926) follows the adventures of a man from our world who acquires the model of an ancient ship and is thereby magically transported into another world where it is full-sized. There he becomes embroiled in the battle between the forces of good and evil. *Seven Footprints to Satan* (1928) is a marginal story about a super-criminal, but *Burn, Witch, Burn!* (1933) and its sequel, *Creep, Shadow, Creep!* (1934) are overtly supernatural. The former was filmed as *The Devil Doll* (1936).

Some incomplete manuscripts were completed by Hannes Bok, but they are unmemorable. Merritt's short stories, including the very good "Three Lines of Old French" (1919) and "THE WOMEN OF THE WOOD" (1924), both of which were collected in *The Fox Woman* (1949). Although the premises of most of his novels have been overtaken by events, they are still very readable, and his influence on the writers of his time and those that followed has been pervasive.

"The Mezzotint" M. R. James (1904)

Some of the most effective horror stories result from mixing bizarre incidents with an otherwise familiar, even humdrum, setting. Williams, the protagonist of this classic tale of the supernatural, has the rather prosaic job of acquiring topographical sketches for a museum. In that capacity he is at-

tracted one day by the sale of a mezzotint of an unknown manor house drawn by an equally unknown artist. Although he considers it an indifferent engraving, he decides to try to identify the subject of the drawing, during the course of which investigation the picture begins to change.

When he first sees the hint of a human figure, he assumes that he just missed it during his earlier examination. That evening he glances at the drawing again as he is preparing for bed and is startled to notice the finely drawn figure of a man crawling on all fours toward the manor house, an image that was certainly not there earlier in the day. In the morning Williams discovers that the figure is gone, but one of the windows is now open. He concludes that the crawling man must have reached the house during the night. Upon subsequent viewings he and his associates witness the abduction of an infant by a grotesque but largely unseen intruder, after which all human figures disappear from the drawing entirely.

They eventually identify the manor house and discover that a child was, in fact, abducted a century earlier, after which the owner completed the mezzotint and promptly died. Further research indicates an old feud, a hanging, and apparently a vengeful return from the grave. James leaves the reader with no explanation of the reason the drawing should reflect past events. The eerie atmosphere is well done, and the image of a static image changing over time has been used by many later horror writers. James himself may have been inspired by Oscar Wilde's THE PICTURE OF DORIAN GRAY (1891).

Michaels, Barbara (1927–   )

Barbara Michaels is one of the pseudonyms used by Barbara Mertz, who has written a large number of mystery and suspense novels, although most of her fantastic fiction has appeared under this single pseudonym. Most of these employed the supernatural to create a sense of menace and mystery and were more atmospheric than substantive, although in some cases the supernatural elements are key to the plot. That is the case in her first fantastic novel, *Ammie, Come Home* (1968), in which a woman is possessed by a restless spirit who wishes to right an old wrong. There are also strong romantic elements, which recur in most of her other titles.

The protagonist of *The Dark on the Other Side* (1970) has an unreliable psychic power that tells her that one of the two men in her life is demonically possessed, but unfortunately neglects to identify which one. A coven of witches decides to use magic to discourage a newcomer in the community in *Prince of Darkness* (1970), but they are defeated by the power of romantic love. *The Crying Child* (1971) has a variety of standard supernatural events—strange sounds in the night, a ghostly child, and other manifestations—but the individual scenes are not drawn together well.

Witch (1973) is quieter but much more effective. A woman moves into a house supposedly haunted by the ghost of a witch, and her scoffing eventually turns to belief. With *House of Many Shadows* (1974) Michaels seems to have settled into a formula. There is another haunted house, whose apparitions urge a new resident to resolve an issue from the past. There is reincarnation in *The Sea-King's Daughter* (1975), but it is peripheral to the plot, which involves an entirely natural danger.

Wait for What Will Come (1978) is much better, another atmospheric story set in a remote house whose new resident hears of a family curse that involves a legendary sea creature. *The Walker in Shadows* (1979) is also a traditional ghost story, but quite well handled, and again the main danger comes from the living rather than the dead. There are ghostly intrusions and witchcraft in *The Wizard's Daughter* (1980) and *Someone in the House* (1981), the latter an intermittently interesting story set in a haunted house, but Michaels seemed to be losing interest in her supernatural themes, which became less relevant with each new novel. *Here I Stay* (1983) is another ghost story, *Be Buried in the Rain* (1985) involves some minor psychic powers, and the much later *Other Worlds* (1999) invokes the spirits of the dead, but Michaels has clearly retreated from the supernatural, leaving behind a dozen very well-written but unremarkable books, only a few which rose above the ordinary.

Miéville, China (1972–)

Modern fantasy fiction presents an interesting problem for new writers who wish to do something innovative. Because its readership is perceived as being very conservative about variations from the standard themes of quests, quasi-medieval settings, court intrigues, and heroic warriors, most new fantasy fiction is remarkably similar to what has already been published. China Miéville managed to blend the traditional with the new in his innovative first novel, *King Rat* (1999), and he has continued to do so ever since. *King Rat* is an extrapolation of the story of the Pied Piper of Hamelin transposed to modern London. The protagonist is a young man unjustly accused of murdering his own father who is rescued from jail by a man with superhuman strength. He discovers the existence of warring inhuman powers hidden from the human race and learns of his own destiny among them.

It was an auspicious debut, and his second novel, *Perdido Street Station* (2001), is even better. The setting is the city-state of New Crobuzon in a world where humans and inhumans live side by side. Miéville avoids the standard creatures of fantasy; there are no elves, fairies, goblins, or dragons. There are instead humanoid insects, a race of flying birdmen, and a legal system that uses magical transformations of an individual's body as a form of punishment. The plot is complex and involves a crime lord who wishes to be immortalized as the subject of a piece of art, a stolen government experiment in magic that results in a dangerous beast, and other complexities, although it is often the city itself that holds the reader's interest. Miéville created an entirely new kind of fantasy world, to which he would return in his next two novels.

Most of the story in *The Scar* (2002) takes place on the oceans surrounding New Crobuzon. Bellis Coldwine sails off into semivoluntary exile after committing dubious acts in the city and has various adventures at sea before becoming a captive of a virtual nation of pirates who have created a floating continent of ships lashed together into a single enormous mass. There is an almost bewildering number of characters, creatures, and unusual settings, but Miéville weaves it all into a single, coherent, and very impressive story.

His most recent novel, *Iron Council* (2004), follows the adventures of a group of rebels unhappy with the government of New Crobuzon. The main plot involves the hijacking of a railroad train. *The Tain* (2003) is a short novel about the creatures who live on the other side of the mirror and what happens when they get tired of mimicking humans. The story moves closer to horror than fantasy, and although very effective, it is not of the same caliber as his longer works. All of Miéville's novels have been strong contenders for the field's various awards. He is an exciting and skilled writer who has quickly acquired a following and is already widely acknowledged as one of the major talents in contemporary fantasy.

The Mist Stephen King (1980)

Horror writers know that it is usually much more effective to suggest the nature of a menace than to describe it graphically and in detail. The things that hide in the shadows, waiting for their chance, are much more terrifying and literarily successful than giant reptiles destroying cities or even predictable vampires rising from their coffins to prey on the living. This short novel by Stephen KING is one of the best illustrations of this principle, with its various creatures lurking in a mysterious mist that overwhelms a small town.

The story opens with a particularly devastating storm that, we later learn, somehow upsets things at a secret government research facility. Like most residents, Dave is clearing away the aftermath, slightly puzzled by the lack of official response to the emergency. The local radio stations are not transmitting. The power is out generally, but he feels no particular concern when he, his son, and a neighbor set out for town, leaving his wife to begin the cleanup. They find long lines everywhere as people try to stock up on supplies, eventually accumulate most of what they need in a local grocery store, and are waiting to check out when things begin to take a darker turn.

Dave had previously noticed a bank of fog or mist on a nearby lake that seemed denser and more distinct than usual, but it did not appear to be a matter of any great concern. However, when the mist moves into the town, everyone caught up in it vanishes, often screaming wildly as they disappear. Although most of the people in the store rush out to escape, a handful remain inside waiting to see what develops. Before long they are under siege, unable to see anything through the windows but quite able to hear the sound of moving things all around them.

Predictably and quickly, the trapped people begin to experience a variety of intense emotions—fear, panic, concern for loved ones, religious piety, confusion, and anger. An effort to repair the store's generator backfires when one of their number is seized by tentacles and carried off into the mist. Unable to confront their attackers directly, the survivors begin to turn on one another, at first only with words and later physically. King uses this small group of people as a way to reflect upon how people in greater numbers react to unknown situations, compressing the stages of terror and distress so that the monsters that lie within us are exposed as just as dangerous as those physical beings lurking just out of sight.

Modesitt, L. E., Jr. (1943–   )

Leland Exton Modesitt, Jr. began writing science fiction in the early 1970s but did not publish fantasy until *The Magic of Recluce* (1991). This was the first in a lengthy series of novels set in a universe where magic works and where Order and Chaos are opposed forces, but one that is logically constructed with rules of magic that provide a sense of orderliness. Although there are sometimes common characters, most of the novels can be read in any order, as they jump around in time and place. The opening volume rather typically describes the emergence of an unlikely hero who discovers he has the power to defeat the currently dominant wizard. Modesitt immediately followed up with *The Towers of Sunset* (1992), actually a prequel, in which the protagonist escapes the threat of an arranged marriage and establishes a new political entity.

Science and magic are intertwined in *The Magic Engineer* (1994). The protagonist is exiled from the lands where Order dominates because of his development of questionable technology, but he finds a new home in the lands of Chaos, where his innovations are welcome. Unlike many fantasy writers, Modesitt does not automatically assume that Order is good and Chaos is evil, suggesting that conflict between opposing viewpoints is essential for progress. Generally, however, the reader is nudged into siding with Order. For example, efforts by Chaos wizards to master the world are rightly defeated in *The Order War* (1995), a battle that continues in *The Death of Chaos* (1995). *Fall of Angels* (1996) changes the scene to a new nation founded by independent minded females on the side of Order, but their effort to create a new society is menaced from the outset. The engineer who helped them leaves to follow his own destiny in *The Chaos Balance* (1997) and has a series of episodic adventures as he seeks a new home.

The White Order (1998) is another coming of age story, but this time the young wizard is on the side of Chaos rather than Order, although even he learns at last that balance is important and that it is preferable that neither side ever win a convincing and final victory. Open warfare erupts in *Colors of Chaos* (1998), with the same young wizard playing a pivotal role in its resolution. The protagonist of *Magi'i of Cyador* (2000) is an impetuous young man who learns maturity during a war while his lover struggles to remain solvent back home. This was the first in a subset of stories set in the distant past before Recluce was founded. *Scion of Cyador* (2000) continues their story, as the young man discovers that by distinguishing himself in action against the enemy, he has given rise to jealousy and secret enemies among his own people. Although Modesitt has added two other fantasy series in recent years, he continues to return periodically to Recluce, such as in *Wellsprings of Chaos* (2004), the story of a personal rivalry between two men that escalates into violence and vengeance, and the forthcoming *Ordermaster* (2005).

Modesitt's second major fantasy effort was the Spellsinger series, which has apparently ended with the fifth volume. The series consists of *The Soprano Sorceress* (1997), *The Spellsong War* (1998), *Darksong Rising* (1999), *The Shadow Sorceress* (2001), and *Shadowsinger* (2002). A woman from our reality is magically transported to Erde, a world where magic exists and is inextricably tied up with music,

which provides the underlying structure for a new magic system. She discovers that her musical talents make her a powerful sorceress here, and during the course of the series she rises to power, becomes head of a nation, and then uses her talents to defend her people from foreign invasion and other threats. This is a more tightly connected series than the Recluce novels and should be read in the order in which they were published.

Modesitt's most recent series, still ongoing, is the Corean Chronicles. It opened with *Legacies* (2002), yet another coming of age story about a boy discovering his magical abilities, although this is much more polished and tightly written than the author's previous similar novels. Escaped from slavery, he becomes a prominent defender of his nation in *Darknesses* (2003), helping to ward off a powerful invasion force. Although he intends to retire, he is forced to go to battle again in *Scepters* (2004) when a fanatic religious cult threatens to overwhelm his people.

Modesitt rarely strays from the familiar in his plotting, and his characters are competently drawn but generally unmemorable. His strength lies in the way in which he creates his imaginary worlds and particularly the structured forms of magic he uses, adding color and a feeling that under these conditions magic might actually work. He superimposes exciting, adventurous plots over this setting, providing reliably entertaining if rather repetitive stories.

Monaco, Richard (1940–)

Richard Monaco, who also writes for the stage and the screen, opened his career in fantasy with a series of Arthurian adventures, starting with *Parsifal, or, A Knight's Tale* (1977), a history of Sir Percival and his adventures after the dissolution of the Round Table and the death of King Arthur. He is a relatively innocent, idealistic, and good natured man whose subsequent adventures fighting evil sorcery and more mundane enemies gradually change him, not entirely for the better. His adventures are continued in *The Grail War* (1979). The two novels are such a thoughtful and skillful rethinking of that portion of the Camelot story that they were nominated for the Pulitzer Prize. Monaco returned to the same setting less successfully with two more novels. *The Final Quest* (1981) describes the infighting and factionalism that ended the unity that had existed under Arthur, and *Blood and Dreams* (1985) returns to the quest for the Holy Grail, this time undertaken by men with less than noble motives.

Monaco used a slightly different setting for *Runes* (1984) and its sequel, *Broken Stones* (1985). The Romans have conquered much of what is now Great Britain, imposing their rule despite the opposition of the druids, who in the first novel are aligned with the forces of evil. A slave girl and a Roman nobleman must make common cause to defeat them. They are forced to acquire more allies in the sequel in an effort to repel the attacks of shadowy creatures from another plane of existence. Although well written, they are not as interesting as his previous work. *Journey to the Flame* (1985) is a sequel to SHE (1886) by H. Rider HAGGARD. An explorer investigates legends of an immortal woman living in a remote, cloistered land and sets out to find her, stumbling into a lost world where magic works.

Monaco's last novel was *Unto the Beast* (1987), which mixes fantasy and horror themes. An inhuman creature who functions essentially as a stand-in for Satan exists independently of time and space, spreading his evil influence through the world by means of selected humans, including Adolf Hitler. Although the novel is a reasonably entertaining occult adventure, the plot is occasionally unfocused. Monaco has written no fantastic fiction since then. A rare short story, "Blood and Dreams" (1982), is also of interest.

"The Monkey's Paw" W. W. Jacobs (1902)

Although the British writer William Wymark Jacobs was a popular and influential writer, it was his crime stories and tales of the seamier side of London that were most often imitated. He wrote a substantial number of weird and supernatural stories as well. Less than half a dozen are still read today, and only this one is widely known. The popularity of this single tale alone, however, makes him a noteworthy figure in horror fiction. It has been adapted in one form or another for a variety of television versions and is one of the most frequently anthologized tales in the English language. The twofold message is clear. Be very careful what you wish for, and refrain from interfering with the natural order of things.

Mr. and Mrs. White and their grown son entertain a visitor, recently returned from service in India, who shows them a mummified monkey's paw that is supposed to have magical properties. He tells them it has the power to grant three wishes but that its purpose is to demonstrate to people that their lives are ruled by fate and that fate cannot be thwarted. After acquiring the paw, Mr. White is reluctant to make a wish, partly because his visitor warned against it and partly because he feels content with what he has. Finally, he decides to wish for a small sum of money, just enough to retire the mortgage on their home. Nothing happens immediately, and they decide it was all just a tall story. The following day their son is killed in an industrial accident, and they receive compensation, exactly the amount he wished for.

More than a week passes before Mrs. White recovers from her grief and has an inspiration. She prevails upon her husband to wish their son alive again, which he does, but he instantly regrets the impulse, since his son has lain in his grave all that time and was, in fact, horribly mutilated by the accident. When they hear an insistent knocking on the door during the night, she hastens to let in their son, but, aghast, Mr. White seizes the paw for the final time and wishes his son back to his grave. A tightly written, efficiently constructed story that delivers a considerable shock even though we never see what lies beyond their door, "The Monkey's Paw" is one of the most familiar horror stories of all time and is a classic not just in the genre, but in literature as a whole.

"The Monster of the Prophecy" Clark Ashton Smith (1932)

Most of Clark Ashton SMITH's fantastic fiction is set in imaginary lands such as Poseidonis, Atlantis, Hyperborea, or Zothique, but occasionally he used a contemporary setting. This, one of his longer and most famous stories, opens with the introduction of its protagonist, Theophilus Alvor, literally a starving poet who is contemplating leaping to his death from the Brooklyn Bridge when he is accosted by a mysterious stranger. His benefactor, Vizaphmal, soon reveals himself to be a wizard from the distant world of Antares, an alien life form only masquerading magically as a human being. Vizaphmal is about to return to his home world and wonders if Alvor would consider joining him, since he has so little use for his own race.

They travel to Satabbor in the Antares system by means of a device that functions as a spaceship, although its explanation is more metaphysical than scientific. Alvor's subsequent experiences on that planet are an odd mix of science and magic. Vizaphmal's people have a rigid caste system and are in some ways quite advanced, but they are divided by a number of religious belief systems, each based on a series of prophecies. Most of those prophecies have, in fact, come to pass. One of the prophecies involves the arrival of a wizard and a monster, the latter minutely described and obviously a human being. Under the terms of the prophecy, Vizaphmal could well become the supreme ruler of his people thanks to Alvor's presence. Alvor is to be the monster of the prophecy.

Everything happens as expected. The king abdicates, and Vizaphmal assumes the throne. All does not go well from that point forward. Religious bickering increases, and another rebellion seems to be imminent. Eventually, Vizaphmal flees, and Alvor is abandoned, captured, and put on trial. He survives various tribulations before finding refuge and the fulfillment of his personal destiny. The story is an unusual blend of images and devices from fantasy with the trappings of science fiction, a mixture that showed up later in the work of Ray BRADBURY, Leigh Brackett, and other writers. The reversal of having a human as a monster in an alien culture instead of vice versa would be repeated to humorous effect by William Tenn in his classic "The Flat-Eyed Monster" (1955).

Monteleone, Thomas F. (1946–   )

From 1973 to 1985 Thomas Monteleone wrote primarily science fiction, turning out entertaining, light adventure novels and short stories without producing anything that really distinguished him. His first horror novel was *Night Things* (1980),

which could also be called science fiction since the furry little creatures, harmless alone but deadly in large numbers, do not have a supernatural origin. *Night Train* (1984) began to move away from the rational to the fantastic. Two investigators decide to uncover the facts about an entire subway train that disappeared during the 1930s. They set off on a claustrophobic journey of discovery under New York City and stumble upon an ancient evil that is already contemplating another attack against the surface world. Monteleone was also turning to horror for his short fiction, such as in "Spare the Child" (1982), and would distance himself increasingly from science fiction.

Monteleone had three horror novels appear in 1987 and wrote only one more science fiction novel before abandoning that field. *Lyrica* is the story of a succubus, an evil female spirit that preys on the life force of men under fairly erotic circumstances. Despite some problems with the pacing, particularly toward the end, the novel works well because of the unusually strong character development. *The Magnificent Gallery* is reminiscent of SOMETHING WICKED THIS WAY COMES (1962) by Ray BRADBURY and THE CIRCUS OF DR. LAO (1935) by Charles Finney in that a traveling circus proves to be more than it appears. The exhibits initially are represented as carrying a warning to selected individuals about dangers that face them, but we eventually learn that rather than revealing the future, the circus attractions are choosing their victims and ensuring that the predictions come to pass. His third novel that year was *The Crooked House,* a collaboration with John Dechancie and an interesting variation on the traditional haunted house story. His next solo book, *Fantasma* (1989), employs an unusual backdrop for supernatural horror, the feud between two organized crime families. A member of one group enlists the aid of a witch who can summon demonic forces and is initially pleased with the results. Unfortunately, such assistance always comes with an unusually high price.

Monteleone's short fiction improved dramatically, particularly in "The Way of the Cross" (1990) and "Roadside Scalpel" (1993), but it was with his next novel, *Blood of the Lamb* (1993), which won the Bram Stoker Award, that he emerged as a major talent. A priest discovers that he has miraculously acquired the power to heal the sick with a touch and even to raise the dead. Although his parishioners believe this to be divine intervention, he has reservations about using this new talent, a hesitation shared by his superiors in the Roman Catholic Church. The significance of the miracles is underscored by the imminent coming of the millennium, now past, and the atmosphere of growing fear and uncertainty is marvelously well developed. Monteleone had clearly found a type of story he could write exceptionally well, and most of his subsequent work similarly mixed the supernatural with religious concerns.

The Resurrectionist (1995) makes use of a similar theme. This time a charismatic politician survives a plane crash and emerges with the power to restore the dead to life. The story develops with very understated melodrama, as the miraculous gift proves to be something of a curse. The politician's career is over because of the controversy surrounding him, and certain elements within the government plot to make use of his abilities to advance their own personal agendas. *Night of Broken Souls* (1997) is more consciously a thriller. Several people begin to experience vivid dreams of their former lives as prisoners in Nazi concentration camps, which turns out to be a foreshadowing of the secretive series of murders carried out by a former war criminal.

The Reckoning (1999) is a sequel to *Blood of the Lamb*. The new pope is actually the Antichrist and is using his authority to destroy or neutralize all the holy artifacts that might be used against him when he moves openly against the world. The scale this time is much wider, but Monteleone's writing skills had improved dramatically during the 1990s, and he delivers a taut, sometimes frightening story. His most recent novel is *Eyes of the Virgin* (2002), another thriller in which a woman falsely accused of murder is enlisted in an effort to retrieve an artifact that could allow direct communication with God.

Monteleone is also the editor of the highly regarded Borderlands anthology series and edited the later volumes jointly with his wife, Elizabeth Monteleone. He founded Borderlands Press, which specializes in horror fiction. Many of his short science fiction stories have been collected, but his short horror fiction, unaccountably, has yet to be gathered together in book form.

Moorcock, Michael (1939–   )

Michael Moorcock has long been one of the leading writers in modern science fiction and fantasy, having won major awards in both fields. He is also one of the hardest to categorize because of his concept of the Multiverse, a greater universe that includes our own and effectively infinite numbers of alternate realities, in some of which magic is real, blending science fiction and fantasy unpredictably. As part of that concept, he has developed the idea of the Eternal Champion, a hero who arises in different times and in different universes, always responding when the forces of evil or chaos threaten. Most of his heroes are manifestations of the same personality, sometimes with very similar names, whether they be Jherek Carnelian, Jerry Cornelius, or Elric of Melnibone. The first part of Moorcock's career in fantasy was primarily sword and sorcery tales, at which he proved his mastery quite early, and his various champions usually prevail through force of arms and the exercise of quick wits in a crisis. In recent years his fantasy has taken on a more literary flavor, and most of the trappings of sword and sorcery have been abandoned. Now his champions use reason, personal loyalty, and careful planning to outwit the villains.

Over the years Moorcock has revised novels, retitled novels, and shuffled the contents of short story collections so that it is very difficult in some of his subsidiary series to definitively list the titles in anything approximating the proper order. He began writing in the 1950s but only became significant and prolific during the 1960s, after which he produced a large amount of both science fiction and fantasy as well as thrillers and contemporary fiction. He also edited the very influential British science fiction magazine *New Worlds* and several anthologies and used at least three pseudonyms, almost always for science fiction. *Sojan* (1977) collects some of his earliest short fantasy work.

Moorcock's first major fantasy hero was Elric, still his most famous character. Elric appeared initially in a series of short adventures, an atypical hero in a barbaric world. He is an albino and not particularly powerful and possesses a magic sword that has a stronger will than his own, compelling him to occasional acts of violence. The early stories appeared in book form as *Stormbringer* (1965), which covered his entire lifetime, so that later volumes were expansions or new interludes. Since new stories have been added irregularly ever since, the sequence keeps changing, and the tone is not consistent from book to book. *Elric of Melnibone* (1972) is chronologically the earliest in the series, a blend of sorcery and court intrigue, and *The Fortress of the Pearl* (1989), which directly follows, is far more introspective and metaphysical. The story involves a quest to steal a jewel that has been hidden in the dreamworld. Similarly, *The Revenge of the Rose* (1991) is a psychological study of Elric and his relationship to his father, whose soul he must rescue after entering hell itself. *The Skrayling Tree* (2003) is the most complex novel in the series, featuring a confrontation between Elric and various other versions of himself from elsewhere in the Multiverse.

Dorian Hawkmoon first appeared in *The Jewel in the Skull* (1967). Like Elric, he is trapped into being a hero, this time by a gem embedded in his head. Even though he knows that he is fated to betray his comrades, he is unable to avert his fate. He battles an insane god in *The Sorcerer's Amulet* (1968, also published as *The Mad God's Amulet*), travels to another reality in *Sword of the Dawn* (1968), rallies his allies against a host of enemies in *The Secret of the Runestaff* (1969), assumes the throne in *Count Brass* (1973), discovers the mutability of time in *The Champion of Garathorm* (1973), and searches the Multiverse for his missing children in *The Quest for Tanelorn* (1975).

Corum, the last of his race, also resembles Elric, although he is more focused on his war against the forces of Chaos. The first three novels, *The Knight of Swords*, *The Queen of Swords*, and *The King of Swords*, all appeared in 1971. A second series consists of *The Bull and the Spear* (1973), *The Oak and the Ram* (1973), and *The Sword and the Stallion* (1974). Corum is an elf, not a human, and since humanity has allied itself with Chaos, he becomes its sworn enemy. The gods are fighting among themselves, and the younger deities such as Odin and Loki are rising to power as Corum com-

pletes a succession of heroic tasks. John Daker, also known as Erekose, is still another manifestation of the common personality, appearing in *The Eternal Champion* (1970), *The Silver Warriors* (1973, also published as *Phoenix in Obsidian*), and *The Dragon in the Sword* (1986). He is revived during a different era in each book and was the first of Moorcock's heroes to recognize his true nature as he battles the enemies of humanity, traverses an ice-covered world, and then confronts evil manifesting itself through Adolf Hitler.

The Von Bek novels hover on the borderline between science fiction and fantasy. *The War Hound and the World's Pain* (1981), *Blood* (1995) and *Fabulous Harbors* (1995), the first of which involves an encounter with Lucifer and his restoration to heaven, all fall into the latter category, while the others are science fiction. Some critics have set the line of demarcation elsewhere. The last title is not a true novel but rather a series of interlinked episodes about individuals who can move from one branch of the Multiverse to another. *Lunching with the Antichrist* (1995) is a collection of short stories related to the Von Bek series.

Several other of Moorcock's novels are sometimes referred to as fantasy. *Gloriana, or the Unfulfill'd Queen, being a Romance* (1978) is an alternate world science fiction novel but also the winner of the World Fantasy Award. *Mother London* (1988) and *The Brothel in Rosenstrasse* (1982), the latter of which is related to the Von Bek books, are either science fiction or mainstream depending upon one's definition. The futuristic satires in the Jerry Cornelius series are technically science fiction as well, although much of what takes place in them is surreal and verges on fantasy. Moorcock has developed into a sophisticated and complex writer who is difficult to describe or classify without considerable disclaimers or explanation.

Although Moorcock's influence on science fiction came chiefly from his editorial work at *New Worlds*, his influence on fantasy, particularly heroic fantasy in Great Britain, comes directly from his own fiction. His protagonists perform their heroics under compulsion and are generally unhappy with their lot, in direct opposition to traditional figures such as CONAN by Robert E. HOWARD or the heroic fantasy of Fritz LEIBER. He has written very little short fantasy that did not fall into one or another of his series since the 1960s, some of which is collected in *The Singing Citadel* (1970). Most of his early fantasy novels have been reissued in omnibus form, including *Hawkmoon* (1992), *Von Bek* (1995), *Corum* (1997), and *Elric* (2001). His early work often appears to be nothing more than light adventure fiction, but Moorcock was even then beginning to tackle philosophical issues such as the nature of good and evil and destiny and duty. His heroes are almost always flawed, and those flaws provide a much greater depth than can be found among similar work by his contemporaries.

Morressey, John (1930–   )

After trying his hand at mainstream fiction and books for young adults, John Morressey became a relatively prolific science fiction writer during the 1970s, turning out several creditable but unexceptional novels. He first turned to fantasy with *Ironbrand* (1980) and its sequels, *Graymantle* (1981) and *Kingsbane* (1982). The trilogy follows the adventures of three brothers who are cheated out of their place as ruling family by an evil wizard who usurps the throne. They set out on a typical quest using a set of magical swords to eventually reclaim their legacy. *Time of the Annihilator* (1985) is similarly predictable, involving an imminent invasion hastened by the death of the local sorcerer.

Morressey finally began to distinguish himself with *A Voice for Princess* (1986), the first of the Kedrigern series. Kedrigern is a wizard who is annoyed by the admission of alchemists into the wizards' guild. He is also bored, so he sets out to find himself a wife, during the course of which he has several humorous adventures. His new wife falls under a spell in *The Questing of Kedrigern* (1987), and he frees her in due course. The twosome then pool their talents to help a princess who has been transformed into a talking sword in *Kedrigern in Wanderland* (1988). These first three novels were surprisingly fresh, as Morressey was clearly more adept at light, humorous adventure than at serious sword and sorcery. *Kedrigern and the Charming Couple* (1990) reprised the previous novel. This time the enchanted princess suffers from lycan-thropy; she turns into a wolf when the moon is full. In *A Remembrance for Kedrigern* (1990) the wizard reluctantly agrees to take part in a plan to track down and destroy a swamp monster feared by the locals, but he makes a surprising discovery that sets him at odds with his fellows.

Morressey's most recent fantasy novel is *The Juggler* (1996), a well done and occasionally interesting but ultimately predictable deal-with-the-devil story. The Kedrigern novels have recently been reprinted in omnibus editions as *The Domesticated Wizard* (2002) and *Dudgeons and Dragons* (2002) and are still his most notable fiction. He continues to write short stories regularly, both fantasy and science fiction, and is long overdue for a collection. The decline in popularity of humorous fantasy after the early 1990s probably brought the Kedrigern series to an early end, unfortunately, because they had been improving steadily from one title to the next.

Morris, Janet (1946–   )

Janet Morris emerged as a prolific and versatile writer in the late 1970s with two brief series of science fiction novels that strongly resembled fantasy as well as short fiction in the Thieves' World shared universe series of original anthologies, starting with "Vashanna's Minion" (1980) and "Man and His God" (1981). She used a recurring character, Tempus, a roguish adventurer who generally finds himself fighting on the side of good, although it is not always easy to tell good from evil. Tempus was a popular enough figure that Morris used him as the protagonist of three novels, followed by a collection of the shorter adventures as *Tempus* (1987).

The original Tempus trilogy takes him out of his familiar setting in Sanctuary, a haven for those seeking to hide from the outside world. In *Beyond Sanctuary* he discovers that his particular talents are much in demand in the outside world. His ambitions take on a greater scope in *Beyond the Veil* (1985), this time causing him to join a group opposing an evil witch who has raised an army of demons. In *Beyond the Wizardwall* (1986) he even becomes an agent of his government, infiltrating the city of a neighboring kingdom to disrupt plans for an invasion and assassination. Three additional book-length adventures followed, the first two in collaboration with Chris Morris. *City at the Edge of Time* (1988), the best in the series, takes Tempus to a distant city whose inhabitants have achieved a form of immortality, but at a terrible cost. *Tempus Unbound* (1989), the weakest of her novels despite an interesting premise, transports Tempus from his own world to our own contemporary America. *Storm Seed* (1990) describes his final battle against the forces of demonic evil.

Most of Morris's remaining fantasy falls into another shared world series, this one set literally in hell. On each of these novels, Morris collaborated with another writer, a pattern that repeated itself in her later science fiction. The Trojan War is fought again in *Kings in Hell* (1987, with C. J. CHERRYH), the poet Homer conducts the reader on a guided tour of the afterlife in *The Little Helliad* (1988), and various characters from different times and places interact in *Explorers in Hell* (1989, with David Drake). In the mid-1990s Morris briefly concentrated on mainstream thrillers before falling silent. After a gap of many years, the Thieves' World anthology series has been resumed, and it is to be hoped Morris will revive what is probably the most famous character to emerge from the earlier volumes.

Morris, William (1834–1896)

William Morris was a British writer, poet, and designer whose fantasy fiction was very influential on J. R. R. TOLKIEN, E. R. EDDISON, and through them on virtually every fantasy writer who followed. His first prose fantasy was "The Hollow Land" (1856), and the first novels to contain marginal fantastic elements were the Viking adventure story *The Roots of the Mountains* (1889) and *The House of the Wolflings* (1889), which involves conflict between Romans and Saxons. *The Glittering Plain* (1891) is more recognizable as a fantasy novel. A traveler visits an imaginary land that claims to be a utopia and whose residents are virtually immortal. The image of a perfect kingdom is an illusion, however, and he is finally forced to flee the secretively repressive government. The novel is an interesting counterpoint to *News from*

Nowhere (1891), a utopian science fiction novel Morris wrote at approximately the same time.

The Wood Beyond the World (1894) more closely resembles modern fantasy. Once again we are introduced to an imaginary world through the eyes of a traveler who stumbles into a dangerous array of personalities, dominated by a witch who decides the outsider should replace her current lover. Violence ensues before the protagonist escapes. His most successful fantasy novel was *The Well at World's End* (1896), so large that it appeared in two volumes when published in paperback. The plot is an episodic quest taking a young man through a variety of locations and adventures, at the end of which he has had his youth restored by magical waters and has found the love of his life. The major innovation was the creation of an entire civilization in a universe not our own and the author's considerable efforts to describe a realistic and plausible imaginary setting.

Morris's subsequent fantasy novels, both published posthumously, were less impressive, though occasionally interesting. *The Sundering Flood* (1897) deals with two lovers in a fantasy world illogically separated by waters narrow enough to be easily crossed. *The Waters of the Wondrous Isles* (1897) contains another series of adventures in a medieval style kingdom. *Golden Wings and Other Stories* (1976) collects many of Morris's short stories, not all of which are fantasy. Although he is not generally popular with modern fantasy readers, his influence on the shape of the genre is beyond measure.

Morrow, James (1947–)

Although James Morrow's early novels are all technically science fiction, he was never interested in technological details or general scientific fact, and much of his work is predicated on the discovery of some new principle that served his literary purpose but that was often not scientifically plausible. He finally turned to outright fantasy with the novel *Only Begotten Daughter* (1990), the first of several openly satiric works focused on Christianity. The setting is the near future. Odd events at a sperm bank appear initially to be some kind of mix up but are eventually explained as divine intervention. Julie Katz's advent is explained as a virgin birth and the Second Coming of Christ, although this time the manifestation is a woman. Her arrival precipitates some minor apocalyptic events, largely at the instigation of a suave devil, who proves to be the motivating force behind fundamentalist religious movements. As the turmoil mounts and general chaos threatens, Katz eventually decides that for the benefit of humanity she must renounce her own nature. Morrow is clearly indicting organized religion and suggesting that we are no more prepared for the coming of the Messiah now than we were 2,000 years ago.

Towing Jehovah (1994) postulates not only that God is dead, but that his corpse is floating in the Atlantic. The Vatican secretly hires an ocean freighter to tow the body to the Arctic, where it can be concealed so that the world at large will not learn the truth. The various incidents that occur during the voyage are generally humorous, but there is a bitter and sarcastic undertone as well. Morrow followed up with two sequels. In *Blameless in Abaddon* (1996), the body has become a tourist attraction, but it has also become the focus of an effort by some to posthumously place God on trial for the many tribulations he placed on humanity while he was alive. The satire becomes considerably less focused in *The Eternal Footman* (1999), with God's skull placed in orbit around the Earth and the old rules of the natural universe beginning to break down.

In a similar vein, Morrow has also written a series of Biblical allegories with satirical twists, many of which are quite biting. These were eventually collected as *Bible Stories for Adults* (1996). "Bible Stories for Adults #17: The Deluge" (1988) won a Nebula Award. *Towing Jehovah* and *Only Begotten Daughter* both won the World Fantasy Award. Morrow has confined himself primarily to short fiction during the past few years, most of which can be found in *The Cat's Pajamas and Other Stories* (2004).

"Mr. Mergenthwirker's Lobblies" Nelson Bond (1937)

This was Nelson Bond's first and is still his most popular short story, although he was well regarded throughout the 15 years when he was most active as a writer. He has written only a handful of short stories since the late 1950s, but there has been renewed interest in his work in recent years. Bond employs a light, almost journalistic tone in his stories, and, in fact, the narrator of this particular one is the newly appointed assistant city editor of an unnamed newspaper who receives an unusual visitor. Mr. Mergenthwirker tells him that he has advance knowledge that a murder will be committed later that day. Initially, the narrator is interested, but when he asks how Mergenthwirker came by his information, his visitor tells him that he often receives such previews of the future from his two invisible companions, Japheth and Henry.

Mergenthwirker is summarily ejected, but the editor learns later that day that a crime was committed exactly as described and that there seems to be no way in which Mergenthwirker could be connected to the matter. He is intrigued but fails to track the man down until he encounters him by chance in a bar. Mergenthwirker sits at a table with four chairs and three beers, and two of the beers slowly disappear even though no one is sitting near them. The editor wants proof, so Mergenthwirker provides advance knowledge in detail of a bank robbery. The tip proves valuable, and the editor realizes he has stumbled onto a gold mine. He attempts to actively cultivate his new friend. Unfortunately, Mergenthwirker is mortally wounded in an accident, after which his last thoughts are of his friends, the "lobblies," and what might happen to them when he is gone. The editor assures him that he will take care of them, and, of course, we know that he will.

Bond initially left what follows to our imagination but later added additional stories as well as adaptations for television and radio. It is still one of the best stories of imaginary friends and may have provided the inspiration for Jimmy Stewart's giant invisible rabbit in the movie *Harvey* (1950). Many of Bond's later stories are technically better written, but none of them captured the simple but direct appeal of his very first published fiction.

"Mrs. Amworth" E. F. Benson (1923)

Although E. F. Benson is remembered today primarily for his novels of manners and other mainstream fiction, he was a friend of M. R. JAMES and possibly as a consequence wrote occasional ghost and horror stories and a handful of novels of the supernatural, none of the latter of which have remained in print. His short stories are much better known, however, and one of the best is this vampire adventure, which in general form is strikingly similar to DRACULA (1898) by Bram STOKER, although the depiction of the vampire is slightly different.

Mrs. Amworth is the widow of a British civil servant who died in India, recently returned to a small English village where she becomes the prime mover in the local society. She is fondly welcomed by everyone except Francis Urcombe, a retired academic who is pursuing private studies of the paranormal. Urcombe finds her mildly distasteful but fascinating, and the antipathy quickly becomes mutual. He raises the subject of vampirism, which he compares to a disease, just before one of the local boys is struck down by an extreme form of anemia. There are bites on the boy's neck, but the local doctors dismiss this as the marks left by a swarm of gnats that have lately been troubling the area. Urcombe and the narrator eventually keep watch over the boy, frustrating Mrs. Amworth, who is, of course, a vampire.

The parallels with Stoker's novel are obvious. Urcombe is Van Helsing, the young boy is Lucy Westenra, and Mrs. Amworth is the new arrival from foreign lands. Benson strays from Stoker's plot line only late in the story. Like Dracula, Benson's vampire can walk about in the daylight, can assume the form of a bat, and is repelled by religious signs. Mrs. Amworth is killed after being struck by an automobile, but her spirit is astrally projected and continues to seek blood. She is finally destroyed when Urcombe opens her grave and drives a shaft through her heart. The story very efficiently accomplishes most of what Stoker achieved with an entire novel, although the tone is oddly matter of fact, and there is very little suspense in the story.

Mundy, Talbot (1879–1940)

Talbot Mundy was the pseudonym of the British writer William Gribbon, who spent his early adult years in India and who later emigrated to the United States, where he eventually became a full-time writer. One of his earliest novels is still his most fa-

mous, *King—of the Khyber Rifles* (1916), which hints at fantasy themes without using them overtly. Mundy wrote two major series of novels, both of which used occasional elements of the fantastic. The first of these involves several British agents in India, including King from the early novel, although they focus on two others, Jeff Ramsden and James Grim. The first of these to employ a fantastic element was *Caves of Terror* (1924), a fairly minor effort, although it introduced the Nine Unknown, a secret group of powerful mystics who we are led to believe are united in the furtherance of mysterious ambitions.

The Nine Unknown (1924) continued their story and identified James Grim, known locally as Jimgrim, as an agent of the group of the title, who turn out to be fighting for good against a cult of Kali worshippers, who represent evil. *The Devil's Guard* (1926, also published as *Ramsden*) moves the battle to Tibet, with rival monasteries as the homes of good and evil, each aided by supernatural forces. The series came to an end with *Jimgrim* (1930, also published as *King of the World*), with Grim traveling to Egypt to defeat an enemy who has created a new type of weapon with which to conquer the world. The series is slightly dated today but still reads remarkably well.

Mundy's second major series was a historical trilogy about Tros, a sea captain who gets involved with Julius Caesar and Cleopatra, among other historical figures. Three novels appeared, although Mundy had planned to write others. These were *Tros of Samothrace* (1925), *Queen Cleopatra* (1929), and *The Purple Pirate* (1930). The first of these was so long that it was broken up into smaller volumes twice for issue in paperback under various titles. Tros is the son of Perseus, and both Greek and druid magic are involved, although for the most part the series is a straightforward historical adventure with Caesar as the primary villain.

Mundy's best single fantasy novel was *Om: The Secret of Ahbor Valley* (1924), a lost world novel. Other nonseries fantasy novels of note include *Full Moon* (1935, also published as *There Is a Door*), also involving a hidden civilization, and *Old Ugly Face* (1939), a marginal thriller involving psychic phenomena in Tibet. Mundy is probably the best known and most successful writer of 20th-century Oriental fantasy adventures.

Munn, H. Warner (1903–1981)

Harold Warner Munn began writing fantasy and horror stories in 1925 with "The Werewolf of Ponkert," still one of his best-known works, later published in book form in 1958 along with a sequel, "The Werewolf's Daughter" (1928), ostensibly as a novel. The story is told from the point of view of a 15th-century shape-changer and is still considered one of the best werewolf stories. Additional stories followed, appearing in book form much later as *In the Tomb of the Bishop* (1979) and *The Master Goes Home* (1979), but none of these matched the quality of the first two.

Munn's first true novel was *King of the World's Edge,* published in magazine form in 1939 but not as a book until 1967. Refugees from the fall of Camelot travel to the west across the ocean and eventually encounter the Aztecs, but in a world where magic actually works. Following the much-belated book publication, Munn revealed the existence of an unpublished sequel, *The Ship from Atlantis* (1967), a very effective story about a ship that ventures into the Sargasso Sea and encounters others stranded there, including one that set sail from legendary Atlantis. The two novels were later published together as *Merlin's Godson* (1976). Late in his career Munn wrote a third in the series, longer than the previous two combined. *Merlin's Ring* (1980) mixes Arthurian and Atlantean legends and chronicles their supposed influence throughout human history.

The Lost Legion (1980) is another historical fantasy but less successfully done. He also wrote several short stories late in his career, both horror and fantasy, including some noteworthy ones including "The Black Captain" (1975) and "The Well" (1976). Munn was inactive for many years and left behind only a comparatively small body of work, but it was of sufficiently high quality to ensure his lasting reputation.

Myth Series   Robert Lynn Asprin (1978–)

Humorous fantasy enjoyed only a brief period of broad popularity in the United States during the 1980s, but after the early 1990s it became obvious that there was room only for Terry PRATCHETT, Piers ANTHONY, and occasional isolated novels by other writers. American readers were more interested in large-scale, sweeping epics involving wars, dark sorcery, and court intrigues. Robert Lynn Asprin had started his Myth series in 1978 with *Another Fine Myth,* but it looked as though the series might stop when the 10th volume appeared in 1994. After a lapse of several years, Asprin resumed the series in 2001, adding three more volumes so far, and the earlier titles have been reprinted as well.

The two major characters in the series, which is set in a farcical alternate world, are Skeeve and Aahz. Skeeve is initially a wizard-in-training whose spells have unforeseeable results, much to the dismay of Aahz, his master, who also happens to be a demon. Their initial adventure is very episodic, pitting them against dragons, an angry mob, and a demon hunter, but they persevere after a series of pun-riddled, slapstick adventures. The second title, *Myth Conceptions* (1980), is more unified. Skeeve accepts a job as court magician, unfortunately in a small kingdom that is about to be invaded. *Myth Directions* (1982) spoofs traditional quest stories. *Hit or Myth* (1983) is less original, reprising the story from the second book, although Skeeve's comic matrimonial escapades are particularly amusing.

Aahz disappears in the last book, so Skeeve goes on an interdimensional search to find him in *Myth-ing Persons* (1985), unwisely crosses a group of professional gamblers in *Little Myth Marker* (1985), and deals with a vampire in *M.Y.T.H. Inc. Link* (1986). The next several titles, *Myth-Nomers and Im-Pervections* (1987), *M.Y.T.H.Inc in Action* (1990), and *Sweet Myth-Tery of Life* (1994), often feel forced and formulaic, and the jokes are considerably less original.

Asprin revived the series with *Myth-Ion Improbable* (2001), one of the better titles in the series, and continued it with *Something M.Y.T.H. Inc* (2003), which includes some biting satire about governments and how they function. The most recent addition is *Myth Alliances* (2003), written in collaboration with Jody Lynn Nye. Asprin has written occasional fantasy outside this series as well, of which the best is *E Godz* (2003), written with Esther FRIESNER.

N

"Nackles" Donald Westlake (1964)

Donald Westlake examines the question of whether gods create people or people create gods in this bitingly satiric tale of the anti–Santa Claus. He opens by pointing out that most of the historical gods have a nemesis, such as God and the devil and the Norse gods and the Frost Giants, and that good and evil are usually portrayed as being locked in a perpetual battle, balancing each other. He then postulates that Santa Claus is, in a sense, a god. He is omniscient, is able to watch and keep track of the activities of every child in the world, and on Christmas Eve obviously has a supernatural power that enables him to be in so many different places simultaneously. Millions of children believe in him, and he rewards good and punishes evil. Letters requesting gifts are the equivalent of prayers, and his attendants are not entirely human. If not a god, he is certainly very like one.

The narrator is troubled by his brother-in-law, Frank, a thoroughly nasty man who once abused the narrator's sister but has behaved reasonably well ever since thanks to a timely beating with a baseball bat. Nevertheless, he is thoroughly despised and a source of terror to his three children, and their domestic arrangements are tense at best. When the kids became old enough to believe in Santa, Frank tried to discipline them by threatening that Santa would leave them no presents, but that was too mild a concept for him, so instead he invented Nackles.

Nackles is the anti-Santa, tall, thin, and dressed in black. He travels through a maze of subterranean tunnels in a carriage drawn by eight white goats, visiting the homes of children who have not behaved so he can stuff them into his sack and later eat them. Frank is so pleased with his creation that he tells other parents, and inevitably some of them adopt the concept as well, so that it spreads almost of its own volition. The first Christmas passes, but the following year Frank's job has gotten worse, he is drinking more, and his temper has become dangerously violent. On Christmas Eve he locks himself in his study, and the following morning he is gone. The author concludes that despite his years, he was still at heart a spoiled, ill-behaved child and that perhaps Nackles became real and spirited him away. Westlake writes in the mystery genre almost exclusively, and this rare venture into the fantastic was originally published under the name Curt Clark.

"Naples" Avram Davidson (1978)

Sometimes the most effective stories are those that avoid being explicit, that paint a detailed landscape in which we become immersed. Then, just when it appears that we understand the place and what is happening in it, the author introduces a concept or an event that suggests that we may have misunderstood everything that has gone before. That is the case with this very prose-conscious story, which won the World Fantasy Award.

"Naples" is set at some unspecified time in the past when Naples was a teeming city filled largely with the poor, when pasta was the main source of sustenance but was almost always eaten plain because no one could afford the ingredients to add a tasty sauce, and when the city itself was a collection of distinct and disparate communities. Into this world comes a handsome young man, a traveler, who passes through the marketplace and enters a secluded alley, followed by a second man whose finances and motives are suspect but who hopes to better his lot by providing his services as a guide.

The two men enter an even darker, drearier part of the city, where even the clothes left to dry on ropes above the streets seem to be either rags or clothing designed for forms not quite human. When the second man begins to falter, the traveler pauses and says something that convinces him to continue onward, and eventually they reach a house whose single resident is an elderly man who seems to be on the brink of death. From him they purchase an ephemeral gift, for there is a second presence in the house, apparently held in a timeless limbo from which the gift of death is absent. It is this deferred death that the traveler has purchased. Davidson is never explicit about the details of the transaction and leaves us to speculate about the nature of what has just passed among the characters, giving us the feeling that we have been granted a glimpse into an entirely different world.

The Narnia Series   *See* THE CHRONICLES OF NARNIA.

"Narrow Valley" R. A. Lafferty (1966)

R. A. Lafferty lived most of his life in Oklahoma, was very familiar with Native American traditions, and even wrote a nonfantastic novel about them, *Okla Hannali* (1972). One of his earliest and best stories is this delightful tale of a Pawnee who is granted 160 acres of land located around a valley, with the proviso that he must pay taxes on it. Clarence Big-Saddle does not like that idea, so he invokes magic that makes his valley wide when he is alone but narrow whenever an intruder enters. He never pays any taxes, and the land, which cannot be entered by outsiders, is eventually listed on the books as officially unclaimed.

Enter the Ramparts, an obnoxious family who want to homestead the property. They stake their claim, then try to visit their new acquisition, only to find a ditch that appears to be five feet across but that is actually half a mile in breadth. The Rampart children decide to explore the valley, even though their father is clearly unsettled by the situation. Appalled at their apparent disappearance, he calls for scientists, news crews, and the military. The scientists develop complex theories to explain the phenomenon, while everyone else sits around helplessly. While all of this is happening outside the valley, the children meet Clarence Little-Saddle, whose father invoked the magic many years in the past.

Clarence is patient at first, waiting for the Ramparts to lose interest or their nerve, like everyone who came before them, but instead their stolidity transforms the valley, which expands to its normal dimensions. Disgruntled, Clarence resorts to Pawnee magic of his own, compelling the valley to narrow again, although he fails to get the incantation exactly right. The Ramparts emerge, terrified, as the valley becomes narrower than ever, and they themselves have been reduced to two dimensions, although they slowly regain their usual form after moving some distance from the area of enchantment. Clarence has his property back, unchallenged, and can make plans to leave it to his own son when he dies. Lafferty gently spoofs the modern compulsion to explain and quantify everything and suggests we might be happier if we just enjoyed things for what they are.

Nathan, Robert (1894–1985)

Robert Nathan wrote a considerable body of fiction over the course of his long writing career, and several of his novels involve fantastic or supernatural themes, although he is rarely thought of as a genre writer. Perhaps his most famous novel is *Portrait of Jennie* (1948), in which an artist meets a young girl in a park and draws her picture. In each subsequent encounter she seems slightly older, until at last he discovers that she was drowned at some point in the past and is not physically present. Nathan never really resolves whether she was a ghost appearing retroactively through time or a child who somehow traveled forward in large increments because of her affection for the protagonist. It was made into a low-key but very effective film. He used a similar theme in *So Love Returns* (1958) and *The Wilderness Stone* (1960), and although his novels sometimes have a less-than-happy ending, his are among the first and best of the time travel romances that have since become something of a subgenre of their own.

Nathan's first significant fantasy novel was *The Bishop's Wife* (1928), which was also made into a popular motion picture. An angel is secretly living among humans, having answered a prayer from a bishop who seeks help in building a new cathedral. The angel falls in love with the man's wife, causing an interesting and doomed love triangle. *There Is Another Heaven* (1929) is a very loose sequel. Angels and demons appear frequently in Nathan's work, although it is not always clear that either side is entirely good or entirely evil. *But Gently Day* (1943) is another time travel story with a hint of paradox, as the traveler interacts with his own ancestors. Lucifer makes a visit to a Halloween party in *The Innocent Eve* (1951), and death personified joins a cruise in *The River Journey* (1949).

The devil changes tactics in *The Devil with Love* (1963), another bittersweet romantic comedy, and Merlin makes an appearance in *The Elixir* (1971). In *Heaven and Hell and the Megas Factor* (1975), an angel and a devil are forced to make common cause. Despite the frequent use of the supernatural, the closest Nathan ever came to true horror was in the very early *The Puppet Master* (1923), in which puppets come to life, and the closest to mainstream fantasy was *Sir Henry* (1955), which involves a dragon. In general, however, his stories are understated, unmelodramatic, thoughtful, and often sentimental. He is probably the most underrated American fantasist.

Neiderman, Andrew (1940–)

Andrew Neiderman wrote conventional thrillers before edging into supernatural horror in the early 1980s, starting with the very marginal *Brainchild* (1981) and the much more effective *Pin* (1981), the basis for a mediocre horror film. The latter novel itself is quite suspenseful, involving an imaginary tutor invented to help comfort two recently orphaned children. The tutor begins to take on a malign life of his own. Four years passed before Neiderman's next horror novel, *Imp* (1985), but that was the first of a steady stream that appeared through the mid-1980s and early 1990s. *Imp* is a variation of the devil's child story, popularized in ROSEMARY'S BABY 1967) by Ira Levin and THE OMEN (1976) by David Seltzer, but with a unique twist. The child in this case lives secretly beneath an old house, protected by the demented woman living above.

Night Howl (1986) is less impressive, although it also turns a familiar theme slightly askew. The protagonist is a young boy whose dog dies and whose spirit returns in a form that allows it to interact with the living, sometimes with deadly consequences. As it becomes more savage, it begins to turn even on its former owner. *Teacher's Pet* (1986) is much more formulaic. The teacher in question is using his gift for the supernatural to literally alter the minds of his students and turn them into virtual puppets he can use to perform various evil acts. The child in jeopardy was a popular theme in horror and suspense fiction at the time, largely because of the success of the novels of V. C. Andrews, and it is therefore interesting to note that following her death, Andrews's family selected Neiderman to continue writing novels in the same vein under the name Virginia Andrews, although none of these involve the supernatural.

Lovechild (1986) is a werewolf story. A teenager has a genetic trait that makes her a kind of rationalized werewolf. At times she is gentle and loving, but on other occasions she is consumed by uncontrollable rage. This transformation gives her superhuman strength and cunning, so she is able to conceal her condition from others. Her problem is to reconcile the two aspects of her personality before she destroys everyone she loves. *Sight Unseen* (1987) is very similar, except that the child in this case is a young boy with the power of clairvoyance. *Surrogate Child* (1988) also covers much of the same ground. This time a distraught family adopts a boy to replace their own after he dies, but the newcomer is not what he seems to be.

Perfect Little Angels (1989) borrows from Ira Levin again, this time *The Stepford Wives* (1972). Someone is using radio waves to control the minds of the population of a small town. Despite a strong start, this is one of the author's weakest books. Oddly enough, it was immediately followed by Neiderman's best novel, *Devil's Advocate* (1990), in which a disgruntled lawyer joins a new law firm and discovers an interesting anomaly. In many cases the defense has been decided upon even before the client has committed a crime, indicating supernatural foreknowledge. The novel was made into a fine movie, but it was followed by the disappointing *Bloodchild* (1990), a vampire novel, and Neiderman's subsequent output would continue to vary between original ideas and overworked formulas.

The *Immortals* (1991) is very similar to *Devil's Advocate* and nearly as good. When the main character's husband takes a job with a company that produces a surprisingly effective treatment for aging, she is initially pleased. When she begins to notice a change in his attitude toward her, she investigates and eventually discovers that he is a candidate for a program that provides immortality through supernatural means and that the price in his case is her murder. *Sister, Sister* (1992) is another evil child story, this time involving conjoined twins with psychic powers, and is relatively undistinguished, but *Need* (1992) is a very original vampire story involving multiple personalities in a single body.

Neiderman's last horror novel before concentrating on the pseudonymous Virginia Andrews thrillers is unfortunately very minor. *After Life* (1993) mixes the walking dead with psychic possession. He returned to horror briefly with *The Dark* (1997), a well-written but unexceptional story in which a psychologist uncovers frightening secrets while treating a patient who has foreknowledge of violent crimes. Neiderman's career as a horror writer was truncated by the decline of that genre during the 1990s and the much more promising prospect of writing pseudonymously within an established thriller franchise. His published novels vary from mediocre to excellent, and at his best he has written some quite original and impressive work.

Nesbit, Edith (1858–1924)

Edith Nesbit began writing children's stories late in the 19th century, only a few of which involve fantastic elements, but her first fantasy novel, FIVE CHILDREN AND IT (1902) became the first of several for which she would subsequently be regarded as one of the most influential early writers of children's fantasy. She combined plausible stories filled with characters who seemed to be real children with a clever sense of invention and an effective sense of humor. In *Five Children and It* the children encounter a sand fairy, a magical being who will grant them one wish per day. Although they give increasing thought to their wishes as the story progresses, most of the results are not entirely what they hoped for. The message is clearly that the things in life that are worth having are not going to come easily, but Nesbit packages the lesson in an engaging and logical story.

The five children returned for two more adventures. In *The Phoenix and the Carpet* (1904) they find a magic carpet and use it to visit the Phoenix, a fabulous creature, and in *The Story of the Amulet* (1906) they travel back through time to ancient Rome and Greece and eventually the lost continent of Atlantis. This trilogy in particular is cited as an influence on Edward EAGER, C. S. LEWIS, and other fantasy writers who followed, and they are certainly the titles for which she is best known, although her most impressive novel is *The Enchanted Castle* (1907). Also of interest is *Wet Magic* (1913), in which children rescue a mermaid and are given a tour of an underwater world, and *The House of Arden* (1907).

Nesbit wrote a number of horror stories early in her career, but they have been largely overlooked in favor of her fantasies. A good selection can be found in *E. Nesbit's Tales of Terror* (1983) and *In the Dark* (2000). Several of her short children's fantasies were collected in *The Last of the Dragons and Some Others* (1972). Her willingness to write for children without patronizing her audience and her gift for mixing serious insights with light humor have had a large if not immeasurable impact on children's literature.

The Neverending Story Michael Ende (1979)

The German writer Michael Ende had already written children's fantasies before producing this classic, most notably *Momo* (1973), in which a girl outwits a mysterious group of people who turn children into adults by forcing them to conform to the rules of time. *The Neverending Story* appeared in German in 1979 and in English in 1983, its immense popularity leading to a disappointing film version in 1984 and two even less interesting sequels. *The Neverending Story* employs an interesting recursive device in that the story, read by young Bastian Bux, turns out to be, in part, the story of his own adventures. Initially, he escapes his own world only metaphorically, reading of the adventures of Atreyu, a young warrior in a magical kingdom who is, unfortunately, unable to defeat the insidious threat hanging over everyone.

Bux is later magically transported into a magical world called Fantastica, which is quite literally disappearing from existence. The queen of that world is personally affected by the magical depletion, although eventually Bux is able to counteract a portion of the curse by giving her a new name and then completes a renewal of that world after a series of quests and adventures during which he makes the transformation from child to adult. The film version concentrated on the first half of the story, and although it is sometimes effective in translating the impact of the book to a different medium, most of the time we are treated to just a succession of episodes involving clever animation and special effects. *The Neverending Story II* (1990) is even less coherent as a story, and *The Neverending Story III* (1994) bears virtually no relationship to the book.

Ende has written occasional young adult fantasy since, most notably *The Night of Wishes, or The Satanarchaeolidealcohellis Notion Potion* (1992), but none of his subsequent work has caught the imagination of his readers as effectively as *The Neverending Story*. Had he embellished his imaginary world, it might have gained the stature of Narnia as created by C. S. LEWIS. As a single novel it is less likely to have a secure position as a modern classic of children's literature, although it certainly merits that stature.

Newman, Kim (1959–)

The film historian and critic Kim Newman began writing fiction during the late 1980s, often under the name Jack Yeovil for novels set within the Warhammer shared universe series. His first book under his own name, *The Night Mayor* (1989), is technically science fiction, although it often feels like fantasy as the characters explore the world of dreams. *Bad Dreams* (1991) was his first overt horror novel. A woman investigates the death of her sister and discovers that the cause was supernatural, a kind of psychic vampire who is drawn to the sister in turn. Vampires soon became a common element in Newman's fiction, but his next novel, *Jago* (1991), deals with a religious cult that manages to tap into the collective unconscious of humanity, giving nightmarish creatures and fears physical form.

Anno Dracula (1992) was the first of Newman's vampire novels set in an alternate world, in this case a Victorian England where vampires are accepted members of society, and Dracula himself is the consort of Queen Victoria and the power behind the throne. The mix of supernatural themes and historical characters is very well managed and the novel itself is very similar to *The Empire of Fear* (1988) by Brian M. STABLEFORD. The first sequel was *The Bloody Red Baron* (1995), set during the equivalent of World War I. Vampires are on both sides of the conflict, and they are able to transform their bodies quite literally into weapons of warfare. *Judgment of Tears* (1998) moves forward to 1959. Dracula has been disgraced and expelled from England, but the mix of human and vampire has now become inextricably interwoven. Not everyone is happy with that fact, however, and someone is methodically assassinating vampires who have achieved positions of prominence. The fourth book in the series, *Dracula Cha Cha Cha* (2000), reprises that same theme less successfully.

Newman's remaining horror novels are well done but less widely known. *The Quorum* (1994) is a modern take on the story of Faust. *Seven Stars* (2000) is a sequel to *Jewel of the Seven Stars* (1903) by Bram STOKER and deals with living mummies and an ancient curse. It is an occult adventure story rather than horror. Newman has also been a prolific short story writer, with notable stories such as "The Big Fish" (1993) and "Out of the Night, When the Full Moon Is Bright" (1994). His collections include *The Original Doctor Shade and Other*

Stories (1994) and *Famous Monsters* (1995). *Where the Bodies Are Buried* (2000) is a collection of interrelated stories about a man who returns from the dead. After a very promising start, Newman's career seems to have slowed considerably since 2000, although he continues to write short fiction of unusually high quality.

"Nightmare at 20,000 Feet" Richard Matheson (1961)

Many of the strongest and most effective horror stories are those that exploit actual fears affecting the reader—claustrophobia, the lurker in the darkness, even the fear of death itself. Richard MATHESON draws on a modern preoccupation for this classic story, the fear of flying. His protagonist, Arthur Wilson, is forced to take an extensive air trip to the West Coast, even though he is terrified by the prospect. The motion makes him airsick, and he spends much of his time imagining horrible things that could happen to him or the airplane. His condition is one that most readers can identify with, at least to a degree, although his behavior is exaggerated. Indicative of the changing times, one element of the plot is no longer plausible—Wilson carries a handgun in his carry-on.

The real trouble starts when he glances out the window and sees what appears to be a living creature moving on the wing. Initially, he wonders if it could be a cat or dog caught there by accident, but he quickly revises his opinion. The form appears to be that of a man, perhaps a mechanic clinging for his life. Wilson calls the stewardess, but there is nothing in sight when she looks through the window. All he has accomplished is to make her suspicious of his state of mind. Deciding that he probably hallucinated the entire thing, he closes the curtains and tells himself to forget about it, but of course that is impossible. When he finally gives in to temptation and opens the curtains again, an inhuman creature is grinning through the window at him, although it disappears immediately when he calls for help. There follows a game of hide-and-seek as Wilson tries to convince the aircraft's crew that there is a gremlin on the wing and that the creature is attempting to sabotage one of the engines.

Since the reader knows about the handgun, Wilson's eventual solution is not a great surprise. He wrenches open the emergency door, nearly causing the plane to crash in the process, and shoots the gremlin before it can finish its sabotage. He is then placed under restraints but is calm now, convinced that when they land the maintenance crew will find evidence to support his claim. Matheson leaves his ending somewhat ambiguous, however, and we can interpret the story literally or assume that it was, in fact, a series of hallucinations brought about by stress. The story is equally chilling regardless of which interpretation the reader prefers.

The Night Stalker Jeff Rice (1973)

This original vampire novel was written almost simultaneously with the production of the television movie version, also by Rice, and can be thought of either as the novel that provided the basis for the movie, or the novelization of the author's screenplay. In either case, it is a surprisingly effective work that fused a traditional, evil vampire with the plot devices of a contemporary thriller, almost a police procedural. The movie was popular enough to spawn a sequel, *The Night Strangler* (1974) and a short-lived but highly regarded television series, *Kolchak, the Night Stalker.* It is interesting to note that the night stalker of the title is not, in fact, the vampire but rather Carl Kolchak, an ornery, disreputable investigative reporter who has an affinity for stories that involve the supernatural.

In the first novel police are puzzled by a series of murders, all involving young women who have lost massive amounts of blood from throat wounds and some of whom have been killed under extraordinary circumstances. Kolchak has the luck to be present when they make their first attempt to apprehend the killer and is as stunned as the police when the suspect displays superhuman strength and an apparent invulnerability to bullets during the course of his escape. Although he remains skeptical, Kolchak gradually begins to believe that their quarry is a genuine, supernatural vampire, but his efforts to convince the authorities backfire, making him even more unpopular than he already was. Ultimately he is forced to act on his own, succeeds in destroying the vampire, but apparently ruins his own life in the process.

The Night Stalker is very effective both as a novel and as a film, although the sequel, *The Night Strangler,* was less satisfying. The villain this time has achieved immortality through an occult rite that involves the sacrifice of human life. The novel takes too long to start unraveling the mystery, and Kolchak's success at the end is anticlimactic and too reminiscent of his first adventure. Rice wrote no further horror novels, but he popularized the image of the reluctant vampire killer and also proved that vampires could be just as frightening on a brightly lit boulevard as they were in a dark and gloomy castle.

The Night We Buried Road Dog Jack Cady
(1993)

Jack CADY is one of those rare writers in any genre who has a genuine feel for the subcultures of America. This novella explores one of those worlds, one inhabited by a small number of people in the Northwest whose primary obsession is automobiles and highways. The narrator is a young man who is the close friend of Brother Jesse, an enigmatic figure who so loved his 20-year-old Hudson that when it finally failed he dug a grave, and conducted a burial service, and now hopes to run a cemetery for the dead cars of other dedicated drivers. Brother Jesse and the narrator are on a prolonged trip cross-country when their path intersects that of the legendary Road Dog, a mysterious character who few people have actually seen, although he is known for the cryptic messages written in an elegant hand that he leaves on the inside walls of restrooms wherever he goes and for the Studebaker in which he races all comers and never loses.

The two are on their way home, each driving his own car, when the narrator begins to see the ghosts of highway fatalities appearing along the side of the road. At first he suspects that they are just hallucinations, but then another vehicle approaches from behind at an impossible rate of speed. He recognizes it as the ghost of the Hudson he watched being buried. Sobered, Brother Jesse slows down and thus escapes injury when the front end suspension fails a short time later. A similar

manifestation several days afterward saves a mutual friend, whose car also concealed a hidden deathtrap. More time passes, and the narrator, alone this time, runs into a man who is apparently Jesse's supposedly dead identical twin but who is, in fact, the fabled Road Dog.

Time passes as the narrator joins the army and has only distant contact with his home. Word leaks out that Jesse did indeed have a twin, which seems to explain that anomaly, but Jesse himself is deteriorating, losing interest in his old life although he is still obsessed with his automobile cemetery. Almost by chance, the narrator stops in a town where Jesse's brother John is well known and where they believe that it is Jesse who is dead. Eventually, we learn that one of the brothers did die, but it is impossible to know which one, because the survivor kept both lives moving forward, balancing one against the other.

Cady's story involves the supernatural, but it is the human characters who take center stage, displaying the great lengths we go to in order to hold on to what we have lost. In addition to winning a Bram Stoker Award, this novella also gained Cady a grant from the National Endowment for the Arts.

Nix, Garth (1963–)

The Australian writer Garth Nix very quickly emerged as one of the most interesting new writers of young adult fantasy starting with *Sabriel* (1995), the first volume of the Abhorsen trilogy, which mixed traditional fantasy elements with darker themes. The young protagonist has been warned to stay away from an area where magic works and where the dead are rumored to walk, but the temptation is too great. There she encounters Abhorsen, whose job is to lay the dead to rest, defeating some genuinely creepy monsters in the process. The story was intense enough to attract a considerable adult audience, as did two sequels. In the first, *Lirael* (2001), another young girl goes on a lonely quest accompanied only by her dog, and in *Abhorsen* (2003) we witness perhaps the ultimate battle between good and evil, with the former trying to sharpen the distinction between life and death and the latter seeking to eliminate the living. Although it appears that the story concluded with this volume, there are hints that further adventures set in this world might be in the offing.

Nix also wrote a much less ambitious series of six books in the Seventh Tower series, consisting of *The Fall, Castle, Aenir, Above the Veil, Into Battle,* and *The Violent Keystone,* all published in 2000 and 2001. The setting is reminiscent of the work of Mervyn PEAKE in that the action takes place within a gigantic castle so large that it is essentially a city, providing a large cast of characters and a wide variety of settings for the young protagonists, who seek a missing magical artifact and battle a number of enemies before recovering it and saving the castle from destruction. It is aimed at a much younger audience than the Abhorsen trilogy and has less appeal for mature readers.

Nix has recently started a new series with *Keys to the Kingdom* (2003) and *Grim Tuesday* (2004), also for young readers. The protagonist is a boy with magical powers who must defeat a succession of interesting villains. Nix's occasional short stories for adults, such as "Under the Lake" (2001) and "Heart's Desire" (2004), indicate that he might find a welcome audience among adults as well as children.

Norton, Andre (Alice Mary Norton)
(1912–2005)

Alice Mary Norton began her writing career producing adventure stories for young adults, mostly in historical settings, during the 1930s. She also turned out her first fantasy novel, *Rogue Reynard* (1947), a minor talking animal story, and then a second, *Huon of the Horn* (1951), but most of her output during the 1950s and early 1960s was science fiction.

It was the publication of *Witch World* in 1963, the first of more than two dozen novels in the WITCH WORLD SERIES written solely or coauthored by Norton with other writers, that has proven to be her most noticeable achievement. The early volumes bear some resemblance to her science fiction and are cast as planetary adventures, but she quickly abandoned all efforts at rationalization and invoked magic and psychic powers in their stead. The series begins in the land of Estcarp, a matriarchy ruled by witches, women with psychic powers, but later volumes move to other regions of

that world and follow separate sets of characters, often with no connection to the other story lines. Individual volumes are set in various times and places and most stand completely alone, sharing a common setting and occasionally characters but with separately resolved plots. In recent years many of the titles in the series have been collaborative efforts and of less interest than earlier titles, but the Witch World novels have had obvious influence on the work of Marion Zimmer BRADLEY and other writers.

The popularity of the series overshadows the fact that Norton wrote a considerable body of fantasy not set in that world. Although most of her work prior to the 1960s had been ostensibly for a young adult audience, her emphasis began to change as she largely abandoned science fiction in favor of fantasy. Only a small portion of her fiction was still designed for younger audiences, such as *Steel Magic* (1965, also published as *Gray Magic*), in which children go through a magic portal into a world where King Arthur and Huon of the Horn battle evil. This was the first of a series of thematically related fantasies, all of which involved some form of magical time travel. *Octagon Magic* (1967), the best of her children's fantasies, follows the adventures of a troubled young girl who discovers that a neighbor's elaborate dollhouse is magical and that she can enter it and travel to a different age. *Fur Magic* (1968) also involves a transformation in which a young boy finds himself magically changed into an animal as well as transported through time.

Norton continued to write occasional children's fantasies through the 1970s, starting with *Lavender Green Magic* (1974), in which children travel back through time to visit a good witch. *Red Hart Magic* (1976) explores similar territory and actually consists of interrelated short stories about young people who have adventures in time thanks to the magic properties of an old inn. One of her most interesting fantasies during this period is the adult novel *The White Jade Fox* (1975), in which a young woman accepts a job as governess in a home that is set in a magical landscape where animals have unusual intelligence and the physical nature of the countryside can change from moment to moment. *Knave of Dreams* (1975) describes the adventures of a young man who wakes up one day in a strange body in a world he has never seen before.

Perilous Dreams (1976) actually consists of four stories with the same character, a woman who can travel to other realities through her dreams. *Wraiths of Time* (1976) is one of her best novels, reminiscent of her earlier historical fiction. A magic amulet conveys the protagonist back through time to ancient Egypt, where she becomes a pivotal player in a battle between the forces of good and evil. *The Opal-Eyed Fan* (1977), *Velvet Shadows* (1977), and *Iron Butterflies* (1980) are all romantic adventure stories with marginal fantastic elements, a curse in the first case and a magical necklace in each of the others. It appeared that Norton's career might be turning in a new direction, but these were the last of her romantic thrillers. A warrior with a magic sword has adventures in an underground world in *Moon Called* (1982), and evil sorcery threatens to overwhelm an imaginary world in *Wheel of Stars* (1983).

Quag Keep (1978) is much more mainstream fantasy. A group of people find themselves literally living in the imagined world of a role-playing game. Starting in the late 1980s many of Norton's novels were collaborations, and the extent of her contributions is unknown. She has continued to produce occasional novels completely her own, however, such as *The Mark of the Cat* (1992), the story of cat people, and *The Hands of Llyr* (1994), whose protagonist has the power to heal with a touch. *Mirror of Destiny* (1995) is one of the best of her later novels, a story in which the friction between industrialization and conservation is mirrored in a conflict between humans and fairies. *Scent of Magic* (1998) is another of her best efforts and employs an unusual concept. It is set in a world whose magic is closely linked to the sense of smell.

In recent years Norton has collaborated with other writers for more than two dozen novels, most of them fantasy. The most notable of these are the Halfblood trilogy, consisting of *Elvenbane* (1991), *Elvenblood* (1995), and *Elvenborn* (2002), all written with Mercedes LACKEY, and *Imperial Lady* (1989) and *Empire of the Eagle* (1993), both written with Susan SHWARTZ. Although not a prolific short story writer, Norton has written a number of good stories, most of which are fantasy. These have been collected in *High Sorcery* (1970), *Dragon Magic* (1972), *The Book of Andre Norton* (1975), and *Moon Mirror* (1988). She will probably always be best known for the Witch World series, but much of her best fantasy has been set outside that world.

"An Occurrence at Owl Creek Bridge"
Ambrose Bierce (1891)

This short Civil War horror story is the best known and most imitated story by Ambrose BIERCE, an unusual figure whose career ended when he disappeared mysteriously in Mexico. Having served in the Civil War himself, Bierce was ideally suited to portray the plight of ordinary soldiers of that period, and the majority of his stories, supernatural and otherwise, are linked to that conflict.

This particular tale opens with a saboteur about to be hanged by Federal forces from the railroad bridge in the title. The condemned man has no friends to plead for him, and the only witnesses to his execution are a company of soldiers drawn up nearby. His name is Peyton Farquhar, a civilian, and Bierce explains that he was tricked into committing an act of sabotage to slow the army's advance, for which he is to be summarily hanged. As the final seconds tick away, he is struck by an apparent slowing of time, a foreshadowing of what is to follow.

The moment comes, and he drops through the ties of the bridge, feeling a sudden burning pain around his neck. Then he is in the water and decides that the rope must have broken at just the right moment. On the verge of drowning, he manages to free his bound arms and remove the noose, but now he faces the possibility of being shot when he appears on the surface. His senses seem preternaturally sensitive as he swims desperately away from the soldiers, who are now shooting at him. Eventually, he eludes them and spends the rest of the day moving through the forest, which seems unusually wild to him, eventually reaching his home town despite the growing pain in his neck and dryness in his mouth. Just as he sees his wife coming to meet him, he feels a sharp pain and loses consciousness.

With the final line, Bierce reveals the truth. All that has happened took place within the split second during which Farquhar fell and had his neck broken, a wish-fulfillment fantasy that replaced the reality of what was happening to him. The idea that a wealth of experience could be compressed into such a small expanse of time has been copied in many forms since, but never more effectively.

O'Day-Flannery, Constance (unknown)

During the past 20 years, the time travel romance has evolved into a subgenre in its own right. Typically, a woman from the present day is transported through some magical or unexplained means to an earlier time and place, where she finds true love, usually in the arms of an aristocrat or a mighty warrior. There have been literally hundreds of novels that used this same plot in recent years, varying widely in narrative quality and historical accuracy. One of the best of the authors working in this particular vein is Constance O'Day-Flannery, whose career started with *Timeless Passion* (1986), in which an automobile accident inexplicably projects a lonely woman back to the pre–Civil War South, where she eventually finds a place and a lover. Two similar novels, *Time Swept Lovers* (1987) and *Time Kissed Destiny* (1987), followed quickly, conforming closely to the original formula.

Time-Kept Promises (1988) added considerably more depth. This time the time traveling woman finds herself in the middle of a reasonably clever murder mystery as well as having to adjust to a different age. The author considers the ramifications of time paradoxes briefly and is clearly more in control of her writing, using more efficiently constructed plots and more realistic characters. *This Time Forever* (1990) continued in the same vein, but for her next novel, she switched to a supernatural theme. In *Once in a Lifetime* (1991) the protagonist is trying to recover from the effects of a recent divorce when the love of her youth shows up to comfort her. This potentially happy outcome is tempered by the fact that he died many years earlier.

A Time for Love (1991) reverted to the time travel formula, and is not particularly distinguished, but *The Gift* (1994), O'Day-Flannery's best novel, also makes use of supernatural elements, although it is not a horror novel. The protagonist has conversations with a dead actress whose image appears on her television screen, helping her find her way through a romantic tangle. *Bewitched* (1995) turns the time travel plot around with often humorous results. A man from the past finds himself in the contemporary world, and his entrenched chauvinism causes considerable difficulties for the woman who eventually falls in love with him. *Anywhere You Are* (1999) treats the same theme more seriously but less successfully, and *Time after Time* (2001) once more sends a contemporary woman back to the Civil War to find love.

Her most recent novel is *Shifting Love* (2004), which is another of her better efforts. This time the love affair is entirely within our own era between a staid businessman and a woman who is concealing a small secret—that she can alter the shape of her body. O'Day-Flannery is clearly at her best when she avoids formula stories and engages her imagination. If she comes to be recognized as a fantasy writer as well as a romantic novelist, her reputation is likely to rise dramatically.

Offutt, Andrew J. (1937–)

Andew Offutt began writing in the 1950s, often under pseudonyms and concentrating mostly on science fiction, although *Jodinareh* (1970, written as John Cleve) is set during the time of Atlantis and is arguably fantasy. Although some of his planetary romances contain many elements common to fantasy adventures, he published only occasional short fantasy stories until 1975, after which most of his books were sword and sorcery tales often making use of characters or situations from the works of Robert E. HOWARD.

The most popular of these were additions to the CONAN series. The career of Howard's most famous character was being expanded by a variety of writers, but Offutt was one of the most effective at recreating the texture and excitement of the originals. His three titles were *Conan and the Sorcerer* (1978), *The Sword of Skelos* (1979), and *Conan the Mercenary* (1980), which make up one connected story in which Conan's soul is imprisoned in a magic jewel and he must accomplish various tasks to reclaim it. Offutt also wrote three novels using Howard's Celtic hero, Cormac Mac Art. A woman must be restored to her rightful throne in *Sword of the Gael* (1975), an evil sorcerer must be overcome in *The Undying Wizard* (1976), and another in *The Sign of the Moonbow* (1977), the best of the three. Offutt added two more novels to the series in collaboration with Keith Taylor, but *When Death Birds Fly* (1980) and *The Tower of Death* (1982) are not as interesting.

Offutt was a regular contributor to the Thieves' World shared universe anthology series and wrote two novels based on his recurring character, *Shadowspawn* (1987) and *The Shadow of Sorcery* (1993), both of which are excellent, as is his War Gods trilogy, consisting of *The Ironlords* (1979), *Shadows out of Hell* (1980), and *The Lady of the Snowmist* (1983), which makes use of all the usual trappings—a quest, a magic sword, meddling gods—to very good advantage. Another trilogy, written with Richard K. Lyon, includes *Demon in the Mirror* (1978), *The Eyes of Sarsis* (1980), and *Web of the Spider* (1981) but is less consistently entertaining.

Offutt's two best fantasy novels are not part of a series. *The Chieftain of Andor* (1976, also published as *The Clansman of Andor*) projects its protagonist into the body of a warrior on a distant world, after which he has a series of exciting and cleverly written adventures. His best fantasy novel is *Deathknight* (1990), which superimposes an intriguing murder mystery onto a fantasy setting. Offutt, who also edited the well regarded Swords Against Darkness anthology series during the 1970s, has been generally inactive in fantasy since 1993 but has recently begun producing new short stories. He was the most consistent of the generation of sword and sorcery writers who flourished during the 1970s, and his skillful storytelling has been missed.

The Omen **David Seltzer** (1976)

When Ira Levin's ROSEMARY'S BABY appeared in 1967, the blend of medieval superstition with a contemporary American setting made the story of the birth of the child of Satan, the Antichrist, unusually plausible and frightening. The novel, written at the same time as the screenplay by the same author, left a particularly lasting impression because it ended just when it might be presumed that the real story would start, with the child still an infant and with his impact on the world only a suggestion. David Seltzer provided a metaphorical sequel with his novel and screenplay, describing several events that take place during the childhood of Damien, the son of Satan, who is protected from his enemies by natural and unnatural allies. The movie was parodied very effectively in *Good Omens* (1990) by Neil GAIMAN and Terry PRATCHETT.

The sequels to *The Omen* are a mixed lot. The next two novels were both based on screenplays and were not by David Seltzer. *Damien* (1978), novelized by Joseph Howard, covers the character's adolescence, his growing realization of the truth, and his use of his powers to eliminate his enemies. *The Final Conflict* (1981), novelized by Gordon McGill, portrays Damien as an adult, the head of a business empire that he uses to promote evil and misery wherever possible, although in the end he is defeated by the forces of good. McGill then added two original novels. In *Armageddon 2000* (1982) we discover that Damien had a son, who has survived and who has organized his followers

to carry on his father's work. He continues his efforts in *The Abomination* (1985) before joining his father in defeat. Further complicating the story line was the 1991 television movie, *The Omen: The Awakening*, in which we discover that Damien also had a daughter and whose young career is unsurprisingly similar to that of her father. The books and films are uneven in quality but have an undeniable power that is perhaps a reflection of the general moral uncertainty of our times.

The Once and Future King **T. H. White** (1958)

The legend of King Arthur and the Knights of the Round Table has had a long and enduring popularity, starting with *Le Morte D'Arthur* by Sir Thomas Malory (1485). Scores of writers have rewritten the story of Arthur, Merlin, and Camelot, sometimes straying a considerable distance from the original legend and even transposing the characters into the present day. Perhaps the most frequently read of all of these, however, is this very long novel by Terence Hanbury WHITE, a portion of which appeared as the animated feature *The Sword and the Stone* (1963) and which also provided the inspiration for the stage play *Camelot* (1960) and the 1967 movie musical of the same name.

The book actually consists of four shorter novels, starting with *The Sword and the Stone* (1938), which tells the story of the young Arthur, his tutelage under Merlin, and his eventual triumph in drawing out a sword magically embedded in stone, a sign indicating that he is destined to be king. The remaining three parts are *The Witch in the Wood* (1939), also known as *The Queen of Air and Darkness, The Ill-Made Knight* (1940), and a previously unpublished conclusion, *The Candle in the Wind*. This last section replaced an earlier version, *The Book of Merlyn*, which White's publishers objected to when he first proposed the combined edition in the 1940s, possibly because of its advocacy of pacifism in the middle of World War II. *The Book of Merlyn* was published on its own in 1977.

The Sword and the Stone is generally considered a children's fantasy, but the themes grow darker and more adult in the later sections. Sir

Lancelot's dalliance with Queen Guinevere and later Mordred's betrayal of Arthur are much more complex and disturbing themes. White remains fairly true to Malory's version although he introduces occasional anachronisms, in part because of the portrayal of Merlin as a man who lives backward through time and therefore knows the future. The tragic ending is perhaps meant to be a reflection of Britain's loss of its ancient innocence and despite the implications in the title that Arthur might one day return, there is no indication in the closing chapters that this is possible. *The Once and Future King* may not be the best single book written about King Arthur, but it is the standard against which all others are compared.

Onions, Oliver (1873–1961)

The British writer Oliver Onions wrote contemporary novels and thrillers in addition to ghost and horror stories, of which the most famous is the short novel THE BECKONING FAIR ONE (1911), one of the best-known ghost stories of all time. It was so good that it overshadowed the rest of his first collection of horror stories, *Widdershins* (1911), which also included "Rouum," the story of a talented man chased by an unknown presence, "Benlian," in which an insane sculptor begins to merge with his work, and "The Rocker," which involves the ghost of a child.

His second collection, *Ghosts in Daylight* (1924), includes one of the earliest stories in which a writer's characters come to life and interact with him, but "The Real People" runs too long, so that the surprising developments are diluted. His third and last collection is *The Painted Face* (1929), whose title story deals at great length with reincarnation. "The Rosewood Door" is another effective ghost story. Most of the contents of the three collections were gathered together as *The Collected Ghost Stories of Oliver Onions* (1935) and a slightly different selection as *Ghost Stories* (2001).

His book-length fantastic fiction has not remained popular, although some of it is quite interesting and ahead of its time. Onions was particularly sensitive to the psychological aspects of horror and used it extensively in his characterization and mood setting. There is an enchanted

suit of clothing in *A Certain Man* (1931), a magic coin that continually returns to its owner in *A Shilling to Spend* (1965), and a man who experiences a reversal of the aging process in *The Tower of Oblivion* (1921). Although his reputation is supported primarily by *The Beckoning Fair One*, his small output of supernatural stories continues to be highly regarded.

"On the Far Side of the Cadillac Desert with the Dead Folks" Joe R. Lansdale (1989)

In 1989 the writing team of John SKIPP and Craig SPECTOR decided to edit an anthology of stories set in the world of George Romero's Living Dead movies, where the dead rise as mindless zombies because of a mysterious and incurable disease. The premise might have resulted in monotonous stories of senseless violence, but the editors challenged their writers to find something original and creative to say, and none did it as well as Joe R. LANSDALE.

The initial shock is over and, as one might expect, people have become inured to the walking dead. They hunt the more powerful males down with rifles, but the women are often muzzled and sold to clubs, where they dance naked in cages for the amusement of the clientele. Civilization as we know it has undergone some strange and never fully explained transformation. Among other things, there was a war between Chevrolet and Cadillac, and the latter and their drivers are half-buried in long rows in the desert separating the wilds from Law Town, which is where the protagonist, a bounty hunter named Wayne, is bringing Calhoun, a fugitive child killer, not that Wayne is a model of decorum, either. He is not averse to kicking his opponent when he is down and actually prefers it that way.

On his way in with his prisoner, Wayne is waylaid by a group of undead who act cooperatively, contrary to anything in his experience, and coexist with two unusual living people as well. They identify themselves as a small and very strange religious order, and one of them claims to have been responsible for the accident that unleashed the plague of living death in the first place. As penance, he has been recruiting and training some of the dead, controlling them by means of brain implants. Calhoun and Wayne eventually reach an accommodation against their common enemy. Lansdale's interpolation and extrapolation from George Romero's original concept combines strong storytelling with graphic, disturbing images and events.

"The Opener of the Way" Robert Bloch (1936)

H. P. LOVECRAFT had an enormous influence on other writers of his time, and not just in those stories they chose to set in his universe. His invocation of older gods, gods that existed during prehistoric times and who were actually alien beings rather than supernatural entities, shows up again and again in short weird fiction during the 1930s and 1940s. Robert BLOCH was one of those who learned from Lovecraft, and in this, one of the most famous of his early short stories, he marries Lovecraftian imagery to an otherwise traditional story of tomb robbers and an ancient Egyptian curse.

Sir Ronald Barton and his son Peter have located a tomb whose innermost secret is guarded by a statue of Anubis, the opener of the way. The elder Barton had long felt mistreated by the authorities, unappreciated for his earlier archaeological efforts as part of a team, so he stole an ancient parchment that provided a clue to the location of this present find. Sir Ronald has investigated Egyptian sorcery in enough depth to have a certain degree of respect for it, but he still disregards warnings that there is a curse on the tomb and all who enter it. According to the manuscript, the tomb contains an image of the first true Anubis, a sort of intermediary between humans and the older gods.

As they draw closer, tension between father and son increases. Sir Ronald is obsessed and secretive, and Peter begins to both worry about his father's sanity and fear for his own safety. Although they have performed all the rituals required, there is one that remains, one that Sir Ronald has not described to his son. At last he reveals the truth, that the tomb can be opened only if he hypnotizes himself and transfers his consciousness into the guardian statue. This he proceeds to do, disregarding the curse, and in that

form he finds himself not only trapped for all of eternity but compelled to viciously murder his own son. Bloch's tale might seem low-key by the standards of today's horror fiction, but when it first appeared it was considered a powerful and effective story. It remains one of his best known.

"The Open Window" Saki (1912)

Saki was the pseudonym used by the British writer Hector Hugh Monroe for his very short, usually barbed, stories, several of which involve elements of the fantastic. This particular tale is one of his shortest and is probably his best known. It is a ghost story, one of the best ever written, but there are no ghosts in it. In fact, the story is technically neither fantasy nor horror at all, although the reader does not know this until the final few paragraphs. There have been many stories and novels in which the reader is led to believe that supernatural events are taking place, only to have them explained away in the final pages, such as *Too Many Magicians* (1959) by Paul Gallico, *The Rim of the Pit* (1964) by Hake Talbot, and *The Shadow Guest* (1971) by Hillary Waugh, but none of them have the intense, convincing impact of this simple little vignette.

The author introduces us to Framton Nuttel, who is recovering from a nervous disorder by spending some time in the country making the acquaintance of some of his sister's friends. He is calling upon one of them when he is left to be briefly entertained by his hostess's niece, Vera. Vera draws his attention to an oversized window, actually a doorway, that has been left open facing the woodland beyond. She describes her aunt's tragedy, losing her husband, her two brothers, and the family dog, all of whom died when they were sucked into a bog three years previously, beyond any hope of even recovering the bodies. Her aunt was so affected that she superstitiously leaves the window open so that they can come in if they should ever return.

Eventually, his hostess appears, chatting about her husband's hunting trip, much to the dismay of Nuttel, who believes her to be mentally ill. Then he notices an expression of horror on Vera's face and follows her eyes out onto the lawn, where three mud-stained figures and a dog are slowly walking toward them. Horrified, he leaps to his feet and runs from the house, much to the consternation of his hostess, for, as we find out presently, Vera made the entire story up. She then shows off her talent for prevarication again by convincing her family that Nuttel had a morbid fear of dogs and that this was why he raced away without explanation. The story is one of the best examples of a twist ending and is noteworthy as well for having concentrated a relatively complex story into a surprisingly short narrative.

P

"Pages from a Young Girl's Journal"
Robert Aickman (1974)

This story's narrator is a precocious young girl traveling through Europe with her parents, from whom she seems quite remote. They have recently arrived in Ravenna, home of Lord Byron, where they are staying with a contessa and her daughter. Despite her skepticism about foreigners, the protagonist feels increasingly sympathetic to and connected with their hostess.

Shortly after noticing an apparent clandestine embrace between the contessa's daughter and one of the servants, the heroine learns to her delight that there will be a large formal party. The story skips the party itself, but in the aftermath the narrator wakens with a small scar on her neck and a bloodstain on her pillow, a sight from which the contessa recoils in horror, although the girl herself dismisses it as inconsequential. Her memories of the party are murky, and she is unusually weak and pale. These symptoms she also dismisses, although the reader will by now have anticipated the revelation yet to come. She does remember having met an older man and fancies herself in love with him.

Her mood of elation changes when her parents inform her that they will be moving on shortly, although she is convinced that her newfound lover will be able to transcend any barrier that might separate them. Other problems arise. She feels faint when about to enter a church, and the sun bothers her more than it did before. There is no escape, however, for the vampire pursues her, visiting her in the night. It is soon evident that she welcomes his visits, even though she understands what is happening to her, perhaps captivated by his supernatural power, perhaps seeking any escape from the life she has been forced to live until now. Even the loss of her reflection and her shadow do not upset her. Ultimately, she has become a willing partner in her own seduction, for at least it offers an escape from a life she finds colorless and boring.

The story was not original in theme or plot, but the unusual viewpoint was striking, the story told from the point of view of the victim, and an unprotesting one at that. We never see the vampire at first-hand because the story is not about him but about the changes that take place in the protagonist's life and her perceptions of those around her. AICKMAN received the World Fantasy Award for the story.

Paine, Michael (unknown)

Occasionally a writer publishes with one or more outstanding works, then disappears from public view suddenly and completely. That was the case with Michael Paine, a byline that first appeared with a very original horror novel, *Cities of the Dead*, in 1988. The protagonist is an Englishman who loses his job in Egypt in 1903 and finds fresh employment acting as a guide for visiting Europeans. Disillusioned and effectively suspended between two worlds, he becomes increasingly involved with the darker side of Egyptian religion, including sorcery, and eventually discovers a plot to raise the dead. Although the bare plot outline sounds like a straightforward occult adventure, Paine uses his inventive imagination to enrich the background. Some of the monstrous figures, for example, are creatures who might have been given life by Jesus Christ himself. The mix of Egyptian lore and Christian beliefs and heresies is skillfully woven together in this highly atmospheric and often vividly realized novel.

Paine drew on many of the same sources for his second novel, *The Colors of Hell* (1990). This time the protagonist is involved in a search for fragments of glass that were forged with the blood of saints, rumored to give them unusual powers. The quest brings him into contact with a secretive order of nuns, who have been concealing something from the outside world ever since they were founded. Paine's third novel is *Owl Light* (1990), which also mixes supernatural horror with religious themes. In the midst of a controversy about the teaching of the theory of evolution at a local school, a town becomes involuntary host to an enigmatic woman who can bring dead animals back to life and command them to perform various acts. She becomes a center of great controversy when she asserts that her powers derive from her pagan beliefs and that this disproves the truth of Christianity.

Paine had quickly established a reputation for intelligent, sometimes controversial, and always engrossing horror thrillers, but he fell silent for the next 15 years. His fourth novel, *Steel Ghosts* (2005), which involves a haunted steel mill, signals a welcome return, a less ambitious but relentlessly suspenseful novel. Michael Paine is the pseudonym for John Curlovich.

"Paper Dragons" James P. Blaylock (1986)

This very unusual short fantasy starts with the narrator waking one morning to find his bedroom infested with blood-red crabs. He chases them out, but they return in greater numbers. The entire area is overrun with them for some time, with the smaller creatures giving way to larger and larger ones, until the last two pass by, each as large as a small automobile. One of the crabs gets into a neighbor's garage and shreds the stuffed dragon that he, Filby, had been keeping safe for a friend, the famous magician Augustus Silver. This world,

we discover, resembles ours only in part, because in this California the nature of matter can be altered so that life and nonlife are no longer separate things. It is possible for a talented magician to take inorganic material and turn it into a living being, such as a dragon.

In anticipation of Silver's arrival, Filby begins constructing a new dragon to replace the old one. As the day approaches, Filby frantically struggles to complete his project, convincing the narrator that he should travel into the city to meet Silver and bring him back. Although he tries to do just that, he fails because Silver has diverted himself on another trip. Then his attempt to visit a town made of discarded dragon parts comes to nought, and he returns to find that Filby is beginning the process of dismantling his dragon, initially to find an apparent fault in the design, but eventually as an act of uncreation. Indeed, none of the characters achieve their goals except a tomato worm that succeeds at last in becoming a moth.

Most fantasy fiction, even that that takes place in magical otherworlds, explains the rules that govern the setting so the reader can feel comfortable within it. BLAYLOCK'S version of our world is more than slightly off kilter, and there are hints that it is even stranger than what we are shown. The things that motivate his characters are just the same, and their failures are just as tragic. Although not prolific at this length, Blaylock has written several memorable short stories, of which this, a World Fantasy Award winner, is his best.

Paxson, Diana L. (1943–)

Diana Paxson started appearing in fantasy anthologies during the late 1970s and published her first novels, *Lady of Light* (1982) and *Lady of Darkness* (1983), a short while later. Both novels are set in Westria, a postapocalyptic version of California in which magic works, and are fairly straightforward tales of a king and his efforts to retain his throne despite the opposition of evil sorcery. Her third novel, *Brisingamen* (1984), is much more interesting. A contemporary woman discovers Freya's necklace, a magical artifact with immense powers. Loki detects its presence as well and returns to the world in order to acquire it and transform things to his liking. This is one of the better contemporary fantasies.

Silverhair the Wanderer (1986) marked the first of several return visits to Westria, a series that improved dramatically as it continued. *The Earthstone* (1987) and *The Sea Star* (1988) describe the transition to a new ruler after a period during which the throne was vacant. *The Wind Crystal* (1990) and *The Jewel of Fire* (1992) are above-average quest adventures in which magic jewels must be acquired from different locations to ensure the kingdom's security.

Paxson continued to demonstrate her ability to write convincingly in a contemporary setting as well as in different historical periods. *White Mare, Red Stallion* (1986) is set in early Scotland and involves a tragic clan rivalry that places a young woman in a position in which she is obligated to kill the man who loves her. *The White Raven* (1988) is a very effective retelling of the story of Tristan and Iseult. Paxson also relied on classical sources in *Serpent's Tooth* (1991), one of her stronger novels, which is based on William Shakespeare's *King Lear*. *The Wolf and the Raven* (1993) is a retelling of the story of Sigfrid and Brunhild, another story of a love affair that crosses clan lines. Their history is continued in *Dragons of the Rhine* (1995) and *The Lord of Horses* (1996). *The Hallowed Isle* (2000), originally published in four volumes, is a new interpretation of the story of King Arthur. Another trilogy, *Master of Earth and Water* (1993), *The Shield Between the Worlds* (1994), and *Sword of Fire and Shadow* (1995), all written with Adrienne Martine-Barnes, is based on Celtic legends.

Paxson also collaborated with Marion Zimmer BRADLEY on some of the latter's novels set in Roman Britain. She was not credited for *The Forest House* (1993) but was listed as a collaborator on *Priestess of Avalon* (2001). Her most recent novel is *Ancestors of Avalon* (2004), based partially on notes left by the late Bradley. Paxson has also written a large number of short stories, several of which are quite good but none of which have at present been collected. She is a reliable, skilled practitioner whose reputation is likely to grow in the years to come.

Peake, Mervyn (1911–1968)

Mervyn Peake's Gormenghast trilogy is one of the most unusual works in the history of fantasy because, despite its enduring popularity, it has almost never been imitated. The uniqueness of Peake's vision and the complexity of his creation set the books apart and have given them a so far unique status in the genre. The trilogy is not entirely consistent, and one might wonder from one volume to the next whether the story is taking place in some obscure corner of our world or in another reality entirely. The three volumes are *Titus Groan* (1946), *Gormenghast* (1950), and *Titus Alone* (1959), the last of which has appeared in two slightly different versions.

Each of the novels is set within the lifetime of Titus Groan, who goes from childhood to maturity to a kind of exile during the course of the work, although he is usually not the central character. The setting is Gormenghast, a castle so immense and convoluted that it is virtually a self-enclosed world with its own culture and laws. There is a very large cast of characters, and the relationships among them are complex and sometimes volatile. Much of the actual story involves the efforts to advance himself made by one of these characters, Steerpike, an ambitious, intelligent, but not entirely honorable man who eventually gets what he deserves. The third volume turns to Titus and is significantly different in tone and structure, often surrealistic. He ventures out of the castle to explore a world that does not appear to be ours, or is ours transformed very strangely in the near future.

Peake died before completing the story, which was to have included at least one more complete book, *Titus Awakes*. A short story, "Boy in Darkness" (1976), is related to the trilogy. A shorter novel, *Mr. Pye* (1953), is set on an island that at times resembles Gormenghast in its social structure. It is an allegorical battle between good and evil, with the title character sprouting angel wings or horns as the situation changes. A handful of other short fantasies have survived but are largely forgotten. Peake's work requires some focus on the part of the reader, as his stories often emerge slowly from his elaborate backgrounds, but they reward the extra effort required.

"The Pear-Shaped Man"   George R. R. Martin
(1987)

This fine story opens with a description of the title character, a repulsive, slovenly, overweight figure about whom we know nothing except for his physical appearance. It is suggested, however, that he is one of a type, that he is not a unique individual. The implications of this become obvious later. Jessie, the protagonist, has recently moved into a new apartment that she is going to share with her friend Angela. She meets him during a cryptic encounter while moving in, a minor incident that troubles her disproportionately, and is not happy to realize that she lives directly above him.

When she next sees him in a supermarket, she asks about him and learns surprisingly little, not even his name, only that his diet is strange and that he is possibly mentally retarded, nor can the other tenants in the building tell her anything other than that he has strange habits and never lets anyone see inside his apartment. Since Jessie works freelance at home doing cover paintings for books, she runs into the pear-shaped man on numerous occasions, and it is clear that he has become attached to her in some fashion, a situation she finds frightening. Her efforts to find out his name so that she can check his background prove completely fruitless.

Her situation worsens when she realizes that some of the pear-shaped man's unpleasant physical features are being replicated in the male figures she is painting, definitely not what is called for on the cover of romance novels. He begins inviting her down to his apartment in the basement to see his "things," an invitation she always declines angrily, but he never takes offense. Her situation continues to deteriorate. The pear-shaped man eats a distinctive snack food that turns up wherever she looks, including mixed into her underwear drawer.

Eventually, Angela's boyfriend convinces her that she needs to confront her fears in order to get past them. Reluctantly, she agrees to try to go down to the pear-shaped man's apartment, where she is promptly invited in, and finds herself in a place every bit as slovenly and tattered as the man himself. Some strange inertia holds her as he approaches, sheds his clothing, and then touches her, and she passes out. Moments later she regains consciousness, now in the body of the pear-shaped man and barely capable of coherent thought, watching in stunned horror as her former body walks out to go on with the life she has lost.

Martin's fiction has consistently avoided commonplace themes and plot devices. The "monster" in this story is not a traditional one, nor is his nature or origin precisely defined. He is, perhaps, symbolic of the way in which we can lose our own identities in our attempt to project the proper image to others. We may not clearly understand what has happened to Jessie or why, but we are left with a distinctly disturbing image. "The Pear-Shaped Man" won the Bram Stoker Award.

Peter Pan   J. M. Barrie   (1904)

The history of the character Peter Pan, created by James Matthew BARRIE, is somewhat complex. Barrie's first version was a play written in 1904 under the title *Peter Pan, or the Boy Who Would Not Grow Up,* and the novel version did not appear until 1911 and was originally called *Peter and Wendy. Peter Pan in Kensington Gardens* (1906) is actually an adaptation of one sequence from an earlier work. Barrie also later wrote a screenplay, but it was not used for any of the subsequent movie versions.

The story has become one of the all-time children's classics, although its status is probably based on the film and television versions rather than the books. Peter is a young boy who is determined never to grow up, a device used more recently to great effect by Harlan Ellison in "JEFFTY IS FIVE" (1977). He manages to avoid ageing by living in Never-Never Land with a band of other children who look to him for leadership. There he leads an adventurous life battling Captain Hook, a villainous pirate with an artificial hand. Wendy Darling joins him briefly but chooses to return to our world, where she grows up. As an adult she is visited by Peter, who is still a boy, and although she cannot return with him, she allows him to take her children to Never-Never Land.

Barrie was not always consistent in the various versions, and in one case Peter's immortality is conferred upon him by fairies. He wrote other work with fantastic elements, but nothing nearly as popular. The first film version appeared in 1924, and it was also a very popular stage play. Dan Barry and Ridley Pearson have recently written a prequel, *Peter and the Starcatchers* (2004).

Pet Sematary Stephen King (1983)

Many of the best horror stories are effective because they avoid the more exotic symbols of horror, instead relying on banal, familiar situations after giving them a bizarre twist. It is far more unsettling to entertain the possibility that a child or a pet could be the source of some monstrous evil than to worry about vampires and other creatures from outside our experience. Stephen KING has learned this lesson well, and in this novel from early in his career, he created one of his most frightening and suspenseful stories, although without a great deal of overt horror.

The story deals with a young couple who have recently purchased a new home in a rural area. They like the house and the neighborhood, and they are both in love with one another and with their children, including their young son, barely a toddler. Their nearest neighbor is a kindly man who unwisely mentions an ancient graveyard built by Native Americans but long since abandoned that has the power to bring the dead back to life. They scoff at the story, but their skepticism changes when their pet cat is killed by a passing vehicle.

The cat returns after being buried in the sacred, or perhaps cursed, ground, showing up unexpectedly. It is recognizably their pet, and at first everything seems to be all right. However, the animal's personality has changed, and not for the better. The protagonist begins to regret the impulse that led him to experiment with the burial ground, and he vows never to repeat the experiment. That resolve holds until their young son is struck and killed by a truck. The boy returns as well, even more twisted and evil, and his father realizes at last that the dead cannot really be recalled and that he needs to destroy this new false life he has caused. Unfortunately, he fails to act quickly enough, and another tragedy follows.

The novel is in many ways an elaboration of the classic story "THE MONKEY'S PAW" (1902) by W. W. Jacobs. In both a loved one is brought back from the dead through magical means, and in both

the result is a curse rather than a blessing. The notion that fate, once arrived, cannot be recalled is a common one in horror fiction, although rarely so effectively demonstrated.

"The Phantom Rickshaw" Rudyard Kipling (1902)

Rudyard Kipling wrote a fair number of fantastic stories, many of them based at least in part on his experiences in British India and his familiarity with local beliefs and legends. His most famous horror tale is this one, which is also set in India, although it is in fact a traditional European ghost story with an exotic setting.

The protagonist is Jack Pansay, who we know from the first few paragraphs has perished after an experience with ghosts. The bulk of the tale is in Pansay's own words, his account of the affliction that cost him his life. He admits from the outset that he has not led the most commendable of lives. He carried on an affair with Agnes Wessington for more than a year, after which he tired of her and became increasingly abusive despite her conviction that it was just a temporary interruption in their relationship. Agnes traveled about in a very recognizable rickshaw, drawn invariably by the same four servants. She was not the healthiest of women, and the collapse of her love affair apparently hastened her decline and eventual death.

Unperturbed by her passing, Pansay becomes engaged to another Englishwoman, Kitty, the daughter of a prominent family. They are out riding together when he first spots the phantom rickshaw, clearly the same one used by Agnes Wessington but visible only to himself. From its interior she calls to him using familiar phrases, but no one else can hear her, either. The first encounter is awkward enough, but when the rickshaw begins to appear more frequently, Pansay's behavior becomes increasingly bizarre. He is taken under a doctor's care and seems to have recovered, but the rickshaw returns when he is released. The torment this causes him leads to a break with his fiancé and a general blackening of his reputation. Ultimately, with his life ruined, Pansay ceases to struggle with his fate, resigning himself to a premature death.

Although the form is that of a traditional ghost story, Kipling tweaked the plot with considerable originality for his time. The ghosts appear in daylight as well as darkness, and they are not overtly menacing. Indeed, it appears that Agnes Wessington's spirit is still deeply in love with the man who wronged her. The concept that too fervent a love might in itself be a kind of curse may have been a reflection of a similar theme in "HOW LOVE CAME TO PROFESSOR GUILDEA" (1900) by Robert Hichens. Another innovation involves the death of the four servants, all of whom contract cholera, so that their spirits might also be present in his visions, a decidedly Eastern touch. Kipling wrote several other ghost and horror stories, but only "THE MARK OF THE BEAST" rivaled this one in quality.

Phantoms Dean R. Koontz (1983)

Dean R. KOONTZ began his career primarily writing science fiction and occasional pseudonymous thrillers. During the 1980s he completed his transition, at least in terms of marketing, to the horror genre, becoming one of the leading names along with Stephen KING, Anne RICE, and Peter STRAUB, but unlike those three, most of his "horror" novels are actually science fiction. A case in point is this, one of his very best and most suspenseful novels, which has all of the atmosphere and many of the devices of supernatural horror but which is completely rationalized.

The story opens with the discovery of a virtually abandoned town in a remote area. Although most of the residents have disappeared without a trace, apparently in the blink of an eye leaving food cooking and machinery in operation, there are remnants left behind that hint that something violent may have happened. The handful of people investigating are subjected to a series of increasingly baffling and terrifying phenomena, including the appearance of odd and malevolent forms of life, none of which seem biologically capable of existing on their own.

The truth is that the town has been visited by an ancient form of life, probably the only one of its kind on Earth, an amorphous mass that lives underground but can shape its body into a variety of forms and even detach parts of itself to act semi-independently. The creature lives by absorbing the physical bodies of other living beings, and in the process it gains their memories. Having devoured an entire town, it has suddenly gained intelligence equivalent to that of human beings and must be outwitted rather than outfought. The 1998 film version, though reasonably loyal to the story, is nevertheless disappointing.

Phillpotts, Eden (1862–1960)

Eden Phillpotts was a British writer who wrote in many different genres, including fantasy, but whose work has been undeservedly overlooked in recent years. He began writing short fantasies late in the 19th century, including *A Deal with the Devil* (1895), which unsurprisingly tells the story of an unwise pact made with Satan and its consequences.

After the turn of the century, Phillpotts wrote several fantasy novels based on Greek and Roman mythology, including *The Girl and the Faun* (1916), *Evander* (1919), *Pan and the Twins* (1922), *The Treasures of Typhon* (1924), and *Arachne* (1927). His best fantasy novel is *The Lavender Dragon* (1923), in which a knight is sent out to slay a dragon but discovers instead that the beast is actually helping people rather than preying upon them. *The Owl of Athene* (1936) also involves the Greek gods but quickly moves into unusual territory, as the gods have to deal with an invasion of Earth by giant crabs. The best of these classically inspired works are *Pan and the Twins*, in which a young Roman man becomes a worshipper of Pan and grows to maturity in a world in which the power of the gods is on the wane, and *Arachne*, which retells the story of the rivalry between Arachne and Athena, in this case based on an intellectual disagreement about the purpose of art. Phillpotts provides the story with a happier ending than in the original.

The Miniature (1926) also makes use of the Greek Gods, this time chronicling their decision to create humanity in their own image. There are some clever ideas, but much of the story is revealed in the form of lengthy dialogues that read more like philosophical essays than a work of fiction. The author's early short fantasies are collected mostly in *Fancy Free* (1901) and *Transit of the Red Dragon* (1903), and his later ones in *Peacock House and Other Mystery Stories* (1926), several of the latter being ghost stories. Phillpotts tended to write slow-paced, philosophical fantasies rather than adventure stories, which may explain his present obscurity, but at his best he was witty and posed a variety of interesting philosophical questions using fantasy elements to place them in a different perspective.

"Pickman's Model" H. P. Lovecraft (1927)

It is, of course, impossible to describe in detail a horror so terrible that it would drive a witness insane, because any such description would necessarily put constraints on the reader's imagination that would make the situation seem impossibly implausible. Writers rely on suggestion to accomplish the same thing, assuring us that were we to actually see what they are describing, our minds would break under the strain, a literary conceit that readers generally find acceptable.

H. P. LOVECRAFT illustrated that fact all too well in this, one of his best stories not set in the context of the Cthulhu Mythos, which dominated his work. The narrator is Thurber, a slightly disreputable art connoisseur who is the last personal confidant of Richard Upton Pickman, an artist who specializes in what Thurber calls "morbid" art, paintings of horrible scenes and ghoulish creatures. One such recent picture, never described, is so loathsome that Pickman is no longer invited to social functions and barely maintains his membership at his club. Pickman, who is descended from a witch who was executed in Salem, is particularly forthcoming with Thurber, who refuses to go along with the general ostracism, and shows him even more ghastly paintings of which the public is unaware.

Thurber becomes so trusted that Pickman confides in him that he has a secret studio in the Back Bay of Boston, an area honeycombed with ancient underground passageways and streets no longer recognized by city officials. There Thurber sees even more grotesque paintings, mostly of ghoulish creatures, some in their lairs, some emerging into the upper world to prey on the living. He

is appalled by the subject matter, but even so he admits to being extraordinarily impressed by Pickman's skill, particularly in the manner in which he depicts the horrid faces, so realistic that it is almost as though living creatures were imprisoned in the canvas and paint.

Even more disturbing is a kind of history of the ghoulish race that can be discerned by examining the paintings. The creatures apparently switch their own young with normal humans, which implies that the ghouls themselves are a devolved, depraved offspring of humanity. There is also a clear implication that Pickman himself is one of these changelings.

While exploring the basement studio, Pickman absents himself briefly to deal with what he claims to be an infestation of rats, although Thurber interprets the sounds of the unseen animals as being those of a much larger creature. He takes fright, absentmindedly snatches at a scrap of paper, and places it, unseen, in his pocket. It is only later that he examines it and discovers that it contains the image of one of the ghouls, but that it is not a drawing at all but a photograph, presumably of the model Pickman used to create his art.

All of the horror in the story is by implication. The ghouls never appear, nor is the protagonist ever in any real danger. Even so, the suggestion that he descended unwittingly into the lair of such obscene creatures is designed to leave the reader with a lingering sense of horror. The story became an episode of the television series *The Night Gallery*.

The Picture of Dorian Gray Oscar Wilde (1891)

The concept of the scapegoat has been with us for a long time and is found in a multitude of cultures. Oscar Wilde conceived of a new form of the scapegoat with this short novel. The title character is a handsome but spoiled man who is having his portrait painted one day when a chance visitor espouses a cynical attitude about life and suggests that hedonism, the pursuit of pleasure, should be our central preoccupation and would be if it were not for the unfortunate side effects of a life of vice and corruption. Gray immediately gives voice to the wish that the bad effects of a dissipated life should be visited upon his portrait rather than himself, and through some means never really explained, that is exactly what happens.

Gray's life becomes increasingly degenerate. He abandons his first mistress so cruelly that she kills herself, escapes vengeance at the hands of her outraged brother, and becomes increasingly disturbed by the horrible transformation evident in his portrait. Although still a determined libertine, he now suspects that he has somehow been duped into a tragic trap and avenges himself by murdering the man who first suggested that he lead the kind of life he has chosen. Ultimately, he decides to change things before it is too late and destroys the painting, but in doing so he kills himself. His body then assumes all of the repulsive features of the painting, which has itself reverted to its original state.

The novel is very unevenly written, the tone varying enormously from beginning to end, and Wilde was not clear about the moral relationship among the characters. Is Gray guilty of having chosen a life of sinfulness, or does the guilt lie with the artist who somehow imbued the painting with the power to tempt Gray away from the life he would otherwise have lived? There have been several attempts to bring the story to the screen, but the 1945 version is the most effective and is fairly faithful to the plot, although it mixes the characters somewhat. The concept of good and evil having separate existences within a single individual was repeated in THE STRANGE CASE OF DR. JEKYLL AND MR. HYDE (1896) by Robert Louis Stevenson.

Pierce, Tamora (1954–)

Almost all of Tamora Pierce's published fantasy to date has been for a young adult audience and, although not all in the same series, has the common setting of her alternate world, Tortall. She made her debut with *Alanna: The First Adventure* (1983), which introduced her main character, a teenaged girl who refuses to accept the limitations placed on her sex. Disguised as a boy, she enters a military school under an assumed name and slowly begins to win the respect of her fellow students. The ongoing effort to conceal the fact that she is female adds considerable complexity, as does her growing

ability to manipulate magic, another secret she conceals from her companions.

Still pretending to be male, she becomes the bodyguard to a prince in *In the Hand of the Goddess* (1984), although he knows her secret. *The Woman Who Rides Like a Man* (1986), the high point in the series, tests her severely when she is captured by barbarian warriors and is also torn between her growing love for two different men. Pierce does not shy away from the internal conflict as well as the physical battles her character must fight. Her romantic entanglements become even more complicated in the final volume in the series, *Lioness Rampant* (1988), but everything is eventually resolved.

Wild Magic (1992), the first book in a new sequence, has another female protagonist, this one a young woman who has a magical ability to communicate with animals, which may prove crucial to her people, who are facing a supernatural threat. She takes the animals' part in *Wolf-Speaker* (1994), becomes involved in negotiations toward peace in *Emperor Mage* (1995), and visits the gods themselves in *The Realm of the Gods* (1996). The Protector of the Small series followed, consisting of *First Test* (1999), *Page* (2000), *Squire* (2001), and *Lady Knight* (2002). Keladry is the first girl to openly begin training as a knight, and her biggest problem consists of the male students, who are determined that she will fail. The series chronicles her early career and the way in which she overcomes obstacles and wins the respect of her colleagues.

Her next series was the Circle of Magic, which includes *Sandry's Book* (1999), *Tris's Book* (1999), *Daja's Book* (2000), and *Briar's Book* (2000). The four novels chronicle a series of adventures of four young friends, each of whom has a different magical power. Their adventures continue in the Circle Opens sequence—*Magic Steps* (2001), *Street Magic* (2002), *Cold Fire* (2003), and *Shatterglass* (2004). Most recently she has begun the Daughter of the Lioness series with *Trickster's Choice* (2003) and *Trickster's Queen* (2004), in which Alanna's daughter is cast in the role of a spy.

Pierce is notable for her use of assertive, competent female characters who refuse to be limited by custom or the lowered expectations of those around them and who find fulfillment through their own accomplishments rather than from the acts of others. Her stories are quite sophisticated, and though aimed at young teens, they find a ready audience among adults as well.

"Pigeons from Hell" Robert E. Howard
(1938)

Robert E. HOWARD, the creator of Conan and some of the best weird adventure fiction in the early part of the 20th century, was primarily a writer of action stories. His protagonists rarely shrank from danger and usually triumphed over it. Although he wrote a fair number of horror stories, his were generally not the brooding, intellectual types of fellow writers such as H. P. LOVECRAFT but followed in much the same pattern as his fantasy fiction. "Pigeons from Hell," perhaps his most famous story of contemporary horror, illustrates this difference.

The protagonist is Griswell, a traveler who camps out in an apparently abandoned house with his friend, John Branner. He wakens from an unsettling dream to hear a strange whistling from the second floor, after which his companion ascends the stairs as though in a trance. A scream follows, after which Branner returns with his skull shattered by the same ax he now holds in his hand, a walking corpse whose horrible aspect drives Griswell out into the darkness. There he conveniently runs into Sheriff Buckner, who understandably finds Griswell's story suspicious. They return to the house and find Branner's now motionless body. It now appears that Griswell must be arrested for the crime. Fortunately, Buckner is both intelligent and courageous, because he uncovers contradictory evidence and attempts to investigate the second floor, retreating when he discovers that his flashlight will not work above the ground level.

The two men learn the history of the house, which was last occupied by the Blassenville sisters, several of whom disappeared mysteriously before the last fled to another part of the country. One of the missing sisters, Celia, was well known for mistreating her servants, and there were rumors of a hidden room in the house and dark magic. Buckner and Griswell consult a voodoo man, who is

promptly killed by a poisonous snake, apparently in retribution for revealing the secret of the "zuvembie," a magically altered woman who is ageless, who can command the dead to walk, and who has various other powers. They believe that one of the servants who was particularly badly treated by Celia had herself transformed so she could wreak her revenge, but when they finally track down the killer—helped by fragments of a diary that show up at an opportune moment—they discover it is Celia herself who was transformed, although against her will.

The story mixes voodoo, a haunted house, and adventure in equal doses. Good does triumph over evil, and Celia clearly deserves her horrible fate. Evil rarely triumphs in Howard's fiction, and this is no exception. The pigeons of the title are symbolic of the damned souls of the Blassenville family and are only peripherally mentioned in the story, suggesting that Howard added them simply to justify using a title he liked.

Pike, Christopher (1954–   )

The American writer Kevin McFadden began writing young adult novels during the 1980s under the name Christopher Pike and has continued to do so ever since. Many of his later titles appeared as part of the Spooksville series, which was the main competition to the Goosebumps books by R. L. STINE and is aimed at preteens, mixing very light horror with farcical humor. The Spooksville series tends to be more serious and is generally much better written than Stine's books, but it is still minor fare and does not satisfy more sophisticated readers. Among the better entries in the series, which ran to more than 20 titles, are *The Haunted Cave* (1995), *The Cold People* (1996), about the power to turn people to ice, and *The Dangerous Quest* (1998), which takes a band of children into the world beyond the mirror.

Pike's novels for teenagers are much more serious and often quite good. His first fantasy title, *Remember Me* (1989), involves time travel, a theme he used several more times. His first story of the supernatural was *The Witch* (1990), although the teenaged witch in this case is on the side of good. *Bury Me Deep* (1991) is a somewhat ambiguous story of the mystery of life after death. Pike wrote several straightforward suspense thrillers, including *The Chain Letter* (1986), but the sequel to this title, *The Ancient Evil* (1992), reveals that the villain was genuinely possessed by a demon. *The Immortal* (1993) pits a teenager against a hostile goddess.

The Last Vampire (1994) is the first volume in a series that proved very popular. A 5,000-year-old vampire poses as a teenager in order to identify a mysterious stalker at a high school. A pair of good vampires investigate a series of brutal killings in the first sequel, *Black Blood* (1994), but the government finds out about their existence and wants to study them in *Red Dice* (1995). The series ended with *Phantom* (1996), in which a female vampire becomes pregnant, with unexpected results.

Pike has also written occasional novels for adult audiences, although not as successfully. A hitchhiker picks up a woman with supernatural powers in *Sati* (1990). *The Season of Passage* (1992) is actually science fiction, although it turns out that the vampires of legend are real; they just happen to live on Mars. *The Cold One* (1995) is the best of his adult horror novels, the story of a beast whose very existence is inimical to humanity. An experiment in mental projection attracts the attention of a supernatural creature in *The Listeners* (1995).

After several years of inactivity, Pike has returned to writing both for adults and for teenagers. *The Blind Mirror* (2003) is a competent but somewhat routine story of demonic activity and murder. In *Alosha* (2004) a teenager discovers that she is fated to be the next queen of the fairies. Pike has always been a considerably better writer than most of the others working in young adult literature, although he has been less successful writing adult fiction. It is too early to determine whether he will yet master the transition.

Pinocchio Carlo Collodi (1881)

There are a handful of children's novels that have become so familiar over the course of time, particularly those that have resulted in one or more motion pictures, that the basic plot elements have become part of our general culture, although often in a form slightly different than that of the original

story. In some cases the original books are read by only a small portion of those who have seen the film version, as is the case with J. M. BARRIE'S PETER PAN (1904) and Carlo Collodi's *Pinocchio*. Collodi was the pseudonym of the Italian writer Carlo Lorenzini, who wrote several other children's fantasies, although none of his other titles has remained popular.

The central human character is Gepetto, a kindly old man who fashions Pinocchio as a puppet and somehow imbues his creation with animation. Pinocchio is childish, but not the clumsy, basically good-natured character in the Disney film. He is troublesome, mean spirited, self-centered, and prone to cruel jokes. It is only over the course of time, when he begins to realize that he is less fortunate than living children and wants to become one, that he slowly learns his lesson. Pinocchio has a variety of adventures in the book, visiting the land of the fairies and other mystical places, escaping after a chase by assassins, and even spending a short time in prison. Ultimately, he redeems himself and even saves Gepetto's life at one point, and the transition to humanity is justified once he has seen the error of his ways.

The Disney film version is also noteworthy for the enhanced use of the character Jiminy Cricket, who became nearly as popular as Pinocchio himself, for the nasty villain Stromboli, and for the famous scene in which the puppet boy's nose grows longer each time he tells an untruth about himself. Clever as it is, some of the punch of the original morality tale was lost during the translation.

Poe, Edgar Allan (1809–1849)

The American writer Edgar Allan Poe was born to wealth. He was educated in England but soon broke with his family and was forced to support himself, which he did in part through his writing. His short but productive career as a writer of prose and poetry had a significant effect on the evolution of short fiction and detective and horror fiction in particular, and on poetry and even science fiction to a lesser extent. He was one of the first writers to emphasize the psychological component of horror, and many of his characters clearly suffer from paranoia and other mental illnesses.

Poe's first published story was "Metzengerstein" (1832), the story of a family rivalry that reaches a critical point of violence, after which a demonic horse appears. Probably the most famous of Poe's horror stories is "The Pit and the Pendulum," which contains no fantastic elements at all and is not even a true story but rather a description of a series of mental tortures followed by a tacked on rescue. He was at his best in "THE FALL OF THE HOUSE OF USHER" (1839), in which a brother and sister are caught in a psychological trap that will eventually doom them both. Another excellent psychological tale is "The Black Cat" (1845), wherein a man murders his wife but inadvertently walls up the family cat when he attempts to conceal the body. The story is generally interpreted to mean that he did so deliberately, if unconsciously, in response to his feelings of guilt. "WILLIAM WILSON" is also one of his most sophisticated stories. The protagonist lives a dissipated life until the mysterious advent of an apparent doppelgänger who exposes his activities but who might actually be his own alter ego.

"The Facts in the Case of M. Valdemar" (1845) involves a man who dies while in a hypnotic trance. The trance state allows him to continue to speak even after death, and he expounds upon the need to experience adversity in order to appreciate pleasure. When finally released, Valdemar immediately subsides into a puddle of corruption. A group of nobles lock themselves in a castle to keep out the plague that is ravaging the countryside in "The Masque of the Red Death" (1842), but the figure that appears at their costume ball is not a welcome guest after all but the personification of the disease they had hoped to avoid. "Morella" (1835) is a story of reincarnation. A strong-willed woman of that name dies, leaving behind her unnamed daughter, who is nearly grown before she recognizes that she is also Morella and promptly dies. Her mother's grave proves to be empty. A similar situation arises in "LIGEIA" (1838), wherein another indomitable woman returns from the grave to supplant the personality of her husband's second wife.

There is a ghost ship of sorts in "Ms Found in a Bottle" (1833). "The Murders in the Rue Morgue," though often included in horror anthologies, is a detective story. Most of Poe's remaining fantastic fiction is minor. "The Devil in the Belfry" (1839) is a mildly humorous story about the appearance of the devil in a small village. The devil also appears in "Never Bet the Devil Your Head" (1841) and in "Bon-Bon" (1832), in the latter case to discuss philosophy, and a demon does likewise in "Silence—A Fable" (1838). Another conversation takes place between supernatural entities in outer space in "Conversation of Einos and Charmion" (1839), and still another with a dead Egyptian in "Some Words with a Mummy" (1845). "Mesmeric Revelation" (1844) was an early treatment of "The Facts in the Case of M. Valdemar." "Eleanora" (1842) is a gentle ghost story.

Many of Poe's stories have been brought to the screen, although often in a form the author might not have recognized. His marginal tales are only curiosities now, but his best work still holds up well and is constantly reprinted. Although all of his fiction can be collected in a single volume, it has been shuffled and arranged in more than 100 separate collections under various titles since it first appeared. Poe also wrote a number of macabre poems, of which "The Raven" is the most famous. He is acknowledged as a classic American writer by mainstream as well as genre critics.

"The Pomegranate Seed" Edith Wharton (1931)

Edith Wharton is best known for her mainstream novels, but she was also the author of a small but highly respected body of short supernatural stories, most involving ghosts, of which this subtle, soft-spoken story is an excellent example. Charlotte and Kenneth Ashby are happily married, her first and his second marriage following the death of his first wife. They are relatively well-off, though not rich; they employ servants, but cannot afford to move to a larger home or to redecorate their present apartment. Kenneth regrets this because Charlotte has no choice but to accept the design of her predecessor, but Charlotte is content and does not feel threatened by his memories of a lost love. She accepts that he will always miss his first wife but knows that he loves her truly.

Everything seems ideal except for one very minor detail. From time to time she finds a letter in the mail, always addressed to her husband, written in the same handwriting, and never bearing a postal stamp. On each occasion he opens the letter in private, then secretes himself away for a while, emerging slightly irritable, although he quickly recovers. It seems at first a small thing, but as time passes and the incidents continue, they begin to worry her. Eventually, she arranges things so that she can watch Kenneth's reaction when he opens the next letter, and she is shocked when he kisses the letter before putting it away.

Although she never doubts his faithfulness, she suspects the existence of a rival and confronts him. Kenneth refuses to say anything about the letters, and the situation escalates to a confrontation and eventually an ultimatum. She finds other things to complain about as well, including the fact that they have not taken a trip since their honeymoon. Kenneth is obstinate at first but eventually agrees to a short vacation. Most readers will have concluded by now that the letters are from his dead wife, which proves to be the case, although Wharton sidesteps the usual melodrama. Kenneth disappears mysteriously, prompting Charlotte to open one of the letters, for even she is now beginning to suspect the truth. However, the letter is unreadable, nearly blank pages with only hints of words written on them in a handwriting so faint that it could only be interpreted by someone who had a long and intimate familiarity with it, someone such as Kenneth.

Wharton skillfully avoids the clichés of the form. There is no violence in the story and no overt horror, and the ghost never actually puts in an appearance. It is nonetheless suspenseful and engrossing and introduces us to a pair of complex characters caught up in an extraordinary and stressful situation. Kenneth's conflicting loyalties place him in an impossible situation, and Charlotte's well-intended efforts to strengthen their relationship actually weaken it. Wharton demonstrates effectively that love can be a destructive force even when it is intended to be otherwise.

"The Pond" Nigel Kneale (1949)

The British writer Nigel Kneale is best known outside Great Britain for his screenplays for the popular series of science fiction films produced for the BBC featuring Quatermass, a senior scientist who overcomes various threats to the world. Kneale also wrote a number of short horror stories, many of them relying entirely on psychological suspense and a few involving elements of the fantastic. The best-known of these is this very short story of supernatural revenge.

The unnamed protagonist is first seen lurking near a small pond where he uses various techniques to lure out the local frogs. He captures the very last frog and takes it back to his hut, where he kills it and prepares it for stuffing to add to his collection. All the other frogs have been posed in human positions with historical costumes in an elaborate stage setting, and this final member is designed to be the star of it all. Kneale describes the process of taxidermy in considerable detail, and the cutting of flesh and breaking of bones become more than just a clinical description but actually a horrible, inhuman procedure.

After darkness falls he is disturbed by the sound of croaking, apparently caused by a fresh influx of frogs to the nearby pond. Intrigued, he sets aside his work and goes to investigate, although the sounds cease entirely when he reaches the edge of the water. He catches a whiff of some noxious odor and is about to leave when he is overcome by the fumes and falls. The scene and viewpoint abruptly switch to the following morning, when a police officer visits the scene, finding the abandoned hut with a fire still burning. He follows the path to the lake and sees what he thinks is the taxidermist crouching naked, but when he moves closer he discovers that the man has been stuffed, preserved, and posed in the position of an oversized frog.

Kneale tells the story quickly and pointedly. If it were any longer, readers would too readily anticipate the ending. Supernatural fiction is often based on the principle of balance—good vs. evil, one debt against another, powers granted but with unpleasant catches. In this case the evil the protagonist inflicted upon the natural world is revisited upon him in like manner.

Powers, Tim (1952–)

After an impressive start writing science fiction, Tim Powers turned to fantasy for his third novel,

The Drawing of the Dark (1979), and most of his subsequent fiction has fallen into that category. The protagonist of his first fantasy tale is ostensibly a bouncer at a tavern but is actually the current incarnation of King Arthur, who is continuing his mission to protect a mystical ruler. The novel marked Powers as a writer to watch, and it was not long before he lived up to the promise. *The Anubis Gates* (1983) is a historical fantasy involving a time traveler who finds himself battling a variety of villains, including one who rules an immense underground kingdom and uses sorcery against his enemies. The blend of traditional and original fantasy elements distinguished this novel from mainstream fantasy without being so strange that readers could not identify with it.

After returning to science fiction briefly, Powers next wrote *On Stranger Tides* (1987), set in the Caribbean during the days of pirates and treasure ships. An accountant finds himself pursuing a new career as a buccaneer, but the pirates he meets are not of the ordinary variety. One is using black magic to advance his aims, including voodoo incantations that give him control of a small army of zombies. More overtly adventurous than most of Powers's other fiction, it is more suspenseful as well. Powers's drift toward the supernatural became even more evident in *The Stress of Her Regard* (1989). As with his other novels, there are major historical figures as characters, this time Lord Byron , Keats, and Shelley, who have taken as their muses a race of vampirelike creatures. When they finally break away and try to continue on their own, they discover that they lack the inspiration to do so.

Powers turned away from historical settings during the 1990s, or at least moved closer to the present. *The Last Call* (1992), which won the World Fantasy Award, is set in an alternate Las Vegas that has been magically transformed after the death of the gangster Bugsy Siegel. The chief protagonist is a gambler who feels he has lost his soul and sets out to recover it. *Expiration Date* (1995) similarly presents an altered Los Angeles. A young boy assimilates the spirit of Thomas Edison and finds himself pursued by others who seek Edison's vitality. Powers invented an entirely new legend of ghosts and possession and transports the reader into a world that is tantalizingly familiar but always a bit skewed. *Earthquake Weather* (1996) is a sequel to both of the previous novels, drawing their threads together as another ghostly possession leads to murder and the brink of yet another magical transformation.

Powers's most recent novel is *Declare* (2001), which alternates between 1960 and the 1940s. The protagonist is a British spy who was involved in a project to destroy a colony of powerful supernatural djinn who lived on Mount Ararat. The first attempt failed, but 20 years later the authorities wish to try again. The novel is complex and involves very intense action, and as always it includes a few historical characters, most notably the spy Kim Philby. It won Powers his second World Fantasy Award. Although Powers rarely writes short fiction, it is almost always worthwhile. Most of his short fantasy can be found in *Night Moves and Other Stories* (2001).

Pratchett, Terry (1948–)

Terry Pratchett's first fantasy novel, *The Carpet People* (1971), is a children's fantasy set in a magical world contained within an otherwise ordinary carpet. He tried science fiction next, but his third novel, *Strata* (1981), is set on another planet where dragons and robots intermingle. That set the stage for *The Colour of Magic* (1983), the first of the DISCWORLD SERIES, which has made up the greatest part of Pratchett's fiction ever since. The Discworld books, which are immensely popular in England and made him that country's single best-selling writer, are set in a magical world that is flat and peopled with a variety of wizards, witches, and other fantastic characters. The books are loosely organized into separate, occasionally overlapping, series, and are marketed primarily for adults, although their wacky humor is equally appealing to younger readers. Some of the more recent titles in the series have been targeted specifically at children. They rely heavily on puns, coincidences, farcical situations, magic spells gone awry, and good intentions gone bad. The villains are villainous, but only to a point, and the heroes are often less than heroic, although they usually try very hard to succeed.

Pratchett also wrote a short series about tiny people known as Nomes. They are introduced in *Truckers* (1990), where we discover that they live hidden in a department store, although their secret is in jeopardy and they may have to move. The Nomes series resembles the BORROWERS SERIES by Mary Norton or the Littles books by John Peterson. They move to a quarry in *Diggers* (1991), but winter catches them by surprise since they have never been exposed to snow before. In *Wings* (1991) they decide to try to emigrate to another planet.

Pratchett also collaborated with Neil GAIMAN for one novel, *Good Omens* (1990), a spoof of the film and book THE OMEN and its various imitators. The devil conceives a son and sends him to be raised on Earth, but the forces of evil lose track of where he is. Raised by a family of very good people, he is not at all what his father expected. Given the success of the Discworld books, which have also led to companion guides, calendars, and other items, it is unlikely that Pratchett will stray too far from that world in the future. He has managed to keep the concept reasonably fresh by moving from one set of characters to another and to different parts of his imaginary world, and to date at least the freshness of the humor has been generally quite dependable.

"Pretty Maggie Moneyeyes" Harlan Ellison (1967)

Kostner is a desperate man who had hoped to alter his situation by winning big in Las Vegas but who instead finds himself down to his last silver dollar. He decides to risk it in the only machine in the casino that takes that particular coin and is surprised when he wins the jackpot of $2,000 and even more surprised because it was not jackpot bars that he saw but very blue eyes that disappeared only when other people arrived on the scene. He takes his winnings and then returns to play another dollar, with the exact same results, much to the consternation of the floor manager. It is only then that his thoughts are touched by those of Margaret Jessie, better known as Maggie.

Maggie grew up grindingly poor and became hardened, determined to escape poverty. She was a flashy, attractive woman who hustles money however she can get it, with sex or guile. She was visiting Las Vegas with her less-than-appealing boyfriend when she impulsively began playing the very same machine and suffered a fatal stroke as she was pulling the lever. Maggie was so immersed in the desire for money that her spirit literally passed into the machine, where it has been waiting for a suitable soul to turn up. Still unsure whether or not this is real, he plays a third time and wins his third jackpot.

By the time he has won his 19th jackpot, the casino management is decidedly unhappy with him, although their own experts assure them that he is not cheating in any way. Only Kostner knows what is really happening, and he is not about to tell, even if he thought anyone would believe him. After all, he really needs the money. The casino suggests that he take a break and offers him a room for the night, and he falls into an exhausted sleep in which Maggie comes to him in a dream professing love. But the following morning, when he plays the machine again for the first time, she strikes through it, killing him and imprisoning him inside the machine. Ellison had warned us that she was a hard, bitter woman, and now he reveals the inevitable consequences.

The story illustrates some of the forces that keep us separate from one another, and on another level it is also a low-key indictment of the lifestyle found in Las Vegas, the constant quest for easy money, and the desire for easy solutions to complicated problems.

"Prey" Richard Matheson (1969)

Richard MATHESON has written for television and the movies so extensively that it should come as no surprise that most of his stories evoke very sharp images. He has also produced some of the most intensely suspenseful stories in the field, classics such as "Duel" and "LITTLE GIRL LOST." This particular story made up one of the segments of the film *Trilogy of Terror* (1975).

Amelia is a young woman living alone, mildly estranged from her dominating mother, who has recently purchased an elaborate doll for her new boyfriend. The doll is an African warrior with a fierce expression and a miniature spear, and the enclosed gift card indicates that he is a hunting fetish with a warrior's spirit trapped inside. Caught in an emotional struggle between her boyfriend and her mother, Amelia tries to calm herself, but in the process accidentally releases the bond that imprisons the warrior spirit. When she looks for the fetish again, it is missing.

A knife disappears from the kitchen, there are strange noises in the apartment, and one of the lights goes off mysteriously. The reader will be well ahead of Amelia by now, who does not recognize the truth even when something begins stabbing her in the calves and ankles, driving her from one room to another. She finally accepts the truth only when she is barricaded in the bathroom trying to stanch the flow of blood from her various wounds. Although she temporarily traps the doll in a suitcase, the security bolt for her apartment door has been damaged and will not open, so she remains trapped. After a number of additional upsets, she finally maneuvers the fetish into the oven, where she burns it to ash.

Just as the reader believes the storm has passed, Matheson changes everything. The spirit of the warrior has finally been driven from the fetish, but now it is lodged in Amelia's body. Amelia calls her mother, invites her over, then picks up a knife to wait for her prey. "Prey" is a pure horror story with no lofty ambitions other than to entertain and perhaps surprise the reader. Matheson's considerable talents for painting a scene of intense action have rarely been displayed as fully.

Prince Caspian C. S. Lewis (1951)

The second volume of the CHRONICLES OF NARNIA by C. S. LEWIS returns the four Pevensie children to that magical realm from our world. Although they remember growing to adulthood when they ruled Narnia, their childhood personalities were apparently restored along with their bodies when their previous adventure ended. Since time runs differently on the two planes, centuries have passed in Narnia, and the castle where they ruled is now an abandoned ruin. The descendants of a band of human pirates, known as Telmarines, have founded a kingdom that has now conquered Narnia. Prince Caspian is the rightful heir to the throne, which has been usurped by Miraz, his

uncle. Miraz originally designates Caspian as his heir, but when the queen becomes pregnant he decides to murder his nephew instead.

The children find Narnia much changed. Most of the animals have lost the power of speech. Those who can still speak have been hunted to near extinction, although when the half-dwarf Doctor Cornelius urges Caspian to flee, he stumbles across a community of them almost immediately. He and the children have a series of adventures, separately at first, while the original inhabitants of Narnia become divided over what the best course might be for them to follow. Some wish to summon Aslan, the mystical lion who saved them in the past, while others prefer the White Witch, who they deem more powerful. Since Aslan is a transparent Christ figure, the Witch is clearly evil personified, and the quarrel has the expected outcome, although only after considerable violence.

Lewis is somewhat inconsistent about the children's status. When one of them challenges Miraz to single combat, he is accepted as a knight despite his age—and, in fact, nearly defeats the usurper, who is eventually betrayed and killed by his own forces. Caspian eventually wins the throne, the talking animals are freed from persecution, Aslan moves behind the scenes, and the villains are all disposed of in proper fashion. *Prince Caspian* is much more cohesive than the first Narnia book, THE LION, THE WITCH, AND THE WARDROBE, although the setting still contains some minor inconsistencies.

The Princess Bride William Goldman (1973)

Only a very talented writer could produce a self-evident spoof of a genre that itself becomes a genre classic. William Goldman, who leaned toward supernatural horror in *Magic* (1976) and who used quasi-rationalized fantastic elements in *Control* (1982) and *Brothers* (1986), adopted many of the elements of popular mainstream fantasy in *The Princess Bride*, but exaggerated them. He interlaces the serious elements in the plot with so much wry humor that the reader knows better than to take the story too seriously. At the same time, his characters are so appealing that we do care what happens to them.

The basis of the story is a love affair. The hero is Westley, a poor boy who falls in love with a beautiful girl and she, Buttercup, with him, though neither admits it. She at least perhaps does not recognize the truth until later in the story. The boy sails off to make his fortune and is captured and reportedly killed by pirates, after which the girl mourns for many years before reluctantly agreeing to marry the local ruler, Prince Humperdinck. His plans are more nefarious, however. He plots her abduction and death even before they are married, hoping to use this as an excuse to launch an expansionist war against an otherwise peaceful neighbor.

To carry out his plan, Humperdinck has hired three dubious characters—Fezzik, reportedly the strongest man in the world, Inigo, the world's greatest swordsman, and Vizzini, who believes himself the most intelligent man alive. They successfully carry off Buttercup, but a mysterious figure follows, defeating each of them in turn and each in their own specialty. Rescued, Buttercup recognizes him as Westley, who has taken over the identity of the now-retired pirate who captured him, and who initially spurns her, believing her to have been disloyal to his memory. Humperdinck captures them both and seems on the verge of victory when two of his former adversaries free Westley and help save the day.

The captive-turned-pirate, the forced marriage, the series of trials Westley undergoes, and other plot elements would have seemed overly familiar by a less-skilled hand, but Goldman's light, amusing treatment makes them fresh and interesting. *The Princess Bride* is a fairy tale for modern readers. The 1987 film version was from Goldman's own screenplay and is, unsurprisingly, very loyal to the original book.

Pullman, Philip (1946–)

Philip Pullman's early novels during the 1970s and 1980s were a mixture of mainstream and often vaguely fantastic elements, although the only clear fantasy title is *Count Karlstein* (1982), a children's book in which a great hunt is conducted at the instigation of a demon. Most of his other novels from this period were young adult suspense stories set during the 19th century, many of which hinted at without being explicit about darker, magical undertones. *Spring Heeled Jack* (1989) came the closest to being fantasy and hinted at the complexity that would become evident with the His Dark Materials trilogy, which was loosely patterned after the works of John Milton.

The trilogy opened with THE GOLDEN COMPASS (1995, also published as *The Northern Lights*). The initial setting is an alternate version of contemporary England, a magical variant reality where every child is paired with a shape-shifting demon that will not assume its final form until its partner reaches maturity, at which point its appearance is dictated by the character of the other. The cast of very well-realized characters is expanded and developed in THE SUBTLE KNIFE (1997) and the concluding volume, THE AMBER SPYGLASS (2000), but only after a series of adventures, quests fulfilled, betrayals, revelations, encounters with ghosts, and other adventures. The trilogy is unusually complex stylistically for young adult literature but was enormously successful nonetheless. "Lyra's Oxford" (2003), published as a chapbook, is related to the trilogy.

Pullman's most recent fantasy novel is considerably less ambitious. *I Was a Rat* (2002) is about a young boy who insists that he has spent part of his life as a rat. Pullman has also written occasional short fantasy fiction and an adaptation of Mary SHELLEY'S FRANKENSTEIN (1818) for the stage. The dramatic success of His Dark Materials has raised expectations for Pullman's subsequent work. To date he seems content to produce lighter fantastic fare, although his nonfantastic Sally Lockhart trilogy, set in the slums of 19th-century London, is a superior young adult mystery sequence.

Q

Quinn, Seabury (1889–1969)

Seabury Quinn was a prolific contributor to the pulp magazines during the 1920s and 1930s, producing scores of short stories for the weird- and occult-oriented magazines. His prose is colorful but simple, his plots are straightforward, and many of his stories seem written to a specific formula. A very large number of these feature Jules de Grandin, a typical occult detective who invariably solves the case, thwarting various mundane and supernatural villains. Quinn's first book appearance was a short novel, *Roads* (1938), which appeared in a limited edition that was reprinted in 1948 and which is a convoluted but inventive story of the origin of Santa Claus. A Viking warrior who becomes immortal is present at the Crucifixion and is eventually magically transformed into a symbol of Christmas. It is not typical of the bulk of his work and is actually more imaginative than most of his supernatural fiction.

The first collection of Jules de Grandin stories was *The Phantom Fighter* (1966), published only a few years before the author's death. The rest of his books appeared posthumously and include the general collection *Is the Devil a Gentleman?* (1970), five volumes of de Grandin short stories, and Quinn's only full-length novel, *The Devil's Bride* (1976, from the 1932 magazine version), which also features the occult investigator. The more recent *Night Creatures* (2003) also assembles nonseries stories.

De Grandin first appeared in "Terror on the Links" (1925), which involves a rather silly plot about the transformation of humans into beasts. He went on to defeat the usual array of supernatural entities, zombies, werewolves, ghosts, and vampires. The vampire in "Restless Souls" (1928) is one of his more interesting opponents, as is the giant snake in "The Tenants of Broussac" (1925). "The Curse of Evarard Maundy" (1928) describes an encounter with a disembodied elemental, and there is a particularly malevolent witch in "Daughter of the Moonlight" (1930). Several of the other stories in the series contain no supernatural elements at all, and the novel, *The Devil's Bride*, though supernatural, verges on the incoherent and is inferior to most of the short fiction.

Of his nonseries stories, "Is the Devil a Gentleman?" (1942) is probably the most interesting, a story of intervention from beyond the grave that raises some interesting moral questions. "The Globe of Memories" (1937) anticipates the current popularity of time travel romances. "The Gentle Werewolf" (1940) is an interesting nonhorrific werewolf story. Although Quinn never produced a single distinguished work, his creation of Jules de Grandin and the success of that character contributed to the popularity of occult detectives, and the collections issued during the 1970s have become collectors' items.

R

Radford, Irene (1944–)

Irene Radford is the pseudonym of Phyllis Ann Karr, who wrote fantasy under that name from 1974 to 1986 and sporadically since, although most of her fantasy fiction since 1994 has been as Radford. After a small number of short stories, Karr published two connected novels, *Frostflower and Thorn* (1980) and *Frostflower and Windbourne* (1982), which feature a sorceress and a warrior who have various adventures, completing a quest in the first and solving a mystery in the second volume. Karr, who is an authority on the subject of King Arthur and Camelot, next turned to that setting for a blend of fantasy and detective fiction in *Idylls of the Queen* (1982), in which Guinevere is framed for a murder. *Wildraith's Last Battle* (1982) resembles the Frostflower novels and is traditional sword and sorcery, but *At Amberleaf Fair* (1986) is another detective story, this one featuring a recurring character from her short fiction, Torin the Toymaker, who must solve the crime in order to prove his own innocence.

From 1986 forward Karr used her own name primarily for Arthurian works such as *The Follies of Sir Harald* (2001), the humorous story of a minor knight at Camelot, and occasional short stories, of which "Babbitt's Daughters" (1995) and "Cold Stake" (1991), a vampire story, are the most interesting. After a gap of several years Karr returned to novels, with the first under the Irene Radford name, *The Glass Dragon* (1994), which began the Dragon Nimbus series. In the opening volume a wizard investigates the mysterious deaths of most of the dragons in the world, a disaster because in their absence magic will not work. The story continues in *The Perfect Princess* (1995) and comes to a temporary conclusion in *The Loneliest Magician* (1996), culminating with the return of the dragons just in time to alter the balance of power and defeat the villains. The series resumed for another series consisting of *The Dragon's Touchstone* (1997), *The Last Battlemage* (1998), *The Renegade Dragon* (1999), and *The Wizard's Treasure* (2000). The story line is very similar, but the story is told on a much broader scale.

The most interesting work to appear under Radford's name is the Merlin's Descendants series, which is obviously influenced by the author's interest in Arthurian history. The premise is that the children of Merlin for generations have had a sacred role in protecting the world from evil. The sequence opens with *Guardian of the Balance* (1999), in which Merlin's daughter realizes her destiny. In *Guardian of the Trust* (2000) two later descendants must use their magical talents to oppose an aristocratic troublemaker with a demon in his ancestry, and in *Guardian of the Vision* (2001) another generation questions its duties and almost falls prey to demonic mischief. Elizabethan werewolves provide the menace in *Guardian of the Promise* (2003), the best in the series to date. One additional title, *Guardian of the Freedom*, was published in 2005.

Karr is also the author of the nonfiction book *The King Arthur Companion* (1983) and completed the unfinished Jane Austen novel *Lady Susan* (1980). Although much of her later work has been more conventional than her earlier efforts, they are more technically polished, and the Merlin's Descendants series in particular is evidence that she is capable of producing significant and worthwhile fiction.

"The Raft"   Stephen King (1982)

Sometimes the best horror and suspense stories are the ones that employ the simplest of concepts. That is certainly the case with this early thriller by Stephen KING, in which four young people find themselves trapped on a raft in the middle of a pretty little pond, isolated from outside contact and unable to escape because of an amorphous but deadly form of life living in the water.

The story opens with the introduction of four college students, two male and two female. Deke is an obvious jock, while Randy is less outgoing, less physically intimidating, and mildly jealous because of the way his date is watching his friend. They are the only ones in the area because it is really too cold for swimming, and, in fact, Randy has some misgivings but is unable to dissuade his companions. Shortly after arriving Randy notices a dark patch in the water, something like an oil slick, and thinks it may have moved toward them deliberately, but he dismisses the thought when he reaches the raft in the center of the pond and climbs up into the cool air. His fears return when he sees the object moving toward Laverne and Rachel, and he almost panics before they have safely arrived at the raft.

Although they appear to be safe now that they are out of the water, Rachel becomes fascinated by some unexplained hypnotic quality radiating from the creature, reaches toward it, and is caught and engulfed by its flesh-dissolving properties. Rachel dies, and the rest react in shock or panic even before they realize that they are trapped. Time passes as the blob investigates the raft, finally reaching up between two segments to touch Deke's foot and eventually kill him. In similar fashion it later claims Laverne, and only Randy lives long enough to see the dawn. But even though he can see the shoreline, where he would be safe, there is no way he can reach it, and the story ends with him finally surrendering to the creature. "The Raft" became

one segment of the motion picture *Creepshow 2* (1987), with a more satisfying though just as downbeat ending.

Rankin, Robert (1949–)

Robert Rankin's unique style of humor moves freely, almost chaotically, from science fiction to fantasy to supernatural, so that labeling his fiction as one or the other is sometimes futile. Although there is a distinctly British tone to his novels, there is little to unify them in the way that Terry PRATCHETT has done with his own work, for example. Most of Rankin's novels are set in our world, but a distinctly skewed version that is only sometimes recognizable.

His first success came with the Brentford Trilogy, consisting of *The Antipope* (1981), *The Brentford Triangle* (1982), and *East of Ealing* (1984). The opening volume introduces us to the Brentford area and its strange characters, jumps around in time a bit, and presents us with a problem involving magic beans. The middle volume is more science fiction than fantasy, involving possible aliens on Earth, and by the concluding volume it is obvious that the prophecies of Revelation are taking place in Brentford, although not quite in the fashion expected. He returned to that setting with *The Sprouts of Wrath* (1988) and later with *Nostradamus Ate My Hamster* (1996) and *The Brentford Chainstore Massacre* (1997), in the latter of which a genetic expert clones a number of copies of Jesus Christ so that he can hand them out to various religions. Another spoof of religion, *The Suburban Book of the Dead* (1993) and *A Dog Called Demolition* (1996), about a talking dog, are less successful, but *The Garden of Unearthly Delights* (1996), in which science and reason are replaced by myth and magic, is often side-splittingly funny.

Demons attempt to take over the world in *Waiting for Godalming* (2001) but find themselves confused into submission. *The Hollow Chocolate Bunnies of the Apocalypse* (2002) is set in Toy Town, the place where toys come to life, but there is a serial killer on the loose, though not one to be taken too seriously. *The Witches of Chiswick* (2003), Rankin's funniest book, postulates that a group of witches have used magic to rewrite history and that many of the adventures we read about in fiction actually happened but were magically erased. The sequel, *Knees Up Mother Earth* (2004) invokes Lovecraftian monsters, but only in order to lampoon them. Rankin's other novels are technically science fiction, but they make use of the same zany viewpoints and far-fetched events as does his fantasy.

"Rappaccini's Daughter" Nathaniel Hawthorne (1844)

Nathaniel Hawthorne is generally remembered for his classic novels such as *The Scarlet Letter* (1850) and *The House of the Seven Gables* (1851), which, though not supernatural, have very grim undertones and explore the darker side of human nature in some detail. Hawthorne exhibited the same tendency in his short fiction, much of which has fantastic content, and the best of which is this one, set some time in the days before Italy became a cohesive nation-state. Giovanni is a young student recently moved to Padua whose room overlooks a verdant but unusual garden tended by his neighbor, Dr. Rappaccini. Rappaccini treats the plants as though they were dangerous creatures, but his lovely daughter Beatrice seems perfectly at ease with them.

A discreet inquiry turns up disturbing information. Rappaccini is acknowledged as a skilled physician and scientist but disliked because of his attitude that the experiment is more important than the subject and because he concentrates on the theory that all cures can be derived from one poison or another. Giovanni is also bothered by Beatrice's apparent immunity to the poisonous plants and eventually by the discovery that her body has somehow become sympathetic to them, acting as a fatal poison to insects and small animals simply by being near them. Despite these signs, he becomes infatuated with her and eventually manages to find a hidden entrance to her garden.

Another scientist, a friend of the family, grows worried when it becomes obvious that Giovanni is in danger. He comes to the young man with a vial containing an antidote that, he thinks, might provide a cure for Beatrice so that she can live nor-

mally among humans once again. Before he can try to help her, he discovers that he, too, has become transformed and that his presence is already poisonous to insects. Outraged, he explodes at Beatrice, berating her cruelly. Calming, he reveals the existence of the antidote, but Beatrice has been so altered that by consuming it, she brings about her own death. In a very real sense, the interference by the outsider was at least as destructive as Rappaccini's own immoral experimentation.

Rawn, Melanie (1954–)

Melanie Rawn is the pseudonym of Ellen Randolph, who has written some nonfantastic fiction under her own name. The Rawn byline first appeared with *Dragon Prince* (1988), a standard though lengthy and detailed mainstream fantasy in which a newly crowned king and his witch wife attempt to unite the various factions of his people behind him. A treacherous noble tries to usurp the throne but is dealt with in the usual fashion. The crown does not rest easy, however, as a conspiracy of sorcerers attempt to displace the king in the sequel, *The Star Scroll* (1988). All of the various conflicts are brought to a head in *Sunrunner's Fire* (1990), the catalyst for victory being the enlistment of a number of dragons on the side of good.

Rawn immediately followed up with a second trilogy set in the same magical universe. The Dragon Star series opens with *Stronghold* (1990), pitting the crown against external enemies this time, an invading army that would be formidable even if it were not helped along by powerful evil sorcery. The situation continues to deteriorate in *The Dragon Token* (1992), with the earlier enemies among the aristocracy allying themselves with the invaders in order to settle old scores. Factions continue to realign themselves in *Skybowl* (1993), ultimately configuring themselves in such a way that the intruders can be repelled and order restored, although only after devastating losses.

Rawn began her third trilogy, the Exiles, with *The Ruins of Ambrai* (1994). All of the humans who were capable of performing magic emigrated from Earth to another world. A war breaks out soon thereafter, and their culture is splintered into a variety of factions. The story continues *in The*

Mageborn Traitor (1997), in which war threatens to erupt again along the lines of two very different schools of magic. The third title in the series, *The Captal's Tower*, has been promised on and off ever since and is now scheduled to appear in 2005. Rawn's remaining novel, *The Golden Key* (1997), written in collaboration with Jennifer ROBERSON and Kate ELLIOTT, is the story of a family of magic practitioners whose tranquility is disturbed by a love affair. Rawn remains a potentially significant figure in the fantasy genre despite her inactivity and may regain her former prominence if her reported intention to return to fantasy is fulfilled.

Reichert, Mickey Zucker (1962–)

Mickey Zucker Reichert made her debut with *Godslayer* (1987), the first in the Bifrost Guardians series, a Norse-derived fantasy that proved to be typical of much of her subsequent work. A Vietnam era soldier is snatched into a world where the Viking gods rule, placed into the body of an elf, and charged with defeating Loki and his allies, which task he eventually accomplishes, at least in part. The focus turns to a professional thief in *Shadow Climber* (1988), and he and his companion defeat and kill Loki, which forces them to seek magical assistance to protect them from the power of Hel, a goddess, in *Dragonrank Master* (1989). The satisfyingly climactic battle comes in *Shadows Realm* (1990), and the hero is returned to his original world in *By Chaos Cursed* (1991), only to discover that he no longer feels at home in a universe without magic.

The Last of the Renshai (1992) started a new series, set in a magical realm on the brink of a war so devastating that the gods themselves may not survive it. The Renshai are a famous warrior race, virtually extinct, and the protagonist is the outsider, a single Renshai whose existence could have enormous implications. Four powerful wizards attempt to maintain order, but one of them dies in *The Western Wizard* (1992), further destabilizing the situation. His replacement tries to restore the balance in *Child of Thunder* (1993), but Ragnarok, the ultimate battle, takes place anyway. Fortunately, the world survives, as we discover in *Beyond Ragnarok* (1995), but fresh troubles ensue including universal sterility in the final volumes *Prince of Demons* (1996) and *Children of Wrath* (1998).

Reichert had also written the apparent standalone novel *The Legend of Nightfall*, in 1993, the considerably less panoramic story of a likeable thief engaged in a dangerous quest. She revived the character for a sequel, *The Return of Nightfall* (2004), in which his new role as adviser to the king takes on a greater significance when the king vanishes. *The Flightless Falcon* (2000) is a less interesting blend of detective story and quest. The Barakhai duo, set in a world where animals speak and a despotic ruler represses them as well as humans, consists of *The Beasts of Barakhai* (2001) and *The Lost Dragons of Barakhai* (2002). She has also written occasional short stories, but none of particular merit. "Nightfall's Promise" (2002) is linked to the Nightfall novels. Reichert has proved to be a reliable source of convincing fantastic adventures who seems most at ease with protagonists who are not part of the establishment, allowing the author to adopt the viewpoint of the outsider in order to examine her various created worlds.

"Rendezvous in Averoigne" Clark Ashton Smith (1931)

The troubadour Gerard de l'Automne, who wanders Europe making music for a living and apparently deflowering local maidens as his avocation, is a guest of a small noble in the region of Averoigne, Smith's mythical European country, when he meets and becomes enamored of Fleurette, a young, vivacious girl who professes to share his attraction. Since her father would certainly not approve, the two lovers decide to meet beyond his view in a wooded area where they can be alone with their love. Unfortunately, they choose a region reputed to be under some mild form of curse because of the proximity of the tomb of one or more practitioners of dark sorcery.

As Gerard approaches the rendezvous, he hears a woman scream and, to his credit he draws his weapon and continues forward. He finds a woman struggling with three bestial men, but when he attempts to intercede they all vanish like phantoms, leaving him in a wooded area that no longer appears familiar. A mysterious and daunting castle dominates the scene, and every effort that Gerard makes to escape leads him inevitably back toward it. When he finally enters he is greeted by the Sieur de Malinbois, a cadaverous man who Gerard instinctively distrusts. Malinbois tells him to leave his staff outside, but the troubadour refuses to relinquish it.

Fleurette and her servants have been similarly trapped, and some restraining magic compels them to cooperate with their host. During the night they discover the truth. Malinbois and his wife are vampires, and their attack on Fleurette's servants leaves them both weak and terrified. Gerard sharpens the end of his staff into a stake, and during the daylight hours he and one of the servants search the castle until they find the one part of it that is not an illusion, an elaborate burial vault containing the unliving bodies of Malinbois and his wife. He dispatches them both, at which point the illusiory castle promptly disappears, setting them all free.

Smith is often identified as an author of weird fiction rather than fantasy or horror, because a large number of his short stories straddle both fields, as is the case with this, one of his finest works, which mixes a common horror theme, vampirism, into a medieval landscape in a story that is, despite its subject matter, light and witty rather than morbid and suspenseful.

The Renquist Series Mick Farren
(1996–2002)

Much of the work of H. P. LOVECRAFT fell into the Cthulhu Mythos series, which straddled the genres of science fiction and horror because its monsters were actually alien beings from the far past who still lived in a kind of alternate universe from which they were constantly attempting to escape. Many other writers have set stories within the framework originated by Lovecraft, some adding details, others exploring it from an entirely new direction, as is the case with William Browning Spencer in *Resume with Monsters* (1994) and *Irrational Fears* (1998) and Paul Di Filippo in *The Steampunk Trilogy* (1994). Mick Farren's previous novels had all been science fiction, although one, *Necron* (1991), included rationalized demons,

when he decided to develop his own take on Lovecraft starting with *The Time of Feasting* (1996).

Vampires traditionally have been evil, although the trend in recent years is to make them romantic heroes or misunderstood and troubled victims. Farren created a small tribe of vampires for this novel led by Renquist, named for the madman in DRACULA (1897) by Bram STOKER, although it is not clear whether this is meant to be anything more than coincidental. Renquist and his followers are neither good nor evil. They protect their own existence, even if that means killing humans. For most of them it is a necessity rather than a sport, and the need to conceal their existence limits their predation. Farren's vampires have some clearly supernatural powers, including a useful immunity to surveillance cameras, although as the series progressed he made desultory attempts to rationalize things.

The opening volume serves primarily to introduce the characters and situation and show us Renquist dealing with a rebellion among his own people. As such, it is an above average but otherwise unremarkable vampire novel. The sequels move the story in a new and surprising direction. In *Darklost* (2000) Renquist discovers that the head of a major commercial enterprise is secretly attempting to open a gateway between universes so that Cthulhu and his minions can return and rule the Earth. Since vampires have no place in that power structure, it is in their best interests to interfere, which they do successfully after a series of well-conceived adventures. We learn more about Cthulhu, actually one of a race of space travelers that Farren describes in far more detail than Lovecraft ever attempted, and there are further revelations in *More Than Mortal* (2001), in which Renquist travels to Scotland after hearing rumors that a coven of witches have wakened Merlin, who is also linked to the aliens.

Farren brought the series to an apparent close with *Underland* (2002), with Renquist recruited by the U.S. government to help defeat the menace of a secret Nazi base beneath the surface of Earth whose inhabitants have allied themselves with an antediluvian reptilian race with super-scientific powers. The Renquist novels are written with tongue firmly in cheek, poking fun at various genre conventions even though the tone of the novels is relentlessly serious. Farren's most recent novel, *Kindling* (2004), is an alternate world fantasy considerably less interesting than the Renquist series.

The Return of the King J. R. R. Tolkien
(1955)

The concluding volume of the Lord of the Rings trilogy finds the various members of THE FELLOW-SHIP OF THE RING scattered and all facing death and destruction. Frodo Baggins and Sam Gamgee are on their way toward the heart of Mordor, determined to destroy the magical ring of evil by throwing it into the molten lava of Mount Doom, thereby thwarting Sauron's plans to rule the world. They are accompanied by Gollum, who alternates between slavishly following Frodo's instructions and malevolently plotting to kill both of the hobbits in order to recover the ring for himself. Frodo is mindful of the fact that Gandalf indicated that even Gollum has a part to play in the unfolding story and is sympathetic to the damage Gollum has suffered because of his obsession.

Gandalf and the remaining two hobbits are on their way to Minas Tirith in an effort to forge an alliance between the major human nations to oppose the legions that Sauron has assembled. Aragorn and Legolas are with the king of Rohan, although their paths will soon diverge. Aragorn eventually turns the tide of battle and lifts the siege of Minas Tirith by enlisting the aid of an army of the dead, a narrative turn that is dramatically effective although perhaps somewhat too convenient. This is a stopgap measure, however, as the forces at Sauron's disposal seem inexhaustible, and the real heroism is that of Frodo and Sam, who overcome one hardship after another before finally achieving their goal.

The film version made a number of changes, including moving incidents back and forth among the three volumes, and it concentrates primarily on the battle scenes. The prolonged anticlimactic ending in the novel becomes even more obvious on the screen as we discover that Frodo can no longer be content in the Shire after all he has seen and done. He leaves Middle Earth forever with Gandalf, Bilbo, and the last of the elves. Despite this small

dramatic flaw, the trilogy is still the finest example of the quest story, although in this case the object is to destroy the magical artifact rather than recover it, and is set in perhaps the most fully realized and detailed imaginary world in all of literature.

Rice, Anne (1941–)

Prior to the 1970s most vampire fiction made no effort to render undead characters as sympathetic. Vampires were evil, dangerous, and often disgusting creatures. Stories describing them in other terms, usually troubled by their bloodthirsty compulsions, were novelties. That all began to change in dramatic fashion with *Interview with the Vampire* (1976) by Anne Rice, the first in her lengthy and ongoing series of vampire novels, most of which involve one particular vampire and his line, Lestat. Rice has also written historical fiction and mild erotica, and there are elements of both of these in her supernatural fiction.

The first novel, cast in the form of a series of conversations, is still the best. It describes the complex relationship among three vampires, the older Lestat, the younger protagonist, and a third, an ageless vampire child. The interactions among these three are complex and fascinating, and the novel is an extraordinary achievement much more satisfying than the 1994 film version. Lestat becomes a rock star in *The Vampire Lestat* (1984) and is somewhat reformed, preying only on people who deserve to die. During this novel and the next, *Queen of the Damned* (1988), Rice develops the folklore of vampires quite elaborately and portrays it as a society just as diverse and divided as our own.

Rice attempted to switch themes for her next novel, *The Mummy* (1989), an uneven story about a mummy brought back to life in contemporary times with predictable mayhem ensuing. *The Witching Hour* (1990), the first in the Mayfair Witches series, uses ghosts and other supernatural phenomena mixed into a very complex family saga set in New Orleans. *Lasher* (1993) and *Taltos* (1994) continue this story in ever-increasing complexity. *Servant of the Bones* (1996) also stands alone, although it has the feel of a Lestat novel. A man is turned into a genie and interacts with a number of humans during the course of centuries. Although all these titles sold quite well, Rice was so firmly associated with vampires that it was inevitable that she would continue the story of Lestat.

Rice returned to vampires for *The Tale of the Body Thief* (1992), a story reminiscent in structure of the first of the Lestat novels. The next, *Memnoch the Devil* (1995), is considerably more interesting, although the narrative bogs down occasionally during the lengthy discussions of the differences between good and evil. *Pandora* (1998) moves the Lestat saga to contemporary Paris, and *The Vampire Armand* (1998) is another retrospective of a vampire's career. A mortal falls in love with a vampire in *Vittorio the Vampire* (1999), thereby sealing his own fate. Perhaps finding it difficult to discover anything new to introduce into the saga, Rice merged it with the Mayfair Witches series in her next, *Merrick* (2000), a dark and complicated story involving voodoo magic, souls searching for bodies, and other occult matters.

Blood and Gold (2001) jumps back in time to ancient Rome, and that setting helps freshen the theme somewhat. *Blackwood Farm* (2002) is the best of her recent novels, the story of a man who has been haunted by a doppelgänger all his life. When he is turned into a vampire, it has an unexpected magical effect on his double as well. Her most recent Lestat novel, *Blood Canticle* (2003), is smoothly written, but the plot is undistinguished.

Although Rice's later novels contain many interesting concepts and individual scenes of considerable merit, they have tended to be very repetitive. Her best work remains her first few novels. Although she did not originate the concept of the romantic vampire, she certainly was responsible for its dramatic rise in popularity, and her influence is obvious in the works of Laurell HAMILTON, Charlaine Harris, and many other authors of vampire romance novels.

"Ringing the Changes" Robert Aickman (1971)

Gerald and Phrynne Banstead have recently married and are finally leaving on their delayed honeymoon. Phrynne insisted they go someplace he had never been before, so Gerald decided on the sea-

port town of Holihaven, even though it was not the usual tourist season. He has misgivings from the outset. The accommodations are less than satisfactory, the people managing the hotel are perpetually drunk, the streets seem deserted, the sea has retreated impossibly far from the shore leaving a rank wasteland behind, and, worst of all, the town churches are ringing their bells incessantly and loudly.

Clearly, something peculiar is going on. One of the local residents tells them that they have come at a bad time, that once a year the villagers peal the bells until they literally wake the dead, who come from the sea and from the graveyard to make merry with the living for a single night. Although skeptical at first, Gerald eventually concedes that something decidedly queer is happening and makes a belated effort to leave town before they are caught. When that fails, he and Phrynne barricade themselves in their room, which is where they are when the bells finally fall silent and they hear people shouting that the dead have awakened.

Sounds of revelry fill the streets. From their window the couple watches as the villagers begin to dance and sing, their numbers augmented by shadowy figures that they do not see clearly. Unfortunately, their locked door is no barrier. Their room is invaded, and Phrynne disappears in the crush, although she is rescued in the nick of time by the same man who warned them earlier. They leave the village then, but Gerald recognizes that the experience has changed Phrynne in some fashion and that the relationship between them will never again be the same as it once was. Aickman does a remarkable job of creating a genuinely eerie and menacing atmosphere, even though almost nothing overt happens. Neither the protagonist nor the reader really "sees" any of the dead, and there is no threat of physical harm. The story illustrates that hints and suggestions can be far more useful than explicit description in creating an effective horror story.

"Rip Van Winkle" Washington Irving (1819)

Rip Van Winkle is one of those characters whose story is so widely known that many readers feel they have read the story even if they have not. It is often misidentified as a tale of the Brothers Grimm or Hans Christian ANDERSEN, but it is, in fact, a short story by Washington Irving, who also wrote "THE LEGEND OF SLEEPY HOLLOW."

The title character is a gentle, likeable, unambitious man living in upstate New York Dutch country some time prior to the American Revolution. He is married to a domineering, nagging wife, and despite his willingness to work hard without pay to help others, he has never been able to make a financial success of his small farm or at any other job he has attempted. Despite this, he is universally liked, even by the town's children and dogs, he appears to lead a completely contented life, and his children seem perfectly happy to follow his example.

Rip is driven from his home and later away from his friends thanks to the intercession of his wife, who is constantly berating him to make more of himself. His final refuge is to take to the woods, hunting with his dog Wolf and enjoying the peace and quiet as he stalks squirrels and other small game. One day Rip encounters a strange man in the woods who leads him to others of his kind who are playing an early version of the game we now call bowling. They are an odd lot, but he risks drinking some of their wine, quite a lot of it, in fact, finally slipping into a deep sleep.

When he wakens he is alone. Even Wolf has gone. He returns to the village, which is larger than he remembered and filled with strangers. Believing himself still befuddled by the wine, he approaches his home, which is a deserted ruin. The portrait of King George III of England has been replaced by one of General George Washington. He discovers that he has been gone 20 years, during which time his friends have died or moved on, his wife has passed away, and his two children are grown. Although it is commonly believed that he was charmed by fairies, the story actually identifies the company in the forest as Henry Hudson and his crew, magically empowered to live outside of time.

Irving anticipated with this story one of the pervasive themes in time travel stories and tales of sleepers wakened from suspended animation. The disorientation that Rip Van Winkle experiences by displacement in time is more unsettling than if he

had been moved through space to a distant land with different customs. One of the particularly effective aspects of the story is that Rip recognizes the subtle changes as well as the obvious ones. The very pace of life has altered. Fortunately, he has little difficulty in settling into his old role and, free of his wife, does so. Contemporary readers might wish for a more definitive ending, but Irving was content simply to present a wondrous situation and describe its consequences. He did so with such skill that the story has become a part of our common heritage.

Roberson, Jennifer (1953–)

During the 1980s fantasy fiction began to take shape as a separate genre. Formerly, a significant portion of mainstream fantasy was written by writers active in other genres, primarily science fiction and romance, and it was marketed as a subset of those fields. Now fantasy fiction was beginning to develop its own corps of writers, and one of the most interesting of these was Jennifer Roberson, whose debut novel, *Shapechangers!* (1984), was the first in what would be the eight-volume Chronicles of the Cheysuli. The Cheysuli are a race with the ability to change shape who share a magical world with humans. Although for many generations their relationship is friendly, that situation is altered at least in part by the events that take place in this opening adventure. One of the Cheysuli elopes with the daughter of the human ruler, and years later the shape-changers have been hunted to the point of extinction by his vengeful soldiers.

Roberson added complexity to her created world in *The Song of Homana* (1985). Although the central plot involves an effort to remove a usurper from the throne, it is the evolving relationship between Cheysuli and humans, some of whom hope to restore the old balance, that fully involves the reader. The situation changes dramatically in *Legacy of the Sword* (1986), with one of the shape-changers poised to assume the throne, and in *Track of the White Wolf* (1987) the new king discovers that few trust him on either side. *A Pride of Princes* (1988) is a less ambitious adventure, and *Daughter of the Lion* (1989) is a rather predictable story about a determined woman faced with an imposed marriage she wishes to avoid. *Flight of the Raven* (1990) and *A Tapestry of Lions* (1992) are entertaining but unexceptional potboilers. Having exhausted most of the potential of her imagined world, Roberson wisely abandoned it at that point.

Roberson's second fantasy series is less ambitious but is generally superior because of the depth of her characterization of its two recurring characters. The Swords series consists of *Sword-Dancer* (1986), *Sword-Singer* (1988), *Sword-Maker* (1989), *Sword-Breaker* (1991), *Sword-Born* (1998), and *Sword-Sworn* (2002). The two protagonists, one male and one female, are both experts with the sword. They are introduced in a fairly routine quest story but become much more vivid in the second volume, in which one must clear her name after she is forced to kill her mentor. Their subsequent adventures compel them to contemplate what is meant by the term *duty* and battle supernatural menaces and an army of fanatics, and they include a shipwreck and abduction by pirates. They eventually discover the secret of the male partner's origin and return to his homeland to fulfill the destiny he never realized awaited him. The series is one of the most intelligent and engaging sword and sorcery epics.

Roberson has also written some historical novels and collaborated with Melanie RAWN and Kate ELLIOTT on *The Golden Key* (1977). Her short fiction has yet to be collected but includes several notable stories, including "The Count of Summer King" (1988), "The Horse Who Would Be King" (1995), and "Guinevere's Truth" (1996). Although still actively writing, she has been regrettably less productive in recent years.

Roberts, John Maddox (1947–)

Although John Maddox Roberts has been actively working in science fiction throughout his career, most of his best work has been in the fantasy and murder mystery fields, the latter primarily a series set in ancient Rome. His first fantasy novel was *King of the Wood* (1983), which pits Vikings against Mongols in North America. His next was *Conan the Valorous* (1985), the first of eight novels he would add to the CONAN SERIES created by

Robert E. HOWARD over the course of the next 10 years, ending with *Conan and the Amazon* (1995). Although Roberts did not recreate Howard's character exactly, making him more intellectual and less inclined to solve every problem by hitting it with a sword, his evocation of the barbaric setting is superior to that of most of the other writers contributing to the series. *Conan the Marauder* (1987) and *Conan the Rogue* (1991) are the best of the set.

The Islander (1990) is the first in an original series set in the Stormlands, a devastated land where magic has emerged following the collapse of technology. The opening volume serves primarily to set the stage and introduce the main character. In *The Black Shields* (1991) he violates a taboo and is forced into exile, but some of his enemies are pursuing him, intending to punish him more dramatically by killing him. *The Poisoned Lands* (1992) follows the career of an ambitious king who seeks to extend his rule to include his neighbors, which leads to the threat of an even wider war in *The Steel Kings* (1993). *Queens of Land and Sea* (1994) brings the sequence to a close.

Roberts's only remaining fantasy novel is his best, *Murder in Tarsis* (1996), in which three unlikely detectives are given the task of solving a politically sensitive murder, with everyone expecting them to fail so that the matter can be forgotten. Unfortunately, the threesome decides to take their job seriously, uncovering more than they bargained for. Roberts's experience writing detective fiction is evident here. His most recent series is alternate history science fiction involving the battle between Rome and Carthage. He has written at least one good fantasy short story, "Arms and the Enchanter" (1992).

"The Rocking-horse Winner"
D. H. Lawrence (1926)
Although D. H. Lawrence is perhaps best known as the author of the once-controversial *Lady Chatterley's Lover* (1928), he is also the author of this, one of the more frequently reprinted short stories of the supernatural. Paul is a young boy growing up in a very difficult family situation. Paul and his sister are treated well, but their mother's affection is

mostly pretense, as she is preoccupied with what she sees as the tragedy of her intellectually and socially impoverished personal life.

Since money, or the lack thereof, is the unmentioned background theme to their lives, Paul finally asks about it and is told that they have little money because his parents are unlucky. Paul has a rocking-horse that he orders to take him to where luck can be found, with no visible effect, although when an uncle asks the horse's name, Paul indicates that it changes from week to week. Coincidentally, perhaps, the previous week's name was that of the winner of a major horse race. The uncle subsequently discovers that Paul, with the aid of one of the servants, has been quietly betting on the horses for some time and has accumulated considerable winnings.

With the uncle's assistance Paul arranges for a substantial part of his money to be funneled back to his mother, hoping that this will lighten the atmosphere at home. Although he does experience a significant improvement in the family's lifestyle, the unspoken wish for more money becomes, if anything, more strident than before, and it is obvious to everyone except the boy that his mother will never be satisfied. Paul rides the rocking-horse furiously awaiting another winner, but as the days pass unsuccessfully he becomes increasingly upset. When he finally does find a winner, the strain has been so much that he falls into a fever and eventually dies.

Paul's mother is clearly the villain of the story, guilty of neglect if not malice. By withholding her love and by obsessing over their perceived poverty, she has created stresses too intense and complex for the boy to resist. To a lesser extent, the uncle and even the servant are also guilty, exploiting the boy's abilities without being seriously concerned about the toll it is taking on him. Ironically, he dies leaving his mother with a small fortune, which she will undoubtedly still consider inadequate for her needs.

Rohan, Michael Scott (1951–   )

After a brief stint writing science fiction, Michael Scott Rohan collaborated with Allan Scott on *Burial Rites* (1986, also published as *The Ice King*),

a dark fantasy in which an ancient superhuman Viking warrior is released from the ice and restored to life, after which he begins a brief reign of terror before finally being destroyed. The tone is much closer to horror than fantasy, one that Rohan largely abandoned for his subsequent work.

The Anvil of Ice (1986) opened the Winter of the World series, set in a magical land that is still caught up in an ice age. A young boy becomes an apprentice wizard and has a series of low-key adventures, setting the scene for *The Forge in the Forest* (1987), in which we are shown the conflict between two rival groups of magic users, each striving for dominance in their ice-clad world. The young wizard rescues an entire isolated city but is given a fresh round of tasks to accomplish in *The Hammer of the Sun* (1989). *The Castle of the Winds* (1998) changes direction, following the adventures of a blacksmith who builds a marvelous suit of armor and then must track down the thief responsible for its disappearance. The chronicles of that world are continued in *The Singer and the Sea* (2000) and, at least for the time being, seem to have ended with *Shadow of the Seer* (2001).

The Spiral series began with *Chase the Morning* (1990), which has a considerably lighter tone. A businessman discovers that our world is the nexus among various realities and that it is possible to move from one to another. An entrepreneur attempts to set up an interreality trading consortium in *The Gates of Noon* (1992) but runs into unexpected difficulties. The negative consequences of the arrangement become more evident in *Cloud Castles* (1993) when hordes of creatures, some demonic, invade the now accessible Earth, and the insanity grows zanier and more general in *Maxie's Demon* (1997).

Rohan also wrote *The Lord of the Middle Air* (1994), in which Sir Walter Scott teams up with a wizard to battle evil, and *A Spell of Empire* (1992), with Allan Scott, set in an alternate Europe. Both novels are very cleverly done. Rohan is a reliable source of entertaining adventure stories, is capable of delivering a wide range of atmospheres, and is particularly adept at creating colorful settings. Despite a period of considerable productivity in the early 1990s, his recent work has appeared only at increasing intervals.

Rohmer, Sax (Arthur Sarsfield Ward)
(1883–1959)

Sax Rohmer was the pseudonym used by Arthur Sarsfield Ward, a prolific writer of thrillers and weird fiction who is best known for the creation of his superintelligent Chinese villain, Dr. Fu Manchu, whose adventures often involve fantastic elements ranging from superscience to the mystical. Fu Manchu first appeared in *The Insidious Dr. Fu Manchu* (1913). He is a criminal mastermind and head of the mysterious international criminal organization known as the Si-Fan, which has more members than the population of many countries. His opponents are two British agents who often seem to defeat him more by luck than intelligence. There are 11 book-length adventures in the series, ending with *Emperor Fu Manchu* (1959), in which he employs giant insects, occult forces, assassins, the revived dead, voodoo, immortality, hypnosis, and other weapons, but always without success.

Although Rohmer is less well known for his other thrillers, many of them involve Asian magic or other occult themes. In *The Quest of the Sacred Slipper* (1913) thugs armed with supernatural powers attempt to seize a slipper that once belonged to Muhammad. A magical painting alters the personalities of people who observe it in *The Yellow Claw* (1915), and a master magician uses a variety of magical powers in the rambling but exciting *Brood of the Witch Queen* (1918). *The Dream Detective* (1920) is a collection of related stories about an occult detective, several of which involve fantasy plot devices, and *The Haunting of Low Fennel* (1920) also contains some supernatural stories.

The Green Eyes of Bast (1920) is Rohmer's best novel outside the Fu Manchu series. The investigation of a series of mysterious murders reveals the existence of a nonhuman race that possesses occult powers. They have become convinced that they are superior to the human race and are entitled to supplant it. *Grey Face* (1924) and *She Who Sleeps* (1928), the latter making use of a revivified mummy, are considerably less interesting, although both have strong supernatural content. Rohmer's

later work is almost exclusively about Fu Manchu and emphasizes superscience rather than the occult. Two recent collections have gathered most of his better uncollected short weird fiction, *The Secret of Holm Peel and Other Strange Stories* (1970) and *The Wrath of Fu Manchu* (1973). His series about a female villain, Sumuru, is often mentioned as fantasy but is not. Rohmer's Asian villains were often imitated in the pulp adventure magazines, but only Fu Manchu has remained popular, featured in several motion pictures and a short-lived television series.

"The Room in the Tower" E. F. Benson
(1912)

This early classic horror tale opens with the author attempting to talk the reader into accepting the fantastic content by first assuring the reader that he, the narrator, is a skeptic. It is not surprising, he asserts, that we occasionally find our dreams repeated in reality. Given the mundane content of most dreams and the fact that they usually involve people we know, it would be more surprising if that were not the case. Having said that, however, the narrator relates a recurring dream he has experienced since childhood in which he finds himself a guest among strangers and is told that he has been given the room in the tower, a place he instinctively know holds a hideous horror. As the dream continues to recur, he remembers more details about the house and the other occupants and notices as well that they seem to age as the years pass, as though the dream were really happening in some alternate existence.

As an adult he is part of a holiday party when he finds himself at the very house of his dreams, although its occupants are entirely different, friendly and cheerful. Nevertheless, his uneasiness grows when he is assigned to stay in the room in the tower, a situation that makes him alternately curious and anxious. In that room he notices a portrait of Julia Stone, the older woman who assigns him that room in his dreams, a woman he instinctively knows is tainted by some insidious evil. When he and his host move the picture, they both find their hands covered with blood, although neither has suffered a wound.

The climax comes that night when the narrator wakens to find the portrait back on the wall and the original, now pale and exuding the stench of death, poised over his bed. He escapes, of course, and lives to tell the story, revealing at the end that the woman committed suicide after a dissolute life and that repeated efforts to bury her have failed. Benson's ghostly image and understated horror might seem quaint by contemporary standards, but the story was considered quite unsettling when it first appeared. The theme of precognition, advance knowledge of events to come, has rarely been handled as effectively.

Rosemary's Baby Ira Levin (1967)

Until the 1970s horror fiction had always been much less popular in the United States than in Europe, and what did appear in book form was either lumped with science fiction or with mystery fiction. Two novels began to change the perception of the genre and paved the way for Stephen KING, Anne RICE, Peter STRAUB, and others. The first of these was this suspenseful novel by an author whose previous book had been a murder mystery. The second was William Peter Blatty's THE EXORCIST (1971). Both novels were best-sellers, and both were quickly made into major motion pictures.

Rosemary's Baby is the story of a young married woman whose husband falls under the influence of a group of seemingly pleasant people living in the apartment house where the couple has just moved. Rosemary is occasionally jealous of her husband's new friendships, but she is soon preoccupied by her pregnancy, which becomes evident shortly after she experiences a horrifying nightmare in which she is sexually assaulted by a demonic creature. Her husband becomes very attentive, and even the neighbors seem unusually concerned about the child's welfare. It is only gradually that she begins to suspect that something is wrong.

Eventually, she discovers the truth, that the dream was real and that she was impregnated by the devil so that his son could be born on Earth to work great evil. Even though she apparently grasps the implications, she is still devoted to the child, although reluctant to accept the assistance of the cultists. Levin even leaves open the possibility that the dream was not real and that she has imagined everything, although that alternative is less obvi-

ous in the film version. The novel ends almost quietly, and the realization that evil has triumphed leaves the reader to speculate about the future.

Perhaps unwisely, Levin wrote a sequel 30 years later. In *Son of Rosemary* (1997) she wakens from a magically induced coma to find that her son has grown to maturity and is now a charismatic figure with an enormous following. Although she is initially relieved to find that he is apparently fighting on the side of righteousness rather than evil, she quickly begins to detect flaws in his character that indicate he is unable to completely escape his father's imprint. Standing on its own, the novel is an interesting thriller, but retrospectively, it dulls the impact of the original novel.

Rosenberg, Joel (1954–   )

Joel Rosenberg, a steady source of enjoyable light fantasy adventure, made his debut with the first volume of the Guardians of the Flame series, *The Sleeping Dragon* (1983), which uses a common plot device of the time, game players caught within the artificial reality of the game they are playing. In this case seven friends have constructed an elaborate fantasy role-playing game whose conflicts often mirror the rough spots in their relationships in the real world. That distinction vanishes when they find themselves trapped in the reality of the game. In *The Sword and the Chain* (1984) they discover that they feel more at home in the imaginary world, and begin to create new lives for themselves and the game-related subplots disappear during the books that followed. In *The Silver Crown* (1985) they create a free state but are hard pressed by the repressive forces of evil, which prefer things to remain as they have been.

The story continues with *The Heir Apparent* (1987) and *The Warrior Lives* (1988), which consolidate and to some extent reprise earlier parts of the series while setting the stage for the next generation to appear. The events in *The Road to Ehvenor* (1991) have moved so far from the original concept that it almost seems to belong in another series. A gap of several years followed before Rosenberg returned to that setting for *The Road Home* (1995), in which a young man's hatred of slavers becomes so fierce that it clouds his judgment. That was followed by a loose, good-humored trilogy consisting of *Not Exactly the Three Musketeers* (1999), *Not Quite Scaramouche* (2001), and *Not Really the Prisoner of Zenda* (2003), which are easily Rosenberg's most rewarding work.

Not all of his fantasy has fallen into this series. *D'Shai* (1991) describes the efforts of an acrobat to clear his name, as a consequence of which he becomes a sort of magical private detective. He returns in *Hour of the Octopus* (1994), an even better sequel, to solve another murder. *The Fire Duke* (1995) introduces the Keeper of the Hidden Ways, which starts in our world but moves quickly to one with Norse overtones, werewolves, and other magical creatures. The protagonist proves to be a catalyst for change in a battle that involves shape-changers, gods, and monsters in two sequels, *The Silver Stone* (1996) and *The Crimson Sky* (1998).

Rosenberg's most recent fantasy novel is *Paladins* (2004), in which a band of knights battles evil. He rarely writes short fiction and has yet to produce anything memorable at that length. His work tends to be most effective when there is a strong element of humor and the tone is light, but he is invariably a convincing storyteller with a productive imagination.

Rowley, Christopher (1948–)

Christopher Rowley began writing science fiction in 1983, producing several space operas mixed with military settings and plots. He switched to fantasy in 1992, and almost all of his fiction since then falls into his two extended series. The first and most popular of these is the Bazil Broketail sequence, which might be described as military fantasy. The title character from the opening novel, *Bazil Broketail* (1992), is an intelligent dragon who, along with his human companion, sets out on a quest to rescue a princess. In the sequel, *A Sword for a Dragon* (1993), Bazil receives a magic sword with which to battle his enemies, of which there are many.

Evil wizards want to supplant the good witches who rule the land in *Dragons of War* (1994), and Bazil's efforts to stop them are hampered by a subplot in which his human friend is

framed for murder. *Battledragon* (1995) involves more warfare and the effort to defeat the nastiest of the evil wizards. Rowley changed the scene for the next in the series, *A Dragon at World's End* (1997), stranding Bazil in a distant land where he comes to the aid of the local people, who are beset by slavers. A fresh war breaks out in *Dragons of Argonath* (1998), and the forces of evil are routed at last in *Dragon Ultimate* (1999), which brought the series to a close. *The Wizard and the Floating City* (1996) is set in the same universe but is a routine quest story that does not involve the recurring characters.

Rowley's second series is less well known but considerably more interesting. In *The Ancient Enemy* (2000) we are introduced to a magical future world where apes have evolved into intelligent beings and where humanity has disappeared, apparently extinct. Trouble arises when rumors of the return of humanity begin to filter through the world. War between the two races breaks out in *The Shasht War* (2001) and spreads rapidly in *Doom's Break* (2002). The magical elements are partially rationalized, and the series could almost be read as science fiction rather than fantasy, similar to the Aldair series by Neal Barrett, Jr. Rowley has the rare ability to make his unusual protagonists—dragons and apes—seem like real and interesting people. Unfortunately, he has a tendency to reuse overly familiar plots and has yet to prove that he can distinguish himself from his peers, although he certainly seems to have the prerequisite writing skills.

Rowling, J. K. (1965–)

Joanne Kathleen Rowling took the publishing world by surprise with the appearance of the first of her Harry Potter series, HARRY POTTER AND THE SORCERER'S STONE (1997, also published as *Harry Potter and the Philosopher's Stone*). Her series of seven projected novels about a young wizard in training and his effort to survive adolescence along with the attacks of an evil magician named Voldemort and his allies has attracted an amazingly large and diverse reading audience, and each new volume has been greeted by long lines at bookstores on their first day of sales.

Rowling introduced her major characters and the ongoing plot in the opening volume and developed both in HARRY POTTER AND THE CHAMBER OF SECRETS (1998), providing hints of the darker scenes that would follow. The third volume, HARRY POTTER AND THE PRISONER OF AZKABAN (1999) has such a complex plot that there was some concern that young readers would not be able to follow its intricacies, but these fears proved to be unfounded. HARRY POTTER AND THE GOBLET OF FIRE (2000) runs more than 700 pages, but readers of all ages took it in stride, as they also did the considerably darker tone that Rowling continues to develop. Good characters die in the course of the story, which makes no effort to disguise the deep cruelty of the villains and the occasional thoughtlessness of even the more admirable characters. HARRY POTTER AND THE ORDER OF THE PHOENIX (2003) is even longer and more convoluted. The sixth book is titled *Harry Potter and the Half Blood Prince*. A seventh and final volume will follow.

In addition to her financial success, Rowling has won considerable critical acclaim and the Hugo Award for best novel of the year. On the other hand, she has encountered some controversy, primarily from parties who are critical of her depiction of magic as anything other than evil and for what is perceived as a disrespectful attitude exhibited by the child characters toward some of the adults. Rowling has also provided some short descriptive books related to the series, including *Quidditch through the Ages* (1999), *Goodbye Privet Drive* (2001), and *Harry at Hogwarts* (2001). Her success has single-handedly given fantasy literature a significant boost. The first three books have all resulted in exceptionally good motion pictures.

Rusch, Kristine Kathryn (1960–)

The very prolific Kristine Kathryn Rusch began writing short stories in the late 1980s, both science fiction and fantasy, won the John W. Campbell Award for best new writer, and has worked in both fields ever since under her own name and using pseudonyms, often in collaboration with Dean Wesley Smith. Her first fantasy title of interest is the short novel *The Gallery of His Dreams* (1991),

a story of magical time travel. *The White Mists of Power* (1991) is more conventional, with a bard and a magician fleeing enemies and seeking refuge despite a dark destiny linked to the former. Rusch's third early fantasy novel is *Afterimage* (1992), a collaboration with Kevin J. Anderson in which the victim of a serial killer is magically changed into his simulacrum and given the task of tracking him down. The novel was reprinted in 1998 as *Afterimage Aftershock*, with the story extended.

Heart Readers (1993) is an interesting story of court intrigue set in a typical fantasy world. The local king is of a line that always has twin sons. The heart readers have the power to mystically examine the two and determine which should be the heir, but an ambitious lord decides to corrupt the process so that he can manipulate the more pliable brother. *Traitors* (1993) is a similar variation from the expected. A man whose family was unjustly executed vows to kill those responsible, including the royal family, but finds his plans going awry when he falls in love with the queen. In 1995 Rusch began the Fey series, which consists of *The Sacrifice* (1995), *The Changeling* (1996), *The Rival* (1997), *The Resistance* (1998), and *Victory* (1998). The series opens with a crisis because the presumed heir to the throne has not experienced a mystical vision that is a prerequisite to the succession. A horde of invaders and a civil war follow, and the conflict is eventually resolved when two races successfully intermarry.

The Black Throne duo includes *The Black Queen* (1999) and *The Black King* (2000), a comparatively minor story about a queen who is in danger of being possessed by an evil spirit. *Fantasy Life* (2003) is much better and is set in a remote part of North America where the creatures of legend still exist. A collection of Rusch's better fantasy short stories appeared as *Stories for an Enchanted Afternoon* (2001). Much of her recent fantasy fiction has been romantic comedy written under the name Kristine Grayson, lightweight but refreshingly clever. A lawyer represents the magician who put Sleeping Beauty to sleep in *Utterly Charming* (2000), a reincarnated princess has trouble controlling her magical powers in *Thoroughly Kissed* (2001), one of Cupid's minions falls in love with a mortal in *Completely Smitten* (2002), and the Fates show up in our world in *Simply Irresistible* (2002) and again in *Absolutely Captivated* (2004). Her romances are reminiscent at times of Robert NATHAN.

During the 1990s Rusch tried her hand at horror fiction with *Facade* (1993) and the much more interesting *Sins of the Blood* (1995), an unusual vampire story in which a professional hunter of the undead becomes emotionally involved with her work. Her best novel of the supernatural is *The Devil's Churn* (1996), an atmospheric story about a woman who worships the spirits of the ocean and possesses the power to reanimate the dead. Unfortunately, Rusch has written only occasional short supernatural fiction since.

Despite her considerable output, which includes a very large number of science fiction novels under her own and other names, Rusch is consistently entertaining and sometimes impressively thoughtful and prose conscious. She adapts well to various styles and appeals to a wide range of audiences.

Russo, John (1939–   )

John Russo was the coauthor with George Romero of the screenplay for the original film *The Night of the Living Dead* (1968) and has subsequently written a number of additional screenplays, some based on his own novels. His first book was the novelization of the Romero-directed movie, published in book form in 1968, and his second novel was *Return of the Living Dead* (1978), based on the screenplay for a film of that title, which he cowrote with several others. Both stories deal with a contagious plague that turns the dead into flesh-eating zombies, and in neither case is there much effort to explain the phenomenon. *Return of the Living Dead* is more clearly satirical, although much of the humor of the film is lost in the text version. Russo wrote a new version of the novel under the same name in 1985.

Midnight (1980) was Russo's first original novel of the supernatural. The children of a man who reportedly could summon demons decide to experiment to find out if they have inherited his abilities. They have, of course, but they summon an entity who is much too powerful for them to control. The plot too closely resembles that of a slasher movie to

be entirely convincing, and the carnival of carnage begins to wear by the final chapters. Russo adapted it as a film. His next, *Black Cat* (1982), is considerably better, the first to indicate that the author might be able to create something more than a fleshed out screenplay. The soul of an evil magician has been reincarnated in the body of a panther, which is revered by a cult living in the American Southwest, where they prey on unsuspecting victims.

The Awakening (1983), also adapted as a film, is a straightforward vampire story with a few interesting twists. Russo returned to the zombie story with *Inhuman* (1986), in which a misguided government operation turns a group of terrorists into virtually unstoppable walking dead. *Voodoo Dawn* (1987), also a motion picture, describes the efforts of a voodoo cult to find a fresh body for the disembodied spirit of their spiritual leader. It is easily Russo's most effective and suspenseful novel. Another voodoo priest raises an army of zombies in an effort to supplant the Mafia in the amusing but disjointed *Living Things* (1988). His most recent horror novel is *Hell's Creation* (1995), in which a woman becomes convinced that her son was fathered by Satan and surrenders him for manipulation by a cult of satanists. Russo is far more likely to be remembered for his motion picture work than for his novels, but his better titles such as *Voodoo Dawn* and *The Awakening* suggest that he might well have been even more successful if he had devoted more time to developing his prose writing skills.

Ryman, Geoffrey (1951–   )

The Canadian writer better known as Geoff Ryman has spent most of his life living in the United Kingdom. His first genre fiction appeared in 1976, and he has since alternated between science fiction and fantasy. His first book-length work, *The Warrior Who Carried Life* (1985), is a fantasy that makes use of many of the standard devices of modern fantasy but uses them for a very unorthodox purpose, emphasizing the self-destructive consequences of revenge. A young woman whose family was brutally assaulted sets out to track down and punish those responsible. *The Unconquered Country* (1986) is technically a work of science fiction, although it strongly resembles a fantasy. In the aftermath of a devastating war, a young girl travels through the much altered landscape and has a series of low-key adventures. *The Child Garden* (1989), also science fiction, won the John W. Campbell Award and the Arthur C. Clarke Award, and it appeared that Ryman was firmly established in that genre.

Ryman did not produce much work for the next few years but returned to fantasy for the novel *Was* (1992), still considered his single most impressive work. It is only marginally fantastic, cast in the form of a realistic look at the young girl who was the supposed prototype for the protagonist of *The WIZARD OF OZ* (1906). Her retreat into fantasy—the land beyond the rainbow—is a psychological escape from a colorless, impoverished background and an abusive guardian.

His most recent fantasy novel is *Lust* (2001), a witty but comparatively weaker story of a man who discovers that he has the power to wish people in and out of existence. *Was* has been produced for the stage, and Ryman has himself been involved with a number of dramatic productions. His small body of very fine short stories are collected in *Coming of Enkidu* (1989) and *Unconquered Countries: Four Novellas* (1994), but both are predominantly science fiction.

S

Saberhagen, Fred (1930–)

Although many writers have written across a broad spectrum of science fiction, fantasy, and horror, most concentrate on one or at most two genres and only dabble in the third. Fred Saberhagen is one of the few who has been steadily active in all three and is particularly well known in science fiction circles for his Berserker series. He started writing in the early 1960s, producing his first fantasy novel in 1968, *The Broken Lands*, the opening title in a series that starts as science fiction set in a distant future when technology has been lost. The two sequels, *The Black Mountains* (1971) and *Changeling Earth* (1973), introduce magic as an alternative to technology. The last novel was revised in 1988 as *Ardneh's World*.

During the 1970s Saberhagen wrote a number of novels about Dracula, starting with *The Dracula Tape* (1975), a memoir by the world's most famous vampire, who asserts that it was all a misunderstanding and that he was just an innocent bystander. The count joins forces with Sherlock Holmes in *The Holmes Dracula File* (1975) and travels to Chicago to oppose the reborn Morgan Le Fay in *An Old Friend of the Family* (1979). Although the series appeared to have been discontinued at this point, Saberhagen decided to add new volumes after a lengthy gap. Dracula falls ill in *A Matter of Taste* (1990) and battles an evil one of his own kind who travels through time in *A Question of Time* (1992). Dracula and Holmes are reunited in *Seance for a Vampire* (1994), and Dracula must battle his own brother in *A Sharpness in the Neck*

(1996). Another lapse followed, ended by *A Coldness in the Blood* (2002), in which Dracula is caught up in a search for mystical artifacts. Although clearly supernatural, most of the novels in this series can be read as fantasy as well as horror.

Saberhagen began the more conventional Swords series with *The First Book of Swords* (1983), set in another world where technology has been displaced by magic. The gods create 12 magical swords, and each title in the series follows the history of one of the swords, ending with *Wayfinder's Story* (1992). *Merlin's Bones* (1995) is an unusual fantasy that starts in the future, with Morgan Le Fay returning yet again, this time to steal a time machine and return to Camelot. *Dancing Bears* (1996) is a noticeable change of pace, the story of a family of "were-bears" in prerevolutionary Russia. Saberhagen's most recent fantasy is the Book of the Gods series, which began with *The Face of Apollo* (1998) and continued in *Ariadne's Web* (2000), *The Arms of Hercules* (2000), *The God of the Golden Fleece* (2001), and *Gods of Fire and Thunder* (2002). The series involves the Greek Gods and, in the final volume, the Norse gods as well and often consists of retellings of famous legends.

Saberhagen has also written a few additional horror novels of note, most significantly *Thorn* (1980), the story of a latter-day sorcerer, and *Dominion* (1982), in which Merlin is brought back to life in the 20th century to battle ancient evil as well as his own human shortcomings. *The Frankenstein Papers* (1986) tells Mary SHELLEY's famous story from the monster's point of view. Saberhagen's supernatural fiction is more properly occult adventure than horror, and his fantasy is generally traditional and adventure oriented. On those occasions when he attempts something at variance from his usual subject matter, as in *Dancing Bears* and *Thorn,* he displays a versatility that might better be exploited in the future.

Sackett, Jeffrey (1949–   )

One of the most frustrating experiences for a reader is to discover a new writer who has evident talent and who seems to improve from one book to the next, but who suddenly stops writing or at least is no longer being published. The crash of the popular horror field during the late 1980s apparently terminated the careers of a number of very fine writers, not the least of whom was Jeffrey Sackett. Sackett made his debut with *Stolen Souls* (1987), the least interesting and most derivative of his novels. A museum acquires seven Egyptian caskets, unaware of the fact that they are cursed and that ancient spirits will be resurrected in each following the sacrifice of seven living people. It was an inauspicious debut, and Sackett might have been no more than a minor footnote if he had not sharpened his skills for his next effort.

Candlemas Eve (1988) is a dramatic improvement. A musician whose career is on the skids meets two strange women whose influence helps him to get his life back on track. Unfortunately, they are using the powers of witchcraft to help him, and in return they want his assistance in avenging themselves against their enemies from previous lifetimes. Although the novel falters in the waning chapters, Sackett displayed much more skill this time at creating plausible, complex characters. This improvement continued in *Blood of the Impaler* (1989), an indirect sequel to DRACULA, (1897) by Bram STOKER. A descendant of Jonathan Harker is tricked into raising Lucy Westenra from the grave and with her help into causing the restoration of Dracula himself. The novel is well constructed and develops a suspenseful atmosphere quickly and effectively. *Mark of the Werewolf* (1990) is somewhat less impressive but still worthwhile. An aging werewolf has decided to destroy

himself, but before he can do so, he is manipulated by a militia group who want to breed superwarriors to further their cause.

Although Sackett had by then honed his writing skills, he continued to use ideas already in common use in the genre. It was with his last and best novel, *The Demon* (1991), that he began to demonstrate original thinking as well as technical competence. The protagonist is Sweet, a retired sideshow geek, a particularly unattractive man who finds it difficult to fit into a normal town because of the obvious animosity of his neighbors. When a series of murders takes place in the area, he immediately becomes a prime suspect and narrowly escapes being lynched even though he is innocent. Unfortunately for his tormentors, their attack has freed the demonic spirit that has been locked within his body and mind for many years, and the result is a killer much more daunting than the one they originally feared. Sweet is a thoroughly realized character, and the plot is filled with surprises. Unfortunately, it was Sackett's last novel.

"Sail On! Sail On!" Philip José Farmer (1952)

Sometimes a fantasy writer takes a very absurd premise, treats it seriously, and the result is a story that sticks firmly in the reader's memory simply because it is so audacious. The science fiction writer Philip José Farmer rarely ventured into fantasy, but this story from early in his career is certainly one of his best. The story opens on the *Santa Maria,* one of Christopher Columbus's ships en route to sail around the world, but Farmer immediately warns us that something is different. For one thing, they have electric lights aboard the ship. For another, they are still in intermittent radio contact with their base back in Europe.

A friar aboard the vessel enters into a discussion of alternate worlds with two members of the crew, leading the reader to believe that the story is simply science fiction set in a world where history did not follow the same course as in our own. Farmer lulls us with additional detail, but then casually lets drop the fact that different-sized objects fall at different rates in this reality, a clear violation of the physics of our own universe. A short time later we learn that the prevailing opinion is that the Earth is shaped like a ball and that only a small minority believe that it is actually flat.

The crew is restless so far from land, and Columbus has promised to turn about if there is no indication of land ahead by the end of the day. During the morning birds are sighted, but they are strange creatures with no legs, as if they spent their entire lives in the sky never coming to earth. Later that day they come to the end of the world, which is indeed flat and which is now the instrument of their doom. Farmer leads the reader to expect one resolution, then offers the most unlikely of them all, and makes it convincing.

Saint Germain Series Chelsea Quinn Yarbro (1978–　)

Although other writers have taken advantage of the fact that vampires are supposed to be immortal to use a recurring character in differing historical situations, most notably Anne RICE and Les DANIELS, Chelsea Quinn YARBRO is the author of the longest and most historically interesting example. She introduced the character of Saint Germain in *Hotel Transylvania* (1978), set during the French Revolution. Although her vampire protagonist is not without his faults, he usually manages to secure the blood he requires without killing his victims, often by seducing women and essentially purchasing their blood with safe and rewarding sexual fulfillment, always described in romantic terms. The human villains are a good deal more repulsive, and Saint German eventually intervenes, gets into trouble, and flees, turning up next in *The Palace* (1978), this time set in 15th-century Florence, where he mingles with the nobility as part of his perpetual quest for knowledge and the acquisition of fine artwork.

It was obvious after the first two books appeared that this was going to be a popular series, although they are not horror novels in any real sense despite the vampirism. Rather, they are historical adventure stories with a touch of the fantastic, sometimes so subsidiary to the plot that it might easily have been left out altogether. *Blood Games* (1980), which moves the scene further back to ancient Rome, introduces the character of Olivia,

who also becomes a vampire and who had her own short-lived spin-off series of novels. The Mongol hordes of Genghis Khan in 13th-century China provide the stage for *Path of the Eclipse* (1981), one of the very best of the early titles in the series. As usual, Saint Germain is relatively powerless to affect the course of history. *Tempting Fate* (1982) moves forward to World War II, but Saint Germain's adventures in Nazi-dominated Europe are not nearly as entertaining as in the previous books.

Yarbro left the series for several years at that point, and when she returned it was to follow Olivia's adventures in Constantinople in *A Flame for Byzantium* (1987) and then back to Rome during the Crusades in *Crusader's Torch* (1988). After *A Candle for D'Artagnan* (1989), however, Yarbro reverted to Saint Germain and has stayed with him ever since. In *Out of the House of Life* (1990) we learn a great deal more about his past, particularly that period during which he lived in Egypt at the height of that country's ancient glory. Most of the previous novels had been set among the nobility, but he finds himself stranded in a very small and constrained society in *Better in the Dark* (1993), this time in 10th-century Germany. He returns to high society in *Darker Jewels* (1993) as an accredited envoy for Poland during the time of Ivan the Terrible.

In *Mansions of Darkness* (1996) Saint Germain decides to escape the threat of the Inquisition by traveling to the New World, where he becomes involved with the Spanish suppression of the Aztecs in one of the best of the later novels. He is an envoy again in *Writ in Blood* (1997), this time serving the czar of Russia in 1910, and is nearly killed for political reasons rather than because of his unique nature. *Blood Roses* (1998) is one of his weakest adventures and is set during the plague in 14th-century France. Olivia does not return in *Communion Blood* (1999), but Saint Germain crosses paths with one of her progeny when he visits Rome during the 17th century. *Come Twilight* (2000) is also one of the better titles. Fooled by his own emotions, Saint Germain turns a 7th-century Spanish woman into a vampire, but she is so changed by the transition that she becomes a threat to both of them.

Saint Germain returns to the land of the Mongols and has his secret exposed in *A Feast in Exile*

(2001), one of the few that revisits a culture. *Night Blooming* (2002) takes place in Europe just before Saint Germain manages to flee from the excesses of the Inquisition. *Midnight Harvest* (2003) moves forward again to the time of the Spanish Civil War, and *Dark Is the Sun* (2004) is set amidst the chaos following the explosion of Krakatowa.

Yarbro has managed to keep the series fresh and interesting by varying the time and place from volume to volume so dramatically and only occasionally repeats major plot elements. The novels appeal to fans of romance and historical fiction as well as those fond of dark fantasy. Various short adventures featuring the same protagonist were collected as *The Saint Germain Chronicles* (1983). The most interesting of the short stories is "Advocates" (1991), written in collaboration with Suzy McKee Charnas and set in a future after vampires have taken over the world. The series has been consistently successful and is ongoing as of this writing. *In the Face of Death* (2001) does not involve Saint Germain but is related to the series.

'Salem's Lot Stephen King (1975)

Vampires have been a staple of horror fiction ever since Bram STOKER created DRACULA (1897), codifying a set of powers and weaknesses of the undead that have been adopted with considerable uniformity by horror writers and horror filmmakers alike. Although many 20th-century American writers had used vampires in their fiction, the creature remained essentially a European creation, and no significant vampire novel even approached the popularity of Stoker's original until Stephen KING chose to attempt it with his second published horror book.

King elected to avoid many of the standard devices of the vampire story. Instead of an urban setting, he used a small town in Maine. (The title is an abbreviation for Jerusalem's Lot.) His vampire, although impressively evil and powerful, is off stage for most of the novel, working primarily through his agent, who opens an antique shop in town as a cover for their activities. King's vampire is not driven off by religious symbols, because it is the faith of the wielder that determines their effect. The vampire's agent, though more or less

human, is himself endowed with supernatural strength and endurance.

The story progresses more by suggestion than overt action for a very long time, and most of the conflict is among the residents of the town, a varied and not always admirable group of people. This would prove to be a trademark of King's novels, the careful development of a strong set of supporting characters, even to the point of extended departures from the main plot in order to develop a particular trait or relationship. Readers were also surprised by the closing chapters, because King again breaks with tradition. His hero fails to save the woman he loves, who is vampirized and eventually destroyed along with most of the rest of her kind. And while the two main protagonists, an adult and a teenaged boy, avoid the fate that is planned for them, the novel ends with the conclusion that they will be running for the balance of their lives, pursued by the surviving vampires.

King demonstrated that it was possible to write a major vampire novel that was not just an imitation of Stoker. His achievement was repeated the very next year when Anne RICE turned the undead into tormented, romantic figures in *INTERVIEW WITH THE VAMPIRE* (1976). The success of these two novels resulted in literally scores, perhaps hundreds, of new vampire novels during the next three decades. King's novel has been filmed twice for television.

Salvatore, R. A. (1959–)

When TSR Publishing began issuing paperback novels as an adjunct to their multiple fantasy role-playing game series, they wanted writers who would work within the comparatively narrow confines of the worlds as created in the games rather than innovative individuals who would generate their own settings and characters. The downside of this was that the end product was repetitive, usually characterless, and attracted little attention outside the gaming community. Fortunately, there was enough of an audience to support the program, which has continued for 20 years and seems healthier than ever. While it is undoubtedly true that many of the authors working in the DRAGONLANCE SERIES and FORGOTTEN REALMS SERIES were less competent than their peers in the mainstream, and probably equally true that the competent ones had few opportunities to show what they were capable of, there were a handful such as Margaret WEIS and Ed GREENWOOD whose work stood out and who used this opportunity to hone their abilities before expanding their careers into other markets.

With the possible exception of Margaret Weis, Robert Anthony Salvatore has been the most successful in establishing himself with mainstream fantasy readers. He continues to write for TSR and is, in fact, one of their best-selling authors, but his best work is now reserved for other publishers. Salvatore debuted with *The Crystal Shard* (1988), the first in the Icewind Dale trilogy, followed by *Streams of Silver* (1989) and *The Halfling's Gem* (1990). One of the characters in that sequence, Drizzt, later became much more prominent in his fiction. The sequence is a typical quest adventure involving a magical gem that has a personality of its own and the usual round of captures and escapes. It is fairly well written, and the trilogy has recently been reprinted in a single volume but is not distinguished enough to suggest that Salvatore was any more promising than his contemporaries at TSR. Much more interesting is a second series from a different publisher, the Black Warlock sequence, consisting of *Echoes of the Fourth Magic* (1990), *The Witch's Daughter* (1991), and, after a long gap, *Bastion of Darkness* (2000). A modern submarine is transported into a distant future when magic has supplanted technology, where they have a series of typical though well-told adventures.

His next several books were for TSR. *Homeland* (1990), *Exile* (1990), and *Sojourn* (1991) make up the Dark Elf series, whose protagonist grows increasingly alienated from his people and eventually escapes to a better world. The Cleric series consists of *Canticle* (1991), *In Sylvan Shadows* (1992), *Night Masks* (1992), *The Fallen Fortress* (1993), and *The Chaos Curse* (1994). This series was the first to provide clear evidence that Salvatore was capable of much better work. The protagonist is a monk who has dedicated his life to the preservation of a library and who battles an ancient evil throughout the series. By now Salvatore was firmly established

as one of the leading writers in the Forgotten Realms series, and with *The Legacy* (1992) he began to develop the culture of the Drow, a variety of elf, and the personality of Drizzt, his most popular recurring character, who reappears in various novels from that point forward. Their underground world is expanded upon in *Starless Night* (1993).

Salvatore ventured outside the TSR world again with the Spearwielder's trilogy, which includes *The Woods out Back* (1993), *The Dragon's Dagger* (1994), and *Dragonslayer's Return* (1995). The three novels, which each stand separately, involve the adventures of a man from our reality who finds a mystical gateway to an alternate world where magic works. Although entertaining adventures, they are actually less substantial than some of his game tie-ins, but it was clear that Salvatore intended to branch out and write in worlds of his own creation rather than continue to dabble in the imaginations of others. He continued to write occasional tie-in novels, but his next substantial work was the Crimson Shadow trilogy, *The Sword of Bedwyr* (1995), *Luthien's Gamble* (1996), and *The Dragon King* (1996). Luthien is an unlikely hero who becomes increasingly disturbed by the cruelties of his new king and eventually becomes the leader of a rebellion against the throne. The king turns out to be a demon. The trilogy is typical mainstream fantasy adventure, but Salvatore's ability to tell a rousing adventure story and create memorable characters was finally beginning to attract attention outside the gaming universe.

The Demon Awakens (1996) and its two sequels, *The Demon Spirit* (1998) and *The Demon Apostle* (1999), propelled Salvatore to the front rank of fantasy writers. An evil demon raises an army of goblins in an attempt to seize control of the land of Corona and is repulsed in three separate but related campaigns. A second trilogy continues the story, consisting of *Ascendance* (2001), *Transcendence* (2002), and *Immortalis* (2003), in which a woman must find the will and the skill to defeat a curse that has turned her son into an agent of evil. Although Salvatore continues to write for the gaming world, now under the imprint Wizards of the Coast, his contributions there are less frequent, though they invariably, as in *Sea of Swords* (2001) and *The Thousand Orcs* (2002), rise above their limited subject matter. The best of his recent work is the atypical *The Highwayman* (2004), a much more restrained adventure with more fully realized characters.

Salvatore has developed from a competent but minor name to one of the leading authors of mainstream fantasy adventure. Although his plots are familiar and he takes few chances in his writing, he clearly has begun to produce more substantial work on a regular basis. His short fiction has been rare and minor, but "The Coach with Big Teeth" (1996) suggests he might also do better at that length in the future.

Sarban (John William Wall) (1910–1989)

Sarban was the pen name of the British diplomat John William Wall, who published only three books but who immediately established himself as one of the premier writers of atmospheric horror fiction. His books include three relatively brief novels and a handful of short stories, most of which have been repeatedly reprinted since their original appearance. The first of his books was *Ringstones and Other Curious Tales* (1951). The title story, a short novel, describes the adventures of Daphne, a young woman who agrees to serve as a kind of governess to three children at the remote Ringstones mansion, named for a circle of standing stones similar to Stonehenge. The children strike her as more than a bit odd, particularly the oldest boy, whose cruel tricks eventually lead her to attempt to leave. When she does so, the very landscape changes around her, foiling her escape, although she ultimately survives. The children, or at least the boy, is apparently not entirely human, perhaps a refugee from the world of fairies.

There were three short stories in the original edition that were dropped for the paperback. The best of these is "Calmahain," in which three children living under unhappy circumstances build a magical boat in which to escape. "The Khan" mixes an unhappy marriage with the appearance of a man who is also a bear, and "Capra" involves a caprice of the god Pan. Although none of these stories are of the same quality as the novella, they are rendered in a rich and entertaining prose and deserve wider dissemination.

The Sound of His Horn (1952) is a more difficult novel to describe. In form it would seem to be science fiction rather than horror, because it is apparently set in a future after the Nazis have won World War II, one in which members of the "lesser" races are hunted as game animals. As a straightforward adventure, this might not be horror at all, but Sarban places the story in a world that seems virtually untouched by technology and that may not be our future at all but rather some strange alternate reality. *The Dollmaker* (1953) is the best of his longer works. A young woman becomes involved with a mysterious man who has created an elaborate world of animated dolls. She eventually discovers that the dolls are magically enlivened by the essences of human beings her "friend" has killed and that she is in line to join the cast.

Sarban's work has recently been reprinted in new editions, including previously uncollected stories. Despite the very small body of work he produced, his reputation has not dimmed with the passage of time. His gift for creating worlds just slightly askew from our own has rarely been equaled.

"Sardonicus" Ray Russell (1960)

Although Ray Russell wrote several excellent short fantasy and horror stories, the one for which he will be best remembered is this tale of a man trapped by his own grotesque past. Robert Cargrave is a prominent 19th-century English physician who specializes in problems involving disorders of the muscles, especially the development and use of relaxants. He is surprised but not displeased to receive a letter from Maude Randall, to whom he had been romantically inclined several years earlier but who had disappeared after her family suffered bankruptcy. She is now married to a man named Sardonicus and living in Bohemia, and she and her husband express their desire to have him visit.

Although not entirely certain what is intended, Cargrave cannot pass up the opportunity to visit Maude, finding her much dispirited and living in a castle built in the shape of a skull. His arrival there is reminiscent of Jonathan Harker's visit to the vampire's castle in DRACULA (1897) by Bram STOKER, almost certainly a conscious effort on the author's part. The story itself reads like a cross between Stoker and Edgar Allan POE, specifically "THE FALL OF THE HOUSE OF USHER" (1839). Her husband, Sardonicus, suffers from a peculiar ailment. The muscles of the lower half of his face are paralyzed in a ghastly grin, a disfigurement both he and Cargrave recognize as being psychological rather than physical and the result of his experience as a young man when he robbed his father's grave and was so shocked by the condition of the body that his face froze in a grimace.

The reason for Cargrave's invitation is now evident, and he attempts to alleviate the problem, knowing full well that it is the man's mind, not his body, that is responsible. Sardonicus has become so disturbed by his situation that he first offers Cargrave his wife for sexual gratification, then threatens her with horrible punishments to induce him to try further treatments. The physician finally agrees, sending for various chemicals and experimenting on animals before indicating he is ready for a human subject. The injections work, and Sardonicus's face relaxes into a normal expression, although his jaw muscles are unresponsive, preventing him from talking. Cargrave assures him this is a temporary condition and leaves, taking Maude and a statement of annulment of their marriage along with him.

It is only years later that he learns of Sardonicus's fate. Although his face was restored to normal, he never regained the use of his jaw muscles and eventually starved to death. His end is doubly ironic, because Cargrave did not inject him with any miraculous experimental drug but with plain water, suspecting that it was the man's mental state that needed treatment. The story is marvelously well balanced, every paragraph contributing to the advancement of the plot, with a clever but logical conclusion that satisfies the reader's sense of justice without blemishing the character of the hero.

Sarrantonio, Al (1952–)

Although Al Sarrantonio sold several short science fiction stories during the early 1980s, his first several novels were all horror. His debut was with *To-*

tentanz (1985), which makes use of the time-honored horror theme of the mysterious carnival most notably used in THE CIRCUS OF DR. LAO (1935) by Charles G. Finney and SOMETHING WICKED THIS WAY COMES (1962) by Ray BRADBURY. Sarrantonio's carnival springs up overnight, and everyone in town is fascinated by it except for one young boy who can see the truth behind the illusion. That same year saw the publication of *Worms*, which borrows its monstrous worms from science fiction, setting them free to prey on humans.

Campbell Wood (1986) displays far more originality. A race of mysterious people live in a remote stretch of woods, They are possibly a kind of fairy, or perhaps the originals from which fairy legends developed, capable of using the trees as weapons against their enemies. Although slow to develop, the story becomes quite engaging once it is underway. Far more impressive is *The Boy with Penny Eyes* (1987), in which an orphan retreats into what appears to be a form of autism but which is actually a sign that he is watching for a supernatural attack. Sarrantonio followed up these two thoughtful, moody horror tales with *Moonbane* (1989), an homage to low-budget science fiction films. The moon is inhabited after all, by werewolves who descend upon the Earth in an all-out invasion. Although the premise cannot be taken seriously, the result is a gleefully gruesome spoof.

A supernatural creature wears humans as masks in *October* (1990), and a powerful entity from another reality turns people into her puppets in *House Haunted* (1991), two satisfying but unremarkable thrillers. *Skeletons* (1992) is to date his most impressive and original novel. Through some unexplained means, all of the skeletons on Earth become animated and attempt to resume their former lives. Lenin and his followers conduct a bloodbath in the former Soviet Union, for example. Serious sequences are mixed with broad satire, but Sarrantonio balances them well enough that the story succeeds on both levels.

His most recent horror novel is the mildly disappointing *Orangefield* (2002, also published as *Hallow's Eve*). Two collections of his short fiction have also appeared, *Toybox* (2000) and *Hornets and Others* (2004). Among his better short fiction are "Under My Bed" (1981), "The Quiet Ones"

(1983), "The Dancing Foot" (1986), and "The Trail of the Chromium Bandits" (1989). He has also edited two major anthologies: *999* (1999) is horror fiction, and *Flights* (2004) is fantasy.

"Satan and Sam Shay" Robert Arthur (1942)

One of the most underrated authors from the pulp era was Robert Arthur, whose clever tales of horror and fantasy had a peculiarly American flavor and whose gift for narrative has ensured his lasting reputation in the field. Perhaps his most famous story is this clever account of an encounter with Satan and the consequences of beating the devil at his own game. Sam Shay is a likeable man, generous, good hearted, and thoughtful, but he has a major shortcoming, at least in the eyes of Shannon Malloy, who hoped to marry him. Sam is a gambler, a fairly successful one who takes chances for the joy of it rather than just to win. Not a day passes that he fails to place at least one bet, and his success is such that he has no need to actually work for a living. Unfortunately, Shannon objects to gambling, and when she finally abandons all hope of reforming him, she returns his ring and resigns herself to finding someone else to marry.

Sam's good fortune continues. His skill at beating the odds is such that several of his friends have insisted that he could place three bets with the devil and win them all, and Satan, intrigued, shows up to find out if it is true. Sam quickly defeats him through some clever word play, and the devil, infuriated, vows that all the forces of hell will be invoked to prevent him from ever winning another bet in his life. Although Sam thinks it was all just a dream when he wakens the following morning, events prove that it was not, as the most unlikely series of circumstances arise to prevent him from winning even the safest of wagers.

There ensues a struggle between Sam and the legions of hell. Sam constructs complex, multilayered, and contradictory bets, all of which fail. The strain is considerable on the other side, however, and so many of the devil's minions are occupied with the task that the general level of temptation in the world drops noticeably. Even worse, the often miraculous interventions required to ensure Sam loses have generated a religious revival. Satan

stubbornly refuses to revoke his vow, but eventually Sam figures out how to profit from it, opening an insurance company and placing bets against his clients, thereby ensuring that they will never need to collect. Shannon agrees to marry him, although only after a bit of connivance on Sam's part, and everyone except the devil lives happily ever after. "Satan and Sam Shay" is a clever story, succinctly told, and has become an acknowledged classic of its type.

Saul, John (1942–)

John Saul's first horror novel appeared in the same year as *THE SHINING* (1977) by Stephen KING, and his subsequent work has often been compared to that of King and Dean R. KOONTZ. Although Saul is generally considered the least original and interesting of the three, he has enjoyed best-seller status for many of his books. He almost always provides a satisfying story, although from time to time his plots do not hold up under close scrutiny. His first novel was *Suffer the Children* (1977), the story of a ghostly child who returns after a century, influencing living children and driving them to commit horrible acts. The wrathful child ghost proved to be a common device in Saul's early novels. His follow-up was *Punish the Sinners* (1978), in which another secret from the past strikes among the students at a girls' school, driving several of them to commit suicide. This proved to be the most suspenseful and convincing of Saul's novels until the 1990s. His third, *Cry for the Strangers* (1979), is only marginally horror and deals with a town so hostile to outsiders that they frequently end up dead. Is it the townspeople or a supernatural force?

Comes the Blind Fury (1980) revisits the concept of the ghost child. This time the angry spirit can assume physical form and pretends to be a visitor, slowly insinuating herself into the community in order to wreak vengeance for her own accidental death years earlier. Saul's young ghosts had used children to strike at adults, but in his next, *When the Wind Blows* (1981), the angry spirit kills her childish allies as well as their parents. *The God Project* (1982, also published as *All Fall Down*) involves children once again, but this time Saul drifted toward a medical thriller. A woman discovers that her child is the subject of an unauthorized and terrifying experiment and takes desperate measures to unmask the plot. His next, *Nathaniel* (1984), is a retreat to more familiar ground, with a young boy falling under the influence of yet another dead child planning vengeance against the living.

The pattern continues with only a slight variation in *Brain Child* (1985). This time a boy who temporarily dies in surgery has his personality supplanted by that of an angry wraith with the usual agenda. Although Saul's technical skills as a writer were improving, the repetitive plots limited his appeal. *Hell Fire* (1986), for example, is well written and relentlessly suspenseful, but the angry ghosts seeking revenge against those that allowed them to die in a fire include a large number of children, and many of the individual scenes feel as though they were rewritten from previous novels. The child protagonist of *The Unwanted* (1987) similarly falls under the sway of an angry supernatural evil.

The Unloved (1988) breaks the pattern slightly, describing the descent of an entire family into madness and violence. The malevolent child in *Creature* (1989) is not a ghost, but he functions in much the same fashion for dramatic purposes. *Sleepwalk* (1990) is a conspiracy story in which a large corporation secretly experiments with the children in a small community, causing the usual inevitable death and destruction. The mystery unfolds in a nicely paced manner, but the logic of the situation does not hold up under scrutiny. *Second Child* (1990), although another story of a child ghost, reverses his usual formula and casts the ghost in the role of protector rather than nemesis.

Darkness (1991) and *Shadows* (1992) both involve threats to children, and both seem well below Saul's usual standards. *Guardian* (1993), another evil child story, is only marginally better. *The Homing* (1994) is actively awful, the story of a serial killer who meets his doom when genetically altered bees invade the bodies of the local children and begin to control their behavior. *Black Lightning* (1995), which also involves a serial killer, is much better, his most successful novel in more than a decade.

In 1996 Stephen King published *The Green Mile* as a series of six small paperbacks, although it was one continuous story, similar to the Blackwater series by Michael McDOWELL published in the middle of the 1980s. Saul and his publishers tried to mimic this success with the Blackstone stories, published in similar fashion in 1997. Each installment of the Blackstone series is a separate story with a separate cast of characters, which robs the series of any dramatic impetus, and the stories themselves are not memorable. Saul finally returned to novel length with *The Presence* (1999), probably his best novel to date, an intriguing mystery involving unusual skeletons and something hiding in the ocean.

His more recent novels have been inconsistent. *The Right Hand of Evil* (1999) returns to the theme of ghostly children, and there is another nasty ghost in the unremarkable *Nightshade* (2000). Elderly people use sorcery to steal life from the young in *Midnight Voices* (2002), and two teenagers find a book of magical spells that really work and use them to get even with their enemies in *Black Creek Crossing* (2004). Saul has developed into a technically competent and sometimes interesting writer who retards his own development by constraining himself to a limited number of themes and settings. At the same time, it must be admitted that it has proven to be a successful strategy for his career and has gained him a solid corps of loyal readers.

Saxon, Peter (1921–1983)

Peter Saxon was a frequently used pseudonym of Wilfrid McNeilly, who also wrote horror fiction as W. A. Ballinger and Errol Lecale, as well as thrillers under other names, and who also shared the Peter Saxon name with other writers, making it impossible to determine with certainty who was responsible for some titles that appeared under that name. The bulk of McNeilly's horror fiction fell into two series, the Guardians series as Peter Saxon and the Specialist series as Errol Lecale.

The Guardians series consists of separate adventures of an organization that has dedicated itself to opposing evil occult powers, sometimes using magic itself to turn the tide. In *The Curse of Rathlaw* (1968) a family with a heritage of sorcery is threatened when one man plots to sacrifice his brother in order to acquire enhanced powers. *Dark Ways to Death* (1968) is a surprisingly complex story about a cult of Satan worshippers who live a secret life concealed beneath a major city. In *The Haunting of Alan Mais* (1968), the best in the series, one of the guardians is supernaturally corrupted during a visit to a haunted house and attacks the organization from within. They travel to Australia to involve themselves in aboriginal magic in *The Killing Bone* (1968) and battle an occult evil that exists simultaneously in more than one age in *Through the Dark Curtain* (1968). *The Vampires of Finistere* (1970) is also quite original, the story of a town overrun by a variety of vampire that lives in the ocean.

The Specialist series, all six written as Errol Lecale, similarly explore a variety of traditional horror themes, with the occult investigator protagonist triumphing over all of his adversaries, but the individual stories, which involve shape-changers, a curse, a ghoul, and other magical terrors are considerably less substantial and more formulaic than the Guardians novels. McNeilly's nonseries efforts vary considerably in quality. *Drums of the Dark Gods* (1966), written as W. A. Ballinger, is a disorganized occult adventure that is frequently implausible but sometimes quite exciting. The cult of Kali is resurgent in *The Darkest Night* (1966), and *Black Honey* (1968) pits modern society against African witchcraft. *Satan's Child* (1967) rather routinely describes the efforts of a magically empowered man to avenge the death of his mother. *The Torturer* (1966) and *Vampire's Moon* (1970) are both routine vampire novels, although well told. *The Disorientated Man* (1966, also published as *Scream and Scream Again*) mixes the supernatural with superscience and was the basis of a bland horror film. McNeilly failed to distinguish himself under any of his various names, but his Guardians series in particular suggested that he was able to bring new ideas to an old venue and turn them into good if not spectacular novels.

Scarborough, Elizabeth Ann (1947–   )

Elizabeth Ann Scarborough started her career writing lightly humorous, traditional fantasies in familiar settings. Her first novel, *Song of Sorcery* (1982), introduces Maggie Brown, a good witch who sets out on various quests, and her career concludes in *The Unicorn Creed* (1983), which was followed by two related novels set in the same universe, *Bronwyn's Bane* (1983) and *The Christening Quest* (1985). The second set of two follows a similar path, although the protagonist's curse—she is incapable of telling the truth—leads to some amusing situations.

Scarborough continued to experiment with settings throughout the 1980s, but for most of that time she continued to use a light, playful style. *The Harem of Aman Akbar* (1984) is an Arabian Nights–style adventure in which one of three wives of a powerful man decides to intervene when her husband is magically transformed. *The Drastic Dragon of Draco, Texas* (1986) anachronistically drops a traditional dragon into a small Texas town, where it is subsequently tamed by a young woman. *The Goldcamp Vampire* (1987) is set in the Yukon during the Gold Rush, a climate ideally suited for an amicable vampire who takes advantage of the extended nights.

Scarborough was firmly established as a writer of light adventure stories when she finally turned to more serious themes. *The Healer's War* (1978), which won the Nebula Award as best novel of the year, describes the transformation of a nurse assigned to duty during the war in Vietnam. Her unsuspected magical talent is detected by a local healer who gives her an amulet that enables her to see through the lies people tell. *Nothing Sacred* (1991) is technically science fiction, but in the sequel, *The Last Refuge* (1992), we discover in the aftermath of a nuclear war that reincarnation and other supposedly fictional concepts are real. An interesting but minor trilogy followed, in which supernatural forces attempt to wipe out folk music, which in some fashion guards humanity. The titles are *Phantom Banjo* (1991), *Picking the Ballad's Bones* (1991), and *Strum Again?* (1992).

The Godmother trilogy, *The Godmother* (1994), *The Godmother's Apprentice* (1995), and *The Godmother's Web* (1998), returns to her earlier light humor, although it has grown more sophisticated and is woven around serious themes. A genuine fairy godmother solves various problems in contemporary America. *The Lady in the Loch* (1998) is more serious, a blend of historical novel and alternate world fantasy in which Sir Walter Scott apprehends a killer seeking to perform a black magic ritual. Some of Scarborough's short fiction has been collected in *Scarborough Faire* (2003). One of her best is "Carol for Another Christmas" (1996), in which Ebenezer Scrooge's ghost visits a modern-day woman.

"The Scent of Vinegar" Robert Bloch (1993)

Although vampires show up in one form or another in the myth systems of a wide variety of cultures, most horror writers follow the model of the European vampire, as created by J. Sheridan LE FANU, Bram STOKER, and others. Robert BLOCH, one of the more prolific and consistently entertaining authors of short horror and suspense fiction, chose to invoke a very different tradition in this Bram Stoker Award–winning story.

Greg Kolmer is a tabloid reporter who thinks he may have stumbled onto a good thing. During an interview with an aging Hollywood star, he learns of the existence of a brothel that was once the secret rendezvous of many influential and now rich movie industry figures, a brothel that eventually switched emphasis to sadomasochism and other extreme fetishes. He also learns that the operator of the brothel, the Marquess, was secretly taping and photographing her clients as part of a plan to blackmail them that never came to fruition. Kolmer then ascertains the approximate location from another man and finds the remote, decaying house. Unfortunately, he also finds the animated corpse of a young Asian woman who removes her own head, sending him racing to safety.

Unfortunately for Kolmer, someone else is on the same trail and knows of his interest. An Asian man who identifies himself as the son of a one-time employee of the brothel holds him at gunpoint, forcing him to return to the abandoned building. He tells Kolmer that the creature is a "penangallan," a Malaysian vampire that hunts by removing its head and that flies around in search of a victim with its entrails hanging below. The penangallan must soak its entrails in vinegar before

returning to its body and is otherwise fairly analogous to European vampires.

They drive a stake through the creature's heart before searching the remainder of the building, where they find only desiccated fragments of the rest of the penangallans, who were all killed and devoured by the one survivor. They also find the remains of the blackmail cache, destroyed beyond any possibility of ever being put to use. Kolmer, suspecting that his partner will kill him to cover his tracks, acts preemptively, but his own escape is thwarted by the penangallan's head, which can survive separately from the now-disabled body.

There are two ways in which a writer can make us care about the fate of a character in a horror story: by making them so likeable that we sympathize with them or so annoying that we are rewarded by their eventual fate. Bloch took the latter route in this case in what is probably the best story from the later part of his long and successful writing career.

Schow, David J. (1955–   )

David Schow quickly established a reputation with the explicit gore and violence of his short stories and, in fact, is credited with having coined the term *splatterpunk* to refer to writers who chose that path. He is also a distinctly regional writer, reflecting Californian settings and attitudes in most of his published fiction. Schow has written only a few novels, thrillers that rely on psychological horror rather than fantastic content, although *Rock Breaks Scissors Cuts* (2003) comes very close to being supernatural. He has also produced a large body of distinctive short fiction, most of it collected in six volumes between 1988 and 2004.

Schow's stories are widely varied in theme and treatment, ranging from quiet and thoughtful to gross-out horror. In "One for the Horrors" (1983) a decaying movie theater shows old films that inexplicably have new and sometimes horrible scenes never shown in the originals. "Coming Soon to a Theater near You" (1984) has a very similar setting, but this time the theater is run by the animated dead. Dinosaurs mysteriously begin reappearing in the world in "Sedalia" (1989), apparently through some magical change in the laws of nature. "Scoop

Makes a Swirly" (1994) takes the reader on a tour of a bizarre underground world and the society an outsider finds there. The protagonist of "Petition" (2001) can hear prayers, sometimes very perverted ones. Other stories of note include "Lonesome Coyote Blues" (1985), "Where the Heart Was" (1993), and "The Thing Too Hideous to Describe" (2004). There is often an element of very twisted humor in his fiction. "Red Light" (1986) won the World Fantasy Award.

The best selection of his work can be found in *Lost Angels* (1990). The recent collection *Zombie Jam* (2004) consists of four stories about zombies, the George Romero variety rather than those associated with voodoo. "Jerry's Kids Meet Wormboy" is the longest and most interesting, set in a post-collapse future in which the zombies have virtually taken over the world. Schow also edited a very good anthology of movie-related horror fiction titled *Silver Scream* (1988). He has recently begun to write more actively following a comparatively inactive period.

The Screwtape Letters C. S. Lewis (1942)

The Screwtape Letters, expanded and reissued in 1961 as *The Screwtape Letters and Screwtape Proposes a Toast,* is a satire cast in epistolary form, that is, it consists entirely of an interchange of letters between two demons, one senior and one junior, with the former, Screwtape, lecturing the latter, Wormwood, on the finer points of seducing and corrupting the souls of the unwary. Lewis pokes fun at a number of human institutions and predispositions, but bureaucracy in all its obstructive and wasteful manifestations is its primary target.

Lewis was not writing specifically for a young adult audience, although the book is frequently employed as a means to stimulate discussion among students on various Christian issues in an entertaining format. One of Lewis's major concerns is temptation toward evil. Those who tempt us away from a righteous life are fearful of being discovered for what they are and anxious to prove they have the power to influence the thoughts and actions of others. The discussions also touch on the attainment of grace, the validity of sincere repentance, and the very nature of good versus evil.

Despite the profundity of the subject matter, Lewis maintains a light, bantering tone throughout that makes his arguments more accessible to the average reader. Lewis also excoriates complacency and advocates a more active role for the genuine believer. The later epilogue, "Screwtape Proposes a Toast," is more controversial, an indictment of the commonly held opinion that everyone should be considered as equals. The examples Lewis provides are often less than convincing and perhaps betray his personal class prejudices.

"Seasons of Belief"   Michael Bishop (1979)

Christmas stories tend to be light and airy, but occasionally a writer decides to look at a darker side of that magical season. Donald Westlake did so with "NACKLES" (1964), the story of the anti–Santa Claus, and Michael Bishop, who has won two Hugo Awards for his science fiction, does so in one of his rare excursions into fantasy and horror. Stefa and Nimbo are brother and sister, five and seven years old, respectively, who want to relieve the pre-Christmas Eve boredom by having their father tell them a story, preferably a scary one. He agrees to do so and tells them about the "grither."

The grither is a one-of-a-kind monster who lives in the Arctic and who kills anyone who mentions his name. When Stefa decides this story is too scary, her mother tells her it is too late to stop because they have already spoken the creature's name. According to their father no one knows exactly what the grither looks like because everyone who has ever seen it has been gobbled up, although illogically he provides a vivid description anyway. Although the grither travels very fast, it needs to hear its name repeated in order to find its prey, so the only chance of surviving is to finish the story quickly. Much to the children's dismay, however, the telephone rings, causing a lengthy delay.

Just as the story is drawing toward its climax, there is a sound at the door, terrifying the children until the newcomers are identified as their grandparents. Their father then assures them that the story was imaginary and that creatures that exist only in their imagination cannot do any harm. But later that evening Stefa, who does believe in the grither, mentions its name one final time, and that is when the grither finally arrives. The author never explains the ending in any detail, leaving it to our own imagination to speculate about what follows. The concept that a strong enough belief can have physical effects on the world is a common one in fantasy and horror, but it has rarely been used to such chilling effect.

The Sentinel Jeffrey Konvitz (1974)

Much American horror fiction at least implicitly has a religious undertone, good versus evil, and often makes it much more explicit and clearly Christian. Vampires are repelled by crosses and holy water, demons cannot enter hallowed ground, and satanists use altered versions of Christian religious rituals. Some of the most famous horror novels have been even more clearly religiously themed. William Peter Blatty's THE EXORCIST (1971) involves the efforts by two priests to expel a demon from a child it has possessed, and THE OMEN (1976), by David Seltzer, involves the coming of the Antichrist. More recently, Thomas F. MONTELEONE used strong religious themes in several novels, including *The Blood of the Lamb* (1993), *The Reckoning* (1999), and *Eyes of the Virgin* (2002).

Jeffrey Konvitz drew on that same resource for his first novel, *The Sentinel* (1974). The story involves a fashion model who moves into a new apartment building. Shortly after meeting one of her neighbors, an enigmatic blind priest, she begins to experience vivid recollections of unpleasant incidents from her past, including her unsuccessful suicide attempts. She is also bothered by the noises caused by other residents in the apartment house, a collection of distorted and unpleasant characters she never sees outside the building. When she finally decides to investigate directly, she discovers that she and the priest are the only tenants and that the others are illusions. That leads to the revelation that the priest is actually guarding a doorway between our world and hell and that the sounds she hears are the demons trying to break through. Even worse, she has not come there by accident but has been manipulated by the church, which plans to use her as a replacement for the priest, who is dying.

Konvitz cowrote the screenplay for the 1977 film version and then added a sequel, *The Guardian* (1979, also published as *Sentinel II* and as *The Apocalypse*), which introduced new protagonists but which is otherwise basically a minor variation of the original story and less effective because we already know what the guardian really does. His only other published novel, *Monster* (1982, also published as *The Beast*), is a relatively suspenseful story of the Loch Ness monster.

Serling, Rod (1924–1975)

Rod Serling will, of course, always be remembered for hosting and writing many of the scripts for the popular television series *The Twilight Zone*, which ran from 1959 through 1964, its title becoming a part of everyday vernacular. The television series won three Hugo Awards for best dramatic presentation. A second series of similarly formatted anthology stories was *Night Gallery*, which ran from 1970 through 1973. Although Serling adapted some stories by other writers, perhaps most notably "IT'S A GOOD LIFE" (1953), by Jerome Bixby, and "LITTLE GIRL LOST" (1953), by Richard MATHESON, he penned a very large proportion of the screenplays and original stories himself. Serling, who also wrote outside the genre, won numerous awards for his dramatic work during his lifetime.

Although Serling was active as a writer beyond the limits of his television career, his strongest and best-remembered works can be found in the three collections of stories he adapted from his own screenplays, *Stories from the Twilight Zone* (1960), *More Stories from the Twilight Zone* (1961), and *New Stories from the Twilight Zone* (1962). They were published in one volume in 1998. Two further collections from *Night Gallery* are of lesser interest. Serling ranged from science fiction to fantasy to horror, but most of his stories share a very similar tone. "The Monsters Are Due on Maple Street" (1960), in which the terrors that spread through a typical suburb prove to be completely imaginary, is typical in that it demonstrates that most of our fears are of our own making.

Serling had a superb talent for suspense, as in "Where Is Everybody?" (1960) and "The Odyssey of Flight 33" (1961), as well as an inventive sense of dark humor, shown in "Mr. Dingle the Strong" (1961) and "The Rip Van Winkle Caper" (1962). He often took elements of popular culture and transformed them, skewering baseball in "The Mighty Casey" (1960) and the traditional western in "The Showdown with Rance McGrew" (1962). Although he usually used modern themes and settings, he occasionally drew upon historical events, as in "The Big Tall Wish (1961) and "Ghost Train." Serling's prose is transparent and workmanlike, and several of his stories might well have become minor classics even if they had been published in print form initially rather than as adaptations of television scripts. As it is, unfortunately, they are generally regarded as shadows of the televised versions rather than artistic works in their own right.

"The Shadow over Innsmouth"
H. P. Lovecraft (1936)

One of the recurring themes in the work of H. P. LOVECRAFT is the physical decay and degradation of human stock, a reflection of his personal reservations about the influx of immigrants in his home city. The most obvious example is in this, one of his very best stories, in which a tourist becomes intrigued when he hears of Innsmouth, a formerly prosperous seaport now home to a small population of inbred, unattractive, insular people who are despised and even feared by outsiders. On a whim he decides to spend a day in the town, despite warnings about their unfriendliness and their strange habits, which include adherence to a religious cult known as the Esoteric Order of Dagon.

Immediately upon arriving he notices a strange similarity among the population. They have rough, scaly skin, misshapen heads, and a tendency to go bald while still very young, and the older residents remain out of sight, presumably hidden in their homes. They also have a fondness for a particularly exotic form of jewelry. Although repulsed by what he sees, the narrator plies one elderly man with whiskey and learns the history of the town, that in generations past the residents abandoned God to worship other deities that live in the sea, but that as part of the deal they interbred with the sea creatures, which explains their

fishlike features. However, he says too much and finally warns his companion to get out of town immediately, to run for his life. Upset though not yet alarmed, the narrator decides to leave but discovers at the last minute that there is no transportation out of town for the rest of the day and that he is stranded.

During the night a party of locals attempts to break into his room. He escapes through a window and is pursued, and during the course of that pursuit he recognizes that some of those chasing him move in a manner that suggests they are no longer entirely human. Although he ultimately eludes them and precipitates an armed assault on the town by the authorities, he has been corrupted by the contact, and the story ends with him resolving to return, to swim down into the harbor, and to find the powerful creatures who transformed the residents of Innsmouth. The story, which is part of Lovecraft's Cthulhu Mythos, was the inspiration for the film *Dagon* (2001).

The Shadowrun Series

Like the FORGOTTEN REALMS, WARHAMMER, and DRAGONLANCE books, this series of novels is based on a role-playing game system, Shadowrun. The setting is a variation of generally urban fantasy set in the near future, which allows magical and technological wonders to be mixed. The basic premise is that our world and one where elves and fairies exist overlap so that England might once again become home to the druids, for example, and dragons and other mythical creatures exist alongside aircraft and corporations.

As with the other series, the Shadowrun books are usually written by a group of writers who specialize in shared-world universes based on game systems, including in this case Nigel Findley, Lisa Smedman, Jak Koke, and Nyx Smith. The most prominent Shadowrun author is Robert Charrette, who has moved on to other publishers with several generic fantasy adventures. A few independently established writers have also contributed to the series, including Mel Odom, Michael Stackpole, and Nick Pollotta.

Some of the titles are light adventures with considerable humor, as is the case with *Never Trust* an *Elf* (1991) and *Choose Your Enemies Carefully* (1991), both by Robert Charrette. Some are cast in the form of tough detective stories such as *House of the Sun* (1995), by Nigel Findley, and disaster thrillers such as *Clockwork Asylum* (1997), by Jak Koke. *Streets of Blood* (1992), by Carl Sargent and Marc Gascoigne, is a more traditional murder mystery, while *The Lucifer Deck* (1997), by Lisa Smedman, is a technothriller. Other titles such as *Worlds Without End* (1995), by Caroline Spector, verge on supernatural horror.

Although to date none of the novels in the series is individually outstanding, they vary enough from one title to the next to keep the reader guessing and make the shared universe a reasonably complex and interesting one. There are no common characters, which detracts from any real sense of continuity, and the settings are also scattered all over the world. This variation helps keep the series reasonably fresh, although it is less likely to hold on to a dedicated group of readers.

Sharp, Margery (1905–1991)

Although Margery Sharp wrote primarily mainstream adult fiction prior to 1959, one of those novels was actually her first fantasy, *The Stone of Chastity* (1940), a marginal piece set in a village where a magical stone that can determine whether women are virginal causes considerable upset when some women object to being subjected to the test. She made no real impact on the fantasy field until 1959, and then primarily for younger reader, when she produced the first adventure of Miss Bianca, *The Rescuers,* and introduced the Rescuers, a band of mice who have taken as their mission the freeing of prisoners of various kinds. In their debut the Rescuers liberate one of their number who is held in a dungeon by a nasty cat, but in the first sequel, *Miss Bianca* (1962), they expand their efforts to come to the aid of a human child.

Their selflessness is put to the test in *The Turret* (1963) because their latest victim is himself a rather horrible character. The mission is more important, however, and predictably the act of kindness has its effect. By *Miss Bianca in the Salt Mines* (1966) the stories had become somewhat formulaic, but the title character and her faithful assistant, Bernard, were

endearing enough to sustain additional volumes, which included trips to Asia in *Miss Bianca in the Orient* (1970), the South Pole in *Miss Bianca in Antarctica* (1971), and back home in *Miss Bianca and the Bridesmaid* (1972).

The next two volumes vary from the formula, concentrating on Bernard, who has various adventures opposing and finally defeating an army of rats in *Bernard the Brave* (1976) and *Bernard into Battle* (1978). Their final adventure was *The Rescuers Down Under* (1991), written in conjunction with the animated film of the same title. There had been a previous animated movie of their adventures, *The Rescuers* (1977), which drew upon multiple books. The Miss Bianca series, particularly the earlier volumes, are among the better children's fantasies, but like many similar books they are probably in the long term doomed to be overshadowed by the film versions.

She H. Rider Haggard (1886)

H. Rider HAGGARD was the master of the lost world adventure, producing almost a dozen of them during his lifetime, the most famous of which was *King Solomon's Mines* (1885), which also featured his most popular recurring character, Allan Quatermain, a great white hunter and explorer. His second-most-famous was Ayesha, the immortal demigoddess of *She*. The chief protagonist is Leo Vincey, the descendant of a woman who lost her love to Ayesha, a white woman who never ages and who lives in a concealed land in a remote part of Asia. Although Ayesha is her proper name, she is known to her people as She Who Must Be Obeyed. Vincey is determined to avenge his ancestor and after several adventures finally finds the lost land. Vincey turns out to be a reincarnation of the long-dead, unfaithful lover, and he, Ayesha, and Vincey's companion are trapped in a repetition of the romantic triangle that resulted in the first tragedy. The plot thickens, and eventually Ayesha attempts to win Vincey's heart by stepping into an immortal flame, but against all expectations it leads to her apparent doom.

Vincey and his wife refuse to believe that Ayesha is dead, and their search many years later comes to fruition in *Ayesha: The Return of She*

(1905). When her old body died, Ayesha was reincarnated in the body of an elderly priestess in yet another lost Asian kingdom, this one ruled by an insane king. Although portrayed as a villain in the first novel, she is redeemed in this one, but once again her end is an unhappy one, for in attempting to express her love for Vincey she inadvertently kills him. *She and Allan* (1920) is actually a prequel to the first two adventures and blends her story line with that of Allan Quatermain, who arrives just in time to become instrumental in the resolution of a power struggle between She and another immortal, this one a male. *Wisdom's Daughter* (1923), the last book Haggard wrote about Ayesha, is a retroactive memoir of her life, how she became immortal, the origins of her doomed love affair, and how she came to the lost land where Vincey found her.

Other writers have attempted sequels and parodies, the only one of which that is of lasting interest is *Journey to the Flame* (1985), by Richard MONACO, in which a pair of expeditions journey to the lost land in search of her secrets. A reasonably loyal but uninspired motion picture version was produced as *She* (1965).

Shea, Michael (1946–   )

Michael Shea's reputation in fantasy and horror fiction would appear to be out of proportion to his output. Over the course of three decades he has produced only seven novels and perhaps two dozen shorter works, and many of them have been openly imitative of Jack VANCE, H. P. LOVECRAFT, and other writers. He is perhaps best known for his character Nifft the Lean, a professional thief in a typical sword and sorcery world who has appeared in three book-length adventures.

Shea's first novel was *A Quest for Simbilis* (1974), a rollicking fantasy adventure set in the same world as the Dying Earth series by Jack Vance. The Dying Earth is set in a distant future in which magic has supplanted technology, but spells are so difficult to control that magicians can possess only a limited number of them at any given time. Adding a new one requires relinquishing an existing one. Shea set his baroque quest story in that world, imitating Vance stylistically as well,

with surprising success for such a new writer. The next several years disappointed his fans, however, because he wrote only a handful of shorter tales during this period, including the very impressive "Polyphemus" (1981). Most of his short fiction from this period and a few later ones have been collected as *Polyphemus* (1988).

Nifft the Lean (1982) signaled the beginning of a relatively productive period in the 1980s and also won the World Fantasy Award. Nifft is a typical roguish thief whose episodic adventures are reminiscent of the heroic fantasy of Fritz LEIBER, although also distinctly Shea's own. Nifft returned for a full-length adventure in *The Mines of Behemoth* (1997), wherein he attempts to steal the valuable fluid secreted by an oversized insect, and in *A'Rak* (2000), in which a city makes a deal with a spider god for protection, then hopes to renege when the terms of payment come due. Nifft also appears in some of Shea's short fiction.

The Color out of Time (1984) is a sequel to *The Color out of Space* (1927) by H. P. LOVECRAFT. Something alien is lying hidden in a lake, altering the physical makeup of anything living that comes within its range. Shea also borrowed from Lovecraft for the novella *I, Said the Fly* (1993), in which various unusual phenomena plague the world. His one remaining novel is *In Yana, the Touch of Undying* (1985), in which a student uncovers the secret of magical alternate worlds and possible immortality. His output has been very sporadic since 1990 but includes some memorable short stories, including "Fast Food" (1994) and "For Every Tatter in Its Mortal Dress" (2000). Although Shea's published fiction is impressive, there remains the feeling that he has much unrealized potential.

Shelley, Mary Wollstonecraft (1797–1851)

Mary Shelley is, of course, most famous for her creation of FRANKENSTEIN (1818), originally *Frankenstein, or the Modern Prometheus*. The genesis was a contest suggested by Lord Byron and Percy Shelley in which the participants each wrote a ghost story, the term then in use for all supernatural tales, after which Mary Shelley wrote her classic tale of the creation of life after being inspired by a dream. The novel is variously claimed by horror and science fiction critics, the latter because the animation of Frankenstein's monster is the result of scientific principles rather than the supernatural. The novel was so gruesome for its time that many believed Shelley, who was still in her teens when she wrote it, was incapable of having produced a work of that nature.

The novel has since become a part of common culture, primarily because of the movies, given that the prose of the original is quite difficult for casual modern readers. Many writers have attempted to write sequels and retellings, including such a diverse lot as Brian W. Aldiss, Christopher Isherwood, Fred SABERHAGEN, and Theodore Rosczak. *FRANKENSTEIN UNBOUND* (1973) by Aldiss includes Mary Shelley herself as a character.

Although Shelley wrote additional novels, none of them involve the fantastic except for *The Last Man* (1826), which is set in a future world following a devastating plague and which is science fiction. She did write a number of short stories, including several that involve ghosts, reanimation, and other wonders. The best of these is "Transformation" (1831), in which a man switches bodies with a demonic dwarf, supposedly for a short period although the dwarf reneges when the time is up. Most of her short fiction was assembled as *Collected Tales and Stories* (1976) and with a slightly different selection as *The Mortal Immortal* (1996). Shelley's reputation stands on a single work, but that work has been immeasurably important in literature in general as well as within the two genres that claim it.

Shepard, Lucius (1947–)

Lucius Shepard began writing fiction in the early 1980s, mostly science fiction although his first novel in that genre, *Green Eyes* (1984), was a rationalized zombie story. His first major effort in fantasy was "The Man Who Painted the Dragon Griaule" (1984), which was followed by two further stories, *The Scalehunter's Beautiful Daughter* (1988) and "Father of Stones" (1989), all set in a magical alternate reality dominated by a dragon so large it contains a small separate society of its own. Shepard's extremely unusual use of what might seem otherwise a typical fantasy attracted considerable attention.

The short novel *Kalimantan* (1990) mirrored some of the themes of Shepard's earlier science fiction, which often involved experimentation with drugs, in this case leading to contact with disembodied spirits. Shepard then turned to the vampire legend and transformed it dramatically in the bizarre and rewarding *The Golden* (1993), wherein a group of the undead live in a vast European castle and must solve the crime when one of their number is murdered. The vampire society is particularly original and rich in detail.

Although Shepard was relatively unproductive during the balance of the 1990s, he returned to the genre with *Valentine* (2002), a somewhat marginal story that postulates that some humans may have the ability to alter the laws of chance. *Louisiana Breakdown* (2003) is an enigmatic novel about a stranded motorist who falls in love with a woman who is the focus of a sort of communal pact with magic. A police officer develops a set of unusual physical symptoms after shooting a suspect in *Floater* (2003) and finds himself caught up in the middle of a voodoo war. The protagonist of *A Handbook of American Prayer* (2003) has his prayers answered, but not by the entity he thought he was addressing. Although all four of these novels are thoughtful, intelligent, and entertaining, they lack the enthusiasm and wider-ranging imagination of his earlier work.

Several of his later short stories are much more memorable than his novels. The best of these are the two thematically related stories in *Two Trains Running* (2004), which involve Shepard's actual experiences researching an article about people who illicitly ride on freight trains. Shepard's short story collection, *The Ends of the Earth* (1991), won a World Fantasy Award but is predominantly science fiction. His recent novels show a definite drift toward mainstream fiction, but much of his short fiction is still clearly aimed at a genre audience.

Sherman, Josepha (unknown)

There are only a handful of authors who can write well for both adult and young adult audiences. Josepha Sherman, whose work is very often based on authentic folklore, is one of those rarities, who has been writing for both markets since the late 1980s. Her very early books for children are of minimal interest, but her first adult novel, *The Shining Falcon* (1989), is an engaging traditional story of a kingdom whose ruler is missing and in whose absence evil magic threatens to hold sway. *The Horse of Flame* (1990) is equally impressive, the story of an immortal but evil sorcerer trapped in a mortal body and determined to seize power. *Child of Faerie, Child of Earth* (1992), for young adults, is also somewhat out of the ordinary, the story of a young fairy who defies his family when he falls in love with a mortal girl, with not always predictable consequences.

Somewhat similar, although for adults, is *A Strange and Ancient Name* (1993), in which a half-human fairy prince undertakes a quest in the world of mortals. In *Windleaf* (1993), again for young readers, a bored young prince rescues a fairy princess, complicating matters for both families. A young man who wishes only to be left in peace is caught between conflicting oaths, one to humans and one to fairies, in *King's Son, Magic's Son* (1994), one of the best of her books for adults. *The Shattered Oath* (1995) and its sequel, *Forging the Runes* (1996), are to date her most impressive accomplishments, the story of an elf who is banished to the world of humans during the days of the Vikings and who makes a place for himself in this, to him, completely alien society. *Son of Darkness* (1998) is also excellent, the story of a woman from our world who discovers that there are magical intrusions in her life and that her destiny is not entirely in her own hands.

Sherman also collaborated with Mercedes LACKEY for three fantasies, *Wheels of Fire* (1992), set in the Serrated Edge series, *Castle of Deception* (1992), a Bard's Tale book, and *A Cast of Corbies* (1994), set in the Bardic Voices sequence. *The Chaos Gate* (1994) by Sherman alone is also in the Bard's Tale series, the story of a wizard who gives up his powers to become a mere bard, although he is forced to come out of retirement to battle an insidious evil. *Rachel the Clever and Other Jewish Folktales* (1993) consists of retellings of magical legends. She has also written two novels about Buffy the Vampire Slayer, both collaborations with Laura Ann Gilman, and a considerable number of

short stories, including "The Old Woman Who Created Life" (1995), "A Question of Faith" (1999), and "The Case of the Headless Corpse" (2004), the latter a very amusing magical murder mystery.

Shetterly, Will (1955–)

Will Shetterly made his debut with the pleasant if unremarkable *Cats Have No Lord* (1985), a blend of mystery and quest story in which a group of elves tries to solve a riddle and finds themselves opposed by an evil force. His next, *Witch Blood* (1986), uses a very similar scheme of conflict, although in this case the protagonist is a human magician who begins to master his powers just in time to avoid being destroyed by a gaggle of villains. Both novels are light entertainments with nothing to distinguish them, and it was only with *The Tangled Lands* (1989) that Shetterly began to demonstrate the potential for more interesting work, an innovative adventure set in a fantasy land that is also a kind of computer-driven virtual reality.

Along with his wife, fellow fantasy writer Emma Bull, Shetterly edited a shared world series of original anthologies that began with *Liavek* (1985) and ended after the fifth volume, *Festival Week* (1990). It is not surprising therefore that Shetterly himself wrote in another shared world, the Borderlands series created by Terri Windling, a magical half-world that acts as the bridge between our reality and another where magic works. His first novel in that setting, *Elsewhere* (1991), is much better than his previous work, even though it is ostensibly for young adult readers. The protagonist is a human runaway who wanders into this nebulous region and makes a new life for himself. Shetterly then expanded a short story into a sequel, *NeverNever* (1993), this time concentrating on a teenager's efforts to find a cure for the curse that changes him periodically into the shape of a wolf. His efforts cause him to cross paths with an exiled fairy prince, and the interaction of the two is very nicely handled.

His subsequent work has not measured up to those two novels, however. *Dogland* (1997) is a likeable but undistinguished contemporary fantasy that is admirable in its efforts to deal with the subject of racial prejudice, but the plot is not consistently strong enough to hold the reader's attention. *Thor's Hammer* (2000) is for children. Shetterly has never been prolific at shorter length but has produced several very fine short stories, including "The Princess Who Kicked Butt" (1993), "Oldthings" (1994), and "Taken He Cannot Be" (1995). He is not likely to build a stronger following unless he begins to appear more regularly. His most recent novel, *Chimera* (2000), is science fiction.

The Shining Stephen King (1977)

With his second novel, 'SALEM'S LOT (1975), Stephen KING produced a vampire novel that was also a major best-seller. With his third, *The Shining*, he did the same for the haunted house story, in this case an entire hotel, although the ghosts are not necessarily those of the dead. The hotel is more properly speaking a "bad place," a physical location that has become a kind of gathering place for evil, where past events and present tensions can generate physical manifestations as well as psychological pressure on those who venture within range.

The Overlook is a large resort hotel cut off from the outside world by snow during the winter and is therefore closed and tenanted only by a caretaker and his family. The previous caretaker became unbalanced and murdered his family, so Jack, a frustrated, alcoholic writer, and his wife and child move in as their last desperate attempt to allow Jack to write his novel. The manifestations of evil start almost at once, although it is only the boy, Danny, who is aware of them at first. Danny has a psychic power that the departing hotel cook refers to as the "shining," an ability to see things invisible to the rest of us, and to communicate telepathically with others, such as the cook, who shares his talent.

Danny becomes increasingly disturbed by the manifestations—a rotting animated corpse in one room, visions of twin girls drenched in blood, topiary shapes that change position, warning messages from an older version of himself—but it is his father, Jack, who becomes most affected by the hotel, his personality seduced by its ingrained evil. The change is slow and insidious, exploiting Jack's flaws and suppressing his good side. He eventually becomes insane and attempts to murder his family, who escape only because of Danny's resourcefulness and the intercession of the sympathetic cook.

The Shining is a powerful book because Jack's collapse and subversion are a genuine tragedy. Through it all he continues to love his son, even when he is driven into fits of insane, murderous fury. Two film versions have appeared. The first, released theatrically in 1980, takes rather cavalier liberties with the plot but is considered one of the great horror films. The second, produced for television in 1997, is more loyal to the original but dramatically less interesting.

Shirley, John (1953–)

John Shirley has built a strong reputation for himself in both science fiction and horror, although it is in the latter direction that he has been moving most recently. Although most of his short fiction during the late 1970s was for science fiction markets, *Dracula in Love* (1979) is a vampire novel, a very unorthodox variation on the original story by Bram STOKER. Shirley concentrates on the ritualistic side of Dracula's bloodletting, with fairly strong sexual content for that time. His leanings toward both genres became more obvious in *City Come A-Walkin'* (1980), set in a future in which the city of San Francisco has become a hotbed of violent forces rapidly descending toward chaos. The spirit of the city manifests itself as a physical being and takes a hand in its own future in a very original, although not entirely convincing, fashion. The novel did garner him considerable attention, however, and is often cited as an early example of cyberpunk, a trend toward urban-based, nihilistic science fiction.

Cellars (1982) is a much more conventional horror tale. Another city is torn apart as a supernatural force possesses literally scores of children, evidence of the reawakening of the cult of Ahriman. It is less original than his previous novels but technically very well done and genuinely scary. Shirley really hit his stride with *In Darkness Waiting* (1988), in which a new cult is revealed to be the offshoot of the awakening of a creature that lies dormant in every human mind, a holdover from prehistory. That same year saw publication of his only true fantasy, *The Black Hole of Carcosa*, a blend of magic and tough detective story set in the world created by J. Michael Reaves in *Darkworld Detective* (1982). Shirley was by now well established, but his output at novel length slowed considerably. His next novel was controversial because of its violent sexual theme. *Wetbones* (1993) involves the direct stimulation of the pleasure and pain centers in the human brain and the consequences when a group uses the ability to manipulate these sensations in order to sexually enslave others.

During the 1980s and 1990s Shirley produced short fiction of consistently high quality, much of it horror, sometimes rationalized and sometimes supernatural. Most of his stories from this period can be found in *Black Butterflies* (1998), *Really, Really, Really, Really Weird Stories* (1999), and *Darkness Divided* (2001). *Black Butterflies* won the Bram Stoker Award for a single-author collection.

Demons (2000) is a short, violent novel set in the near future and is horror rather than science fiction. Demons have overrun the world, and the surviving humans face a variety of horrible fates at their hands. The novel was reprinted under the same title in 2002, but with a second, book-length sequel included. Discorporate creatures manipulate the lives of human beings in *The View from Hell* (2001), and an actor is overwhelmed by visions of supposedly imaginary entities in *And the Angel with Television Eyes* (2001). Shirley's fiction often takes chances, and he is rarely satisfied with writing a predictable story. Sometimes the results are less successful, but in most cases he has proven to be an exciting and innovative writer who often startles his readers with unexpected and occasionally bizarre twists.

"Shottle Bop" Theodore Sturgeon (1941)

The magic shop is a standard device in contemporary fantasy, a store where magical objects can be bought, although usually with a concealed catch. The protagonist of this classic by Theodore Sturgeon has been recently spurned by the woman he has been wooing and is generally a failure, to a large extent through his own shortcomings. He enters the odd little shop on a whim and is told by

the unusual proprietor that he sells bottles with things in them, anything, in fact, that you could possibly want. Although skeptical, a touch of magic convinces him something odd is going on, and he leaves with a small bottle in his possession, one that the proprietor insists will cure his problems. Once outside, he decides that it was all a hoax, but nonetheless he holds on to the bottle and brings it home with him.

Predictably, he gives in to temptation and drinks the contents, not expecting any actual results, but after which he discovers he has a strange new ability. In an interesting anticipation of the movie *The Sixth Sense* (1999), he can now see dead people, the ghosts of those who died with some act incomplete, tied to their old existence until they somehow accomplish it and usually unwilling to accept the fact that they are actually dead. Sympathetic to their plight, he tries to help and eventually opens a business as a psychic consultant, conveying messages back and forth to the land of the dead. The one complication to his new talent is that while he can see ghosts, ghosts cannot see him, although they can hear his voice.

Unfortunately, he decides to give in to temptation and taunt some former acquaintances who never thought he would amount to anything. He places a bet with one of them that he can summon a frightening ghost and then spends a night with him in a haunted house. The resident spirit, a typical malevolent entity, arrives, and despite the narrator's intercession, causes the other man to die of shock. This use of his talent for such a mean purpose results in its immediate loss. Visible to the angry ghost, the narrator dies horribly and, we realize now, is telling this story from beyond the grave. Despite the somewhat horrific ending, the tone of the story is surprisingly light, suggesting an allegory about wasting one's talents rather than an attempt to horrify the reader.

"The Shunned House" H. P. Lovecraft (1937)

Many of the stories by H. P. LOVECRAFT are set in his native Providence, Rhode Island, and involve actual places and structures, many of which survive to this day. That is the case with the building in "The Shunned House," still a rental property on Benefit Street, although none of its recent residents have ever experienced the horrible effects described in this story, one of the best of his non-Cthulhu Mythos tales. Although the narrator and his uncle eventually play a part in the resolution of the mystery, the first half is essentially a fictional history of the house, built in the 18th century on a plot of land that was formerly used as a graveyard. Its original owners and their servants all suffered from some form of debilitating ailment, anemia, fevers, and such. All the children died young or were stillborn, their mother succumbed to insanity, and the other adults were similarly affected in some fashion.

The house quickly acquired a reputation of being unhealthy, although nothing specific was ever found except a faint, unpleasant smell and a tendency for fungus to grow in the raised cellar. There were no sightings of ghosts or other apparitions, but rumors spread anyway that it was a bad place. When the original family had all died or moved on, it experienced a short, unhappy period as a rental property before falling completely vacant and slowly subsiding into decay.

The narrator noticed much of this as a young boy growing up nearby, but it was not until he was an adult that his uncle, a physician, confided in him the results of his detailed study of the house and his conclusion that it was the focus for some influence beyond the knowledge of science. There are indications of a kind of vampirism—the anemia, certain wounds on the throat, and other factors—but clearly this was not a traditional case. Rather, as we discover, an ancient evil being has been buried under the property, and its lingering influence seeps up through the ground to affect the minds and bodies of those in close proximity. Their initial effort to neutralize this influence has disastrous consequences, and the uncle dies. The narrator perseveres, digging down to the remains and then destroying them with carbolic acid.

The story takes place with no dialogue and minimal characterization, a technique at which Lovecraft excelled, presenting the story as though it were a contemporary account rather than a piece of fiction. The details he provides about the history of the building and the individuals who lived in it are elaborate and credible, leaving the reader with the impression that while the events in the story might not have actually happened, they certainly could have.

Shwartz, Susan M. (1949–)

Although some of Susan Shwartz's short fiction from the 1980s is fantasy, it was with the Heirs of Byzantium series that she first attracted serious attention in that field. Like most of her fantasy, the series is strongly enhanced by her background in historical studies. The sequence opened with *Byzantium's Crown* (1987), set in an alternate history in which the capital of the Roman Empire has been moved to Byzantium and in which magic still works, although it is already decidedly in decline by the end of the series. The story in the opening volume and the immediate sequel, *The Woman of Flowers* (1987), chiefly involves the difficulties caused for the rightful heirs following the usurpation of the throne. In *Queensblade* (1988) the role of magic is examined in more depth, and the world is changed forever in *Silk Roads and Shadows* (1988). Although the surface story is a familiar one, Shwartz enriches her world with such convincing background material that it seems fresh and new.

Her next fantasy novel was *Imperial Lady* (1989), an Asian fantasy written with Andre NORTON. They collaborated again on *Empire of the Eagle* (1993), a very fine historical fantasy in which a Roman legion wanders into unknown territory and interacts with strange foreign cultures. Although only marginally fantasy, it is a very moving and, as always, well-researched story. *The Grail of Hearts* (1992) is the best of her fantasy novels, a reexamination of the story of Sir Parsifal from the legend of King Arthur. Shwartz has a genuinely original concept of the story and surpasses almost every other Arthurian writer in making that period seem historically accurate.

Shwartz's most recent novels of interest are the two volumes of the Constantinople duo consisting of *Shards of Empire* (1996) and *Cross and Crescent* (1997). As Constantinople falls to the army of barbarians besieging it, a disgruntled nobleman seeks allies with which to oppose the rise of evil sorcery. The ensuing battle for control of the city takes place on many levels, some of which involve magical rivalries. The balance of her subsequent fantasy has been at shorter length, mostly light adventure and humor, although "The Refuge of Firedrakes" (1996) and "One Wing Down" (1999) are quite good. Her most recent novels have been science fiction, but it seems likely that she will return to historical fantasy, where her greatest strengths lie.

"The Signalman" Charles Dickens (1866)

It is not generally known that Charles Dickens wrote other ghost and horror stories in addition to his acknowledged classic, A CHRISTMAS CAROL (1843), but there are nearly two dozen of them, of which this is the most famous and most frequently reprinted. The unnamed narrator happens one evening to make the acquaintance of a signalman, an intelligent individual admittedly employed below the level of his ability performing the lonely task of signaling passing trains with news or warnings. On the night of their first acquaintance, the signalman acts very oddly, as though responding to sounds and sights invisible to everyone else, and he offers no explanation.

Puzzled but interested in his new friend, the narrator suggests that he return the following night, to which the other agrees, requesting only that he refrain from speaking or gesturing during his approach. This also strikes the narrator as odd, but he conforms. The following night he hears the reason. A few months earlier the signalman had seen an apparition, accompanied by an eerie sounding of a bell, who appeared to be waving a warning. A short time later there was a major train accident at the very same spot, which might have been dismissed as coincidence if that same apparition had not made a subsequent appearance on another occasion, this time anticipating the tragic death of a young woman aboard a different train.

The spectral figure has appeared for a third time, and the signalman is very distressed, unable to figure out what disaster it is warning him about this time. The narrator remains skeptical and suggests that they consult a physician. He returns to meet his friend at the end of the latter's shift, only

to see an actual living man perform the very gestures that were ascribed to the apparition earlier. Arriving on the scene he learns that the signalman has been killed, struck by a passing train. Although by contemporary standards the ending might seem tame, it was written in a time when people were a lot less certain about the impossibility of supernatural intervention in the affairs of the living, and this quiet tale of precognition would have been most unsettling.

The Silmarillion J. R. R. Tolkien (1977)

In most cases writers of fantasy fiction must first create the world in which their story is set and then make it credible to the reader. At its simplest form this consists of naming places, deciding upon the kinds of creatures who make up the population, and developing at least a rough idea of their culture and government, usually establishing a set of rules about how magic works. Few writers go to the elaborate lengths of J. R. R. TOLKIEN, who created a long, detailed history for each of his many separate cultures, complete with sets of historical episodes and legends. Much of this material has been gathered together as *The Silmarillion*, which can be considered a companion volume to The Lord of the Ring rather than a prequel.

Although *The Silmarillion* was published long after the trilogy, it was actually a work in progress from shortly after World War I, and was compiled in its present form from Tolkien's papers after his death. The background, culture, and history of Middle Earth were worked out in elaborate detail over the course of many years and became the setting for THE HOBBIT (1937) and later the trilogy about Frodo's quest to destroy the ring of Sauron. *The Silmarillion* is a history of a fictional world rather than a cohesive novel, a collection of fables and stories about the shaping of that world, the exploits of some of its more famous inhabitants, and a general description of the civilization that arose there.

The book opens with an account of the creation of the universe in which the stories are set, followed by four additional sections, the most important of which is that involving the "silmarils." The silmarils are magic jewels that were coveted by humans long before the events in the Ring trilogy, a desire that caused a fatal rift between their race and that of the elves. The conflict eventually results in war, and it is only after considerable destruction that the Dark Lord is defeated and the threat ended, although it is later revived in altered form with the rise of Sauron.

Based on other notes left by Tolkien, his son Christopher later published a multivolume series of histories of Middle Earth. Other associated material by Tolkien senior was also published in two volumes as *The Book of Lost Tales* (1983). In combination with *The Silmarillion*, these additional titles provide the most complete history of a fictional reality ever written.

The Silver Chair C. S. Lewis (1953)

The fourth book of the CHRONICLES OF NARNIA by C. S. LEWIS is cast in the form of the traditional fantasy quest, an adventure in which Eustace Scrubb, the human boy who appeared first in THE VOYAGE OF THE "DAWN TREADER," along with a new character from our world, Jill Pole, are transported to the world of Narnia. The two are lamenting the bullying tactics of their schoolmates when they are summoned to that magical land by Aslan, the mystical Christ figure who appears in the form of a lion. Aslan gives the children a series of signs to watch for. Jill gets them confused, and Eustace is too impatient to listen to her at critical moments.

Caspian is still king, but his death is imminent. The future of Narnia is in jeopardy because Caspian's son, Prince Rilian, has been missing for many years, and every effort to find him has met with failure. The signs given to the children will supposedly save the day, but only if the children have faith in them and understand their sometimes unclear meanings. They set out on their own rescue mission, even though that will take them into the territory of the potentially hostile giants in search of a ruined city under which Rilian may be imprisoned. They encounter a woman in green who gives them supposedly helpful advice, although even unsophisticated readers will likely suspect her motives. She is, in fact, the chief villain, the Emerald Witch who is responsi-

ble for Rilian's captivity and who also appears in the form of a serpent. The children fall in with the giants as guests for a feast, unaware of the fact that they are meant to be the main course, until they fortuitously stumble across a cookbook with a recipe for humans, which seems inconsistent with the author's previous statement that humans, were unknown in that world until quite recently.

Although they have consistently misread the signs, Eustace and Jill reach the underground city and encounter the Knight, who is blindly loyal to the Emerald Queen except for one hour each night when he is confined to an enchanted silver chair during a spell of "madness," which we and eventually the children recognize as his only moment of actual sanity. The children release him, the spell is broken, and the Knight is revealed as Prince Rilian, although another confrontation with the witch queen nearly reverses their victory. *The Silver Chair* had the most complex plot in the series at that point and was of much more interest to adult readers than the previous volumes.

Silverlock John Myers Myers (1949)

John Myers Myers spent most of his life writing historical novels and nonfiction, but his reputation rests almost entirely on this single fantasy novel. *Silverlock* is as much a game as a story, because the protagonist, Silverlock, survives a shipwreck and then experiences an episodic series of adventures in the land of Commonwealth, which is actually the sum total of all fictional worlds created by the human imagination. The very large cast of characters includes a large number of figures from other works of fiction, although they are generally disguised and sometimes unrecognizable.

His encounters are often quite cleverly done, although the book never really holds together as a novel. Readers should have no difficulty picking out the more obvious characters—Robin Hood, Robinson Crusoe, Beowulf, Don Quixote, and Circe, for example—but others are sufficiently obscure to evade easy identification. To remedy this, there exists *The Silverlock Companion* (1961), edited by Fred Lerner, which explains all the allusions and reveals the concealed identities.

A later book, *The Moon's Fire-Eating Daughter* (1991), is structured similarly, this time in the form of a journey through time as well as space, during which the reader is introduced to a bewildering string of historical characters, mostly authors, similarly disguised in some cases but more readily deciphered. The individual adventures are considerably less entertaining. Myers's only remaining genre novel is the marginal *The Harp and the Blade* (1941), which has some minor fantastic content. Although *Silverlock* remains an intellectual exercise as much as a work of fiction, it has continued to enjoy popularity among those readers interested in literary fantasy and has garnered some favorable attention from critics outside the genre.

Simmons, Dan (1948–)

Dan Simmons has written successfully in both science fiction and horror, winning several awards in each genre. He started writing during the early 1980s, producing several memorable short stories during the first few years, most of which were later collected as *Prayers from Broken Stones* (1990). His first novel was *The Song of Kali* (1985), in which an American is spending what he expects to be a boring few weeks in Calcutta but which turns into a much livelier adventure when he stumbles into a conspiracy involving an ancient text that might have the power to bring Kali back into the world. Although only a marginal occult adventure, the novel won the World Fantasy Award and immediately raised expectations about Simmons's future work.

His next novel was no disappointment. *Carrion Comfort* (1989) is based on a much shorter work originally published in 1983. Although sometimes characterized as a vampire novel, it falls into that category only thematically. The fantastic element involves a small group of people who have the power to displace the personalities of others, using these captive bodies as their tools. The power makes them arrogant, but they are also easily bored and engage in constant internecine warfare using their victims as weapons and spending their lives thoughtlessly. The novel is arguably science fiction, since Simmons makes some efforts to explain their abilities as a human mutation, but

the atmosphere is clearly horror. The novel won the Bram Stoker Award.

Summer of Night (1991) is very reminiscent of Stephen KING. A group of children prove wiser than adults when they recognize that there is an evil presence in the local school building and persevere despite the reanimated dead and other opposition. Although the novel is more predictable than most of Simmons's other fiction, the characterization of the young protagonists is particularly well handled, and the evil entity, though somewhat slow in making an appearance, is suitably nasty. Several scenes excised from the book version later appeared as the chapbook *Banished Dreams* (1996). Simmons continued to write occasional short stories, and two additional collections appeared during the early 1990s, *Going After the Rubber Chicken* (1991) and *Lovedeath* (1993).

His second roundabout assault on the vampire story was *Children of the Night* (1992), the title derived from Dracula's term for his faithful wolves. The novel is set in Romania, the traditional homeland of Dracula and vampirism, but in the present day following the collapse of the communist government. Since the Ceauşescu regime refused to acknowledge the existence of AIDS while it was in power, the aftermath includes thousands of orphans bearing the disease, most of them confined to horrifyingly terrible conditions in poorly staffed and financed state run institutions. An American doctor trying to help discovers a child with an unusual immune system, after which he is pursued by mysterious men who seem to be immune to bullets. The eventual revelation that the child is the son of Dracula himself is followed by a satisfyingly heroic rescue.

Simmons wrote primarily science fiction during the rest of the 1990s as well as a mainstream novel about Ernest Hemingway, and only one additional horror novel, the interesting but uneven *Fires of Eden* (1994). The construction of a new resort in the Hawaiian Islands precipitates a battle among traditional Hawaiian gods and demons, the story alternating between the present and Mark Twain's somewhat similar experiences a century earlier. The background mythos is interesting. The horrors are decidedly nontraditional, but the story lacks the cohesiveness of Simmons's other novels.

His most recent book-length horror is *A Winter Haunting* (2002), the direct sequel to *Summer of Night*, whose characters Simmons had occasionally used in other works already. One of the survivors of that earlier book has grown up, becomes a professional writer, and returns to his hometown after a series of personal and emotional crises, where he is confronted by apparitions of people from his past. Although quieter than the author's previous novels, it is very effectively creepy.

His short fiction is almost always rewarding. *Prayers from Broken Stones* won the Bram Stoker Award for a single-author collection, and "This Year's Class Picture" (1992) and "Dying in Bangkok" (1995) also won Stokers. Other stories of note include "The River Styx Runs Upstream" (1982), "Entropy's Bed at Midnight" (1993), and "Sleeping with the Teeth Women" (1993). Simmons is undeniably one of the major voices in science fiction and might claim the same position in horror fiction if he writes in the field more frequently than he has in recent years.

"Skeleton" Ray Bradbury (1945)

Mr. Harris is a hypochondriac frustrated by his doctor's refusal to take his complaints seriously, particularly his most recent one, that his bones are aching unnaturally. When the doctor dismisses him with a lecture, he turns to Mr. Munigant, a self-professed bone specialist although not a doctor, a man who seems much more sympathetic to his new client's complaints. Munigant sends him home with some literature that Harris studies, apparently realizing for the first time the complexity of his bone structure and considerably distressed with the emotional implications of the fact that he is walking around with a genuine skeleton inside him, a knowledge he had possessed all his life without ever actually considering it and that now strikes him as vulgar at best, horrible at worst.

The more Harris thinks about it, the more he becomes convinced that his skeleton is alien and an intruder rather than a part of him. He begins to believe that he and his skeleton are locked in a battle for control of his body, and when he begins to lose weight, he interprets that as a plot by his enemy to slough off its fleshy envelope. The turmoil grows steadily until, desperate, Harris finally appeals to Mr. Munigant again. Munigant visits him at home, and we learn the truth about him. He is not a human being at all but a creature who can literally consume the bones of a living creature, leaving the flesh and organs untouched. Mr. Harris is finally free, and his wife arrives home to find him still living but now an oversized jellyfish unable to move. Although the body of the story prepares the reader for an eventual crisis, it is only in the final scene that one realizes that Harris's problems are not just psychological.

Skipp, John (1957–) and Craig Spector (1958–)

The writing team of John Skipp and Craig Spector remained together for less than 10 years and produced only seven novels, one of them a movie novelization, but their impact was so significant that their joint byline became synonymous with the splatterpunk school of horror writing, characterized by extremely shocking, explicit violence. Unlike most of their imitators, however, they understood that descriptions of death and mutilation could not sustain a book-length work and that it was necessary to create a plausible setting with sympathetic characters so that the explosions of visceral horror meant something to the reader other than just random images of blood and gore.

Although both writers published a handful of short stories alone, some as early as 1982, they were still virtually unknown when they were tapped to novelize *Fright Night* (1985), an above-average vampire movie in which a teenager discovers that his new neighbor is an undead creature but, predictably, cannot convince any adult that he is telling the truth. Their first original novel followed the next year. *The Light at the End* (1986) is set in New York City, or more properly beneath it, as a creature that is a kind of physical personification of the evil that accumulates in urban landscapes haunts the subways and sewer system, claiming several victims and destroying them in horrible ways. The graphic death scenes were an instant source of controversy, masking the fact that the story is in many ways quite subtle and complex.

The Cleanup (1987) starts as a wish-fulfillment fantasy. A young man who feels as though he has been victimized by everyone he has ever met, with some justification, discovers that he has a supernatural power that enables him to strike back. He believes that he is acting morally, because he targets criminals, muggers, rapists, and so on rather than innocent people. Unfortunately, the more he uses his new powers, the more his own personality changes, corrupted by what he mistakenly believes to be his obligation to society. The indictment of vigilantism is quite obvious, and the dissolution of the protagonist's personality is absorbing and convincing.

The Scream (1988) is in some ways more inventive but less interesting. An ancient Asian horror reaches America, and its victims are destroyed in unusually horrible ways. A fast-paced and surprising thriller, it sometimes becomes so caught up in its bizarre imagery that the story suffers, although in the long run it remains a remarkable achievement, possibly the epitome of splatterpunk. *Dead Lines* (1989), on the other hand, adapts several short stories into an episodic "novel" in which the new tenant in an apartment finds several old manuscripts and reads them, slowly becoming affected by their evil aura.

The Bridge (1991) borrowed its plot from low-budget science fiction films. A toxic waste dump gives birth to a new form of life, an amorphous creature that kills and absorbs all other life it encounters, growing so quickly that it poses a menace to the entire world. Although the plot is exciting, it lacks the originality of their previous work and feels very much like a movie novelization. Their final novel together, *Animals* (1993), also borrowed from traditional themes, in this case having its protagonist fall in love with a woman who is actually a werewolf, leading to a very interesting love triangle when her shape-changing boyfriend objects.

Skipp and Spector also edited two highly regarded anthologies of short stories set in the universe of George Romero's Living Dead movies. *The Book of the Dead* (1989) and *Still Dead* (1992) were to have been followed by a third volume, but publishing problems and the breakup of the writing team prevented it from ever appearing. They also collaborated on the screenplay for *The Nightmare on Elm Street: The Dream Child* (1989), certainly the most interesting movie in that series.

Both writers have continued to work sporadically on their own. Spector is the author of two nonsupernatural thrillers. Skipp collaborated with Mark Levinthal for *The Emerald Burrito of Oz* (2000), a very strange novel in which a portal opens between our world and Oz, resulting in a power struggle for control of the government of that magical world. Skipp's "Now Entering Monkeyface" (1998) is also worthwhile.

"The Skull of the Marquis De Sade" Robert Bloch (1945)

Horror fiction is replete with stories in which a particularly evil person manages to leave behind some trace of himself or herself to wreak further havoc even after he or she is gone. The most common form is, of course, the ghost story, but there are others in which lingering traps, spells, curses, or other supernatural phenomena serve much the same purpose. Robert BLOCH has a slightly different take in this, one of his most famous stories.

Christopher Maitland is a collector of odd items, things he cannot display publicly because of their unusual nature or the less-than-strictly-legal methods he uses to acquire them. He is reading a very old book bound in human skin when one of his suppliers appears unexpectedly, bearing a very unusual item for which he asks a substantial price. It is, according to his claim, the actual polished skull of the Marquis De Sade, who, in addition to his sexual fantasies, investigated and engaged in sorcery. The skull is very extraordinary in that it has an expression of sober contemplation rather than the usual wide grin. Maitland is skeptical, particularly when the other man, Marco, promptly drops his price, insisting that the skull makes him uneasy.

Maitland defers a decision and after a night filled with dreams of death and torture consults a fellow collector who tells him he once owned the very same skull, that it was stolen from him, and that he was glad to see it go despite its authenticity and uniqueness. During the night outsiders would break in, apparently to conduct arcane rites with the skull, but even these interlopers had no intention of actually possessing it. Convinced, Maitland goes to Marco's home but finds the man murdered, his throat torn out apparently by his own guard dog. Maitland takes the skull and hurries away to avoid involvement, pleased with his new acquisition.

Later that same evening he realizes that there was no blood on the dog's mouth, which puzzles him, but he dismisses the thought and goes to bed. During the night the skull rolls across the floor and bounces up onto the bed, and Maitland dies in the same fashion, to be found in the morning with the skull, now grinning conventionally, sitting on his chest. This is an example of the strong strain of morality in modern horror fiction. Evil acts will eventually be rewarded appropriately.

Sleator, William (1945–   )

William Sleator began writing novels for young readers in 1972 and concentrated on science fiction, fantasy, and horror for most of those titles. His first book, *Blackbriar* (1972), is a surprisingly intense novel about two teenagers who investigate a mysterious, possibly haunted house. The somewhat similar *Into the Dream* (1979) also balances two teenaged protagonists, this time a pair who discover that they are sharing the same dream, or perhaps nightmare. *Fingers* (1983) is also complex enough to entertain adult readers. Another teenager convinces his brother, a musician, that his talent has become enhanced by the spirit of a long-dead musical artist. The hoax slowly becomes less amusing when there is mounting evidence that the ghost of the dead man is, in fact, influencing the teenager.

The Boy Who Reversed Himself (1986) takes its young protagonist through a mirror into the bizarre world that exists on the opposite side. *The Spirit House* (1991) and its sequel, *Dangerous Wishes* (1996), are much lighter in tone. In the first an exchange student from Thailand brings along some unusual baggage, playful Thai spirits. In the second another teenager searches for a missing talisman whose recovery might end a prolonged spate of bad luck experienced by his family. He is aided by a Thai student with a magically enhanced computer. *Boltzmon!* (1990) also invokes a

magical creature for some light-hearted adventure, but less successfully.

Rewind (1999) is entertaining but less original than Sleator's other novels. A teenager dies in an accident and is given the opportunity to relive his life and correct his mistakes. *The Boxes* (2000), a new take on Pandora's Box, seems to demand a sequel because of its unresolved ending. The story concerns a young girl who opens a mysterious box despite orders to the contrary, releasing a horde of crablike creatures who may or may not be evil. The ensuing chaos is very entertaining, but the story is not tied up well in the final chapter. A boy finds a gateway to a magical world in *Marco's Millions* (2001), and another finds immortality in *The Boy Who Couldn't Die* (2004), although there is a catch. There is always a catch.

Sleator is a very reliable source of slightly dark fantasy novels for young adults. He avoids patronizing his readers and writes with sufficient sophistication and detail to entertain mature tastes as well as his target audience. At his least interesting he produces competent renditions of familiar stories. At his best he creates unique characters and unusual situations and explores the possibilities inherent in these combinations.

"Slime" Joseph Payne Brennan (1953)

The monster story has fallen into disrepute in written science fiction, although moviemakers are still fond of the device. Stories of alien life forms, even from other planets, are now generally lumped with horror fiction even if they are completely rationalized in some manner, and while science fiction is outside the scope of this book, there are some stories that make such a cursory effort at explaining the creature's origins that they are appropriately considered here. One of the best of these is this tale of an eons-old creature thrown up from the bottom of the ocean by an undersea earthquake. The monster is a blob, a shapeless mass that consumes every animal it encounters, in much the same manner as the similar creature in the motion picture *The Blob* (1958), likewise immune to bullets and the only one of its kind.

Since BRENNAN's slime monster originated in the depths of the ocean, it is physically repelled by light and so only hunts during the hours of darkness, emerging from a swamp to kill cattle, wildlife, and eventually people. Predictably, the only man to suspect the truth early on is greeted with disbelief by the authorities, who attribute the disappearances to a human killer. The usual sequence of events follows, though enlivened by Brennan's crisp, lyrical prose—he is also the author of several volumes of poetry. A search is made, but there are no bodies to recover. The magnitude of the danger becomes obvious only after one deputy is killed and another is driven nearly insane with fear. There is a particularly exciting chase and conclusion, with flame throwers destroying the monster just as it is about to escape into the ocean.

"Slime" is in the tradition of such classic stories as "Dune Roller" (1951) by Julian May and "IT" (1940) by Theodore Sturgeon and like these stories is written in a noticeably restrained and nonmelodramatic fashion, almost as though it were a news account rather than a piece of fiction. *PHANTOMS* (1983) by Dean R. KOONTZ also uses a very similar explanation for the origin of his amorphous monster, which travels under the land rather than the sea but is otherwise remarkably similar. It is in some ways atypical of Brennan's work, which tended to be more sedate and intellectual.

"The Small Assassin" Ray Bradbury (1946)

Several writers have explored the potential consequences of malevolent children whose capacity for evil is suggested by the fact that they are too young to be subject to the moral restraints we instill in them as they grow older. Stories of this kind generally involve preteens and sometimes toddlers, but rarely infants, since it is generally assumed that infants are too physically impotent to provide much of a menace. The physical weakness of the child is usually compensated for in some fashion, such as with the magical powers of creation invoked in "IT'S A GOOD LIFE" (1953), by Jerome Bixby, or possibly with the aid of an adult accomplice.

Ray BRADBURY took the concept to its extreme with this nasty little story of the Leiber family. Alice has just delivered their first child, a son, but she is immediately estranged from the baby, who she believes tried to kill her while still in the womb. Her husband, David, and the family physician, Jeffers, both believe this is a temporary condition brought on by stress and post partum depression, but as the days pass she refuses to lavish any affection on the child, who David admits does act a bit peculiarly. His suspicions do not carry any weight at first, not even when one of the baby's toys is mysteriously placed at the top of the staircase, nearly causing him a serious fall, and he dismisses the feeling that someone is watching them in their bedroom one night as just a dream-spawned illusion.

David is recalled from a business trip after Alice allegedly attempts to kill the child. Distraught, he is preoccupied with her condition and fails to notice other warning signs. Eventually, he comes home to find her dead, having fallen down the staircase after tripping on another misplaced toy. Only then does he begin to believe the truth, but Dr. Jeffers dismisses his conclusions as the result of shock and administers a powerful sedative. When he returns to check on his patient, he discovers that someone has turned on the gas and that David is now dead also. More to the point, the wind has blown the door to the nursery closed so that the infant, who is now openly revealed to be mobile and intelligent, could not return to the crib and provide the illusion of innocence.

Although Bradbury wisely stops short of the implied final scene, Jeffers recognizes the truth and sets about killing the monster child. Bradbury wrote his own screen adaptation for the *Ray Bradbury Theater* production, shuffling the order of events and for some reason reversing the manner of the Leibers's deaths. The story was almost certainly part of the inspiration for the 1974 film *It's Alive* and the two subsequent sequels.

Smith, Clark Ashton (1893–1961)

Also noted as a poet, Clark Ashton Smith wrote more than 100 fantasy stories, most published in pulp magazines such as *Weird Tales* during the 1920s and 1930s, but no novels. Although he was a correspondent of H. P. LOVECRAFT, his own fiction tended more toward fantasy than horror and was frequently set in one or another of his imaginary lands, Hyperborea, Zothique, Posedonis,

Averoigne, and others. His fiction is highly descriptive and prose conscious, and many of his stories are little more than tours of exotic landscapes or descriptions of unusual and bizarre objects or events. Much of his short fiction was reprinted in hardcover by Arkham House during the 1940s, reassembled by Ballantine Books for mass-market paperbacks during the 1970s, and reshuffled and reprinted by a variety of publishers since. Although a few of his stories are technically science fiction, the vast majority make no attempt to rationalize the wonders they contain.

Smith was highly influential not only in the fantasy field but also in science fiction, in which writers such as C. L. Moore and Leigh Brackett were moved to imitate his decaying societies, often setting them on distant worlds. His own stories take the reader on a trip to a wondrous otherworld such as in "THE CITY OF THE SINGING FLAME" (1931) or to a far distant future when Earth is unrecognizable and magic again holds sway, such as in "THE ABOMINATIONS OF YONDO" (1926). He describes a horrifying physical transformation in "UBBO-SATHLA" (1933) and shows a civilization in decline in "The Empire of the Necromancers" (1932). His terrors could be familiar, traditional ones such as the vampires in "A RENDEZVOUS IN AVEROIGNE" (1931), mindless forces of nature such as the flesh devouring plants in "The Seed from the Sepulchre" (1933), or distorted versions of familiar creatures such as the malevolent toads in "Mother of Toads" (1938). Even his occasional science fiction stories set on other worlds, such as "The Vaults of Yoh-Vombis (1932) are simply different venues for the same type of story he normally set on Earth.

Smith's enduring popularity is evident from the frequency with which he is reprinted. The most recent collections of his work are *A Rendezvous in Averoigne* (1988), *Strange Shadows* (1997), and *The Emperor of Dreams* (2002).

Smith, Guy (1939–   )

It would be easy to dismiss the very prolific Guy Smith as a minor hack writer who churned out new horror novels with relentless regularity and little entertainment value, and it is undoubtedly true that no single novel of his has ever achieved either best-seller status or critical acclaim. Smith works very much in the manner of the pulp authors of the 1930s and 1940s, writing to a set of limited formulas, peopling his books with shallowly described characters and often predictable terrors, and rarely challenging the reader to think about the content beyond the surface plot. Judged in those terms, he comes off rather better. He writes in a clear, no-nonsense prose style, his plots are coherent and plausible given their initial premise, his characters have understandable if shallow motives, and he delivers exactly what the reader expects.

Smith first began writing with *Werewolf by Moonlight* (1974), a lightweight horror story about a werewolf stalking the English moors. It was followed by two similar sequels, *Return of the Werewolf* (1977) and *Son of the Werewolf* (1978). His second published novel was *The Sucking Pit* (1975), a story of mysterious incidents taking place in the vicinity of a pit of quicksand. Next came *The Slime Beast* (1975), a predictable gruesome monster story followed by a novelization of the minor horror film *The Ghoul* (1976). Smith had established himself quickly as a reliable if not exceptional horror writer.

His next novel inaugurated his longest and most successful series. The premise of *Night of the Crabs* (1976) is that a new breed of carnivorous crab appears off the coast of Great Britain, creatures capable of coming ashore in large numbers, fearless, and able to attack and subdue larger creatures, including people. This unlikely situation continued in *Killer Crabs* (1978), *The Origin of the Crabs* (1979), *Crabs on the Rampage* (1981), *Crabs' Moon* (1984), and *Crabs: The Human Sacrifice* (1988). In each case the crabs are repulsed but not defeated, and in the final volume a new religious cult begins to worship them. Smith used the nature-in-uprising-against-humanity theme in several other novels, most notably *Bats Out of Hell* (1978), one of his best, in which a plague of vampire bats becomes even more threatening when it is discovered that they are carrying a new plague. Swarms of insects threaten the world in *Locusts* (1979), and in *Carnivore* (1990) the villain uses magic to turn the entire natural world against humanity.

One of Smith's better novels of the supernatural is *Deathbell* (1980), in which a cursed bell foretells horrible events whenever it tolls. A sequel, *Demons* (1987), is less interesting. The ghosts of victims of Nazi atrocities exact revenge in *Satan's Snowdrop* (1980), and voodoo is used to bypass security at a nuclear missile base in *Warhead* (1986). *Wolfcurse* (1981) is a predictable werewolf story, but *Manitou Doll* (1981), which invokes Native American magic, has some innovative plot twists. *Doomflight* (1981) matches modern weapons against druidic magic. *Entombed* (1982) is a satisfying ghost story, and *The Wood* (1985) is a surprisingly lively story of people who cross the paths of a satanic cult. *The Neophyte* (1986) is a novel of witchcraft, as is the much better *Witch Spell* (1993). A thoroughly awful child plagues his babysitters with stories about his powerful mentor in *The Dark One* (1995). *Dead End* (1996), another of his better novels, involves a house that is supposedly home to the dead, a reputation the protagonist scoffs at until he sees his dead girlfriend in the house. The story is much more atmospheric than Smith's earlier work and suggests that he might have developed into a better writer if he had not been content to produce formula fiction. *Water Rites* (1997), in which evil lives concealed beneath the placid surface of a lake, is also notably better than Smith's previous work.

Smith, who also wrote novelizations of several fantasy films for children, has generally chosen quantity over quality, although there is a certain minimal level of quality below which he has never descended. Not surprisingly, he is generally at his best when he breaks from his usual formulas and tries something new. Although never a literary writer, he is skilled at plot construction, provides adequate characterization to involve the reader, and almost invariably ends with a rousing and satisfying climax.

Smith, L. J. (unknown)

Lisa James Smith is the author of several supernatural thriller series for young adults, the earliest of which includes a relatively unmemorable series about a teenaged girl who battles sorcery in this and other worlds. The best in that sequence is *Night of the Solstice* (1987). Smith failed to hit her stride until she started the Vampire Diaries series with *The Awakening* (1991). The setting is a typical high school, but the female protagonist has a problem. She is attracted by each of two brothers, one of whom is good and one evil, even though both are secretly vampires. Their adventures continue in *The Struggle* (1991), *The Fury* (1991), and *Dark Reunion* (1992), ending with the teenager's conversion to vampirism and the final battle between the siblings.

Smith followed with the Secret Circle trilogy, *The Initiation*, *The Captive*, and *The Power*, all published in 1992. This time the teenaged protagonist is tempted by the powers of witchcraft. She is offered a place in a coven that professes to practice only good magic, but she suspects that might not be the case, particularly when the animosity of some of the other witches leads to supernatural danger. The sequence is a bit more complex than that of the Vampire Diaries, with more depth to the characters and a less clear-cut choice between good and evil. The Forbidden Game trilogy appeared in 1994, *The Hunter*, *The Chase*, and *The Kill*. A group of teenagers find themselves menaced by Julian, an evil spirit who uses a magical game to transport them to his realm, where they must compete to save their lives and souls. All three installments are cleverly done, and Julian is a particularly effective villain. *The Strange Power* (1994) and *The Possessed* (1995) follow the adventures of a group of teenagers with psychic powers.

Smith then launched the 10-volume Night World series with *Secret Vampire* (1996), bringing it to an apparent conclusion with *Strange Fate* (1998). The loosely arranged series assumes that the world of the supernatural lies quite close to ours and pits various human characters against vampires both good and evil and other creatures of the darkness. The best in the series are *Dark Angel* (1996) and *The Chosen* (1997). Smith has been inactive since the end of this series, but many of her books remain in print. Her fans would certainly welcome her return.

Smith, Thorne (1892–1934)

If he had written only the single novel *Topper* (1926), James Thorne Smith would probably still be remembered fondly. As it is, he also wrote several other humorous fantasies, most of them rather bawdy at the time they were published, although they are quite tame by contemporary standards. Topper is an older man who finds his life complicated by the presence of the ghosts of the Kerbys, tragically killed in an accident. He is the only person who can see or hear them, and Mrs. Kerby's tendency to wear transparent or even invisible clothing proves to be a considerable trial for him. He returns in *Topper Takes a Trip* (1932), retired and moved to the country for some peace and quiet, which he fails to achieve because the Kerbys follow him there and bring along a number of their ghostly friends to boot.

Most of Smith's other novels contain some element of fantasy as well. In *The Stray Lamb* (1929) the protagonist is turned into a succession of different animals by the intercession of a minor god. A husband and wife exchange identities and bodies in *Turnabout* (1931) for a series of farcical adventures before they both discover that they were happier the way they were to start with. Smith's least successful novel is *The Night Life of the Gods* (1931), wherein a man discovers the power to bring statues to life and soon finds himself hosting a rather ribald party attended by the Greek gods and goddesses. His last completed fantasy novel is *The Glorious Pool* (1934), which substitutes a swimming pool for the fountain of youth. A set of older people find their youth restored with not entirely happy results, and they are forced to deal with an animated statue as well.

Rain in the Doorway (1933) and *Skin and Bones* (1933) also contain some fantasy elements, but they are all rationalized in some fashion. Smith left an incomplete manuscript at his death, which was completed by Norman Matson as *The Passionate Witch* (1941), to which Matson later added a sequel, *Bats in the Belfry* (1942). The first novel was the basis for a movie, as was *Turnabout*. *Topper* spawned a movie and a television series.

"Smoke Ghost" Fritz Leiber (1941)

Fritz LEIBER was an extremely accomplished writer who proved his ability to write in a number of genres and voices, from science fiction to heroic fantasy to contemporary horror. His horror fiction is often difficult to characterize, however, because he generally avoided the genre's clichés, believing that moldering castles, wailing ghosts, and blood-sucking vampires were horrors for an older generation. If the supernatural exists, he suggested, then it is a response to the minds of the current generation, and those manifestations would take a very different form in a modern urban environment. His work reflects this philosophy, with witches using their powers as part of campus politics in *Conjure Wife* (1953), for example, and a haunted revolver in "The Automatic Pistol" (1940).

Perhaps the best example of this is "Smoke Ghost," in which Catesby Wran, a businessman, discovers a ghostly creature whose image is a reflection of his time. He spots the specter during the daylight from the window of his commuter train lying like an abandoned sack on a distant rooftop, somehow conveying over that distance a sense of disquiet and filth. As the days pass he notices that the form is moving closer, one roof at a time, and he becomes convinced that it is being attracted to him personally and that it is somehow a source of menace. At the same time he becomes acutely aware of dust and dirt in his immediate environment, uncertain whether it has recently increased or whether he has just become more sensitized to it.

Wran, we discover, was trained by his rather dotty mother as a medium and even demonstrated some rudimentary psychic powers when examined by a delegation of university researchers as a child, although he has long since abandoned that activity and has only a shadowy memory of it. It is this, perhaps, that has made him sensitive to the smoke ghost. He wonders about its motivation and comes to dread the sight of it more with each passing day, although he is confident that it cannot physically harm him, at least not directly.

Although he is right, he underestimates the danger. The smoke ghost invades the mind of his secretary, effectively possessing her and threatening his life, which he saves only by promising to worship the creature. Satisfied, it lets him live and restores the secretary to her right mind. Just as Leiber's modern ghost has taken on a different form, it also has a different nature. Rather than the spirit of a dead individual, it is an amalgamation of mass emotions, despair, ambition, fear, and anxiety. Other writers have similarly attempted to update the traditional devices of horror fiction, usually with far less success.

Something Wicked This Way Comes
Ray Bradbury (1962)

Although Ray BRADBURY has been a prolific writer since the 1940s, he has only occasionally written novels, and of his supernatural novels, only this one was not written for children, although the chief protagonist is a child. The premise of the story has been used in one form or another in a variety of fine stories before and since, including THE CIRCUS OF DR. LAO (1935), by Charles G. Finney, *The Dreaming Jewels* (1950), by Theodore Sturgeon, and later in *Blind Voices* (1978), by Tom Reamy, and *The Magnificent Gallery* (1987), by Thomas F. MONTELEONE. The setting is a typical small midwestern town, a common time and place for Bradbury, whose residents have their lives changed forever when a traveling carnival arrives unexpectedly.

The carnival of Mr. Dark is not a source of merriment and joy, despite its gaudy signs and lavish promises. The carousel can add or subtract years from your life, and the other attractions also have their hidden dangers. As the people who attend begin to disappear, only the young protagonist, who has spied on the carnival's personnel, suspects the truth, that the carnival is an elaborate trap, and typically it takes a while before he convinces one of the adults, his father, that he is telling the truth.

Intermingled with the melodrama is a subtler story. The victims of the carnival are not so much coerced as seduced. They are overcome by the evil chiefly because of their own shortcomings, their wishes to be young, or wealthy, or powerful, or just to be loved. Although Mr. Dark and his minions are eventually foiled, they are symptoms of a greater ill that Bradbury and the reader know cannot be so easily remedied. A portion of the novel is based on a much earlier short story, "The Black Ferris" (1948), which is sufficiently different to be an interesting sidebar to the novel. A reasonably loyal motion picture version was released in 1983, but the tension and atmosphere of the novel did not transfer to the screen particularly well.

"Sometimes They Come Back"
Stephen King (1974)

Memories of unpleasant encounters with schoolyard bullies are common in our culture, but it took a writer like Stephen KING to explore the really terrifying possibility that we might not be free of them even in maturity. The protagonist of this early story is a high school teacher, Jim Norman, recently recovered from a nervous breakdown, who watched four thugs murder his older brother when he himself was only nine years old. Although the incident is far in his past, he has never been able to escape it and is on the verge of experiencing it all over again.

One of the classes he is teaching is a typical parking lot for jocks, malcontents, and oddballs, a reading class whose participants really do not want to be there and whose teacher is hard pressed to maintain his own interest. Norman is particularly unhappy with one student, Chip Osway, who makes veiled threats and is constantly belligerent. Osway becomes a relatively minor problem when one of the other students is run down by a hit-and-run driver and replaced in class by Robert Larson, a supposed transfer from Milford High School. Larson is the spitting image of one of the boys who killed Jim's brother, and his presence and attitude revive old fears.

When a second student dies, her seat is filled by another transfer from Milford, another disrespectful troublemaker and also a duplicate of a second member of the gang of killers. Jim is convinced now that this is not a coincidence but cannot explain how the young thugs could remain the same age until he checks with a retired policeman and discovers that three of the foursome were killed in an automobile accident not long after the murder. Sure enough, another death is followed by the arrival of the third member of the gang, and they make no secret of the fact that they are back from the dead to complete some unfinished business: that Jim was supposed to have died as a child.

When Jim's wife is run down and killed by a hit-and-run driver, he is driven to an experiment with the occult. He performs a violent, forbidden ritual in order to defeat the threesome and send them back to hell, but even as they disappear, he realizes that his victory might not be permanent, because "sometimes they come back." Although King never wrote a follow-up, the 1991 film version was later followed by two sequels, *Sometimes They Come Back Again* (1996) and *Sometimes They Come Back . . . for More* (1999), but the sequels diluted the impact of the first rather than enhanced it.

Somtow, S. P. (1952–   )

S. P. Somtow is the pen name of Somtow Sucharitkul, a native of Thailand although he has lived most of his life abroad. In addition to his fantasy and horror, he has written a considerable amount of science fiction, mostly under his real name. The majority of his horror and fantasy, which often draws on his cultural background, has appeared under this pseudonym. His first major horror fiction was *Vampire Junction* (1984), which mixes vampires with rock and roll. The vampire rock singer protagonist later returned in two sequels, *Valentine* (1992) and *Vanitas* (1995), but the original is by far the best of the three volumes.

His next horror novel was *Forgetting Places* (1987), a quietly suspenseful novel in which a teenager begins receiving e-mails from his dead brother. Although he originally believes it to be a cruel prank, he eventually comes to believe that he is actually communicating with the land of the dead. *Darker Angels* (1997) is his best book-length horror for adults, an evocative story of voodoo magic and a man who visits Civil War battlefields in order to raise the dead. *The Vampire's Beautiful Daughter* (1997) is a very offbeat, cleverly done story for young adults.

Somtow's fantasy is much less varied than his horror fiction. *The Shattered Horse* (1986) is a historical fantasy set shortly after the fall of Troy. *The Fallen Country* (1986, as Sucharitkul) is much better, even though it is for young adults. The protagonist lives partly in our world and partly in one locked under a sheath of ice where magic works. The Riverrun trilogy consists of *Riverrun* (1991), *Forest of the Night* (1992, also published as *Armorica*), and *Yestern* (1996), the last of which appeared only as part of the omnibus *Riverrun Trilogy*. A young man from our world battles sorcery and other dangers both in our world and in another reality. The next two young adult fantasies appeared

under the name Sucharitkul. A young American boy becomes a trainee magician in *The Wizard's Apprentice* (1993), and a similar young protagonist has less overt contact with magic in *Jasmine Nights* (1994).

The Pavilion of Frozen Women (1996) assembles some of the best of the author's short supernatural fiction. A second collection, *Dragon's Fin Soup* (1998), is mostly fantasy. *Tagging the Moon* (2000) is an interesting collection of classic fairy tales retold in the form of horror stories. Somtow won a World Fantasy Award for the novella *The Bird Catcher*, in 1992.

The Sonja Blue Series Nancy Collins (1989–2002)

By 1989 the popularity of vampire fiction had already increased so dramatically that it was hard to believe any writer could find some radically new approach to the form. There were good vampires as well as bad, happy ones and others tormented by their new condition, vampire detectives and vampire lovers, and vampires in just about every other situation readers might imagine. Nancy COLLINS not only found a new niche, but scored highly with her debut novel, *Sunglasses after Dark* (1989), which introduced Sonja Blue and which won the Bram Stoker Award for first novel.

Sonja is a violent mental patient diagnosed as having a split personality. After she escapes from custody, we discover that she is not crazy and that she really is a vampire, though not modeled along traditional lines. She is also capable of seeing the invisible world of magical beings and events that takes place in and around human society, completely concealed from the rest of us. Her half-human, half-vampire nature suspends her between two very different worlds, in both of which she has to find a way to survive. Her second adventure was *In the Blood* (1991), not quite as remarkable but still very good, this time causing her to make common cause with a private detective as they seek to track down the local vampire lord.

Vampire turns vampire hunter in *Paint It Black* (1995), an episodic and only intermittently interesting follow-up. *A Dozen Black Roses* (1996) is considerably better, set in an urban neighborhood that has been abstracted from the rest of the world, but the main plot dealing with the rivalry between two vampire clans does not provide a particularly gripping story. The fifth in the series, *Darkest Heart* (2002), is very reminiscent of *In the Blood*, perhaps reflecting the author's lessening interest in supernatural fiction. She has subsequently indicated her intention to abandon the genre entirely. Three of the five books in the series are skillfully written and fully engaging, and the first, in particular, is one of the modern classics of horror fiction and probably was an influence on Laurell HAMILTON and others who use the supernatural as just another magic system in their dark fantasies.

A Spell for Chameleon Piers Anthony (1977)

After starting his writing career as a mildly controversial science fiction writer, Piers ANTHONY turned most of his attention to humorous fantasy starting in the late 1970s. Funny fantasy had never been very popular in the United States, although it enjoys more popularity in England, but during the 1970s and early 1980s, several writers including Craig Shaw GARDNER, Esther FRIESNER, and John Dechancie delivered a flurry of varied comical adventures. The British writer Terry PRATCHETT was also building a following. The subgenre imploded shortly thereafter, leaving only Pratchett and Anthony in strong positions.

Most of Anthony's humorous fantasy falls within the Xanth series, now nearly 30 volumes long. The sequence started with *A Spell for Chameleon*, which unfortunately is probably the single best title in the series, although there are occasional sequels of nearly the same quality. The protagonist is Bink, a likeable young character who is the only person without any apparent magical talent in a world where it is an integral part of life. Bink consults the good magician Humfrey, whose magic tells him that Bink is a person of great importance in the world, perhaps just as important as the evil wizard Trent, who has villainous designs on the world. If Bink cannot prove that he has a magical talent by his 25th birthday, he will by law be expelled into our universe, known as Mundania.

Xanth itself is a magical world that is only slightly connected to our own, a place where all the creatures of legend exist. In fact, the legends in our own world originated because inhabitants of that other realm occasionally strayed across the barrier into our reality. People from our world also occasionally cross in the opposite direction, although a shield has been erected to prevent further migrations and disruptions. Bink eventually discovers his magical talent and saves the day, returns in a few further volumes, but soon disappeared from the series in favor of a more diverse and ever-changing series of protagonists. Although the Xanth books have become very formulaic, the opening volume has a charming sense of innocence and an atmosphere of good humor all too rare in modern fantasy.

The Spellsinger Series Alan Dean Foster (1983–1994)

Although Alan Dean Foster is known primarily for his science fiction, he is also the author of a significant number of fantasy novels, some of them quite unusual. His longest-running and most popular series is his most conventional, transporting a likeable young man from our world into a fantasy realm starting with *Spellsinger* (1983). Predictably, he quickly accumulates a small party of companions for his adventures, but they are an unusual lot, including an intelligent otter and a magic turtle. The first volume serves mostly to introduce the characters, setting, and main conflict and does not stand well alone, requiring the sequel, *The Hour of the Gate* (1984), to resolve the situation, allowing him space to complete various quests and forge an alliance against the inevitable magical threat to the world.

In *The Day of the Dissonance* (1984), one of the party of friends falls seriously ill, and only a magical cure will suffice, which is retrieved after a mildly exciting series of adventures. There is considerably more substance in *The Moment of the Magician* (1984), in which a new villain arises to challenge the world, and yet another quest must be undertaken. *The Paths of the Perambulator* (1985) accelerates things and provides some quite innovative variations of standard fantasy devices. This particular cycle of adventures comes to an end with *The Time of the Transference* (1986), appropriately with another quest, this time an effort to mend a broken musical instrument with magical powers.

Two later additions were less interesting. *Son of Spellsinger* (1993) introduces the next generation, but the adventures are largely repetitive. *Chorus Skating* (1994) is similarly light, although the segments involving a weird, evil rock group are amusing. The Spellsinger books are good-humored adventures in which there is never any serious doubt that good will prevail in the end. The first six novels in the series have been collected in omnibus volumes as *Season of the Spellsong* (1985) and *Spellsinger's Scherzo* (1987). Most of Foster's other fantasy novels are inconsequential, but The Journey of the Catechist trilogy is quite original, although sometimes rambling.

Springer, Nancy (1948–)

Nancy Springer is one of the minority of fantasy writers who demonstrate a clear evolution in theme and setting during the course of their careers. She began writing with *The Book of Suns* (1977), a pleasant formulaic fantasy about a quest in a land of elves, but as the years passed she moved away from exotic otherworlds and times and concentrated on contemporary fantasy, usually with a feminine viewpoint and primarily for young adults, although she continues to enjoy an adult audience for that same work.

Her first major fantasy was the sequence consisting of *The White Hart* (1979), *The Silver Sun* (1980, a completely rewritten version of *The Book of Suns*), *The Silver Sun* (1981), *The Sable Moon* (1982), *The Black Beast* (1982), and *The Golden Swan* (1983), published in an omnibus edition as *The Book of Vale* (1984). All five books are well written but rather conventional adventures involving quests, the battle for a throne, and evil sorcery. Springer seemed destined to become one of the many authors mining this particular literary vein, and her next few novels did little to change this impression. *Wings of Flame* (1985) chronicles the efforts by a small number of heroic figures to deflect the force of an evil invader, and *Chains of Gold* (1986) follows the adventures of two fugitives who flee their homeland pursued by various enemies, human and inhuman.

The Sea King trilogy also was not markedly different, although it was much more ambitious and noticeably better written, consisting of *Madbond* (1987), *Mindbond* (1986), and *Godbond* (1988). A supernatural force menaces the future of an entire world, so another group of heroes battle shape-changing infiltrators and a reincarnated goddess to save the day. It was with *Apocalypse* (1989) that Springer began to change her perspective and branch out into new territory. A small Pennsylvania town whose economy is on the skids encounters even greater problems when the legendary Four Horsemen appear, and an uncertain young woman tentatively turns to magic. Although the plot is ostensibly one of good versus evil, Springer was much more interested in developing her human characters and portraying how they react under stress. Most of her fiction from this point forward used a contemporary real-world setting. *The Hex Witch of Seldom* (1989), which bears strong similarities in setting and characterization, is an almost equally impressive novel.

Although the majority of Springer's later work was for young adults, she did write two additional adult titles. In *Larque on the Wing* (1994) a contemporary woman is confronted by a manifestation of her younger self, who takes her on a voyage of inner discovery, a reversal of the device used in A CHRISTMAS CAROL (1843) by Charles Dickens. An angel comes to earth in *Metal Wings* (1994) and discovers that his appearance is so memorable that the only life he is suited for among humans is as a rock star. Despite some humorous overtones, Springer treats the theme quite seriously.

Springer's young adult fantasy novels are intelligently written and potentially rewarding to readers of all ages. *Red Wizard* (1990) is the least interesting, placing a boy from our world in an alternate reality where magic works. *Damnbanna* (1992) is a thoughtful, low-key short novel about a woman's encounter with a mystical creature. *The Friendship Song* (1992) is a very moving story about the friendship between two teenaged girls, one of whom is facing an emotional crisis because her father is remarrying, with their situation complicated by their discovery of genuine magic. Springer turned to humor with *Fair Peril* (1996), in which a young girl kisses a frog that changes into a prince who has considerable difficulty fitting into our world. *I Am Mordred* (1998) is a rare recent excursion from the contemporary world, a reimagining of one of the more complex relationships in the story of King Arthur, that between Arthur and his son Mordred, raised by Morgan Le Fay to hate his father. A magical bird transforms a woman's life in *Plumage* (2000).

Springer began writing for even younger children after 2000, primarily her series of nonfantastic Rowan Hood books about a young girl in the time of Robin Hood. She has also written a sizeable body of short fiction, including fine stories such as "The Black Angel" (1995) and "Transcendance" (1997). Her only collection, *Chance and Other Gestures of the Hand of Fate* (1987), contains comparatively lesser work, and a more recent selection is long overdue.

"Sredni Vashtar" Saki (1911)

By the very nature of the form, many horror stories are ambiguous. The psychological state of the characters is of far more importance in most horror fiction than it is in any other genre because it is the feelings of fear and revulsion that we explore through this type of story. The fear of death is an almost universal quality, and it is through tales of terror that we are able to face death in its most awful forms and come to terms with it. Horror writers frequently suggest that it is our fear that causes external events to seem so horrible rather than those events themselves. This particular story, for example, can be read as supernatural or not, because Saki never explicitly tells us what happens; readers will have no difficulty filling in the gaps themselves, although not necessarily in the same manner.

The protagonist is a 10-year-old boy, Conradin, orphaned and living with his adult cousin, Mrs. De Ropp, whom he also refers to generically as the "woman." There is a deep and abiding, though unspoken, hatred between the boy and his guardian. His health is not good, and both she and the doctor have declared that he will not live to adulthood, which might certainly prove to be the case given the stifling atmosphere in which he lives. Mrs. De Ropp does not think of herself as a cruel person, but she acknowledges that she takes delight in frustrating Conradin's wishes, although always justifying her actions as being in his best interests.

Conradin has a secret, a tool shed in which he keeps a domestic hen and a ferret, both caged and the latter smuggled in. When Mrs. De Ropp notices that he spends a great deal of time there, she investigates and promptly disposes of the hen, although she initially overlooks the ferret. Enraged at this further incursion into his world, Conradin begins worshiping the ferret, who he dubs Sredni Vashtar, praying to him to come to his aid. All of this seems doomed to come to nothing, however, because Mrs. De Ropp knows that there is still something in the shed that draws Conradin to it. She ventures there again, and the boy is caught between despair and a furtive hope that the ferret god will grant him his freedom. And, of course, that is exactly what happens. The ferret is released and kills Mrs. De Ropp before escaping. Did the creature actually answer his suppliant's prayers, or was it just a coincidental accident? Saki, the pseudonym of H. H. Munro, leaves that conclusion to the individual reader.

Stableford, Brian M. (1948–   )

Although Brian Stableford began writing professionally in 1965, most of his early work was science fiction, and his first fantasy, a young adult novel, did not appear until more than 10 years later. *The Last Days of the Edge of the World* (1978), is an agreeable rearrangement of familiar fairy tale concepts, with a young girl forced to accept an arranged marriage, an alliance between wizards and the local ruler, and the quest by a suitor to accomplish a series of tasks. It would be another 10 years before Stableford wrote his first fantasy for adults, a rationalized horror novel set in an alternate reality where vampires are real and have become an accepted and powerful part of European society. Their vampirelike nature is explained in scientific rather than supernatural terms, so arguably Stableford still had not produced an adult fantasy.

The David Lydyard trilogy followed almost immediately and is clearly fantasy. In *The Werewolves of London* (1990) several godlike beings, or possibly some variety of angel, are wakening from an age-long sleep to interfere in human affairs during the Victorian era, and a secret society of werewolves is battling them. The series continued with *The Angel of Pain* (1991) and *The Carnival of Destruction* (1994), with more of the sleepers wakening and using humans as tools with which to examine the world. The trilogy is a major accomplishment, but its complexity tends to discourage casual readers.

Young Blood (1992) is a more conventional present-day vampire story, notably, for the depth with which the author examines the various characters who discover that they are no longer human. *The Hunger and Ecstasy of Vampires* (1996) is science fiction, despite its title, although Stableford's treatment may be of interest to horror fans. His most recent fantasy novel is *Year Zero* (2002), an offbeat satire and kitchen sink novel in which a contemporary woman has a series of surreal encounters with everything from angels and demons to aliens from outer space.

A good selection of Stableford's fantasy fiction can be found in *Fables and Fantasies* (1996). Among his better stories are "Judas Story" (1975), "Slumming in Voodooland (1991), "Seers" (1997), and "The Devil's Comedy" (2002). He has also written four heroic fantasy novels set in the Warhammer role-playing game universe under the pen name Brian Craig. Although primarily a science fiction writer, his occasional horror fiction has gathered considerable praise.

Stallman, Robert (1930–1980)

Although Robert Stallman's writing career was cut short by his premature death, he left behind an unusual set of three books that has ensured that his name will not soon be forgotten. The trilogy consists of *The Orphan* (1980), *The Captive* (1981), and *The Beast* (1982, also published as *The Book of the Beast*). A cursory examination would lead the casual reader to believe that these are novels about a werewolf, but Stallman actually took that legend and stood it on its head. The opening volumes reveal the birth of the beast, a powerful, predatory animal whose origin is never explained and whose powers are never rationalized. The beast is the

central figure from that point forward, not a human who can turn into a beast but a beast who can alter his form and take the guise of a human.

The limitations on the beast's powers of transformation are unusual. It can violate the law of conservation of mass and energy by becoming a human child, but it cannot imitate an imaginary or living human, only those who have recently died. As part of the process of self-preservation the beast creates a second personality in its own mind, and there is sometimes conflict between the two personae. Most of the series then consists of the beast's attempts to learn how to be human and the occasional difficulties arising from his split nature. There is a melodramatic subplot in which the beast rescues his human wife and child from a band of neo-Nazis and the revelation in the final book that there are other shape-changers in the world, though most are not like the beast. The beast achieves his destiny at last, although the final volume is not as coherent as the first two, probably because Stallman died before he had completed revising it. The trilogy is a particularly remarkable achievement since Stallman had written no previous fiction.

Stasheff, Christopher (1944–)

Christopher Stasheff is best known as the author of the very long Warlock series, which is science fiction rather than fantasy but should also be of interest to fantasy readers because it is set on a planet whose physical laws and technology have been contrived to make it appear that magic works. Stasheff began writing the series in 1969, but it was not until 1986 that his first actual fantasy novel appeared.

Her Majesty's Wizard (1986) was the first volume of the Wizard in Rhyme series, the individual volumes of which share a common setting but sometimes use entirely different casts of characters. In the first a man from our world discovers that by reciting certain poetry he can be magically transported into a typical fantasy world. His lighthearted, lightweight adventures are often caused by his own blundering in this and the belated sequel, *The Oathbound Wizard* (1993). A different protagonist takes the stage in *The Witch Doctor*

(1994), battling an evil sorceress, a plot repeated with only slight variations in the next, *The Secular Wizard* (1995). One of the newcomers returns to his home reality in *My Son, the Wizard* (1997). *The Feline Wizard* (2000) changes the tone of the series, featuring a cat who is also an accomplished wizard as the central character. The most recent volume is *The Haunted Wizard* (2000).

The Star Stone duo is atypically quite serious and perhaps not surprisingly more interesting. The two volumes are *The Shaman* (1995) and *The Sage* (1996). The backdrop this time is a magical world where humans are a subordinate species dominated by inhuman creatures, one of whom decides to help humans achieve their own destiny. His most recent novel, *Saint Vidicon to the Rescue* (2005), appears to stand alone. A computer expert is investigating the appearance of bibilical text in computer files where it does not belong when he discovers the existence of Saint Vidicon, a new saint dedicated to protecting computer users from a variety of pitfalls. The novel is an expansion of an idea that first appeared in "The Afterlife of Saint Vidicon" (2004).

Stasheff's short fantasy fiction has been partially collected in *Sir Harold and the Monkey King* (1993) and *Mind out of Time* (2003). Like his novels, the stories tend to be mild adventure mixed with sometimes obvious humor. His best effort at this length is "Sir Harold and the Hindu King" (1995). Stasheff is one of a small group of writers who have successfully built a career based primarily on humorous fantasy and science fiction.

Stewart, Mary (1916–   )

Mary Stewart began her writing career with a series of very popular romantic thrillers between 1955 and the 1970s that spawned scores of imitators at the time but that are now less well remembered than her Arthurian romances. Her first fantasy novel was *The Crystal Cave* (1970), which broke from tradition by concentrating on the character of Merlin, in this case a young man whose life is forever altered when he begins to develop magically enhanced perception. *The Hollow Hills* (1973) encompasses the most familiar parts of the legend, Arthur's rise to the throne, his management of the Round Table, and his transformation of Britain. Stewart reveals all of this through the eyes of Merlin, who, from off stage, is actually the architect for most of what takes place. The device of stepping outside the central frame of the story was adapted by many other writers, including A. A. Attanasio, Marion Zimmer BRADLEY, and Diana L. PAXSON. The original concept was for a trilogy ending with *The Last Enchantment* (1979), which follows the death of Arthur with Merlin's own ruminations about his own future. Despite its not entirely cheerful conclusion, it is the single best of Stewart's novels. *The Wicked Day* (1983) returns to that setting to tell the story of Mordred, Arthur's rebellious son. *The Prince and the Pilgrim* (1995) is also peripherally related.

Stewart returned to the thriller format during the 1970s and 1980s, although two of her suspense novels are also fantasy. The protagonist of *Touch Not the Cat* (1976) has a telepathic link with a man she has never met, and *Thornyhold* (1988), although not properly a haunted house story, involves the psychic effects on a tenant originating from events in the past. A young girl with the power to heal others upsets the religious establishment in *Grace* (1989), and *Rose Cottage* (1997) also involves some ambiguous psychic phenomena. Stewart also wrote three fantasies for children. A young girl discovers that she is a witch in *The Little Broomstick* (1971), the reader takes a tour of the zodiac in *Ludo and the Star Horse* (1974), and two children with a magic amulet help a man escape the curse of the werewolf in *A Walk in Wolf Wood* (1980). Stewart's Arthurian novels are among the best and most influential in that subgenre, but her contemporary fantasies are also quite entertaining.

Stine, R. L. (1943–   )

Robert Lawrence Stine started writing books for young readers in the 1970s and had produced a considerable number of titles under his own and other names before switching to suspense and horror for both teens and preteens at the end of the 1970s. The popularity of that form was such that he was soon turning out an amazing volume of works, most of it gathered into two separate series, although the Fear Street books for young adults were only loosely interrelated, and the Goosebumps series for younger readers had no common thread at all.

Many of the Fear Street books involve no fantastic or supernatural elements, but the Goosebumps books almost always include some kind of monster. The Fear Street novels generally have deeper characterization and a more serious tone, and the violence is less cartoonish, although the subset The Ghosts of Fear Street is much like the Goosebumps series, with plots involving fish that mutate and leave their fishbowl and similar absurdities. Fear Street novels typically follow the viewpoint of a teenager, usually a girl, who faces some sort of threat. In *Bad Dreams* (1994), for example, the protagonist is troubled by recurring dreams of a horrifying murder and tries to disavow her clairvoyant power. The plots are often standard horror themes restructured for young characters and are often somewhat less than plausible. An ancient curse affects the current generation in *The Burning* (1993), and a high school experiment gone awry reanimates the dead in *The Bad Girl* (1998). *The First Horror* (1994) is a predictable haunted house tale, and *Goodbye Kiss* (1992) involves a standard vampire. Many others are variations on familiar ghost stories. The best of the Fear Street novels are *The New Evil* (1994), in which an evil spirit preys on cheerleaders, and *The Perfect Date* (1996), a ghost story.

The Goosebumps books are considerably less serious, even when they involve equally horrifying themes. With titles such as *The Cuckoo Clock of Doom* (1995), *Eat Cheese and Barf* (1996), *It Came from Beneath the Sink* (1995), *How I Got My Shrunken Head* (1996), and *The Blob That Ate Everyone* (1997), it is obvious that Stine did not want his stories to seem too frightening. Other titles are quite obviously mild satires of other horror novels or films, such as *The Abominable Snowman of Pasadena* (1995), *Bride of the Living Dummy* (1998), *Invasion of the Body Squeezers* (1998), *The Haunted Car* (1999), and *Jekyll and Heidi* (1999).

Despite the superficiality of many of the Goosebumps novels, Stine occasionally incorporated clever ideas. *Stay Out of the Basement* (1992) demonstrates that experimentation has an effect on the experimenter as well as the subject. An obsessed music teacher attempts to build the perfect student in *Piano Lessons Can Be Murder* (1993). *Let's Get Invisible* (1993) proves that having a supernatural power is not necessarily a good thing. Phantom dogs bedevil the new kid in town in *The Barking Ghost* (1995). *Revenge of the Lawn Gnomes* (1995) also has some genuinely funny sequences.

The Goosebumps series eventually metamorphosed into the very similar Goosebumps 2000 and then The Nightmare Room, but by the end of the 1990s it was obvious that the boom in young readers' horror had ended. Several episodes from the series were filmed for television. Stine continues to write in this vein at a much lower volume but continues to sell at that level even after his many competitors have disappeared from the book stores entirely. Stine's horror novel for adults, *Superstitious* (1995), involves a woman who discovers that a college professor's interest in the occult is more than just academic and has a connection to a series of brutal murders in the area. It is competently done but unremarkable. *Nightmare Hour* (1999) is a collection of unrelated stories.

Many parents and teachers looked askance at the Goosebumps novels during the height of their popularity. They sported garish covers that gave them a comic-book appearance, and their titles and themes suggested death, corruption, and horrible events. They were for a time immensely popular, and while some critics contend that their later decline was because the stories became more rushed and repetitive, the truth is probably that the fad had crested and would have receded no matter how well written the later volumes had been. Stine's closest rival was Christopher PIKE, who has begun writing novels for adults in recent years, but Stine has so far declined to follow suit other than with his one book in that area.

Stoker, Bram (1847–1912)

Bram Stoker is, of course, best known as the author of DRACULA (1897), which defined the vampire for modern horror fiction and whose central figure has probably appeared in more motion pictures than any other fictional character, as well as scores of novels continuing his adventures or providing alternate versions of his history. Although Stoker began writing professionally while still young and was employed for a time by J. Sheridan LE FANU, who wrote another classic vampire novel, *Carmilla* (1871), his work prior to Dracula was largely inconsequential and nonfantastic, although *Under the Sunset* (1882) is a collection of dark fairy tales and a few short pieces, notably "The Primrose Path" (1875), that involve the supernatural.

Dracula, which was also adapted as a stage play, is certainly Stoker's masterpiece, and the deadly count has joined the handful of fictional characters—including Frankenstein's monster, Dr. Fu Manchu, Tarzan, Dr. Jekyll and Mr. Hyde, and a few more—who have become so deeply rooted in our culture, in large part because of motion picture renditions, that they have an existence separate from their original works. Stoker went on to write several more novels, some of them supernatural, but they never even approached the quality of his vampire tale, although some of the later books are still quite readable.

The Mystery of the Sea (1902) is a deservedly forgotten novel of psychic insight, but *The Jewel of the Seven Stars* (1903), in which the disembodied spirit of an ancient Egyptian woman tries to reanimate her age long comatose body, is reasonably good and is periodically reprinted, although it is rather slow moving until the closing chapters. It was the basis for the film *The Awakening* (1980) and has inspired, at least in part, several others involving mummies and Egyptian magic. *The Lady of the Shroud* (1909) has most of its fantastic content rationalized at the end. The woman who the reader has been led to believe is a vampire actually is not, although the psychic events are genuine.

The closest Stoker came to repeating his success at book length is the very atmospheric *Lair of the White Worm* (1910, also published as *Garden of Evil*), which blends shape-changing, possession, an underground monster, and a strange cult into a sometimes confusing but occasionally very suspenseful story. The 1988 movie version, though not particularly loyal, is considerably more coherent. Stoker wrote no further novels of the supernatural. His short fiction has been collected in various combinations as *Dracula's Guest* (1914), of which the title story is an excerpt dropped from the novel, *The Bram Stoker Bedside Companion* (1973), and *Midnight Tales* (1990). The best of his short stories are "The Judge's House" (1891) and "The Squaw" (1893).

"The Strange High House in the Mist"
H. P. Lovecraft (1931)

Although H. P. LOVECRAFT is primarily remembered as a writer of horror fiction, he also wrote several fantasy stories, most of them just as original as his weird fiction, including the short novel *The Dream Quest of Unknown Kadath* (1943). This particular story, although technically set somewhere in the fringes of the Cthulhu Mythos sequence, which mixed horror and science fiction, is much lighter in tone and only peripherally suggests anything horrid or menacing.

Several of Lovecraft's stories center on structures, whether they be "THE SHUNNED HOUSE" (1937), the unearthly buildings of *At the Mountains of Madness* (1936), or a mausoleum such as "In the Vault" (1932). The house in this particular story is perched atop a very high, reportedly inaccessible, cliff adjacent to the decaying fishing village of Kingsport. There are many rumors about the structure, supposedly home to an ageless entity who speaks to the mist and looks into other worlds, but no one has ever seen the tenant. Few even like to talk about it.

The situation remains unchanged until the arrival of Thomas Olney and his family. Olney is curious and asks questions until he has heard all the variations of the story. Unconvinced that the cliff is unassailable, he eventually finds a way to reach the top, where he is briefly frightened by sounds within the house until he is invited in by an apparently perfectly human tenant with whom he spends the day in conversation. He returns to Kingsport at dusk, but everyone can tell that the man who came down is not the same as the one who went up. He has lost his sense of imagination, perhaps overloaded by what he discovered from that strange high observer.

Like many of Lovecraft's tales, the story is told completely without dialogue, and the only character about whom we learn anything substantial is Olney himself. It is designed to invoke a sense of wonder and mystery about the universe, to tell us that even in the most prosaic settings, there can be an element of magic, and that by knowing the extent of that magic, we might lose something of our own enthusiasm for life. Lovecraft is not saying that there are some things humans was not meant to know, but rather that we need to understand that there is a price to be paid for that knowledge.

Straub, Peter (1943–)

Along with Stephen KING, Anne RICE, and Dean R. KOONTZ, Peter Straub has dominated the American horror fiction scene for more than two decades. He made his debut in the genre with *Julia* (1975, also published as *Full Circle*), a very intelligent and convincing modern ghost story. After a young girl dies tragically in an accident, her mother is subject to particularly cruel apparitions that initially appear to be illusions founded in her guilt but that are soon revealed to be a genuinely supernatural intervention. There is an even more malevolent ghost in *If You Could See Me Now* (1977), this time a wronged woman returning from the grave to exact vengeance on her unfaithful lover. But it was with GHOST STORY (1979) that Straub became one of the dominant voices in horror fiction. *Ghost Story* is a large, complex novel with unusually well-developed characters and a very unconventional type of ghost who can change her appearance and manifest herself physically so that she can interact with the living, even during daylight, rather than lurking in the shadows, nebulous, indistinct, and physically impotent. The 1981 film version did an above-average job of translating the story to the screen. The book did for the ghost story what Stephen King had earlier done for vampires in 'SALEMS' LOT (1975).

Straub's next fantasy novel was *Shadowland* (1980), considerably narrower in scope, in which two young people live with an authentic magician in rural New England waiting for him to decide to which of them he will pass on his talent and knowledge. This was followed by the much more ambitious *The Floating Dragon* (1982), which mixes ancient supernatural evil in the form of a kind of disembodied spirit, the dragon, with a rather implausible science fiction device, a chemical spill

that causes those affected to begin to dissolve from within. Portions of the novel are extremely effective, while other sections seem less coordinated or credible. Three subsequent loosely related novels have ambiguous or no fantastic content at all but are still associated with the genre. These are *Koko* (1988), *Mystery* (1990), and *The Throat* (1993). *The Hellfire Club* (1996) is not fantasy, either.

Straub returned to the supernatural with *Mr. X* (1999), a chilling story about a man who experiences a precognitive vision of murder on his birthday every year until he finally reaches the year in which the events are to take place. He followed with two related novels, *Lost Boy, Lost Girl* (2003) and *In the Night Room* (2004). In the first a teenager's obsession with a house once owned by a serial killer leads to his discovery of a ghostly girl who exists in another reality. The second novel concerns a horror writer who learns that at least one of his characters has come to life and that what he writes can affect her reality. He is, in fact, the author of *Lost Boy, Lost Girl*. Both novels are more contemplative and less melodramatic than Straub's earlier supernatural novels, but both involve fascinating mysteries.

With Stephen King Straub collaborated on *The Talisman* (1984), set partly in our world and partly in a parallel reality in which werewolves and other magical elements exist. The story is basically an extended quest, not always tightly plotted but filled with fascinating tidbits and side trips. The two authors added a very belated sequel, *Black House* (2001), in which an evil force from the other world uses a serial killer in ours as its agent in the theft of a number of children. Although less imaginative, the sequel is otherwise a much better book, tightly plotted and suspenseful.

Straub has won numerous fantasy and horror awards. His novels *The Throat*, *Mr. X*, and *Lost Boy, Lost Girl* all won the Bram Stoker Award, as did the collection *Magic Terror* and the story "Mr. Clubb and Mr. Cuff." His marginally fantastic novel *Koko* won the World Fantasy Award, as did the short story "The Ghost Village." Several other short stories are worth special mention, including "The Juniper Tree" (1988), "The Fee" (1994), and the short novel *Pork Pie Hat* (1994). *Houses without Doors* (1990) contains some of his best shorter fiction. *Mrs. God* (1990), a novella, is particularly good.

Strieber, Whitley (1945–)

Although Whitley Strieber has become a more polished writer during the course of his career, his two most interesting works are his first two novels, particularly the first, *WOLFEN* (1978). The premise of the novel, not revealed until after the two protagonists investigate a series of mysterious deaths and find themselves running for their own lives, is that a race of canine creatures with an intelligence at least equal to that of humans and with physical prowess superior to any ordinary wolf, has been living hidden on the fringes of human society since prehistory. The wolfen prey on those who will not be missed, the homeless, the lost, and the insane, which requires that they live in cities rather than in the country. When the two human detectives learn the truth, they are marked for death by the pack, whose primary motivation is to survive, and they only manage to avoid their fate by coming to an accommodation with the creatures. The novel is extremely suspenseful, involves an interesting pair of characters, and was an original and radically new interpretation of the werewolf legend.

Strieber followed up with *The Hunger* (1981), which would eventually be his first novel about Miriam Blaylock, a charming but deadly vampire. Although Strieber used some of the traditional trappings of the vampire story, he created a dramatically different mythos. Only the female vampires are ageless and unchanging. The males gradually wither over time, and although they never truly die, they become ghostlike, powerless, and relegated to a perpetual tortured inactivity. To avoid loneliness Blaylock must periodically seek a new human male to transform into a partner, although the eventual fate of each is inevitable. Both *The Hunger* and *Wolfen* were turned into surprisingly good horror movies.

Strieber's next novel, *Black Magic* (1982), was marketed as horror but is actually a technothriller with no fantastic content. *The Night Church* (1983) has another interesting premise, a cult that plans to use modern breeding techniques to create a race uniquely suited to worship Satan, but despite some individual sequences that are quite exciting, the pace of the novel is erratic. *Catmagic* (1986) is technically more successful, a story of modern witchcraft. Amanda Walker is surprised to discover that she is potentially a powerful magic wielder and then horrified to learn that her abilities have made her the target for secretive groups who wish to use her powers to advance their own agendas. Despite her misgivings, she learns to master the art of witchcraft in order to defend herself in this tightly plotted, effective story of the supernatural.

Strieber abandoned horror fiction for several years, returning with *The Wild* (1991), a short and unpredictable story about a man transformed into a werewolf. *Unholy Fire* (1992) followed, which is less inventive but handled very skillfully. The protagonist is a priest who has had recent doubts about his vocation and whose worldview is shattered when one of his parishioners dies in a horrible way, after which he discovers that she led a life of remarkable depravity. Having decided that he should have done something to save her, he begins to investigate her death and learns of the existence of a serial killer. He eventually discovers that the murderer has been possessed by an entity that literally escaped from hell. *The Forbidden Zone* (1993) is about a bad place, an area subject to some evil force that manifests itself in various ways, some of them apparently violating the laws of nature. An unlikely hero solves the mystery and finds a way to neutralize the area before its influence can spread throughout the world.

Except for a short story or two, Strieber produced no new supernatural fiction after 1993 until 2001. That lapse ended with *The Last Vampire* (2001) and *Lilith's Dream* (2002), both vampire novels, the first a further adventure of Miriam Blaylock. She is caught up in a duel of wits with a wily Interpol agent who eventually tracks her down, although not with the results he expected. In *Lilith's Dream* an ancient vampire who has not walked the Earth in hundreds of years finally rises and has considerable difficulty adjusting to the dramatic changes that have taken place.

Strieber is a talented, inventive horror writer whose work is always interesting, although he seems to have grown less ambitious with the passage of years. His occasional short fiction remains uncollected but includes some very fine stories such as "Properties of the Beast" (1992) and "Open Doors" (1997). He has also written several science fiction novels and some nonfiction, although none of his nonhorror work approaches the stature of his supernatural novels.

The Subtle Knife Philip Pullman (1997)

This is the middle volume of the His Dark Materials trilogy that began with THE GOLDEN COMPASS and concluded with THE AMBER SPYGLASS. Although ostensibly targeted at a young adult audience, the books employ such sophisticated language, imaginative extrapolation, and well-drawn characters that they have become, if anything, even more popular with adults. Lyra Belacqua returns to join forces with a new protagonist, Will Parry, a 12-year-old boy from our world whose father disappeared while exploring the Arctic and whose mother is under psychiatric care. Mysterious strangers have been asking about his father, and when he accidentally kills one of them, Will becomes a fugitive. Then, in a scene reminiscent of ALICE IN WONDERLAND (1865), by Lewis CARROLL, he follows a cat through an invisible gateway into Lyra's world.

Together and separately the two children experience a series of adventures, while the underlying plot slowly advances around them. Lyra is surprised to meet a child who is not bonded to a demon, since that is unheard of in her world. For his part, Will is confused by the strangeness around him, particularly in the city of magpies, a region ruled by children. Serafina Pekkala, a witch, and other characters from the previous volume show up, along with several new ones, the most significant of whom is Mary Malone, a scientist. There are also some new creatures, the Specters, and another magical artifact, the subtle knife of the title, which allows its wielder to cut windows between realities. Once again, Philip PULLMAN demonstrates that he is ready to kill off major characters, sometimes surprisingly so, and there is considerable violence this time as well as a cliffhanger ending in which Lyra is kidnapped.

Some readers and reviewers were troubled by the concept of a war against God in a children's book. The author rarely describes anything or anyone as wholly good or wholly evil, and that ambiguity is what makes his characters so rich. Some of the religious undertones drawn from Milton's *Paradise Lost* become more manifest this time, and we learn that Lyra faces a challenge that could determine the fate of worlds. Although the novel suffers from some of the structural necessities of the middle volume of a trilogy—no clear ending and the assumption that the reader knows what has gone before—it is still a remarkable achievement and a major work of children's fantasy.

"The Surly Sullen Bell" Russell Kirk (1962)

The conservative columnist and commentator Russell Kirk wrote a small but well-respected body of short horror and ghost fiction, the best of which has recently been reprinted as *Ancestral Shadows* (2004). The best-known of these is "The Surly Sullen Bell," the title taken from one of the sonnets of William Shakespeare, referring to the tolling of a bell to announce the passage of a soul from this life to the next. The protagonist is Frank Loring, who receives an unusual request from the man who married the woman Loring had loved many years earlier, inviting him to have dinner at their home.

Loring finds the Schumachers to be a most unusual couple. Nancy is much as he remembers her. He discovers he is still in love with her, but she has become seriously ill and is almost an invalid. Godfrey is a charming host and a doting husband and seems perfectly happy taking care of his ailing wife. In his absence she tells Loring that her husband is intrusive and insistent and that his desire to possess her has become so inflamed that he wishes to gain access even to her past, which is why he tendered the invitation to Loring, her one-time suitor. Schumacher also claims to have abandoned traditional religion in favor of a much more powerful mysticism, which sounds distinctly like the occult, but Loring dismisses this as a harmless idiosyncrasy.

After taking his leave, Loring experiences what may be a hallucination, but which might also be the result of a magical manipulation of his mind. This ambiguity becomes more vivid after ensuing visits, culminating with the final one, during which Nancy tells him that he lost her to Godfrey only because he refused to fight for her. That night he learns to fight, because he is pursued by a form of astral projection from Godfrey that chases him into a remote part of a slum, where he collapses, having also been poisoned. Realizing the truth at last, Loring finally finds the strength to fight, overcomes the spectral follower, and saves his own life, although it proves to have been too late for Nancy.

Kirk's story clearly cautions us not to wait too long to stand up for our own interests and those of others about whom we might care. Nancy's death is tragic, but out of that tragedy Loring presumably learns a lesson that will stay with him for the rest of his life.

Swann, Thomas Burnett (1928–1976)

Thomas Burnett Swann was a poet and academic most of whose novels are essentially set in our historical past, although a version of the past where magic works and the creatures of legend all existed. Swann jumped around considerably in time, even within series of related novels, but an underlying theme of most of his work is that modern civilization is a very mixed blessing, namely that technology, nationalism, and modern religions have driven something valuable from the Earth and cost us more than we have gained.

Swann first attracted attention with two long stories, "WHERE IS THE BIRD OF FIRE?" (1962), set during the founding of Rome, and "The Dolphin and the Deep" (1963). They were followed by *Day of the Minotaur* (1964, also published as *The Blue Monkeys*), in which the last minotaur on Earth tries to live out the rest of his life peacefully in a magical forest but is constantly intruded upon by sometimes well-meaning but always distracting outsiders. Another excellent short story, "The Manor of Roses" (1965), was followed by his second novel, *The Weirwoods* (1967), set in a prehistoric period in which humans are not the only intelligent species on Earth and a few still have the good sense to listen to the teachings of an older but disappearing race.

Swann largely abandoned short stories after his next novel, *Moondust* (1968), also set in Roman times but more properly science fiction since its shape-changing character is apparently from another planet. The short fiction was then collected in two volumes, *The Dolphin and the Deep* (1968) and *Where Is the Bird of Fire?* (1970). *The Forest of Forever* (1971) recounts the earlier life of Eunostos, the minotaur, when his situation was happier. *The Goat without Horns* (1971), his only novel set in the 20th century, is also arguably science fiction because it deals with the relationship between a human and a dolphin in rationalized terms, although the mood is very much that of fantasy.

Green Phoenix (1972) is a loose sequel to *The Weirwoods*, describing the last days of the elder race that faces extinction during the time of the siege of Troy. In *Wolfwinter* (1973) a woman is repelled by her husband's plans for their child and retreats into a world of magic and fauns during the days of the Roman Empire. *How Are the Mighty Fallen* (1974) is more bitter in tone, set in biblical Israel and dealing with lost love and disgrace. Swann's increasing dissatisfaction with the modern world was perhaps best demonstrated in his next novel, *The Not-World* (1975), in which we discover that the ancient race that preceded humans has not become entirely extinct and that a handful survive in a magically protected miniature world in a forest in Great Britain, enjoying all these benefits of the natural world that humanity has lost.

Lady of the Bees (1976) is an expanded version of "Where Is the Bird of Fire?" that provides considerably more background and deeper characterization but adds little to the actual story. *Will-o-the-Wisp* (1976) casts the poet Robert Herrick as its protagonist, suggesting that his verse was inspired by his ability to sense the existence of magical alternate realities. A prince sets out on a magical journey through ancient Egypt in *The Minikins of Yam* (1976), and in *The Gods Abide* (1976) another traveler seeks the river Styx in a Europe where Christianity is rapidly replacing the old pagan religions and banishing magic from the world.

The Tournament of Thorns (1976) suggests that magic might have lingered on in some form until the Middle Ages, but the novel is unusually dispirited and slow paced. Swann's last significant novel was much more upbeat. *Cry Silver Bells* (1977) is the third adventure of Eunostos, although chronologically the first, set during a much happier time when his existence was not a source of wonderment. Swann's last novel, *Queens Walk in the Dust* (1977), was published posthumously and is not as polished as his other books.

Swann's fantasies generally avoid physical violence. Much of the conflict results from the differing attitudes of people, either individually or as a culture, and the damage inflicted is more likely to be emotional and psychological. His depictions of the ancient world are unrealistically romanticized, but the results are frequently charming. Despite his popularity, he was rarely imitated and never very successfully, and he remains a distinct if muted voice in the genre.

"The Sword of Welleran"   Lord Dunsany
(1908)

Lord DUNSANY was a master at condensing a story to its essentials. This short fantasy epic would have occupied many another writer for at least three volumes without adding anything significant to the central plot. The setting is the city of Merinma, which once dominated the land for many miles in every direction but which has become decadent after the death of Welleran and its other legendary heroes. Now it is withdrawn and isolated from the lands it once ruled, which are dominated by various barbarian leaders. These violent tribes have avoided striking back at their one-time oppressor despite the almost casual defensive system that is all that remains of Merinma's former might, dissuaded because they have long believed that the famous heroes of Merinma, Welleran being the foremost, are immortal and still protect the city. The heroes themselves helped preserve this superstition by choosing to throw themselves into an inaccessible ravine when their time came, so that no one has ever seen their bodies. Only Welleran's famous sword remains to show the man ever really lived.

The outsiders' fear begins to ebb over the years until finally two condemned criminals agree to slip into Merinma and find out the truth. They arrive and discover that the figures they have feared are statues and that the heroes are long gone, and they return to report the good news in exchange for a pardon. Once they know the truth, the various tribes set aside their current rivalries to create a unified army with which to conquer the city they have long feared. It seems likely they will succeed, but the spirit of Welleran and his fellows quite literally return from the dead. Dismayed by what they see and frustrated by their inability to intervene directly, they invade the dreams of the locals, bestirring them to take up the old arms and wait in readiness, and one particular young man, Rold, is chosen by Welleran himself to seize the fabled sword and lead the attack.

Although the battle goes in their favor and the enemies of Merinma are routed, Dunsany deliberately dilutes the sense of triumph. Rold is appalled by the carnage and wonders what they were fighting for that was worth so many lives. In only a few pages, Dunsany created one of the enduring classics of heroic fantasy, a model for the many writers who would follow in his footsteps.

T

Tarr, Judith (1955–)

Judith Tarr began writing fantasies during the 1980s, initially in a fairly traditional format, but her interest in history has become a progressively more significant influence on her work, which quickly evolved into historical novels with varying degrees of fantasy content, sometimes almost undetectable. Her debut came with two trilogies, both appearing between 1985 and 1989. The first includes *The Isle of Glass* (1985), *The Golden Horn* (1985), and *The Hounds of God* (1986). During the age of Richard the Lionheart, war between humans and fairies seems inevitable, and the latter prevail upon a human monk to act as their representative. The story moves to the besieged city of Constantinople in the middle volume, and a duel between sorcerers dominates the climax. Two more volumes were added later, *Alamut* (1989), in which a warrior falls in love with a sorceress who for her part is determined to destroy him. A halfling and a human sorceress seek dispensation to marry in *The Dagger and the Cross* (1991), which puts them squarely in the middle of a political and cultural struggle.

The second trilogy consists of *The Hall of the Mountain King* (1986), in which a man lays claim to a throne, arousing the wrath of a goddess in addition to his political enemies, *The Lady of Han-Gilen* (1987), in which a female warrior joins the fray, and *A Fall of Princes* (1988), wherein the situation must be resolved by warfare. Tarr returned to this setting for *Arrows of the Sun* (1993), which also involves a contested throne, *Spear of Heaven* (1994), which expands the boundaries of her imagined world, and *Tides of Darkness* (2002), which encompasses a myriad of interconnected universes.

Tarr began to mix stand-alone novels with series from this point forward. *A Wind in Cairo* (1989), still one of her best, is set in ancient Egypt. The protagonist crosses paths with a sorceress, who changes him into the form of a horse, in which guise he has various adventures. *Ars Magica* (1989) chronicles the life of an apprentice magician who steals his master's books of knowledge and eventually rises to a prominent position in the Christian church. *Lord of the Two Lands* (1993) deals with the conquests of Alexander the Great and has only minor fantastic content. *His Majesty's Elephant* (1993) pits a young boy and a magical elephant against a sinister plot to assassinate Charlemagne.

White Mare's Daughter (1998) was the first of three related novels. In the first a goddess incarnates herself in order to pay a visit to a prehistoric culture that is ruled by women. In the second, *Lady of Horses* (2000), a young woman challenges the cultural mandate that says that only boys should be taught to ride horses. A female warrior helps lift a curse set upon a king in *Daughter of Lir* (2001) in a somewhat disappointing final volume. Although there had been feminist elements in some of Tarr's earlier novels, they are a much more dominant theme this time. She later used a very similar situation as the basis for her historical romance *The Mountain's Call* (2004), which appeared under the pen name Caitlin Brennan.

Kingdom of the Grail (2000) is set some time after the death of Arthur and the fall of Camelot. Merlin is a prisoner until he is rescued by the legendary Roland. *Pride of Kings* (2001) is one of her best books and returns to the time of Richard the Lionheart. He has been offered the throne of Faerie in addition to his authority in Great Britain but turns it down, setting in motion a crisis that will cause unrest in both worlds. He reconsiders in *The Devil's Bargain* (2002), responding to the depredations of an evil sorcerer. Their battle finally concludes in *House of War* (2003).

Rite of Conquest (2004) is somewhat similar in structure to the Richard novels. This time the protagonist is William the Conqueror, who has hidden magical powers that he learns to use thanks to the intercession of a perceptive governess. Another incarnated goddess walks abroad in ancient Egypt in *The Shepherd Kings* (2001). Tarr invokes Alexander the Great again in *Queen of the Amazons* (2004), this time describing his encounter with a culture in which women serve as warriors.

Tarr's short fiction has yet to be collected and includes several good stories, including "Piece de Resistance" (1986), "Death and the Lady" (1992), and "I Sing the Maiden" (1992), but she seems most comfortable at book length and with historical rather than contemporary or completely imaginary settings. Tarr also collaborated with Harry TURTLEDOVE for *Household Gods* (1999), which pokes considerable fun at the romantic images of the past portrayed in time travel romance novels. A woman from our time finds herself back in ancient Rome and, while initially pleased, discovers that the drawbacks far outweigh the advantages.

"The Tell-Tale Heart" Edgar Allan Poe
(1843)

The narrator of this particularly spooky story by Edgar Allan POE confesses from the outset that he has been ill but insists that his illness led to a heightening of his senses rather than their confusion and that his hearing has become unusually acute in recent days. By the end of the second paragraph, we already understand much of his character and the background for what is to come.

He has become obsessed with an old man, who he freely admits he loved and who had done him no harm. The elderly man has a deformed eye that upsets the narrator, who is clearly insane, because of which he decides to kill his friend.

He approaches during the night on several occasions, but since the old man is always asleep and has his eyes closed, it is impossible to act. The narrator is determined to strike when the eye is open and aware, because it is the eye and not the old man that he hates. One night he slips slightly as he is spying, and the old man wakens, after which the two are frozen like statues in anticipation. When at last the narrator allows a little light into the room, he sees that the eye is open and knows that his opportunity has come at last. In the dark and silence, the only thing he can hear is the beating of the other man's heart.

At last he strikes, driven even madder by the heartbeat, killing the old man and then dismembering his body. The severed remains are concealed beneath the floorboards, and all signs of struggle are removed. Unfortunately, the disturbance was heard by the neighbors, and the police arrive. The narrator is able to put them at their ease and convince them that nothing untoward has happened. While they are speaking, however, he begins to hear the rhythmic beating of a heart, a sound that upsets him to the point he finally confesses his guilt.

The resolution can be read ambiguously, although it is probable that Poe meant us to understand that the deathly heartbeat was imaginary rather than supernatural. Guilt and its effect on unhealthy minds is a recurring theme in his work. Although this is one of Poe's shortest stories, it manages to incorporate more insight into the human mind as well as a fully realized atmosphere of horror than most contemporary horror writers can manage with an entire novel.

Tepper, Sheri S. (1929–)

Sheri Tepper made an immediate favorable impression with her first published fantasy fiction, the True Game series, which began with *King's Blood Four* (1983), set in a world that is actually an elaborate game. All the inhabitants are governed by the rules except a handful of exceptions, who exist to provide random elements. The protagonist is a shape-changer who returns in *Necromancer Nine* (1983) to search for another of his kind who has disappeared, Mavin Manyshaped, who would later become the main character in the series. *Wizard's Eleven* (1984) is another lighthearted quest story with a plot enlivened by the unique nature of the imaginary world in which it takes place.

The next three titles were *The Flight of Mavin Manyshaped, The Search of Mavin Manyshaped,* and *The Song of Mavin Manyshaped,* all published in 1985 and comprising a loose trilogy within the larger frame story. They tell the story of Mavin, who sets out on a series of quests and resolves conflicts peculiar to those who are not bound to a single physical form. *Jinian Footseer* (1985) is the first in another trilogy set within the True Game universe, this one considerably darker in tone. A powerful magical force has arisen that could bring the elaborate game of existence to an abrupt end. Jinian gets caught in the middle when Order and Chaos renew their long-standing war in *Dervish Daughter* (1986), and she becomes the pivot around which the conflict is finally resolved in *Jinian Star-Eye* (1986).

Not all of Tepper's fantasies are set within the True Game universe. *The Revenants* (1984) is a very similar quest adventure in another created world. The Marianne Trilogy—*Marianne, the Magus, and the Mantichore* (1985), *Marianne, the Madame, and the Momentary Gods* (1988), and *Marianne, the Matchbox, and the Malachite Mouse* (1989)—starts as a contemporary fantasy. A college student is troubled when magical creatures begin appearing on campus, which eventually leads to the revelation that she has come to our reality from a world very similar to that of the True Game. She manages to conceal her secret, learns a serious lesson about the dangers of tampering with time, and becomes a playing piece in an elaborate game in order to return a magical artifact to its rightful owner.

Tepper's novels began to grow darker in tone during the middle of the 1980s and have generally been more serious and occasionally polemic ever since. She wrote two very good horror novels, *Blood Heritage* (1986) and *The Bones* (1987), the former about an obsessively rational man who

must embrace magic to defeat a demonic force menacing his family, and the latter, which is much the better of the two, about a woman who discovers human remains on her property and slowly gets caught up in an investigation of occult rites and human sacrifice. *The Awakeners* (1987), which was also published in two volumes as *Northshore* and *Southshore,* has a strongly feminist theme. A priestess grows disenchanted with the ways in which her society functions and begins to speak out, after which she discovers she has attracted the attention of ruthless and powerful enemies.

Beauty (1991) is her best fantasy novel, an elaborate and inventive retelling of the story of the Beauty and the Beast. *A Plague of Angels* (1993) is set in a version of Earth from which most of the human race has disappeared, leaving the survivors to struggle to find their place in a reality increasingly dominated by inhuman creatures, many of whom have magical powers. The elements of science fiction were indicative of a shift in her interest, which became obvious during the balance of the 1990s.

Tepper has written primarily science fiction and detective fiction since 1993, although *The Visitors* (2002), set in a postapocalyptic future, involves the emergence of partially rationalized ogres and other creatures from inside the Earth, and some of her other novels in that genre involve technology that approaches magic. Her last horror novel, *Still Life* (1989), was written under the pen name E. E. Horlak, an interesting story about an artist whose paintings are imbued with a supernatural power. She rarely writes short fiction, but "The Gardener" (1988) suggests she might be quite successful at that length.

"The Terror of Blue John Gap"   Sir Arthur Conan Doyle (1910)

Although Sir Arthur Conan Doyle is, of course, best known as the author of the Sherlock Holmes stories, he also wrote the single most famous of all lost civilization novels, *The Lost World* (1912). His fondness for the concept that there might be forms of life living on Earth unbeknownst to man did not begin there, however, for he proposed another hidden ecology in this earlier short story about a monster who lives secretly right within the English countryside.

Dr. James Hardcastle is resting from an illness in the countryside when he hears rumors of a legendary creature that lives in Blue John Gap. The gap is an old Roman mine where they excavated Blue John, a valuable mineral, but which has been abandoned for centuries and is now shunned by the locals, who believe it is the home of a monster that steals their sheep at night. Hardcastle is skeptical but intrigued by a strange sound he hears from the shaft, and in due course he secures candles and matches in order to explore the tunnels. Unfortunately, he slips and falls into a stream of water during his first expedition and finds himself sitting in the dark with wet matches and no idea how to return to the surface. His only hope seems to be to dry the matches, but while trying to do so he becomes aware that he is no longer alone, that some large animal has come down to drink.

Hardcastle escapes injury and later manages to light his candle and climb out of the mine, but he fails in his efforts to convince the authorities that there really is something preying on sheep and, unfortunately, at least one local man. Determined to end the menace, he secures a rifle and more reliable lighting and returns, surprising and wounding the creature, although he himself is seriously injured and rendered unconscious in the process. When he recovers he has been rescued by the villagers, who have also used massive stones to block the shaft of the mine so that the creature can never again venture out onto the surface. The reader might justifiably wonder why they had not taken these steps earlier.

The monster story is a major part of horror fiction, usually supernatural, sometimes rationalized, and sometimes just mysterious. Doyle makes a perfunctory effort to justify his creature as the denizen of an underground cave system, even describing it as completely blind, but the story is not dependent on a scientific explanation. Surprisingly, although this is one of Doyle's very best non-Holmes stories, it is rarely reprinted.

Tessier, Thomas (1947–)

Thomas Tessier's first novel, *The Fates* (1978), is an unusual and maddeningly uneven horror novel in which the danger originates with a mysterious force or entity that quite literally rips its victims apart. Although it is finally driven into inactivity, it is neither destroyed nor positively identified, an ending somewhat too ambiguous for many readers. It also involves a surprisingly large cast of characters for such a short novel, none of whom are very deeply developed. His second effort, *The Nightwalker* (1979), takes a very different approach, describing the protagonist's slow descent into insanity and homicidal fury in great detail and establishing Bobby as a vivid though repulsive character. The fantastic content is quite limited this time and equally nontraditional. Bobby may be succumbing to a supernatural force and turning into an inhuman monster, although we never learn that for certain, but since one of the other characters is a genuine clairvoyant, the premise of the story certainly allows for either interpretation.

Phantom (1982) is far more conventional. A young boy explores an abandoned building that is home to restless and sometimes angry spirits. The novel is a quiet, modernized ghost story that derives most of its impact from descriptions of the boy's reactions to what he discovers and his growing isolation from the world of the living. Most of Tessier's fiction from that point forward consists of nonsupernatural thrillers, but he returned to fantastic horror with *Fog Heart* (1997), one of the best horror novels of the 1990s. The story involves two sisters, one of whom is a genuine medium, their relationship with each other and with their clients, and their dangerous involvement with a man who is secretly determined to commit a murder.

Tessier has never been particularly prolific and has produced only a few short stories, most of them collected in *Ghost Music* (2000), but they are of almost uniformly high quality. The stories range from conventional supernatural to oddball fantasy. Among the best are "I Remember Me" (1994), in which humans lose their memory because of a new virus, "Food" (1988), wherein an obsession with eating leads to a terrifying transformation, and "La Mourante" (1997), a distressing but convincing story of a living person who falls in love with a zombie because the latter is so pliable. Tessier's fiction comes only at unfortunately long intervals. Even his lesser works have interesting elements, and his better stories are beautifully written and hard to forget.

"That Hell-Bound Train" Robert Bloch (1986)

By the 1980s it seemed unlikely that anyone could find a new twist to the deal-with-the-devil story, let alone write one that would win a major award, but Robert BLOCH, the author of *Psycho* and literally hundreds of short stories in a variety of genres, proved equal to the task. His story, which won the Hugo Award, the only story of the supernatural ever to do so, describes the life of Martin, whose father was a railroad man who died while Martin was young and whose mother ran off, abandoning him to grow up in an orphanage. Martin emerged as a young man without prospects but with an affinity for the railroads, so he becomes a bindlestiff, living much of his life hiding on railroad cars and occasionally working for poor wages or stealing when that seems easier.

Martin remembers a song his father used to sing about a phantom train that carries the souls of the damned to hell, and one night as he is considering letting himself be converted by the Salvation Army a mysterious dark train roars up and stops nearby. The conductor steps down, limping on one misshapen foot, his hat askew because of a pair of horns. The world has changed, and there is no shortage of damned souls, so the devil usually does not engage in deals as he did in the past. However, he is particularly interested in not losing Martin to the Salvation Army, so he offers him one wish in exchange for damnation. After due consideration Martin asks for the ability to arrest time once, planning to do so when he achieves a certain level of happiness. The devil agrees and then sulks away in evident disappointment when Martin indicates that by using his wish, he can hold off his damnation forever.

The reader is not likely to be fooled; the devil has an ace up his sleeve. Martin decides to improve his life so that he can enjoy it when he stops time. He cleans up, gets a good job and becomes educated, married, and eventually wealthy. He keeps waiting for things to get just a little bit better and adds children and a mistress. Alas, things begin to go badly after that. His wife divorces him and takes the kids, and he loses his job and is bankrupted. Chastened, he decides to rebuild just enough to be tolerable and then use his wish, but somehow he has grown old, and his health is not what he would like it to be. Destitute and friendless, he suffers a stroke, and just as he is about to invoke his wish anyway, he hesitates and dies.

The devil shows up promptly and admits that he knew what would happen because it had happened many times before. Martin grudgingly concedes defeat and boards the train, but at the last minute he decides to use his wish at last, trapping the devil on a train ride that will never end and ensuring himself an endless future in an environment that he always loved. Thus, both parties to the deal are victorious, and both are cheated in part of what they hoped to acquire.

"They Bite" Anthony Boucher (1943)

Most of Anthony Boucher's published fiction is in the mystery genre, even though he was the editor of *The Magazine of Fantasy & Science Fiction* for many years. The majority of his remaining stories are science fiction, but he also wrote this chilling little story of murder and horror set somewhere in the southwestern corner of the United States. The protagonist is Hugh Tallant, who is apparently spying on a military training camp in the desert at some point during World War II. Tallant's efforts are complicated by the chance arrival of Morgan, an old acquaintance who suspects his real motives but who is more interested in blackmail than in advising the authorities.

Tallant is camped out near a deserted adobe structure, which he discovers is the focus of long-standing unpleasant rumors about a family of people, if they are people, named the Carkers, who lived there at one time and who apparently waylaid travelers and ate them. The Carkers were supposedly wiped out on two separate occasions, but the locals still avoid the area. Tallant dismisses the legend as a tall tale or practical joke, even though he himself has on at least one occasion spotted something in the desert that seemed almost but not quite human.

The legend gives him an idea, however. He invites Morgan over to discuss their arrangements, then murders him and drags the body into the adobe building, confident that no one will find it there for at least several years. Inside he notices what appears to be the mummified body of a child, but the creature wakens and attacks him. Even after Tallant severs the thing's head with a machete, its teeth remain locked onto his hand. Even worse, the bite has a peculiar ache that probably means some form of venom was injected. Desperate, he cuts his own hand off at the wrist. Weak and barely able to stand, he stumbles outside just in time to see the creature's mate coming his way.

The idea of a secret, inhuman race living among us is a common one in horror fiction, starting with vampires and werewolves and running the gamut to transformed children, such as in *The Children of the Island* (1983), by T. M. WRIGHT, *Shadow Child* (1987), by Joe Citro, and Rick HAUTALA's *Little Brothers* (1988), which postulates the existence of a species very much like those in this classic story. Some form of cannibalism is usually involved.

"The Thing in the Cellar"   David Keller
(1932)

One of the recurring themes in horror fiction is that the innocence of a child might somehow allow him or her to detect evils of which adults are unaware. One of the earliest and most powerful of these stories is this disturbing piece from *Weird Tales* magazine. The author introduces the cellar of the title even before we meet his characters. It is an unusual construction that appears to be too large for the house that rests on top of it and parts of which are blockaded by debris so substantial that portions have not been entered for more than a hundred years. The latest owners of the house are the Tuckers, whose infant son, Tommy, is often reduced to hysterics when he is in the kitchen, particularly if the door to the basement is unlocked or open.

Although his parents expect him to grow out of his formless fear, Tommy's dread of the cellar increases as he learns to crawl, then walk, and then talk. Although he refuses to explain just what it is that frightens him, he will not remain alone in the kitchen and absolutely will not venture into the basement, even when accompanied by an adult. His father in particular begins to wonder if there is something wrong with the boy, and when he reaches school age the parents take him to a doctor, to whom the boy finally confides his conviction that there is something in the basement, something he has never seen but that can hurt him.

The doctor unwisely decides that the boy is simply too pampered and suggests locking him alone in the kitchen with the basement door secured open on the assumption that by finally facing his greatest fear he will overcome it. His parents decide to try this approach, though with some misgivings, and the doctor himself has second thoughts after conferring with a colleague. He arrives in the middle of the experiment and urges that it be stopped, but it is too late. The boy's mutilated body is found lying at the top of the cellar stairs. John Collier used a very similar device but with a much different ending for "THUS I REFUTE BEELZY" (1941), but whereas Collier's story is whimsical, Keller's is tragic.

Thompson, Ruth Plumly   (1891–1976)

When L. Frank BAUM wrote THE WIZARD OF OZ (1900) and then followed up with more than a dozen sequels, it seemed he had exhausted the possibilities of that world. The stories and their characters were so popular, however, that imitators and parodies sprang up on every side as well as a large number of pastiches by writers including John R. Neill, Eric Shanower, Jack Snow, and Donald Abbott. The most successful of these was Ruth Plumly Thompson, who wrote 18 book-length Oz novels between 1915 and 1938 with more total words than Baum, although the last was not published until 1976.

Thompson started with *Pirates in Oz* (1915), which introduces Peter, Thompson's recurring child protagonist, who must help defend the city against the armies of the Gnome King. More titles followed using both existing and new characters and settings. The Scarecrow discovers that he is entitled to the throne of a distant land in *The Royal Book of Oz* (1921). *Kabumpo in Oz* (1922) introduces possibly Thompson's most popular Oz character, Kabumpo the magical elephant. She rapidly expanded her own cast of characters and generally abandoned those created by Baum, but she endeavored to keep the same general tone, usually successfully.

A few of her titles stand out, although eventually they became repetitive, just as had been the case with Baum's later novels. In *Jack Pumpkinhead of Oz* (1929), Peter uses a magic coin to return to the other side of the rainbow in time to help save the Emerald City from being conquered by the Red Baron of Baffleburg. Thompson invents several new and amusing characters in this one, including a gryphon who has lost his voice. The title character in *Handy Mandy of Oz* (1937) is improbably equipped with seven functional arms. A horse with telescoping legs battles a sea serpent in *The Giant Horse of Oz* (1928), and *The Cowardly Lion of Oz* (1923) sees that Baum character locked up in a zoo and in need of rescue.

Thompson wrote very little other fiction, but a collection of her shorter work was recently published as *Sissajig and Other Surprises* (2003). Thompson was never as polished a writer as Baum or even some of the others who added to the Oz story, but she had the most consistently inventive imagination and created several memorable characters.

Through the Looking Glass Lewis Carroll (1871)

The popularity of Lewis CARROLL's *ALICE IN WONDERLAND* (1865) logically resulted in a sequel relating Alice's further adventures, published under several variations of the title *Through the Looking Glass*. In her first outing Alice entered a fabulous, irrational world by following an unusual rabbit down his hole, but this time she steps through a magical mirror to visit the world that exists behind the glass. Although Carroll engaged his wild imagination as fully as before, there was an underlying pattern to this novel because it is based very loosely on a classic chess game. The two novels are frequently confused in readers' minds, however, although the sequel is generally of more interest to adult readers.

As with the first book, Carroll included memorable characters and poetry. "The Walrus and the Carpenter" and "Jabberwocky" are both from *Through the Looking Glass*. Alice finds herself this time in a fabulous land where everything is the opposite of what she would ordinarily expect. The birds are capable of speech, the kings and queens are all a bit mad, and she herself becomes a pawn in an elaborate chess game that involves a variety of unusual characters such as Tweedledee and Tweedledum, Humpty Dumpty, and other familiar figures from nursery rhymes. Although Alice eventually becomes a queen herself, she is frustrated by

the very strict rules in this reality and becomes more than slightly rebellious. Along with the first volume, with which it is often jointly published, this is one of the true classics of children's fantasy.

"Thus I Refute Beelzy" John Collier (1941)

John Collier had a very unique, intense, and witty story technique that has rarely been imitated. This very short tale is probably his most famous, one that initially bears a strong resemblance to "SREDNI VASHTAR" (1911), by Saki, although Collier has a different twist at the end and his story lacks the ambiguity of the other. Both involve young boys who are living a solitary life among adults who are theoretically affectionate but quietly cruel and smothering in their relationship. Saki's protagonist lives with a guardian, but Collier's is the son of a presumably happily married couple with a good income and a nice home.

The young Simon Carter prefers his own company to that of other children, engaging in a series of mysterious rituals that his parents interpret to be part of an elaborate game. Although his mother is perfectly willing to tolerate this behavior, Simon senior, who prefers to be known as Big Simon as opposed to Little Simon, has decided that he is an expert on the psychological development of his son and is also determined that the boy shall have no secrets, no world of his own. He insists upon details of the game and is told that his son plays with a mysterious being known as Beelzy, who is invisible to everyone else and whose shape and nature vary from visit to visit.

Big Simon assumes that Beelzy is an imaginary companion, but rather than accept that fact and tolerate it, he decides that Little Simon must acknowledge that it is all make believe. Uncharacteristically, Little Simon balks, refuses to cooperate, and warns his parents that Beelzy will protect him. Unimpressed, Big Simon orders him to his room, where he plans to follow shortly to administer a spanking. Moments after he climbs the stairs his wife hears a terrible scream and investigates, but all that is ever found of her husband is a single foot still in its shoe, as though it had been bitten off. Collier sets the reader up for the predictable revelation that Beelzy is, in fact, imaginary and then quietly but effectively demonstrates otherwise in a single sentence.

"Tight Little Stitches in a Dead Man's Back" Joe R. Lansdale (1986)

After-the-bomb stories are almost always the province of science fiction writers, but occasionally someone finds a way to turn that device into a tale of fantasy and horror. Joe R. LANSDALE has one of the most fertile imaginations in the genre, and he used that premise for this very bizarre story about two survivors, the narrator, Paul Marder, and his wife, Mary, who are among the very few to emerge from the fallout shelters into a transformed world. Mary hates her husband because of his former job, working in the missile industry, and blames him for the war and the death of their daughter. Every night she embellishes an elaborate tattoo of her daughter's face on his back, and he submits despite the pain because he, too, suffers from guilt.

It is the details of that world that make this fantasy. The oceans have disappeared, but whales, sharks, and even some fish have managed to alter their bodies so that they can live and move about on the empty sea beds. Strange oversized lizards prowl a landscape where unusual plants provide a menace of their own. It is humans who look out of place in this setting, and most of them feel that way. The greatest threat lies in the rose vines, which have become intelligent, malevolent creatures. They insinuate themselves into corpses and partially animate them, attempting to lure more victims into the trap. Paul and Mary are besieged in a lighthouse, one of the few structures to survive the war, with dwindling supplies and little hope.

Paul has a vision one evening, or perhaps a visitation. Lansdale never tells us whether he is imagining the sight of his dead daughter because of his own feeling of guilt or whether she is some variation of a ghost. The latter seems more likely because it appears that her presence has somehow physically altered the tattoo on his back. A short time later he discovers that the vines have managed to find an entry point into the lighthouse and that his wife has been attacked and is dead. Ultimately, he decides not to fight any more and to ac-

cept death by letting the animated corpse of Mary embrace him one last time.

Lansdale's indictment of the mentality that believes nuclear weapons make sense is effective, if sometimes heavy-handed. The story suggests no opportunity for redemption; a mistake on this scale cannot be atoned for adequately. What makes it particularly memorable is the uniquely bizarre imagery with which he gives depth to his nightmarish postapocalyptic world, where violence and beauty are so intertwined that they are no longer distinguishable.

"Tlon, Uqbar, Orbis Tertius" Jorge Luis Borges (1961)

The Argentinean writer Jorge Luis Borges is the author of a considerable number of intelligent, fantastic stories, many of which, like this one, have no characters in the usual sense of the term. The narrator is simply relating the history of a series of events that begin with the discovery of a single volume of a common encyclopedia. This particular volume varies slightly from all other copies of the same book in that it includes a lengthy article on the fictional country of Uqbar. Uqbar, whose geographical location is quite vague, is an unusual nation whose culture is based entirely on idealistic principles. The article describes its history under the guise of a fictional world, Tlon.

The book is explained away in various fashions as a hoax or as part of a plan by a secret organization to create a fictional world in incredible detail for purposes of their own. Much of the ensuing text is a discussion of some of the attributes of this mythical world. The language has no nouns, and objects are seen as a succession of experiences rather than isolated in time. Time itself is a more important delimiter than space. Fiction exists, but a story must contain all possible resolutions in order to be complete. Reality is mutable in the sense that strong enough expectations will lead to physical results. If a group is told to dig up artifacts that do not actually exist, the artifacts will appear as if they had been there all the time, created by the credibility of the diggers. Contrarily, items that are forgotten begin to lose their detail over time, eventually disappearing entirely.

What might be an interesting philosophical discussion turns into genuine fantasy only in the final few pages. More volumes of the encyclopedia begin turning up, revealing increased detail about the imaginary world, and other artifacts follow. The world slowly becomes aware of the existence of Tlon until this supposedly fictional reality begins to replace the familiar one. We learn at the end that the narrator is now living in what has become Tlon, and the old world of humanity is now the fiction. The story is filled with exotic, thought-provoking ideas and speculations.

Tolkien, J. R. R. (1892–1973)

John Ronald Reuel Tolkien will, of course, be remembered primarily for the Lord of the Rings trilogy—THE FELLOWSHIP OF THE RING (1954), THE TWO TOWERS (1954), and THE RETURN OF THE KING (1955), as well as the associated novel, written earlier, THE HOBBIT (1937). His development of an elaborate, extended history accompanied by minutely detailed descriptions of his many human and nonhuman civilizations in Middle Earth gives the books a feeling of authenticity rarely equaled in fantasy fiction. His influence on authors who followed is immeasurable. There are those who have directly imitated him such as Terry BROOKS and others who have adopted one aspect of his work, as is the case with the many authors who contribute to the FORGOTTEN REALMS fantasy world series. His work remained relatively unknown until the 1960s, when mass-market paperback editions propelled him to superstar status, and his work has maintained its preeminent position ever since. There has been no other single work as influential on other fantasy writers.

Tolkien wrote other fantasy fiction, although nothing else as ambitious or as successful. The short Farmer Giles of Ham (1949) is a pleasant, likable story about a farmer who tames a dragon. Smith of Wooton Major (1976) is similarly low key, almost in the style of a traditional fairy tale. His several short stories and a few related articles have been collected in various combinations as The Tolkien Reader (1966) and Sir Gawain and the Green Knight, Pearl, and Sir Orfeo (1975), and fragments and sketches appeared in book form as Unfinished

Tales (1980) and with others added as The Book of Lost Tales (1983) in two volumes. His only other effort at a full-length fantasy was the far less successful The Silmarillion (1977), which is actually a mesh of interrelated stories chronicling the history of Middle Earth. Roverandom (1998) is a short children's story about a dog magically transformed into a toy. Although some of his other fiction demonstrates flashes of the scope and vision of his best-known work, the plots are less dramatic and are at times bogged down by the same depth of detail that worked so effectively in the Lord of the Rings. With the exception of Farmer Giles of Ham, which is an underrated gem, Tolkien's short fiction is of only minor interest and would have been forgotten if he had not also written his masterpiece.

Tremayne, Peter (Peter Ellis) (1943–)

Peter Tremayne is the pseudonym of the writer and Celtic expert Peter Ellis, who has written horror and fantasy as well as science fiction and detective stories. His first novel in the horror genre was The Hound of Frankenstein (1977), a slight but amusing addition to that saga in which the obsessed Doctor Frankenstein reanimates a dead dog, which escapes to cause trouble in the surrounding countryside. This was quickly followed by Dracula Unborn (1977, also published as Bloodright), the memoirs of Dracula's son Mircea recounting his days as a Balkan nobleman. He next wrote The Vengeance of She (1978), a sequel to the lost world adventure novel SHE (1886), by H. Rider HAGGARD, but it was notably inferior to another sequel, Journey to the Flame (1985), by Richard MONACO.

Tremayne's next few books were almost all conventional potboilers, ranging from science fiction to horror. He continued the story of Dracula in The Revenge of Dracula (1978) and Dracula My Love (1980), the last of which is one of Tremayne's best books. Others such as Zombie! (1978) are competently written but predictable. His best horror novel from this period is The Morgow Rises (1982). After 1980 he turned to traditional fantasy, drawing on his background in Celtic lore for The Fires of Lan-Kern (1982) and its sequels, The Destroyers of Lan-Kern (1982) and The Buccaneers of Lan-Kern (1983), using traditional myths as the basis for updated stories. *Raven of Destiny* (1984) is similarly based on the legend of an ancient Celtic warrior and explorer, and *Island of Shadows* (1991), the best of his sword and sorcery work, features a female warrior in ancient Britain. *Ravenmoon* (1988) is a very impressive work that blends traditional fantasy and horror, mixing themes and moods in a historical setting. Druids identify a newborn child as the embodiment of a terrible curse and exert considerable effort to ameliorate the child's impact.

Although Tremayne has written no fantasy or horror novels for more than a decade, concentrating instead on his detective series, he continues to contribute occasional outstanding short stories, including "The Specter of Tullyfane Abbey" (2001) and "The Bridge of Sighs" (2002). A good selection of Tremayne's short fantasy fiction appeared as *My Lady of Hy-Brasil* (1987), while *The Aisling* (1992) has a much darker tone. His success in the mystery genre has deprived the fantasy and horror field of one of its potentially outstanding writers.

"A Tropical Horror" William Hope Hodgson (1904)

With personal experience of the sea in his background, it is not surprising that several of the better horror stories of William Hope HODGSON are set entirely or in part aboard oceangoing vessels, as is the case with this early, exceptionally intense monster story. The protagonist is one of several sailors aboard the *Glen Doon* who are faced with imminent death when their ship is boarded by a sea serpent, never described in exact detail but clearly an oversized snake with tentacles and claws. The creature dominates the deck, driving the protagonist and a young boy into hiding in a metal-walled structure while the others aboard escape below deck or up into the rigging.

The serpent is intelligent, powerful, and patient. It manages to pluck some of the men from the rigging, although others climb beyond its reach. The captain organizes a counterattack using their signal cannon, which wounds the beast but not seriously enough to drive it off, and it responds by killing its attackers. On more than one occasion the protagonist believes that the creature has re-

turned to the sea because it remains silent for so long, on one occasion even jostling the vessel to suggest that it had gone over the side, but in every case it is waiting for them to emerge.

The siege is finally lifted by another physical attack on the serpent, but by then all but the protagonist have died, even the men in the rigging, who have succumbed to exposure after two days without water or shelter. The story is told in the present tense, a device that conflicts with its journalistic prose style and an affectation Hodgson abandoned for the bulk of his work. Writers as diverse as Peter Benchley, Mel Odom, and Piers ANTHONY wrote entire novels involving an undersea creature's predation on humans, but Hodgson delivers much of the same impact in only a few pages.

"Trucks" Stephen King (1973)

Sometimes horror stories are well grounded in logic and seem completely plausible. Authors often exert great efforts to convince us that the irrational is rational, that vampires could exist even though they would quickly multiply and overwhelm the living population, that ghosts haunt houses even though there has never been any serious evidence that this is true, and so on. Some horror is, in fact, technically science fiction. Monsters could be mutations, visitors from outer space, or genetically engineered. This verisimilitude is designed to draw the reader more completely into the fictional world so that we can share the emotions of the characters. On the other hand, there are occasional stories that seize on some interesting but totally implausible device and run with it, as is the case with this short but intense story by Stephen KING.

Much of the action has already taken place when the story opens. All the trucks and buses in the world have become animate and hostile to humans. The protagonist is one of a handful of survivors trapped in a gas station and convenience store on a highway while a number of trucks prowl the parking lot, waiting to run down anyone who strays outside. A terrified man promptly and unwisely abandons cover and is knocked into a ditch, an incident designed to make certain the reader understands what is happening. The situation rapidly deteriorates from that point on. Although they have food and water to last for weeks, the besieged group is thrown into a crisis when the power goes off, limiting how long the former will last and preventing them from pumping the latter. Then a bulldozer shows up and threatens to knock down the building unless the people come out and fuel the trucks, the various vehicles communicating their desires improbably by honking their horns in Morse code.

There were two film versions. The first and better of the two was *Maximum Overdrive* (1986), which was fairly loyal to the original story, although the characters come across as more admirable, making an attempt to rescue the injured man, an action they choose not to take in the original. The remake, *Trucks* (1997), is considerably less interesting. "Trucks" is a Frankenstein story, with humanity threatened by its own creations. It also seems likely that the story is at least in part intended to be a satire of the Living Dead zombie movies by George Romero and others, which have an equally inexplicable basis for the collapse of the world and also follow the adventures of a small group held under siege by numerous deadly enemies. Despite a rather superficial plot, the story leaves the reader with distinct and lasting images.

Tuck Everlasting Natalie Babbitt (1975)

Natalie Babbitt, a poet and author, is one of the small group of children's novelists whose work has found a sizeable audience among adult readers as well, possibly because of her ability to evoke a fairy tale quality that is absent from the work of most of her contemporaries. She has written several fantasies, including two linked collections of stories, *The Devil's Storybook* (1974) and *The Devil's Other Storybook* (1986); presented a gentle, heart-warming ghost story in *The Eye of the Amaryllis* (1977); and created a magical kingdom in *The Search for Delicious* (1969). Her most important work, however, is *Tuck Everlasting,* produced as a motion picture in 2002 and 1981.

The story is set in early 19th-century America in the mythical town of Treegap. The Foster family owns a stretch of woods that no one ever enters because it has a vaguely disreputable reputation, but 10-year-old Winnie Foster is eventually trapped by circumstances and discovers that there is a family, the Tucks, living concealed within that forest. The Tucks have another secret. Hidden nearby is a spring, essentially the fountain of youth, from which they all drank at one time in the past. Winnie initially believes that their immortality is a great blessing, but it has frozen them in time at the age they were when they drank the water, preventing them from living a normal life.

The Tucks eventually convince her that immortality is a curse rather than a blessing. If the fountain's existence were known to outsiders, it would cause a disastrous upheaval. The Tucks themselves will never be able to mingle with normal people because their differences would eventually become obvious, so they have hidden themselves away and live a narrowly circumscribed life. Unfortunately, no situation is perpetually stable. A mysterious man who has heard about the fountain and wants to market its water is trying to confirm the rumors, and that leads to death and near discovery.

In addition to being a very fine story in itself, *Tuck Everlasting* provides an excellent case for the cycle of life in nature. Death is presented as a natural and necessary process required to make room for new life.

The Turn of the Screw Henry James (1898)

This short novel by Henry James is a strong contender for the best ghost story of all time. A governess takes a job at a large estate where she is put in charge of two children, Flora and Miles, but is forbidden to speak to their presumed father. Although she is initially happy with her position despite the unusual circumstances, she begins to have reservations after seeing a mysterious figure on the property who she eventually decides is the ghost of a former valet employed at the estate.

A second apparition appears, a woman, who the governess instinctively knows is evil and eventually identifies as the ghost of the previous governess, who left her position under a cloud, apparently because of an affair between herself and the valet. The two ghosts are apparently seeking to gain influence over the children and have been at least partially successful, because they both begin to exhibit uncharacteristic behavior inappropriate for their age and inconsistent with their personalities. The ensuing struggle is complex and subtle, with neither side emerging completely victorious. The governess manages to save the girl, but in the process the boy dies, presumably to join the valet in the afterlife.

Given James's more famous fiction, it was inevitable that this story would also be subject to minute scrutiny, interpreted as an allegory of sexual awakening, and the ambiguous ending obviously fails to clarify matters. Although the most common interpretation is that the governess provides an accurate and truthful summary of what happened and that the ghosts are genuine, there are other interpretations that have been championed by some critics, including speculation that the governess may have imagined the entire thing, since no one else but the children seems aware of the ghosts, and they were clearly under her influence. A third interpretation assumes that the ghosts are real but that they are invoked by the governess rather than the children, which explains her ability to see them when others cannot.

James wrote a few other short supernatural tales, including most notably "The Romance of Certain Old Clothes" (1868), "Owen Wingrave" (1892), and "The Third Person" (1900), but none of his other works rivals *The Turn of the Screw*.

Turtledove, Harry (1949–   )

Although Harry Turtledove did not become a prolific writer until the middle of the 1980s, he debuted with two sword and sorcery novels in 1979, *Wereblood* and its sequel, *Werenight*, both under the pen name Eric Iverson. They are both routine quest adventures, well written but certainly not suggestive of the talent he would display only a few years later. His real fantasy career started with *The Misplaced Legion* (1987) and *An Emperor for the Legion* (1987), the first two installments in the Videssos series. An entire Roman legion inadvertently passes into an alternate reality where magic works and after various trials and tribulations is instrumental in ensuring that the true ruler of the land of Videssos is installed on the throne. Two more volumes followed quickly, *The Legion of Videssos* (1987), in which the Romans

are framed and charged with treason, and *Swords of the Legion* (1987). The series proved to be very popular right from the outset, a lively set of adventures given depth by Turtledove's historical accuracy and strong narrative skills.

Turtledove continued to add to the series until *Videssos Besieged* (1998), but many of the later volumes are repetitious accounts of stolen thrones and magical wars. Turtledove's novels as Eric Iverson were reprinted in one volume under his own name, after which he added superior sequels. *Prince of the North* (1994) has an old hero come out of retirement and battle new enemies, human and supernatural, and *King of the North* (1996) pits the ruler of a typical primitive sword and sorcery kingdom against malevolent gods. *Fox and Empire* (1998) brings back an old enemy and nearly causes the loss of a throne.

Some of Turtledove's best fantasy novels do not fall within a series. *The Case of the Toxic Spell Dump* (1993) is unlike any of Turtledove's other fantasy novels, set in an alternate Los Angeles where magic and not technology is the key to urban life. The protagonist is an agent of the "Environmental Perfection Agency" whose job is to prevent pollution by the waste product of old spells. The blend of humor and a hint of a tough detective story mesh well, and the result is one of Turtledove's very best books. *Thessalonica* (1997) is also very good, set during the collapse of the Roman Empire, when legendary creatures as well as humans seek to find safer ground on which to survive the growing chaos. *Between the Rivers* (1998) has a clever premise. Some time in prehistory the human race was divided into two civilizations, each dominated by a specific god. One of the gods became lax and allowed his subjects to think for themselves and seek new knowledge, and when they decided that they no longer needed the help of a god, their decision upsets the order of things.

Into the Darkness (1999) inaugurated a new series, one that was quite original in concept, although the later volumes have added little to the original premise. In a fantasy world divided into many nations, large and small, where magic functions in the place of technology, a war breaks out between two superpowers. Flying dragons serve as aircraft, and other magical analogies are drawn.

There is a large cast of characters whose story spreads over the course of several books, the most recent being *Out of the Darkness* (2004), which appears to have brought the series to an end. *Sentry Peak* (2000) similarly transposes the American Civil War to a fantasy world, this time with a black majority holding white slaves and a war between two halves of a nation to determine their fate. The war continues in *Marching through Peachtree* (2001) and *Advance and Retreat* (2002). Turtledove has also added to the CONAN series based on a character created by Robert E. HOWARD with *Conan of Venarium* (2004), set very early in the barbarian warrior's career.

Turtledove collaborated with Judith TARR for *Household Gods* (1999), a time travel story in which a contemporary woman discovers that ancient Rome was not what she expected it to be. The popularity of Turtledove's alternate history science fiction novels has resulted in his directing most of his recent work in that direction. The majority of his short stories are also in that field, although "The Gentleman of Shade" (1988) is an interesting Jack the Ripper story in which we discover that the serial killer was actually a vampire. Turtledove is a reliable source of fast-paced, action-filled adventure stories but often fails to develop his characters fully and switches viewpoints so often that the reader might become lost.

Tuttle, Lisa (1952–   )

From the beginning of her career, Lisa Tuttle established herself as a writer who ignored what was popular in a genre, preferring to write intelligent and thoughtful stories that were not quite what her readers expected. She has been primarily interested in the psychology of her characters rather than the physical events happening around them, examining serious themes against a supernatural or even surreal backdrop. Much of her later fiction in particular incorporates feminist themes, although never dogmatically.

She first began selling regularly in the 1970s, primarily science fiction, although one of the best of her early short stories is "The Horse Lord" (1978), a horror story. She largely abandoned science fiction and moved to horror after 1980, and

her first full-length novel in that genre, *Familiar Spirit*, appeared in 1983. Although it is structured as a haunted house story—a woman moves into a new home and is altered by the influence of a disembodied spirit resident in the house—the story unfolds primarily through the mind of the protagonist, with few overt signs of the spirit's presence.

Gabriel (1987) also employs a traditional device, in this case an ambiguous reincarnation. The central character is a woman whose great love died while still young. When she encounters her lost lover's nine-year-old son, she sees in him many of the traits of his father and begins to believe he may share the same soul. *Lost Futures* (1992) is very difficult to categorize. The protagonist dreams vividly of alternate realities based on different choices she might have made. The experience is disturbing enough when it is confined to her dreams but becomes terrifying when she finds herself cast adrift while awake. *Pillow Friend* (1996) is lighter in tone but still heavily character driven. A young girl learns that she is heir to a magical power that can give her anything she desires, but eventually she learns that everything also has a price. Her most recent novel is *The Mysteries* (2005), in which a private detective investigating a missing person discovers that ancient Celtic magic might be responsible for the disappearance.

Much of Tuttle's most effective work can be found among her short stories, which have been collected as *A Nest of Nightmares* (1986), *Memories of the Body* (1992), *Panther in Argyll* (1996), and *Ghosts and Other Lovers* (2002). Many of her stories mix supernatural and science fiction elements. "Treading the Maze" (1981), "From Another Country" (1986), "The Spirit Cabinet" (1988), "The Walled Garden" (1989), "Turning Thirty" (1993), and "The Mezzotint" (2003) are all of outstanding quality. Because of her low output of novels, Tuttle's name is not as familiar with most readers as it deserves to be, but she is known within the genre as a skilled and reliable writer with a powerful talent for looking inside the human mind.

The Two Towers J. R. R. Tolkien (1954)

The middle volumes of trilogies are usually perceived to be the weakest portion of a story. Typically, the first title introduces the characters, setting, and plot, all of which are new and presumably of interest to the reader. The closing title contains the climax, resolves the various conflicts, and brings everything to a more or less satisfying close. The middle volume has the most difficult job, because it must sustain the interest of the story while usually making the situation increasingly difficult for the protagonists and accomplish all of this without becoming repetitive. Even more of a challenge is the ending, which necessarily leaves the reader hanging in metaphorical mid-air.

In *The Two Towers*, the middle volume of the Lord of the Rings trilogy by J. R. R. TOLKIEN, the author provides a subsidiary climax that brings closure to certain portions of the plot but that leaves the greater issues unresolved. Saruman the White has betrayed Middle Earth by allying himself with Sauron, the evil entity who rules Mordor and plans to conquer the rest of the world. Sauron's plans are progressing in part because of the unwillingness of his enemies to act in common cause, a situation that will not be resolved completely until the final volume. Gandalf, now transformed and more powerful after his battle with the Balrog, has returned to help unify the opposition, but even he is powerless to help Frodo and Sam, who are now alone on their quest to carry the ring to Mount Doom and destroy it. They are alone except for Gollum, of course, who is alternately their guide and their enemy.

One of Tolkien's underlying themes is that the natural world is despoiled by modern technological society, and we see this most clearly in the sequences involving the Ents, gigantic creatures who oversee the shrinking forests, who speak to the trees, and who are finally stirred to take part in the developing battle only when it becomes obvious that Saruman no longer honors the existence of the natural world. There are heroic deeds, and the hobbits Pip and Merry gain some maturity by addressing their own responsibilities. *The Two Towers* may seem at times to wander a bit from the central plot, but the disparate threads are all being positioned so that they can be drawn into a closer weave in *The Return of the King*.

U

"Ubbo-Sathla" Clark Ashton Smith (1973)

Clark Ashton SMITH was one of several writers who occasionally set their stories within the Cthulhu Mythos created by H. P. LOVECRAFT. Smith had created more than one recurring setting of his own, including the prehistoric civilization of Hyperborea, which he links to Lovecraft's creation in this tale. Like many of Smith's stories, the plot is secondary to the images and concepts he describes, which is not surprising given his background in poetry. The initial protagonist is Paul Tregardis, a contemporary man who finds a strange crystal in a curio shop and identifies it as a magical artifact mentioned in *The Book of Eibon*, a fictional tome Smith created in the fashion of Lovecraft's *Necronomicon*.

According to the manuscript, the jewel was used by a Hyperborean sorcerer named Zon Mezzamalech to explore the past in search of the technology used by a race of ancient godlike beings who once ruled the Earth, analogous if not identical to those in Lovecraft's mythos. While contemplating this Tregardis falls into a stupor during which his personality is briefly supplanted by that of the sorcerer, although Tregardis has no memory of this afterward. Although he vows never to touch the crystal again, it lures him into further trances, during which he regresses ever further, losing his original identity and following Zon Mezzamalech back to a time before humanity evolved on Earth. Their combined personality merges with many others as the process continues, finally ending with a glimpse of an amorphous protoplastic shape that is the source of all other forms of life on Earth. The process so completely absorbs Tregardis that at the end even his physical body is translated to another existence.

The theme is clearly that there are some things about which we are better left ignorant. Although Tregardis indulges simple curiosity rather than any overt desire to acquire power, he is doomed simply by virtue of having interposed himself among forces too powerful to control. This is a common outcome in Smith's fiction, which is designed to deflate our opinion that the universe is our playground.

"The Ultimate Egotist" Theodore Sturgeon (1941)

Although this story comes from early in the career of Theodore Sturgeon and is missing the skillful plotting and scene construction that would mark his later work, it is one of his cleverest ideas, and the author's obvious enthusiasm for his subject shines through the sometimes awkward construction. Woodie, the narrator, is so proud of himself that he believes everything in the world and everyone in it is effectively just a figment of his imagination, existing simply to make his life more interesting. One day he tells his girlfriend, Judith, that anything he refuses to believe in will simply not exist. An argument ensues, friendly at first, with Judith attempting to convince him that the fact that Siam exists even though he has never seen it proves his theory wrong, but he counters that Siam is real only on his sufferance and that it would vanish completely if he stopped believing in it.

He only partly believes this himself, but when Judith begins to get angry, he jokingly offers to prove his point by wishing a tree out of existence. To their mutual surprise, he succeeds and is unable to restore it because once it is gone, he clearly cannot believe in its existence, because it has none. Judith is alternately intrigued and alarmed, but Woodie relishes his sudden power and experiments by picturing a rival lying injured on the floor. Reality changes accordingly. Predictably, things begin to get out of hand because he cannot stop himself from being skeptical about certain things. An unlikely looking fish results in the extinction of the entire species. Certain laws of nature make no sense to him, but he consciously stops thinking about them in order not to introduce further chaos into the world.

The story then makes a significant digression in the form of Drip, Woodie's paranoid friend. Woodie is now able to see the world through his eyes for some reason and discovers that Drip has manufactured an entire ecology of horrible monsters that are visible and tangible only to him. Appalled, Woodie stops believing in Drip, thereby disposing of both him and his creations, but that opens the floodgates of disbelief. He begins to consider the possibility that the entire universe is just a dream, and when Judith walks out on him his last anchor is lost. Ultimately, he wonders if he himself is just a creation of his own imagination, and the final sentence of the story is, significantly, left uncompleted.

Sturgeon makes playful use of a familiar philosophical issue. Despite a plot structure that rambles, "The Ultimate Egotist" has undeniable power and remains one of the author's most memorable, if not technically impressive, works. Ursula K. LE GUIN would use the concept of the ultimate egotist with only a slight change in structure for her science fiction novel *The Lathe of Heaven* (1971).

"The Upper Berth" F. Marion Crawford
(1894)

Oceangoing vessels have been a popular setting for ghost and horror stories ever since "The Rime of the Ancient Mariner," by Samuel Taylor Coleridge. Writers such as William Hope HODGSON and Frederick Marryatt wrote classic ghost stories set at sea, but neither ever surpassed this enigmatic tale of a haunted stateroom. The story is framed in a familiar manner, a group of men swapping stories, of which this one proves to be the best. Brisbane is a quiet but impressive man, and his account of his last voyage aboard the *Kamtschatka* is truly frightening.

He suspects something is wrong from the outset when the steward expresses surprise that Brisbane has been assigned to stateroom 105. Although he declines to be specific, he hints that bad things have happened there in the past. Brisbane is not easily cowed, however, and declines to move even when the ship's doctor informs him that the three previous passengers from that particular stateroom all threw themselves over the rail at night and perished. Fortunately, he takes the lower berth, because his cabin mate leaps from his berth in the middle of the night and rushes out, never to be seen again. Perhaps even more unsettling is the porthole in the cabin, which opens and locks itself in place even when firmly closed.

Brisbane is intrigued rather than frightened and declines an offer from the captain to be relocated. The captain then volunteers to keep watch with him during the night, and the two observe a series of strange events, the opening of the porthole, an unusual odor, and a conviction that something conscious is suddenly present in the upper berth. Although they both survive, Brisbane is at last convinced that he is witnessing the uncanny and vows never to set foot near the stateroom again. Although Crawford never explains the reason for the haunting and refrains from describing the horrors in any detail, the suggestive hints and sense of supernatural dread are particularly well handled in what is probably his best single story.

V

"The Valley of the Worm" Robert E. Howard (1934)

Although Robert E. HOWARD occasionally wrote stories set within the Cthulhu Mythos created by his fellow writer H. P. LOVECRAFT, he was more at ease with stories of heroes and bold deeds than with quiet, atmospheric horror. This particular story incorporates the best of both worlds, a combination of sword and sorcery adventure and brooding ancient horrors. The narrator is a contemporary man who insists that he is able to remember incidents from the lives of his former incarnations, all the way back through prehistoric times. One of those incarnations was as Niord, a hero so great that later legends, including those of Beowulf, Siegfried, and Perseus, were actually based on real events in the life of the earlier hero.

Niord was an Aryan, a precursor of the Vikings, and part of a tribe that migrated across the primitive world in search of a new homeland. After battling the Picts, they settle nearby and fashion a friendship with their former adversaries, who warn them against entering a particular valley, which they believe to be cursed. Their tribe has grown quite large, however, and a small group wishes to break off and found their own line, a schism that takes place amiably although Niord, or rather his future counterpart James Allison, knows that such fragmentation eventually leads to conflict. No such conflict will take place this time because the splinter group chooses to settle in the forbidden valley. When Niord ventures there to visit them a short time later, he finds the village destroyed and all the inhabitants dead, torn apart as though by some savage animal.

The entity responsible is an enormous serpent, identified by one of the Picts as the god of an even more ancient people. Accompanied by a kind of humanoid familiar, the serpent lives hidden in the soil of the valley and emerges to kill those who trespass there. Determined to avenge his friends, Niord waits and confronts the beast, eventually slaying it, although he loses his own life in the process. The serpent is not a conventional earthly animal but a primordial alien force similar to those of Lovecraft's mythos and may have been intended as another aspect of them. As is the case with many of Howard's stories, his depiction of ancient warriors and their physical prowess is not entirely credible, but his ability to create genuinely heroic figures has rarely been equaled.

"The Valley Was Still" Manly Wade Wellman (1939)

This fantastic Civil War story, which is sometimes reprinted under the title "The Still Valley," is typical of the best work of Manly Wade WELLMAN, who drew upon his knowledge of American history and folklore extensively in his fiction, particularly the Silver John series. The protagonist is Joseph Paradine, a Confederate soldier who has been assigned the task of locating a unit of the Union army known to be in the area and suspected to be hiding in the town of Channon in a small valley. Surveillance from a distance proves unsatisfactory, so he proceeds alone and on horse-back, although his mount grows increasingly nervous during the descent and refuses outright to enter the town limits.

Paradine continues on foot and is astounded to find the entire Union brigade lying in the street, as though they had all died in a single instant. When he examines their bodies, however, he discovers that they are still somehow alive although not breathing and remain impervious to his efforts to waken them. His shouting also fails to bring out the local townspeople and, oddly, seems to have no echo. He is growing increasingly nervous when another man appears suddenly, identifying himself as Teague, the local witch man.

Teague has a book of spells, one of which he used to place the Union soldiers into a magical coma from which only he can waken them, although he did so only after the local population had fled the area. He was never well respected and apparently did not grasp the extent of his powers until now, but having flexed his conjuring muscle, he is determined to do more. Teague plans to immobilize the rest of the Union army in similar fashion, thus assuring a successful outcome to the war, and he wants Paradine to help him.

Paradine has two strong reservations, however. First, Teague is clearly a megalomaniac who wishes to establish himself as leader of the Confederacy in return for his services. Second, and perhaps more important, he recognizes that in all such magical deals there is always a price to pay somewhere down the road, and the cost almost always outweighs the benefits. He waits for his chance, then kills Teague, releases the soldiers from the spell, and burns the book so that neither he nor anyone else will ever be tempted to use it. Years later, after the war is over, he insists that the crucial battle of the war did not take place in Virginia at all, but in the town of Channon. Wellman's story is constructed like the folk tales of Paul Bunyan and Davy Crockett, simply plotted and with a clearly stated theme.

Vance, Jack (1916–   )

Although the vast majority of Jack Vance's published work is science fiction, his most famous cre-

ation is his fantasy series set in a far future when the sun is fading, technology has largely disappeared, and the world is once again ruled by magic. The first several episodes appeared as *The Dying Earth* (1950), clearly influenced by the work of Clark Ashton SMITH but employing a unique prose style and a very clever wit that has occasionally been imitated but never with much success. Vance proved to be a successful writer of otherworld adventures, and he did not return to the dying earth series until after more than a decade, with a second set of episodes collected as *The Eyes of the Overworld* (1966), which introduced the recurring character Cugel, a not particularly admirable but quick-witted wanderer who survives a series of harrowing encounters. Another long interval ensued, during which Vance allowed Michael SHEA to write a sequel, *A Quest for Simbilis* (1974), but Vance later produced his own sequel, *Cugel's Saga* (1983), followed promptly by *Rhialto the Marvelous* (1984), a series of episodes about another character, this one a wizard. The four separate titles were reissued in one volume as *Tales of the Dying Earth* (2000), unquestionably one of the masterpieces of modern fantasy.

Vance's second set of fantasy novels is much more conventional and more serious in tone. The Lyonesse trilogy, which includes *Suldrun's Garden* (1983), *The Green Pearl* (1985), and *Madouc* (1989), is set in Europe sometime prior to the days of King Arthur. The Elder Isles are a hotbed of political and military plotting as various would-be rulers each seek preeminence over the others. A young princess unexpectedly becomes the fulcrum by means of which the contending forces are reconciled.

Many of the stories incorporated into the Dying Earth series stand well on their own. Other fantasies worth noting are "Green Magic" (1963), in which a very unusual method is employed to spy on a fantasy world. "Noise" (1952) is also excellent, as is "The Narrow Land" (1967) and "Chateau D'If" (1950). Most of Vance's non–Dying Earth fantasies can be found in *The Fantasy Realms of Jack Vance* (1979) or in his predominantly science fiction collections *Eight Phantasms and Magics* (1970) and *The Narrow Land* (1982). Several of his science fiction novels, most notably *The Dragon Masters* (1963) and *The Last Castle* (1967), are constructed and narrated very much like fantasy.

"The Vanishing American"   Charles Beaumont (1955)

Charles BEAUMONT was one of the most talented short story writers in the fantasy and horror genres and would probably be a considerably more familiar name if his career had not been so short. Among his many classic stories is this tale of an average man, so average, in fact, that in some ways he ceases to exist as a distinct human being.

Mr. Minchell works as an accountant in a very large company, so large that he has not spoken to his boss in a decade and so anonymously that no one even acknowledges him when he greets them. One evening his alienation from his surroundings reaches a critical point—he literally cannot be seen. He first suspects something when the elevator operator fails to acknowledge his presence, but it is his 47th birthday. He is too interested in getting home to his family to worry about it. Before he arrives his grasp on reality grows even weaker. He is able to purchase items, but in such an impersonal fashion that the vendor never even looks in his direction. Minchell stops for a drink and cannot see his own reflection in a mirror, although he dismisses this as an optical illusion.

When he arrives home he can no longer deny that something is wrong. His wife and son do not respond to him, and when he looks in the bathroom mirror, all he can see is an anonymous smudge. Shaken, he goes for a walk, during which he begins to realize that the dehumanizing, monotonous, and demeaning facts of his life have literally taken away everything that has made him real and human. He experiments and confirms that he is effectively invisible.

Depressed and frightened, he happens to walk past the local library and notices the large carved lion he had always wanted to ride when he was a child. As an adult it would be beneath his dignity to be seen conducting himself in that way, but now that he is invisible, he decides to indulge himself. That single act of individuality and willfulness is sufficient to restore his identity. He is suddenly visible again and attracts a small crowd of curious and envious onlookers.

Beaumont's point is obvious. The mechanization and conformity of modern life steal that part of ourselves that makes us distinct individuals, and it is only by asserting the things that make us different, however small, that we can recover our individuality. Bentley LITTLE reprised this theme in *The Ignored* (1997), suggesting an entire hidden culture of people who have vanished from mainstream consciousness, and the concept was also adapted as one of the better episodes of the television series *Buffy the Vampire Slayer.*

Varney the Vampyre, or, The Feast of Blood   James Malcolm Rymer (1845)

Although the Scottish writer James Malcolm Rymer is generally credited as the author of this long, rambling vampire novel published in serial form in more than 100 installments, it is possible that some portions were written by his fellow writer Thomas Pecket Prest. The plot is very straightforward and extremely repetitive, with the undead Mortimer, who fought against Cromwell's forces and later fell under a curse after killing his own son, changing his name to Varney and preying on a steady succession of victims, enough to make each weekly installment lurid if not entirely logical.

The story is filled with familiar scenes and devices from the penny dreadfuls of that time, a missing body, chases, visits to mausoleums, and mysterious figures appearing and disappearing in the darkness. Varney is not particularly competent as a vampire, and by contemporary standards some of his antics are almost comical. Eventually, he is thwarted so effectively that, in despair, he travels to Italy and throws himself into Mount Vesuvius.

Varney the Vampyre was the single major vampire novel for more than 20 years, eclipsed only by CARMILLA (1871), by J. Sheridan LE FANU, and, of course, later by DRACULA (1897), by Bram STOKER. It was largely forgotten until the renewed popularity of vampire fiction raised its profile. Marvel Comics used his character briefly in 1990, but there is nothing distinctive enough about Rymer's creation to make Varney more than a historical curiosity.

Viriconium Series   M. John Harrison (1971–1984)

The Viriconium series by the British writer M. John Harrison is set on a far future Earth where technology has been displaced by magic, in much the same fashion as in the Dying Earth series by Jack VANCE. Whereas Vance uses that venue for lighthearted though clever adventures, Harrison has a much more serious attitude, and his stories often draw upon sword and sorcery devices, although with a very distinct flavor and certainly far more attention to literary values than is common in that form.

The first book in the series is *The Pastel City* (1971), which establishes this setting quite colorfully. Viriconium is one of the last surviving cities, ruled by a queen and menaced by external enemies, chiefly those living in underground warrens. Although the opening novel can be read as science fiction, since the promised magic fails to materialize, the intent and tone of the series is clearly inclined toward the metaphysical rather than the scientific. *A Storm of Wings* (1980) is in one sense very similar, although this time the enemy is a swarm of oversized and unusually intelligent locusts. Harrison adds an extra level of interest by alternating between human and locust viewpoints.

The Floating Gods (1983, also published as *In Viriconium*) is the last novel in the series. A lonely artist seeks to find his own personal way in a city beset by plague, rampant crime, and the gradual decay of its institutions. A fourth volume, *Viriconium Nights* (1984), whose contents differ from edition to edition, is a collection of stories using that setting. The four volumes were published in a combined edition as *Viriconium* (1988). The best of the short stories are "Viriconium Nights" (1981), "The Lords of Misrule" (1984), and "The Luck in the Head" (1983).

Harrison has not added to the series since the 1980s and has written only intermittent fantasy, although *The Course of the Heart* (1992) is quite good. His reputation remains high because the Viriconium series is one of the very small handful of story sequences of a dying earth to rise above the level of simple fantasy adventure.

"The Voice in the Night"   William Hope Hodgson (1907)

Although William Hope HODGSON wrote many tales of terror set at sea, this quiet tale in which nothing violent occurs is his most famous and most chilling. A fishing schooner is lying becalmed one night when the crew is hailed by a mysterious voice from a small boat requesting that they provide some food for the rower, a man, and the woman he left behind on a nearby uncharted island. Although the fishermen are perfectly happy to provide the supplies, they are puzzled by the speaker's unwillingness to approach the boat or to allow them to shine a light in his direction. Nevertheless, they place food in a box and push it off, for which charity they receive shouted thanks.

Hours pass, and the man returns, still remaining out of sight. Having restored his strength, he agrees to tell them his story. He and his wife were survivors of the sinking of another vessel, unhappily named *The Albatross*, who managed to contrive a raft and subsequently drifted about until they encountered a derelict ship. The ship was deserted, but the larder was stocked. The only bad aspect of the situation was the profuse growth of fungus, in some places piled up into man-sized lumps. Their efforts to clear even part of the ship came to naught, because the fungus always returned within hours, and they eventually decided to move to the nearby island, which was also heavily overgrown with the same substance.

Their situation soon worsened. They began to run short of food, surviving primarily on occasional fish they managed to catch. Even worse, spots of the fungus appeared on their skin, and although they removed it on each occasion, the infection appeared to be growing. Then the man discovered that his wife had started eating the fungus, which proved to be mildly addictive, and although he convinced her stop, it seemed likely that starvation would overcome their aversion. Days later, while exploring the interior of the island, the man encountered a clump of fungus that moved and realized that it was what remained of one of the crew of the derelict ship. He and his wife are doomed to the same fate, and they cannot come close to the fishermen for fear of spreading the infection even further.

Hodgson offers no hope for his characters. They are literally doomed to lose their humanity, if not their lives. The story led to several imitations, most notably "Fungus Isle" (1923), by Philip M.

Fisher Jr., and the 1963 Japanese horror film *Attack of the Mushroom People,* also released under several other names.

Volsky, Paula (1950–)

Although Paula Volsky's first fantasy novel, *The Curse of the Witch Queen* (1982), was clever and memorable, four years passed before her next book appeared. The story is basically a simple quest story, but Volsky embellished the plot and the characters considerably through the device of a web of curses, including one that causes the protagonist to overeat compulsively and gain weight. In order to free himself from the curse he agrees to perform a dangerous mission for his king. Her second novel was the opening volume in the Sorcerer's Lady trilogy, *The Sorcerer's Lady* (1986), which was followed by *The Sorcerer's Heir* (1988) and *The Sorcerer's Curse* (1989). The trilogy describes the problems a young woman faces when told her marriage to a sorcerer has been arranged over her objection and despite her concern that the sorcerer wants more than just a wife. She becomes reconciled to him, but following his murder she and her son become fugitives, although he eventually regains his birthright. The familiar plot elements are intermingled with several lively twists and turns.

The Luck of Relian Kru (1987) is a similarly pleasant but generally unsurprising fantasy adventure enlivened by some inventive humor and a memorable protagonist but still not able to rise above the blandness of its subject matter. Volsky was much more successful with *Illusion* (1991), the first book of Vonahr, a fantasy of intrigue and adventure set in an innovatively realized fantasy world whose aristocratic rulers have recently been overthrown. At times Vonahr resembles 18th-century Europe, but a version filled with magic and with unusual technological devices that give the series a very distinct flavor. Volsky later added an even better sequel, *The Grand Illusion* (2000), in which her fabulous land faces destruction at the hands of barbarian invaders. In an effort to find a powerful defensive weapon, the protagonist travels to a distant land to learn the secret of sentient fire.

There is another battle for political power in *The Wolf in Winter* (1993), this time with a thor-

oughly unlikable protagonist who commits various crimes in his effort to seize power. Once again, Volsky develops her background in great detail so that it feels like a real place. *The Gates of Twilight* (1996) and its sequel, *The White Tribunal* (1997), are set in the city of Lis Folaze, where magic has been outlawed and the pogroms against it are used also to punish political enemies and to expropriate personal fortunes. The second novel is particularly intense, involving a man's decision to make a pact with a demon in order to strike back at his enemies. Volsky has not had a new book in several years but still enjoys an enviable reputation. Her short Lovecraftian story "The Giant Rat of Sumatra" (1996) is also excellent.

The Voyage of the "Dawn Treader" C. S. Lewis (1952)

Only two of the four Pevensie children, Lucy and Edmund, return to Narnia for the third book in the famous children's series by C. S. LEWIS, although they are accompanied by a new recurring character, Eustace Scrubb, their obnoxious and unimaginative cousin. The three are drawn in by a magical picture of an oceangoing galley this time and find themselves aboard the *Dawn Treader,* King Caspian's most impressive ship. Caspian is searching the uncharted regions of the world in an effort to discover the fate of several lords who took his father's side when the throne of the Telmarines was usurped and who went into voluntary exile. Lewis wrote a much more conventional quest story this time, cast in the form of a marvelous journey that is reminiscent of the adventures of Sinbad the Sailor.

Eustace is unhappy with everything, of course, and complains incessantly. He becomes the particular foil of a talking mouse warrior, who is the most interesting character in the book, although most readers will recognize early on that Eustace is fated to recognize the error of his ways. The Christian symbolism is more obvious as well. Aslan, the lion-shaped Christ figure, appears exclusively to young Lucy for most of the book, and she becomes his unofficial prophet. Just in case we miss the significance, Aslan later appears in the guise of a lamb.

Their adventures are much more exciting than in the first two volumes. Part of the company is captured by slavers on a remote island, and Caspian uses an ingenious trick to free his comrades and reform the local government. A storm drives them to another uncharted island, where Eustace is magically transformed into a dragon, in which form he rejoins his comrades, who fortunately are easily convinced of his true nature. His subsequent difficulties teach him the value of human companionship, and although his behavior is not completely above reproach thenceforward, he is much improved company when he is finally restored, thanks to Aslan's intervention.

More adventures follow, including an encounter with a sea serpent, magical water that turns things into gold, and an island inhabited by invisible servants who may or may not have deserved their fate. On yet another island one's darkest dreams may come true. They eventually reach the end of the world, rescue some of the missing nobles, and discover the fate of the others. Then the visitors from our world are returned to their homes. The third installment involves a much more adult fantasy theme and is far more inventive than the first two volumes in the series.

Wagner, Karl Edward (1945–1994)

Karl Edward Wagner began selling short stories during the early 1970s, about equally distributed between supernatural horror and heroic fantasy. During the latter half of the 1970s he concentrated on sword and sorcery, but after 1980 his output turned increasingly toward horror fiction and continued in that vein until his death. Wagner's recurring fantasy hero is a barbarian warrior named Kane, described somewhat in the mode of the CONAN series by Robert E. HOWARD, although Kane is much more likely to use his brains to extricate himself from a situation than was Conan. When Wagner added his own novel to the Conan series, *The Road of Kings* (1979), he superimposed many of Kane's attributes on Howard's character, and the result is a much more complex novel than most of the others appended to that series.

Kane made his first book-length appearance in *Darkness Weaves* (1970, also published in abridged form as *Darkness Weaves with Many Shades*), which collects some of his shorter adventures into an episodic narrative. Three more adventures appeared as *Death Angel's Shadow* (1973). Two full-length novels followed. *Bloodstone* (1975) has Kane finding an artifact that provides access to a magical power left behind by an ancient civilization. The best of Kane's adventures is *Dark Crusade* (1976), wherein Kane must take a leadership role to help defeat an army of religious fanatics led by an insane but charismatic criminal. More short pieces are woven together as *Night Winds* (1978), and a collection of his miscellaneous adventures later appeared as *The*

Book of Kane (1985). In addition to the Conan novel, Wagner wrote one other book set in a world created by Howard. *Legion from the Shadows* (1976) is a suspenseful story of Bran Mak Morn, a heroic figure in ancient Britain who helps the Pictish people defend themselves from evil magic.

Wagner also edited several anthologies, including 15 volumes of the *Year's Best Horror* series from DAW books from 1980 to 1994 as well as others in both the fantasy and horror genres. His own short horror fiction is collected in *In a Lonely Place* (1983), *Why Not You and I?* (1987), and *Exorcisms and Ecstasies* (1997). The last title won a Bram Stoker Award for a single-author collection. His short story "Beyond Any Measure" (1982) won the World Fantasy Award. Other notable short stories include "But You'll Never Follow Me" (1990), the Civil War horror story "Hell Creek" (1993), and the Lovecraftian "I've Come to Talk with You Again" (1996).

Wakefield, H. R. (1888–1964)

The British ghost and horror story writer Herbert Russell Wakefield never produced a novel of the fantastic, although he did write a handful of detective thrillers at that length, and his short stories have been shuffled around into various anthologies, giving the impression that he was much more prolific than is actually the case. He is one of the more underrated writers of his period, however, for his work was consistently well done and occasionally matched the quality of M. R. JAMES, Arthur

MACHEN, and other more familiar names. His first collection, *They Return at Evening*, appeared in 1928, although his two best-known are *The Clock Strikes Twelve* (1939) and *Strayers from Sheol* (1961). The most comprehensive sampling of his work can be found in *The Best Ghost Stories of H. Russell Wakefield* (1978).

The vast majority of Wakefield's horrors were ghosts, usually vengeful ones who had committed suicide and were thus condemned to remain on Earth. One of his best stories, "He Cometh and He Passeth By" (1928) was clearly an imitation of the classic "CASTING THE RUNES" (1911), by M. R. James, in which a magician's curse employs Oriental sorcery. In "Professor Pownall's Oversight" (1928) the ghost of a murdered chess player returns to finish his match with the rival responsible for his death. "Old Man's Beard" (1929) similarly has a murder victim returning, this time to haunt his killer's wife. "Blind Man's Bluff" (1929) and "The Cairn" (1929) both involve protagonists who disregard warnings to avoid bad places, with predictable consequences.

"The Frontier Guards" (1931) is an above-average haunted house tale, and "Damp Sheets" (1931) is a clever though formulaic story of ghostly revenge. "Mr. Ash's Studio" (1932) is an unusual haunted house story variation involving oversized ghostly moths. There is a were-hyena in "Death of a Poacher" (1935), and "Jay Walkers" (1940) is a very clever ghostly revenge variation in which jay-walking ghosts precipitate automobile accidents. "The Gorge of the Churels" (1951) is atypical of Wakefield's work, a lurid tale of creatures that seize and kill children. "Immortal Bird" (1961) is a story of psychological haunting with an ambiguous ending. Although Wakefield never reached the first rank of ghost story writers and often repeated themes and situations, he had a powerful talent for creating an atmosphere of quiet disturbance, and scenes from his stories often linger in the reader's memory even long after the plot is forgotten.

Walton, Evangeline (1907–1996)

Although Evangeline Walton began writing quite early, only a small amount of her fiction was actually published when it was first written, and some of her short stories published during the 1970s under her name were actually written 40 years earlier. Her first fantasy novel was published as *The Virgin and the Swine* (1936) and was marketed as an historical novel, in which field she published two more books during the 1950s. It was not until *The Virgin and the Swine* was reissued under the title *The Island of the Mighty* in 1970 that she attracted the attention of fantasy readers, which is surprising since the novel is one of the very best retellings of Welsh legends, organized into a consistent and very effective narrative. The novel draws on the fourth portion of the Mabinogion, the complex cycle of Welsh myth, and describes the coming of age of the children of a goddess.

Walton wrote a second book based on the Mabinogion, which finally saw print in 1971. *The Children of Llyr* also follows a group of children caught up in a war between Britain and Ireland, which claims the lives of most of them. Walton then wrote two more books based on the remaining two segments of the Mabinogion, *The Song of Rhiannon* (1972) and *Prince of Annwn* (1974). The first is an elaborate, romantic tale of magic and personal loyalty, and the second is a straightforward quest story.

At the time of Walton's death, she had finished only the first volume of a new trilogy based on Greek mythology. *The Sword Is Forged* (1984) is an entertaining story but fails to measure up to her Welsh stories, which have recently been collected in an omnibus edition as *The Mabinogion Tetralogy* (2002). Walton also published one horror novel, *Witch House* (1945), in which rather typically a family is compelled by the terms of a will to live in a haunted house and hires an exorcist to rid the building of the resident malevolent spirits. Although relatively unknown, it is one of the best of its type and has now had editions from at least six different publishers. Her short fiction is generally of minor interest, of which "Above Ker-Is" (1978) is the best.

War for the Oaks Emma Bull (1987)

Although Emma Bull has been writing fantasy for more than two decades, she has produced a very small body of work, only three fantasy novels, one collaboratively, and a handful of uncollected short stories. Despite her small output, she retains her position as an important figure in contemporary fantasy primarily because of her first novel, *War for the Oaks,* which established many of the standard elements of urban fantasy and the idea that our world and that of another realm of magic might overlap at some point.

The protagonist is Eddi McCandry, who recently broke up with her rock musician lover and is now trying to found a new band in Minneapolis. One night she encounters a "phouka," a magical being who can appear either as a human or as a kind of dog, who informs her that she has been chosen to serve as the fulcrum for the battle between the Seelie and Unseelie courts, light and dark, good and evil, who are at war in the realm of elves and fairies but whose battle has spilled over into our world. Bull's fairies and elves are not gentle, meek creatures. They are, in fact, very much like humans except that they do not seem to be capable of feeling much emotion, although Eddi attempts to explain their significance among humans.

With misgivings and considerable skepticism, Eddi eventually accepts the truth of the situation, and, in fact, her new band develops into a source of a powerful magic that helps turn the tide of battle. Although the plot has been reprised by many authors since, few have equaled Bull's simple, direct approach, and even fewer have created a character as believable as Eddi McCandry. Bull went on to write other fantasy in a similar vein, including *Finder* (1994), set in the Borderlands shared universe series, which in itself owes at least part of its original concept to *War for the Oaks.* The SHADOWRUN role-playing game system and an extensive series of tie-in novels published during the 1990s follow a similar pattern, mixing elves with an urban environment and adding advanced technology. Other writers of urban fantasy include Mercedes LACKEY, Tanya HUFF, Megan Lindholm.

Warhammer Series

The Warhammer role-playing game system, like many of its rivals, has spun off a line of novels using the basic setting and sometimes ongoing characters for a series of original adventures, mostly novel-length but also including occasional collections of short stories. The Warhammer series has a particularly wide range of settings because it is split into two distinct branches. The first takes place on a primitive, barbaric Earth where magic works and good and evil are usually differentiated without difficulty. Heroes are quick with their wits as well as their weapons, and villains are usually either monsters or users of dark magic. Novels in this branch are basically sword and sorcery, more in the tradition of Robert E. HOWARD than J. R. R. TOLKIEN, which thereby distinguishes them from the otherwise similar tie-in novels in the FORGOTTEN REALMS or DRAGONLANCE series.

The other branch is set in the distant future, when humanity has spread to the stars and intermingles with alien races, although aliens are generally not a major plot device in the novels. Although the setting seems to be science fiction, this version of the future is dominated by a battle between humans on the side of good and those ranged with demons that exist among the stars, genuinely supernatural beings rather than aliens. Most of the novels closely approximate military science fiction, spending a great deal of their time describing battles in space or on distant worlds, and thus are of less interest to fantasy readers.

Although there is some crossover, writers tend to stay within their preferred branches. Most of the authors of the Warhammer novels have not had books published elsewhere, unless in another shared universe series. There have been exceptions, however, and sometimes notable ones. The most significant of these is Ian Watson, a well-respected science fiction writer whose Warhammer books *Draco* (1990), *Harlequin* (1994), and *The Chaos Child* (1995) make up the Inquisition War trilogy, which leans very clearly toward science fiction. As Brian Craig, Brian STABLEFORD wrote four Warhammer novels that are more clearly fantasy, *Plague Daemon* (1990) and *Storm Warriors* (1991) and later *Wine of Dreams* (2000) and *Zaragoz* (2002). Although not approaching the stature of Stableford's novels under his own name, they are all superior sword and sorcery tales, particularly *Wine of Dreams.*

David Ferring, the pen name for the science fiction writer Dav Garnett, has also wrote one of the better titles in the series, *Konrad* (1990), along with two sequels. The best of those authors who work almost exclusively within the Warhammer universe is Dan Abnett, whose Eisenhorn trilogy, *Xenos* (2001), *Malleus* (2002), and *Hereticus* (2003), is particularly good. Other homegrown writers of interest are William King, Graham Mc-Neill, and Gav Thorpe. Although it seems unlikely that a Warhammer novel will ever achieve widespread acclaim, the series provides a consistent stream of tolerable to quite good sword and sorcery stories, and it is entirely possible that some of the authors who learn their craft within this framework will later expand their horizons and create original work in their own imagined worlds.

Watership Down Richard Adams (1972)

Talking-animal fantasy novels have historically been aimed at very young readers, although a few, such as THE WIND IN THE WILLOWS (1908), by Kenneth Grahame, have also proven to be successful entertainments for adult readers. The major difference between traditional animal fantasies and this novel is that Adams does not describe his rabbit society in human terms but constructed it based on the way rabbits actually live. The plot is an extended multipart quest. Following predictions of a major catastrophe in their present warren, which is, in fact, an accurate forecast of the plans of a human land developer, a small group of rabbits set out to find a new home for themselves and do so in a place called Watership Down. In order to make their new warren complete, they need females, who they locate in yet other warrens, although one of them is dominated by evil. Adams creates an entire culture for his rabbits, consistent with their behavior in the real world, including games, a form of religion, and even a few words peculiar to their culture.

Animals figure significantly in Adams' later books, but never with as great an impact. Bears are prominent in *Shardik* (1974), there are intelligent dogs in *The Plague Dogs* (1977), and *Traveler* (1988) is narrated by General Robert E. Lee's horse. Adams also wrote a collection of short pieces, *Tales from Watership Down* (1996), set in the same world. An animated feature was made in 1978, and Adams wrote a shorter, alternate version of the story released as *The Watership Down Film Picture Book* (1978). The book was also the basis for a short-lived animated television series in 1999.

Watership Down's success helped create an ongoing market for animal fantasies designed for a broader audience than simple children's books. Among the many to follow in its footsteps, or rabbit tracks, are the rodents of the Redwall series by Brian JACQUES, farmyard animals in *The Book of the Dun Cow* (1978), by Walter Wangerin, moles in *Duncton Wood* (1980) and several sequels by William Horwood, cats in *Tailchaser's Song* (1985), by Tad WILLIAMS, foxes in *Hunter's Moon* (1989), by Garry Kilworth, and birds in *One for Sorrow, One for Joy* (2005), by Clive Woodall. *Watership Down* has become an acknowledged classic for children and continues to be a rewarding experience for older readers.

Watt-Evans, Lawrence (1954–)

Although Lawrence Watt-Evans made his first professional sale in 1975, he did not have any impact in fantasy fiction until he began the Lords of Dus series with *The Lure of the Basilisk* (1980). Each of the four novels in the series involves the protagonist, a warrior named Garth, in another quest adventure. In the opening volume he must outwit invisible bandits as well as a creature whose gaze turns men into stone in order to retrieve a magical artifact. The pattern is repeated in *The Seven Altars of Dusharra* (1981), *The Sword of Bheleu* (1983), and *The Book of Silence* (1984). Although the stories are not particularly original, Watt-Evans employed a lighter-than-usual authorial touch than most of his contemporaries, which made his early work stand out. Although technically sword and sorcery, they sometimes approach the style of traditional fairy tales. A shorter sequence included only two titles, *The Cyborg and the Sorcerers* (1992) and *The Wizard and the War Machine* (1987), mixing science fiction themes and magic, a blend the author would return to in future novels. In this case, a cyborg lands on a planet where magic works and has several adventures, providing a mild spoof of military science fiction in the process.

The Misenchanted Sword (1985) started the Ethshar sequence, to which he has added titles intermittently ever since. The hero accepts a magical sword that instills its bearer with a kind of immortality, although the spell has several unexpected surprises and consequences. The Ethshar books share a common setting but rarely common characters. *With a Single Spell* (1987) provides a new version of the story of the ill-prepared apprentice wizard and the consequences of his blunders. *The Unwilling Warlord* (1989) is the best of the early Ethshar novels. A merchant is kidnapped and told that he must arrange to win a war against a superior force or forfeit his life, a task at which he eventually and creatively succeeds. After failing to find a vocation as a wizard, a young man takes up dragon hunting and almost loses his life in *Blood of a Dragon* (1991), and another innocent out to make his fortune spends time with a winged girl who appears to be more experienced than she lets on in *Taking Flight* (1993). A thief tries to imitate a wizard's spell and gets unexpected results in *The Spell of a Black Dagger* (1994).

By the early 1990s Watt-Evans was well established as one of the leading writers of light fantasy adventure as opposed to the multivolume disguised historical epics that dominated the field. He demonstrated his willingness to experiment with another cross-genre trilogy, *Out of This World* (1994), *In the Empire of Shadow* (1995), and *The Reign of the Brown Magician* (1996). The story this time spreads across three different realities, our own, one in which a comic-book style galactic empire rules the universe, and a third that is a typical fantasy world except that it has been overwhelmed by an evil supernatural force that wants to extend its rule into the other universes, even though the laws of nature act differently in each. There are times when the anachronisms are quite amusing, but overall the trilogy is too inconsistent in tone to be entirely successful.

His more recent work has been more serious in tone and more technically impressive. *Touched by the Gods* (1997) follows the exploits of a man literally chosen by the gods to lead his people to victory over an invading army of the undead. *Night of Madness* (2000) is an Ethshar novel. All of the magic in the world is divided among various schools of study, all of whom are outraged when a mysterious phenomenon allows some individuals to practice multiple forms. *Ithanalin's Restoration* (2002) is Watt-Evans's most humorous book, the story of a curse gone wrong and the difficulties involved when a house full of furniture becomes animate.

By far his most impressive series of novels is the trilogy *Dragon Weather* (1999), *The Dragon Society* (2001), and *Dragon Venom* (2003). The only survivor of a village whose residents were massacred by dragons escapes from slavery, grows to maturity, then launches a long-term plan to wreak vengeance on an elite group of powerful humans who are responsible for the death of his family and who have entered into a bizarre magical pact with the dragons, ensuring their own extended longevity in return for protecting the creatures from human interference. The protagonist is the most skillfully drawn of all the author's characters, and the ethical problems he faces in his quest are genuinely thought provoking.

Watt-Evans's only horror novel, *The Nightmare People* (1990), is unusually original, but unfortunately it appeared just as the horror market was collapsing. The protagonist suspects that all the other tenants in his apartment building have been replaced by a new kind of supernatural creature, and he is right. Watt-Evans also collaborated with Esther FRIESNER for the humorous fantasy novel *Split Heirs* (1993). His short stories have tended to be science fiction rather than fantasy or horror, although "The Frog Wizard" (1993) is quite clever, and "Worthy of His Hire" (1995) is a good vampire story. A recurring theme in his novels is the loss of innocence, either through corruption or through experience, but his characters always emerge as winners, though sometimes they are embittered by the process.

"A Way of Thinking" Theodore Sturgeon (1953)

This particularly biting story achieves most of its effects by suggestion rather than the explicit descriptions found in splatterpunk but is no less powerful because of that. The narrator starts by describing an acquaintance, Kelley, whose mind works very differently from that of most other people when faced with a problem to be solved, usually approaching from a direction directly opposite the usual one. Whereas most of us would see a wheel that needs to be removed from a shaft, Kelley sees a shaft that needs to be freed from a wheel. This odd viewpoint becomes critical as the story progresses.

The narrator encounters Kelley by chance after a gap of several years and finds him nursing his brother Hal, who is suffering from a series of inexplicable injuries. His bones break with no apparent cause, and he appears to be on the verge of death. The only clue to the cause is the odd-looking Haitian doll he gave to his ex-girlfriend, from whom he parted under extremely unpleasant circumstances. Although the narrator and Hal's doctor are skeptical about the possibility that voodoo could work without the victim knowing about it and becoming psychologically convinced that he was dying, they can think of no other explanation. The doctor's efforts to retrieve the doll fail, but the narrator is more imaginative. Pretending to be drunk, he approaches the girl, Charity, and allows himself to be invited up to her apartment, where he does, in fact, find several voodoo dolls, but it is apparent to him that Charity has no magical powers. He also discovers that the doll she named after Hal is missing and realizes that Kelley has anticipated him and burglarized the apartment.

Hal dies the same day, and Kelley promptly appears at the narrator's apartment. It is clear that Charity was not directly responsible because her other dolls were all ineffectual, but the specific doll he has in his possession may be the original magical creation upon which all others were based. Kelley leaves the doll in his friend's charge and disappears, and during the months that follow the doll undergoes several horrible transformations. Its limbs are broken, and it smells of putrefaction. The narrator fails to realize the implications until a young woman dies in a nearby hospital exhibiting the exact same wounds after insisting that her assailant kept calling her Dolly. It is only then that the reader understands the indirect and horrible fashion in which Kelley has exacted revenge for the death of his brother.

Weis, Margaret (1948–   )

Margaret Weis's career started in the middle of the 1980s, when she began collaborating with Tracy Hickman on a series of novels based on the DRAGONLANCE role-playing game system, with Weis doing the bulk of the writing and Hickman drawing on a background in game design. Their first joint venture was a trilogy consisting of *Dragons of Winter Night* (1984), *Dragons of Autumn Twilight* (1984), and *Dragons of Spring Dawning* (1985). A group of humans, elves, and other folk gather together to battle and eventually defeat an evil power in a manner very reminiscent of the Lord of the Rings trilogy by J. R. R. TOLKIEN. They followed up with a second trilogy about those characters who had survived the first round of adventures, this time sending them back through time for *Time of the Twins, War of the Twins,* and *Test of the Twins,* all published in 1986. The second trilogy is noticeably inferior, poorly paced, hastily constructed, and with even less characterization than their first effort.

Their third trilogy includes *Doom of the Darksword, Triumph of the Darksword,* and *Forging the Darksword,* all published in 1988. The premise is more interesting in this fantasy world. Since virtually everyone has some magical talent, those who do not are viewed as handicapped and are shunned. The protagonist flees to another land where he discovers the wonders of technology, builds a weapon that neutralizes magic, and then returns, eventually bringing weapons from our reality. For the most part, the series is much better written, and the concept is original enough to compensate for some of the repetitive sequences. Their next trilogy, *The Will of the Wanderer, The Paladin of the Night,* and *The Prophet of Akhran,* appeared in 1990 and blends elements from Arabian Nights–style adventures with legends of the Greek gods. There is a war raging among the gods, one of whom wishes to become ascendant and displace all the others. The battlefield is Earth, but since the gods cannot intervene directly in the works of humanity, they must work through subtle influence and the efforts of their particular champions.

Their next collaborative effort was a much longer series, starting with *Dragon Wing* (1990). The Death Gate series is set in a fantasy realm divided into separate areas with unique sets of physical rules, although there is considerable crossover among them. The seventh and final volume was *The Seventh Gate* (1994), which resolves the battle by various parties to seize control of the gateways among the realities in their efforts to rule them all. Next came another trilogy, *Dragons of Summer Flame* (1995), *Dragons of a Fallen Sun* (2000), and *Dragons of a Vanished Moon* (2002), yet another epic struggle between good and evil, the latter in this case consisting of an army of invaders. Although deliberately imitative of Tolkien's work, as were most of the other Dragonlance tie-in novels, Weis and Hickman are markedly superior in concept and execution to most of the other writers working in this particular milieu.

After 1995 their collaborations were sporadic. Weis and later Hickman began to write novels on their own and for other publishers. Some of Weis's novels were science fiction rather than fantasy, and she also occasionally collaborated with her husband, Don Perrin, and others. With Hickman she wrote several more collaborations at longer intervals, one of which added a belated adventure to the Darksword series, *Legacy of the Darksword* (1997), which pits a hero with a magic sword against alien invaders. They mixed magic and superscience for *The Mantle of Kendis-Dai* (1997, also published as *Starshield Sentinels*) and its sequel, *Nightsword* (1998), but the blend does not work well. Their most recent collaborative work is another trilogy based on another role-playing game, consisting of *Well of Darkness* (2000), *Guardians of the Lost* (2001), and *Journey into the Void* (2003). The opening volume does a very good job of developing the relationship between a spoiled prince and his whipping boy, but the story soon evolves into another quest to defeat an inimical magical force.

Weis has written three Dragonlance novels with Don Perrin. *The Doom Brigade* (1996) is quite good and follows the adventures of a band of retired soldiers who hear rumors of a treasure and decide to get rich. *Brothers in Arms* (1999) is a direct sequel to *The Soulforge* (1998), the earlier adventures of the apprenticed wizard who now gets caught in the middle of a war. Their third and best collaboration is the humorous *Draconian Measures* (2000), a sequel to *The Doom Brigade,* with the heroes still trying to settle down and carve out a new life. *Dark Heart* (1998), written with David Baldwin, is very atypical of her work, a blend of magic and police procedural. It was announced as

the first volume in a series, but no subsequent titles have yet appeared. *Mistress of Dragons* (2003) and its sequel, *The Dragon's Son* (2004), are set in another fantasy world and involve the efforts of the children of humans and dragons to prevent another devastating war.

Although Weis is certainly the most successful of the Dragonlance authors, her work in mainstream fantasy has been less well received, possibly because most of it so closely resembles her tie-in work. She clearly has the potential to produce more interesting fiction, and there have been signs in recent years that she is trying to expand her range. Her short stories have also been restricted almost entirely to game-related scenarios, but "The Legend of Jesse James" (1999) suggests she might be able to do better in that format as well.

Wellman, Manly Wade (1903–1986)

Manly Wade Wellman began writing for *Weird Tales* and other pulp magazines during the 1920s, although during the late 1930s and throughout the 1940s the bulk of his fantastic work was in science fiction and most of his novels were mysteries or westerns. The most interesting of his early stories are the adventures of John Thunstone, a kind of psychic detective who drew upon a deep knowledge of American folklore, and isolated tales such as "The Devil Is Not Mocked" (1943), in which a unit of German soldiers unwisely occupies Dracula's castle, and "THE VALLEY WAS STILL" (1939, also published as "Still Valley"), reminiscent of the work of Ambrose BIERCE. "For Fear of Little Men" (1939) draws upon Native American legends, as does "The Hairy Thunderer" (1960). Most of the better stories from this period were collected as *Worse Things Waiting* (1973).

Wellman's most important work is his sequence about John the Wanderer, or Silver John, a folk singer who wanders the hills of rural North Carolina defeating a variety of supernatural menaces, which often draws upon authentic folk ballads for inspiration. Wellman started this series with "O Ugly Bird" (1951) and followed-up with several excellent short stories, including "The Desrick on Yando" (1952), "Vandy Vandy" (1953), "Old Devlins Was A-Waiting" (1957), and "Wonder As I

Wander" (1962). These early short episodes were collected as *Who Fears the Devil?* (1963). Later in his career Wellman began writing book-length adventures that are invariably entertaining but lack some of the charm of the shorter pieces. The Silver John novels are *The Old Gods Waken* (1979), *After Dark* (1980), in which a hidden race of nonhumans are found to be living in Appalachia, *The Lost and the Lurking* (1981), whose menace is a modern-day witch, *The Hanging Stones* (1982), which proves that developers should be careful not to offend the "real" owners of remote plots of land, and *The Voice from the Mountain* (1985).

What Dreams May Come (1983) and *The School of Darkness* (1985) revived John Thunstone, whose earlier short adventures were collected as *Lonely Vigils* (1981). *The Beyonders* (1977) is a less successful stand-alone novel in which creatures from another dimension invade Appalachia and are eventually repulsed. Wellman was a very prolific writer, much of whose early work has been deservedly forgotten. At his best he wrote effective, efficiently plotted short stories that move directly to their point, and his Silver John books and stories are a unique and underestimated blend of folklore and contemporary supernatural themes.

Wells, Angus (1943–)

Although the majority of Angus Wells's published fiction has not been in the fantasy field, he has been an intermittent contributor whose work has shown very obvious development with experience. His first appearance was under the name Richard Kirk for the Raven series of sword and sorcery fantasies that began with *Swordsmistress of Chaos* (1978), written in collaboration with Robert HOLDSTOCK. Wells wrote two of the four sequels, and Holdstock penned the remaining titles.

Wells wrote no further fantasy until *Wrath of Ashar* (1988), the first volume of the Kingdoms trilogy. The god Ashar is a tyrant who wishes to deprive humans of their freedom. He is opposed by the Lady, another godlike being, who like Ashar cannot intervene directly but uses human servants to carry out her wishes. The hero is blinded at the end of the first novel and must travel into a kind of

otherworld to confront his assailant in the second volume, *The Usurper* (1989). The battle is finally resolved in *The Way Beneath* (1990). The rather similar Godwars trilogy, *Forbidden Magic* (1991), *Dark Magic* (1992), and *Wild Magic* (1993) followed. This time the malevolent god is insane but asleep. Unfortunately, a villainous wizard is determined to waken him, and a band of adventurers has to overcome an exciting if somewhat familiar array of villains and dangerous situations in order to foil his plot.

Lords of the Sky (1994) was the first of Wells's novels to demonstrate an ability to rise above genre clichés. His magical land is divided into nations, one of which has recently developed a primitive form of aircraft, just as the international situation drifts toward war. The novel is far more introspective than his earlier work, and Wells takes much greater pains to create his imagined world in depth and detail. He also tackles moral questions about warfare and duty to one's country in a refreshing and intelligent fashion. *Exile's Children* (1995) and *Exile's Challenge* (1996) are essentially one continuous story. Another fabulous land is threatened by external invasion, and in the aftermath former slaves seek to find a new role for themselves. *Yesterday's Kings* (2001), complete in itself, is more conventional, the story of a beleaguered people seeking a magical defense against their enemies. Although Wells sometimes settles for providing superficial backgrounds and characterization, he is at his best when he takes the time to flesh-in his creation. With more than 70 nonfantasy novels to his credit, he has certainly proved that he can be prolific, but his fantasy has so far only hinted at his writing talents.

Wells, Martha (1964–)

Although Martha Wells has not been a prolific writer since her debut in 1993, she has proved herself to be one of the most inventive new fantasy writers and has quietly gained a loyal following. Her first novel was *The Element of Fire* (1993), which on its surface is yet another story of the struggle for control of a throne, in this case occupied by a weak king who lacks the will and skill to resist his enemies. The plot is very complex, with an evil sorcerer adding to the mix. We see the action through the eyes of a captain of the guard who joins forces with the king's half-human sister to ensure that the castle's magical defenses are maintained during the chaotic days that follow. The real charm of the novel is the interplay between these two characters, both of whom are feisty but flawed. The novel also introduces the land of Ile-Rien, the setting for most of Wells's subsequent work.

Her second novel, *The City of Bones* (1995), is an Arabian Nights–style adventure, except that the protagonist discovers evidence of a lost technology and we realize this might be a distant future, magically transformed Earth. *The Death of the Necromancer* (1998) returns to Ile-Rien and is a remarkably fine book. The protagonist is the head of a gang of thieves who poses as a necromancer as part of his elaborate plot for vengeance against a powerful aristocrat. Unfortunately, he runs afoul of a genuine necromancer, and his plans go partly awry. The characters are lively, the dialogue witty, and the action at times hectic.

Wheel of the Infinite (2000) uses a much less familiar setting, a culture in which the spirits of the departed are still present. A disgraced priestess is told to investigate the apparent sabotage of the sacred wheel that provides structure to reality, find out who is responsible, and correct the situation before disaster strikes. Much more somber in tone than her other novels and a bit dense in the opening chapters, the story rewards the patient reader. Her two most recent novels, *The Wizard Hunters* (2003) and *The Ships of Air* (2004), are both set in Ile-Rien. In the first a small group of people are trying to discover the secrets of an invading race who have blockaded their world but are diverted when they find themselves inadvertently transported to another reality. In the second the engaging female protagonist leads a group of insurgents determined to expel the enemy from their world. The third and perhaps final volume in this series has not been announced as of this writing. Wells is a skilled writer whose greatest strength is her ability to create interesting, likable characters and to place them in created worlds that are original without being too farfetched to be credible.

"The Wendigo" Algernon Blackwood (1910)

The Wendigo is a traditional spirit of the wilderness in Canada, a mysterious creature whose physical appearance is not clearly defined and whose powers are equally vague. The Wendigo lures its victims away from their companions by calling to them, although its voice is inaudible to everyone else. It can lift its prey into the air and is fond of burning their feet. Possibly because of the vagueness of its particular mythos, the Wendigo has never been a common plot element in horror fiction, but it is also possible that this early story by Algernon BLACKWOOD covers the ground so thoroughly that there is little new to say on the subject, although *Where the Chill Waits* (1991), by T. Chris Martindale, recreates the eerie atmosphere of Blackwood's story quite effectively.

A party of hunters has been searching for moose in a particularly remote part of Canada, but without success. Determined to change their luck, the party splits in two and moves to fresher territory. One pair consists of a guide and a brash young man, the former of whom begins to act very strangely after an unusual odor wafts through their camp one evening. An eerie atmosphere of dread begins to overtake the hunters, and the guide behaves inconsistently, sometimes cheerful and effusive, sometimes withdrawn and clearly frightened. When the young man hears the guide crying in his sleep, he is particularly disturbed. Then a strange, nonhuman voice seems to be calling the guide's name, and eventually he runs off, leaving his charge to fend for himself.

The hunter trails his guide, whose tracks change shape, are accompanied by those of an unknown beast of enormous size, then disappear as though he were lifted into the air and carried off. He eventually rejoins the other half of the party, who are convinced that he suffered from illusions caused by stress. They attempt to find the missing guide, but their efforts appear doomed to failure. The guide then returns to their camp unexpectedly and behaves quite unnaturally, and in due course we realize that it is not the guide at all but a duplicate created by the Wendigo. Blackwood was particularly skilled at creating an eerie atmosphere, and "The Wendigo" is his masterpiece.

"The Werewolf" Captain Frederick Marryatt (1839)

Although most of the traditional monsters of horror fiction have appeared in a number of classic stories, the werewolf, or lycanthrope, has generally been relegated to a less interesting, formulaic list of titles. Most of the werewolf stories that prove memorable usually involve some sort of transformation of the original legend, sometimes changing it almost completely. It could be argued, for example, that DR. JEKYLL AND MR. HYDE (1886), by Robert Louis Stevenson, is a kind of werewolf story, and Dean R. KOONTZ rationalized the concept of shape-changing creatures in *Shadowfires* (1987) and *Midnight* (1989). The best traditional werewolf story is THE WEREWOLF OF PARIS (1933), by Guy Endore, but a close runner-up is this much shorter but very effective piece by the author of *The Phantom Ship* (1839), the best story ever written about the *Flying Dutchman*.

Krantz is a serf who flees his native Transylvania after he catches his wife scandalously entertaining a nobleman and kills them both. He is accompanied by his three children, Caesar, Marcella, and Hermann, the last of whom is the narrator. His experience has made him somewhat misogynistic, and he frequently mistreats Marcella. They are living in a remote part of Germany when a wolf appears outside their cabin. Krantz pursues it, but it eludes him. Instead, he meets a man and his daughter, Christina, who are also exiles from Transylvania. He offers them shelter for the night, becomes obsessed with Christina, and eventually asks to marry her. Her father agrees, but only if he is allowed to perform the marriage rite, which includes references to evil magic and a curse should Krantz ever harm her.

The children are not pleased with their stepmother, but life continues tolerably until they notice that Christina sneaks out of the cabin at night, and later they can hear a wolf outside their window. Eventually Caesar, the oldest, follows her, but he never returns. His mangled body is retrieved in the morning. Krantz is grief stricken and buries the boy deep in the ground, but during the night the grave is disturbed and the body even further mutilated. Only the children suspect that Christina was involved, but even they fail to grasp the full truth.

Some time later Krantz and Hermann are working outdoors when Marcella is attacked inside the cabin by a white wolf, which escapes before Krantz can shoot it. The girl dies soon after and is buried beside the remains of her brother. Hermann instinctively understands now that Christina and the wolf are the same, so he waits, and when she ventures outside that night he wakens his father, who surprises his wife in the act of devouring the girl's body. He shoots and kills her, after which he learns that the curse is unavoidable and that retribution will be visited on Hermann as well.

Marryatt was writing before the modern interpretation of the werewolf legend was formulated, so Christina is vulnerable to ordinary bullets rather than silver ones. The reference to Transylvania as the source for inhuman creatures predates Bram STOKER's use of that region by more than half a century. Despite the age of the story, it is as readable today as it was when it was first published.

The Werewolf of Paris Guy Endore (1933)

Guy Endore was an American novelist and screenwriter whose sole memorable work is this still-unequaled werewolf story, which mixes the supernatural with satirical humor. Supposedly, the novel is based in part on an actual French maniac and serial killer who cannibalized his victims. Bertrand Caillet is the werewolf, apparently born in 19th-century France already subject to the taint, although Endore never offers any real explanation for his condition other than a suggestion that it is the consequence of vague sins committed by his ancestors. As a child he began to exhibit bizarre behavior, including howling like a wolf, and as he grows older he becomes increasingly bellicose, violently attacking other people and scandalizing his family. He also begins to alter his shape after darkness and hunts like an animal.

The protagonist is another Frenchman, Aymar Galliez, who makes largely ineffectual efforts to moderate Bertrand's behavior. The Franco-Prussian War breaks out, Paris is under siege, and Bertrand finds the chaos and violence particularly well suited for his needs. He claims human as well as animal victims and occasionally stores grisly snacks under his bed for later consumption. There is also a priceless scene in which a family kills and eats the family dog and then opines that the missing pet would really have enjoyed the leftovers.

Bertrand is not an entirely disagreeable character. He falls in love, although his proclivity to violence makes consummation difficult, and is eventually arrested and confined in an asylum, where he eventually manages to commit suicide. Endore spends a considerable amount of time satirizing social life among the upper classes of France, sometimes distracting the reader from the central story. Flawed as it is, however, it was the first skillfully written werewolf novel and has few rivals even today.

West, Michelle (1963–)

Michelle Sagara West first began publishing fantasy fiction as Michelle Sagara with *Into the Dark Lands* (1991), the first volume in the Sundered series. It is a straightforward and well-written story about a world threatened with a magical conflict between good and evil. A seeress has a vision of a young woman who could alter the balance of power toward the side of good, but evil appears to triumph in the opening volume. The evil ruler seeks to waken his magically sleeping bride in *Children of the Blood* (1992), which will allow him to tighten his grip over his subjects. A new champion for good enters the fray in *Lady of Mercy* (1993), and the one-time lovers square off for the final battle in *Chains of Darkness, Chains of Light* (1994). Although nothing out of the ordinary, the Sundered series is solid, action-filled fantasy adventure, and the author did a respectable job of rendering her characters and placing them in a coherent and convincing story. Several short stories also appeared under the Sagara byline, but she reverted to Michelle West for most of her subsequent fiction.

As West she has written two sequences of fantasy novels, both of which are of considerably more merit. The first is a two-part sequence consisting of *Hunter's Oath* (1995) and *Hunter's Death* (1996). A god of the hunt has proved to be a beneficent patron for an imaginary nation, but in return for his gifts and protection the citizens are required to conduct an annual hunt with a member of the aristocracy as the prey. The background premise provides an unusual setting, and the two books are a significant step up from her earlier work.

Even more impressive is her remaining series of novels, the Sun Sword, which started with *Broken Crown* (1997) and ran to six volumes, each of them quite long even for the fantasy field. The opening title introduces a very complex world in which two powerful nations have been long-standing rivals, an animosity that takes a dangerous turn when magic is introduced into the mix. *The Uncrowned King* (1998) follows the adventures of a young aristocrat who discovers that he is the target of a band of demonic assassins. Open warfare seems to be imminent in *The Shining Court* (1999), but those leaders of one nation who have allied themselves with demonic forces begin to have second thoughts about the wisdom of their decision. The validity of their concerns is proven in *Seas of Sorrows* (2001) and *The Riven Shield* (2003). A mystical weapon promises to turn the tide of battle in the conclusion, *The Sun Sword* (2004). West proved with this series that she can take a typical fantasy adventure format and use it to produce major character-driven novels. Her short fiction, though less impressive, is similarly competent. Her only collection to date is *Speaking With Angels* (2003).

"What Was It?" Fitz-James O'Brien (1859)

Fitz-James O'Brien was an Irish immigrant who died of wounds suffered during the Civil War. He left behind no novels but a number of short stories, of which this tale of an invisible stranger is the most famous. A landlady and most of her tenants relocate to a new building, even though the house has a reputation of being haunted. They are, in fact, disappointed when weeks pass with no unusual events taking place and have decided that the rumors are just as false as they expected when one of their number, the narrator, is attacked in his bed one evening by an assailant of unusual strength. He manages to overcome and capture the other, but when he lights a candle, he is shocked to discover that the creature in his grasp is entirely invisible.

With the assistance of one of the other lodgers, the creature is subdued and tied up. No one else in the house wants anything to do with it, and several of the tenants eventually move out.

The twosome endeavor to understand the nature of their prisoner, who demonstrates no ability to talk. It is shaped like a human, although oddly muscular and contorted. They are entirely unable to understand its nature or origin, however, and it eventually dies of starvation despite their best efforts to find something that will sustain it.

Part of the story's thrust is based on a conversation between the two men in which they speculate about the greatest element of terror, that is, the one thing that is more frightening than anything else. The author seems to be suggesting that no familiar fear has that quality, that it must be fear of something completely unknown and unknowable, although in fact the two men show no fear at all once the creature is secured and unable to harm them. Their efforts to understand it, including making a mold of its body, have resulted in the story being described occasionally as science fiction, but, in fact, O'Brien never offers even the faintest hint about the invisible attacker's origin and makes no effort to rationalize its existence.

Wheatley, Dennis (1897–1977)

The British writer Dennis Wheatley produced a fairly large number of thrillers, about equally split between espionage stories and tales of black magic and the occult, with occasional forays into science fiction. Wheatley's first novel of the supernatural was *The Devil Rides Out* (1935), one of his best and part of the Duke de Richleau series, not all of which involve the supernatural. A band of friends discover that one of their number has fallen under the influence of a modern-day sorcerer, so they kidnap him in order to break the villain's control. By doing so they become the targets of his dark magic. The same group returns in *Strange Conflict* (1941), this time traveling to the astral plane, where they battle the disembodied forces raised by Nazi agents who have recruited the help of a voodoo practitioner who uses his ability to function outside of his body in order to spy on allied planning during World War II. The duke and his friends have one further occult adventure, *Gateway to Hell* (1970). One of their circle abruptly undergoes a change of character, embezzles the family fortune, and flees to South America. They pursue him and discover that

he has fallen under the mystical influence of a cult of satanists who are using his wealth to help them precipitate a supernatural catastrophe.

The Haunting of Toby Jugg (1948), despite the title, is not a ghost story. Toby Jugg is a powerful and wealthy man, though an invalid, who begins to experience incidents of a supernatural origin that initially make him doubt his sanity, although eventually he realizes that he is the target of a cabal of black magicians who wish to replace him with a doppelgänger in order to acquire his power. Through other magical means he is cured and eventually takes the initiative, destroying his enemies. *To the Devil—A Daughter* (1953) is about the corruption of innocence. A young woman assumes an entirely different personality after darkness falls, as though she were possessed by some evil spirit. The novel was considered sexually suggestive for its day, although it is innocuous by contemporary standards. A series of chases and escapes in much the same vein as the Duke de Richleau series follows, and a fairly loyal film version was produced in 1976. Wheatley wrote a sequel, *The Satanist* (1960), a kitchen sink novel filled with espionage and the occult, plots to explode nuclear weapons in England, devil worshippers, a conjured imp, and other subplots. The novel is exciting but at times almost incoherent.

The Ka of Gifford Hilary (1956) is his only other significant novel of the supernatural. A financier is apparently murdered by a mysterious new weapon, but although his body is functionally dead, his personality has been set free and roams about spying out secrets before finally returning to reanimate his own corpse and tell all. Several other novels have fantastic elements, but they are usually subsidiary to the main plot. *The Rape of Venice* (1959), part of Wheatley's Roger Brook historical adventure series, involves genuine satanists and evil manifestations. One of his later exploits, *The Irish Witch* (1973), does as well. *They Used Dark Forces* (1964), part of the Gregory Sallust spy series, involves supernatural weapons employed against Adolf Hitler. There is genuine voodoo in *The White Witch of the South Seas* (1968), another Sallust story.

Wheatley's short fiction is generally slight, although "The Snake" (1943) is an effective story of

African magic. His only collection is *Gunmen, Gallants, and Ghosts* (1943), which contains only a handful of horror stories. Some of his science fiction novels might also be of interest to fantasy readers, including *The Fabulous Valley* (1934) and *The Man Who Missed the War* (1945), both of which are lost world novels, *The Lost Continent* (1938, also published as *Uncharted Seas*), and *They Found Atlantis* (1936), the last of which involves the discovery of an ancient, though abandoned, civilization. Wheatley probably never thought of himself as a genre writer but borrowed from science fiction and horror fiction to enliven his otherwise conventional thrillers. His best novels tend to be from early in his career. Wheatley was not widely known outside Great Britain until the 1960s and 1970s, when he enjoyed a brief period of renewed popularity, and many of his books appeared in softcover in the United States. Interest in his work has been sporadic since his death, but he is generally recognized as the most popularly successful writer of occult adventure novels.

"Where Is the Bird of Fire?" Thomas Burnett Swann (1962)

Most of Thomas Burnett SWANN's fantasy fiction is set in the ancient world and suggests that in the early days of civilization, the creatures that we now think of as mythological were real. The development of more complex human civilizations eventually drained the magic from the world, and they retreated into other realms or ceased to exist entirely. This particular story is set at the time of the founding of Rome and is told from the point of view of Sylvan, a fawn, who is befriended by Remus.

The brothers are living among a group of shepherds after escaping death in infancy at the hands of the usurper of Alba Longa, where their grandfather, the rightful king, is still held as a prisoner. They have made some attempts to organize an army, but there are few able to answer the call. They appear doomed to failure. Swann uses the two brothers to illustrate two contending human urges. Romulus is ambitious and pragmatic. He wants to be the ruler of Alba Longa, and he is willing to recruit thieves and rascals into his army if that is what it takes to succeed. The other forest folk, such as fauns, are of no interest to him except as sparring partners for his warriors in training. Remus, on the other hand, wishes justice for the people of Alba Longa and also for the animals and other forest creatures.

Remus is particularly upset when a hive of bees he has been cultivating sickens. To find a cure he and Sylvan visit the dryad, Mellonia, with whom Remus falls in love, much to the dismay of a now jealous Sylvan. Romulus has become impatient, however, and decides the time is right to strike. Remus prevails upon him to wait while he infiltrates in disguise to speak to the imprisoned king, but he is discovered and imprisoned. Mellonia then agrees to help with the attack, calling swarms of bees and a pack of wolves to drive off the soldiers. The usurper dies, Remus is freed, but to the dismay of Romulus, their grandfather announces his intention to rule for the remainder of his life rather than abdicate.

The brothers then decide to found a new city, but they quarrel over its location and the future of the less reputable of Romulus's followers. Romulus lies to get his way, and two of his followers rape and kill Mellonia. The quarrel becomes more heated, and Romulus, unthinking, strikes Remus a fatal blow. He then announces his intention to mitigate his crime by making the new city, Rome, a messenger of freedom and knowledge as well as a military force. Sylvan recognizes his good intentions but knows that the true outcome will be different, that humanity has chosen a path that will forever diverge from the older ways. Swann shared this exaggerated fondness for pastoral settings with many other fantasy writers, including J. R. R. TOLKIEN and C. S. LEWIS. This long story would later be expanded into the novel *Lady of the Bees* (1976) without adding anything significant to the core story.

"The Whimper of Whipped Dogs" Harlan Ellison (1973)

Harlan Ellison has long enjoyed a reputation for generating intense emotional responses with his fiction, which is certainly the case in this, one of his few overtly supernatural tales. The story opens with a vividly described murder patterned after the famous Kitty Genovese case, in which a woman was murdered after a prolonged struggle in a public place, her cries for help ignored by dozens of witnesses who could not be bothered to do even so much as call the police. Ellison used that incident to speculate about a new form of horror, one that is generated by the shortcomings of human nature.

The protagonist is Beth O'Neill, one of those who watched without acting in this latest incident. At one point she sensed that the scene was also being observed by some intelligence other than human, although she could not put a name to it. She also paid attention to several of the other witnesses at the time and noticed that in some cases they seemed to derive a kind of metaphysical nourishment from the violence. Despite her own complicity, she is only mildly troubled, not necessarily by guilt, but sufficiently that her actions in the days that follow are atypical. She starts dating another of the witnesses and stays with him even after he begins to act abusively, although eventually he seems to sense something in her that drives them apart.

Her life quickly begins to change. The rudeness, cruelty, and ugliness around her begin to affect Beth's own actions. Everything comes to a climax when she returns to her apartment one night and walks in on a burglar, who attacks her, drags her out onto the balcony, and is clearly going to strangle her. That is when she finally realizes the truth, that the masses of people jammed into the city have generated a ferment of emotions that has given life to a new god, one who demands violent sacrifices and the devotion of its followers. On the verge of death, she prays to this new spirit to spare her and kill the burglar instead, and she is suddenly free as her attacker is lifted into the air by an unseen force and literally torn apart.

The story is meant to be an entertainment, but Ellison is also openly indicting an unfortunate aspect of modern life, our willingness to lower our own standards to echo the attitudes and behavior of those around us. It is not the city or the god that is at fault in the story, but the failure of people to live up to their own ideals.

White, T. H. (1906–1984)

Terence Hanbury White will always be best remembered for *The Once and Future King* (1958), which actually consists of several shorter novels that together provide a comprehensive retelling of the legend of King Arthur and Camelot. His early work includes some minor science fiction and a collection of supernatural stories, *Gone to Ground* (1935, also published in shorter form as *The Maharajah and Other Stories*).

The Once and Future King includes somewhat revised versions of three previous titles, *The Sword and the Stone* (1938), *The Witch in the Wood* (1939), and *The Ill-Made Knight* (1940), with a fourth segment that did not appear separately. The original version of that portion of the saga was later published as *The Book of Merlyn* (1977), and *The Witch in the Wood* was retitled *The Queen of Air and Darkness*. *The Sword and the Stone* was brought to the screen by Disney Studios in 1963, and the series as a whole was loosely adapted as the musical *Camelot* in 1967. The first volume, which covers Arthur's childhood, is a part of his life missing from Thomas Malory's *Le Morte D'Arthur*. It is ostensibly written for children, although that has not prevented generations of adults from enjoying it as well. Merlin is Arthur's tutor, a man who has been living backward through time and actually came originally from the present day. The later volumes are darker and more mature, and White's reservations about the morality of warfare become more evident. Unlike many versions of the Camelot story, which treat it as a form of historical saga with little or no magic, White's version is filled with spells, magical transformations, curses, prophecies, and the supernatural. The series is probably the single most widely read version of Camelot, and the section about Sir Lancelot, *The Ill-Made Knight*, is particularly well done.

Although *Mistress Masham's Repose* (1946), a children's story, is relatively unknown, it is a very fine semisequel to GULLIVER'S TRAVELS (1726), by Jonathan Swift. A group of Lilliputians, extremely tiny people, were brought to England by Gulliver and are secretly living in a garden, where they are discovered by a young girl who attempts to turn them into pets. *The Elephant and the Kangaroo* (1947) is a less interesting children's book in which a new flood threatens, and an Irishman declares himself the new Noah. White's remaining fiction is outside the genre, although *Earth Stopped* (1934) and *The Master* (1958) are science fiction.

Williams, Tad (1957–   )

The success of WATERSHIP DOWN (1972), by Richard Adams, demonstrated that it was entirely possible to write a fantasy novel with no human characters and have it become a best-seller. Various domestic and wild animals were soon featured in similarly constructed novels, even moles, with varying degrees of success and not a few dismal failures. One of the few clear winners was *Tailchaser's Song* (1985), which introduced Tad Williams to fantasy readers, an epic fantasy involving cats. Despite its popularity, however, Williams abandoned the animal fantasy promptly, and his next novel was *The Dragonbone Chair* (1988), the first volume in a more mainstream trilogy continued in *The Stone of Farewell* (1990) and concluded in *To Green Angel Tower* (1993), the last of which was so long that it was published in two volumes, subtitled *Siege* and *Storm*. The trilogy is an epic fantasy clearly imitative of the Lord of the Rings by J. R. R. TOLKIEN but with a much more complex understanding of the complexities of war and politics. The characters are neither entirely good nor entirely bad, and the issues are not a clear-cut battle between good and evil.

Williams's next major project was the Otherland series, which started with *City of Golden Shadow* (1996) and concluded with *Sea of Silver Light* (2001). A group of travelers wanders through a series of universes, each with its own set of natural laws, sometimes pursued by their enemies and sometimes simply trying to find the way back to their original reality. Although less integrated as a single story, the series is filled with fascinating creations and imaginative settings. *The War of the Flowers* (2002), although not related to the Otherland books, similarly describes its protagonist's journey into other worlds. *Shadowmarch* (2004) launched a new epic fantasy sequence, the shape of which can only be guessed at at this point, although once again Williams has built an immense, detailed, and realistic imagined world for his characters to play in.

The very atypical *Caliban's Hour* (1994) is a much shorter work and stands alone, a retelling of Shakespeare's *The Tempest* providing fresh perspective on the characters. He also collaborated with Nina Kiriki HOFFMAN on *Child of an Ancient City* (1992), a very unusual story of an encounter with a vampire in an Arabian Nights–style setting. Although not a prolific short story writer, Williams has proved his ability at that length as well with stories such as "The Burning Man" (1998), "Not with a Whimper Either" (2002), and "The Happiest Dead Boy in the World" (2004), but he appears more comfortable when he has the luxury of an entire novel or series of novels in which to develop his plot and characters.

Williamson, Chet (1948–   )

The decline of the horror fiction market in the 1990s changed or ended the careers of many writers, some deservedly so. Chet Williamson, who began writing in the 1980s, had easily established himself as one of the most interesting new writers in the genre, but he has appeared only sporadically since the early 1990s. After debuting with a handful of short stories, Williamson produced his first novel, *Soulstorm* (1986), whose premise sounds like an elderly retread. A group of diverse individuals are offered a bounty to spend a night in a haunted house, where they encounter a variety of ghosts before discovering the true purpose of their visit. Just when the reader thinks the plot has settled down, Williamson adds a new twist to keep the tension level high.

His second novel, *Ash Wednesday* (1987), is also a ghost story, but a very unconventional one. In the small town of Merrivale, the ghosts of everyone who has died there appear one night, locked in their final moments of life. The inhabitants respond in various ways, some having their own lives transformed by the experience and others reacting badly. Despite the presence of ghosts, this is more fantasy than horror, for the apparitions pose no threat to the characters. They are in danger only because of their own personal flaws in this thoughtful and insightful novel. *Lowland Rider* (1988) is somewhat more explicit and suspenseful but no less original. When his family is murdered the protagonist explores the world of the homeless and the criminal in a major city, seeking answers and discovering the presence of a supernatural force within the city, but one with a surprising nature. There had been hints of theological speculation in Williamson's earlier work, but in this case the divine intervention is direct and unmistakable, although it takes a rather unexpected form.

Dreamthorp (1989) is not as impressive, although the relationship between the two protagonists fighting a demonic influence is skillfully done. *Reign* (1990) is much better, a story about a doppelgänger. Members of a theatrical troupe are being attacked by a mysterious figure that appears to be the protagonist, although we eventually discover that it is actually a duplicate of him consisting of all of his baser impulses and fears, reminiscent of DR. JEKYLL AND MR. HYDE (1888), by Robert Louis Stevenson. *City of Iron* (1998) opened a series of novels about a team of occult investigators who believe that the abduction of an artist is part of a plot by satanists to introduce major supernatural evil into the world. They return to track down a demon in *Empire of Dust* (1998) and battle the forces of hell itself in *Siege of Stone* (1999). Although their enemies are supernatural, the series is more adventure than horror.

Williamson has also written fantasy, although with a noticeably dark tone. *Mordenheim* (1994) is set in the shared world Ravenloft series and is essentially a retelling of the story of FRANKENSTEIN (1818), by Mary SHELLEY, in a different setting. *Second Chance* (1995) is a minor time travel fantasy. *Murder in Cormyr* (1996) is a murder mystery set in another shared world universe, with a wizard as a detective. He also wrote a tie-in novel to the Crow movies, *Clash by Night* (1998), with the undead avenger returning to eliminate a band of brutal terrorists. Although Williamson's tie-in novels are much better than most similar efforts, they are not nearly as impressive as his original work. *Hell* (1995), a tie-in to a computer game, is technically science fiction but is set in a future where technology results in the creation of what are essentially demons.

Williamson's short fiction is equally quirky and interesting, although to date only a single collection, *Figures in Rain* (2002), has appeared. Many of his horror stories have no supernatural content and involve ordinary people who justify their own cruelty and avarice to themselves, sometimes in quite creative ways. Among his best are "From the Papers of Helmut Hecker" (1990), "The Bookman" (1991), "Coventry Carol" (1994), and "A Fly Called Jesus" (1996). His insights into human psychology, his willingness to tackle complex moral and ethical issues, and his gift for creating novel situations and images make him one of the most interesting writers of the last 20 years.

Williamson, J. N. (1932–   )

J. N. Williamson's first novel appeared in 1979, but he soon proved to be astonishingly prolific, with nearly three dozen horror novels published over the course of the next 15 years as well as a number of short stories. *The Ritual* (1979) introduced Martin Ruben, a parapsychologist who communicates with a minion of Satan while investigating a case of apparent possession. Ruben also appears in *Premonition* (1981), in which he travels to a remote island where a health resort is offering immortality, but only in exchange for eternal slavery to a supernatural being. His final appearance is in *Brotherkind* (1982), which blends the supernatural with science fiction. The Men in Black, normally associated with flying saucers, are actually harbingers of a new form of life, a blend of human and nonhuman traits.

The Houngan (1980, also published as *Profits*) mixes voodoo with modern business and is probably the best of Williamson's early novels, restrained and neatly plotted. Other novels from this period such as *The Tulpa* (1981) and *Queen of Hell* (1981) rather more routinely examine standard horror themes such as possession and reincarnation. *Horror House* (1981) is the most interesting of several haunted house novels, this one set in a building that was at one time investigated by Thomas Edison, with negative results, but that now appears to be home to genuine angry spirits. It is less hastily written than most of Williamson's other work from the early 1980s and includes some genuinely suspenseful sequences.

Williamson then launched two series, one involving vampires and the other set within Minnifield House. The vampire novels are *Death-Coach* (1981), *Death-Angel* (1981), *Death-School* (1982), and *Death-Doctor* (1982), all involving a lamia, or female vampire, who comes to a small midwestern town hoping to establish a sanctuary for herself and her kind. Each book is complete in itself, and one must wonder why she kept returning to the same area after each defeat. The stories are otherwise brisk and convincing, and Williamson's evil protagonist is his single most memorable character. The Minnifield House books are *Ghost Mansion* (1981) and *Horror Mansion* (1982), both predictable tales of hauntings, but the first has some genuine chills.

Most of the next several novels are minor, although *Playmates* (1982) does a good job of describing the consequences when imaginary companions become real, and *Ghost* (1984) is an intriguing ghost story told from the point of view of a disembodied and somewhat confused ghost. There were larger gaps between Williamson's novels at this point, and that may account for the fact that the later ones are considerably more controlled and better plotted. *The Longest Night* (1985), for example, is on the surface just a story of a serial killer whose victims' ghosts linger after their deaths, but the author expends considerable effort to make their suspended existence, caught between life and death, seem real and tragic. *Evil Offspring* (1987) is less contemplative, the story of an ancient evil reawakened, but is considerably more exciting and adventurous than most of Williamson's earlier novels.

Ghosts and the details of their existence recur frequently in Williamson's later work, though most of these are minor. *The Night Seasons* (1991) is the best of the novels from the latter part of his career. *The Monastery* (1992), although very uneven, is also at times quite effective. *Don't Take Away the Light* (1993), another ghost story, delves deeper into the psychological state of its child protagonist than any previous work by Williamson, and *Bloodlines* (1994) is a rather unconventional vampire story. Williamson may have been tempted to explore new ideas and territory but still felt compelled to anchor his stories with some standard supernatural device. His most recently published novel, *Affinity* (2001), suggests that the trend may have continued if Williamson had continued to write, because it is a quite unusual story about a man whose memories are slowly being supplanted by those of another personality. It appears likely to be his last book.

Most of Williamson's short fiction has been collected in *The Naked Flesh of Feeling* (1991), *The Fifth Season* (1993), and *Frights of Fancy* (2000). "The Gap Nearly Closed Today" (1987) and "The Land of Second Chance" (1991) are his two best short stories. He also edited the well-regarded *Masques* anthology series of original horror. Although it would be easy to dismiss Williamson's fiction as derivative, he was to some extent the epitome of the wave of popularity mainstream horror enjoyed during the 1980s, producing familiar stories that rarely challenged the reader but that almost always entertained.

"William Wilson" Edgar Allan Poe (1840)

The doppelgänger is more commonly found in European horror fiction than in American, but Edgar Allan POE wrote what is certainly the best-known example. The story anticipates DR. JEKYLL AND MR. HYDE (1888), by Robert Louis Stevenson, in that the narrator and his doppelgänger move to opposite poles, one living a life of honor and the other one of disgrace. He introduces himself as William Wilson but insists this is not his real name. He describes in detail his childhood education in England, apparently based on Poe's own experiences, during which he rose to dominate all of his schoolmates except for a second boy of the same name and exact same birthday. Although the two were themselves aware of their intense rivalry, the rest of the school was oblivious, or so Wilson tells us.

The narrator appears to have been the primary aggressor, visiting various petty torments on the other boy until the latter retaliated by deliberately imitating his rival, dressing in the same fashion and even mimicking his manner of speaking, although hampered by his mysterious and suggestive inability to speak above a whisper. Readers might suspect that the second boy is imaginary, but there are other hints that imply this cannot be the case. The rest of the school reportedly believes them to be related, for example. In any case, Wilson is moved to Eton and later learns that Wilson number two has also left school, although under different circumstances.

The next several years prove to be very difficult. The doppelgänger shows up at Eton just in time to expose Wilson as he cheats at cards, forcing him to withdraw from school. The narrator spends the next few years in various parts of Europe living a dissolute lifestyle of drink and gambling, constantly pursued by his former victim. At last there is a confrontation at a party, followed by a sword fight in which he kills his doppelgänger and realizes that by doing so he has also killed himself. Whether the blood is literally his and he has committed suicide, or whether by killing the other man he has become a murderer is never revealed with certainty.

The story can be interpreted in various fashions. At one extreme, the entire sequence of events may be a product of Wilson's guilty imagination. Although there are indications that the external world does recognize his alter ego's existence, we have only the narrator's word for that corroborative evidence. Certainly he has led a life of such dishonor and dissolution that it is entirely possible his guilt has become on some level unbearable. At the opposite extreme, the second Wilson may have been intended as his double from the outset, sent by some unknown power to balance his life and to bring retribution. A third interpretation is that the two were, in fact, originally distinct individuals, although through luck and coincidence very similar in appearance, and that their childhood rivalry caused the second Wilson to imitate his tormentor so completely that some sort of physical and metaphysical change did, in fact, take place, making the two somehow one. Regardless of the interpretation, the story remains one of the most effective tales of psychological horror ever written.

"The Willows" Algernon Blackwood (1907)

The possibility that the world is not what it seems, that we are not as much in control of human destiny as we think we are, has appealed to horror and science fiction writers as diverse as H. P. LOVE-CRAFT and Robert A. Heinlein. This early story by the British writer Algernon BLACKWOOD is one of the earliest and most effective to suggest that we may share the planet with beings so far in advance of ourselves that we can only perceive faint hints of their existence and that we would be better off if we avoided being noticed in return. It was almost certainly an influence on Lovecraft's Cthulhu

Mythos stories, which in turn have inspired scores of other writers.

The unnamed narrator and his friend, identified only as the Swede, are taking a prolonged trip by canoe down the Danube and have reached a relatively unpopulated part of Hungary when a violent storm threatens to swamp their small boat. Despite warnings from the few people they encounter, they choose to shelter on a large island covered by willow trees, even after the narrator senses an unspecific psychic menace. As the hours pass the sense of danger grows much stronger, perceived by both, although in different ways. One has a vision in the darkness of a long stream of nonhuman intelligences rising from the ground to disappear into the sky and suspects that the willows have actually moved, encroaching on their camp. The Swede keeps his own counsel, but it is evident that he has also been affected by the atmosphere of the island.

The threat in this story is not directly inimical. It is so different from humans that motivations are impossible to perceive. On the one hand, they are unwelcome on the island, but on the other, events conspire to prevent them from leaving. Their canoe is sabotaged, and their minds are affected so that they are hesitant to attempt an escape. The Swede is convinced that a sacrifice is required, while the narrator is less certain. Their escape is equally subject to chance. Another man passes through the area and is killed under mysterious circumstances. Blackwood's story is frightening not so much because of what happens as because of what it suggests, that on a cosmic scale, the fate of individual humans, or humanity as a whole, may not be particularly significant.

Wilson, F. Paul (1946–)

The physician and writer F. Paul Wilson began publishing science fiction in the early 1970s and wrote primarily in that field for the next 10 years. His first significant book outside the genre was *The Keep* (1981), a clever and very tautly written thriller set during World War II. In German occupied eastern Europe a unit of military and gestapo officials occupy a decaying castle as their temporary base, but some of the soldiers disturb magical wards that imprison an evil entity. The incidents that follow suggest that the creature is a vampire, but it is actually a very different entity, one shrewd enough to make use of the Germans to further its own plans. Although the link is at times tenuous, *Reborn* (1990) is a sequel that borrows from science fiction. The protagonist is the clone of a dead scientist, and that makes him the target of a group of religious fanatics who believe that he is the Antichrist. The creature from the keep returns late in the book, and an equally strong but virtuous enemy renews the battle. Two more installments followed, *Reprisal* (1991), set decades later after the creature has established himself, and *Nightworld* (1992), which is so filled with apocalyptic battles that the reader becomes rather jaded.

Wilson's second supernatural series has a much smaller scope but is far more interesting and consistently entertaining. Repairman Jack is a man who has managed to remove all records of his existence from the system, living by performing odd jobs, usually bending if not breaking the law, sometimes using violence, and concealing his existence by means of several false identities. Although Jack does not shrink from breaking the law when he thinks it justified, he has ethical standards and only accepts job when he feels the issues are, if not morally defensible, at least neutral. He first appears in *The Tomb* (1984), which started a separate strain of linked stories that also culminate in *Nightworld*. In this case Jack is hired for two separate jobs that seem unrelated but that will eventually merge, a formula that repeats itself throughout the series. The supernatural threat this time is a ship full of Indian demons who are suitably dispatched, although some of their number escape.

Jack's second adventure, *Legacies* (1998), is only marginally fantastic, but in *Conspiracies* (2000) he discovers that the demonic creatures he defeated once before are after him again. Blood from those creatures can be used to concoct a new drug that turns ordinary people into homicidal killers in *All the Rage* (2000), and yet another drug causes users to share a dangerous group persona in *Hosts* (2001). In *The Haunted Air* (2002) Jack investigates a building haunted by the spirits of murdered children, sacrificed by a cult that sought immortality through human sacrifice. *Gateways* (2003), the

weakest of the series, involves a woman who can magically summon a mysterious swamp creature. The most recent installment is *Crisscross* (2004). The Repairman Jack series is currently being developed for the movies.

Wilson has also written several nonseries novels, many of them medical thrillers. *The Touch* (1986) is in that mode but has some fantastic content as well. *Midnight Mass* (1990), a short novel set in a world dominated by vampires, was expanded dramatically in 2004 and released as a disappointing film that same year. Most of Wilson's short fiction has also been supernatural horror, much of which was assembled as *The Barrens and Others* (1992). Among his better short works are "Buckets" (1989), "Pelts" (1990), and "Good Friday" (1999). He is a skilled, reliable writer who is at his best when his supernatural menaces are comparatively low-key, allowing him to concentrate on his well-drawn and usually likeable protagonists.

The Wind in the Willows Kenneth Grahame (1908)

Kenneth Grahame's only full-length novel for children is the most important, and probably best written, talking animal fantasy ever written, although some critics suggest it may have been intended for adults, since it is quite complex and at times digresses into philosophical discussions deemed to be over the heads of children. In fact, two chapters have been dropped from some editions to streamline the story. Although Grahame's protagonists are animals, they behave and live in a society that is essentially a mirror of our own. Toad, the most interesting of the characters, is obsessed with automobiles, particularly fast and flashy ones, a failing that eventually gets him arrested.

Toad's companions and rescuers, Badger, Rat, and Mole, were all brought to life on the screen in the 1949 Disney animated version and two more recent films, and unlike many children's fantasies, the images from the novel seem to have remained vivid with most adults. Their antics are comic, but the story demonstrates the values of friendship and loyalty and the pitfalls of acting impulsively and unwisely. Even the villainous weasels are appealing characters.

Grahame wrote only a few other pieces of fiction, some of which is fantasy. *The Golden Age* (1895) and *Dream Days* (1898) are collections of short stories of varying quality, many of them fantasy for children. The best of these is the novella *The Reluctant Dragon*, published separately in 1938, the story of a young boy who finds a dragon and befriends it despite its fearsome appearance. Although his other work is clearly inferior to *The Wind in the Willows*, it is frequently reprinted.

"The Wish" Roald Dahl (1951)

There are only a handful of writers who are consistently able to look at the world from a child's point of view and use that vision to create stories that reflect that very distinct perspective. Lewis CARROLL and Daniel Manus Pinkwater both come to mind, and so does Roald Dahl, who wrote for both children and adults and whose CHARLIE AND THE CHOCOLATE FACTORY (1964) became the popular film *Willy Wonka and the Chocolate Factory*. Although in most cases he used this talent exclusively for his younger audiences, on this occasion he enjoyed the best of both worlds, a story decidedly for adults but that depends on an interpretation of the world that only a child could truly believe in.

The only character in the story, which is quite short, is a young boy initially found standing at one end of an enormous carpeted room. The carpet is an elaborate, almost chaotic, tangle of three colors, black, red, and yellow. The boy contrives a game for himself. The red areas are lava, the black areas are snakes, and only the yellow portions can be safely traversed. His goal is to get from one end of the room to the other without touching the two dangerous colors, and he decides that if he does so, he will be rewarded by the gift of a puppy on his upcoming birthday.

An arduous crossing follows, with one near-mishap after another. Halfway across he realizes he is committed, but the game has become so real that he feels genuine panic when he nearly falls, and the black sections in particular seem to be moving of their own volition. And then, of course, he does finally falter, and our last glimpse of him is as his hand passes into the dark mass. Dahl wisely does not describe what follows but simply leaves us with the image of his mother searching fruitlessly for her son. This quiet, understated little nightmare is brief and to the point and captures perfectly one of the irrational but common terrors of childhood.

Witch World Series Andre Norton (1963–2005)

Although Andre NORTON began her career as a science fiction writer, she turned to fantasy almost exclusively shortly after publishing *Witch World* (1963), the first in a very long series now totaling 25 novels plus a handful of shared world anthologies. The first novel is set in Estcarp, a land ruled by benevolent witches, although later volumes take place in different parts of her imaginary land, with the characters frequently changing from book to book. The conflict in the opening volume is between the witches and another race, the Kolder, who are importing technological weapons from their own universe in order to shift the balance of power. Simon Tregarth, an adventurer from our world, finds himself in Witch World and helps defeat the invaders, falling in love with a prominent witch in the process. Since loss of innocence results in loss of magical powers, the witch faces a difficult choice when she discovers that she is also in love with him.

Although the novel is complete in itself, it was so popular that Norton began producing sequels. The Kolder launch a fresh attack in *Web of the Witch World* (1964) and are similarly repulsed, and Norton turned to a new cast of characters for the third, *Year of the Unicorn* (1965), a much slower-paced novel about a young woman who finds herself pledged in marriage to a shape-changer as part of a political deal. This is a far more traditional fantasy theme, handled with no distinction, and may not have originally been intended to be part of the series. Norton then introduced the children of Tregarth and the witch, Jaelithe, in *Three Against the Witch World* (1965), who rebel against the rather overly structured society of Estcarp and choose exile. They have separate adventures in *Warlock of the Witch World* and (1967) *Sorceress of the Witch World* (1968), and a similar young man goes through a rite of passage in *The Crystal Gryphon* (1972).

Norton began falling into a formula from this point forward, rewarding her fans with more of the same but rarely providing anything new as she explored her fantasy world. There are quests, battles to control thrones, and wars against evil sorcerers, with sometimes a hint of romance, although Norton rarely explores the latter in any detail. The best of the later adventures include *Zarsthor's Bane* (1978) and *The Warding of Witch World* (1996). Although most of the other novels are individually undistinguished, Norton's creation clearly had a very strong appeal to a large number of readers.

Spell of the Witch World (1972) and *Lore of the Witch World* (1980) are collections of short adventures. Norton also edited *Tales of the Witch World,* three volumes published between 1987 and 1990, and *Four from the Witch World* (1989), which allowed other writers to use her creation. Late in her career Norton coauthored several additional Witch World novels with other writers, including A. C. Crispin, P. M. Griffin, Mary Schaub, Patricia Matthews, Sasha Miller, and Lyn McConchie.

The Wizard of Oz L. Frank Baum (1900)

This classic children's novel, first published as *The Wonderful Wizard of Oz,* was to dominate the career of L. Frank BAUM even as it has become one of the dominant books in children's literature. Although Baum wrote occasional children's fantasies not set in the land of Oz, some of them quite good, he never again achieved the success of Dorothy's first trip to Oz. He eventually wrote 13 full-length sequels and a handful of shorter pieces, expanding the lives of his characters as well as introducing new ones and exploring ever farther from the Emerald City.

The characters of the Cowardly Lion, the Scarecrow, and the Tin Woodman have become a part of our general cultural heritage, their images sharpened by the 1939 film version, which remained reasonably loyal to the book, although first-time readers who have seen the film version may be surprised at how much was invented for the screen. Dorothy arrives in Oz and is assigned a quest, to accomplish which she gathers a group of companions, a formula very familiar to adult fantasy readers. The color and liveliness of Oz is contrasted sharply to the desolation and dullness of

Kansas, Dorothy's home. The movie suggests that Oz may have been a dream, but the books make it clear that her adventures are genuine.

Baum's first sequel, *The Land of Oz* (1904), is one of the better ones, following the adventures of three human children in the land beyond the rainbow. *Ozma of Oz* (1907) introduced another recurring character, Princess Ozma, *Dorothy and the Wizard of Oz* (1908) takes the reader on a tour of an underground world, and *The Tin Woodman of Oz* (1981) follows the exploits of the Tin Woodman, who sets off on a journey of his own. Most of the rest of the books involve an attempt to conquer the Emerald City, usually by a rival king who is rather easily defeated.

Several other authors continued the series following Baum's death, the most prominent and prolific of whom was Ruth Plumly THOMPSON. Other Oz writers include Donald Abbott, Eric Shanower, John R. Neill, Jack Snow, David Hulan, and Robin Hess. At least two Oz novels have been intended for adults, *A Barnstormer in Oz* (1982), by Philip Jose Farmer, and *The Emerald Burrito of Oz* (2000), by John SKIPP and Mark Levinthal. Several films have been based at least in part on the Oz books, including *The Wizard of Mars* (1964), which moves the story to another planet, *The Wiz* (1978), a musical set in Harlem, and the very underappreciated *Return to Oz* (1985).

Wolfe, Gene (1931–)

Since Gene Wolfe's professional background is in engineering, it is not surprising that he has written a considerable body of science fiction, although in general he avoids dwelling on technology to such a degree that much of the science in his science fiction also feels very much like magic. Although he was selling regularly as early as the mid-1960s, his first significant fantasy did not appear until a decade later. *Peace* (1975) is an ambiguous, nonlinear narrative that is cast in the form of the posthumous memoirs of a man responsible for multiple murders who appears to be haunting a house, although that is never explicitly stated. *The Devil in a Forest* (1977), for young adults, is similarly light on fantasy, written as a murder mystery in a medieval setting. *Free Live Free* (1984) is more clearly fantastic, involving time travel and self-redemption, but as is the case with almost everything Wolfe writes, the treatment is unique, the prose distinctive, and the plot intricate and subtle.

Wolfe next wrote a fantasy duo that is similarly unconventional, *Soldier of the Mist* (1986) and *Soldier of Arete* (1989), published together as *Latro in the Mist* (2003). The setting is ancient Greece. Latro is a soldier, but in the opening volume he has lost all of his memory earlier than the previous day. He has a number of adventures spread across the Mediterranean world, during which he has authentic visions of gods and ghosts and proves himself to be a genuine hero, although Wolfe rarely dwells on the physical heroics. *There Are Doors* (1988) is closer to mainstream fantasy. The protagonist encounters and falls in love with a goddess from another reality and pursues her, having various adventures. *Castleview* (1990) is a contemporary fantasy in which the world of the fairies is sometimes accessible to humans. The strength of these last two in particular is in the prose and the author's gift for creating exotic images and unusual characters. Wolfe's most recent book-length fantasy is another duo, *The Knight* (2004) and *The Wizard* (2004), actually a single novel in two volumes. A young boy wakens to find himself in the body of a mature warrior in a fantasy world. The dichotomy is resolved through a series of almost lyrical encounters and adventures.

Wolfe has moved significantly away from science fiction and toward fantasy during the past decade in short fiction as well as novels. *Innocents Aboard* (2004) brought together much of his short fantasy, including fine tales such as "A Traveler in Desert Lands" (1999) and "A Pocket Full of Diamonds" (2000), but many more excellent stories remain uncollected. His prose is often difficult for casual readers, although a careful reading is almost always suitably rewarded. He is certainly one of the most distinctive stylists working in fantasy today, and if he is not frequently imitated it is because the bar is set dauntingly high.

Wolfen Whitley Strieber (1978)

Whitley STRIEBER's debut horror novel relied in part on misdirection, because the title and some of the early events strongly suggest that the danger comes from one or more werewolves living in a rundown section of a major city. When two people are viciously attacked and killed and their bodies mutilated, a massive police investigation is launched, but from the outset we know that this is not going to be a smooth operation, that there are internal conflicts and departmental rivalries and intrigues that are going to hamper progress.

As if the situation is not bad enough, the detective George Wilson is distracted by his relationship with a younger woman, Becky Neff, also a detective, who is married to another police officer currently suspended because of a suspicion of corruption. Wilson eventually begins to believe that there is something extraordinary going on, something less prosaic than an insane killer, and his investigation eventually leads to the revelation that the wolfen—wolves with an intelligence equal or superior to humans and the ability to move with blinding speed—have secretly been living in small colonies since prehistory, hidden from humans because of their almost supernatural abilities and their resemblance to wolves. They seek prey among the homeless, mentally ill, and unwary, killing and eating their victims and hiding the bodies. Since the ones they choose are rarely missed, they avoid the kind of attention that would have been generated by killing others, a choice that recent events appear to contradict. They have also moved into the cities because, paradoxically, they are better able to survive there, where many potential victims exist, than in the countryside, where their appearance might otherwise put them at a disadvantage.

The tension begins to build when the detectives discover the truth, because now they are the hunted rather than the hunters. Naturally, they are unable to convince anyone else that they are right. The wolfen are determined to protect the secret of their existence, but their pursuit ends with a surprising twist. The movie version in 1981 was only intermittently loyal to the original book, although it contains several very evocative scenes that capture some of the sense of awe that Strieber meant the reader to feel for the wolfen. Although he would become more technically able as his career progressed, Strieber was never able to duplicate the impact of his first novel.

"The Woman Who Loved the Moon"
Elizabeth A. Lynn (1981)

Although Elizabeth LYNN is not one of the most pro-lific fantasy writers, her work is highly regarded in the field, and she has won two World Fantasy Awards, for the novel *Watchtower* (1981) and for this short story. Lynn's work often contains a very strong feminist viewpoint, although she never allows the subtext to overpower her story's entertainment value. This particular story, which has very much the flavor of a classic fairy tale, is no exception.

Kai Talvela is one of three sisters from Issho who have trained themselves as fearless and feared warriors, each specializing in a different weapon. They would normally have many suitors, for they are all beautiful, but each has vowed never to marry a man who cannot best them with their particular chosen weapon. Since each is unsurpassed, they keep mostly their own company. Although they are not particularly boastful, others speak freely about their beauty, insisting that even the moon pales in comparison, a challenge to the gods not unlike those sprinkled through Greek mythology.

One day they encounter a stranger, another female warrior who identifies herself as Sedi. When one of the sisters challenges her to a friendly match with quarterstaffs, the others expect her to win as she always does. Surprisingly, she not only loses but receives a blow that wreaks such internal damage that she dies within the day. A year passes, the surviving sisters encounter Sedi again, the second sister challenges her with spears, and within the hour she is lying dead on the ground. Only Kai is left, and it is she who learns the truth, that Sedi is actually a personification of the moon, incarnated on Earth because she was offended by her unfavorable comparison to the sisters.

Kai sets off to find Sedi, resigned to her own death, but this time the outcome is different. Sedi falls in love with Kai and allows her to win, and the two become lovers, living isolated in time from the rest of the world. When Kai finally decides that she wishes to see her family, only her mother is still alive, a very elderly woman, although Kai herself has not aged during the 50 years that have passed. Sedi reluctantly allows her to leave, and Kai returns. Her mother dies, and she finds herself alone among a people she does not know and who are nervous in her presence. Her loyalty is proved, however, because even after she herself dies her ghost returns periodically to help protect the people of Issho. Lynn packs a surprisingly large amount of story into relatively few words and describes complex interpersonal relationships economically and with a feeling of genuine emotion.

"The Women of the Woods" A. Merritt
(1924)

Abraham MERRITT was the author of a half dozen of the best early fantasy adventures, most of them novels about lost civilizations. He rarely wrote short fiction. Most of it was relatively minor, but at least one of his stories is powerful enough to rank with his novels. The story is told from the point of view of McKay, an ex-airman recovering from trauma experienced during the recently ended war. He is vacationing in a rural part of Europe, a mostly forested region with a small inn and, nearby, the decaying lodge of the Polleau family, a father and two grown sons.

McKay loves the trees, particularly those in one region where they seem to have human personalities and where he experiences visions of them as men and women, and he sometimes believes that they speak to him, that they are seeking his help. He also notices that the Polleaus are systematically destroying the trees, either by cutting or burning, and realizes in time that there is an animosity between the family and the forest that he openly compares to warfare. In fact, one might interpret his visions as illusions brought on by his disturbed mental state.

The situation escalates quickly. While cutting down a tree in McKay's favorite area, one of the Polleau sons is hit by a stray branch and loses an eye. Spectral women, manifestations of the trees, urge McKay to kill the woodcutters, but he recoils from that idea and instead attempts to purchase that portion of their land that is most precious to him in order to keep the trees safe. The Polleaus refuse, the patriarch openly asserts that McKay is under the influence of the trees, and eventually McKay is goaded into killing one of the sons. His guilt is concealed by a fallen tree that wipes out the family and disguises the fatal wound, but the innkeeper suspects something of the truth and asks him to leave.

The story is of interest because none of the parties involved is entirely evil or entirely guiltless, and the analogy to warfare is strong. The age-long enmity between the Polleaus and the forest has become a reason in itself for their continuing struggle, and McKay's reluctance to participate mirrors the acquiescence of soldiers in a conflict that may not directly concern them.

The World of Darkness Series

Although there are many shared world universes for fantasy game players, most based on role-playing games such as WARHAMMER, FORGOTTEN REALMS, and DRAGONLANCE, the same is not true for horror fiction. By their very nature, horror stories are not usually amenable to becoming parts of series, even within the output of single writers, because normally either the evil or the protagonist is vanquished in the end. Those that do exist are usually based on movies or television shows such as *Buffy, the Vampire Slayer, Angel, Charmed,* and *The Crow.* The one exception to this rule has been the World of Darkness series from White Wolf, although even in this case the treatment of the novels, despite the inclusion of vampires, werewolves, and other supernatural creatures, is more that of fantasy than horror.

The central premise of the World of Darkness is that vampires, werewolves, and other supernatural creatures exist in our world and have since historic times, hidden from us and living in their own elaborate societies. They are neither all evil nor all good, and there are frequent tensions and battles among their factions, which are generally arranged in tribes or clans. Some of the novels are set in the past, most notably a trilogy set in Victorian Europe by Philippe Boulle consisting of *A Morbid Initiation* (2002), *The Wounded King* (2003), and *The Madness of Priests* (2003), which features vampires as well as a coven of evil sorcerers, but most have a contemporary, urban setting.

As with most fantasy tie-in series, the novels are written primarily by authors who specialize in that setting or who write otherwise only in similarly constructed shared universes. The World of Darkness has attracted several writers who have proved successful outside the genre, including Edo Van Belkom, David Niall Wilson, Richard Lee Byers, Scott Ciencin, James Moore, Tim Waggoner, and Owl GOINGBACK, although they are generally newer or young writers just beginning to establish themselves. The best single World of Darkness novel is *Beyond the Shroud* (1996), by Rick HAUTALA, an atypical story in which a man visits the land of the dead and a novel that may not originally have been written for this market at all. A large subset of books is named after specific vampire clans, including *Ventrue* (1999), by Gerhod Fleming, *Tremere* (2004), by Sarah Roark, and *Lasombra* (1999), by Richard Dansky, but the individual titles vary considerably in quality and not widely in plot. They do not need to be read in any particular order.

There have also been several anthologies of stories using the same general setting. Like other shared world universes, the restrictions imposed by the frame create something of a handicap for the writers, but in this case they are loose enough that there remains the potential for original and more impressive work in the future.

The Worm Ouroboros E. R. Eddison (1922)

The least-remembered of the British academics who wrote fantasy novels during the middle of the 20th century is E. R. EDDISON, known to J. R. R. TOLKIEN and C. S. LEWIS and in many ways their literary superior. Eddison's masterpiece is *The Worm Ouroboros,* an unusual epic fantasy, although his other three fantasy novels, a loosely organized trilogy, are distantly related. The frame story for *Worm* is awkward and is dropped after the opening chapter, in which the observer, Lessingham, is magically transported to the planet Mercury, where all of the action is theoretically set.

The world is divided into nations, Demonland, Pixyland, Impland, and so forth, although the inhabitants are all human, and the names are essentially meaningless except to distinguish one from the other. Witchland is the major power but is ethically compromised, while Demonland is home to most of the heroes and is clearly morally superior. When the witches attempt to subjugate the demons, the dispute is decided by a physical contest in which the king of the witches is killed, although he is immediately restored to life in his homeland. He then uses magic to defeat and scatter the demons, who must rescue their missing champion if they are to have any hope of regaining their freedom. They eventually do so, but only after considerable trouble, and when they finally defeat the witches, they are saddened at the prospect of no further heroic deeds. The gods therefore cause the situation to revert to its original state, hence the title, which refers to the snake that devours its own tale.

The associated trilogy consists of *Mistress of Mistresses* (1935), *A Fish Dinner in Memison* (1941), and the unfinished *The Mezentian Gate* (1958). The setting is Zimiamvia, which is referred to in passing in *Worm*. Lessingham dies and is reborn there as adviser to one of the parties striving for the throne. Although there is significant magic—visions, shape-changing, and a kind of time travel—it is primarily a novel of intrigue and court politics. The second title is actually a prequel in which the king still lives and has the magical ability to create other worlds, including the one in which Lessingham originates. The final title, though incomplete, is readable thanks to detailed summaries that Eddison had written. The story starts even earlier but concludes with the death of the king.

It would be a mistake to dismiss the books as typical heroic fantasy. Eddison's use of language is superb, and his ability to create a large cast of fascinating characters is almost unequalled in fantasy fiction. The physical action may be too slow-paced for casual readers, but the many-leveled text rewards those who devote sufficient effort.

Wrede, Patricia (1953–)

Some writers establish a pattern with their first book and rarely vary from it, while others tend to diversify as they grow more experienced. Patricia Wrede falls somewhere in between, because her books have steadily improved in quality while only slowly evolving in scope and theme. She made her debut with *Shadow Magic* (1982), which introduced the world of Lyra and its inhabitants. As is the case

in most of her novels, the protagonist is female, a young woman who discovers that the myths of that country have begun to take on a form of reality. *Daughter of Witches* (1984) is a somewhat similar adventure concerning a city that allows everyone to enter, but is picky about whom it chooses to let depart. A young witch discovers that magic has both its good and bad sides. *The Seven Towers* (1984), not set in Lyra, is relatively uninteresting, but *The Harp of Imach Thyssel* (1985) is a very fine story about a man who finds a magic harp and then discovers that it is a very mixed blessing. *Caught in Crystal* (1987) continues the darker tone, with a mysterious entity stirring to wakefulness after a long sleep, but Wrede waited several years before returning to Lyra for *The Raven Ring* (1994), a stirring but imitative quest story.

Talking to Dragons (1985) is for young readers and is basically a coming-of-age story with a boy taking a legendary sword and facing various dangers in an enchanted forest. In many ways it is much more effective than Wrede's adult novels, and she later wrote a three-volume prequel, *Dealing with Dragons* (1990, also published as *Dragonsbane*), *Searching for Dragons* (1991, also published as *Dragon Search*), and *Calling on Dragons* (1993). The trilogy is lighter in tone than the first novel. Wrede also produced an admirable version of Snow White and the Seven Dwarves in *Snow White and Rose Red* (1989), ostensibly for adults but actually accessible to all reading levels.

Mairelon the Magician (1991) is a fairy tale set in Regency England, drawn from traditional plots and themes but developed in an unpredictable and very rewarding fashion. It was with this novel and another sharing the same setting, *The Magician's Ward* (1997), that Wrede proved she could be a formidable addition to the roster of contemporary fantasy writers. Both novels demonstrate her growing skill and self-confidence. Wrede also collaborated with Caroline Stevermer for two other books set in a magical alternate Regency England. *Sorcery and Cecilia* (1888) is a superior young adult fantasy, and the long-delayed sequel, *The Grand Tour* (2004), is even better, one of the best young adult novels of the past 10 years, with the protagonists foiling a plot to magically seize control of all of Europe.

Unfortunately, just as Wrede began to be recognized for her considerable talents, she also became much less productive. Other than "Stronger Than Time" (1994), most of her short fiction has been minor, usually set in worlds shared with other writers. Her only collection is *Book of Enchantments* (1996).

Wright, T. M. (1947–   )

The premise of most of T. M. Wright's novels is that the world as we know it conceals secrets that only occasionally surface, but when they do those who perceive the underlying truth are forever changed. He established this with his first novel, *Strange Seed* (1978), whose protagonist is newly married and lives in a house surrounded by dense woods. To her dismay her husband begins to retreat into his own interior world at the same time that she begins to catch glimpses of mysterious children playing in the woods, except she is not entirely sure that they really are children. Wright added two loose sequels. The site of the first novel has been cleared and turned into a housing project in *Nursery Tale* (1982). One of the new tenants is a woman who experiences a series of visions, including some involving ghosts, which she initially believes to be illusions brought on by her pregnancy. When the neighbors' children begin to disappear, one of the ghosts reveals the truth, that they were victims of an inhuman race to whom the area is sacred. *The Children of the Island* (1983) is even more explicit. The childlike figures are actually the remnants of an ancient race that lived in Manhattan whose survivors have concealed themselves from humanity for generations.

The Woman Next Door (1981) is similarly unsettling. Another happily married woman notices that people near her have been changing ever since a new neighbor moved in. Her son's imaginary playmate has become more aggressive, her husband has started acting flirtatiously with other women, and the new neighbor seems to know things she could not possibly have learned in the normal course of things. Wright seemed content to reshuffle similar images and themes for his next few novels as well. *The Playground* (1982) involves evil children, real ones this time, in this case possessed by demons after some of the adults in the area unwisely experimented with the occult. *Carlisle Street* (1983) also involves ghostly children, but Wright seemed to have exhausted the possible variations of his usual theme, and after a strong opening, the novel wanders awkwardly toward its ending. On the other hand, *A Manhattan Ghost Story* (1984) is remarkably effective, one of his best novels, placing enigmatic ghosts in an urban setting and avoiding most of the clichés of that form. *The Waiting Room* (1986), which has a very similar theme, is even better and is still his single most impressive work. One of the characters inadvertently crosses the border between the living and the dead, although still alive, and seeks help in order to return fully to the world of the living.

Wright employed more conventional themes for some of his novels during this period, producing competent but unmemorable stories such as *The People of the Dark* (1985), which involves another haunted place, and two werewolf novels under the name F. W. Armstrong, *The Changing* (1985) and *The Devouring* (1987). The first of these innovatively has the creature choosing his victims from among the members of middle management, but the treatment is otherwise conventional. *Island* (1988) is another story of a bad place, in this case a remote lake. *The Place* (1989), his weakest novel, involves a standard serial killer and a potential victim who is psychically linked to him.

His next novel was more experimental, a trend that has continued. In *Boundaries* (1990), the protagonist is robbed of closure when the murderer of his sister commits suicide. Determined to discover what caused her death, he uses an experimental drug to penetrate into the land of the dead. Wright used the same concept in reverse for *Goodlow's Ghosts* (1993), in which a murdered man's spirit returns to solve the mystery of his own death. *The School* (1990) is something of a return to his beginning, following the efforts of two people to reopen a school that is haunted by the ghosts of children.

The Last Vampire (1991) is not entirely successful but has an interesting concept. A vampire 50 years from now, reflects on the possibility that he may be the last of his kind in a world of humans. *Little Boy Lost* (1992) is a somewhat murky novel about an archaeologist whose family undergoes a supernatural transformation. *The Ascending* (1994) initially appears to be a variation of *The Place*, with the protagonist psychically linked to a killer, but changes direction when we discover that the killer's original personality has been supplanted.

Possibly due to the decline of the horror market in the 1990s, Wright fell silent for seven years and has only recently returned with a spate of new novels. *Sleapeasy* (2001) is stranger than any of his previous work. Its main character dies and wakens in a new life, cast in the role of a private detective in a world not quite our own. *The House on Orchid Street* (2003) resembles his earlier novels, the story of a house that is somehow supernaturally connected to a series of murders in the past. A police officer with an affinity for the dead draws upon that resource in *Laughing Man* (2003), and ghostly lovers meet in *Cold House* (2003). It does not seem likely that Wright will ever write a best-selling horror novel because his plots tend not to be completely straightforward and linear, and most of his horrors are very subtle and understated. He does have a very strong following among hard-core horror fans, in part because he provides such a clear alternative to the more homogenized mainstream horror.

Wurts, Janny (1953–   )

The fantasy artist Janny Wurts's first novel, *Sorcerer's Legacy* (1982), is a very traditional high-fantasy novel in which a woman is rescued from the dungeons by a sorcerer but later finds herself on her own, caught in the middle of familiar court intrigues and magical schemes. Although the plot is occasionally awkwardly constructed, there are sections that move quite well. Her next project was much more ambitious and better constructed, however, the Cycle of Fire trilogy consisting of *Stormwarden* (1984). *Keeper of the Keys* (1988), and *Shadowfane* (1988). A sorcerer is accused of a terrible crime and gains limited freedom at the behest of a sorceress, who enlists him in her campaign to rid the world of a variety of demon that preys upon humans. As the story progresses Wurts introduces

elements borrowed from science fiction and implies that the magic is a form of mental power acquired by merging with unusual crystals, brought to this planet by an alien race. The demons are aliens as well and must be stopped before they continue their plans of expansion and conquer all of humanity. Despite the attempts to rationalize the situation, which is reminiscent of *The Storm Lord* (1976), by Tanith LEE, the trilogy is clearly fantasy by intent.

The Master of White Storm (1992) is an episodic adventure that reads more like a collection of linked stories, culminating in the construction of a daunting castle. Wurts does a much better job of characterization, however, possibly having learned from her experience coauthoring a trilogy with Raymond E. FEIST, *Daughter of the Empire* (1987), *Servant of the Empire* (1990), and *Mistress of the Empire* (1992). Her growing willingness to explore the personalities of her characters is even more evident in her next, *The Curse of the Mistwraith* (1993), the first part of the Wars of Light and Shadow. Two rival princes are forced to put aside their personal rivalries to combine arms against a supernatural creature that threatens their world. The sequel, *The Ships of Merior* (1995), is so large that it is sometimes split into two titles, the second part as *Warhost of Vastmark* (1995). Although the mistwraith was destroyed, its legacy is a magical curse that causes the two allies to become violently disposed toward each other, throwing the world into war. Their animosity spills over into other domains and threatens the entire world in *Fugitive Prince* (1997). The climax came in *Grand Conspiracy* (2000).

Wurts's most recent novel, *To Ride Hell's Chasm* (2002), is a competently told but overly familiar quest story. Her short fiction is generally slight, and the best of her fantasy stories are contained in *That Way Lies Camelot* (1994), although many of the stories are science fiction. In general, Wurts has proved to be a competent writer whose better work suggests she may be capable of more serious endeavors but who has yet to produce a book that will separate her prominently from her peers.

"Xelucha" **M. P. Shiel** (1896)

Matthew Phipps Shiel was a prolific British writer whose most famous work, *The Purple Cloud* (1901), is usually regarded as science fiction despite its metaphysical theme. This became more evident in the film version, *The World, The Flesh, and the Devil* (1959), which strayed considerably from the original story. Shiel wrote in a number of genres, including a considerable number of supernatural stories, of which his best known is "Xelucha," which deals with a sort of universal female principle.

The narrator is Merimee, a man who admits freely to living the life of a sybarite. He sleeps by day and wanders through London at night, enjoying clubs and parties, usually under the influence of drugs or strong drink and often accompanied by women of low repute. Merimee has recently been disturbed by the death of a long-time friend, Cosmo, whose final letter brings to mind a woman named Xelucha who died of cholera some 10 years earlier. Merimee had been romantically involved with Xelucha for some time, although he no longer remembers her face but does recall that she had seemed to him the epitome of feminity. He does remember her personality, which was unusually assertive and flamboyant. Merimee also ponders the statement that "vitality is not material," not realiz-

ing how it will soon be brought home to him with great force.

One night he is wandering alone when he encounters a mysterious, attractive woman who invites him to her apartment for a sumptuous feast and vintage wine. She offers no name and will not let him touch her even fleetingly. When they arrive the food and drink are excellent, but she refrains from taking any herself, instead engaging Merimee in a sometimes abstruse philosophical discussion in which she claims that creation is a function of will, that he knows far less than he believes he does, and that the true torment of hell is the constant envy of those who remain in the land of the living.

It is late in the argument when Merimee notices that the woman's clothing has unaccountably changed. The woman then identifies herself as Xelucha, or at least her spirit. When Merimee tries to grasp her she vanishes in a puff of filth and fetid odors, and he collapses and loses consciousness. When he recovers he finds the room filthy and disorderly and realizes the fineries and the refreshments were all an illusion. Technically speaking, "Xelucha" is a ghost story, but the presence who used that name is more a generic amalgamation of the souls of collective womanhood than of any particular individual.

Yarbro, Chelsea Quinn (1942–)

There is no question that the work for which Chelsea Quinn Yarbro is best known is her SAINT GERMAIN vampire series, which began with *Hotel Transylvania* (1978) and continues today. Saint Germain is a benevolent vampire, an intellectual who deplores cruelty and takes blood without killing, usually concealing his true nature and living as a productive member of society. Each novel takes place in a different historical period, and the stories are as much about the times and places as they are about the vampire, whose special condition is sometimes irrelevant to the plot. In this series as well as in her other fantasy and supernatural fiction, Yarbro often underlines the violence and cruelty that dominate our history, and her characters sometimes seem to accept their travails as just a necessary part of life rather than as wrongdoing.

Yarbro began writing professionally in the late 1960s, and most of her work for the next 10 years was science fiction or detective stories. Her first nonseries horror novel was an adaptation of the film *Dead and Buried* (1980), in which a renegade coroner finds a way to restore the dead to life and turns an entire community into zombies. She later novelized another horror film, *Nomads* (1984). Her next, *Sins of Omission* (1980), in which a woman struggles to control her psychic abilities, is murky and slow paced. It was her last attempt to write book-length contemporary horror for seven years.

The Godforsaken (1983) attempts to adapt the Saint Germain formula to werewolves, in this case suggesting that the condition is caused by a curse during the age of the Spanish Inquisition. The lack of a likable protagonist and a sometimes slow-moving plot weaken the novel considerably, and her next historical horror novel, *A Mortal Glamour* (1985), set in a 14th-century convent, is only marginally more interesting. Yarbro returned to a contemporary setting with *Fire Code* (1987), in which a supernatural entity equivalent to a basilisk is set free to attack and destroy using the power of fire. It is one of Yarbro's fastest paced novels and considerably better than her other nonvampire supernatural fiction.

Yarbro devoted most of her writing time to Saint Germain during the 1990s but eventually tried another historical horror novel. *The Angry Angel* (1998) is the origin story of one of Dracula's wives, describing a young girl's reaction to a disembodied voice that she initially believes to be that of an angel, although she later has reservations. *Soul of an Angel* (1999) similarly describes the fate of an aristocratic young woman who flees from her family to avoid an arranged marriage and falls under the influence of Count Dracula.

Yarbro's first fantasy novel was *To the High Redoubt* (1985), a typical magical world adventure in which a young woman discovers, with mixed feelings, that she possesses the potential to be a sorceress. *A Baroque Fable* (1986) is a complete change of pace, a lightly humorous fantasy that includes several of the usual devices, including a troublesome dragon, a feisty young woman, and a wizard who is not entirely in control of his spells. *Dark Light* (1999) is standard sword and sorcery fare, although the vampire magician protagonist is an interesting character. Her two best fantasy novels are *Monet's Ghost* (1997), in which a teenager receives the power to physically enter the worlds depicted in paintings, and *Ariosto* (1980), based in part on *Orlando Furioso* (1516) by Ariosto, an epic poem, although in this case the hero has visions of himself in a future America.

A good selection of Yarbro's short supernatural fiction appeared as *Signs and Portents* (1986). *Apprehensions and Other Delusions* (2003) is more slanted toward fantasy. "The Creatures That Walked in Darkness" (1993) and "In the Face of Death" (2000) are among her very best at that length, as is "The Spider Glass" (1991), a Saint Germain story. No other writer of fantasy or horror has used settings from so many different times, places, and cultures. Although the results have not been uniformly successful, the majority, particularly the vampire novels, succeed in making their settings and characters come to life.

"The Yellow Wallpaper" Charlotte Perkins Gilman (1890)

The early feminist author Charlotte Perkins Gilman, author of one of the first feminist utopian novels, *Herland* (1914), wrote very little fantasy or horror fiction, but one of her few short horror tales has been an acknowledged classic almost from the time of its first publication. It is story like "WILLIAM WILSON" (1840) by Edgar Allan POE that concentrates so completely on the psychology of the narrator-protagonist that the events described could be either supernatural or delusional.

The narrator in this case is a woman married to a domineering physician who insists that she suffers from a nervous condition and micromanages her life to such an extent that she barely has one. They have temporarily rented a house and are sleeping in a former nursery decorated with yellow wallpaper that she initially finds hideous and vaguely disturbing because of its odd pattern but that later fascinates her. There is evidence that the former residents found the paper equally upsetting, which is the closest we have to actual proof that something paranormal is taking place. The house is run by her sister-in-law, who even takes care of

their infant child, and she is forbidden even the strain of writing, although the present account proves that she does so when unobserved.

The first hint we receive that something is wrong is that she sees people from her window who are clearly invisible to everyone else, although even she admits she may be daydreaming. The wallpaper becomes an increasing obsession, particularly when she begins to perceive the pattern as bars that restrain the spirit of an unknown woman, who can only escape in the darkness but must return at sunrise. Determined to solve the pattern and free the prisoner, she becomes increasingly introverted, develops paranoid feelings toward the other people in the house, and finally locks herself in her room. She strips the last of the paper from the wall and then informs her husband that she is now the woman from behind the pattern.

The symbolism is very obvious. Trapped in her own life by the pattern imposed by her husband, she "escapes" through a series of rebellious acts. Whether this breakdown was inherent in her situation or whether the wallpaper possessed some latent power to influence the mind of the living is left to the reader's interpretation.

Yolen, Jane (1939–)

Jane Yolen is something of a publishing phenomenon, particularly in children's literature, although she has also proven her ability to write for adults with equal skill. Since starting her career in the 1960s, she has published more than 100 books, many of them fantasy, but also in several other areas, including poetry, picture books, nonfiction, and science fiction. The publisher Harcourt Brace established the Jane Yolen Books imprint for several years, under which name she published a number of overlooked fantasies by other writers. She also edited the short-lived but highly respected Xanadu series of original anthologies of fantasy short stories during the 1990s as well as several other collections.

The border between Yolen's adult and young adult novels is not always clear, and even some of her children's books appeal to much older readers. Her best novel is *Briar Rose* (1992), which is only marginally fantasy. She used the basic situation of the classic fairy tale Sleeping Beauty and recast it in rationalized form, set during the days of the Holocaust in Nazi-dominated Europe. She used a very similar setting for a young adult novel that also highlights the horrors of that age, *The Devil's Arithmetic* (1988), which involves time travel. *Cards of Grief* (1984) also mixes genres, in this case using a world where magic works as background and introducing outsiders in the form of curious visitors from another planet.

Sister Light, Sister Dark (1988) addresses a very powerful theme. The young protagonist believes that she is fated to become a sort of messiah for her people, a future that is daunting as well as flattering, although the reader might suspect that she is simply being fooled by a series of coincidences. Her life becomes far more complex and dangerous, and the issue is not resolved until the sequel, *White Jenna* (1989), the two books later combined as *The Book of Great Alta* (1990). After several years Yolen added a third volume, *The One-Armed Queen* (1998), in which Jenna's hold on the throne is troubled not only by rival political factions and outside interests but by her own restless children.

Other novels of interest to older readers include *The Magic Three of Solatia* (1974), which consists of four related stories wherein various characters learn how to control magical powers, and *Merlin's Book* (1986), a collection of stories in an Arthurian vein although mostly dealing with Merlin. Yolen also made use of the legend of Merlin for children in her Young Merlin trilogy, which includes *Passager* (1996), *Hobby* (1996), and *Merlin* (1997), as well as in *The Dragon's Boy* (1990) and *Merlin and the Dragons* (1997). *The Mermaid's Three Wisdoms* (1978) is a touching story about a deaf girl who makes friends with a mermaid. *Neptune Rising* (1982) is a collection of stories and poems about "merpeople" and the sea and contains some of her most memorable tales. One of her darker stories is *The Wild Hunt* (1995), set in a fantasy realm that is dominated by fear of a band of mysterious huntsmen.

Most of her children's books can also prove rewarding for a wider range of readers. Yolen has a genuine flair for fairy tales, and whether she is retelling old favorites or creating new ones, there is always a sense of authenticity about her worlds and

their characters. Some of her best include a series of collections of stories and poems on specific fantastic subjects, starting with *Here There Be Dragons* (1993), followed by *Here There Be Unicorns* (1994), *Here There Be Witches* (1995), and *Here There Be Angels* (1996), each of which mixes prose and verse. *Twelve Impossible Things before Breakfast* (1997) is one of the best of her many collections of short stories.

The Tartan Magic series includes *The Wizard's Map* (1999), *The Pictish Child* (1999), and *The Bagpiper's Ghost* (2002), in which children visiting in Scotland find a magic deck of cards that connects them to a sorcerer from another age. Other titles of particular merit are *The Transfigured Hart* (1975) and *Wings* (1991), which retells the story of Daedalus and Icarus. Her recent *Sword of the Rightful King* (2003) is another return to the world of King Arthur and Camelot. Although Yolen is clearly best known as a writer for children, she has a large and loyal following among readers of all ages and is one of the most important names in contemporary fantasy.

"Yours Truly, Jack the Ripper" Robert Bloch (1943)

The real-life Jack the Ripper, who terrorized London in 1888, was undoubtedly a mortal person, but that has not prevented a number of writers from ascribing supernatural powers to him and placing him in a variety of situations and settings, even including an episode of the television series *Star Trek* and another episode in the world of *Babylon 5*. There have been entire anthologies of short stories featuring the London killer or very similar characters, including *The Harlot Killer*, edited by Allan Barnard (1953), *Red Jack*, edited by Martin Harry Greenberg, Charles Waugh, and Frank McSherry (1988), and *Ripper!*, edited by Gardner Dozois and Susan Casper (1988). Robert BLOCH, who also wrote a novel about the real incidents, *Night of the Ripper* (1984), is the author of the most famous short story about the most famous serial killer of all time.

The setting is contemporary Chicago. Sir Guy Hollis works at the British Embassy, but he is more interested in his life-long obsession, an effort to track down Jack the Ripper, who he believes is a sorcerer who murders his victims as part of a sacrifice to appease evil powers that grant him immortality in exchange. He consults the psychiatrist John Carmody, who initially doubts his sanity, because he believes that Carmody can provide an introduction into that milieu of Chicago society where the Ripper is most likely to conceal himself. Hollis has analyzed scores of killings in various locations and is convinced that the next Ripper murder will take place within two days somewhere in the city of Chicago.

Carmody reluctantly agrees, and the two attend a party where Hollis announces his intentions and invites the Ripper to kill him during a brief period when the lights are all turned off. There is no response, and Hollis grows increasingly concerned that he is wasting his time and will be too late to prevent another death. He and Carmody begin to drink, and Hollis reveals that he is descended from one of the Ripper's victims and that he will not be dissuaded from his goal. It is only then that Carmody realizes that Hollis will never become so discouraged that he will abandon his quest, so he kills him, revealing that he is, in fact, the Ripper and that the theory that he has been granted extended life is true. Perceptive readers might well have anticipated the ending despite some clever red herrings, but even having done so, the neat way in which Bloch ties everything together is impressive.

Z

Zelazny, Roger (1937–1995)

Roger Zelazny enjoyed an enviable reputation as a writer of both science fiction and fantasy, and the latter is dominated by the AMBER SERIES, two sets of five novels each involving the struggle among family members who rule an alternate reality known as Amber. The series began with *Nine Princes in Amber* (1969) and concluded with *Prince of Chaos* (1991), although it has been extended recently by John Gregory Betancourt. The popularity of the Amber novels has somewhat overshadowed Zelazny's other fantasy, some of which is equally well done.

Jack of Shadows (1971) was clearly inspired in part by the Dying Earth stories of Jack VANCE. In the very distant future the Earth has stopped rotating and is divided into two very different cultures, one ruled by magic and one by technology. Jack is a professional thief, a charmer, and a man with his own code of honor who is equally at ease on both sides of the demarcation line. Amber novels dominated the balance of the 1970s, but Zelazny ventured into new territory with *Changeling* (1980), which borrowed some of the plot elements from the first Amber novel and its sequel, *Madwand* (1981). A prince exiled to our world from another returns to reclaim his heritage despite the opposition of several wizards. Zelazny had also been writing a series of related short fantasies that were collected as *Dilvish the Damned* (1982). He proved that even the most familiar plot devices could be given a fresh look in *The Changing Land* (1981), in which a warrior who escaped from hell is caught between battling wizards in the land of the living.

During the latter half of the 1980s, Zelazny began writing the second series of Amber novels, and his other fantasies were relatively minor and mostly collaborations. *A Dark Traveling* (1987) is for young adults and features a pair of siblings, one a werewolf, the other a witch. *The Black Throne* (1990), written with Fred SABERHAGEN, uses Edgar Allan POE as its protagonist. *The Mask of Loki* (1990), with Thomas T. Thomas, draws on Norse mythology. Three titles written with Robert Sheckley are humorous: *Bring Me the Head of Prince Charming* (1991), *If at Faust You Don't Succeed* (1993), and *A Farce to Be Reckoned With* (1995), of which the first is the best. *Lord Demon* (1999), with Jane LINDSKOLD, is the story of a relatively benign demon living hidden within human society.

Zelazny's last solo fantasy novel was *A Night at the Lonesome October* (1993), a charming story of a Victorian-era tavern that is the gathering site for various magical characters. The plot is rather thin, but the varied characters interact cleverly and amusingly. "The Last Defender of Camelot" (1979) is his best single short fantasy. The posthumous collection *Manna from Heaven* (2003) contains several short fantasies, including some Amber material not included in the novels. "The Unicorn Variations" (1981) won a Nebula Award. Zelazny was one of the leading writers associated with the New Wave movement in science fiction during the 1960s and became one of the most popular new fantasy writers during the 1970s. The Amber novels in particular set a standard by which similar fantasy adventures are still measured.

Zettel, Sarah (1966–)

Although Sarah Zettel began writing stories for fantasy and horror markets as early as 1990, her first several novels were science fiction space adventures. It was not until 2002 that she turned to book-length fantasy. Her next four novels were all in that genre, however, and, like several other new writers, she now appears to have moved to the more lucrative fantasy market completely. *The Sorcerer's Treason* (2002) is the first in the Isavalta sequence, which draws heavily on Russian and Asian mythologies, and starts with Bridget, a woman from our reality having visions of another world and then encountering someone who claims to be from there who tells her she is destined to save that world. Although she is dubious, she is subsequently conveyed across the barrier between realities and only then learns that things are not entirely as she was led to believe. The magic system is unusual enough to be interesting in its own right, and the protagonist is well drawn, although the slow-moving plot in the opener is not a new one. There is a battle over the succession to the throne, various factions involved in the usual court politics, and two opposing sorcerers.

The pace picks up considerably in *Usurper's Crown* (2003), although much of the conflict is covert. Zettel adds a considerable dose of romance as the interloper from our world becomes involved with one of the sorcerers, but the focus remains on the battle to control the empress through argument or magic. The sequence comes to an apparent close with *The Firebird's Vengeance* (2004). Bridget discovers that her daughter, presumed dead, is very much alive, but her joy is balanced by the realization that this can be used as a weapon against her. Nevertheless, she sets out to search two realities in order to find her in an unusually well done quest adventure.

Zettel's commitment to fantasy appears to be ongoing. Her latest series began with *In Camelot's Shadow* (2004), in which a young girl is befriended by Sir Gawain and brought back to Camelot for safety and shelter. Unfortunately, unbeknownst to her, she is still under a spell of dark magic and is an innocent agent of a dark power seeking to undermine King Arthur's rule. The romantic elements are more obvious this time but never become sloppy or overly sentimental. In the sequel, *In Camelot's Honor* (2005), the battle spreads with the revelation that Morgaine is the motive force behind a plot against King Arthur and Camelot. Additional titles in this series seem to be a distinct possibility.

The following terms have specialized meanings within the horror or fantasy fields that may not be readily apparent.

alternate history Although alternate history stories are usually science fiction, some writers have recently begun to use settings that resemble our own world as it might have evolved if magic were real and if history had taken a different course at some time in the past. Examples are *Strange Cargo,* by Jeff Barlough, set in a world where the Ice Age never ended, and the Age of Unreason trilogy, by J. Gregory Keyes.

Cthulhu Mythos The partly rationalized supernatural backdrop of most of H. P. Lovecraft's best fiction. His basic premise was that the Earth was once ruled by loathsome aliens with near magical powers who were expelled to another universe but still seek to return and dominate humanity. A wide variety of authors have expanded on Lovecraft's original creation, including Brian Lumley, Fred Chappell, and Colin Wilson.

dark fantasy A term usually applied to stories that blend themes of fantasy and horror. The supernatural adventures of Laurell Hamilton, whose vampires are an accepted part of society in her alternate universe, are an example of dark fantasy. The term is sometimes expanded to include much or all of supernatural fiction, but it loses its utility when so applied.

high fantasy Fantasy novels set in another reality, possibly linked to ours, usually one where magic works. Society normally consists of nobles and warriors, kings and princes, castles and quests. The works of Robert Jordan, George R. R. Martin, and Terry Goodkind are typical high fantasy.

multiverse The concept that ours is just one of many universes, in some of which magic works, and among which travel may be possible through one means or another. The most detailed of these is the overall background for most of the individual fantasy series by Michael Moorcock, most of whose heroes are different manifestations of the same personality in different realities.

mythos A set of magical or supernatural rules that are used as the backdrop for a series of stories and/or novels by one or more authors. The best-known example is the Cthulhu mythos of H. P. Lovecraft. Most shared world series written by multiple authors employ some form of common mythos.

quest fantasy A story whose main plot requires that the protagonist accomplish one or more tasks, usually to retrieve a valuable object or rescue a prisoner. The most famous example is the Lord of the Rings trilogy by J. R. R. Tolkien, which varies the formula somewhat in that the quest in this case is to rid the protagonist of an object rather than to acquire it.

shape-changers Intelligent creatures who can magically alter their form into other shapes. Werewolves are shape-changers, but many others have wider ranging abilities. In fantasy fiction they are not necessarily inimical to humans. The Cheysuli in Jennifer Roberson's fantasy novels are a prime example. Also referred to as shape-shifters.

shared universe   A situation in which several authors write stories with a common setting, although usually not with any common characters, as distinguished from writers continuing or adding to a series by a deceased author. Shared universes are frequently collections of short stories, such as the Thieves' World series, edited by Robert Lynn Asprin and Lynn Abbey.

splatterpunk   A term applied to writers who specialize in visceral, erotic horror that employs shock and revulsion to evoke an emotional response. Writers generally associated with splatterpunk include John Skipp, Craig Spector, and Edward Lee.

steampunk   Stories usually set in Victorian England, or a variation of Victorian England, that often blend magic and science, such as in *Homunculus*, by James P. Blaylock, although some examples are science fiction rather than fantasy.

sword and sorcery   Originally applied to fantasy adventures set in a primitive world, sometimes prehistoric Earth, usually pitting barbarian heroes against evil sorcerers. The term is sometimes intended to include most contemporary fantasy using a quasi-medieval setting, i.e.,
swords rather than firearms, although most of this is more properly high fantasy. Robert E. Howard and Fritz Leiber are two of the most prominent writers of sword and sorcery.

tie-ins   Stories or novels written to fit into a story line or fantasy world created in another medium, such as television, movies, and most commonly role-playing games and computer games. The most obvious examples are the multiauthor Dragonlance, Forgotten Realms, and Warhammer novel series. They should be distinguished from novelizations, which adapt a movie or television script into book form.

timeslip   Most commonly romance novels in which a character from our era is transported by some magical means back to an earlier period. Sometimes used in reverse, with a person from the past magically carried forward to the present. The most famous of these is the Voyager series by Diana Gabaldon.

urban fantasy   Although technically any fantasy novel set within a city, the term is more properly applied to stories in which our world overlaps at one or more points with that of a fantasy realm, these points located within a major city populated by elves and fairies who sometimes cross the border. One of the earliest and most influential was *War for the Oaks* by Emma Bull.

BRAM STOKER AWARD WINNERS

These are given annually by members of the Horror Writers' Association and include some titles that are crime or suspense but contain no fantastic elements.

1987

Novel: Misery by Stephen King tied with *Swan Song* by Robert R. McCammon

First Novel: The Manse by Lisa Cantrell

Long Fiction: The Pear Shaped Man by George R. R. Martin tied with *Dead* by Alan Rodgers

Short Fiction: "The Deep End" by Robert R. McCammon

Collection: The Essential Ellison by Harlan Ellison

1988

Novel: The Silence of the Lambs by Thomas Harris

First Novel: The Suiting by Kelley Wilde

Long Fiction: Orange Is for Anguish, Blue for Insanity by David Morrell

Short Fiction: "The Night They Missed the Horror Show" by Joe R. Lansdale

Collection: Charles Beaumont: Selected Stories by Charles Beaumont

1989

Novel: Carrion Comfort by Dan Simmons

First Novel: Sunglasses after Dark by Nancy Collins

Long Fiction: With Dead Folks by Joe R. Lansdale

Short Fiction: "Eat Me" by Robert R. McCammon

Collection: Collected Stories by Richard Matheson

1990

Novel: Mine by Robert R. McCammon

First Novel: The Revelation by Bentley Little

Long Fiction: Stephen by Elizabeth Massie

Short Fiction: "The Calling" by David B. Silva

Collection: Four Past Midnight by Stephen King

1991

Novel: Boy's Life by Robert R. McCammon

First Novel: The Cipher by Kathe Koja tied with *Prodigal* by Melanie Tem

Long Fiction: The Beautiful Uncut Hair of Graves by David Morrell

Short Fiction: "Lady Madonna" by Nancy Holder

Collection: Prayers to Broken Stones by Dan Simmons

1992

Novel: Blood of the Lamb by Thomas F. Monteleone

First Novel: Sineater by Elizabeth Massie

Long Fiction: Aliens: Tribes by Stephen Bissette tied with *Found in a Harlequin Romance* by Joe R. Lansdale

Short Fiction: "This Year's Class Picture" by Dan Simmons

Collection: Mr. Fox and Other Feral Tales by Norman Partridge

1993

Novel: The Throat by Peter Straub

First Novel: The Thread That Binds the Bones by Nina Kiriki Hoffman

Novella: Mephisto in Onyx by Harlan Ellison tied with *The Night We Buried Road Dog* by Jack Cady

Novelet: Dying in Bangkok by Dan Simmons

Short Fiction: "I Hear the Mermaids Singing" by Nancy Holder

Collection: Alone with the Horrors by Ramsey Campbell

1994

Novel: Dead in the Water by Nancy Holder
First Novel: Grave Markings by Michael A. Arnzen
Long Fiction: The Scent of Vinegar by Robert Bloch
Short Fiction: "Cafe Endless: Spring Rain" by Nancy Holder
Collection: The Early Fears by Robert Bloch

1995

Novel: Zombie by Joyce Carol Oates
First Novel: The Safety of Unknown Cities by Lucy Taylor
Long Fiction: Lunch at the Gotham Cafe by Stephen King
Short Fiction: "Chatting with Anubis" by Harlan Ellison
Collection: The Panic Hand by Jonathan Carroll

1996

Novel: The Green Mile by Stephen King
First Novel: Crota by Owl Goingback
Long Fiction: The Red Tower by Thomas Ligotti
Short Fiction: "Metallica" by P. D. Cacek
Collection: The Nightmare Factor by Thomas Ligotti

1997

Novel: Children of the Dust by Janet Berliner and George Guthman
First Novel: Lives of the Monster Dogs by Kirsten Bakis
Long Fiction: The Big Blow by Joe R. Lansdale
Short Fiction: "Rat Food" by Edo van Belkom and David Nickle
Collection: Exorcisms and Ecstasies by Karl Edward Wagner

1998

Novel: Bag of Bones by Stephen King
First Novel: Dawn Song by Michael Marano
Long Fiction: Mr Clubb and Mr Cuff by Peter Straub
Short Fiction: "The Dead Boy at Your Window" by Bruce Holland Rogers
Collection: Black Butterflies by John Shirley
Anthology: Horrors!: 365 Scary Stories edited by Stefan Dziemianowicz, Martin H. Greenberg, and Robert Weinberg

1999

Novel: Mr. X by Peter Straub
First Novel: Wither by J. G. Passarella
Long Fiction: Five Days in April by Brian A. Hopkins tied with *Mad Dog Summer* by Joe R. Lansdale
Short Fiction: "Aftershock" by F. Paul Wilson
Collection: The Nightmare Chronicles by Douglas Clegg
Anthology: 999: New Stories of Horror and Suspense edited by Al Sarrantonio

2000

Novel: The Traveling Vampire Show by Richard Laymon
First Novel: The Licking Valley Coon Hunters Club by Brian A. Hopkins
Long Fiction: "The Man on the Ceiling" by Melanie and Steve Rasnic Tem
Short Fiction: "Gone" by Jack Ketchum
Collection: Magic Terror by Peter Straub
Anthology: The Year's Best Fantasy and Horror: 13th Annual Collection edited by Ellen Datlow and Terri Windling

2001

Novel: American Gods by Neil Gaiman
First Novel: Deadliest of the Species by Michael Oliveri
Long Fiction: "In These Final Days of Sales" by Steve Rasnic Tem
Short Fiction: "Reconstructing Amy" by Tim Lebbon
Collection: The Man with the Barbed Wire Fists by Norman Partridge
Anthology: Ends of the Earth edited by Brian A. Hopkins

2002

Novel: The Night Class by Tom Piccirilli
First Novel: The Lovely Bones by Alice Sebold
Long Fiction: "El Dia de Los Muertos" by Brian A. Hopkins tied with "My Work Is Not Yet Done" by Tom Ligotti
Short Fiction: "The Misfit Child Grows Fat on Despair" by Tom Piccirilli
Collection: One More for the Road by Ray Bradbury
Anthology: The Darker Side edited by John Pelan

2003

Novel: Lost Boy, Lost Girl by Peter Straub
First Novel: The Rising by Brian Keene
Long Fiction: "Closing Time" by Jack Ketchum
Short Fiction: "Duty" by Gary A. Braunbeck
Collection: Peaceable Kingdom by Jack Ketchum
Anthology: Borderlands 5 edited by Elizabeth and Thomas Monteleone

2004

Novel: In the Night Room by Peter Straub
First Novel: Covenant by John Everson tied with *Stained* by Lee Thomas
Long Fiction: "The Turtle Boy" by Kealan-Patrick Burke
Short Fiction: "Nimitseahpah" by Nancy Etchemendy
Collection: Fearful Symmetries by Thomas F. Monteleone
Anthology: The Year's Best Fantasy and Horror, 17th Annual edited by Ellen Datlow, Kelly Link and Gavin Grant

WORLD FANTASY AWARD WINNERS

This annual award is given for fantasy and horror titles, although on occasion winners have been more properly science fiction.

1975

Novel: The Forgotten Beasts of Eld by Patricia A. McKillip
Short Fiction: "Pages from a Young Girl's Journal" by Robert Aickman
Collection/Anthology: Worse Things Waiting by Manly Wade Wellman

1976

Novel: Bid Time Return by Richard Matheson
Short Fiction: "Belsen Express" by Fritz Leiber
Collection/Anthology: The Enquiries of Doctor Esterhazy by Avram Davidson

1977

Novel: Doctor Rat by William Kotzwinkle
Short Fiction: "There's a Long Long Trail A-Winding" by Russell Kirk
Collection/Anthology: Frights edited by Kirby McCauley

1978

Novel: Our Lady of Darkness by Fritz Leiber
Short Fiction: "The Chimney" by Ramsey Campbell
Collection/Anthology: Murgunstrumm and Others by Hugh Cave

1979

Novel: Gloriana by Michael Moorcock
Short Fiction: "Naples" by Avram Davidson
Collection/Anthology: Shadows edited by Charles L. Grant

1980

Novel: Watchtower by Elizabeth A. Lynn
Short Fiction: "Mackintosh Willy" by Ramsey Campbell tied with "The Woman Who Loved the Moon" by Elizabeth A. Lynn
Collection/Anthology: Amazons edited by Jessica Amanda Salmonson

1981

Novel: The Shadow of the Torturer by Gene Wolfe
Short Fiction: "The Ugly Chickens" by Howard Waldrop
Collection/Anthology: Dark Forces edited by Kirby McCauley

1982

Novel: Little, Big by John Crowley
Novella: The Fire When It Comes by Parke Godwin
Short Fiction: "The Dark Country" by Dennis Etchison tied with "Do the Dead Sing?" by Stephen King
Collection/Anthology: Elsewhere edited by Terri Windling and Mark Alan Arnold

1983

Novel: Nifft the Lean by Michael Shea
Novella: Confess the Seasons by Charles L. Grant tied with *Beyond Any Measure* by Karl Edward Wagner
Short Fiction: "The Gorgon" by Tanith Lee
Collection/Anthology: Nightmare Seasons by Charles L. Grant

1984

Novel: The Dragon Waiting by John M. Ford
Novella: Black Air by Kim Stanley Robinson

Short Fiction: "Elle Est Trois (La Mort)" by Tanith Lee

Collection/Anthology: *High Spirits* by Robertson Davies

1985
Novel: *Mythago Wood* by Robert Holdstock tied with *Bridge of Birds* by Barry Hughart

Novella: *The Unconquered Country* by Geoff Ryman

Short Fiction: "Still Life with Scorpion" by Scott Baker tied with "The Bones Wizard" by Alan Ryan

Collection/Anthology: *Clive Barker's Books of Blood Volumes I, II, III* by Clive Barker

1986
Novel: *Song of Kali* by Dan Simmons

Novella: *Nadleman's God* by T. E. D. Klein

Short Fiction: "Paper Dragons" by James P. Blaylock

Collection/Anthology: *Imaginary Lands* edited by Robin McKinley

1987
Novel: *Perfume* by Patrick Suskind

Novella: *Hatrack River* by Orson Scott Card

Short Fiction: "Red Light" by David J. Schow

Collection/Anthology: *Tales of the Quintana Roo* by James Tiptree, Jr.

1988
Novel: *Replay* by Ken Grimwood

Novella: *Buffalo Gals, Won't You Come Out Tonight?* by Ursula K. Le Guin

Short Fiction: "Friend's Best Man" by Jonathan Carroll

Collection/Anthology: *The Architecture of Fear* edited by Kathryn Cramer and Peter D. Pautz tied with *Dark Descent* edited by David G. Hartwell

1989
Novel: *Koko* by Peter Straub

Novella: *The Skin Trade* by George R. R. Martin

Short Fiction: "Winter Solstice, Camelot Station" by John M. Ford

Collection/Anthology: *The Year's Best Fantasy: First Annual Collection* edited by Ellen Datlow and Terri Windling

1990
Novel: *Lyonesse: Madouc* by Jack Vance

Novella: *Great Work of Time* by John Crowley

Short Fiction: "The Illusionist" by Steven Millhauser

Collection/Anthology: *The Year's Best Fantasy: Second Annual Collection* edited by Ellen Datlow and Terri Windling

1991
Novel: *Only Begotten Daughter* by James Morrow tied with *Thomas the Rhymer* by Ellen Kushner

Novella: *Bones* by Pat Murphy

Short Fiction: "A Midsummer Night's Dream" by Neil Gaiman and Charles Vess

Collection: *The Start of the End of It All and Other Stories* by Carol Emshwiller

Anthology: *Best New Horror* edited by Stephen Jones and Ramsey Campbell

1992
Novel: *Boy's Life* by Robert R. McCammon

Novella: *The Ragthorn* by Robert Holdstock and Garry Kilworth

Short Fiction: "The Somewhere Doors" by Fred Chappell

Collection: *The Ends of the Earth* by Lucius Shepard

Anthology: *The Year's Best Fantasy & Horror: Fourth Annual Collection* edited by Ellen Datlow and Terri Windling

1993
Novel: *Last Call* by Tim Powers

Novella: *The Ghost Village* by Peter Straub

Short Fiction: "This Year's Class Picture" by Dan Simmons tied with "Graves" by Joe Haldeman

Collection: *The Sons of Noah and Other Stories* by Jack Cady

Anthology: *Metahorror* edited by Dennis Etchison

1994
Novel: *Glimpses* by Lewis Shiner

Novella: *Under the Crust* by Terry Lamsley

Short Fiction: "The Lodger" by Fred Chappell

Collection: *Alone with the Horrors* by Ramsey Campbell

Anthology: *Full Spectrum 4* edited by Lou Aronica, Amy Stout, and Betsy Mitchell

1995
Novel: *Towing Jehovah* by James Morrow

Novella: *Last Summer at Mars Hill* by Elizabeth Hand

Short Fiction: "The Man in the Black Suit" by Stephen King

Collection: *The Calvin Coolidge Home for Dead Comedians* and *A Conflagration Artist* both by Bradley Denton

Anthology: *Little Deaths* edited by Ellen Datlow

1996

Novel: *The Prestige* by Christopher Priest

Novella: *Radio Waves* by Michael Swanwick

Short Fiction: "The Grass Princess" by Gwyneth Jones

Collection: *Seven Tales and a Fable* by Gwyneth Jones

Anthology: *The Penguin Book of Modern Fantasy by Women* edited by Susan Williams and Richard Glyn Jones

1997

Novel: *Godmother Night* by Rachel Pollack

Novella: *A City in Winter* by Mark Helprin

Short Fiction: "Thirteen Phantasms" by James P. Blaylock

Collection: *The Wall of the Sky, the Wall of the Eye* by Jonathan Lethem

Anthology: *Starlight 1* edited by Patrick Nielsen Hayden

1998

Novel: *The Physiognomy* by Jeffrey Ford

Novella: *Streetcar Dreams* by Richard Bowes

Short Fiction: "Dust Motes" by P. D. Cacek

Collection: *The Throne of Bones* by Brian Mc-Naughton

Anthology: *Bending the Landscape: Fantasy* edited by Nicola Griffith and Stephen Pagel

1999

Novel: *The Antelope Wife* by Louise Erdich

Novella: *The Summer Isles* by Ian R. McLeod

Short Fiction: "The Specialist's Hat" by Kelly Link

Collection: *Black Glass* by Karen Joy Fowler

Anthology: *Dreaming Down-Under* edited by Jack Dann and Janeen Webb

2000

Novel: *Thraxas* by Martin Scott

Novella: *The Transformation of Martin Lake* by Jeff VanderMeer tied with *Sky Eyes* by Laurel Winter

Short Fiction: "The Chop Girl" by Ian R. McLeod

Collection: *Moonlight and Vines* by Charles De Lint tied with *Reave the Just and Other Tales* by Stephen R. Donaldson

Anthology: *Silver Birch, Blood Moon* edited by Ellen Datlow and Terri Windling

2001

Novel: *Declare* by Tim Powers tied with *Galveston* by Sean Stewart

Novella: *The Man on the Ceiling* by Steve Rasnic Tem and Melanie Tem

Short Fiction: "The Pottawatomie Giant" by Andy Duncan

Collection: *Beluthahatchie and Other Stories* by Andy Duncan

Anthology: *Dark Matter* edited by Sheree R. Thomas

2002

Novel: *The Other Wind* by Ursula K. Le Guin

Novella: *The Bird Catcher* by S. P. Somtow

Short Fiction: "Queen for a Day" by Albert E. Cowdrey

Collection: *Skin Folk* by Nalo Hopkinson

Anthology: *The Museum of Horrors* edited by Dennis Etchison

2003

Novel: *The Facts of Life* by Graham Joyce tied with *Ombria in Shadow* by Patricia A. McKillip

Novella: *The Library* by Zoram Zivkovic

Short Fiction: "Creation" by Jeffrey Ford

Collection: *The Fantasy Writer's Assistant and Other Stories* by Jeffrey Ford

Anthology: *The Green Man* edited by Ellen Datlow and Terri Windling tied with *Leviathan 3* edited by Jeff VanderMeer and Forrest Aguirre

2005

Novel: Tooth and Claw by Jo Walton

Novella: "A Crowd of Bone" by Greer Gilman

Short Fiction: "Don Ysidro" by Bruce Holland Rogers

Collection: Bibliomancy by Elizabeth Hand

Anthology: Strange Tales edited by Rosalie Parker

Bibliography of Fantasy and Horror Fiction

Note that only titles that fall into the categories of fantasy or supernatural fiction are included. Many authors have also been published in the science fiction or mystery/suspense genres as well, and these titles are sometimes labeled incorrectly, particularly in the horror genre, which has grown to include psychological horror and some mainstream thrillers.

ABBEY, LYNN
Daughter of the Bright Moon (1979)
The Black Flame (1980)
The Guardians (1982)
Unicorn and Dragon (1987)
Conquest (1988, also published as *The Green Man*)
The Forge of Virtue (1991)
The Wooden Sword (1991)
The Temper of Wisdom (1992)
Beneath the Web (1994)
The Brazen Gambit (1994)
Cinnabar Shadows (1995)
The Rise and Fall of a Dragon King (1996)
Siege of Shadows (1996)
Simbul's Gift (1997)
Planeswalker (1998)
Jerlayne (1999)
The Nether Scroll (2000)
Out of Time (2000)
Sanctuary (2000)
Behind Time (2001)
Taking Time (2004)
Down Time (2005)

AICKMAN, ROBERT
We Are for the Dark (1951, with Elizabeth Jane Howard)

Dark Entries (1964)
The Late Breakfasters (1964)
Powers of Darkness (1966)
Sub Rosa (1968)
Cold Hand in Mine (1975)
Tales of Love and Death (1977)
Painted Devils: Strange Stories (1979)
Intrusions: Strange Tales (1980)
Night Voices (1985)
The Model (1987)
The Wine Dark Sea (1988)
The Unsettled Dust (1990)
Collected Strange Stories (1999)

ALEXANDER, LLOYD
Time Cat (1961, also published as *Nine Lives*)
The Book of Three (1964)
Coll and His White Pig (1965)
The Black Cauldron (1965)
The Castle of Llyr (1966)
The Truthful Harp (1967)
Taran Wanderer (1967)
The High King (1968)
The Marvelous Misadventures of Sebastian (1970)
The Foundling and Other Tales of Prydain (1973)
The Wizard in the Tree (1975)
The First Two Lives of Lukas-Kasha (1978)
Westmark (1981)
The Beggar Queen (1984)
The Illyrian Adventure (1986)
The Eldorado Adventure (1987)
The Drackenberg Adventure (1988)
The Jedera Adventure (1989)
The Philadelphia Adventure (1990)
The Remarkable Journey of Prince Jen (1991)
The Iron Ring (1997)

ANTHONY, MARK
Kindred Spirits (1991)
Crypt of the Shadowking (1993)
Tower of Doom (1994)
Curse of the Shadowmage (1995)
Escape from Undermountain (1996)
Beyond the Pale (1998)
The Keep of Fire (1999)
The Dark Remains (2001)
Blood of Mystery (2002)
The Gates of Winter (2003)
The First Stone (2004)

ANTHONY, PIERS
Kiai! (1974, with Roberto Fuentes)
Mistress of Death (1974, with Roberto Fuentes)
The Bamboo Bloodbath (1974, with Roberto Fuentes)
Ninja's Revenge (1975, with Roberto Fuentes)
Amazon Slaughter (1976, with Roberto Fuentes)
Hasan (1977)
A Spell for Chameleon (1979)
The Source of Magic (1979)
Castle Roogna (1979)
God of Tarot (1980)
Vision of Tarot (1980)
Faith of Tarot (1980)
Split Infinity (1980)
Blue Adept (1981)
The Magic of Xanth (1991)
Centaur Isle (1982)
Double Exposure (1982)
Juxtaposition (1982)
Ogre, Ogre (1982)
On a Pale Horse (1983)
Dragon on a Pedestal (1983)
Night Mare (1983)
Bearing an Hourglass (1984)
Crewel Lye (1984)
With a Tangled Skein (1985)
Golem in the Gears (1986)
Wielding a Red Sword (1986)
Being a Green Mother (1987)
Tarot (1987)
Out of Phaze (1987)
Vale of the Vole (1987)
Dragon's Gold (1987, with Robert E. Margroff)
The Shade of the Tree (1987)
Heaven Cent (1988)
Robot Adept (1988)
Serpent's Silver (1988, with Robert E. Margroff)

The Man from Mundania (1989)
Pornucopia (1989)
Unicorn Point (1989)
Through the Ice (1989, with Robert Kornwise)
Isle of View (1990)
And Eternity (1990)
Phaze Doubt (1990)
Firefly (1990)
For Love of Evil (1990)
Orc's Opal (1990, with Robert E. Margroff)
Chimaera's Copper (1990, with Robert E. Margroff)
Mercycle (1991)
Question Quest (1991)
Virtual Mode (1991)
Fractal Mode (1992)
Final Magic (1992, with Robert E. Margroff)
Mouvar's Magic (1992, with Robert E. Margroff)
Across the Frames (1992, with Robert E. Margroff)
The Color of Her Panties (1992)
Harpy Time (1993)
If I Pay Thee Not in Gold (1993, with Mercedes Lackey)
Chaos Mode (1993)
Killobyte (1993)
Geis of the Gargoyle (1995)
A Roc and a Hard Place (1996)
Yon Ill Wind (1996)
The Willing Spirit (1996, with Alfred Tella)
Faun and Games (1997)
Zombie Lover (1998)
Quest for the Fallen Star (1998, with Richard Goolsby and Alan Riggs)
Xone of Contention (1999)
Dream a Little Dream (1999, with Julie Brady)
Demons Don't Dream (2000)
The Dastard (2000)
The Secret of Spring (2000, with Jo Anne Taeusch)
The Gutbucker Quest (2000, with Ron Leming)
DoOon Mode (2001)
Swell Foop (2001)
Up in a Heaval (2002)
Cube Route (2003)
Quest for Magic (2003)
Havoc (2003)
Currant Events (2004)
Pet Peeve (2005)

APPLEGATE, K. A.
Enter the Enchanted (1999)
Land of Loss (1999)

Realm of the Reaper (1999)
Search for Senna (1999)
Understanding the Unknown (2000)
Discover the Destroyer (2000)
Fear the Fantastic (2000)
Gateway to the Gods (2000)
Inside the Illusion (2000)
Brave the Betrayal (2000)
Mystify the Magician (2001)
Entertain the End (2001)

AYCLIFFE, JONATHAN
Naomi's Room (1991)
Whispers in the Dark (1992)
Vanishment (1994)
The Matrix (1995)
The Lost (1996)
The Talisman (1999)
A Shadow on the Wall (2000)
A Garden Lost in Time (2004)

BAILEY, ROBIN WAYNE
Frost (1983)
Skull Gate (1985)
Bloodsongs (1986)
Enchanter (1989)
The Lake of Fire (1989)
Nightwatch (1990)
The Lost City of Zork (1991)
Brothers of the Dragon (1992)
Flames of the Dragon (1994, also published as *Straight on Till Mourning*)
Triumph of the Dragon (1995)
Shadowdance (1996)
Swords against the Shadowland (1998)
Wyvernwood (2004)
Talisman (2004)
Undersky (2005)

BANGS, JOHN KENDRICK
Roger Camerden: A Strange Story (1887)
Toppleton's Client (1893)
The Water Ghost and Others (1894)
A Houseboat on the Styx (1895)
The Pursuit of the Houseboat (1897)
Ghosts I Have Met and Some Others (1898)
The Enchanted Typewriter (1899)
Mr. Munchausen (1901)
Olympian Nights (1902)
Over the Plum Pudding (1901)

The Autobiography of Methuselah (1909)
Jack and the Check-Book (1911)

BARKER, CLIVE
Books of Blood Volume 1 (1984)
Books of Blood Volume 2 (1984)
Books of Blood Volume 3 (1984)
Books of Blood Volume 4 (1985, also published as *The Inhuman Condition*)
Books of Blood Volume 5 (1985, also published as *In the Flesh*)
Books of Blood Volume 6 (1985, also published as *Cabal*)
The Damnation Game (1985)
Weaveworld (1987)
The Great and Secret Show (1989)
The Hellbound Heart (1991)
Imajica (1991)
The Thief of Always (1992)
Everville (1994)
Sacrament (1996)
Galilee (1998)
The Essential Clive Barker (1999)
Coldheart Canyon (2001)
Abarat (2002)

BAUDINO, GAEL
Dragon Sword (1988)
Duel of Dragons (1989)
Strands of Starlight (1989)
Gossamer Axe (1990)
Dragon Death (1992)
Maze of Moonlight (1993)
Shroud of Shadow (1993)
Strands of Sunlight (1994)
O Greenest Branch! (1995)
Branch and Crown (1996)
The Dove Looked In (1996)
Spires of Spirit (1997)

BAUM, L. FRANK
The Wizard of Oz (1900, also published as *The Wonderful Wizard of Oz* and *The New Wizard of Oz*)
The Surprising Adventures of the Magical Monarch of Mo (1900, also published as *A New Wonderland*)
American Fairy Tales (1901)
Dot and Tot of Merryland (1901)
The Life and Adventures of Santa Claus (1902)
The Enchanted Island of Yew (1903)

The Land of Oz (1904, also published as *The Marvelous Land of Oz*)

Queen Zixi of Ix (1905)

Ozma of Oz (1906, also published as *Princess Ozma of Oz*)

Dorothy and the Wizard of Oz (1908)

The Road to Oz (1909)

The Emerald City of Oz (1910)

The Sea Fairies (1911)

Sky Island (1912)

The Patchwork Girl of Oz (1913)

Tik-Tok of Oz (1914)

The Scarecrow of Oz (1915)

Rinkitink in Oz (1916)

The Lost Princess of Oz (1917)

The Tin Woodman of Oz (1918)

The Magic of Oz (1919)

Glinda of Oz (1920)

Policeman Bluejay (1981)

Little Wizard Stories of Oz (1994)

Twinkle Tales (2005)

BEAGLE, PETER S.

A Fine and Private Place (1960)

The Last Unicorn (1968)

The Fantasy Worlds of Peter S. Beagle (1978)

The Folk of the Air (1986)

The Innkeeper's Song (1993)

The Unicorn Sonata (1996)

Giant Bones (1997)

Tamsin (1999)

A Dance for Emilia (2000)

The Rhinoceros Who Quoted Nietzsche and Other Odd Acquaintances (2003)

BEAUMONT, CHARLES

Yonder (1958)

The Hunger and Other Stories (1958, also published as *Shadow Play*)

Night Ride and Other Journeys (1960)

The Magic Man (1965)

The Edge (1966)

The Best of Beaumont (1982)

The Howling Man (1992, also published as *Charles Beaumont: Selected Stories*)

A Touch of the Creature (1999)

BELLAIRS, JOHN

The Pedant and the Shuffly (1968)

The Face in the Frost (1969)

The House with a Clock in Its Walls (1973)

The Figure in the Shadows (1975)

The Letter, the Witch, and the Ring (1976)

The Treasure of Alpheus Winterborn (1978)

The Curse of the Blue Figurine (1983)

The Mummy, the Will, and the Crypt (1983)

The Spell of the Sorceror's Skull (1984)

The Dark Secret of Weatherend (1984)

The Revenge of the Wizard's Ghost (1985)

The Eyes of the Killer Robot (1986)

The Lamp from the Warlock's Tomb (1988)

The Chessmen of Doom (1989)

The Trolley to Yesterday (1989)

The Secret of the Underground Room (1990)

Mansion in the Mist (1992)

The Ghost in the Mirror (1993, with Brad Strickland)

Vengeance of the Witchfinder (1993, with Brad Strickland)

The Drum, the Doll, and the Zombie (1994, with Brad Strickland)

The Doom of the Haunted Opera (1996, with Brad Strickland)

Johnny Dixon in the Hands of the Necromancer (1996, with Brad Strickland)

The Bell, the Book, and the Spellbinder (1997, with Brad Strickland)

The Wrath of the Grinning Ghost (1999, with Brad Strickland)

BERGSTROM, ELAINE

Shattered Glass (1989)

Blood Alone (1990)

Blood Rites (1991)

Daughter of the Night (1992)

A Tapestry of Dark Souls (1993)

Mina (1994, as Mira Kiraly)

Baroness of Blood (1995)

Leanna (1996, as Mira Kiraly)

Madeline (1996, as Mira Kiraly)

The Door through Washington Square (1998)

Blood to Blood (2000)

Nocturne (2003)

BIERCE, AMBROSE

Cobwebs from an Empty Skull (1874)

Tales of Soldiers and Civilians (1891, also published as *Eyes of the Panther*)

Can Such Things Be? (1893)

In the Midst of Life (1898)

Fantastic Fables (1899)

The Collected Writings of Ambrose Bierce (1946)
Ghost and Horror Stories of Ambrose Bierce (1964)
The Complete Short Stories of Ambrose Bierce (1985)
The Civil War Stories of Ambrose Bierce (1988)
An Occurrence at Owl Creek Bridge and Other Stories (1995)
The Moonlit Road and Other Ghost and Horror Stories (1998)

BLACKWOOD, ALGERNON

The Empty House and Other Ghost Stories (1906)
The Listener and Others (1907)
John Silence: Physician Extraordinary (1908)
Jimbo: A Fantasy (1909)
The Lost Valley and Others (1910)
The Human Chord (1910)
The Centaur (1911)
Pan's Garden (1912)
Incredible Adventures (1914)
The Promise of Air (1914)
Ten Minute Stories (1914)
Julius LeVallon: An Episode (1916)
The Wave (1916)
Tales of the Mysterious and the Macabre (1917, also published as *Day and Night Stories*)
The Bright Messenger (1921)
The Wolves of God and Other Fey Stories (1921)
Tongues of Fire and Other Sketches (1924)
Ancient Sorceries and Other Stories (1927)
The Dance of Death and Other Tales (1927)
Strange Stories (1929)
Dudley and Gilderoy (1929)
The Willows and Other Queer Tales (1934)
The Fruit Stoners (1934)
Shocks (1935)
The Tales of Algernon Blackwood (1938)
The Doll and One Other (1946)
Selected Short Stories of Algernon Blackwood (1946)
Selected Tales of Algernon Blackwood (1948)
Tales of the Uncanny and Supernatural (1949)
In the Realm of Terror (1957)
Tales of Terror and the Unknown (1964, also published as *The Insanity of Jones and Other Tales*)
The Best Ghost Stories of Algernon Blackwood (1973)
The Best Supernatural Tales of Algernon Blackwood (1973)
Tales of Terror and Darkness (1977)
A Mysterious House (1987)
The Magic Mirror: Lost Supernatural and Mystery Stories (1989)
The Complete John Silence (1998)

Pan's Garden (2000)
John Silence: Ancient Sorceries (2002)
John Silence: A Psychical Invasion (2002)
The Wendigo (2002)
The Willows (2002)

BLAYLOCK, JAMES P.

The Elfin Ship (1982)
The Disappearing Dwarf (1983)
The Digging Leviathan (1984)
Homunculus (1986)
The Pink of Fading Neon (1986)
Land of Dreams (1987)
The Shadow on the Doorstep, with Trilobyte (1987)
Two Views of a Cave Painting & The Idol's Eye (1987)
The Last Coin (1988)
The Stone Giant (1989)
The Magic Spectacles (1991)
The Paper Grail (1991)
Lord Kelvin's Machine (1992)
Night Relics (1994)
All the Bells of Earth (1995)
Winter Tides (1997)
The Rainy Season (1999)
Thirteen Phantasms and Other Stories (2000)

BLOCH, ROBERT

The Opener of the Way (1945)
Sea Kissed (1945)
Pleasant Dreams (1960)
Nightmares (1961)
Blood Runs Cold (1961)
Yours Truly, Jack the Ripper (1962, also published as *The House of the Hatchet*)
More Nightmares (1962)
Bogey Men (1963)
Horror 7 (1963)
The Skull of the Marquis de Sade (1965)
Tales in a Jugular Vein (1965)
Chamber of Horrors (1966)
Living Demons (1967)
Dragons and Nightmares (1969)
Bloch and Bradbury (1969, with Ray Bradbury)
It's All in Your Mind (1971)
King of Terrors (1976)
The Best of Robert Bloch (1977)
Cold Chills (1977)
Out of the Mouths of Graves (1978)
Strange Eons (1979)
Such Stuff as Screams Are Made Of (1979)
Mysteries of the Worm (1981)

The Twilight Zone: The Movie (1983)
Midnight Pleasures (1987)
Bitter Ends (1988)
Final Reckonings (1988)
Last Rites (1988)
Fear and Trembling (1989)
The Jekyll Legacy (1990, with Andre Norton)
Lori (1990)
The Early Fears (1993)
Flowers from the Moon and Other Lunacies (1998)
The Devil With You! (1999)
Hell on Earth (2000)
One More for the Road (2002)

BOSTON, LUCY M.

The Children of Green Knowe (1954)
The Chimneys of Green Knowe (1958, also published as
    The Treasure of Green Knowe)
The River at Green Knowe (1959)
A Stranger at Green Knowe (1961)
An Enemy at Green Knowe (1964)
Guardians of the House (1974)
The Stones of Green Knowe (1976)
Adventures at Green Knowe (1979)

BOYER, ELIZABETH

The Sword and the Satchel (1980)
The Elves and the Otterskin (1981)
The Thrall and the Dragon's Heart (1982)
The Wizard and the Warlord (1983)
The Troll's Grindstone (1986)
The Curse of Slagfid (1989)
The Dragon's Carbuncle (1990)
The Lord of Chaos (1991)
The Clan of the Warlord (1992)
The Black Lynx (1993)
Keeper of the Cats (1995)

BOYLL, RANDALL

After Sundown (1989)
Shocker (1990)
Mongster (1991)
Chiller (1992)
Demon Knight (1995)
Katastrophe (2000)

BRADBURY, RAY

Dark Carnival (1947)
The Illustrated Man (1951)
The October Country (1955)
The Day It Rained Forever (1959)

A Medicine for Melancholy (1959)
The Small Assassin (1962)
Something Wicked This Way Comes (1962)
Bloch and Bradbury (1969, with Robert Bloch)
The Halloween Tree (1972)
Long After Midnight (1975)
The Stories of Ray Bradbury (1980)
Quicker Than the Eye (1996)
Driving Blind (1997)
From the Dust Returned (2001)
One More for the Road (2002)
Bradbury Stories (2003)

BRADLEY, MARION ZIMMER

Dark Satanic (1972)
In the Steps of the Master (1973)
Drums of Darkness (1976)
The House between the Worlds (1980)
The Mists of Avalon (1982)
Web of Darkness (1983)
Web of Light (1983)
The Inheritor (1984)
Night's Daughter (1985)
Warrior Woman (1985)
Lythande (1986)
Fall of Atlantis (1987)
The Firebrand (1987)
Witch Hill (1990)
Black Trillium (1990, with Julian May and Andre
    Norton)
The Forest House (1993)
Ghostlight (1995)
Tiger Burning Bright (1995, with Julian May and Andre
    Norton)
Lady of Trillium (1995)
Witchlight (1996)
Glenraven (1996, with Holly Lisle)
Gravelight (1997)
Lady of Avalon (1997)
The Gratitude of Kings (1997)
Heartlight (1998)
Priestess of Avalon (2001, with Diana L. Paxson)

BRAMAH, ERNEST

The Wallet of Kai Lung (1900)
Kai Lung's Golden Hours (1922)
Kai Lung Unrolls His Mat (1928)
The Kai Lung Omnibus (1936)
The Return of Kai Lung (1937, also published as *The
    Moon of Much Gladness*)
Kai Lung Beneath the Mulberry Tree (1940)

The Celestial Omnibus (1963)
Kai Lung: Six (1974)

BRANDNER, GARY

The Howling (1977)
Howling II (1978, also published as *The Return of the Howling*)
Walkers (1980, also published as *Death Walkers*)
Hellborn (1981)
Cat People (1982)
Quintana Roo (1984, also published as *Tribe of the Dead*)
The Brain Eaters (1985)
Howling III (1985)
Carrion (1986)
Cameron's Ghost (1987, also published as *Cameron's Terror*)
Floater (1988)
Doomstalker (1989)
Rot (1999)

BRENNAN, JOSEPH PAYNE

Nine Horrors and a Dream (1958)
The Dark Returners (1959)
Scream at Midnight (1963)
Nightmare Need (1964)
Stories of Darkness and Dread (1973)
The Casebook of Lucius Leffing (1973)
The Chronicles of Lucius Leffing (1977)
Acts of Providence (1979, with Donald Grant)
The Shapes of Midnight (1980)
Creep to Death (1981)
Evil Always Ends (1983)
The Borders Just Beyond (1986)
The Adventures of Lucius Leffing (1989)

BRITE, POPPY Z.

Lost Souls (1992)
Drawing Blood (1993)
Wormwood (1996, also published as *Swamp Foetus*)
Are You Loathesome Tonight? (1998)
The Lazarus Heart (1998)
The Seed of Lost Souls (1999)
Self Made Man (1999)
The Devil You Know (2003)

BROOKS, TERRY

The Sword of Shannara (1977)
The Elfstones of Shannara (1982)
The Wishsong of Shannara (1985)
Magic Kingdom for Sale—Sold! (1986)
The Black Unicorn (1987)

Wizard at Large (1988)
The Scions of Shannara (1990)
The Druid of Shannara (1991)
The Elf Queen of Shannara (1992)
Hook (1992)
The Talismans of Shannara (1993)
Tangle Box (1994)
Witches' Brew (1995)
First King of Shannara (1996)
Running with the Demon (1997)
A Knight of the Word (1998)
Angel Fire East (1999)
Ilse Witch (2000)
Antrax (2001)
Morgawr (2002)
The Heritage of Shannara (2003)
Jarka Ruus (2003)
Tanequil (2004)
Strahon (2005)

BRUST, STEVEN A.

Jhereg (1983)
To Reign in Hell (1984)
Yendi (1984)
Brokedown Palace (1986)
Teckla (1987)
The Sun, the Moon, and the Stars (1987)
Taltos (1988, also published as *Taltos and the Paths of the Dead*)
Phoenix (1990)
The Phoenix Guards (1991)
Taltos the Assassin (1991)
Gypsy (1992, with Megan Lindholm)
Agyar (1993)
Athyra (1993)
Five Hundred Years After (1994)
Orca (1996)
Freedom and Necessity (1997, with Emma Bull)
Dragon (1998)
The Book of Jhereg (1999)
Issola (2001)
The Book of Taltos (2002)
The Paths of the Dead (2002)
The Book of Athyra (2003)
The Lord of Castle Black (2003)
Sethra Lavode (2004)

BUNCH, CHRIS

The Far Kingdoms (1993, with Allan Cole)
The Warrior's Tale (1994, with Allan Cole)
Kingdoms of the Night (1995, with Allan Cole)

The Seer King (1997)
The Demon King (1998)
The Warrior King (1999)
The Empire Stone (2000)
Corsair (2001)
Storm of Wings (2002)
Knighthood of the Dragon (2003)
The Last Battle (2004)

CABELL, JAMES BRANCH (NOTE THAT ALL OF THE POICTESME TITLES ARE INCLUDED, SOME OF WHICH ARE NOT FANTASY.)
The Eagle's Shadow (1904)
The Line of Love (1905)
Gallantry (1907)
Chivalry (1909)
The Cords of Vanity (1909)
The Soul of Melicent (1913)
From the Hidden Way (1914)
The Rivet in Grandfather's Neck (1915)
The Certain Hour (1916)
The Cream of the Jest (1917)
Beyond Life (1919)
Jurgen (1919)
Domnei (1920, also published as *The Soul of Melicent*)
Figures of Earth (1921)
The Jewel Merchants (1921)
The Lineage of Lichfield (1922)
The High Place (1923)
Straws and Prayerbooks (1924)
The Music from Behind the Moon (1926)
The Silver Stallion (1926)
Something about Eve (1927)
The White Robe (1928)
Smirt: An Urbane Nightmare (1934)
Smith: A Sylvan Interlude (1935)
Smire: An Acceptance in the Third Person (1937)
There Were Two Pirates (1946)
The Witch Woman (1948)
The Devil's Own Son (1949)
The Nightmare Has Triplets (1972)

CADY, JACK
The Well (1980)
The Jonah Watch (1981)
McDowell's Ghost (1982)
Dark Dreaming (1991, as Pat Franklin)
The Sons of Noah and Other Stories (1992)
Embrace of the Wolf (1993, as Pat Franklin)
Street (1994)
The Off Season (1995)

The Night We Buried Road Dog (1998)
The Haunting of Hood Canal (2001)
Ghosts of Yesterday (2003)

CAMPBELL, RAMSEY
The Inhabitant of the Lake and Less Welcome Tenants (1964)
Demons by Daylight (1973)
The Doll Who Ate His Mother (1976)
The Height of the Scream (1976)
The Bride of Frankenstein (1977, as Carl Dreadstone)
Dracula's Daughter (1977, as Carl Dreadstone)
The Wolfman (1977, as Carl Dreadstone)
The Parasite (1980, also published as *To Wake the Dead*)
The Nameless (1981)
Through the Walls (1981)
Dark Companions (1982)
Incarnate (1983)
Night of the Claw (1983, originally as by Jay Ramsay, also published as *The Claw*)
Cold Print (1985)
Obsession (1985)
The Hungry Moon (1986)
Black Wine (1986)
Dark Feasts (1987)
Ghostly Tales (1987)
Scared Stiff (1987)
The Influence (1988)
Fine Frights (1988)
Ancient Images (1989)
The Midnight Sun (1990)
The Count of Eleven (1991)
Waking Nightmares (1991)
Uncanny Banquets (1992)
Alone with the Horrors (1993)
The Long Lost (1993)
Strange Things and Stranger Places (1994)
Nazareth Hill (1996, also published as *The House on Nazareth Hill*)
Far Away and Never (1996)
The Last Voice They Hear (1998)
Ghosts and Grisly Things (2000)
Meddling with Ghosts (2001)
Pact of the Fathers (2001)
The Darkest Part of the Woods (2002)
Told by the Dead (2003)
The Overnight (2005)

CARROLL, JONATHAN
The Land of Laughs (1980)
The Voice of Our Shadow (1983)

Bones of the Moon (1987)
Sleeping in Flame (1988)
A Child Across the Sky (1989)
Black Cocktail (1990)
Outside the Dog Museum (1991)
From the Teeth of Angels (1994)
The Panic Hand (1995)
The Marriage of Sticks (1999)
The Wooden Sea (2001)
White Apples (2002)
Glass Soup (2005)

CARROLL, LEWIS
Alice in Wonderland (1865)
Through the Looking Glass (1871)
Alice's Adventures Underground (1886)
Sylvie and Bruno (1889)

CARTER, LIN
The Wizard of Lemuria (1965, also published as *Thongor and the Wizard of Lemuria*)
Thongor of Lemuria (1966, also published as *Thongor and the Dragon City*)
The Flame of Iridar (1967)
Thongor against the Gods (1967)
Thongor in the City of Magicians (1968)
Thongor at the End of Time (1968)
Conan of the Isles (1968, with L. Sprague De Camp)
Lost World of Time (1969)
Thongor Fights the Pirates of Tarakus (1970)
Quest of Kadji (1971)
Conan the Buccaneer (1971, with L. Sprague De Camp)
The Black Star (1973)
Invisible Death (1975)
The Nemesis of Evil (1975)
The Volcano Ogre (1976)
Conan of Aquilonia (1977, with L. Sprague De Camp)
The Wizard of Zao (1978)
Conan the Swordsman (1978, with L. Sprague De Camp and Bjorn Nyberg)
Conan the Liberator (1979, with L. Sprague De Camp)
Tara of the Twilight (1979)
Lost Worlds (1980)
The Earth-Shaker (1982)
Conan the Barbarian (1982, with L. Sprague De Camp)
Kesrick (1982)
Dragonrouge (1984)
Kellory the Warlock (1984)
Horror Wears Blue (1987)
Mandricardo (1987)
Callipygia (1988)

The Conan Chronicles (1989, with L. Sprague De Camp and Robert E. Howard)
The Xothic Legend Cycle (1997)
Lin Carter's Anton Zarnak: Supernatural Sleuth (2002)

CAVE, HUGH B.
Murgunstrumm and Others (1977)
Legion of the Dead (1979)
The Nebulon Horror (1980)
The Evil (1981)
Shades of Evil (1982)
The Corpse Maker (1988)
Disciples of Dread (1989)
The Lower Deep (1990)
Lucifer's Eye (1991)
Death Stalks by Night (1995)
Bitter/Sweet (1996)
The Door Below (1997)
Isle of the Whisperers (1999)
The Dawning (2000)
The Lady Wore Black and Other Weird Cat Tales (2000)
The Evil Returns (2001)
The Restless Dead (2003)

CHAPMAN, VERA
The Green Knight (1975)
King Arthur's Daughter (1976)
The King's Damosel (1976)
Blaedud the Birdman (1978)
Miranty and the Alchemist (1983)
The Three Damosels (1983)
The Notorious Abbess (1993)
The Enchantresses (1998)

CHERRYH, C. J.
The Dreamstone (1983)
The Tree of Swords and Jewels (1983)
Arafel's Saga (1983, also published as *Ealdwood*)
Legions of Hell (1987)
Kings in Hell (1987)
The Paladin (1988)
Rusalka (1989)
Wizard Spawn (1989, with Nancy Asire)
A Dirge for Sabis (1989, with Leslie Fish)
Reap the Whirlwind (1989, with Mercedes Lackey)
Chernevog (1990)
Yvgenie (1991)
The Goblin Mirror (1992)
Faery in Shadow (1994)
Fortress in the Eye of Time (1995)
The Dreaming Tree (1998)

Fortress of Eagles (1998)
Fortress of Owls (1999)
The Fortress of Dragons (2000)

CHETWYND-HAYES, R.

The Dark Man (1964, also published as *And Love Survived*)
The Unbidden (1971)
Cold Terror (1973)
The Elemental (1974)
Terror by Night (1974)
The Monster Club (1975)
The Night Ghoul and Other Grisly Tales (1975)
Tales of Fear and Fantasy (1977)
The Cradle Demon and Other Stories of Fantasy and Terror (1978)
The Awakening (1980)
The Fantastic World of Kamtellar (1980)
The Partaker: A Novel of Fantasy (1980)
Tales of Darkness (1981)
Tales from Beyond (1982)
The Other Side (1983, also published as *Tales from the Other Side*)
A Quiver of Ghosts (1984)
Tales from the Dark Lands (1984)
Ghosts from the Mists of Time (1985)
The Grange (1985, also published as *The King's Ghost*)
Tales from the Haunted House (1986)
Tales from the Shadows (1986)
Dracula's Children (1986)
The House of Dracula (1987)
The Haunted Grange (1988)
Tales from the Hidden World (1988)
Curse of the Snake God (1989)
Dominique (1989)
Kepple (1992)
The Psychic Detective (1993)
Hell Is What You Make It (1994)
Shudders and Shivers (1995)
The Vampire Stories of R. Chetwynd-Hayes (1996)
Shocks (1997)
Looking for Something to Suck and Other Vampire Stories (1998)
Frights and Fancies (2002)

CLARK, SIMON

Blood and Grit (1990)
Nailed by the Heart (1995)
Blood Crazy (1996)
Darker (1996)
King Blood (1997)

Vampyrrhic (1998)
Salt Snake and Other Bloody Cuts (1998)
Judas Tree (1999)
Darkness Demands (2001)
The Stranger (2002)
Vampyrrhic Rites (2003)
Exorcising Angels (2003, with Tim Lebbon)
In the Skin (2004)

CLAYTON, JO

Moongather (1982)
Moonscatter (1983)
A Bait of Dreams (1985)
Changer's Moon (1985)
Drinker of Souls (1986)
Blue Magic (1988)
A Gathering of Stones (1989)
The Soul Drinker (1989)
Wild Magic (1991)
Wildfire (1992)
Dancer's Rise (1993)
Serpent Waltz (1994)
Drum Calls (1997)
Drum Warning (1997)
Drum into Silence (2002, with Kevin Murphy)

CLEGG, DOUGLAS

Goat Dance (1989)
Breeder (1990)
Neverland (1991)
Dark of the Eye (1994)
The Children's Hour (1995)
Bad Karma (1998, as Andrew Harper)
The Halloween Man (1998)
The Nightmare Chronicles (1999)
Mischief (2000)
Naomi (2000)
You Come When I Call You (2000)
Infinite (2001)
Nightmare House (2002)
The Hour Before Dark (2002)
The Necromancer (2003)
The Attraction (2004)
The Priest of Blood (2005)
The Abandoned (2005)

COLLINS, NANCY

Sunglasses after Dark (1989)
Tempter (1990)
In the Blood (1991)
Cold Turkey (1992)

Wild Blood (1993)
Nameless Sins (1994)
Paint It Black (1995)
Midnight Blue (1995)
Walking Wolf (1995)
A Dozen Black Roses (1996)
Angels on Fire (1998)
Lynch (1999)
Avenue X and Other Dark Streets (2001)
Knuckles and Tales (2001)
The Darkest Heart (2002)
Dead Roses for a Blue Lady (2002)
Dead Man's Hand (2004)

CONSTANTINE, STORM
Hermetech (1991)
Sign for the Sacred (1993)
Calenture (1994)
Stealing Sacred Fire (1995)
Stalking Tender Prey (1995)
Scenting Hallowed Blood (1996)
Three Heralds of the Storm (1998)
The Oracle Lips (1999)
Sea Dragon Heir (2000)
The Crown of Silence (2000)
Way of Light (2001)
The Thorn Boy and Other Dreams of Dark Desire (2002)
The Grimoire of Deharan Magick: Kiaran (2004)

COOK, GLEN
A Shadow of All Night Falling (1979)
All Darkness Met (1980)
October's Baby (1980)
The Swordbearer (1982)
The Black Company (1984)
Shadows Linger (1984)
The Fire in His Hands (1984)
The White Rose (1985)
With Mercy toward None (1985)
Annals of the Black Company (1986)
Reap the East Wind (1987)
Sweet Silver Blues (1987)
Bitter Gold Hearts (1988)
Cold Copper Tears (1988)
An Ill Fate Marshalling (1988)
The Garrett Files (1989)
The Tower of Fear (1989)
Shadow Games (1989)
The Silver Spike (1989)
Old Tin Sorrows (1989)
Dread Brass Shadows (1990)

Dreams of Steel (1990)
Sung in Blood (1990)
Red Iron Nights (1991)
Deadly Quicksilver Lies (1994)
Petty Pewter Gods (1995)
Bleak Seasons (1996)
She Is the Darkness (1997)
Faded Steel Heart (1999)
Water Sleeps (1999)
Soldiers Live (2000)
Angry Lead Skies (2002)
The Tyranny of the Night (2005)
Whispering Nickel Idols (2005)

COOK, HUGH
Wizard War (1986, also published as *The Wizards and the Warriors*)
The Hero's Return (1987)
The Questing Hero (1987)
The Wordsmiths and the Warguild (1987)
The Oracle (1987, also published as *The Women and the Warlords*)
Lords of the Sword (1988, also published as *The Walrus and the Warwolf*)
The Wicked and the Witless (1989)
The Wishstone and the Wonderworkers (1990)
The Wazir and the Witch (1990)
The Werewolf and the Wormlord (1991)
The Witchlord and the Weaponmaster (1992)
The Worshippers and the Way (1992)

COOPER, LOUISE
The Book of Paradox (1973)
Blood Summer (1976)
Lord of No Time (1977)
In Memory of Sarah Bailey (1977)
Crown of Horn (1981)
The Initiate (1985)
The Outcast (1996)
The Master (1987)
Mirage (1987)
Nemesis (1988)
The Thorn Key (1988)
Inferno (1988)
Nocturne (1990)
Infanta (1990)
The Deceiver (1991)
The Pretender (1991)
Avatar (1991)
The Sleep of Stone (1991)
Troika (1991)

Revenant (1992)
The Avenger (1992)
Aisling (1993)
The Deceiver (1993)
Eclipse (1994)
Star Ascendant (1994)
Moonset (1995)
Daughter of Storms (1996)
Firespell (1996)
Blood Dance (1996)
Sacrament of Night (1997)
Keepers of Light (1998)
The Spiral Garden (2000)
The Dark Caller (2000)
Short and Scary (2002)
Gathering Storm (2004)

COOPER, SUSAN
Over Sea, Over Stone (1965)
The Dark Is Rising (1973)
Greenwitch (1974)
The Grey King (1975)
Seaward (1976)
Silver on the Tree (1977)
Seaward (1983)
The Boggart (1993)
Green Boy (2002)

COSTELLO, MATTHEW J.
Sleep Tight (1987)
Fate's Trick (1988)
Beneath Still Waters (1989)
Wizard of Tizare (1990)
Midsummer (1990)
Child's Play 2 (1990)
Wurm (1991)
Child's Play 3 (1991)
Darkborn (1992)
Garden (1993)
The Seventh Guest (1995, with Craig Shaw Gardner)
Maelstrom (1999)
The Unidentified (2002)
Missing Monday (2004)

COVILLE, BRUCE
The Foolish Giant (1978)
Eyes of Tarot (1983)
Spirits and Spells (1983)
Waiting Spirits (1984)
Sarah and the Dragon (1984)
Amulet of Doom (1985)

The Ghost Wore Gray (1988)
The Unicorn Treasure (1988)
Monster of the Year (1989)
The Ghost in the Third Row (1989)
The Monster's Ring (1989)
Jeremy Thatcher, Dragon Hatcher (1991)
The Ghost in the Big Brass Bed (1991)
Jennifer Murdley's Toad (1992)
Goblins in the Castle (1992)
The Dragonslayers (1994)
Monster of the Year (1994)
Oddly Enough (1994)
Into the Land of the Unicorns (1994)
Sarah's Unicorn (1995)
The World's Worst Fairy Godmother (1996)
The Skull of Truth (1997)
A Glory of Unicorns (1998)
Odder Than Ever (1999)
Song of the Wanderer (2001)
Juliet Dove, Queen of Love (2003)
The Dragon of Doom (2004)

COYNE, JOHN
The Legacy (1979)
The Piercing (1979)
The Searing (1980)
Hobgoblin (1981)
The Shroud (1983)
The Hunting Season (1987)
Fury (1989)
Child of Shadows (1990)

CROWLEY, JOHN
The Deep (1975)
Little, Big (1981)
Aegypt (1987)
Antiquities (1993)
Love and Sleep (1994)
Daemonomania (2000)

CUNNINGHAM, ELAINE
Elfshadow (1991)
The Radiant Dragon (1992)
Elfsong (1994)
Daughter of the Drow (1995)
The Unicorn Hunt (1995)
Silver Shadows (1996)
Tangled Webs (1996)
Thornhold (1998)
Evermeet (1998)
The Dream Spheres (1999)

The Magehound (2000)
The Floodgate (2001)
The Wizardwar (2002)
Windwalker (2003)
Shadows in the Darkness (2004)

DAHL, ROALD

Gremlins (1943)
Someone Like You (1948)
Some Time Never (1949)
Kiss, Kiss (1960)
The Collected Short Stories of Roald Dahl (1961)
James and the Giant Peach (1961)
Willy Wonka and the Chocolate Factory (1964)
The Magic Finger (1966)
Fantastic Mr. Fox (1970)
Charlie and the Great Glass Elevator (1972)
Danny, the Champion of the World (1975)
Tales of the Unexpected (1979)
More Tales of the Unexpected (1980, also published as *Further Tales of the Unexpected*)
The Witches (1983)
The Complete Adventures of Charlie and Mr. Willie Wonka (1987)
The Best of Roald Dahl (1990)
The Minpins (1991)
The Roald Dahl Treasury (1997)

DALKEY, KARA

The Curse of Sagamore (1986)
Euryale (1988)
The Nightingale (1988)
The Sword of Sagamore (1989)
Little Sister (1996)
Goa (1996)
Bijapur (1997)
Steel Rose (1997)
The Heavenward Path (1998)
Bhagavati (1998)
Crystal Sage (1999)
Genpei (2000)

DANIELS, LES

The Black Castle (1978)
The Silver Skull (1979)
Citizen Vampire (1981)
Yellow Fog (1988)
No Blood Spilled (1991)
Don Sebastian Vampire Chronicles (1994)

DAVIDSON, AVRAM

The Island under the Earth (1969)
The Phoenix and the Mirror (1969)
Peregrine: Primus (1971)
Ursus of Ultima Thule (1973)
Peregrine: Secundus (1981)
Collected Fantasies (1982)
Virgil in Averno (1987)
Marco Polo and the Sleeping Beauty (1988, with Grania Davis)
The Boss in the Wall (1998, with Grania Davis)
Everybody Has Somebody in Heaven (2000)
The Other Nineteenth Century (2001)

DEAN, PAMELA

The Secret Country (1985)
The Hidden Land (1986)
The Whim of a Dragon (1989)
Tam Lin (1990)
The Dubious Hills (1994)
Juniper, Gentian, and Rosemary (1998)

DE CAMP, L. SPRAGUE

The Incomplete Enchanter (1941, with Fletcher Pratt)
The Land of Unreason (1942, with Fletcher Pratt)
The Carnelian Cube (1948)
The Castle of Iron (1950, with Fletcher Pratt)
The Undesired Princess (1951)
Tales from Gavagan's Bar (1953, with Fletcher Pratt)
The Tritonian Ring (1953)
Solomon's Stone (1957)
The Return of Conan (1957, with Bjorn Nyberg)
Wall of Serpents (1960, with Fletcher Pratt)
Conan the Adventurer (1966, with Robert E. Howard)
Conan the Usurper (1967, with Robert E. Howard)
The Goblin Tower (1968)
Conan of the Isles (1968, with Lin Carter)
Conan the Freebooter (1968, with Robert E. Howard)
The Reluctant Shaman (1970)
Conan the Buccaneer (1971, with Lin Carter)
The Clocks of Iraz (1971)
The Fallible Fiend (1973)
The Compleat Enchanter (1975, with Fletcher Pratt)
Conan of Aquilonia (1977, with Lin Carter)
Conan the Swordsman (1978, with Lin Carter and Bjorn Nyberg)
The Purple Pterodactyls (1979)
Conan the Liberator (1979, with Lin Carter)

Conan and the Spider God (1980, with Robert E. Howard)

Conan: The Flame Knife (1981, with Robert E. Howard)

Conan the Barbarian (1982, with Lin Carter)

The Unbeheaded King (1983)

The Reluctant King (1985)

The Incorporated Knight (1987, with Catherine Crook De Camp)

The Honorable Barbarian (1989)

The Complete Compleat Enchanter (1989, with Fletcher Pratt, also published as *The Intrepid Enchanter*)

The Pixilated Peeress (1991, with Catherine Crook De Camp)

Sir Harold and the Gnome King (1991)

DEE, RON

Blood Lust (1990)

Descent (1991)

Dusk (1991)

Blood (1993)

Blind Hunger (1993, as David Darke)

Horrorshow (1994, as David Darke)

Sex and Blood (1994)

Succumb (1994)

Shade (1994, as David Darke)

Last Rites (1996, as David Darke)

DEITZ, TOM

Windmaster's Bane (1986)

Fireshaper's Doom (1987)

Darkthunder's Way (1989)

The Gryphon King (1989)

Sunshaker's War (1990)

Soulsmith (1991)

Stoneskin's Revenge (1991)

Dreambuilder (1992)

Wordwright (1993)

Above the Lower Sky (1994)

Ghostcountry's Wrath (1995)

The Demons in the Green (1996)

Landslayer's Law (1997)

Bloodwinter (1999)

Warstalker's Track (1999)

Springwar (2000)

Summerblood (2001)

Warautumn (2002)

DE LINT, CHARLES

Hedgework and Guessery (1981)

Moonheart (1984)

The Riddle of the Wren (1984)

Mulengro (1985)

The Harp of the Grey Rose (1985)

Yarrow (1986)

Ascian in Rose (1987)

Jack the Giant Killer (1987)

Greenmantle (1988)

Wolf Moon (1988)

Valley of Thunder (1989)

Westlin Wind (1989)

Svaha (1989)

Drink Down the Moon (1990)

The Hidden City (1990)

The Dreaming Place (1990)

Ghostwood (1990)

Angel of Darkness (1990, originally as by Samuel Key)

Our Lady of the Harbour (1991)

The Little Country (1991)

From a Whisper to a Scream (1992, originally as by Samuel Key)

Spiritwalk (1992)

Dreams Underfoot (1993)

The Wishing Well (1993)

Into the Green (1993)

Memory and Dream (1994)

The Wild Wood (1994)

The Ivory and the Horn (1995)

Jack of Kinrowan (1995)

Trader (1997)

Someplace to Be Flying (1998)

Moonlight and Vines (1999)

Forests of the Heart (2000)

The Onion Girl (2001)

Tapping the Dream Tree (2002)

Spirits in the Wires (2003)

DENNING, TROY

Waterdeep (1989, as Richard Awlinson)

Dragonwall (1990, as Richard Awlinson)

The Parched Sea (1991, as Richard Awlinson)

The Verdant Passage (1991)

The Amber Enchantress (1992)

The Crimson Legion (1992)

The Obsidian Oracle (1993)

The Cerulean Storm (1993)

The Ogre's Pact (1994)

The Titan of Twilight (1995)

The Giant among Us (1995)

The Veiled Dragon (1996)
Pages of Pain (1997)
Crucible: The Trial of Cyric the Mad (1998)
Faces of Deception (1998)
Beyond the High Road (1999)
The Oath of Stonekeep (1999)
Death of the Dragon (2000, with Ed Greenwood)
The Siege (2001)
The Summoning (2001)
The Sorcerer (2002)

DERLETH, AUGUST
Someone in the Dark (1941)
Something Near (1945)
Lurker at the Threshold (1945)
Dark of the Moon (1947)
Not Long for This World (1948)
The Survivor and Others (1957)
The Mask of Cthulhu (1958)
Dark Mind, Dark Heart (1962)
The Trail of Cthulhu (1962)
Lonesome Places (1962)
Mr. George and Other Odd Persons (1964)
Colonel Markesan and Less Pleasant Persons (1966, with Mark Schorer)
Shadow out of Time and Other Tales of Horror (1968, with H. P. Lovecraft)
The Shuttered Room and Other Tales of Horror (1970, with H. P. Lovecraft)
Dark Things (1971)
Watchers out of Time (1974)
Dwellers in Darkness (1976)
In Lovecraft's Shadow (1998)
Quest for Cthulhu (2000)

DEXTER, SUSAN
The Ring of Allaire (1981)
The Sword of Calandra (1985)
The Mountains of Channadran (1986)
The Wizard's Shadow (1993)
The Prince of Ill Luck (1994)
The Wind-Witch (1994)
The True Knight (1996)
Moonlight (2001)

DICKINSON, PETER
The Weathermonger (1968)
Heartsease (1969)
The Devil's Children (1970)
The Gift (1974)

The Changes (1975)
The Blue Hawk (1976)
Tulku (1979)
Healer (1983)
A Box of Nothing (1985)
Merlin's Dreams (1988)
Time and the Clockmice (1993)
The Lion Tamer's Daughter and Other Supernatural Stories (1997)
The Ropemaker (2001)
Water (2002, with Robin McKinley)
Tears of the Salamander (2003)

DISCH, THOMAS
The Businessman (1984)
The Brave Little Toaster (1986)
The Brave Little Toaster Goes to Mars (1988)
The M.D. (1991)
The Priest: A Gothic Romance (1995)
The Sub (1999)

DONALDSON, STEPHEN R.
Lord Foul's Bane (1977)
The Illearth War (1977)
The Power That Preserves (1977)
The Wounded Land (1980)
The One Tree (1982)
White Gold Wielder (1983)
The Mirror of Her Dreams (1986)
A Man Rides Through (1987)
The First Chronicles of Thomas Covenant the Unbeliever (1983)
Daughter of Regals and Other Tales (1984)
Reave the Just and Other Stories (1998)
The Runes of the Earth (2004)

DOUGLAS, CAROLE NELSON
Six of Swords (1982)
Exiles of the Rynth (1984)
Keepers of Edanvant (1987)
Heir of Rengarth (1988)
Seven of Swords (1989)
Cup of Clay (1991)
Seed upon the Wind (1992)

DRAKE, DAVID
The Dragon Lord (1982)
From the Heart of Darkness (1983)
Dagger (1988)
The Sea Hag (1988)

Vettius and His Friends (1989)
Explorers in Hell (1989, with Janet Morris)
The Enchanted Bunny (1990)
Old Nathan (1991)
To Bring the Light (1996)
Lord of the Isles (1997)
Queen of Demons (1998)
Servant of the Dragon (1999)
Mistress of the Catacombs (2001)
The Tyrant (2002, with Eric Flint)
Goddess of the Ice Realm (2003)
Master of the Cauldron (2004)

DUANE, DIANE
The Door into Fire (1979)
So You Want to Be a Wizard (1983)
The Door into Shadow (1984)
Deep Wizardry (1985)
Keeper of the City (1989, with Peter Morwood)
Support Your Local Wizard (1990)
High Wizardry (1990)
The Door into Sunset (1992)
A Wizard Abroad (1993, also published as *Wizardry*)
Book of Night with Moon (1997)
To Visit the Queen (1999)
The Wizard's Dilemma (2001)
A Wizard Alone (2002)
Stealing the Elf King's Roses (2002)
Sword and Dragon (2002)
Wizard's Holiday (2003)

DUNCAN, DAVE
A Rose-Red City (1987)
The Coming of Wisdom (1988)
The Destiny of the Sword (1988)
The Reluctant Swordsman (1988)
The Magic Casement (1990)
Emperor and Clown (1991)
Faery Lands Forlorn (1991)
Perilous Seas (1991)
The Cutting Edge (1992)
The Reaver Road (1992)
The Stricken Field (1993)
Upland Outlaws (1993)
The Living God (1994)
The Cursed (1995)
Past Imperative (1995)
The Hunter's Haunt (1995)
Demon Sword (1995, as Ken Hood)
Present Tense (1996)

Future Indefinite (1997)
Demon Rider (1997, as Ken Hood)
The Gilded Chain (1998)
Demon Knight (1998, as Ken Hood)
Lord of the Fire Lands (1999)
Sir Stalwart (1999)
The Crooked House (2000)
Sky of Swords (2000)
Paragon Lost (2002)
Impossible Odds (2003)
The Jaguar Knights (2004)

DUNSANY, LORD
The Gods of Pegana (1905)
Time and the Gods (1906)
The Sword of Welleran and Other Stories (1908)
Dreamer's Tales (1910)
The Book of Wonder (1912)
The Food of Death (1915, also published as *Fifty One Tales*)
The Last Book of Wonder (1916, also published as *Tales of Wonder*)
Tales of War (1918)
Tales of Three Hemispheres (1919)
Unhappy Far Off Things (1919)
Don Rodriguez (1922)
The King of Elfland's Daughter (1924)
The Charwoman's Shadow (1926)
The Blessing of Pan (1926)
The Travel Tales of Mr. Joseph Jorkens (1931)
The Curse of the Wise Woman (1933)
Jorkens Remembers Africa (1934)
Jorkens Has a Large Whisky (1940)
The Fourth Book of Jorkens (1948)
The Man Who Ate the Phoenix (1949)
The Strange Journeys of Colonel Polders (1950)
Little Tales of Smethers and Other Stories (1952)
Jorkens Borrows Another Whisky (1954)
The Sword of Welleran and Other Tales of Enchantment (1954)
At the Edge of the World (1970)
Beyond the Fields We Know (1972)
Gods, Men, and Ghosts (1972)
Over the Hills and Far Away (1974)
The Ghosts of the Heaviside Layer and Other Fantasms (1980)
The Hashish Man and Other Stories (1996)
The Complete Pegana (1998)
Collected Jorkens (2004)
In the Land of Time and Other Fantasy Tales (2004)

DURGIN, DORANNA
Dun Lady's Jess (1996)
Changespell (1997)
Touched by Magic (1997)
Wolf Justice (1998)
Barrenlands (1998)
Wolverine's Daughter (2000)
Seer's Blood (2000)
A Feral Darkness (2001)
Changespell Legacy (2002)
Dark Debts (2003)

EAGER, EDWARD
Half Magic (1954)
Knight's Castle (1956)
Magic by the Lake (1957)
The Time Garden (1958)
The Well-Wishers (1960)
Seven Day Magic (1962)

EDDINGS, DAVID
Pawn of Prophecy (1982)
Queen of Sorcery (1982)
Magician's Gambit (1983)
Castle of Wizardry (1984)
Enchanter's End Game (1984)
The Belgariad (1985)
Guardians of the West (1987)
Demon Lord of Karanda (1988)
King of the Murgos (1988)
The Diamond Throne (1989)
Sorceress of Darshiva (1989)
The Ruby Knight (1990)
The Sapphire Rose (1991)
The Seeress of Kell (1991)
Domes of Fire (1992)
The Shining Ones (1993)
The Elenium (1993)
The Losers (1993)
The Hidden City (1994)
Belgarath the Sorcerer (1995, with Leigh Eddings)
Polgara the Sorceress (1996, with Leigh Eddings)
The Redemption of Althalus (2000, with Leigh Eddings)
Regina's Song (2002, with Leigh Eddings)
The Elder Gods (2003, with Leigh Eddings)
The Treasured One (2004, with Leigh Eddings)

EDDISON, E. R.
The Worm Ouroboros (1922)
Mistress of Mistresses (1935)
A Fish Dinner at Memison (1941)
The Mezentian Gate (1958)
Zimiamvia: A Trilogy (1992)

EDGHILL, ROSEMARY
The Sword of Maiden's Tears (1995)
The Cup of Morning Shadows (1995)
The Cloak of Night and Daggers (1997)
The Empty Crown (1997)
Met by Moonlight (1998)
The Shadow of Albion (1999, with Andre Norton)
Leopard in Exile (2001, with Andre Norton)
Beyond World's End (2001, with Mercedes Lackey)
Spirits White As Lightning (2001, with Mercedes Lackey)
The Warslayer (2002)
Paying the Piper at the Gates of Dawn (2003)
Vengeance of Masks (2003)
Mad Maudlin (2003, with Mercedes Lackey)

ELLIOTT, KATE
The Labyrinth Gate (1988, as Alis A. Rasmussen)
The Golden Key (1997, with Jennifer Roberson and Melanie Rawn)
King's Dragon (1997)
Prince of Dogs (1998)
The Burning Stone (1999)
Child of Flame (2000)
The Gathering Storm (2003)
In the Ruins (2005)

ELROD, P. N.
Bloodcircle (1990)
Bloodlist (1990)
Lifeblood (1990)
Art in the Blood (1991)
Fire in the Blood (1991)
Blood on the Water (1992)
I, Strahd (1993)
Red Death (1993)
Death and the Maiden (1994)
Death Masque (1995)
Dance of Death (1996)
Jonathan Barrett, Gentleman Vampire (1996)
A Chill in the Blood (1998)
The War against Azalin (1998)
The Dark Sleep (1999)
Lady Crymsyn (2000)
Keeper of the King (2000, with Nigel Bennett)
Quincey Morris, Vampire (2001)
His Father's Son (2001, with Nigel Bennett)

The Vampire Files (2003)
The Adventures of Myhr (2003)
Cold Streets (2003)
Siege Perilous (2004, with Nigel Bennett)
Song in the Dark (2005)

EMERSON, RU
The Princess of Flames (1986)
To the Haunted Mountains (1987)
In the Caves of Exile (1988)
On the Seas of Destiny (1989)
The Calling of the Three (1990)
Masques (1990)
Spell Bound (1990)
Two in Hiding (1991)
One Land, One Duke (1992)
The Craft of Light (1993)
The Sword and the Lion (1993, as Roberta Cray)
Fortress of Frost and Fire (1993, with Mercedes Lackey)
The Art of the Sword (1994)
The Science of Power (1995)
The Empty Throne (1996)
The Thief of Hermes (1997)
The Huntress and the Sphinx (1997)
Go Quest, Young Man (1999)
Questward Ho! (1999)
Against the Giants (1999)
How the Quest Was Won (2000)
Keep on the Borderlands (2001)

ETCHISON, DENNIS
The Fog (1980)
Halloween II (1981, as Jack Martin)
The Dark Country (1982)
Halloween III (1982, as Jack Martin)
Videodrome (1983, as Jack Martin)
Red Dreams (1984)
Darkside (1986)
The Blood Kiss (1988)
Shadow Man (1993)
California Gothic (1995)
Double Edge (1997)
The Death Artist (2000)
Talking in the Dark (2001)

EULO, KEN
The Brownstone (1980)
The Bloodstone (1981)
The Deathstone (1982)
Nocturnal (1983)

The Ghost of Veronica Gray (1985)
The House of Caine (1988)
Manhattan Heat (1991)
Claw (1994)

FARRIS, JOHN
King Windom (1967)
When Michael Calls (1967)
The Fury (1976)
All Heads Turn When the Hunt Goes By (1977, also
    published as *Bad Blood*)
The Uninvited (1982)
Son of the Endless Night (1984)
Wildwood (1986)
The Axman Cometh (1989)
Scare Tactics (1989)
Fiends (1990)
The Fury and the Terror (2001)
The Fury and the Power (2003)
Elvisland (2004)
Phantom Nights (2005)

FEIST, RAYMOND E.
Magician (1982)
Silverthorn (1985)
Magician: Apprentice (1985)
Magician: Master (1986)
A Darkness at Sethanon (1986)
Daughter of the Empire (1987, with Janny Wurts)
Faerie Tale (1988)
Prince of the Blood (1989)
Servant of the Empire (1990, with Janny Wurts)
The King's Buccaneer (1992)
Mistress of the Empire (1992, with Janny Wurts)
Shadow of a Dark Queen (1994)
Rise of a Merchant Prince (1995)
Rage of the Demon King (1997)
Shards of a Broken Crown (1998)
Krondor: The Betrayal (1998)
Krondor: The Assassins (1999)
Krondor: Tears of the Gods (2000)
Honoured Enemy (2001, with William R. Forstchen)
King of Foxes (2002)
Murder in Lamut (2002, with Joel Rosenberg)
Talon of the Silver Hawk (2003)
Jimmy the Hand (2003, with S. M. Stirling)
Exile's Return (2004)

FORD, JEFFREY
Vanitas (1988)

The Physiognomy (1997)
Memoranda (1999)
The Beyond (2001)
The Portrait of Mrs. Charbuque (2002)
The Fantasy Writer's Assistant and Other Stories (2002)

FOWLER, CHRISTOPHER
City Jitters (1987)
More City Jitters (1988, also published as *City Jitters Two*)
Roofworld (1988)
The Bureau of Lost Souls (1989)
Rune (1990)
Sharper Knives (1992)
Red Bride (1992)
Darkest Day (1993)
Spanky (1994)
Flesh Wounds (1995)
Dracula's Library (1997)
Personal Demons (1998)
Uncut (1999)
Breathe (2004)

FRANCE, ANATOLE
Thais (1890)
The Well of Santa Clara (1903)
Penguin Island (1909)
Revolt of the Angels (1914)
Great Novels of Anatole France (1914)

FRIESNER, ESTHER
Mustapha and His Wise Dog (1985)
New York by Knight (1986)
The Silver Mountain (1986)
Spells of Mortal Weaving (1986)
Harlot's Ruse (1986)
The Witchwood Cradle (1987)
Druid's Blood (1988)
Elf Defense (1988)
Here Be Demons (1988)
The Water King's Laughter (1989)
Demon Blues (1989)
Sphynxes Wild (1989)
Hooray for Hellywood (1990)
It's Been Fun (1991)
Gnome Man's Land (1991)
Harpy High (1991)
Unicorn U (1992)
Yesterday We Saw Mermaids (1992)
Wishing Season (1993)
Split Heirs (1993, with Lawrence Watt-Evans)

Majyk by Accident (1993)
Majyk by Design (1994)
Majyk by Hook or Crook (1994)
Child of the Eagle (1996)
Playing with Fire (1997)
Up the Wall & Other Tales of King Arthur and His Knights (2000)
E Godz (2003, with Robert Lynn Asprin)

FROST, GREGORY
Lyrec (1984)
Tain (1986)
Remscela (1988)
Crimson Spear (1998)
Fitcher's Brides (2002)
Attack of the Jazz Giants and Other Stories (2005)

GABALDON, DIANA
Outlander (1991, also published as *Cross Stitch*)
Dragonfly in Amber (1992)
Voyager (1994)
Drums of Autumn (1996)
The Fiery Cross (2001)

GAIMAN, NEIL
Good Omens (1990, with Terry Pratchett)
Angels and Visitations: A Miscellany (1993)
Neverwhere (1996)
Smoke and Mirrors (1998)
Stardust (1999)
American Gods (2001)
Coraline (2002)

GARDNER, CRAIG SHAW
A Malady of Magics (1986)
A Multitude of Monsters (1986)
A Difficulty with Dwarves (1987)
The Lost Boys (1987)
A Night in the Netherhells (1987)
The Exploits of Ebenezum (1987)
An Excess of Enchantments (1988)
Wishbringer (1988)
A Disagreement with Death (1989)
Slaves of the Volcano God (1989)
The Wanderings of Wuntvor (1989)
Bride of the Slime Monster (1990)
Revenge of the Fluffy Bunnies (1990)
The Other Sinbad (1991)
The Cineverse Cycle (1991)
A Bad Day for Ali Baba (1991)

The Last Arabian Night (1993, also published as *Scheherazade's Night Out*)
Dragon Sleeping (1994, also published as *Raven Walking*)
Dragon Waking (1995)
The Seventh Guest (1995, with Matthew J. Costello)
Dragon Burning (1996)
Return to Chaos (1998)
Leprechauns (1999)
The Changeling War (1999, as Peter Garrison)
The Sorcerer's Gun (1999, as Peter Garrison)
The Magic Dead (1999, as Peter Garrison)
Dark Mirror (2004)

GARNER, ALAN
The Weirdstone of Brisingamen (1960, also published as *The Weirdstone: A Tale of Aldery*)
The Moon of Gomrath (1963)
Elidor (1965)
The Owl Service (1967)
Hamish Hamilton Book of Goblins (1969)
Red Shift (1973)
Fairytales of Gold (1980)
Alan Garner's Book of British Fairy Tales (1984)
A Bag of Moonshine (1986)

GARTON, RAY
Seductions (1984)
Darklings (1985)
Invaders from Mars (1986)
Live Girls (1987)
Crucifax (1988)
Crucifax Autumn (1988)
Warlock (1989)
The Nightmares on Elm Street (1989, as Joseph Locke)
Methods of Madness (1990)
Lot Lizards (1991)
The New Neighbor (1991)
Dark Channel (1992)
Kiss of Death (1992, as Joseph Locke)
Game Over (1993, as Joseph Locke)
Vampire Heart (1994, as Joseph Locke)
Deadly Relations (1994, as Joseph Locke)
Pieces of Hate (1996)
All That Glitters (1998)
Been There, Done That (1998, as Joseph Locke)
Resurrecting Ravanna (2000)
The Folks (2001)
Zombie Love (2003)
Night Life (2004)

GEMMELL, DAVID
Legend (1984, also published as *Against the Horde*)
The King beyond the Gate (1985)
Waylander (1986)
Wolf in Shadow (1987, also published as *The Jerusalem Man*)
Ghost King (1988)
Last Sword of Power (1988)
Knights of Dark Renown (1989)
The Lost Crown (1989)
The Last Guardian (1989)
Quest for Lost Heroes (1990)
Lion of Macedon (1990)
Dark Prince (1991)
Drenai Tales (1991)
Morningstar (1992)
Stones of Power (1992)
In the Realm of the Wolf (1992, also published as *Waylander II*)
The First Chronicles of Druss the Legend (1993)
Druss the Legend (1994)
Bloodstone (1994)
Ironhand's Daughter (1995)
The David Gemmell Omnibus (1995)
The Second Chronicles of Druss the Legend (1995)
The Hawk Eternal (1996)
The Complete Chronicles of the Jerusalem Man (1996)
Winter Warriors (1997)
Echoes of the Great Song (1997)
Midnight Falcon (1999)
Hero in the Shadows (2000)
Ravenheart (2001)
Stormrider (2002)
Drenai Tales Volume 2 (2002)
White Wolf (2003)
The Swords of Light and Day (2004)
Lord of the Silver Bow (2005)

GENTLE, MARY
Hawk in Silver (1977)
Rats and Gargoyles (1990)
Architecture of Desire (1991)
Grunts (1992)
Left to His Own Devices (1994)
Ash 1: A Secret History (1997)
The Wild Machines (1998)
Carthage Ascendant (2000)
Ash: A Secret History (2000)
1610: A Sundial in a Grave (2003)
White Crow (2003)
Cartomancy (2004)

GODWIN, PARKE

Firelord (1980)
A Cold Blue Light (1983, with Marvin Kaye)
Beloved Exile (1984)
The Fire When It Comes (1984)
The Last Rainbow (1985)
A Truce with Time (1988)
Sherwood (1992)
Robin and the King (1993)
Return to Nottingham (1993)
The Tower of Beowulf (1995)
The Lovers (1999)

GOINGBACK, OWL

Crota (1996)
Shaman Moon (1997)
Darker Than Night (1999)
Evil Whispers (2001)
Breed (2002)

GOLDEN, CHRISTIE

Vampire of the Mists (1991)
Dance of the Dead (1992)
The Enemy Within (1994)
Instrument of Fate (1996)
King's Man and Thief (1997)
Lord of the Clans (2001)
The Books of Verold (2001)
On Fire's Wings (2004)

GOLDEN, CHRISTOPHER

Of Saints and Shadows (1994)
Angel Souls and Devil Hearts (1995)
The Lost Army (1997)
Halloween Rain (1997, with Nancy Holder)
Of Masques and Martyrs (1998)
Blooded (1998, with Nancy Holder)
Child of the Hunt (1998, with Nancy Holder)
Sins of the Fathers (1999)
Strangewood (1999)
Immortal (1999, with Nancy Holder)
Out of the Madhouse (1999, with Nancy Holder)
Ghost Roads (1999, with Nancy Holder)
Songs of Entropy (1999, with Nancy Holder)
Pretty Maids All in a Row (2000)
Prophecies (2001)
Prowlers (2001)
Predator and Prey (2001)
Straight on 'Til Morning (2001)
Laws of Nature (2001)

Dark Times (2001)
King of the Dead (2001)
Original Sins (2001)
Oz: Into the Wild (2002)
The Wisdom of War (2002)
The Ferryman (2002)
Wild Things (2002)
Monster Island (2003, with Thomas E. Sniegoski)
Gathering Dark (2003)
The Bones of Giants (2004)
The Boys Are Back in Town (2004)
The Nimble Man (2004, with Thomas E. Sniegoski)
The Un-Magician (2004, with Thomas E. Sniegoski)
Dragon Secrets (2004, with Thomas E. Sniegoski)
Ghostfire (2005, with Thomas E. Sniegoski)
The Tears of the Furies (2005, with Thomas E. Sniegoski)
Wildwood Road (2005)

GOLDSTEIN, LISA

The Red Magician (1982)
The Dream Years (1986)
Daily Voices (1989)
Tourists (1989)
Strange Devices of the Sun and Moon (1993)
Summer King, Winter Fool (1994)
Travelers in Magic (1994)
Walking the Labyrinth (1996)
Dark Cities Underground (1999)
The Alchemist's Door (2002)

GOODKIND, TERRY

Wizard's First Rule (1994)
Stone of Tears (1995)
Blood of the Fold (1996)
Temple of the Winds (1997)
Soul of the Fire (1999)
Faith of the Fallen (2000)
Debt of Bones (2001)
The Pillars of Creation (2001)
Naked Empire (2003)
Chainfire (2005)

GOUDGE, ELIZABETH

The Middle Window (1935)
Smoky House (1940)
Henrietta's House (1945)
The Little White Horse (1946)
The White Witch (1958)
Linnets and Valerians (1964)

GRANT, CHARLES L.

The Curse (1977)
The Hour of the Oxrun Dead (1977)
The Eve of the Hound (1977, as Deborah Lewis)
Voices out of Time (1977, as Deborah Lewis)
The Sound of Midnight (1978)
Kirkwood Fires (1978, as Deborah Lewis)
The Last Call of Mourning (1979)
River Witch (1979, as Felicia Andrews)
The Wind at Winter's End (1979, as Deborah Lewis)
Moon Witch (1980, as Felicia Andrews)
Mountain Witch (1980, as Felicia Andrews)
The Grave (1981)
A Glow of Candles and Other Stories (1981)
Tales from the Nightside (1981)
The Nestling (1982)
Nightmare Seasons (1982)
The Bloodwind (1982)
The Soft Whisper of the Dead (1982)
Night Songs (1984)
The King of Satan's Eyes (1984, as Geoffrey Marsh)
The Dark Cry of the Moon (1985)
The Tea Party (1985)
The Orchard (1986)
Blood River Down (1986, as Lionel Fenn)
The Pet (1986)
The Long Night of the Grave (1986)
The Tail of the Arabian Knight (1986, as Geoffrey Marsh)
Agnes Day (1987, as Lionel Fenn)
For Fear of the Night (1987)
The Patch of the Odin Soldier (1987, as Geoffrey Marsh)
The Seven Spears of W'dch'ck (1988, as Lionel Fenn)
The Fangs of the Hooded Demon (1988, as Geoffrey Marsh)
Dialing the Wind (1989)
In a Dark Dream (1989)
Fire Mask (1991)
Something Stirs (1991)
Stunts (1991)
Kent Montana and the Once and Future Thing (1991, as Lionel Fenn)
668: The Neighbor of the Beast (1992, as Lionel Fenn)
The Mark of the Moderately Vicious Vampire (1992, as Lionel Fenn)
Daughter of Darkness (1992, as Simon Lake)
Something's Watching (1993, as Simon Lake)
Death Cycle (1993, as Simon Lake)
He Told Me To (1993, as Simon Lake)
Goblin (1994)

Jackals (1994)
The Black Carousel (1995)
Whirlwind (1995)
Symphony (1997)
Web of Defeat (1997, as Lionel Fenn)
Chariot (1998)
Genesis (1998)
In the Mood (1998)
The Hush of Dark Wings (1999)
Winter Knight (1999)
Riders in the Sky (1999)
Hunting Ground (2000)
When the Cold Wind Blows (2001)

GREEN, SHARON

The Far Side of Forever (1987)
Lady Blade, Lord Fighter (1987)
Hellhound Magic (1989)
Dawn Song (1990)
Werewolf Moon (1993)
The Hidden Realms (1993)
Silver Princess, Golden Knight (1993)
Dark Mirror, Dark Dreams (1994)
Enchanting (1994)
Wind Whispers, Shadow Shouts (1995)
Convergence (1996)
Game's End (1996)
Competitions (1997)
Challenges (1998)
Betrayals (1999)
Prophecy (1999)
Haughty Spirit (1999)
Intrigues (2000)
Deceptions (2001)
Destiny (2002)

GREEN, SIMON R.

Hawk and Fisher (1990, also published as *No Haven for the Guilty*)
Winner Takes All (1991, also published as *Devil Take the Hindmost*)
Blue Moon Rising (1991)
The God Killer (1991)
Guard against Dishonor (1991)
Wolf in the Fold (1991, also published as *Vengeance for a Lonely Man*)
The Bones of Haven (1992, also published as *Two Kings in Haven*)
Blood and Honor (1992)
Down among the Dead Men (1993)

Shadows Fall (1994)
Haven of Lost Souls (1999)
Swords of Haven (1999)
Beyond the Blue Moon (2000)
Fear and Loathing in Haven (2000)
Drinking Midnight Wine (2001)
Agents of Light and Darkness (2003)
Something for the Nightside (2003)
Nightingale's Lament (2004)
Hex and the City (2005)
Paths Not Taken (2005)

GREENWOOD, ED

Spellfire (1988)
Crown of Fire (1994)
Elminster: The Making of a Mage (1994)
Cloak of Shadows (1995)
Shadows of Doom (1995)
All Shadows Fled (1995)
Stormlight (1996)
Cormyr (1996, with Jeff Grubb)
To Sleep with Evil (1996, with Andria Hayday)
Elminster in Myth Drannor (1997)
The Mercenaries (1998)
The Diamond (1998, with J. Robert King)
The Temptation of Elminster (1998)
Silverfall (1999)
The Kingless Land (2000)
Death of the Dragon (2000, with Troy Denning)
Elminster in Hell (2001)
The Vacant Throne (2001)
Hand of Fire (2002)
A Dragon's Ascension (2002)
The Dragon's Doom (2004)
The Silent House (2004)

GRESHAM, STEPHEN

Moon Lake (1982)
Half Moon Down (1985)
The Shadow Man (1986)
Dew Claws (1986)
Midnight Boy (1987)
Night Touch (1988)
Runaway (1988)
Abracadabra (1988)
Demon's Eye (1989)
Blood Wings (1990)
The Living Dark (1991)
Just Pretend (1994, as J. V. Lewton)
Called to Darkness (1995, as J. V. Lewton)

In the Blood (2001)
Dark Magic (2002)
Haunted Ground (2003)
The Fraternity (2004)

HAGGARD, H. RIDER

She (1886)
The World's Desire (1890, with Andrew Lang)
Eric Brighteyes (1891)
Ayesha: The Return of She (1905)
The Yellow God (1908)
The Ghost Kings (1908, also published as *The Lady of the Heavens*)
Morning Star (1910)
Red Eve (1911)
The Mahatma and the Hare (1911)
The Wanderer's Necklace (1913)
The Ivory Child (1916)
She and Allan (1920)
Smith and the Pharoahs and Other Tales (1920)
The Ancient Allan (1920)
Wisdom's Daughter (1923)
Treasure of the Lake (1926)
Allan and the Ice-Gods (1927)
Five Adventure Novels (1951)
Lost Civilizations (1953)
The Best Short Stories of H. Rider Haggard (1981)
The Classic Adventures (1986)
Love Eternal (2003)

HAMBLY, BARBARA

The Time of the Dark (1982)
The Walls of Air (1983)
The Armies of Daylight (1983)
Ladies of Mandrigyn (1984)
Dragonsbane (1985)
The Silent Tower (1986)
The Unschooled Wizard (1987)
The Witches of Wenshar (1987)
Those Who Hunt the Night (1988, also published as *Immortal Blood*)
Darkmage (1988)
The Silicon Mage (1988)
Beauty and the Beast (1989)
The Dark Hand of Magic (1990)
Song of Orpheus (1990)
The Magicians of Night (1991)
The Rainbow Abyss (1991)
Sun-Cross (1992)
Dog Wizard (1992)

Bride of the Rat God (1994)
Stranger at the Wedding (1994, also published as *The Sorcerer's Ward*)
Traveling with the Dead (1995)
Mother of Winter (1996)
Icefalcon's Quest (1998)
Dragonshadow (1999)
Knight of the Demon Queen (2000)
Magic Time (2001, with Marc Alan Zicree)
Sisters of the Raven (2002)

HAMILTON, LAURELL
Nightseer (1992)
Guilty Pleasures (1993)
Laughing Corpse (1994)
The Lunatic Cafe (1995)
Death of a Darklord (1995)
Circus of the Damned (1995)
Bloody Bones (1996)
The Killing Dance (1997)
Blue Moon (1998)
Club Vampyre (1998)
Burnt Offerings (1998)
Black Moon Inn (1998)
The Midnight Cafe (1998)
The Obsidian Butterfly (1999)
A Kiss of Shadows (2000)
Narcissus in Chains (2001)
A Caress of Twilight (2002)
Cerulean Sins (2003)
Incubus Dreams (2004)
Seduced by Moonlight (2004)
A Stroke of Midnight (2005)

HANCOCK, NIEL
Greyfax Grimwald (1977)
Faragon Fairingay (1977)
Calix Stay (1977)
Squaring the Circle (1977)
Circle of Light (1977)
Dragon Winter (1978)
Across the Far Mountain (1982)
The Plains of the Sea (1982)
On the Boundaries of Darkness (1982)
The Road to the Middle Islands (1983)
The Fires of Windameir (1985)
The Sea of Silence (1987)
A Wanderer's Return (1988)
The Bridge of Dawn (1991)

HAUTALA, RICK
Moondeath (1980)
Moonbog (1982)
Night Stone (1986)
Little Brothers (1988)
Moonwalker (1989)
Dead Voices (1990)
Winter Wake (1990)
Cold Whisper (1991)
Dark Silence (1992)
Ghost Light (1993)
Shades of Night (1995)
Beyond the Shroud (1996)
The Mountain King (1996)
The Hidden Saint (1999)
Bedbugs (2000)
The White Room (2001, as A. J. Matthews)
Cold River (2003)
Looking Glass (2004, as A. J. Matthews)
Follow (2005, as A. J. Matthews)

HAWKE, SIMON
Jason Lives: Friday the 13th Part IV (1986)
Friday the 13th (1987)
The Wizard of Fourth Street (1987)
Friday the 13th Part II (1988)
Friday the 13th Part III (1988)
The Wizard of Whitechapel (1988)
The Wizard of Sunset Strip (1989)
The Wizard of the Rue Morgue (1990)
The Samurai Wizard (1991)
The Nine Lives of Catseye Gomez (1991)
The Wizard of Santa Fe (1991)
The Reluctant Sorcerer (1992)
The Inadequate Adept (1993)
The Wizard of Lovecraft's Cafe (1993)
The Wizard of Camelot (1993)
The Outcast (1993)
The Nomad (1994)
The Seeker (1994)
The Broken Blade (1995)
The Iron Throne (1995)
The Ambivalent Magician (1996)
War (1996)
The Last Wizard (1997)

HERBERT, JAMES
The Rats (1974, also published as *The Deadly Eyes*)
The Fog (1975)
The Survivor (1976)

Fluke (1977)
The Spear (1978)
Lair (1979)
The Dark (1980)
The Jonah (1981)
Shrine (1983)
Domain (1984)
Moon (1985)
Magic Cottage (1986)
Sepulchre (1987)
Haunted (1988)
Creed (1990)
Portent (1992)
The Ghosts of Sleath (1995)
Others (1999)
Once (2002)
Nobody True (2004)

HOBB, ROBIN

Harpy's Flight (1983, as Megan Lindholm)
The Limbreth Gate (1984, as Megan Lindholm)
The Windsingers (1984, as Megan Lindholm)
Wizard of the Pigeons (1986, as Megan Lindholm)
Wolf's Brother (1988, as Megan Lindholm)
The Reindeer People (1988, as Megan Lindholm)
Luck of the Wheels (1989, as Megan Lindholm)
A Saga of the Reindeer People (1989, as Megan Lindholm)
Cloven Hooves (1991, as Megan Lindholm)
Gypsy (1992, as Megan Lindholm, with Steven Brust)
Assassin's Apprentice (1995)
Royal Assassin (1996)
Assassin's Quest (1997)
Ship of Magic (1998)
Mad Ship (1999)
Ship of Destiny (2000)
Fool's Errand (2002)
Golden Fool (2003)
Fool's Fate (2004)
Soldier Son (2005)

HODGE, BRIAN

Dark Advent (1988)
Oasis (1989)
Nightlife (1991)
Deathgrip (1992)
The Darker Saints (1993)
Shrines and Desecrations (1994)
The Convulsion Factory (1996)
Prototype (1996)

Falling Idols (1998)
Lies and Ugliness (2002)

HODGSON, WILLIAM HOPE

The Boats of the Glen Carrig (1907)
The House on the Borderland (1907)
The Ghost Pirates (1909)
Poems and the Dream of X (1912)
The Night Land (1912)
Carnacki, the Ghost Finder (1913)
Men of the Deep Waters (1914)
The House on the Borderland and Other Novels (1946)
Deep Waters (1967)
Out of the Storm (1975)
Masters of Terror Volume 1 (1977)
A Dream of X (1977)
Spectral Manifestations (1984)
The Haunted Pampero (1991)
Demons of the Sea (1992)
Terrors of the Sea (1996)
Down Among the Weeds (1997)
The Boats of the Glen Carrig and Other Nautical Adventures (2003)

HOFFMAN, NINA KIRIKI

Legacy of Fire (1990)
Courting Disasters and Other Strange Affinities (1991)
Unmasking (1992)
Child of an Ancient City (1992, with Tad Williams)
The Thread That Ties the Bones (1993)
The Silent Strength of Stones (1995)
Why I'm Not Afraid of Ghosts (1997)
I Was a Sixth Grade Zombie (1998)
A Red Heart of Memories (1999)
Past the Size of Dreaming (2001)
A Fistful of Sky (2002)
A Stir of Bones (2003)
Time Travelers, Ghosts, and Other Visitors (2004)

HOLDSTOCK, ROBERT

Legend of the Werewolf (1976, as Robert Black)
The Satanists (1976, as Robert Black)
The Bull Chief (1977, as Chris Carlsen)
Shadow of the Wolf (1977, as Chris Carlsen)
Swordsmistress of Chaos (1978, as Richard Kirk with Angus Wells)
Necromancer (1978)
A Time of Ghosts (1978, as Richard Kirk)
Lords of the Shadows (1979, as Richard Kirk)
The Horned Warrior (1979, as Chris Carlsen)

In the Valley of Statues (1982)
Nighthunter (1983, as Robert Faulcon also published as
  The Stalking)
The Talisman (1983, as Robert Faulcon)
The Ghost Dance (1983, as Robert Faulcon)
The Shrine (1984, as Robert Faulcon)
Mythago Wood (1984)
The Hexing (1984, as Robert Faulcon)
The Emerald Forest (1985)
The Labyrinth (1987, as Robert Faulcon)
Death Angel (1988, as Robert Black)
Lavondyss (1988)
The Bone Forest (1991)
The Hollowing (1993)
Merlin's Wood (1994)
Ancient Echoes (1996)
Unknown Regions (1996, also published as *The Fetch*)
Gate of Ivory, Gate of Horn (1997)
Celtika (2001)
The Iron Grail (2002)

HOLT, TOM

Expecting Someone Taller (1987)
Who's Afraid of Beowulf? (1988)
Flying Dutch (1991)
Ye Gods (1992)
Here Comes the Sun (1993)
Faust Among Equals (1994)
Grailblazers (1994)
Djinn Rummy (1995)
Odds and Gods (1995)
My Hero (1996)
Paint Your Dragon (1996)
Open Sesame (1997)
Bitter Lemmings (1997)
Wish You Were Here (1998)
Only Human (1999)
Snow White and the Seven Samurai (2000)
Valhalla (2000)
The First Tom Holt Omnibus (2001)
Nothing But Blue Skies (2001)
Little People (2002)
Expecting Beowulf (2002)
Falling Sideways (2002)
The Second Tom Holt Omnibus (2002)
The Divine Comedies (2003)
The Portable Door (2003)
In Your Dreams (2004)
Earth, Air, Fire, and Custard (2005)

HOWARD, ROBERT E.

Skull-Face and Others (1946)
Conan the Conqueror (1950, also published as *The
  Hour of the Dragon*)
The Sword of Conan (1952)
The Coming of Conan (1953)
King Conan (1953)
Conan the Barbarian (1954)
Tales of Conan (1955, with L. Sprague De Camp)
The Dark Man and Others (1963, also published as *The
  Dead Remember*)
Conan the Adventurer (1966, with L. Sprague De
  Camp and Lin Carter)
Conan the Usurper (1967, with L. Sprague De Camp
  and Lin Carter)
King Kull (1967, with Lin Carter)
Conan (1967, with L. Sprague De Camp and Lin
  Carter)
Conan the Warrior (1967, with L. Sprague De Camp
  and Lin Carter)
Conan the Wanderer (1968, with L. Sprague De Camp
  and Lin Carter)
Wolfshead (1968)
Red Shadows (1968)
The Moon of Skulls (1969)
Bran Mak Morn (1969)
The Moon of Skulls (1969)
Conan of Cimmeria (1969, with L. Sprague De Camp
  and Lin Carter)
The Hand of Kane (1970)
Solomon Kane (1971)
The Lost Valley of Iskander (1974)
Worms of the Earth (1974)
Tigers of the Sea (1974)
The People of the Black Circle (1974)
Conan in the Tower of the Elephant (1975)
A Witch Shall Be Born (1975)
Red Nails (1975)
The Tower of the Elephant (1975)
The Book of Robert E. Howard (1976)
The Second Book of Robert E. Howard (1976)
*Pigeons from Hell and Other Weird and Fantastic
  Adventures* (1976)
The Grim Land and Others (1976)
Rogues in the House (1976)
The Shadow Kingdom (1976)
The Swords of Shahrazar (1976)
The Valley of the Worms and Others (1976)
Marchers of Valhalla (1977)

The People of the Black Circle (1977, with L. Sprague
    De Camp and Lin Carter)
Conan of Aquilonia (1977, with Lin Carter)
Three Bladed Doom (1977)
The Robert E. Howard Omnibus (1977)
The Sowers of Thunder (1977)
The Sword Woman (1977)
Black Canaan (1978)
Kull (1978)
Skulls in the Stars (1978)
Skull-Face (1978)
Black Canaan (1978)
Queen of the Black Coast (1978)
Sons of the White Wolf (1978)
Black Colossus (1979)
The Howard Collector (1979)
Jewels of Gwahlur (1979)
The Hills of the Dead (1979)
The Gods of Bal-Sagoth (1979)
Hawks of Outremer (1979)
The Road to Azrael (1979)
The Treasure of Tranicos (1980, with L. Sprague De
    Camp and Lin Carter)
Lord of the Dead (1981)
The Adventures of Lal Singh (1985)
Robert E. Howard's Kull (1985)
The Pool of the Black One (1986)
Cthulhu—The Mythos and Other Kindred Horrors
    (1988)
Cormac Mac Art (1995)
Beyond the Borders (1996)
Eons of the Night (1996)
Trails in Darkness (1996)
The Conan Chronicles Volume I (2000)
The Essential Conan (2001)
The Conan Chronicles Volume II (2001)
Nameless Cults (2001)
The Bloody Crown of Conan (2004)
The Savage Tales of Solomon Kane (2004)
The Coming of Conan the Barbarian (2004)
The Black Stranger and Other American Tales (2005)
Bran Mak Morn: The Last King (2005)

HUBBARD, L. RON
Death's Deputy (1948)
Slaves of Sleep (1948)
Triton and Battle of Wizards (1949)
Fear & Typewriter in the Sky (1951)
From Death to the Stars (1952)
Typewriter in the Sky (1952)

Fear (1957)
Fear and The Ultimate Adventure (1968)
Slaves of Sleep and Masters of Sleep (1993)

HUFF, TANYA
Child of the Grove (1988)
Gate of Darkness, Circle of Light (1989)
The Last Wizard (1989)
The Fire's Stone (1990)
Blood Lines (1991)
Blood Trail (1992)
Blood Pact (1993)
Blood Price (1993)
Sing the Four Quarters (1994)
Fifth Quarter (1995)
Scholar of Decay (1995)
No Quarter (1996)
Blood Debt (1997)
Summon the Keeper (1998)
What Ho, Magic (1998)
Wizard of the Grove (1999)
Stealing Magic (1999)
The Quartered Sea (1999)
The Second Summoning (2001)
Of Darkness, Light, and Fire (2001)
Long Hot Summoning (2003)
Relative Magic (2003)
Smoke and Shadows (2004)
Smoke and Mirrors (2005)

HUGHART, BARRY
Bridge of Birds (1984)
The Story of the Stone (1988)
Eight Skilled Gentlemen (1991)
Chronicles of Master Li and Number Ten Ox (1998)

HUTSON, SHAUN
Skull (1982)
Spawn (1983)
Erebus (1984)
Shadows (1985)
Relics (1986)
Victims (1987)
Slugs (1987)
Assassins (1988)
Captives (1991)
Renegades (1991)
Heathen (1992)
Deadhead (1993)
White Ghost (1994)

Lucy's Child (1995)
Stolen Angels (1996)
Deathday (1996, as Robert Neville)
Purity (1997)
Compulsion (2001)
Hybrid (2002)
Hell to Pay (2003)
Necessary Evil (2004)

JACKSON, SHIRLEY
The Lottery (1949)
The Sundial (1958)
The Haunting of Hill House (1959)
The Magic of Shirley Jackson (1966)
Come Along with Me (1968)
The Lottery and Other Stories (1991)
Masterpieces of Shirley Jackson (1996)
Just an Ordinary Day (1997)

JACQUES, BRIAN
Redwall (1986)
Mossflower (1988)
Mattimeo (1989)
Mariel of Redwall (1991)
The Redwall Trilogy (1991)
Seven Strange and Ghostly Tales (1991)
Salamandaston (1993)
Martin the Warrior (1994)
The Outcast of Redwall (1995)
The Bellmaker (1995)
The Pearls of Lutra (1996)
The Great Redwall Feast (1996)
The Long Patrol (1997)
The Quest (1997)
The Warrior (1997)
Redwall Abbey (1998)
Marlfox (1999)
The Legend of Luke (1999)
Lord Brocktree (2000)
Friend and Foe (2000)
A Redwall Winter's Tale (2000)
Badgers (2001)
Castaways of the Flying Dutchman (2001)
Taggerung (2001)
Otters (2002)
Triss (2002)
Angel's Command (2003)
Loamhedge (2003)
Captain Snow (2004)
Sparra's Kingdom (2004)

Treachery (2004)
Rakkety Tam (2004)
Shrews (2005)
High Rhulain (2005)

JAKES, JOHN
Brak the Barbarian (1968)
Brak the Barbarian vs the Mark of the Demons (1969)
Brak the Barbarian vs the Sorceress (1969)
The Last Magicians (1969)
The Fortunes of Brak (1970)
Mention My Name in Atlantis (1972)
Brak: When the Idols Walked (1978)
Excalibur! (1980, with Gil Kane)

JAMES, M. R.
Ghost Stories of an Antiquary (1904)
More Ghost Stories of an Antiquary (1911)
A Thin Ghost and Others (1919)
The Five Jars (1922)
A Warning to the Curious and Other Ghost Stories (1925)
Wishing Well (1928)
The Collected Ghost Stories of M. R. James (1931, also published as *The Penguin Complete Ghost Stories of M. R. James*)
Thirteen Ghost Stories (1935)
The Best Ghost Stories of M. R. James (1944)
Selected Ghost Stories of M. R. James (1944)
Book of the Supernatural (1979, also published as *The Book of Ghost Stories*)
The Illustrated Ghost Stories of M. R. James (1986)
M. R. James (1987)
Casting the Runes and Other Stories (1987)
The Fenstanton Witch and Others (1999)
A Pleasing Terror (2001)

JONES, DIANA WYNNE
Wilkins' Tooth (1973, also published as *Witch's Business*)
The Ogre Downstairs (1974)
Cart and Cwidder (1975)
Dogsbody (1975)
Eight Days of Luke (1975)
Power of Three (1976)
Drowned Ammet (1977)
Charmed Life (1977)
The Magicians of Caprona (1979)
The Spellcoats (1979)
The Homeward Bounders (1981)

The Time of the Ghost (1981)
Witch Week (1982)
Archer's Goon (1984)
Fire and Hemlock (1984)
Warlock at the Wheel and Other Stories (1984)
Howl's Moving Castle (1986)
A Tale of Time City (1987)
The Lives of Christopher Chant (1988)
Castle in the Air (1990)
Aunt Maria (1991, also published as *Black Maria*)
A Sudden Wild Magic (1992)
The Crown of Dalemark (1993)
Stopping for a Spell (1993)
Hexwood (1993)
Everard's Ride (1995)
Minor Arcana (1996)
The Tough Guide to Fantasyland (1996)
Deep Secret (1997)
The Dark Lord of Denholm (1998)
Puss in Boots (1999)
Believing Is Seeing (1999)
Year of the Griffin (2000)
The Chronicles of Chrestomancy (2001)
Mixed Magics (2001)
Stealer of Souls (2002)
The Merlin Conspiracy (2003)

JORDAN, ROBERT
Conan the Defender (1982)
Conan the Invincible (1982)
Conan the Triumphant (1983)
Conan the Unconquered (1983)
Conan the Victorious (1984)
Conan the Magnificent (1984)
Conan the Destroyer (1984)
The Eye of the World (1990)
The Great Hunt (1990)
The Dragon Reborn (1991)
The Shadow Rising (1992)
The Fires of Heaven (1993)
Lord of Chaos (1994)
A Crown of Swords (1996)
The Conan Chronicles (1996)
Path of Daggers (1998)
The Further Chronicles of Conan (1999)
Winter's Heart (2000)
From the Two Rivers (2002)
To the Blight (2002)
Crossroads of Twilight (2003)
The Hunt Begins (2004)

New Spring: The Novel (2004)
Threads in the Pattern (2004)

JOYCE, GRAHAM
Dreamside (1991)
Dark Sister (1992)
House of Lost Dreams (1993)
Requiem (1995)
The Tooth Fairy (1998)
Stormwatcher (1998)
Separate Skins (1998, with Mark Morris)
Indigo (2000)
Smoking Poppy (2001)
Black Dust (2001)
The Limits of Enchantment (2004)

KAY, GUY GAVRIEL
The Summer Tree (1984)
The Darkest Road (1986)
The Wandering Fire (1986)
Tigana (1990)
A Song for Arbonne (1992)
The Lions of Al-Rassan (1995)
Sailing to Sarantium (1999)
Lord of Emperors (2000)
The Sarantine Mosaic (2001)
The Last Light of the Sun (2004)

KENNEALY-MORRISON, PATRICIA
The Copper Crown (1984)
The Throne of Scone (1986)
The Silver Branch (1988)
The Hawk's Gray Feather (1990)
The Oak above the Kings (1994)
The Hedge of Mist (1996)
Blackmantle (1997)
The Deer's Cry (1998)

KERR, KATHARINE
Daggerspell (1986)
Darkspell (1987)
The Bristling Wood (1989, also published as *Dawnspell: The Bristling Wood*)
The Dragon Revenant (1990, also published as *Dawnspell: The Southern Sea*)
A Time of Exile (1991)
A Time of Omens (1992)
Days of Blood and Fire (1993, also published as *A Time of War*)

Days of Air and Darkness (1994, also published as *A Time of Justice*)
The Red Wyvern (1997)
The Black Raven (1998)
The Fire Dragon (2001)
The Gold Falcon (2004)

KEYES, J. GREGORY

Waterborn (1996)
The Blackgod (1997)
Newton's Cannon (1998)
A Calculus of Angels (1999)
Empire of Unreason (2000)
The Shadows of God (2001)
The Briar King (2003)
The Charnel Prince (2004)

KING, STEPHEN

Carrie (1974)
'Salem's Lot (1975)
The Shining (1977)
The Stand (1978)
Night Shift (1978)
The Dead Zone (1979)
Firestarter (1980)
Cujo (1981)
The Gunslinger (1982, also published as *The Dark Tower*)
Christine (1983)
Pet Sematary (1983)
Thinner (1984, originally as by Richard Bachman)
The Talisman (1984, with Peter Straub)
The Eyes of the Dragon (1984)
The Silver Bullet (1985)
Skeleton Crew (1985)
It (1986)
Tommyknockers (1987)
The Drawing of the Three (1987)
The Dark Half (1989)
Four Past Midnight (1990)
The Waste Lands (1991)
Needful Things (1991)
Nightmares and Dreamscapes (1993)
Insomnia (1994)
Rose Madder (1995)
Desperation (1996)
The Regulators (1996)
Wizard and Glass (1996)
Coffey on the Mile (1996)
Two Dead Girls (1996)

Coffey's Hands (1996)
Night Journey (1996)
The Mouse on the Mile (1996)
The Bad Death of Edward Delacroix (1996)
The Green Mile (1997)
Bag of Bones (1998)
Storm of the Century (1999)
The Girl Who Loved Tom Gordon (1999)
Hearts in Atlantis (1999)
The Little Sisters of Eluria (1999)
Dreamcatcher (2001)
Black House (2001, with Peter Straub)
Everything's Eventual (2002)
From a Buick 8 (2002)
Wolves of the Calla (2003)
Song of Susanna (2004)
The Dark Tower (2004)

KLASKY, MINDY L.

The Glasswright's Apprentice (2000)
The Glasswright's Progress (2001)
The Glasswright's Journeyman (2002)
Season of Sacrifice (2002)
The Glasswright's Test (2003)
The Glasswright's Master (2004)

KLEIN, T. E. D.

The Ceremonies (1984)
Dark Gods (1985)

KNAAK, RICHARD A.

The Legend of Huma (1988)
Firedrake (1989)
Ice Dragon (1989)
Shadow Steed (1990)
Wolfhelm (1990)
The Shrouded Realm (1990)
Kaz the Minotaur (1990)
Children of the Drake (1991)
Dragon Tome (1992)
King of the Grey (1993)
The Crystal Dragon (1993)
Dragon Crown (1994)
The Janus Mask (1995)
Frostwing (1995)
Land of the Minotaurs (1996)
Dutchman (1996)
The Horse King (1997)
Reavers of the Blood Sea (1999)

Ruby Flames (1999)
The Citadel (2000)
Day of the Dragon (2001)
Legacy of Blood (2001)
The Kingdom of Shadow (2002)
Night of Blood (2003)
The Well of Eternity (2004)
The Demon Soul (2005)
The Burning (2005)

KOJA, KATHE

The Cipher (1991)
Bad Brains (1992)
Skin (1993)
Extremities (1998)
The Blue Mirror (2004)

KOONTZ, DEAN R.

The Crimson Witch (1971)
The Haunted Earth (1973)
Invasion (1974, as Aaron Wolfe)
Night Chills (1976)
The Vision (1977)
The Face of Fear (1977, as Brian Coffey)
Watchers (1977)
Whispers (1980)
The Funhouse (1980, as Owen West)
The Mask (1981, as Owen West)
The Eyes of Darkness (1981, as Leigh Nichols)
The House of Thunder (1982, as Leigh Nichols)
Phantoms (1983)
Darkfall (1984, also published as *Darkness Comes*)
The Door to December (1985, as Leigh Nichols)
Twilight Eyes (1987)
Shadowfires (1987, as Leigh Nichols)
Oddkins (1988)
Midnight (1989)
The Bad Place (1990)
Servants of the Twilight (1990, also published as *Twilight*)
Cold Fire (1991)
Three Complete Novels (1991)
Dragon Tears (1992)
Hideaway (1992)
A Dean Koontz Omnibus (1993)
Winter Moon (1994, expanded version of *Invasion*)
Strange Highways (1995)
Ticktock (1996)
Santa's Twin (1996)
Sole Survivor (1997)

Fear Nothing (1998)
Seize the Night (1999)
From the Corner of His Eye (2000)
The Face (2003)
Odd Thomas (2003)
Robot Santa (2004)
Life Expectancy (2004)
The Taking (2004)
Prodigal Son (2005, with Kevin J. Anderson)

KOTZWINKLE, WILLIAM

The Leopard's Tooth (1976)
Doctor Rat (1976)
Fata Morgana (1977)
The Ants Who Took Away Time (1978)
Christmas at Fontaine's (1982)
Great World Circus (1983)
Hearts of Wood and Other Timeless Tales (1986)
The Exile (1987)
The Midnight Examiner (1989)
The Hot Jazz Trio (1989)
The Bear Went over the Mountain (1996)

KRINARD, SUSAN

Prince of Dreams (1996)
Prince of Shadows (1996)
Prince of Wolves (1996)
Twice a Hero (1997)
Body and Soul (1998)
Touch of the Wolf (1999)
Once a Wolf (2000)
Secret of the Wolf (2001)
The Forest Lord (2002)
To Catch a Wolf (2003)
Shield of the Sky (2004)

KURTZ, KATHERINE

Deryni Rising (1970)
Deryni Checkmate (1972)
High Deryni (1973)
Camber of Culdi (1976)
Saint Camber (1978)
Camber the Heretic (1981)
Lammas Night (1983)
The Bishop's Heir (1984)
The King's Justice (1985)
The Chronicles of the Deryni (1985)
The Quest for Saint Camber (1986)
The Deryni Archives (1986)
The Harrowing of Gwynedd (1989)

Deryni Magic (1990)
The Adept (1991, with Deborah Turner Harris)
King Javan's Year (1992)
The Lodge of the Lynx (1992, with Deborah Turner Harris)
The Templar Treasure (1993, with Deborah Turner Harris)
The Bastard Prince (1994)
Dagger Magic (1995, with Deborah Turner Harris)
Two Crowns for America (1996)
Death of an Adept (1996, with Deborah Turner Harris)
The Temple and the Stone (1998, with Deborah Turner Harris)
King Kelson's Bride (2000)
St Patrick's Gargoyle (2001)
The Temple and the Crown (2001, with Deborah Turner Harris)
In the King's Service (2003)

KUSHNER, ELLEN
The Enchanted Kingdom (1986, with Judith Mitchell)
Swordspoint (1987)
Thomas the Rhymer (1990)
St Nicholas and the Valley Beyond (1994)
The Fall of the Kings (2002, with Delia Sherman)

KUTTNER, HENRY
The Dark World (1964)
The Mask of Circe (1977)
Elak of Atlantis (1985)
Prince Raynor (1987)
The Book of IOD (1995)

LACKEY, MERCEDES
Arrow's Flight (1987)
Arrows of the Queen (1987)
Arrow's Fall (1988)
Oathbound (1988)
Oathbreakers (1989)
Burning Water (1989)
Magic's Pawn (1989)
Reap the Whirlwind (1989, with C. J. Cherryh)
Children of the Night (1990)
Magic's Price (1990)
Magic's Promise (1990)
The Last Herald Mage (1990)
Knight of Ghosts and Shadows (1990, with Ellen Guon)
Jinx High (1991)
By the Sword (1991)
Winds of Fate (1991)

Elvenbane (1991, with Andre Norton)
The Lark and the Wren (1992)
Summoned to Tourney (1992, with Ellen Guon)
Born to Run (1992, with Larry Dixon)
Winds of Change (1992)
Wheels of Fire (1992, with Josepha Sherman)
Castle of Deception (1992, with Josepha Sherman)
The Robin and the Kestrel (1993)
Prison of Souls (1993, with Mark Shepherd)
When the Bough Breaks (1993, with Holly Lisle)
Winds of Fury (1993)
Fortress of Frost and Fire (1993, with Ru Emerson)
If I Pay Thee Not in Gold (1993, with Piers Anthony)
Sacred Ground (1994)
Storm Warning (1994)
A Cast of Corbies (1994, with Josepha Sherman)
Chrome Circle (1994, with Larry Dixon)
The Black Gryphon (1994, with Larry Dixon)
Vows and Honor (1994)
The Eagle and the Nightingale (1995)
Elvenblood (1995, with Andre Norton)
The White Gryphon (1995, with Larry Dixon)
Firebird (1996)
Storm Breaking (1996)
Storm Rising (1996)
The Silver Gryphon (1996, with Larry Dixon)
The Fire Rose (1996)
Four and Twenty Blackbirds (1997)
The Free Bards (1997)
Owlflight (1998, with Larry Dixon)
Oathblood (1998)
Bedlam's Bard (1998, with Ellen Guon)
Fiddler Fair (1998)
Owlsight (1998, with Larry Dixon)
Owlknight (1999, with Larry Dixon)
The Chrome Borne (1999, with Larry Dixon)
The River's Gift (1999)
Werehunter (1999)
The Black Swan (1999)
Brightly Burning (2000)
Take a Thief (2001)
Beyond World's End (2001, with Rosemary Edghill)
Serpent's Shadow (2001)
Spirits White As Lightning (2001, with Rosemary Edghill)
Exile's Honor (2002)
The Shadow of the Lion (2002, with Eric Flint and Dave Freer)
Elvenborn (2002, with Andre Norton)
The Gates of Sleep (2002)
Exile's Valor (2003)

Mad Maudlin (2003, with Rosemary Edghill)
The Outstretched Shadow (2003, with James Mallory)
This Rough Magic (2003, with Eric Flint and Dave Freer)
Joust (2003)
Alta (2004)
Phoenix and Ashes (2004)
The Fairy Godmother (2004)
To Light a Candle (2004, with James Mallory)
This Scepter'd Isle (2004, with Roberta Gellis)
Ill Met by Moonlight (2005, with Roberta Gellis)
Sanctuary (2005)

LANG, ANDREW
The Princess Nobody: A Tale of Fairy Land (1894, also
    published as *In Fairyland*)
That Very Mab (1885, with May Kendall)
The Gold of Fairnilee (1888)
The Blue Fairy Book (1889)
The World's Desire (1889, with H. Rider Haggard)
The Red Fairy Book (1890)
The Green Fairy Book (1892)
The Yellow Fairy Book (1894)
The Grey Fairy Book (1900)
The Violet Fairy Book (1901)
The Crimson Fairy Book (1903)
The Brown Fairy Book (1904)
The Orange Fairy Book (1906)
The Olive Fairy Book (1907)
The Lilac Fairy Book (1910)
The Rainbow Fairy Book (1993)

LANSDALE, JOE
Dead in the West (1986)
The Nightrunners (1987)
The Drive-In (1988)
The Drive-In 2 (1989)
By Bizarre Hands (1989)
Stories by Mama Lansdale's Youngest Boy (1991)
Dark at Heart (1992)
Bestsellers Guaranteed (1993)
Writers of the Purple Rage (1994)
A Fist Full of Stories (1997)
Triple Feature (2000)
The Long Ones (2000)
For a Few Stories More (2002)
Bumper Crop (2004)

LAURIA, FRANK
Doctor Orient (1970)
Raga Six (1972)

Lady Sativa (1973)
Baron Orgaz (1974)
The Priestess (1978)
The Seth Papers (1979)
The Foundling (1984)
Blue Limbo (1991)
End of Days (1999)

LAWHEAD, STEPHEN
In the Hall of the Dragon King (1982)
The Warlords of Nin (1983)
The Sword and the Flame (1984)
Taliesin (1987)
Merlin (1988)
Arthur (1989)
The Paradise War (1991)
The Silver Hand (1992)
The Endless Knot (1993)
Pendragon (1994)
Grail (1997)
The Iron Lance (1998)
Avalon (1999)
The Black Rood (2000)
The Mystic Rose (2001)

LAWS, STEPHEN
Ghosttrain (1985)
Spectre (1986)
The Wyrm (1987)
The Frighteners (1990)
Darkfall (1992)
Gideon (1993)
Voyages into Night (1993)
Macabre (1994)
Daemonic (1995)
Somewhere South of Midnight (1996)
Chasm (1997)
The Midnight Man (1999)
Fear Me (2004)

LAYMON, RICHARD
The Cellar (1980)
The Woods Are Dark (1981)
Out Are the Lights (1982)
Nightmare Lake (1983, as Carl Laymon)
Night Show (1984)
Beware! (1985)
Allhallow's Eve (1986)
The Beast House (1986)
Flesh (1987)

Tread Softly (1987, also published as *The Dark Mountain* as Richard Kelly)
Resurrection Dreams (1988)
Funland (1989)
The Stake (1990)
Darkness Tells Us (1991)
One Rainy Night (1991)
Alarms (1993)
Out Are the Lights and Other Tales (1993)
A Good Secret Place (1993)
Bite (1996)
Body Rides (1996)
Fiends (1997)
The Midnight Tour (1998)
Once upon a Halloween (2000)
The Traveling Vampire Show (2000)
Dreadful Tales (2001)
Friday Night in Beast House (2001)
To Wake the Dead (2003)

LEE, EDWARD

Ghouls (1988)
Incubi (1991)
Coven (1991)
Succubi (1992)
The Chosen (1993)
Creekers (1994)
Sacrifice (1995, as Richard Kinion)
Splatterspunk: The Micah Hayes Stories (1998, with John Pelan)
Shifters (1998, with John Pelan)
The Ushers (1999)
City Eternal (2001)
Monstrosity (2002)
Infernal Angel (2003)
Teratologist (2003, with Wrath James White)
Sleep Disorder (2003, with Jack Ketchum)
Messenger (2004)
Flesh Gothic (2005)

LEE, TANITH

The Dragon Hoard (1971)
Animal Castle (1972)
Princess Hyunchatti and Some Other Surprises (1972)
The Castle of Dark (1973)
Companions on the Road (1975)
The Storm Lord (1976)
The Winter Players (1976)
East of Midnight (1977)
Volkhavaar (1977)

Death's Master (1979)
Night's Master (1979)
Shon the Taken (1979)
Sabella, or The Blood Stone (1980)
Kill the Dead (1980)
Sometimes, after Sunset (1980)
Delusion's Master (1981)
Unsilent Night (1981)
Lycanthia, or The Children of Wolves (1981)
Prince on a White Horse (1982)
Cyrion (1982)
Red As Blood, or Tales from the Sisters Grimm (1983)
Anackire (1983)
The War of Vis (1984)
Tamastara or the Indian Nights (1984)
Tales from the Flat Earth (1987)
Sung in Shadow (1993)
The Gorgon and Other Beastly Tales (1985)
Dreams of Dark and Light (1986)
Delirium's Mistress (1986)
Dark Castle, White Horse (1986)
Night's Sorceries (1987)
The White Serpent (1988)
The Book of the Damned (1988)
Madame Two Swords (1988)
The Book of the Beast (1989)
Forests of the Night (1989)
A Heroine of the World (1989)
The Blood of Roses (1990)
The Book of the Dead (1991)
Black Unicorn (1991)
The Secret Books of Paradys 1 & 2 (1991)
Dark Dance (1992)
Elephantasm (1993)
The Book of the Mad (1993)
The Secret Books of Paradys 3 & 4 (1993)
Nightshades: Thirteen Journeys into Shadow (1993)
Personal Darkness (1993)
Heart-Beast (1993)
Gold Unicorn (1994)
Darkness, I (1994)
Louisa the Poisoner (1995)
Reigning Cats and Dogs (1995)
Vivia (1995)
When the Lights Go Out (1996)
Red Unicorn (1997)
Faces under Water (1998)
Law of the Wolf Tower (1998, also published as *Wolf Tower*)
Saint Fire (1999)

Islands in the Sky (1999)
White As Snow (2000)
A Bed of Earth (2002)
Wolf Wing (2002)
Wolf Queen (2002)
Mortal Suns (2003)
Piratica (2004)
Cast a Bright Shadow (2004)
Venus Preserved (2005)

Le Fanu, J. Sheridan

Ghost Stories and Tales of Mystery (1851)
Carmilla (1871)
In a Glass Darkly (1872)
The Purcell Papers (1880)
The Watcher and Other Weird Stories (1894)
Madam Crowl's Ghost and Other Tales of Mystery (1923)
Green Tea and Other Ghost Stories (1945)
A Strange Adventure in the Life of Miss Laura Mildmay (1947)
Sheridan Le Fanu: The Diabolic Genius (1959)
Best Ghost Stories (1964)
The Best Horror Stories (1970)
Vampire Lovers and Other Stories (1970)
Carmilla and the Haunted Baronet (1970)
Irish Ghost Stories of Sheridan Le Fanu (1973)
Ghost Stories and Mysteries (1975)
The Hours After Midnight (1975)
The Illustrated J. S. Le Fanu (1988)
Ghost and Horror Stories (1990)
Carmilla and Other Tales of Mystery (1996)
Spalatro: Two Italian Tales (2001)
Schalken the Painter and Others (2002)
The Haunted Baronet and Other Ghost Stories (2003)

Le Guin, Ursula K.

A Wizard of Earthsea (1968)
The Tombs of Atuan (1971)
The Farthest Shore (1972)
Orsinian Tales (1976)
Earthsea (1977)
Malafrena (1979)
The Beginning Place (1980, also published as *Threshold*)
Catwings (1988)
Catwings Return (1989)
Tehanu (1990)
The Earthsea Quartet (1993)
Wonderful Alexander and the Catwings (1994)
Tales of the Catwings (1996)

The Other Wind (2001)
Tales from Earthsea (2001)
Gifts (2004)

Leiber, Fritz

Night's Black Agents (1947)
Conjure Wife (1952)
Two Sought Adventure (1957)
Shadows with Eyes (1962)
The Swords of Lankhmar (1968)
Swords against Wizardry (1968)
Swords in the Mist (1968)
Night Monsters (1969)
Swords and Deviltry (1970)
Swords against Death (1970)
Rime Isle (1977)
Swords and Ice Magic (1977)
Heroes and Horrors (1978)
Bazaar of the Bizarre (1978)
Our Lady of Darkness (1978)
Ghost Light (1984)
The Knight and Knave of Swords (1988)
The Three of Swords (1989)
Swords' Masters (1990)
Ill Met in Lankhmar (1995)
Lean Times in Lankhmar (1996)
The Dealings of Daniel Kesserich (1996)
Return to Lankhmar (1997)
Farewell to Lankhmar (1998)
Dark Ladies (1999)
Thieves' House (2001)
The First Book of Lankhmar (2001)
The Second Book of Lankhmar (2001)
The Smoke Ghost and Other Applications (2001)
The Black Gondolier and Other Stories (2001)
Day Dark, Night Bright (2002)

Lewis, C. S.

The Screwtape Letters (1942)
The Great Divorce (1945)
The Lion, the Witch, and the Wardrobe (1950)
Prince Caspian (1951)
Voyage of the Dawn Treader (1952)
The Silver Chair (1953)
The Horse and His Boy (1954)
The Magician's Nephew (1956)
Till We Have Faces (1956)
The Last Battle (1956)
The Chronicles of Narnia (1973)
Boxen (1985)

LIGOTTI, THOMAS

Songs of a Dead Dreamer (1986)
Grimscribe (1990)
The Agonizing Resurrection of Victor Frankenstein and Other Gothic Tales (1994)
Noctuary (1994)
The Nightmare Factory (1996)
My Work Is Not Yet Done (2002)
Sideshow and Other Stories (2003)

LINDSKOLD, JANE

Brother to Dragons, Companion to Owls (1994)
The Pipes of Orpheus (1995)
When the Gods Are Silent (1997)
Changer (1998)
Lord Demon (1999, with Roger Zelazny)
Legends Walking (1999)
Through Wolf's Eyes (2001)
Wolf's Head, Wolf's Heart (2002)
The Dragon of Despair (2003)
The Buried Pyramid (2004)
Wolf Captured (2004)
Child of a Rainless Year (2005)

LISLE, HOLLY

Fire in the Mist (1992)
When the Bough Breaks (1993, with Mercedes Lackey)
Bones of the Past (1993)
The Rose Sea (1994, with S. M. Stirling)
Minerva Wakes (1994)
Mind of the Magic (1995)
Mall, Mayhem, and Magic (1995, with Chris Guin)
Sympathy for the Devil (1996)
Thunder of the Captains (1996, with Aaron Allston)
The Devil and Dan Cooley (1996, with Walter Spence)
Glenraven (1996, with Marion Zimmer Bradley)
Hell on High (1997, with Ted Nolan)
Wrath of the Princes (1997, with Aaron Allston)
Diplomacy of Wolves (1998)
Vengeance of Dragons (1999)
Courage of Falcons (2000)
The Secret Texts (2001)
Vincalis the Agitator (2002)
Memory of Fire (2002)
The Wreck of Heaven (2003)
Gods Old and Dark (2004)
Midnight Rain (2004)
Talyn (2005)

LITTLE, BENTLEY

The Revelation (1990)
The Mailman (1991)
The Summoning (1993)
University (1994, also published as *Night School*)
The Store (1996)
Dominion (1996, also published as *The Dark Dominion*)
Houses (1997, also published as *The House*)
The Ignored (1997)
Guests (1998)
The Walking (2000)
The Town (2000)
The Association (2001)
The Collection (2002)
The Return (2002)
The Policy (2003)
The Resort (2004)

LOFTING, HUGH

The Story of Doctor Dolittle (1920)
The Voyages of Doctor Dolittle (1922)
Doctor Dolittle's Post Office (1923)
Doctor Dolittle's Circus (1925)
Doctor Dolittle's Zoo (1925)
Doctor Dolittle's Caravan (1926)
Doctor Dolittle's Garden (1927)
Doctor Dolittle in the Moon (1928)
The Twilight of Magic (1930)
Gub Gub's Book (1932)
Doctor Dolittle's Return (1933)
Doctor Dolittle and the Secret Lake (1948)
Doctor Dolittle and the Green Canary (1950)
Doctor Dolittle's Puddleby Adventures (1952)

LONG, FRANK BELKNAP

The Hounds of Tindalos (1946)
The Horror from the Hills (1963)
The Dark Beasts (1964)
To the Dark Tower (1969, as Lyda Belknap Long)
Fire of the Witches (1971, as Lyda Belknap Long)
The Shape of Fear (1971, as Lyda Belknap Long)
House of the Deadly Nightshade (1972, as Lyda Belknap Long)
The Night of the Wolf (1972)
The Black Druid and Other Stories (1975)
The Early Long (1975)
The Rim of the Unknown (1978)
Night Fear (1979)
Escape from Tomorrow (1995)
The Eye above the Mantle and Other Stories (1995)

LOVECRAFT, H. P.

The Outsider and Others (1943)
At the Mountains of Madness (1943)
Beyond the Wall of Sleep (1943)
The Weird Shadow over Innsmouth and Other Stories of the Supernatural (1944)
Marginalia (1944)
The Dunwich Horror (1945)
The Lurker at the Threshold (1945)
The Lurking Fear (1947, also published as *Cry Horror!*)
The Dunwich Horror and Other Weird Tales (1945)
Best Supernatural Stories of H. P. Lovecraft (1945)
Something about Cats and Other Pieces (1949)
The Case of Charles Dexter Ward (1951)
The Haunter of the Dark (1951)
The Dream Quest of Unknown Kadath (1955)
The Survivor and Others (1957, with August Derleth)
Dreams and Fancies (1962)
The Dunwich Horror and Others (1963)
The Colour out of Space (1964)
The Lurking Fear and Other Stories (1964)
Dagon and Other Macabre Tales (1965)
Three Tales of Horror (1967)
The Shadow out of Time and Other Tales of Horror (1968, with August Derleth)
The Shuttered Room and Other Tales of Horror (1970, with August Derleth)
The Doom That Came to Sarnath (1971)
The Tomb and Other Tales (1971)
The Shadow over Innsmouth and Other Stories of Horror (1971)
The Occult Lovecraft (1975)
The Dream Cycle of H. P. Lovecraft: Dreams of Terror and Death (1995)
The Road to Madness (1996)
The Annotated Lovecraft (1997)
Tales of H. P. Lovecraft (1997)
The Loved Dead (1997)
More Annotated H. P. Lovecraft (1999)
The Call of Cthulhu and Other Weird Stories (1999)
The Shadow out of Time (2001)
The Thing on the Doorstep and Other Weird Stories (2001)
From the Pest Zone (2003)
The New York Stories (2003)

LUMLEY, BRIAN

The Caller of the Black (1971)
Beneath the Moors (1974)
The Burrowers Beneath (1974)

The Transition of Titus Crow (1975)
The Horror at Oakdeene and Others (1977)
Khai of Ancient Khem (1981, also published as *Khai of Khem*)
Psychomech (1984)
Psychosphere (1984)
Psychamok (1985)
Hero of Dreams (1986)
Ship of Dreams (1986)
Necroscope (1986)
Mad Moon of Dreams (1987)
The Compleat Crow (1987)
Demogorgon (1987)
Elysia (1989)
The Source (1989)
Vamphyri (1989)
Iced on Aran (1990)
Deadspeak (1990)
The House of Cthulhu and Other Tales of the Primal Land (1991)
The Complete Khash (1991)
Deadspawn (1991)
Tarra Khash: Hrossak! (1991)
Sorcery in Shad (1991)
Blood Brothers (1992)
The Last Aerie (1993)
Last Rite (1993)
Fruiting Bodies and Other Fungi (1993)
Bloodwars (1994)
Return of the Deep Ones (1994)
Dagon's Bell and Other Discords (1994)
The Second Wish and Other Exhalations (1995)
Necroscope: The Lost Years (1995)
Necroscope: The Lost Years 2 (1996, also published as *Resurgence*)
Necroscribe (1997)
Titus Crow (1997)
Brian Lumley's Mythos Omnibus (1997)
A Coven of Vampires (1998)
Necroscope Invaders (1999)
Necroscope Defilers (2000)
The Whisperer and Other Voices (2001)
Necroscope Avengers (2001)
Beneath the Moors and Darker Places (2002)
Harry Keogh: Necroscope and Other Weird Heroes (2003)
The House of Cthulhu (2005)

LYNN, ELIZABETH

Watchtower (1979)
The Dancers of Arun (1979)

The Northern Girl (1980)
The Woman Who Loved the Moon and Other Stories (1981)
The Silver Horse (1984)
Tales from a Vanished Country (1990)
The Chronicles of Tornor (1998)
Dragon's Winter (1998)
Dragon's Treasure (2004)

MACAVOY, R. A.
Tea with the Black Dragon (1983)
Damiano (1984)
Damiano's Lute (1984)
Raphael (1984)
The Book of Kells (1985)
Twisting the Rope (1988)
The Gray Horse (1987)
A Trio for Lute (1988)
Lens of the World (1990)
King of the Dead (1991)
The Belly of the Wolf (1993, also published as *The Winter of the Wolf*)

MACDONALD, GEORGE
Phantastes (1858)
At the Back of the North Wind (1870)
The Princess and the Goblin (1871)
The Princess and Curdie (1882)
The Portent (1885, also published as *The Lady of the Mansion*)
Lilith (1895)
Visionary Novels (1954)
The Complete Fairy Tales of George MacDonald (1961)
Evenor (1972)
The Gifts of the Child Christ (1973)
The Golden Key and Other Fantasy Stories (1980)

MACHEN, ARTHUR
The Chronicle of Clemendy (1888)
The Great God Pan and the Inmost Light (1894)
The Three Impostors (1895, also published as *Black Crusade*)
The House of Souls (1906)
The Hill of Dreams (1907)
The Angel of Mons, the Bowmen, and Other Legends of War (1915)
The Great Return (1915)
The Sixth Sense (1915)
The Terror (1917)
The Shining Pyramid (1923)

Tales of the Strange and Supernatural (1926)
The Green Round (1933)
The Cosy Room and Other Stories (1936)
The Great God Pan and Other Weird Tales (1943)
Holy Terrors (1946)
Tales of Horror and the Supernatural (1948)
The Strange World of Arthur Machen (1960)
The Novel of the Black Seal and Other Stories (1965)
The Novel of the White Powder and Other Stories (1965)
A Fragment of Life (2001)
The White People (2003)

MARTIN, GEORGE R. R.
Fevre Dream (1982)
Armageddon Rag (1983)
Portraits of His Children (1987)
A Game of Thrones (1996)
A Clash of Kings (1997)
A Storm of Swords (2000)
Quartet (2001)

MASTERTON, GRAHAM
The Manitou (1975)
The Djinn (1977)
The Devils of D-Day (1978)
The Sphinx (1978)
Charnel House (1978)
Revenge of the Manitou (1979)
The Wells of Hell (1980)
The Hell Candidate (1980, as Thomas Luke)
The Heirloom (1981, as Thomas Luke)
Pariah (1983)
Tengu (1983)
Picture of Evil (1985, also published as *Family Portrait*)
Death Trance (1986)
Night Warriors (1986)
Death Dream (1988)
Mirror (1988)
Feast (1988, also published as *Ritual*)
Walkers (1990)
Black Angel (1991)
Night Plague (1991)
The Burning (1991, also published as *The Hymn*)
Burial (1992)
Prey (1992)
Master of Lies (1992)
The Sleepless (1993)
Flesh and Blood (1994)
Fortnight of Fear (1994)
Spirit (1995)

Rook (1996)
Flights of Fear (1996)
Faces of Fear (1996)
The House That Jack Built (1996)
Tooth and Claw (1997)
The Chosen Child (1997)
The House of Bones (1998)
The Terror (1998)
Rook & Tooth and Claw (1999)
Manitou Man (1999)
Snowman (2000)
Bonnie Winter (2001)
The Doorkeepers (2001)
Trauma (2002)
Swimmer (2002)
Charnel House and Other Stories (2002)
A Terrible Beauty (2003)
The Hidden World (2003)
Genius (2003)
The Devil in Gray (2004)
Darkroom (2004)
Unspeakable (2004)
Holy Terror (2004)

MATHESON, RICHARD

I Am Legend (1954, also published as *The Omega Man*)
A Stir of Echoes (1958)
Shock (1961)
Shock II (1964)
Shock III (1966)
Shock Waves (1970)
Hell House (1971)
Bid Time Return (1975, also published as *Somewhere in Time*)
What Dreams May Come (1978)
Shock IV (1980)
Earthbound (1982, as Logan Swanson)
Collected Stories (1989)
Seven Steps to Midnight (1993)
Nightmare at 20,000 Feet (2002)
Offbeat (2002)
Come Fygures, Come Shadowes (2003)
Duel (2003)

McCAMMON, ROBERT

Baal (1978)
Night Boat (1980)
Bethany's Sin (1980)
They Thirst (1981)
Mystery Walk (1983)

Usher's Passing (1984)
Swan Song (1987)
Stinger (1988)
The Wolf's Hour (1989)
Blue World (1989)
Boys' Life (1991)
Gone South (1992)

McDOWELL, MICHAEL

The Amulet (1979)
Cold Moon over Babylon (1980)
The Elementals (1981)
Katie (1982)
The Levee (1983)
Rain (1983)
The War (1983)
The Flood (1983)
The Fortune (1983)
The House (1983)

McKIERNAN, DENNIS L.

The Darkest Day (1984)
The Dark Tide (1984)
Shadows of Doom (1984)
The Brega Path (1986)
Trek to Kraggen-Cor (1986)
Dragondoom (1990)
The Eye of the Hunter (1992)
Voyage of the Fox Rider (1993)
Tales of Mithgar (1994)
Caverns of Socrates (1995)
The Dragonstone (1996)
Into the Forge (1997)
Into the Fire (1998)
The Iron Tower (2000)
Silver Wolf, Black Falcon (2000)
The Silver Call (2001)
Once upon a Winter's Night (2001)
Red Slippers (2004)
Once upon a Summer Day (2005)

McKILLIP, PATRICIA A.

The House on Parchment Street (1973)
The Throne of the Erril of Sherill (1973)
The Forgotten Beasts of Eld (1974)
Heir of Sea and Fire (1976)
The Riddle-Master of Hed (1976)
The Night Gift (1976)
Harpist in the Wind (1979)
Stepping from the Shadows (1982)

The Changeling Sea (1988)
The Sorceress and the Cygnet (1991)
The Cygnet and the Firebird (1993)
Something Rich and Strange (1994)
The Book of Atrix Wolfe (1995)
Winter Rose (1996)
Song for the Basilisk (1998)
Riddle Master (1999, also published as *Riddle of Stars*)
The Tower at Stony Wood (2000)
Ombria in Shadow (2002)
In the Forests of Serre (2003)
Alphabet of Thorn (2004)
Old Magic (2005)
Harrowing the Dragon (2005)

McKINLEY, ROBIN
Beauty (1978)
The Door in the Hedge (1981)
The Blue Sword (1982)
The Hero and the Crown (1984)
The Outlaws of Sherwood (1988)
Deerskin (1993)
A Knot in the Grain and Other Stories (1994)
Rose Daughter (1997)
The Stone Fey (1998)
Spindle's End (2001)
Water (2002, with Peter Dickinson)
Sunshine (2003)

McNALLY, CLARE
Ghost House (1979)
Ghost House Revenge (1981)
Ghost Light (1982)
What About the Baby? (1983)
Somebody Come and Play (1987)
Addison House (1988)
Come into the Darkness (1989)
Hear the Children Calling (1990)
Cries of the Children (1992)
Stage Fright (1995)
Good Night, Sweet Angel (1996)
Blood Relations (1997)

McNAUGHTON, BRIAN
Satan's Love Child (1977, revised as *Gemini Rising*)
Satan's Mistress (1978, revised as *Downward to Darkness*)
Satan's Seductress (1980, also published as *Worse Things Waiting*)
Satan's Surrogate (1982)

Throne of Bones (1997)
Nasty Stories (2000)
Even More Nasty Stories (2000)

MERRITT, A.
The Moon Pool (1919)
The Ship of Ishtar (1926)
Seven Footprints to Satan (1928)
The Face in the Abyss (1931)
Dwellers in the Mirage (1932)
Burn Witch Burn (1933)
Creep Shadow Creep (1935, also published as *Creep Shadow*)
The Metal Monster (1946)
The Fox Woman and the Blue Pagoda (1946, with Hannes Bok)
The Black Wheel (1948, with Hannes Bok)
The Fox Woman (1949)
The Women of the Wood and Other Stories (2003)

MICHAELS, BARBARA
Ammie, Come Home (1968)
The Dark on the Other Side (1970)
Prince of Darkness (1970)
The Crying Child (1971)
Witch (1973)
House of Many Shadows (1974)
The Sea-King's Daughter (1975)
Wait for What Will Come (1978)
The Walker in Shadows (1979)
The Wizard's Daughter (1980)
Someone in the House (1981)
Here I Stay (1983)
Be Buried in the Rain (1985)
Other Worlds (1999)

MIEVILLE, CHINA
King Rat (1999)
Perdido Street Station (2001)
The Scar (2002)
The Tain (2003)
Iron Council (2004)
Collected Stories (2005)
Looking for Jake (2005)

MODESITT, L. E., JR.
The Magic of Recluce (1991)
The Towers of Sunset (1992)
The Magic Engineer (1994)
The Death of Chaos (1995)

The Order War (1995)
Fall of Angels (1996)
The Chaos Balance (1997)
The Soprano Sorceress (1997)
The White Order (1998)
Colours of Chaos (1998)
The Spellsong War (1998)
Darksong Rising (1999)
Magi'i of Cyador (2000)
Scion of Cyador (2000)
The Shadow Sorceress (2001)
Legacies (2002)
Shadowsinger (2002)
Darknesses (2003)
Scepters (2004)
Wellspring of Chaos (2004)
Ordermaster (2005)
Ghosts of Columbia (2005)
Alector's Choice (2005)

MONACO, RICHARD
Parsifal, or, A Knight's Tale (1977)
The Grail War (1979)
The Final Quest (1981)
Runes (1984)
Blood and Dreams (1985)
Broken Stone (1985)
Journey to the Flame (1985)
Unto the Beast (1987)

MONTELEONE, THOMAS
Night Things (1980)
Night Train (1984)
Lyrica (1987)
The Crooked House (1987, with John DeChancie)
The Magnificent Gallery (1987)
Fantasma (1989)
Blood of the Lamb (1993)
The Resurrectionist (1995)
Night of Broken Souls (1997)
The Reckoning (1999)
Eyes of the Virgin (2002)

MOORCOCK, MICHAEL
Stormbringer (1965)
The Jewel in the Skull (1967)
The Stealer of Souls (1967)
Sword of the Dawn (1968)
Sorceror's Amulet (1968, also published as *The Mad God's Amulet*)

The Secret of the Runestaff (1969, also published as *The Runestaff*)
The Eternal Champion (1970)
The Singing Citadel (1970)
The King of Swords (1971)
The Queen of Swords (1971)
The Knight of Swords (1971)
Elric of Melnibone (1972)
The Dreaming City (1972)
Count Brass (1973)
The Silver Warriors (1973, also published as *Phoenix in Obsidian*)
The Jade Man's Eyes (1973)
The Oak and the Ram (1973)
The Bull and the Spear (1973)
The Champion of Garathorm (1973)
The Sword and the Stallion (1974)
The Quest for Tanelorn (1975)
The Sailor on the Seas of Fate (1976)
Sojan (1977)
The Weird of the White Wolf (1977)
The Vanishing Tower (1977, also published as *The Sleeping Sorceress*)
The Bane of the Blacksword (1977)
The Prince with the Silver Hand (1977)
The Chronicles of Corum (1977)
The Golden Barge (1979)
The War Hound and the World's Pain (1981)
The Dragon in the Sword (1986)
The City in the Autumn Stars (1986)
The Revenge of the Rose (1991)
Hawkmoon (1992)
Blood (1994)
Lunching with the Antichrist (1995)
Von Bek (1995)
Fabulous Harbors (1995)
The War amongst the Angels (1997)
Corum (1997)
The Dreamthief's Daughter (2001)
Elric (2001)
The Skrayling Tree (2003)
The White Wolf's Son (2005)

MORRESSEY, JOHN
Ironbrand (1980)
Graymantle (1981)
Kingsbane (1982)
Time of the Annihilator (1985)
A Voice for Princess (1986)
The Questing of Kedrigern (1987)

Kedrigern in Wanderland (1988)
A Remembrance for Kedrigern (1990)
Kedrigern and the Charming Couple (1990)
The Juggler (1996)
The Domesticated Wizard (2002)
Dudgeon and Dragons (2003)

MORRIS, JANET
Beyond the Veil (1985)
Beyond Sanctuary (1985)
Beyond the Wizardwall (1986)
Tempus (1987)
Kings in Hell (1987, with C. J. Cherryh)
City at the Edge of Time (1988, with Chris Morris)
The Little Helliad (1988, with Chris Morris)
Tempus Unbound (1989, with Chris Morris)
Explorers in Hell (1989, with David Drake)
Storm Seed (1990)

MORRIS, WILLIAM
The House of the Wolflings (1889)
The Roots of the Mountains (1889)
The Glittering Plain (1891)
The Wood beyond the World (1894)
The Well at the World's End (1896)
The Sundering Flood (1897)
The Water of the Wondrous Isles (1897)
Golden Wings and Other Stories (1976)
Early Romances (2004)

MORROW, JAMES
Only Begotten Daughter (1990)
Towing Jehovah (1994)
Blameless in Abaddon (1996)
Bible Stories for Adults (1996)
The Eternal Footman (1999)
The Cat's Pajamas and Other Stories (2004)

MUNDY, TALBOT
The Nine Unknown (1924)
Caves of Terror (1924)
Om: The Secret of Ahbor Valley (1924)
Tros of Samothrace (1925)
The Devil's Guard (1926, also published as *Ramsden*)
Queen Cleopatra (1929)
Black Light (1930)
Jimgrim (1930, also published as *Jimgrim Sahib* and as *King of the World*)
Full Moon (1935, also published as *There Was a Door*)
The Purple Pirate (1935)

Old Ugly Face (1939)
Helene (1967)
Tros (1967)
Helma (1967)
Liafail (1967)
Lud of Lunden (1976)

MUNN, H. WARNER
The Werewolf of Ponkert (1958)
King of the World's Edge (1967)
The Ship from Atlantis (1967)
Merlin's Ring (1974)
Merlin's Godson (1976)
In the Tomb of the Bishop (1979)
The Master Goes Home (1979)
The Lost Legion (1980)

NATHAN, ROBERT
The Puppet Master (1923)
Jonah (1925, also published as *Son of Ammitai*)
The Bishop's Wife (1928)
There Is Another Heaven (1929)
The Enchanted Voyage (1937)
Portrait of Jennie (1939)
But Gently Day (1943)
The River Journey (1949)
The Married Look (1950, also published as *His Wife's Young Face*)
The Innocent Eve (1951)
The Train in the Meadow (1953)
Sir Henry (1955)
So Love Returns (1958)
The Wilderness Stone (1960)
The Devil with Love (1963)
The Fair (1964)
Stonecliff (1967)
Mia (1971)
The Elixir (1971)
The Summer Meadows (1973)
Heaven and Hell and the Megas Factor (1975)

NEIDERMAN, ANDREW
Brainchild (1981)
Pin (1981)
Imp (1985)
Night Howl (1986)
Teacher's Pet (1986)
Love Child (1986)
Sight Unseen (1987)
Surrogate Child (1988)

Perfect Little Angels (1989)
Devil's Advocate (1990)
Bloodchild (1990)
The Immortals (1991)
Sister, Sister (1992)
Need (1992)
After Life (1993)
The Dark (1997)

NESBIT, EDITH
Grim Tales (1893)
Something Wrong (1893)
The Book of Dragons (1899)
Nine Unlikely Tales for Children (1901)
The Five Children and It (1902)
The Phoenix and the Carpet (1904)
The Story of the Amulet (1906)
The Enchanted Castle (1907)
The House of Arden (1908)
Harding's Luck (1909)
Fear (1910)
Wet Magic (1913)
The Five Children (1950)
The Last of the Dragons and Some Others (1972)
E. Nesbit's Tales of Terror (1983)
In the Dark (1988)

NEWMAN, KIM
Drachenfels (1989, as Jack Yeovil)
Silver Nails (1989, as Jack Yeovil)
Bad Dreams (1991)
Jago (1991)
Beasts in Velvet (1991, as Jack Yeovil)
Anno Dracula (1992)
Genevieve Undead (1993, as Jack Yeovil)
The Original Doctor Shade and Other Stories (1994)
The Quorum (1994)
Orgy of the Blood Parasites (1994, as Jack Yeovil)
The Bloody Red Baron (1995)
Famous Monsters (1995)
Judgment of Tears (1998)
Andy Warhol's Dracula (1999)
Dracula Cha Cha Cha (2000)
Seven Stars (2000)
Unforgivable Stories (2000)
Where the Bodies Are Buried (2000)

NIX, GARTH
Sabriel (1995)
Castle (2000)

The Fall (2000)
The Violet Keystone (2001)
Into Battle (2001)
Above the Veil (2001)
Lirael (2001)
Aenir (2001)
Abhorsen (2003)
Keys to the Kingdom (2003)
Grim Tuesday (2004)

NORTON, ANDRE
Rogue Reynard (1947)
Huon of the Horn (1951)
Witch World (1963)
Web of the Witch World (1964)
Year of the Unicorn (1965)
Steel Magic (1965, also published as *Gray Magic*)
Three Against the Witch World (1965)
Octagon Magic (1967)
Warlock of the Witch World (1967)
Sorceress of the Witch World (1968)
Fur Magic (1968)
High Sorcery (1970)
The Crystal Gryphon (1972)
Spell of the Witch World (1972)
Dragon Magic (1972)
The Jargoon Pard (1974)
Lavender-Green Magic (1974)
Knave of Dreams (1975)
The White Jade Fox (1975)
The Book of Andre Norton (1975)
Perilous Dreams (1976)
Wraiths of Time (1976)
Red Hart Magic (1976)
Trey of Swords (1977)
The Opal-Eyed Fan (1977)
Velvet Shadows (1977)
Zarsthor's Bane (1978)
Quag Keep (1978)
Seven Spells to Sunday (1979, with Phyllis Miller)
Iron Butterflies (1980)
Lore of the Witch World (1980)
Ten Mile Treasure (1981)
Horn Crown (1981)
Gryphon in Glory (1981)
Moon Called (1982)
'Ware Hawk (1983)
Wheel of Stars (1983)
Gryphon's Eyrie (1984, with A. C. Crispin)
House of Shadows (1984, with Phyllis Miller)

Ride the Green Dragon (1985, with Phyllis Miller)
The Gate of the Cat (1987)
The Magic Books (1988)
Moon Mirror (1988)
Imperial Lady (1989, with Susan Shwartz)
Wizards' Worlds (1989)
Black Trillium (1990, with Marion Zimmer Bradley and Julian May)
Storm of Victory (1991, with P. M. Griffin)
Elvenbane (1991, with Mercedes Lackey)
Flight of Vengeance (1992, with Mary Schaub and P. M. Griffin)
The Mark of the Cat (1992)
Songsmith (1992, with A. C. Crispin)
Golden Trillium (1993)
Empire of the Eagle (1993, with Susan Shwartz)
The Hands of Llyr (1994)
On Wings of Magic (1994, with Patricia Mathews and Sasha Miller)
Annals of the Witch World (1994)
Mirror of Destiny (1995)
Elvenblood (1995, with Mercedes Lackey)
The Key of the Keplian (1995, with Lynn McConchie)
Tiger Burning Bright (1995, with Marion Zimmer Bradley and Julian May)
The Warding of Witch World (1996)
The Magestone (1996, with Mary Schaub)
Scent of Magic (1998)
Ciara's Song (1998, with Lynn McConchie)
The Shadow of Albion (1999, with Rosemary Edghill)
To the King a Daughter (2000, with Sasha Miller)
The Gates to Witch World (2001)
Knight or Knave (2001, with Sasha Miller)
Leopard in Exile (2001, with Rosemary Edghill)
Elvenborn (2002, with Mercedes Lackey)
A Crown Disowned (2002, with Sasha Miller)
Mark of the Cat & Year of the Rat (2002)
Lost Lands of Witch World (2004)
The Duke's Ballad (2004, with Lynn McConchie)
Dragon Blade (2005, with Sasha Miller)
Three Hands for Scorpio (2005)

O'DAY-FLANNERY, CONSTANCE
Timeless Passion (1986)
Timeswept Lovers (1987)
Time Kissed Destiny (1987)
Time-Kept Promises (1988)
This Time Forever (1990)
Once in a Lifetime (1991)
A Time for Love (1991)

The Gift (1994)
Bewitched (1995)
Anywhere You Are (1999)
Time after Time (2001)
Shifting Love (2004)

OFFUTT, ANDREW J.
Jodinareh (1970, as John Cleve)
Sword of the Gael (1975)
The Undying Wizard (1976)
Chieftain of Andor (1976, also published as *Clansman of Andor*)
The Sign of the Moonbow (1977)
Conan and the Sorceror (1978)
Demon in the Mirror (1978, with Richard K. Lyon)
The Ironlords (1979)
The Sword of Skelos (1979)
The Eye of Sarsis (1980, with Richard K. Lyon)
Conan the Mercenary (1980)
Shadows out of Hell (1980)
When Death Birds Fly (1980, with Keith Taylor)
Web of the Spider (1981, with Richard K. Lyon)
The Tower of Death (1982, with Keith Taylor)
The Lady of the Snowmist (1983)
Shadowspawn (1987)
Deathknight (1990)
The Shadow of Sorcery (1993)

ONIONS, OLIVER
Widdershins (1911, also published as *The First Book of Ghost Stories*)
The Tower of Oblivion (1921)
Ghosts in Daylight (1924)
The Painted Face (1925)
A Certain Man (1931)
The Collected Ghost Stories of Oliver Onions (1935)
Bells Rung Backward (1953)
A Shilling to Spend (1965)
Ghost Stories (2001)
Tragic Casements (2001)

PAINE, MICHAEL
Cities of the Dead (1988)
The Colors of Hell (1990)
Owl Light (1990)
Steel Ghosts (2005)

PAXSON, DIANA L.
Lady of Light (1982)
Lady of Darkness (1983)

Brisingamen (1984)
Silverhair the Wanderer (1986)
White Mare, Red Stallion (1986)
The Earthstone (1987)
The Paradise Tree (1987)
The White Raven (1988)
The Sea Star (1988)
The Wind Crystal (1990)
Serpent's Tooth (1991)
Mistress of the Jewels (1991)
The Jewel of Fire (1992)
The Wolf and the Raven (1993)
Master of Earth and Water (1993, with Adrienne Martine-Barnes)
The Forest House (1993, uncredited collaboration with Marion Zimmer Bradley)
The Shield between the Worlds (1994, with Adrienne Martine-Barnes)
The Dragons of the Rhine (1995)
Sword of Fire and Shadows (1995, with Adrienne Martine-Barnes)
The Lady of Horses (1996)
The Book of the Cauldron (1999)
The Book of the Spear (1999)
The Book of the Sword (1999)
The Book of the Stone (2000)
The Hallowed Isle (2000)
Priestess of Avalon (2001, with Marion Zimmer Bradley)
Ancestors of Avalon (2004)

PEAKE, MERVYN
Titus Groan (1946)
Gormenghast (1950)
Titus Alone (1950)
Mr. Pye (1953)

PHILLPOTTS, EDEN
A Deal with the Devil (1895)
My Laughing Philosopher (1896)
Fancy Free (1901)
Transit of the Red Dragon (1903)
The Girl and the Faun (1916)
Evander (1919)
Pan and the Twins (1922)
The Lavender Dragon (1923)
The Treasures of Typhon (1924)
The Miniature (1926)
Peacock House and Other Mystery Stories (1926)
Arachne (1927)
Alcyone (1930)

The Owl of Athene (1936)
Golden Island (1938)
The Hidden Hand (1952)

PIERCE, TAMORA
Alanna: The First Adventure (1983)
In the Hands of the Goddess (1984)
The Woman Who Rides Like a Man (1986, also published as *The Girl Who Rides Like a Man*)
Lioness Rampant (1988)
Wild Magic (1992)
Wolf-Speaker (1994)
Emperor Mage (1995)
Realms of the Gods (1996)
First Test (1999)
Sandry's Book (1999)
Tris's Book (1999)
Page (2000)
Daja's Book (2000)
Briar's Book (2000)
Squire (2001)
Magic Steps (2001)
Lady Knight (2002)
Street Magic (2002)
Cold Fire (2003)
Trickster's Choice (2003)
Trickster's Queen (2004)
Shatterglass (2004)

PIKE, CHRISTOPHER
Remember Me (1989)
Sati (1990)
See You Later (1990)
The Witch (1990)
Bury Me Deep (1991)
The Ancient Evil (1992)
The Season of Passage (1992)
The Immortal (1993)
Black Blood (1994)
The Return (1994)
The Last Vampire (1994)
The Haunted Cave (1995)
The Cold One (1995)
Howling Ghost (1995)
The Listeners (1995)
Red Dice (1995)
The Last Story (1995)
The Witch's Revenge (1996)
The Secret Path (1996)
The Little People (1996)

The Hidden Beast (1996)
The Cold People (1996)
The Dark Corner (1996)
The Deadly Past (1996)
Time Terror (1996)
The Visitor (1996)
The Wicked Cat (1996)
The Wishing Stone (1996)
Phantom (1996)
Invasion of the No-Ones (1996)
Night of the Vampire (1997)
The Thing in the Closet (1997)
The Evil House (1997)
The Living Dead (1998)
The Dangerous Quest (1998)
Creature in the Teacher (1999)
The Blind Mirror (2003)
Alosha (2004)

POE, EDGAR ALLAN

Tales of the Grotesque and Arabesque (1840)
The Tales (1845)
Tales of Mystery and the Imagination (1855)
The Selected Works of Edgar Allan Poe (1880)
The Assignation and Other Tales (1884)
Selections from Edgar Allan Poe (1885)
Tales (1888)
The Choice Works of Edgar Allan Poe (1889)
The Popular Tales of Edgar Allan Poe (1891)
Weird Tales (1895)
The Prose Tales (1897)
The Fall of the House of Usher and Other Tales of the Imagination (1899)
Edgar Allan Poe (1901)
The Best Tales of Edgar Allan Poe (1903)
Tales of Mystery (1903)
Prose Tales of Mystery and Imagination (1903)
Stories and Poems (1904)
Edgar Allan Poe's Tales (1904)
Poe's Tales (1906)
Selected Poems and Tales of Edgar Allan Poe (1906)
Three Tales (1907)
Short Stories (1908)
Selected Tales of Mystery (1909)
The Gold Bug and Other Selections (1912)
The Murders in the Rue Morgue and Other Stories (1920)
Poe (1922)
The Masque of the Red Death and Other Stories (1924)
The Purloined Letter and Other Tales (1924)
Poems and Tales by Edgar Allan Poe (1924)

Uncanny Tales (1925)
Tales of Imagination and Science (1926)
The Works of Edgar Allan Poe (1927)
Poe's Short Stories (1927)
The Book of Poe (1929)
Tales Grotesque (1931)
The Best Known Works of Edgar Allan Poe (1931)
Representative Selections (1935)
Some Tales of Mystery and Imagination (1938)
The Complete Tales and Poems of Edgar Allan Poe (1938)
The Gold Bug and Other Stories (1940)
Mystery and Imagination (1940)
Great Tales and Poems of Edgar Allan Poe (1940)
The Black Cat and Other Short Stories (1943)
Selected Stories (1944)
The Best of Edgar Allan Poe (1945)
Complete Stories and Poems (1946)
The Pit and the Pendulum (1948)
Tales of Effect (1948)
The Centenary Poe (1949)
Selected Poetry and Prose of Edgar Allan Poe (1951)
Selected Short Stories (1952)
Selected Tales (1956)
The Portable Edgar Allan Poe (1957)
The Gold Bug (1960)
Eight Tales of Terror (1961)
Descent into the Maelstrom (1961)
The Fall of the House of Usher (1961)
Poe's Tales of Terror (1962)
Great Tales of Horror (1964)
Poe's Tales of Mystery and Terror (1967)
Eighteen Best Stories of Edgar Allan Poe (1967)
The Pit and the Pendulum and Five Other Tales (1967)
Bizarre and Arabesque (1967)
Fantastic Tales (1969)
The Great Works of Edgar Allan Poe (1970)
Visions of Darkness (1971)
Complete Tales and Poems (1975)
The Illustrated Edgar Allan Poe (1976)
The Short Fiction of Edgar Allan Poe (1976)
Forty-Two Tales (1979)
Famous Tales of Mystery and Horror (1980)
The Edgar Allan Poe Bedside Companion (1980)
The Tell-Tale Heart and Other Writings (1982)
Edgar Allan Poe's Dark Dreams (2002)
Great Tales of Edgar Allan Poe (2003)

POWERS, TIMOTHY
The Drawing of the Dark (1979)
The Anubis Gates (1983)

On Stranger Tides (1987)
The Stress of Her Regard (1989)
Last Call (1992)
Expiration Date (1995)
Earthquake Weather (1996)
Declare (2001)
Night Moves and Other Stories (2001)
Strange Itineraries (2005)

PRATCHETT, TERRY
The Carpet People (1971)
Strata (1981)
The Colour of Magic (1983)
The Light Fantastic (1986)
Equal Rites (1987)
Mort (1987)
Sourcery (1988)
Wyrd Sisters (1988)
Pyramids (1989)
Guards, Guards (1989)
Eric (1990)
Truckers (1990)
Moving Pictures (1990)
Good Omens (1990, with Neil Gaiman)
Diggers (1991)
Reaper Man (1991)
Wings (1991)
Witches Abroad (1991)
Small Gods (1992)
Interesting Times (1994)
Lords and Ladies (1994)
Johnny and the Dead (1994)
Soul Music (1994)
The Witches Trilogy (1994)
Maskerade (1995)
Men at Arms (1996)
Feet of Clay (1996)
Hogfather (1996)
Jingo (1997)
The Last Continent (1997)
Carpe Jugulum (1998)
Death Trilogy (1998)
Rincewind the Magician (1999)
City Watch Trilogy (1999)
The Fifth Elephant (2000)
The Gods Trilogy (2000)
The Truth (2000)
The Last Hero (2001)
Thief of Time (2001)
The Rincewind Trilogy (2001)
The Amazing Maurice and His Educated Rodents (2001)

Night Watch (2002)
The Wee Free Men (2003)
The Bromeliad Trilogy (2003)
Monstrous Regiment (2003)
A Hatful of Sky (2004)

PULLMAN, PHILIP
Count Karlstein (1982)
Spring Heeled Jack (1989)
The Golden Compass (1997, also published as *Northern Lights*)
The Subtle Knife (1997)
The Amber Spyglass (2000)
I Was a Rat! (2002)
Lyra's Oxford (2003)
In the Shadow of the Ark (2005)

QUINN, SEABURY
Roads (1938)
The Phantom Fighter (1966)
Is the Devil a Gentleman? (1970)
The Adventures of Jules de Grandin (1976)
The Casebook of Jules de Grandin (1976)
The Skeleton Closet of Jules de Grandin (1976)
The Devil's Bride (1976)
The Hellfire Fires of Jules de Grandin (1976)
The Horror Chambers of Jules de Grandin (1977)
Night Creatures (2003)

RADFORD, IRENE
Frostflower and Thorn (1980, as Phyllis Ann Karr)
Frostflower and Windbourne (1982, as Phyllis Ann Karr)
The Idylls of the Queen (1982, as Phyllis Ann Karr)
Wildraith's Last Battle (1982, as Phyllis Ann Karr)
At Amberleaf Fair (1986, as Phyllis Ann Karr)
The Glass Dragon (1994)
The Perfect Princess (1995)
The Loneliest Magician (1996)
The Dragon's Touchstone (1997)
The Last Battlemage (1998)
The Renegade Dragon (1999)
Guardian of the Balance (1999)
The Wizard's Treasure (2000)
Guardian of the Trust (2000)
Guardian of the Vision (2001)
The Follies of Sir Harald (2001, as Phyllis Ann Karr)
The Gallows in the Greenwood (2002, as Phyllis Ann Karr)
Guardian of the Promise (2003)
Guardian of the Freedom (2005)

RANKIN, ROBERT
The Antipope (1981)
The Brentford Triangle (1982)
East of Ealing (1984)
The Sprouts of Wrath (1988)
The Suburban Book of the Dead (1993)
The Garden of Unearthly Delights (1996)
A Dog Called Demolition (1996)
Nostradamus Ate My Hamster (1996)
Brentford Chainstore Massacre (1997)
Waiting for Godalming (2001)
The Hollow Chocolate Bunnies of the Apocalypse (2002)
The Witches of Chiswick (2003)
Knees Up Mother Earth (2004)
The Brightonomicon (2005)

RAWN, MELANIE
Dragon Prince (1988)
The Star Scroll (1989)
Stronghold (1990)
Sunrunner's Fire (1990)
The Dragon Token (1992)
Skybowl (1993)
Exiles: The Ruins of Ambrai (1994)
The Mageborn Traitor (1997)
The Golden Key (1997, with Jennifer Roberson and Kate Elliott)
The Capital's Tower (2005)

REICHERT, MICKEY ZUCKER
Godslayer (1987)
Shadow Climber (1988)
Dragonrank Master (1989)
Shadows Realm (1990)
By Chaos Cursed (1991)
The Last of the Renshai (1992)
The Western Wizard (1992)
The Legend of Nightfall (1993)
Child of Thunder (1993)
Beyond Ragnarok (1995)
Prince of Demons (1996)
The Children of Wrath (1998)
Spirit Fox (1998, with Jennifer Wingert)
The Flightless Falcon (2000)
The Bifrost Guardians (2000)
The Beasts of Barakhai (2001)
The Lost Dragons of Barakhai (2002)
The Return of Nightfall (2004)

RICE, ANNE
Interview with the Vampire (1976)
The Vampire Lestat (1984)

The Queen of the Damned (1988)
The Mummy (1989)
The Witching Hour (1990)
The Tale of the Body Thief (1992)
Lasher (1993)
Taltos (1994)
Memnoch the Devil (1995)
Servant of the Bones (1996)
Pandora (1998)
The Vampire Armand (1998)
Vittorio the Vampire (1999)
Merrick (2000)
Blood and Gold (2001)
Blackwood Farm (2002)
Blood Canticle (2003)

ROBERSON, JENNIFER
Shapechangers! (1984)
The Song of Homana (1985)
Legacy of the Sword (1986)
Sword-Dancer (1986)
Track of the White Wolf (1987)
A Pride of Princes (1988)
Sword-Singer (1988)
Daughter of the Lion (1989)
Sword-Maker (1989)
Flight of the Raven (1990)
Sword-Breaker (1991)
A Tapestry of Lions (1992)
Scotland the Brave (1996)
The Golden Key (1997, with Melanie Rawn and Kate Elliott)
Sword-Born (1998)
Children of the Lion (2001)
The Lion Throne (2001)
Shapechanger's Song (2001)
Sword Sworn (2002)

ROBERTS, JOHN MADDOX
King of the Wood (1983)
Conan the Valorous (1985)
Conan the Champion (1987)
Conan the Marauder (1987)
Conan the Bold (1989)
The Islander (1990)
The Black Shields (1991)
Conan the Rogue (1991)
The Poisoned Lands (1992)
Conan and the Treasure of Python (1993)
The Steel Kings (1993)
Queens of Land and Sea (1994)

Conan and the Manhunters (1994)
Conan and the Amazon (1995)
Murder in Tarsis (1996)

ROHAN, MICHAEL SCOTT
Burial Rites (1986, with Allan Scott as Michael Scot, also published as *The Ice King*)
The Anvil of Ice (1986)
The Forge in the Forest (1987)
The Hammer of the Sun (1988)
Chase the Morning (1990)
The Gates of Noon (1992)
A Spell of Empire (1992, with Allan Scott)
Cloud Castles (1993)
The Lord of Middle Air (1994)
Maxie's Demon (1997)
The Castle of the Winds (1998)
The Singer and the Sea (2000)
Shadow of the Seer (2001)

ROHMER, SAX
The Insidious Doctor Fu-Manchu (1913, also published as *The Mysterious Doctor Fu-Manchu*)
The Quest of the Sacred Slipper (1913)
The Yellow Claw (1915)
The Hand of Fu Manchu (1917, also published as *The Si-Fan Mysteries*)
Brood of the Witch Queen (1918)
The Dream Detective (1920)
The Haunting of Low Fennel (1920)
The Green Eyes of Bast (1920)
Grey Face (1924)
She Who Sleeps (1928)
Daughter of Fu Manchu (1931)
The Mask of Fu Manchu (1932)
The Bride of Fu Manchu (1933, also published as *Fu Manchu's Bride*)
The Bat Flies Low (1935)
President Fu Manchu (1936)
The Drums of Fu Manchu (1939)
The Island of Fu Manchu (1941)
Shadow of Fu Manchu (1948)
Re-Enter Fu Manchu (1957)
Emperor Fu Manchu (1959)
The Secret of Holm Peel & Other Strange Stories (1970)
The Wrath of Fu Manchu (1973)

ROSENBERG, JOEL
The Sleeping Dragon (1983)
The Sword and the Chain (1984)

The Silver Crown (1985)
The Heir Apparent (1987)
The Warrior Lives (1988)
D'Shai (1991)
The Road to Ehvenor (1991)
Hour of the Octopus (1994)
The Road Home (1995)
The Fire Duke (1995)
The Silver Stone (1996)
The Crimson Sky (1998)
Not Exactly the Three Musketeers (1999)
Not Quite Scaramouche (2001)
Murder in Lamut (2002, with Raymond E. Feist)
Not Really the Prisoner of Zenda (2003)
Paladins (2004)

ROWLEY, CHRISTOPHER
Bazil Broketail (1992)
A Sword for a Dragon (1993)
Dragons of War (1994)
Battledragon (1995)
The Wizard and the Floating City (1996)
A Dragon at World's End (1997)
Dragons of Argonath (1998)
Dragon Ultimate (1999)
The Ancient Enemy (2000)
The Shasht War (2001)
Doom's Break (2002)

ROWLING, J. K.
Harry Potter and the Sorcerer's Stone (1997, also published as *Harry Potter and the Philosopher's Stone*)
Harry Potter and the Chamber of Secrets (1999)
Harry Potter and the Prisoner of Azkaban (1999)
Harry Potter and the Goblet of Fire (2000)
Harry Potter and the Order of the Phoenix (2003)
Harry Potter and the Half-Blood Prince (2005)

RUSCH, KRISTINE KATHRYN
The Gallery of His Dreams (1991)
The White Mists of Power (1991)
Afterimage (1992, with Kevin J. Anderson)
Heart Readers (1993)
Traitors (1993)
Facade (1994)
Sins of the Blood (1995)
Fey: The Sacrifice (1995)
The Devil's Churn (1996)
Fey: The Changeling (1996)
The Rival (1997)

Afterimage Aftershock (1998, with Kevin J. Anderson)
The Resistance (1998)
Victory (1998)
The Black Queen (1999)
The Black King (2000)
Utterly Charming (2000, as Kristine Grayson)
Stories for an Enchanted Afternoon (2001)
Thoroughly Kissed (2001, as Kristine Grayson)
Completely Smitten (2002, as Kristine Grayson)
Fantasy Life (2003)
Absolutely Captivated (2004, as Kristine Grayson)

RUSSO, JOHN
Night of the Living Dead (1974)
Return of the Living Dead (1978)
Midnight (1980)
Black Cat (1982)
The Awakening (1983)
Return of the Living Dead (1985)
Inhuman (1986)
Voodoo Dawn (1987)
Living Things (1988)
Day of the Dead (1988, with George Romero)
Hell's Creation (1995)
The Warrior Who Carried Life (1985)
The Unconquered Country (1986)
Was (1992)
Lust (2001)

SABERHAGEN, FRED
The Broken Lands (1968)
The Black Mountains (1971)
Changeling Earth (1973, revised in 1988 as *Ardneh's World*)
The Dracula Tape (1975)
The Holmes Dracula File (1978)
Empire of the East (1979)
An Old Friend of the Family (1979)
Dominion (1982)
The Complete Book of Swords (1983)
The First Book of Swords (1983)
The Second Book of Swords (1983)
The Third Book of Swords (1984)
The Frankenstein Papers (1986)
Woundhealer's Story (1986)
Sightblinder's Story (1987)
Stonecutter's Story (1988)
The Lost Swords (1988)
Coinspinner's Story (1989)
Farslayer's Story (1989)

A Matter of Taste (1990)
Mindsword's Story (1990)
Thorn (1990)
Wayfinder's Story (1992)
Dracula (1992, with James V. Hart)
A Question of Time (1992)
Seance for a Vampire (1994)
Merlin's Bones (1995)
A Sharpness on the Neck (1996)
Dancing Bears (1996)
The Face of Apollo (1998)
Ariadne's Web (2000)
The Arms of Hercules (2000)
Vlad Tapes (2000)
God of the Golden Fleece (2001)
Gods of Fire and Thunder (2002)
A Coldness in the Blood (2002)

SACKETT, JEFFREY
Stolen Souls (1987)
Candlemas Eve (1988)
Blood of the Impaler (1989)
Mark of the Werewolf (1990)
The Demon (1991)

SALVATORE, R. A.
The Crystal Shard (1988)
Streams of Silver (1989)
Echoes of the Fourth Magic (1990)
Exile (1990)
Homeland (1990)
The Halfling's Gem (1990)
Sojourn (1991)
The Witch's Daughter (1991)
Canticle (1991)
In Sylvan Shadows (1992)
The Legacy (1992)
Night Masks (1992)
Starless Night (1993)
The Fallen Fortress (1993)
The Woods Out Back (1993)
The Chaos Curse (1994)
The Dragon's Dagger (1994)
Siege of Darkness (1994)
The Sword of Bedwyr (1995)
Dragonslayer's Return (1995)
The Dragon King (1996)
The Demon Awakens (1996)
Passage to Dawn (1996)
Luthien's Gamble (1996)

The Demon Spirit (1998)
The Silent Blade (1998)
The Cleric Quintet (1999)
The Demon Apostle (1999)
The Spine of the World (1999, with Philip Athans)
Bastion of Darkness (2000)
Servant of the Shard (2000)
The Icewind Dale Trilogy (2000)
Ascendance (2001)
Mortalis (2001)
Sea of Swords (2001)
The Thousand Orcs (2002)
Transcendence (2002)
Immortalis (2003)
Legacy of the Drow (2003)
The Lone Drow (2003)
The Highwayman (2004)
Spearwielder's Tale (2004)
The Two Swords (2004)
Brotherhood of the Lost (2005, with James Lowder)

SARBAN (JOHN WILLIAM WALL)

Ringstones and Other Curious Tales (1951)
The Sound of His Horn (1952)
The Dollmaker (1953)
Ringstones (1961)
The Sound of His Horn and the King of the Lake (1999)
The Dollmaker and Other Tales of the Uncanny (1999)
The Sacrifice and Other Stories (2002)

SARRANTONIO, AL

Totentanz (1985)
The Worms (1985)
Campbell Wood (1986)
The Boy with Penny Eyes (1987)
Moonbane (1989)
October (1990)
House Haunted (1991)
Skeletons (1992)
Toybox (2000)
Orangefield (2002, also published as *Hallow's Eve*)
Hornets and Others (2004)

SAUL, JOHN

Suffer the Children (1977)
Punish the Sinners (1978)
Cry for the Strangers (1979)
Comes the Blind Fury (1980)
When the Wind Blows (1981)
The God Project (1982. also published as *All Fall Down*)
Nathaniel (1984)

Brain Child (1985)
Hell Fire (1986)
The Unwanted (1987)
The Unloved (1988)
Creature (1989)
Sleepwalk (1990)
Second Child (1990)
Darkness (1991)
Shadows (1992)
Guardian (1993)
The Homing (1994)
Black Lightning (1995)
Ashes to Ashes: The Dragon's Flame (1997)
Asylum (1997)
Twist of Fate: The Locket (1997)
In the Shadow of Evil: The Handkerchief (1997)
The Day of Reckoning: The Stereoscope (1997)
Eye for an Eye: The Doll (1997)
The Presence (1997)
The Blackstone Chronicles (1998)
The Right Hand of Evil (1999)
Nightshade (2000)
Midnight Voices (2002)
Black Creek Crossing (2004)

SAXON, PETER

The Darkest Night (1966)
The Torturer (1966)
Drums of the Dark Gods (1966, as W. A. Ballinger)
Satan's Child (1967)
Scream and Scream Again (1967, also published as *The Disorientated Man*)
Dark Ways to Death (1968)
Through the Dark (1968)
The Haunting of Alan Mais (1968)
The Killing Bone (1968)
Black Honey (1968)
The Curse of Rathlaw (1968)
Vampire's Moon (1970)
The Vampires of Finistere (1970)
Tigerman of Terrahpur (1973, as Errol Lecale)
Castledoom (1974, as Errol Lecale)
The Severed Hand (1974, as Errol Lecale)
The Death Box (1974, as Errol Lecale)
Zombie (1975, as Errol Lecale)
Blood of My Blood (1975, as Errol Lecale)

SCARBOROUGH, ELIZABETH ANN

Song of Sorcery (1982)
The Unicorn Creed (1983)
Bronwyn's Bane (1983)

The Harem of Aman Akbar (1984)
The Christening Quest (1985)
The Drastic Dragon of Draco, Texas (1986)
The Goldcamp Vampire (1987)
Songs from the Seashell Archives (1987)
The Healer's War (1988)
Phantom Banjo (1991)
Picking the Ballad's Bones (1991)
Nothing Sacred (1991)
Last Refuge (1992)
Strum Again? (1992)
The Godmother (1994)
The Godmother's Apprentice (1995)
Carol for Another Christmas (1996)
The Godmother's Web (1998)
The Lady in the Loch (1998)
Scarborough Faire (2003)

SCHOW, DAVID
Lost Angels (1990)
Seeing Red (1990)
Crypt Orchids (1998)
Eye (2001)
Rock Breaks Scissors Cut (2003)
Zombie Jam (2004)

SERLING, ROD
Stories from the Twilight Zone (1960)
More Stories from the Twilight Zone (1961)
New Stories from the Twilight Zone (1962)
From the Twilight Zone (1970)
Night Gallery (1971)
Night Gallery 2 (1972)
The Twilight Zone: The Complete Stories (1998)

SHARP, MARGERY
The Stone of Chastity (1940)
The Rescuers (1959)
Miss Bianca (1962)
The Turret (1963)
Miss Bianca in the Salt Mines (1966)
Miss Bianca in the Orient (1970)
Miss Bianca in the Antarctic (1971)
Miss Bianca and the Bridesmaid (1972)
Bernard the Brave (1976)
Bernard into Battle (1978)
The Rescuers Down Under (1991)

SHEA, MICHAEL
A Quest for Simbilis (1974)
Nifft the Lean (1982)

The Color out of Time (1984)
In Yana, the Touch of Undying (1985)
Polyphemus (1987)
I, Said the Fly (1993)
The Mines of Behemoth (1997)
A'Rak (2000)
The Incompleat Nifft (2000)

SHELLEY, MARY
Frankenstein, or a Modern Prometheus (1818)
The Mortal Immortal (1996)

SHEPARD, LUCIUS
The Scalehunter's Beautiful Daughter (1988)
Kalimantan (1990)
The Golden (1993)
Valentine (2002)
Louisiana Breakdown (2003)
Floater (2003)
A Handbook of American Prayer (2003)
Two Trains Running (2004)
Eternity and Other Stories (2005)

SHERMAN, JOSEPHA
The Dark Gods (1989)
The Shining Falcon (1989)
The Horse of Flame (1990)
Child of Faerie, Child of Earth (1992)
Castle of Deception (1992, with Mercedes Lackey)
Wheels of Fire (1992, with Mercedes Lackey)
Rachel the Clever and Other Jewish Folktales (1993)
A Strange and Ancient Name (1993)
Windleaf (1993)
The Chaos Gate (1994)
King's Son, Magic's Son (1994)
Gleaming Bright (1994)
Once upon a Galaxy (1994)
A Cast of Corbies (1994, with Mercedes Lackey)
The Shattered Oath (1995)
Forging the Runes (1996)
Son of Darkness (1998)
Visitors (1999, with Laura Ann Gilman)
Deep Water (2000, with Laura Ann Gilman)

SHETTERLY, WILL
Cats Have No Lord (1985)
Witch Blood (1986)
The Tangled Lands (1989)
Elsewhere (1991)
NeverNever (1993)

Dogland (1997)
Thor's Hammer (2000)

SHIRLEY, JOHN
Dracula in Love (1979)
City Come A-Walkin' (1980)
Cellars (1982)
In Darkness Waiting (1988)
The Black Hole of Carcosa (1988)
Wetbones (1993)
Black Butterflies (1998)
Really, Really, Really, Really Weird Stories (1999)
Demons (2000)
Darkness Divided (2001)
The View from Hell (2001)
And the Angel with Television Eyes (2001)

SHWARTZ, SUSAN
Byzantium's Crown (1987)
The Woman of Flowers (1987)
Queensblade (1988)
Silk Roads and Shadows (1988)
Imperial Lady (1989, with Andre Norton)
The Grail of Hearts (1992)
Empire of the Eagle (1993, with Andre Norton)
Shards of Empire (1996)
Cross and Crescent (1997)

SIMMONS, DAN
Song of Kali (1985)
Carrion Comfort (1989)
Prayers from Broken Stones (1990)
Summer of Night (1991)
Going After the Rubber Chicken (1991)
Children of the Night (1992)
Lovedeath (1993)
Fires of Eden (1994)
Banished Dreams (1996)
A Winter Haunting (2002)

SKIPP, JOHN AND SPECTOR, CRAIG
Fright Night (1985)
The Light at the End (1986)
The Cleanup (1987)
The Scream (1988)
Dead Lines (1989)
The Bridge (1991)
Animals (1993)
The Emerald Burrito of Oz (2000, John Skipp only,
    with Mark Levinthal)

SLEATOR, WILLIAM
Blackbriar (1972)
Into the Dream (1979)
Fingers (1983)
The Boy Who Reversed Himself (1986)
The Spirit House (1991)
Dangerous Wishes (1996)
Boltzmon! (1999)
Rewind (1999)
The Boxes (2000)
Marco's Millions (2001)
The Boy Who Couldn't Die (2004)

SMITH, CLARK ASHTON
Double Shadow and Other Fantasies (1933)
Out of Space and Time (1942)
Lost Worlds (1944)
Genius Loci and Other Tales (1948)
The Abominations of Yondo (1960)
Tales of Science and Sorcery (1964)
Other Dimensions (1970)
Zothique (1970)
Hyperborea (1971)
Xiccarph (1972)
Poseidonis (1973)
The City of the Singing Flame (1981)
The Last Incantation (1982)
The Monster of the Prophecy (1983)
Untold Tales (1984)
A Rendezvous in Averoigne (1988)
Strange Shadows (1997)
The Emperor of Dreams (2002)

SMITH, GUY N.
Werewolf by Moonlight (1974)
The Sucking Pit (1975)
Sleeping Beauty (1975)
Snow White and the Seven Dwarfs (1975)
The Legend of Sleepy Hollow (1976)
The Ghoul (1976)
Night of the Crabs (1976)
The Slime Beast (1976)
Return of the Werewolf (1977)
Killer Crabs (1978)
The Son of the Werewolf (1978)
Locusts (1979)
The Origin of the Crabs (1979)
Bats out of Hell (1979)
Satan's Snowdrop (1980)
Deathbell (1980)

Thirst (1980)
Manitou Doll (1981)
Doomflight (1981)
Wolfcurse (1981)
Crabs on the Rampage (1981)
The Lurkers (1982)
The Pluto Pact (1982)
The Graveyard Vultures (1982)
Cannibal Cult (1982)
Entombed (1982)
The Blood Merchants (1982)
Blood Circuit (1983)
The Undead (1983)
The Druid Connection (1983)
Accursed (1983)
Crabs' Moon (1984)
The Walking Dead (1984)
Throwback (1985)
The Wood (1985)
Cannibals (1986)
The Neophyte (1986)
Abomination (1986)
Snakes (1986)
Warhead (1986)
Bloodshow (1987)
Demons (1987)
Alligators (1987)
The Plague (1987)
Fiend (1988)
The Master (1988)
The Island (1988)
Crabs: The Human Sacrifice (1988)
The Camp (1989)
The Festering (1989)
Mania (1989)
Phobia (1990)
The Unseen (1990)
Carnivore (1990)
The Resurrected (1991)
Witch Spell (1993)
The Dark One (1995)
Dead End (1996)
Water Rites (1997)
The Busker (1998)

SMITH, L. J.
The Night of the Solstice (1987)
Heart of Valor (1990)
The Fury (1991)
The Awakening (1991)

The Struggle (1991)
The Captive (1992)
Dark Reunion (1992)
The Initiation (1992)
The Strange Power (1994)
The Hunter (1994)
The Chase (1994)
The Kill (1994)
The Power (1995)
The Possessed (1995)
Secret Vampire (1996)
Spellbinder (1996)
Daughters of Darkness (1996)
Dark Angel (1996)
Black Dawn (1997)
The Chosen (1997)
Soulmate (1997)
The Huntress (1997)
Strange Fate (1998)

SMITH, THORNE
Topper (1926, also published as *The Jovial Ghosts*)
The Stray Lamb (1929)
The Night Life of the Gods (1931)
Turnabout (1931)
Topper Takes a Trip (1932)
The Glorious Pool (1934)
The Passionate Witch (1941, with Norman Matson)
The Thorne Smith Three Bagger (1943)

SOMTOW, S. P.
Vampire Junction (1984)
The Shattered Horse (1986)
The Fallen Country (1986, as Somtow Sucharitkul)
Forgetting Places (1987)
Moon Dance (1990)
Riverrun (1991)
Valentine (1992)
Forest of the Night (1992, also published as *Armorica*)
The Wizard's Apprentice (1993, as Somtow Sucharitkul)
Jasmine Nights (1994, as Somtow Sucharitkul)
Vanitas (1995)
The Pavilion of Frozen Women (1996)
Yestern (1996)
The Riverrun Trilogy (1996)
Darker Angels (1997)
The Vampire's Beautiful Daughter (1997)
Dragon's Fin Soup (1998)
Temple of Night (1999)
Tagging the Moon (2000)

SPRINGER, NANCY
The Book of Suns (1977)
The White Hart (1979)
The Silver Sun (1980)
The Sable Moon (1981)
The Black Beast (1982)
The Golden Swan (1983)
The Book of Vale (1984)
Wings of Flame (1985)
Chains of Gold (1986)
Chance and Other Gestures of the Hand of Fate (1987)
Madbond (1987)
Mindbond (1987)
Godbond (1988)
Apocalypse (1989)
The Hex Witch of Seldom (1989)
Red Wizard (1990)
Damnbanna (1992)
The Friendship Song (1992)
Larque on the Wing (1994)
Metal Angel (1994)
Fair Peril (1996)
I Am Mordred (1998)
Plumage (2000)

STABLEFORD, BRIAN
The Last Days of the Edge of the World (1978)
The Empire of Fear (1988)
The Werewolves of London (1990)
Plague Daemon (1990, as Brian Craig)
Zaragoz (1990, as Brian Craig)
Storm Warriors (1991, as Brian Craig)
Angel of Pain (1991)
Young Blood (1992)
The Carnival of Destruction (1993)
Fables and Fantasies (1996)
Wine of Dreams (2000, as Brian Craig)
Year Zero (2002)

STALLMAN, ROBERT
The Orphan (1980)
The Captive (1981)
The Beast (1982, also published as The Book of the Beast)

STASHEFF, CHRISTOPHER
Her Majesty's Wizard (1986)
The Oathbound Wizard (1993)
Sir Harold and the Monkey King (1993)
The Witch Doctor (1994)

The Secular Wizard (1995)
The Shaman (1995)
The Sage (1996)
My Son, the Wizard (1997)
The Feline Wizard (2000)
The Haunted Wizard (2000)
Mind Out of Time (2003)
Saint Vidicon to the Rescue (2005)

STEWART, MARY
The Crystal Cave (1970)
The Little Broomstick (1971)
The Hollow Hills (1973)
Ludo and the Star Horse (1974)
Touch Not the Cat (1976)
The Last Enchantment (1979)
A Walk in Wolf Wood (1980)
The Wicked Day (1983)
Thornyhold (1988)
Grace (1989)
The Prince and the Pilgrim (1995)
Rose Cottage (1997)

STINE, R. L.
The New Girl (1989)
Haunted (1990)
The Boyfriend (1990)
The Secret Bedroom (1991)
The Third Evil (1992)
Goodnight Kiss (1992)
Monster Blood (1992)
Say Cheese and Die (1992)
Stay Out of the Basement (1992)
Welcome to Dead House (1992)
The Second Evil (1992)
Be Careful What You Wish For (1993)
The Werewolf of Fever Swamp (1993)
Welcome to Camp Nightmare (1993)
The Burning (1993)
The Ghost Next Door (1993)
The Haunted Mask (1993)
The Girl Who Cried Monster (1993)
Piano Lessons Can Be Murder (1993)
Night of the Living Dummy (1993)
Let's Get Invisible (1993)
Monster Blood II (1994)
Attack of the Mutants (1994)
One Day at Horrorland (1994)
Deep Trouble (1994)
Bad Dreams (1994)

The New Evil (1994)
Phantom of the Auditorium (1994)
Say Cheese and Die—Again (1994)
The Scarecrow Walks at Midnight (1994)
Go Eat Worms! (1994)
The Beast (1994)
Ghost Beach (1994)
My Hairiest Adventure (1994)
Why I'm Afraid of Bees (1994)
You Can't Scare Me! (1994)
Return of the Mummy (1994)
The First Horror (1994)
The Abominable Snowman of Pasadena (1995)
Horror at Camp Jellyjam (1995)
Night of the Living Dummy II (1995)
A Shocker on Shock Street (1995)
Monster Blood III (1995)
The Barking Ghost (1995)
The Cuckoo Clock of Doom (1995)
Superstitious (1995)
Switched (1995)
A Night in Terror Tower (1995)
The Headless Ghost (1995)
It Came from beneath the Sink (1995)
Revenge of the Lawn Gnomes (1995)
A New Fear (1996)
Tick Tock You're Dead (1996)
Trapped in Bat Wing Hall (1996)
Attack of the Aqua Apes (1996)
Calling All Creeps! (1996)
Attack of the Jack-O-Lanterns (1996)
The Beast from the East (1996)
Revenge of the Shadow People (1996)
The Dark Secret (1996)
The Deadly Experiments of Dr. Eeek (1996)
The Deadly Fire (1996)
Bad Hare Day (1996)
Eat Cheese and Barf (1996)
How to Kill a Monster (1996)
Stay out of the Bathroom (1996)
Night in Werewolf Woods (1996)
Who's Been Sleeping in My Grave? (1996)
House of Whispers (1996)
The Ooze (1996)
The Perfect Date (1996)
How I Got My Shrunken Head (1996)
Night of the Living Dummy III (1996)
Vampire Breath (1996)
Egg Monsters from Mars (1996)
Legend of the Lost Legend (1996)

Escape from the Carnival of Horrors (1996)
The Evil Moon (1996)
Hide and Shriek (1996)
Ghost Camp (1996)
The Face (1996)
Deep Trouble II (1997)
My Best Friend Is Invisible (1997)
Beware, the Snowman (1997)
The Curse of Camp Cold Lake (1997)
The Haunted School (1997)
The Blob That Ate Everyone (1997)
I Live in Your Basement (1997)
Chicken Chicken (1997)
Don't Go to Sleep (1997)
How I Learned to Fly (1997)
Werewolf Skin (1997)
Triple Header Book 1 (1997)
Fright Camp (1998)
Attack of the Graveyard Ghouls (1998)
The Bad Girl (1998)
Creature Teacher (1998)
Cry of the Cat (1998)
Are You Terrified Yet? (1998)
Headless Halloween (1998)
Revenge R Us (1998)
Bride of the Living Dummy (1998)
Invasion of the Body Squeezers (1998)
I Am Your Evil Twin (1998)
Be Afraid—Be Very Afraid (1999)
Horrors of the Black Ring (1999)
Brain Juice (1999)
The Haunted Car (1999)
Jekyll and Heidi (1999)
The Mummy Walks (1999)
Nightmare Hour (1999)
Return to Ghost Camp (1999)
Return to Horrorland (1999)
The Werewolf in the Living Room (1999)
Scream School (1999)
Don't Forget Me (2000)
Locker 13 (2000)
My Name Is Evil (2000)
Liar Liar (2000)
Camp Nowhere (2001)
Shadow Girl (2001)
They Call Me Creature (2001)
The Howler (2001)
The Sitter (2003)
Have You Met My Ghoulfriend? (2004)
Little Camp of Horrors (2004)

One Night in Doom House (2004)
Who Let the Ghosts Out? (2004)
Ghouls Gone Wild (2005)
Freaks and Shrieks (2005)

STOKER, BRAM

Under the Sunset (1882)
Dracula (1897)
The Mystery of the Sea (1902)
The Jewel of the Seven Stars (1903)
The Lady of the Shroud (1909)
Lair of the White Worm (1911, also published as *Garden of Evil*)
Dracula's Guest (1914)
The Bram Stoker Bedside Companion (1973)
Midnight Tales (1990)

STRAUB, PETER

Julia (1975, also published as *Full Circle*)
If You Could See Me Now (1977)
Ghost Story (1979)
Shadowland (1980)
The Floating Dragon (1982)
The Talisman (1984, with Stephen King)
Wild Animals (1984)
Houses Without Doors (1990)
Mr. X. (1999)
Pork Pie Hat (1999)
Magic Terror (2000)
Black House (2001, with Stephen King)
Lost Boy, Lost Girl (2003)
In the Night Room (2004)

STRIEBER, WHITLEY

The Wolfen (1978)
The Hunger (1981)
The Night Church (1983)
Cat Magic (1986)
The Wild (1991)
Unholy Fire (1992)
The Forbidden Zone (1993)
The Last Vampire (2001)
Lilith's Dream (2002)

SWANN, THOMAS BURNETT

Day of the Minotaur (1966)
The Weirwoods (1967)
Moondust (1968)
The Dolphin and the Deep (1968)
Where Is the Bird of Fire? (1970)

The Forest of Forever (1971)
The Goat without Horns (1971)
Green Phoenix (1972)
Wolfwinter (1972)
How Are the Mighty Fallen (1974)
The Not-World (1975)
Lady of the Bees (1976)
Will-o-the-Wisp (1976)
The Minikims of Yam (1976)
The Gods Abide (1976)
The Tournament of Thorns (1976)
Cry Silver Bells (1977)
Queens Walk in the Dust (1977)

TARR, JUDITH

The Golden Horn (1985)
The Isle of Glass (1985)
The Hall of the Mountain King (1986)
The Hound and the Falcon (1986)
The Hounds of God (1986)
The Lady of Han-Gilen (1987)
Avaryan Rising (1988)
A Fall of Princes (1988)
Alamut (1989)
A Wind in Cairo (1989)
Ars Magica (1989)
The Dagger and the Cross (1991)
Arrows of the Sun (1993)
Lord of the Two Lands (1993)
His Majesty's Elephant (1993)
Spear of Heaven (1994)
White Mare's Daughter (1998)
Household Gods (1999, with Harry Turtledove)
Kingdom of the Grail (2000)
Lady of Horses (2000)
Daughter of Lir (2001)
Pride of Kings (2001)
The Shepherd Kings (2001)
Devil's Bargain (2002)
Tides of Darkness (2002)
Avaryan Resplendent (2003)
House of War (2003)
Rite of Conquest (2004)
Queen of the Amazons (2004)
The Mountain's Call (2004, as Caitlin Brennan)

TEPPER, SHERI S.

King's Blood Four (1983)
Necromancer Nine (1983)
Wizard's Eleven (1984)

The Revenants (1984)
The Flight of Mavin Manyshaped (1985)
The Search of Mavin Manyshaped (1985)
The Song of Mavin Manyshaped (1985)
The True Game (1985)
Jinian Footseer (1985)
Marianne, the Magus, and the Mantichore (1985)
Jinian Star-Eye (1986)
Blood Heritage (1986)
The Chronicles of Mavin Manyshaped (1986)
Dervish Daughter (1986)
The Awakeners (1987)
Southshore (1987)
Northshore (1987)
The End of the Game (1987)
The Bones (1987)
Marianne, the Madame, and the Momentary Gods (1988)
Marianne, the Matchbox, and the Malachite Mouse (1989)
Beauty (1991)
A Plague of Angels (1993)

TESSIER, THOMAS
The Fates (1978)
The Nightwalker (1979)
Phantom (1982)
Fog Heart (1997)
Ghost Music (2000)

THOMPSON, RUTH PLUMLY
Pirates in Oz (1915)
The Royal Book of Oz (1921)
Kabumpo in Oz (1922)
The Cowardly Lion of Oz (1923)
Grampa in Oz (1924)
The Lost King of Oz (1925)
The Hungry Tiger of Oz (1926)
The Gnome King of Oz (1927)
The Giant Horse of Oz (1928)
Jack Pumpkinhead of Oz (1929)
The Yellow Knight of Oz (1930)
The Purple Prince of Oz (1932)
Ojo in Oz (1933)
Speedy in Oz (1934)
The Wishing Horse of Oz (1935)
Captain Salt in Oz (1936)
Handy Mandy in Oz (1937)
The Silver Princess in Oz (1938)

The Enchanted Island of Oz (1976)
Sissajig and Other Surprises (2003)

TOLKIEN, J. R. R.
The Hobbit (1937)
Farmer Giles of Ham (1949)
The Fellowship of the Ring (1954)
The Two Towers (1954)
The Return of the King (1955)
The Tolkien Reader (1966)
Smith of Wooton Major and Farmer Giles of Ham (1967)
The Lord of the Rings (1968)
Sir Gawain and the Green Knight, Pearl, and Sir Orfeo (1975)
The Silmarillion (1977)
Unfinished Tales (1980)
The Book of Lost Tales (1983, in two volumes)
Roverandom (1998)

TREMAYNE, PETER
The Hound of Frankenstein (1977)
The Vengeance of She (1978)
The Revenge of Dracula (1978)
The Curse of Loch Ness (1979)
Bloodright (1980, also published as *Dracula Unborn*)
Dracula My Love (1980)
Zombie! (1981)
The Morgow Rises (1982)
The Destroyers of Lan-Kern (1982)
The Fires of Lan-Kern (1982)
The Buccaneers of Lan-Kern (1983)
Raven of Destiny (1984)
Kiss of the Cobra (1984)
My Lady of Hy-Brasil (1987)
Ravenmoon (1988, also published as *Bloodmist*)
Island of Shadows (1991)
The Aisling (1992)
Dracula Lives! (1993)

TURTLEDOVE, HARRY
Wereblood (1979, as Eric Iverson)
Werenight (1979, as Eric Iverson)
An Emperor for the Legion (1987)
The Legion of Videssos (1987)
Swords of the Legion (1987)
The Misplaced Legion (1987)
Krispos of Videssos (1991)
Krispos Rising (1991)
The Case of the Toxic Spell Dump (1993)
Krispos the Emperor (1994)

Prince of the North (1994)
The Stolen Throne (1995)
Hammer and Anvil (1996)
King of the North (1996)
Thessalonica (1997)
The Thousand Cities (1997)
Between the Rivers (1998)
Fox and Empire (1998)
Videssos Besieged (1998)
Into the Darkness (1999)
Wisdom of the Fox (1999)
Household Gods (1999, with Judith Tarr)
Darkness Descending (2000)
Tale of the Fox (2000)
Sentry Peak (2000)
Marching through Peachtree (2001)
Through the Darkness (2001)
Rulers of the Darkness (2002)
Advance and Retreat (2002)
Conan of Venarium (2003)
Jaws of Darkness (2003)
Out of the Darkness (2004)
The Time of Troubles (2005)

TUTTLE, LISA
Familiar Spirit (1983)
A Nest of Nightmares (1986)
Gabriel (1987)
Lost Futures (1992)
Memories of the Body (1992)
Panther in Argyll (1996)
Pillow Friend (1996)
Ghosts and Other Lovers (2002)
The Mysteries (2005)

VANCE, JACK
The Dying Earth (1950)
The Eyes of the Overworld (1966)
The Fantasy Realms of Jack Vance (1979)
Green Magic (1979)
Cugel's Saga (1983)
Lyonesse (1983, also published as *Suldrun's Garden*)
Rhialto the Marvelous (1984)
The Green Pearl (1985)
Madouc (1989)
Tales of the Dying Earth (2000)

VOLSKY, PAULA
The Curse of the Witch-Queen (1982)
The Sorcerer's Lady (1986)

The Luck of Relian Kru (1987)
The Sorcerer's Heir (1988)
The Sorcerer's Curse (1989)
Illusion (1991)
The Wolf of Winter (1993)
The Gates of Twilight (1996)
The White Tribunal (1997)
The Grand Ellipse (2000)

WAGNER, KARL EDWARD
Darkness Weaves (1970, also published as *Darkness Weaves with Many Shades*)
Death Angel's Shadow (1973)
Bloodstone (1975)
Dark Crusade (1976)
Legion from the Shadows (1976)
Night Winds (1978)
The Road of Kings (1979)
In a Lonely Place (1983)
The Book of Kane (1985)
Why Not You and I? (1987)
Unthreatened by the Morning Light (1989)
Exorcisms and Ecstasies (1997)

WAKEFIELD, H. RUSSELL
They Return at Evening (1928)
Old Man's Beard (1929, also published as *Others Who Returned*)
Imagine a Man in a Box (1931)
Ghost Stories (1932)
A Ghostly Company (1935)
The Clock Strikes 12 (1939)
Strayers from Sheol (1961)
The Best Ghost Stories of H. Russell Wakefield (1978)
Reunion at Dawn (2000)

WALTON, EVANGELINE
The Island of the Mighty (1936, also published as *The Virgin and the Swine*)
Witch House (1945)
The Children of Llyr (1971)
The Song of Rhiannon (1972)
Prince of Annwn (1974)
The Sword Is Forged (1984)
The Mabinogion Tetralogy (2002)

WATT-EVANS, LAWRENCE
The Lure of the Basilisk (1980)
The Seven Altars of Dusarra (1981)
The Cyborg and the Sorcerers (1982)

The Sword of Bheleu (1983)
The Book of Silence (1984)
The Misenchanted Sword (1985)
With a Single Spell (1987)
The Wizard and the War Machine (1987)
The Unwilling Warlord (1989)
The Nightmare People (1990)
The Blood of a Dragon (1991)
The Rebirth of Wonder (1992)
The Spell of the Black Dagger (1993)
Split Heirs (1993, with Esther Friesner)
Taking Flight (1993)
Out of This World (1994)
In the Empire of Shadow (1995)
The Reign of the Brown Magician (1996)
Touched by the Gods (1997)
Dragon Weather (1999)
Night of Madness (2000)
The Dragon Society (2001)
Ithanalin's Restoration (2002)
Dragon Venom (2003)
Worlds of Shadow (2003)

WEIS, MARGARET

Dragons of Winter Night (1984, with Tracy Hickman)
Dragons of Autumn Twilight (1984, with Tracy Hickman)
Dragons of Spring Dawning (1985, with Tracy Hickman)
Test of the Twins (1986, with Tracy Hickman)
Time of the Twins (1986, with Tracy Hickman)
War of the Twins (1986, with Tracy Hickman)
Doom of the Darksword (1988, with Tracy Hickman)
Dragonlance Chronicles (1988, with Tracy Hickman)
Triumph of the Darksword (1988, with Tracy Hickman)
Dragonlance Legends (1988, with Tracy Hickman)
Forging the Darksword (1988, with Tracy Hickman)
The Paladin of the Night (1989, with Tracy Hickman)
The Will of the Wanderer (1989, with Tracy Hickman)
The Prophet of Akhran (1989, with Tracy Hickman)
Elven Star (1990, with Tracy Hickman)
Dragon Wing (1990, with Tracy Hickman)
Fire Sea (1991, with Tracy Hickman)
Serpent Mage (1992, with Tracy Hickman)
Hand of Chaos (1993, with Tracy Hickman)
Into the Labyrinth (1993, with Tracy Hickman)
The Second Generation (1994, with Tracy Hickman)
The Seventh Gate (1994, with Tracy Hickman)
Dragons of Summer Flame (1995, with Tracy Hickman)
The Doom Brigade (1996, with Don Perrin)

Testament of the Dragon (1997)
Legacy of the Darksword (1997, with Tracy Hickman)
The Mantle of Kendis-Dai (1997, with Tracy Hickman, also published as *Starshield: Sentinels*)
Nightsword (1998, with Tracy Hickman)
The Soulforge (1998)
Dark Heart (1998, with David Baldwin)
Brothers in Arms (1999, with Don Perrin)
Dragons of a Fallen Sun (2000, with Tracy Hickman)
Draconian Measures (2000, with Don Perrin)
Well of Darkness (2000, with Tracy Hickman)
Guardians of the Lost (2001, with Tracy Hickman)
Dragons of a Vanished Moon (2002, with Tracy Hickman)
Journey into the Void (2003, with Tracy Hickman)
Mistress of Dragons (2003)
The Annotated Legends (2003, with Tracy Hickman)
The Dragon's Son (2004)
Master of Dragons (2005)

WELLMAN, MANLY WADE

Who Fears the Devil? (1963)
Worse Things Waiting (1973)
The Beyonders (1977)
The Old Gods Waken (1979)
After Dark (1980)
Lonely Vigils (1981)
The Lost and the Lurking (1981)
The Hanging Stones (1982)
What Dreams May Come (1983)
The Voice from the Mountain (1985)
The School of Darkness (1985)
Cahena: A Dream of the Past (1986)
Valley So Low (1987)
John the Balladeer (1988)
The Third Cry to Legba and Other Invocations (2000)
The Devil Is Not Mocked and Other Warnings (2001)
Fearful Rock and Other Precarious Locales (2001)
Owls Hoot in the Daytime and Other Omens (2003)
Sin's Doorway and Other Ominous Entrances (2003)

WELLS, ANGUS

Swordsmistress of Chaos (1978, as Richard Kirk, with Robert Holdstock)
The Frozen God (1978, as Richard Kirk)
A Time of Dying (1979, as Richard Kirk)
Wrath of Ashar (1988)
The Usurper (1989)
The Way Beneath (1990)
Forbidden Magic (1991)

Dark Magic (1992)
Wild Magic (1993)
Lords of the Sky (1994)
Exile's Children (1995)
Exile's Challenge (1996)
Yesterday's Kings (2001)

WELLS, MARTHA

The Element of Fire (1993)
The City of Bones (1995)
The Death of the Necromancer (1998)
Wheel of the Infinite (2000)
The Wizard Hunters (2003)
The Ships of Air (2004)

WEST, MICHELLE

Into the Darklands (1991, as Michelle Sagara)
Children of the Blood (1992, as Michelle Sagara)
Lady of Mercy (1993, as Michelle Sagara)
Chains of Darkness, Chains of Light (1994, as Michelle
    Sagara)
Hunter's Oath (1995)
Hunter's Death (1996)
Broken Crown (1997)
The Uncrowned King (1998)
The Shining Court (1999)
Sea of Sorrows (2001)
The Riven Shield (2003)
Speaking with Angels (2003)
The Sun Sword (2004)

WHEATLEY, DENNIS

The Devil Rides Out (1935)
Strange Conflict (1941)
Gunmen, Gallants, and Ghosts (1943)
The Haunting of Toby Jugg (1948)
To the Devil—a Daughter (1953)
The Ka of Gifford Hilary (1956)
The Black Magic Omnibus (1956)
The Rape of Venice (1959)
The Satanist (1960)
They Used Dark Forces (1964)
The White Witch of the South Seas (1968)
Gateway to Hell (1970)
The Irish Witch (1973)

WHITE, T. H.

Gone to Ground (1935, also published as *The
    Maharajah and Other Stories*)
The Sword in the Stone (1938)

The Witch in the Wood (1939)
The Ill-Made Knight (1940)
The Elephant and the Kangaroo (1947)
Mistress Masham's Repose (1947)
The Once and Future King (1958)
The Book of Merlyn (1977)

WILLIAMS, TAD

Tailchaser's Song (1985)
The Dragonbone Chair (1988)
The Stone of Farewell (1990)
Child of an Ancient City (1992, with Nina Kiriki
    Hoffman)
To Green Angel Tower (1993)
Caliban's Hour (1994)
City of Golden Shadow (1996)
River of Blue Fire (1998)
Mountain of Black Glass (1999)
Sea of Silver Light (2001)
The War of the Flowers (2002)
Shadowmarch (2004)

WILLIAMSON, CHET

Soulstorm (1986)
Ash Wednesday (1987)
Lowland Rider (1988)
Dreamthorp (1989)
Reign (1990)
Mordenheim (1994)
Second Chance (1995)
Murder in Cormyr (1996)
City of Iron (1998)
Empire of Dust (1998)
Clash by Night (1998)
Siege of Stone (1999)
Figures in Rain (2002)

WILLIAMSON, J. N.

The Ritual (1979)
The Houngan (1980, also published as *Profits*)
Ghost Mansion (1981)
The Tulpa (1981)
Premonition (1981)
Queen of Hell (1981)
Horror House (1981)
The Banished (1981)
Death-Angel (1981)
Death-Coach (1981)
Horror Mansion (1982)
Playmates (1982)

The Evil One (1982)
Death-Doctor (1982)
Death-School (1982)
Brotherkind (1982)
The Dentist (1983)
Babel's Children (1984)
The Offspring (1984)
Ghost (1984)
The Longest Night (1985)
Noonspell (1987)
Evil Offspring (1987)
Dead to the World (1988)
Shadows of Death (1989)
Black School (1989)
Hell Storm (1990)
The Naked Flesh of Feeling (1991)
The Night Seasons (1991)
The Monastery (1992)
Don't Take Away the Light (1993)
The Fifth Season (1993)
Bloodlines (1994)
The Haunt (1999)
Frights of Fancy (2000)
Affinity (2001)

WILSON, F. PAUL

The Keep (1981)
The Tomb (1984)
The Touch (1986)
Midnight Mass (1990, expanded 2004)
Reborn (1990)
Reprisal (1991)
Nightworld (1992)
The Barrens and Others (1992)
Legacies (1998)
All the Rage (2000)
Conspiracies (2000)
Hosts (2001)
The Haunted Air (2002)
Gateways (2003)
Crisscross (2004)

WOLF, GARY

Who Censored Roger Rabbit? (1981)
Who P-P-P-Plugged Roger Rabbit? (1991)

WOLFE, GENE

Peace (1975)
The Devil in a Forest (1977)
Free Live Free (1984)

Soldier of the Mist (1986)
There Are Doors (1988)
Soldier of Arete (1989)
Castleview (1990)
Latro in the Mist (2003)
Innocents Aboard (2004)
The Knight (2004)
The Wizard (2004)

WREDE, PATRICIA

Shadow Magic (1982)
Daughter of Witches (1983)
The Seven Towers (1984)
The Harp of Imach Thyssel (1985)
Talking to Dragons (1985)
Caught in Crystal (1987)
Sorcery and Cecilia (1988, with Caroline Stevermer)
Snow White and Rose Red (1989)
Dealing with Dragons (1990, also published as *Dragonsbane*)
Mairelon the Magician (1991)
Searching for Dragons (1991, also published as *Dragon Search*)
Calling on Dragons (1993)
The Raven Ring (1994)
Book of Enchantments (1996)
The Enchanted Forest Chronicles (1996)
The Magician's Ward (1997)
Shadows over Lyra (1997)
The Grand Tour (2004, with Caroline Stevermer)

WRIGHT, T. M.

Strange Seed (1978)
The Woman Next Door (1981)
Nursery Tale (1982)
The Playground (1982)
Carlisle Street (1983)
The Children of the Island (1983)
A Manhattan Ghost Story (1984)
The People of the Dark (1985)
The Changing (1985, as F. W. Armstrong)
The Waiting Room (1986)
The Devouring (1987, as F. W. Armstrong)
Island (1988)
The Place (1989)
Boundaries (1990)
The School (1990)
The Last Vampire (1991)
Little Boy Lost (1992)
Goodlow's Ghosts (1993)

The Ascending (1994)
Sleapeasy (2001)
The House on Orchid Street (2003)
Laughing Man (2003)
Cold House (2003)

WURTS, JANNY

Sorcerer's Legacy (1982)
Stormwarden (1984)
Daughter of the Empire (1987, with Raymond Feist)
Keeper of the Keys (1988)
Shadowfane (1988)
Servant of the Empire (1990, with Raymond Feist)
Mistress of the Empire (1992, with Raymond Feist)
The Master of White Storm (1992)
The Curse of the Mistwraith (1993)
That Way Lies Camelot (1994)
Warhost of Vastmark (1995)
Ships of Merior (1995)
Fugitive Prince (1997)
The Cycle of Fire (1999)
Grand Conspiracy (2000)
To Ride Hell's Chasm (2002)

YARBRO, CHELSEA QUINN

Hotel Transylvania (1978)
The Palace (1978)
Blood Games (1980)
Dead and Buried (1980)
Sins of Omission (1980)
Ariosto (1980)
Path of the Eclipse (1981)
Tempting Fate (1982)
The Saint Germain Chronicles (1983)
The Godforsaken (1983)
Nomads (1984)
A Mortal Glamour (1985)
To the High Redoubt (1985)
A Baroque Fable (1986)
Signs and Portents (1986)
Firecode (1987)
A Flame in Byzantium (1987)
Crusader's Torch (1988)
A Candle for D'Artagnan (1989)
Out of the House of Life (1990)
Better in the Dark (1993)
Darker Jewels (1993)
Mansions of Darkness (1996)
Writ in Blood (1997)
Monet's Ghost (1997)

The Angry Angel (1998)
Blood Roses (1998)
Communion Blood (1999)
The Soul of an Angel (1999)
Dark Light (1999)
Come Twilight (2000)
A Feast in Exile (2001)
In the Face of Death (2001)
Night Blooming (2002)
Apprehensions and Other Delusions (2003)
Midnight Harvest (2003)
Dark Is the Sun (2004)
States of Grace (2005)

YOLEN, JANE

The Wizard of Washington Square (1969)
The Magic Three of Solatia (1974)
The Girl Who Cried Flowers and Other Tales (1974)
The Transfigured Hart (1975)
The Moon Ribbon and Other Tales (1976)
The Hundredth Dove and Other Tales (1977)
The Mermaid's Three Wisdoms (1978)
The Lady and the Merman (1979)
Dreamweaver (1979)
Neptune Rising (1982)
Tales of Wonder (1983)
Cards of Grief (1984)
The Whitethorn Wood and Other Magicks (1984)
Dragonfield and Other Stories (1985)
Merlin's Booke (1986)
The Devil's Arithmetic (1988)
Sister Light, Sister Dark (1988)
The Faery Flag (1989)
White Jenna (1989)
The Books of Great Alta (1990)
The Dragon's Boy (1990)
The Wizard's Hall (1991)
Wings (1991)
Briar Rose (1992)
Storyteller (1992)
Here There Be Dragons (1993)
Here There Be Unicorns (1994)
Here There Be Witches (1995)
The Wild Hunt (1995)
Passager (1996)
Hobby (1996)
Here There Be Angels (1996)
Merlin (1997)
Merlin and the Dragons (1997)
Twelve Impossible Things before Breakfast (1997)

The One Armed Queen (1998)
Here There Be Ghosts (1998)
The Pictish Child (1999)
The Wizard's Map (1999)
Child of Faerie, Child of Earth (2000)
Boots and the Seven Leaguers (2000)
The Bagpiper's Ghost (2002)
Hippolyta and the Curse of the Amazons (2002, with
    Robert J. Harris)
Sword of the Rightful King (2003)
The Young Merlin Trilogy (2004)
Pay the Piper (2005, with Adam Stemple)

ZELAZNY, ROGER
Nine Princes in Amber (1969)
Jack of Shadows (1971)
The Guns of Avalon (1972)
Sign of the Unicorn (1975)
The Hand of Oberon (1976)
The Courts of Chaos (1978)
The Chronicles of Amber (1979)
Changeling (1980)
Madwand (1981)
The Changing Land (1981)
Dilvish, the Damned (1982)

Trumps of Doom (1985)
Blood of Amber (1986)
A Dark Traveling (1987)
Sign of Chaos (1988)
Knight of Shadows (1989)
Wizard's World (1989)
The Mask of Loki (1990, with Thomas T. Thomas)
The Black Throne (1990, with Fred Saberhagen)
Bring Me the Head of Prince Charming (1991, with
    Robert Sheckley)
Prince of Chaos (1991)
A Night in the Lonesome October (1993)
If at Faust You Don't Succeed (1993, with Robert
    Sheckley)
A Farce to Be Reckoned With (1995, with Robert
    Sheckley)
Lord Demon (1999, with Jane Lindskold)
Manna from Heaven (2003)

ZETTEL, SARAH
The Sorcerer's Treason (2002)
The Usurper's Crown (2003)
The Firebird's Vengeance (2004)
In Camelot's Shadow (2004)
In Camelot's Honor (2005)

SELECTED BIBLIOGRAPHY OF SECONDARY SOURCES

There exists, of course, an extensive number of volumes about fantasy and horror literature: critical works, historical analyses, biographies, memoirs, and philosophical discussions. One could assemble a small library focused exclusively on the life and work of J. R. R. Tolkien. Although the following list is far from comprehensive, it includes many useful titles and provides a cross section of what is available.

Ashley, Michael, *Algernon Blackwood*. Westport, Conn.: Greenwood, 1987.

Barron, Neil, ed., *Fantasy Literature: A Reader's Guide*. New York: Garland, 1990.

———. *Horror Literature: A Reader's Guide*. New York: Garland, 1990.

Bleiler, Everett F. *The Guide to Supernatural Fiction*. Kent, Ohio: Kent State University Press, 1983.

Cannon, Peter, ed. *Lovecraft Remembered*. Sauk City, Wisc.: Arkham House, 1998.

Carter, Lin. *Imaginary Worlds*. New York: Ballantine, 1973.

Clute, John, and John Grant. *The Encyclopedia of Fantasy*. New York: St Martin's Press, 1997.

Collings, Michael R. *The Work of Stephen King*. San Bernardino, Calif.: Borgo, 1996.

De Camp, L. Sprague, Catherine Crook De Camp, and Jane Whittington Griffin. *Dark Valley Destiny*. New York: Bluejay, 1983.

Grant, Donald, ed. *Talbot Mundy: Messenger of Destiny*. West Kingston, R.I.: Donald Grant, 1983.

Greenberg, Martin Harry, Ed Gorman, and Munster, Bill, ed. *The Dean Koontz Companion*. New York: Berkley, 1994.

Helfers, John, and Denise Little ed. *The Valdemar Companion*. New York: DAW, 2001.

Jones, Stephen, and Kim Newman. *Horror: 100 Best Books*. New York: Carroll & Graf, 1998.

Joshi, S. T. *Lord Dunsany*. Westport, Conn.: Greenwood, 1998.

Karr, Phyllis Ann, *The Arthurian Companion*. Oakland, Calif.: Green Knight, 2001.

Krulik, Theodore. *The Complete Amber Sourcebook*. New York: AvoNova, 1996.

Matheson, Richard, and Ricia Mainhardt, eds. *Appreciations of the Master*. New York: Tor, 1995.

Moore, Doris Langley. *E. Nesbit: A Biography*. New York: Chilton, 1966.

Pringle, David, *Modern Fantasy*. London: Peter Bedrick, 1988.

———, ed. *St. James Guide to Fantasy Writers*. Detroit: St James Press, 1996.

———, ed. *St. James Guide to Horror, Ghost, & Gothic Writers*. Detroit: St. James Press, 1998.

Raeper, William. *George MacDonald*. Batavia, Ill.: Lion, 1987.

Schweitzer, Darrell, ed. *Discovering Classic Fantasy Fiction*. San Bernardino, Calif.: Borgo, 1996.

Skal, David J. *The Monster Show*. London: Penguin, 1993.

Tyler, J. E. A. *The Complete Tolkien Companion*. New York: Thomas Dunne, 2004.

INDEX

Note: **Boldface** page numbers indicate main entries.